HEARTS
—*of*—
IRON

THE EPIC STRUGGLE OF THE
1ST MARINE DIVISION FLAME TANK PLATOON
KOREAN WAR 1950-1953

JERRY RAVINO & JACK CARTY

TURNER

Turner Publishing Company

445 Park Avenue, 9th Floor
New York, NY 10022

200 4th Avenue North, Suite 950
Nashville, TN 37219

www.turnerpublishing.com

Hearts of Iron:
The Epic Struggle of the 1st Marine Division, Flame Tank Platoon, Korean War, 1950-1953

Cover design by Mike Penticost
Cover photo courtesy of Jack Carty

Library of Congress Cataloging-in-Publication Data

Ravino, Jerry.
Hearts of iron : the epic struggle of the 1st Marine Division Flame Tank Platoon, Korean
War, 1950-1953 / Jerry Ravino and Jack Carty.
    p. cm.
ISBN 978-1-59652-780-5
1. United States. Marine Corps. Division, 1st. Tank Battalion, 1st. Flame Platoon. 2.
Korean War, 1950-1953--Regimental histories--United States. 3. Korean War, 1950-
1953--Tank warfare. 4. Flame throwers--Korea--History--20th century. 5. Flame
throwers--United States--History--20th century. I. Carty, Jack. II. Title.
DS919.R39 2011
951.904'242--dc22

                                    2010051924

Printed in the United States of America

11 12 13 14 15 16 17 18—0 9 8 7 6 5 4 3 2 1

Previously published in hardcover as Flame Dragons of the Korean War © 2003

Contents

Preface

I was relaxing in our Seminole, Florida, condominium, looking over photographs of flame tanks and crews that I had recently received from friends and associates who were interested in our book, *Hearts of Iron*.

It was a Saturday morning, January 21, 2002, to be exact, and my mind was forty-nine years from then.

When the phone rang, I went to it casually, my thoughts still on the pictures that took me back to the Korean War. When I picked up the receiver, little could I have imagined that I truly was going to be jolted back in time.

"Mr. Ravino?"

"Yes," I answered. The voice on the other end of the line was not familiar.

"My name is Scott McAdams."

It took a few seconds for the name to register . . . the last name.

I still wasn't sure what I was hearing. But my mind was racing. So was my blood pressure. I began shaking, and I felt my forehead moisten with sweat.

As I was trying to collect myself, I heard the man's voice:

"I'm the youngest of the three McAdams brothers. I understand you served with my father during the Korean War and that you were with him when he died?"

My memory exploded, with bits and pieces of the day nearly forty-nine years ago when Lt. Michael McAdams was killed by a Chinese rocket piercing the turret of his flame tank that was sitting just in front of our tank at the base of a small hill called Kum gok.

I was speechless, completely taken by surprise, by this strange voice.

"Are you that person?" the man asked.

I managed to catch my breath, finally!

"Yes I am, Scott."

I needed some time to regain my composure, and took another deep breath.

"Scott, please give me a moment to get into a chair. This is overwhelming."

"Certainly, Mr. Ravino. I understand . . . and take your time." I realized, this man must be going through similar emotions.

I had been looking for Lt. McAdams' family for years, more so recently since this book began to dominate my mind. I thought I had tracked them down, once, in California. But I had not received a reply to my inquiry. I continued to run into a dead end.

Now, out of nowhere came this telephone call from Scott McAdams.

The adrenaline was rushing through me. I was trying to sort my emotions, and it was not easy.

Lt. McAdams had told us when he first took over the Flame Platoon in Korea, that he had three sons, and he had never seen the youngest, who was only six months old at the time. Now, this son was on the other end of the line. There was no doubt in my mind, he was going to want to know all about his father, particularly how he had died.

What was I going to tell this boy? Could I explain the gory details of his father's death? Then, I realized: he's not a boy now, he's an adult, forty-nine years old. It still was hard to get the thought of a young child out of my mind.

I began telling Scott McAdams about Lt. Michael McAdams, his father. I told him he had been assigned as commanding officer of nine flame-throwing tanks—the Flame

Platoon, Headquarters Company, First Tank Battalion, First Marine Division—about a month before he died.

"Let me add here, Scott," I said, "your father was transferred to our platoon from battalion reconnaissance and came to us with the reputation as a highly respected officer."

I knew he wanted the whole story of what happened to his father, but I was having trouble deciding how much I should tell him.

I described Operation Clambake, how the four flame tanks were left out in the open of no man's land, how his father's lead tank was hit and immobilized. How we managed to get the tank back to our own MLR with his father's body still in it. I was beginning to feel choked up as I came to the point of telling this man just how the lieutenant died.

It was not going to be easy for me, nor for him. I decided not to go into detail at this time. I explained that we got the tank back to safety behind the MLR (main line of resistance), and I helped take his father's body out of the tank. I did not elaborate that he had been decapitated.

I got through it. I don't know how.

There was a pause on the other end of the line. After a moment, Scott spoke.

"First of all, Mr. Ravino, I want to thank you and the other Marines for the respect you showed my father."

To my surprise, he told me he and his brothers had been trying for years to find someone who could tell them about their father.

"You are the first fellow Marine we've located in all these years," he said, his voice hinting the emotion he was experiencing. "So, we have a lot of questions."

He explained that he and his brother Ian—the Lieutenant's middle son—lived in St. Augustine, Florida, and their older brother, Michael Junior, lived in North Carolina.

This was another jolt for me. "I've been searching for your family for years, Scott, as far away as California," I said, "and it turns out that we live here in the same state."

Imagine that!

That short conversation—less than five minutes—seemed to be enough for both of us for the moment. Scott asked if he and his family could meet me. I was overwhelmed by his request, but quickly collected myself.

"Yes . . . yes, of course!"

Through a series of e-mails with Scott's wife, Lynn, we arranged that they and Ian drive down here to Seminole for dinner with me and my wife, Nona, in two weeks. Ironically, the date would be February 2—one day shy of forty-nine years since Lt. McAdams was killed in action.

It was obvious that the McAdams family, naturally, wanted as much information as they could find on their father, and it would be easier if it could be done in personal conversation with me.

Attached to one of the e-mails Lynn McAdams had sent was a picture of her father-in-law, a handsome young Marine officer in dress blues. Staring at that photo brought tears to my eyes. However, as much as it hurt to remember the circumstances of his death, this chance to meet with his family brought a measure of comfort that is hard to explain. I could only hope that our connection would bring as much comfort and solace to Lt. McAdams' sons.

I was like a caged animal, prancing up and down the sidewalk that Saturday morning, waiting for them to arrive. Finally, around noon, they were here. Seeing them in person was very emotional, and introductions were a little uneasy at first. But it wasn't long before we were embracing each other and walking into our home for the dinner Nona had prepared.

I felt obliged to toast First Lt. Michael McAdams and the occasion of this special meeting with his family—after all these years. I could feel a mood of serenity and thanksgiving around the table. Inwardly, my silent prayer was to remain calm through it all. I knew there were going to be many questions for all of us, and some of the answers were not going to be easy.

While the conversation through dinner was casual, I could not keep thoughts of the impending, more serious conversation from running through my mind.

By the time we retired to the living room, my twenty years of counseling—some of it involving family issues—began to take hold. I felt sure I would be able to handle what was ahead. But I was not totally ready when Scott began telling his story.

"Jerry," he began, "when my father was killed in Korea, I was only six months old, so I never had a chance to meet him. My oldest brother Michael remembers very little about him. The same for Ian."

I was shocked to hear what he told us next.

"As we understand the events following our father's death: When our mother received the notification, she abandoned us. We went to live with her father for three years until he died of heart disease."

I was curious.

"Did you ever find the reason for this?"

Ian responded: "We truly don't know why."

After their grandfather's death, the three boys were sent to an orphanage in Hershey, Pennsylvania. There were 250 boys in that facility, but the McAdams brothers managed to stay together most of the time.

When Scott was ten years old, Ian, eleven, and Michael Junior, twelve, their mother visited the boys and took them on a two-week vacation.

"But that was the last time we saw her," Scott said.

When their mother died two years ago in California, the three brothers all traveled west to attend the services.

"You do realize how very proud your father would have been of you boys," I told them.

"We hope so, Jerry," Scott replied. "We have done the best we could do."

Silence took over the room for several seconds. Then I thought the time had come to tell them whatever they wanted to know.

"Well, what and how much do you want to know about your father?"

"Everything," they replied in unison.

"We need to hear the whole story about him," Scott said, "from you and anybody else that knew him."

I started from the beginning: when Lt. McAdams first came to the Flame Platoon . . . that he was the finest officer I ever met in the Marine Corps . . . that he respected his men and the men respected him . . . that he explained to us why he thought we had to fight the Communists and the reason we were in Korea.

"He was an officer and gentleman in the finest tradition of the Marine Corps. We in the Flame Platoon knew we had a hard-charger and were very proud to serve with your father. He always carried himself, even in combat, with dignity and courage."

The men and Lynn listened without interruption. Now came the toughest part: explaining the details of Operation Clambake, Kum gok, and their father's death.

I told them everything—the Lieutenant's tank leading the way in no man's land; their father getting out of his tank, while under fire, to untangle barbed wire from the track and point out positions for the other three flame tanks to take; the rocket driving through his tank's turret, severing his head and mortally wounding the loader; another rocket coming from the other side and injuring his bow gunner and driver; what happened during the rest of the three-hour battle; how the tank was retrieved; the torment I experienced when I had to help lift the Lieutenant's body from the tank.

"But he was one of us, a Marine tanker, and we owed that respect to our commanding officer."

I could see the sadness in their faces as I related what happened. I prayed silently that the hurt I was adding to the hurt they had carried all these years was not too much for them.

Then I told them their father was one of the major reasons this book was being written. I showed them pictures of the flame tanks. They had never seen a flame tank before.

I think many of their questions have been answered.

I have remained in contact with the McAdams family, and we will meet again. Ian, in a subsequent e-mail to me, may have said it best: "You have given all of us a new breath of life. Thank you."

Words can't describe what that meeting meant to me. Like the imbedded memories of Operation Clambake, I will never forget what I heard when I picked up the phone that day almost forty-nine years later:

"Mr. Ravino? My name is Scott McAdams."

Lt. Michael McAdams' three sons—Ian Andrew, Alan Scott, and Michael Lawrence, Jr.—were cared for by their maternal grandfather after the Lieutenant was killed in action in 1953. Three years later, their grandfather died and the boys were sent to the Hershey (Pennsylvania) Home for Boys, where this picture was taken in the 1960s. (Photo Courtesy McAdams Family)

Michael Lawrence McAdams, a World War II–enlisted Marine, who became a mustang lieutenant and Flame Platoon commanding officer, was killed in action at Kum gok during Operation Clambake on 3 February 1953. (Photo Courtesy McAdams Family)

Prologue

The Flame Tank

The First Tank Battalion, which served in Korea once the First Marine Division was brought up to full strength, complied with the Marine Corps prescribed table of organization (T.O.). There were four tank line companies—A (Able), B (Baker), C (Charlie), D (Dog)—each comprised of 25 M26 Pershings (later M46 Pattons) in platoons of five tanks apiece.

There was Headquarters and Service Company. Attached were the Flame Platoon's nine double-barreled (105mm howitzer and CWS-POH5 Flame Gun) M4A3E8 Shermans—three in each of three sections. Service Company, which had nine Shermans, specially equipped with dozer blades, or bow-mounted tripod boons for lifting disabled tanks, or their bulky parts. Service Company also had special flatbed tractor-trailers for hauling disabled pigirons.

Every tank in the First Tank Battalion had a letter and number on each side of its turret. The letter referred to the company or platoon. In the line companies, A31 was the command tank in the Third Platoon, Able Company. In the Flame Platoon, "F" for "Fox" correlated with "Flame." Thus, F11 was first tank in the first section of the Flame Platoon. The Flame Platoon's nine tanks were numbered F11, F12, F13, F21, F22, F23, F31, F32, and F33 and used the phonetic "Fox" for the call letter.

The M4A3E8 medium tank, often called the "Easy Eight" in U.S. Army armored outfits, was the most recent version of 49,234 Shermans that were produced during World War II. The M4 Sherman was the most widely used tank in Europe and the Pacific.

The nine flame tanks inherited by the First Tank Battalion for the Korean had been designated for use in the planned invasion of Japan in 1945. They were sent to Okinawa just prior to the end of World War II, but devastation of Hiroshima and Nagasaki by the A-bomb finally brought an end to hostilities. That, fortunately for millions of Americans, canceled the invasion, and the flame tanks returned to Hawaii for further development.

Army flame tanks did most of the work in the Pacific islands campaigns, but they were not as sophisticated, nor did they have the main armament—like a 105mm, or a 75mm cannon—to protect themselves.

The First Tank Battalion roamin' candles were a much-improved version.

This Sherman was a medium tank weighing between 30 and 35 tons, depending on the equipment. It was more than 19 feet long, 8-1/2 feet wide, and 9 feet high, powered by a V-8 500-horse Ford radial air-cooled gasoline engine. It had a five-forward speed and reverse clutch-activated transmission, and was turned by a pair of waist-high right and left brake levers that locked the particular track when pulled back.

"By the book," the M4A3E8 had maximum speed of 24 mph. But some Flame Tankers were known to get it up to 30 mph on a good flat road. Its 180-gallon fuel capacity could take it at least 100 miles, depending on the terrain. The "E8" model was improved with a volute spring suspension and 23-inch-wide tracks, 4 inches wider than earlier models. Forward sprockets pulled the tracks over two top idler wheels and under three sets of four bogey wheels.

This version, among 1,445 E8s to roll out of the Michigan Tank Armor Production

Arsenal in Detroit, was specifically designed with the POA-CWS-H5 (Pacific Ocean Area-Chemical Warfare Service-Hawaii [Version 5]) flame gun for use on the Japanese mainland. The island war in the Pacific had proven the worth of flame-throwing tanks in evicting fanatical Japanese defenders from fortified caves, bunkers, and pill boxes, which often were impervious to small arms and artillery. Similar enemy tactics had been expected in Japan.

When the Korean War broke out and the First Marine Division was activated, one of the first orders of business for the First Tank Battalion was the formation of the Flame Platoon under Headquarters Company command.

These tanks had variable fire ability, maybe not as powerful, but more lethal than any rolling armament in the war. Without question, it was one of the most effective close-combat tanks ever to roll out of the Detroit production plant, even though the use of its main armament—the 105mm cannon—was restricted because there were only a half dozen rounds of ordnance available. Since the normal storage area for cannon shells was in the hull below the turret, the flame tank used that area for napalm storage tanks.

Creative Flame Tankers midway through the Korean War rigged extra brackets in some turrets to carry four or five more rounds. By the time the war entered its third year, one tank commander (T.C.) began cramming more than 20 rounds of 105mm in the turret. Eventually, 25 rounds became a standard load on missions where flame tanks made short runs to firing positions.

Normally, the Sherman tank had a five-man crew—driver, bow-machine gunner (often called the assistant driver), 105-gunner, loader, and tank commander. With the flame gun in the turret, space was sparse and the crew was reduced to four Marines. The "gunner" was eliminated, the duties of firing the 105 and flame gun assumed by the tank commander.

The POA-CWS-H5 flame gun was mounted to the right of 105mm howitzer. To the left of the cannon was a 30-caliber machine gun in a fixed position coaxially in line with the cannon. Another 30-caliber machine gun was in the hands of the bow gunner in the lower right compartment opposite the driver. Atop the turret were two mounts for the 50-caliber machine gun. One was between the two hatches, the other to the rear and right of the tank commander's opening. It had 360 degrees capability, as did the turret, which could be traversed full circle. Each of the four-man crew carried a .45-caliber pistol, and a Thompson sub machine gun was bracketed in the tank commander's area of the turret. The turret also contained a satchel of hand 30 to 40 hand grenades.

Communication was by intercom radio, which was on frequency with other tanks and/or command posts. The radio also was linked to a bustle phone on the back of the tank where infantry could converse with the T.C.

Because the two napalm storage tanks consumed much of the space under the turret deck—normally used for closeting 105mm ordnance—the flame tank could only carry its artillery shells in the turret. The ordnance was carried in brackets fixed on the deck of the turret where 105 shells were strapped. Early in 1952, one enterprising tank commander rigged four extra brackets in F22 to increase turret's capacity to 10 rounds.

After the Flame Platoon became more active with indirect fire missions that summer, trailers were hooked to the tanks to carry more than 50 rounds of 105 ordnance. With the tank stationary, the ordnance would be passed up by hand to the loader and tank commander in normal indirect firing missions.

Mounted to the right of the 105, the flame gun relied on many components to deliver its load, not the least of which were two standard CO_2 cylinders stacked and bracketed to the bulkhead to the right of the bow gunner. A two-way regulator was attached to the cylinders to control the pressure at 280 PSI (pounds per square inch).

The bow gunner had the job of opening the valves of the two cylinders and setting the regulator at the prescribed pressure. With a short section of flex hose—necessary because of the way a moving tank bounced around—coming from the regulator, it tied into a one-half-inch stainless-steel line that ran to the two storage tanks below the deck of the turret. The tanks are filled with napthenic and palmitic acids used to thicken gasoline. That's napalm!

The steel line was connected spider-like to the tops of the tanks, allowing each to be pressurized concurrently. Once the CO_2 entered the storage containers, a blanket of pressure began forming in the tops of the vessels, forcing the napalm jelly to the bottom. It was another method of pumping a batch of slurry out of the bottom of a container, or containers, without the use of a pump.

Another half-inch stainless-steel line, similarly connected spider-like to the bottoms of the tanks, allowed the pressurized napalm to be carried to the engine compartment. There, the jelly entered the tail of a "Y" fitting. Two lines of three-quarter-inch copper tubing split off the top of the "Y" to form coils around each the engine's hot manifolds, heating the napalm to hasten its flow toward the flame gun.

Once the napalm exited the heat exchangers, it flowed through the top of another "Y" fitting into a single stainless-steel line that carried it to the shroud of the flame gun tube. There, the line was impeded by a ballcock. It was ready to become a very lethal dose of extremely hot orange-burning jelly.

Before the napalm was sent to the shroud, the tank commander stepped on a switch by his left foot. It started "Little Joe," a small pump, forcing raw gasoline from a two-gallon holding tank to the end of the gun tube. With a free hand, the tank commander hit another switch in front of him. It triggered a magnito, causing a spark plug—an ordinary plug used in the everyday car—to arc and ignite the gasoline.

It was time to introduce the napalm to the gun.

The tank commander activated a small lever, and the ballcock in the napalm line was released, allowing the now-pressurized fluid to flow into the shroud. Quickly, it was ignited by flaming gasoline swirling within shroud. With the pressure of the CO_2 behind it, a rod of scorching orange napalm, about the diameter of a baseball, jettisoned from the gun—instantaneously spreading havoc among anything, or anyone in its path up to 100 or more yards out.

Early in the war, the refueling process of the napalm storage containers was a manual operation. The batch was mixed in 55-gallon drums—usually away from the tank parks because of the danger of spontaneous ignition. The naphtha and palmetic acids in salt-form were poured by hand into the 55-gallon drum, and gasoline from a supply truck would be pumped into it. Flame tank crewmen would stir the concoction with a big hand paddle. The formula was mostly subjective to trial and error. If it came out of the gun too loose, the flame would fan and lose distance. If it was too thick, it would loop and retard the range.

Some tank commanders—experimenting—would add and subtract gasoline and/or the salts until they felt they had the correct consistency. Test firing was the only way to get it near right. The T.C.s had to keep track of their experiments, but once they were able to get the rod of flame out in the 100-yard range, the formula was memory-locked. No two flame guns fired alike, which meant there might be a different mix for each tank.

Once mixed, the loose jelly-like substance was hand-pumped into the Sherman's storage tanks through an intake line below the pistol port, on the left side of the tank turret.

By the third year of the Korean War, the flame tanks pulled up to a flat-bed truck to get their load of napalm. The special rig was accompanied by a gasoline tanker, which would pump raw fuel into the mix. The truck was much like a small chemical factory on wheels. It had three makeup tanks, pumps, agitators, gauges, safety ground straps, and a nozzled pumping line to feed the napalm into the storage tanks.

Although the gasoline was pumped in, the salts were added manually from large containers. It would take less than an hour to refuel one flame tank with 290 gallons of napalm once the mix was considered ready. Crews always made sure ground straps were hooked up to absorb any spark from friction.

The Sherman M4A3E8 flame-throwing tank was an extremely lethal weapon. Although the flame thrower was its primary weapon, it was designed so that its crew had enough other armament to adequately defend it, or unleash another form of mayhem at the enemy—particularly with its main armament, the 105mm howitzer—and the supplementary machines guns.

The Sherman tank was the darling of World War II, and not only for the Marine Corps that used it exclusively in the Pacific. In George Forty's *United States Tanks of World War II Action,* it was called "the Tank that Won the War." Forty wrote:

> It was the most widely used tank of World War II, and, while it was not up to the best German tanks in firepower or armored protection, it was without doubt the most important Allied tank of the war. The Sherman was produced in such quantity as to dwarf the productions of any other AFV (Armored Fighting Vehicle), a staggering total of 49,234 Sherman gun tanks of all types being produced by the United States.
> The Sherman made up for its deficiencies . . . by its straight forward design, ease of maintenance, ruggedness and reliability . . . it was simple to manufacture and simple to operate, two factors which counted for a great deal in a country with little pre-war tank building experience and a large conscript army to train from scratch.

The Sherman was also a very popular in the Korean War, even preferred by some veterans over the newer M26 Pershings and M46 Pattons.

Clay Blair, author of *The Forgotten War,* emphasized the fact that of the Eighth Army's 670 tanks:

> (317) were World War II-vintage medium Shermans (76-mm gun). Despite the older and smaller gun, many tankers, including World War II combat veterans Tom Dolvina and Bill Rodgers (recently promoted from command of the 70th Tank battalion to be Eighth Army armor officer), much preferred a version of the Sherman known as the M4A3E8 (the "Easy Eight") to the Pattons [M-46]. It was sturdy and reliable, was highly maneuverable, and had moderate fuel consumption and a "wide track" which gave "good flotation" in the rice paddies. Both Dolvin and Rodgers had been offered Pattons for their battalions, but both had declined them in favor of Easy Eights.

This was early in the war when the Pattons, then considered the Cadillacs of tanks, were offered to the Army as replacements for their Shermans and M26 Pershings. The Marine Corps' First Tank Battalion line companies didn't get its first Pattons until the winter of 1951-'52. That was typical of how the Marines were supplied much of the time—with leftovers from the Army, or whatever the Army didn't want. Leatherneck line-tank companies entered the war with hand-me-down Army Pershings.

Most of the Flame Tankers didn't have to read books to be convinced they were rumbling around Korea in a damn good piece of equipment. Often, it was an unrequited love affair.

Organization of the Flame Platoon

Midway through the summer of 1950, nine uniquely equipped M4A3E8 Sherman tanks, each with main armament of a 105 millimeter howitzer cannon and POA-CWS H5 napalm-firing flame gun, were being organized as a military unit for the first time in the long history of the United States Marine Corps.

Officially, they were listed in the Marine Corps table of organization as Flame Platoon, Headquarters Company, First Tank Battalion, First Marine Division, Fleet Marine Force. At that time, the Flame Platoon was little known and untested in battle. But it didn't take long before those nine tanks became very much a part of the historic battle to blunt the first hot confrontation of a Cold War that had begun to show signs of frost after the end of World War II.

It was the Korean War!

It doused us like one of those sudden summer storms: no warning. Instantly, it was a torrential downpour of the North Korean People's Army flooding over the 38th Parallel, which separated the Communist upper half of the little-known peninsula, and the shaky democratic south being weakly protected by an ill-prepared and underdeveloped Republic of Korea army. The umbrellas for this kind of storm were collecting mold somewhere in storerooms of the United States Defense Department, despite the fact the U.S. was the newly anointed world leader. That the U.S. had inherited the mantle of global protector was a legacy earned by leading the Allies to victory in the *Big One*—World War II—only five years before.

But in the euphoria of prosperity, and confidence that the world had suffered enough of war, there was little left of the mighty military juggernaut that had brought us through the bad times of the early 1940s.

Before this new storm, a few clouds had sent showers from the political sky off in the distance. But there was no lightning, only muted thunder that didn't seem to disturb many of us. Russia, our great ally in World War II, however, had been busy the last five years, refrigerating the Cold War that would chill us for forty-some years. Yet no one appeared to be paying much attention—not even the United Nations, the world's newest so-called peacekeeper, which emerged from World War II but was a relative toddler in the big peoples' politics.

We were enjoying the good times in the summer of 1950. The guys from *the Big One* had long since returned home. New families were growing, colleges were overflowing, the economy was booming, and none of us were thinking about another war. The powers-that-be in Washington certainly weren't! Politicians had cut our military to the bones. The Navy hit a brick wall trying to convince Congress it needed to keep its carriers up to date to maintain a first line of defense. The relatively new Air Force was just spreading its wings. Soldiers were enjoying soft garrison duty that the emaciated Army was providing.

The United States Marine Corps, which had built six divisions to evict the Japanese from islands all over the Pacific Ocean, was reduced to less than one division.

Fortunately, the Marine Corps remained true to its tradition. Despite drastic cut-backs in men and equipment, it maintained its philosophy of strict training—particularly its infantry—ever cognizant of its heritage to be ready when summoned because no one else was able to answer.

When Korea erupted, General Clifton B. Cates, Commandant of the Marine Corps, wasted no time. He advocated immediate use of the Fleet Marine Force. But he couldn't get anywhere with the Joint Chiefs of Staff, to which the Marine Corps had not yet been admitted. Still, General Cates instructed his staff to begin preparations to have his Marines ready for war. Convincing Admiral Forrest P. Sherman of his mission, he urged the Chief of Naval Operations and his superior to "back door" a message to Gen. Douglas MacArthur, Commander in Chief, Far East: if the Marines were needed, they would have a brigade with air support ready to go.

It wasn't long before the Joint Chiefs got the word:

"Request immediate assignment – Marine Regimental Combat Team and supporting Air Group for duty this command – MacArthur."

It was the quickly formed First Provisional Marine Brigade that answered and began plugging holes in the dike along the Pusan Perimeter after being rushed to the Land of the Morning Calm in early August of 1950. It was a little more than a month after the war exploded when the Brigade bolstered the faltering, badly trained elements of the Eighth U.S. Army and disorganized Republic of Korea troops.

Meanwhile, the feverish reorganization and upgrading of the First Marine Division at Camp Pendleton, California, was an around-the-clock textbook illustration of how to quickly mobilize a ready-to-go military force.

That's where the newest unit of the United States Marine Corps—the Flame Platoon—came to life. Flame tanks were not an unknown quantity, but the Flame Platoon was. Versions of the flame-throwing tank had been used extensively in World War II, particularly in the island hopping around the Pacific. But these tanks were attached, singularly or in small groups, to infantry units. They were not an entity of their own. It was toward the end of the war in the Pacific that their true value was envisioned as a unit operating under a specific command.

Commanding officers of the Fifth and First Tank Battalions came to this conclusion separately, when they saw the effects of using an attachment of flame tanks working with Marine ground units during the bitter fighting in the Pacific. Previously, only one or two of the fire-shooters, attached to one of the tank line companies, would be summoned to rout deeply dug-in Japanese troops. Although the war ended before the battalion commanders were able to put their theories to work, the idea had taken hold.

The outline of a Flame Platoon came with recommendation that the tanks not only be equipped with a flamethrower, but also have enough armament—something more than machine guns—to protect themselves. Further, a platoon of nine of these hybrid multi-weapon pieces of rolling armor would be part of each tank battalion in the Corps.

However, at that point in World War II, there were no main armament flame tanks available to either the Marines or Army. Thus, there was a call for a tank that not only could send burning napalm more than 100 yards into enemy strongholds but also have the firepower of a 75 mm or 105mm cannon to defend itself. These were to be used in the projected invasion of Japan.

The atom bomb and its devastation of Hiroshima and Nagasaki negated their need in World War II. But that did not cancel their development.

Flame-throwing tanks, as we knew them in the Korean War, had been nurtured in the womb of the Chemical Warfare Service (CWS), and their development continued within the body of the Pacific Operation Area (POA) in Hawaii during the mid to late 1940s. By the time the Korean War erupted, they were up for adoption in Honolulu.

The United States Marine Corps became the proud parent of nine of these specially designed babies, and a Flame Platoon was born to the First Tank Battalion when the First Marine Division gathered its fighting family for the historic Inchon Landing. The Flame Platoon got its baptism of fire when three of the versatile Shermans went into Wolmi-do Island and helped secure the key terrain during the preliminary phase of that historic battle.

Flame tanks weren't pretty like the First Tank Battalion's letter-companies' sleek M26 Pershing models, or the more modern M46 Pattons, which would come along later in the war. Flame tanks were pudgy Sherman M4A3E8s with a couple of ugly, but lethal, snouts protruding from their coaxial shield. One of the snouts was a stubby 105mm cannon sticking out of the left side of the shield, and the other a napalm-projecting flame gun mounted to the right of it. On occasion, they were referred to as the "double-barreled shotguns" of the First Tank Battalion.

And maybe these old M4s needed a 50-yard head start to win a 100-yard race with the Pershings—give them 75 yards when it came to the fluid-drive Pattons. But these pigirons were proven tough long before the more modern class of tanks came along. Their ancestors had won their spurs in Europe and the islands of the Pacific. The Sherman was respected as "the tank that won World War II."

As for this special fiery brand of Sherman, Marines proved them equally tough when push came to shove in that place called the Land of the Morning Calm.

Yes, there were times when the Flame Platoon could be perceived as the pesky *kid brothers* of the First Tank Battalion, tagging along after their siblings—Able, Baker, Charlie, and Dog companies—wondering when the big guys were going to let them into the game. But it didn't take them long to prove their mettle.

The Flame Platoon never got a lot of notice outside of Korea, and often its scrimmages were relegated to a terse clipped notation about one of these *kid brothers* in the official after-action reports sent down to Division, and on to EUSAK (Eighth U.S. Army Korea).

The Korean War was a deadly game, to say the least, but Flame Tankers proved they could stand up with the best of them when they got their first-at-bat at Wolmi-do during the pre-invasion operation of the Inchon Landing. Yongdong-Po, then Seoul, were anything but a playground, but they made things hot there, too. Then came the breakout from the Chosin Reservoir, and they helped their *big brothers* slug it out with Chinese Communist Forces as the First Marine Division broke out of Yudam-ni, through Hagaru and Koto-ri to Hamhung and Hungnam.

These Flame Dragons would help turn back the 1951 Chinese winter and spring offensives, know the frustration in one of the many attempts to dislodge *Luke the Gook* from his *Castle* on Hill 1052 in the East Central Mountains during the winter of '52. After the First Marine Division returned to the Western Front that March, Flamers really got into it. They paid dearly in Operation Clambake, a deadly mission designed to destroy enemy positions and take prisoners at Kum gok.

By then, they no longer were the *kid brothers* in the First Tank Battalion. The Flames often led the way into no man's land against Chinese Communists Forces' positions and were no less bloodied than the rest of the tank family.

We Flame Tankers, like many of our Korean War comrades, have had very little to say in the past. Following the example of our predecessors from World War II, we just tried to do our jobs. We came home without any fanfare to reunite with loved ones, go back to work, marry, and raise families. Even to those closest to us, most of us never talked much, if at all, about our experiences in Korea. Maybe that's why it quickly became the Forgotten War.

Now, most of us well into our seventies—we think it's about time our Flame Platoon claims its proud niche in history. It's time we talked—about the combat, the fear, the death of fellow tankers, the havoc we caused, and what we survived.

Our story is unique because the majority of Flame Tankers were not born to be Flame Tankers. We were not even trained to be Flame Tankers. We came from a myriad of other units within the Corps. Most of our paths to the Platoon were unusual, and totally unpredictable. Once we got there, however, there was a deep appreciation for our fortune. And that will be told in the stories of what was going on around us as the First Marine Division etched yet another brilliant chapter in its long and storied history.

Though it has been some fifty years past the fact, this is our story—as memory best serves us and others who helped remind us. Hopefully, the half-century has not clouded recollections of the most important details, or that time has embellished beyond actuality what happened to us in the Land of the Morning Calm from 15 September 1950 until 27 July 1953.

Unfortunately, there are many stories missing—either taken to eternity by those who could have told us more, or still bound in personal memory banks that we could not unlock. Time and attrition have exacted a toll on the full story of the Flame Platoon, but we have plenty to offer on behalf of one of the most unique combat units in Marine Corps history.

We rode as tall and as proud as any tanker, in any war.

Introduction

O livieri, Ravino! Sound off!"

Jerry Ravino and Jimmy Olivieri, young and somewhat bewildered Marine PFCs from the south side of Boston, who became fast friends after they enlisted with the Mayor John B. Hynes Platoon in a 1952 recruiting drive the previous October, were briefly jolted from their misery.

It was another one of the S.O.P (standard operating procedure) moments so common in the United States Marine Corps—never expect the expected to happen.

It was raining like hell somewhere in western Korea—monsoon season—but the booming and flashes of light off to the north were not thunder and lightning. It was 2 September 1952, and only a few hours since the two young Marines debarked from the USS *General Walker* with a couple thousand other Gyrenes in the 24th Replacement Draft from Camp Pendleton, California. The Korean War was already more than two years old, and young men, many of them not even out of their teens, were constantly filling the Replacement Drafts and being sent to the Land of the Morning Calm.

After PFCs Ravino and Olivieri had survived boot camp in Platoon 113 (the Mayor John B. Hynes Platoon) at Parris Island, they—like most Marine recruits of the early 1950s—were sent to Camp Pendleton in Oceanside, California, for infantry training. Like some of their predecessors, they got additional Landing Vehicle Track (LVT) or tank training at neighboring Camp Delmar, across U.S. 101 on the Southern California coast.

Depending on the particular mode of training, they left Delmar for Korea qualified to operate either an LVT or a tank. Ravino and Olivieri completed LVT training. So when they knew they were going to Korea, they figured to be replacements for a landing craft outfit.

It was when the USS *General Walker* had approached Inchon Harbor that they got their first surprise. A gunny sergeant was roaming the ship calling out names. When he found Olivieri, Ravino, and several others, he handed them cards with the numbers *1811* printed on them.

"What the hell is this, Sarg?" Ravino asked, realizing the 1811 is the MOS (Military Occupational Specialty) for tank crewmen.

"First Tank Battalion, First Marine Division," was the curt reply.

"But we've been trained in amphibs," snapped Ravino. "Somebody made a mistake."

"Just do as you're told and no questions asked."

That's the Marine Corps. You learn real quick: *Yours is not to reason why.*

After coming ashore on landing craft similar to what they thought they'd be assigned to before getting their 1811 cards, Ravino and Olivieri were herded onto an old Pullman-type train with hundreds of other replacements headed for the First Marine Division command post for assignment to outfits.

"This thing should be in a junkyard," Ravino cracked as he looked at the train. The entire beach was clouded with smoke as the vintage locomotive chugged out of the freight yard. It was the start of an uncomfortable and mysterious trip north.

Part way through a long tunnel, which reduced light to pitch black, the train jolted to a stop. The Marines heard their first sounds of real war, a burst of rapid rifle fire.

"What the hell is going on?"

They never did find out what had happened, and the train again began to build up steam, lurching forward out of the tunnel. When the Marines finally got their eyes adjusted to daylight, the train was passing through a village. It was the Americans' first real sight of Korean people. It provoked an immediate impression of what war can do to human beings. Peasants were begging for food, clothing, whatever the naïve young Marines were willing to throw to them.

Finally, the train reached its destination—Munsan-ni, the railhead near the First Marine Division CP. There were more tracks ahead, but word came filtering through the aging cars that bridges were out. This was the end of the line for now.

"Line up when your name is called."

A sergeant somewhere among the milling Marines was trying to make order out of confusion. About that time, several six-bys—the six-axle staple of military transportation since World War II—pulled up near the group of confused men. It had begun to rain heavily, and ponchos were hurriedly unpacked from 782 gear. The Marines were experiencing their first monsoon.

"They're going to the First Tank Battalion," barked the sergeant, pointing to the trucks. "So load up when I call your name."

PFCs Ravino and Olivieri responded to the call, throwing their gear over the tailgate of one of the trucks, and climbed aboard with a dozen other confused replacements. The convoy of trucks finally got underway, but by the time it twisted and turned and bounced its way several miles to the First Tank Battalion CP, Ravino, Olivieri, and the rest of the new tankers were drenched, tired, and downright miserable. Climbing down from the back of the six-by into the muck, their first thought was some hot food and getting into a tent to change into dry utilities.

Not yet!

"*Olivieri, Ravino! Sound off!*"

"Here, sir," they shouted in unison to the order from another sergeant, who gave no indication that he was the least bit concerned how lousy the dozen or so men standing around him were feeling. They were confused, soaked, and chilled to the bone in a strange land. It was more than a little depressing.

The only thing they were sure of—there was a damn good chance they were going to be in harm's way very soon, maybe never getting out of this damned hole called Korea.

The sergeant knew all of this. He'd been there once. He experienced the same frustrating feeling when he came to the Land of the Morning Calm. But he wasn't showing any compassion to the new replacements. *It'll get worse, Boots,* he had to be thinking to himself, *and you're supposed to be Marines. You will put up with it, or pay the price.*

PFC Olivieri and PFC Ravino wouldn't have liked what the sergeant was thinking, if they could have read his mind. *Boots,* a not-so-flattering reference to recruits going through boot camp, was a term they heard so often at Parris Island. Once they graduated from that torture, they no longer were *Boots.* But salty NCOs with time in the Corps weren't shy about thinking of untested replacements as *Boots* in a war zone.

Like it or not, Olivieri and Ravino, you're here and there's not enough sympathy to go around for all you Boot replacements.

The two friends had reached the First Tank Battalion CP of the First Marine Division, Eighth U.S. Army Korea. They were now part of the massive United Nations military force brought together within the last year to do something about marauding North

Korean People's Army and the insurgence of the Communist Chinese Forces.

Welcome to the miserable Korean War, Marines.

"Get on that truck over there. You two are going to Flames."

Ravino and Olivieri looked at each other, now beginning to doubt very much that they were going to be in a tank outfit.

"What the hell does that mean?" Ravino muttered to his buddy. "Flames?"

"We going to the infantry? We going to be carrying those flame guns with all that fuel on our backs?"

"Oh, great," Olivieri cracked. "It's not bad enough they just made us tankers; now we're going to infantry, and up on the line at that."

If there is one thing that is drilled, shouted, pushed, stomped, and firmly imbedded into every Marine recruit's skinned head, it's the creed: Every Marine is an infantryman—first and foremost. It is his basic education in boot camp, and unequivocal primary training once out from under a drill instructor's oppressive and stringent presence.

You are 0300—*infantry*. You never get rid of that 0300 MOS (Military Occupational Specialty). Even if a Marine gets specialized training in tanks, or LVTs, or artillery, or cook school, and picks up another primary MOS, he still holds that 0300. The Corps doesn't care if you drive a tank. If the Corps decides it needs another gravel-crunching foot Marine, you have been trained to be a gravel-crunching foot Marine, *first*.

With that fact firmly implanted in Olivieri's mind, he had every reason, under the circumstances, to think he and his buddy were heading for an infantry line company. He also had not-so-pleasant visions they'd be charging up hills with five-gallon expeditionary cans—full of lethal napalm—strapped to their backs, and hunks of pipe in their hands that shoot flaming jelly at Gooks.

"Well," he thought aloud, "we did get infantry training . . ."

"Screw it," Ravino snapped, "I'm so miserable, I could care less."

Standing in the rain in front of another sergeant who tells them they're "going to Flames," Ravino and Olivieri just assumed that those 1811 cards didn't mean a damn thing. They both figured they were the newest infantry cherries being sent out to mush mud and swallow dust somewhere along the front lines in Western Korea.

As ordered, they climbed into another six-by. Oddly, they were the only two Marines aboard.

"Well, Vin," Olivieri cracked, "at least we have a truck to ourselves."

"Ha, ha," Ravino mocked.

Olivieri hung the name "Vin" (as in "Vinny") on his friend a long time ago. Ravino never asked why; he just thought it might have been because of their Italian heritage and accepted it as a token of their friendship.

As the canopied six-by headed north, bouncing and sloshing up a very bad dirt road, Olivieri turned to his buddy with worry in his voice.

"Vin, what the hell are they doing sending us to the infantry . . . and flame-throwers?"

Ravino, also feeling concern, could only think about being out in the middle of nowhere, exposed to the enemy while squirting fire from that damn contraption.

"Guys that carry those flame guns . . . as soon as they open up, they're a quick target."

"Vin, what the hell were we picked for?" Olivieri asked again, now aware Ravino looked scared.

"I don't know, and I don't give a shit at this point."

The ride bumped and dragged on for thirty or forty minutes, before the truck finally chugged to a halt. When it did stop, the two young Marines saw flashes of light in the sky further north. It was artillery, and the sound was becoming much louder. They were convinced they were about to join the infantry with a very good chance of getting their asses shot off.

"What the hell did we take LVT training for," Olivieri asked rhetorically, "if we're going to carry napalm on our backs and crawl up hills to squirt fire at Gooks?"

That rainy September night near the western front, just above what had become popularly known as the 38th Parallel, the two Boston Marines weren't quite sure what to expect.

"What was that river we crossed, Vinny?" asked Olivieri.

"I don't know, but it was a long pontoon bridge," Ravino replied. The river happened to be the Imjin Gang, and the bridge—the Spoonbill Bridge—would be one Ravino and Olivieri would cross many times over the next twelve months.

The truck began to move again.

It took the six-by about fifteen more minutes, twisting and turning along the muddy road before it finally started to slow down. They could see tents, and make out some old tanks not too far away. Their consternation was growing as the truck pulled up to the side of one of the large squad tents.

"Grab your gear," the driver said. "End of the line."

As they hopped over the tailgate, they realized this was some kind of a tank outfit, but they still couldn't figure out what the hell was going on. It was late, and they had been riding in the dark for hours. They were pooped, wet, and thoroughly confused.

"You two, Olivieri and Ravino," ordered a Lieutenant who looked a little pissed off—maybe because these two guys had disturbed his sleep. But his tone soon mellowed. "Come into the tent," he said, motioning to the crude wooden doorway on the large squad tent that had been converted to a mess hall. "Have some hot coffee, if you want."

"No, sir," Ravino replied. "We just as soon dry off and hit the rack, if that's possible. We're drenched."

"Okay by me," the lieutenant said.

"Well, this is tank country, but 'Flames?'" Ravino questioned his buddy, still not getting the connection to the last word. PFCs Jerry Ravino and Jimmy Olivieri were just another pair of befuddled Marines who had completed a confusing circuitous route to the Flame Platoon, Headquarters Company, First Tank Battalion, First Marine Division.

"Sir, we still don't know where or what unit we're in."

"Fill you in with all the scoop in the morning."

Hell, thought Ravino, same old shit.

The confusion and consternation that rattled Ravino and Olivieri was S.O.P.—the Marine Corps way.

Yours is not to reason why . . .

The proud legacy with which they were being entrusted that autumn of 1952 had been etched far and wide since the Flame Platoon first entered combat on the beaches of Wolmi-do Island at the end of Flying Fish Channel outside the monstrous seawalls of Inchon Harbor.

It was an unlikely assortment of call-ups from neighborhood Marine Corps Reserve outfits—many of them veterans of World War II—who began recording the unit's history. They wrote it while rolling through Wolmi-do, the port city of Inchon, and into the street fighting of Seoul. They cut it into ice and snow in the treacherous subzero ranges of the Taebaek Mountains during the breakout from the Chosin Reservoir. When ice thawed into mud, and the mud turned into choking dust the next spring, they wrote new chapters in villages at Hoensong, Hong Chon, the Hwachon Reservoir. Replacements who arrived as the war entered its second year, made a notation on the Kanmubong Ridge in the notoriously ragged mountains of East Central Korea.

Ravino, Olivieri, and their buddies in those Flame Dragons would accept that little-known but proud legacy in the third and final year of the war. And they would inscribe their own bloody niche—perhaps the bloodiest—when they took four flame tanks into Operation Clambake, a mission that was anything but a picnic. It was a deal gone bad, deadly bad.

Their introduction to flame tanks was not unlike that which greeted most of the guys who were assigned to this specialized outfit. Like the two young men from Boston, the majority of Marines coming into the Flame Platoon knew very little, if anything at all, about these uniquely-rigged M4A3E8 Sherman tanks. It was hands-on training, often in the face of the enemy in the early going.

Even young tankers who went through the training at Los Flores Tank Park in Camp Pendleton were told little, if anything, about the flame tank. If they were lucky enough to see the movie *Halls of Montezuma,* which was filmed at Pendleton around 1950, there was a scene showing a tank firing flame into a hill.

If the Marine Corps ever put out a manual on the flame tank, it never got to Korea. It would be hard to find a Flame Tanker who ever saw one in the Land of the Morning Calm. Guys became Flame Tankers learning on the job, taught by NCOs—mostly corporals and sergeants. And when PFCs became NCOs, they continued to pass that knowledge on to other replacements coming in under them.

But on that miserable night in September 1952, PFCs Ravino and Olivieri could only *try* to make sense of all consternation that boiled within them, like so many of their predecessors who had made it to the Flame Platoon in similar confusion. They only knew it was the Marine Corps way.

Yours is not to reason why . . . yours is to do . . . if need be, die!

What the Hell Is Korea?!

The strange word puzzled Jack Carty, a twenty-one-year-old sportswriter, when he first heard it. He was walking by the wire room cubicles near the editorial room of the *Courier-Post* newspaper in Camden, New Jersey, when he noticed a couple of editors hovering over the clattering United Press and International News Service teletype machines.

Normally, editors didn't bother to wander away from their desks to monitor teletype machines unless something big was brewing. The wire rooms were usually the domain of copyboys, whose many jobs included stripping sheets of news emanating all around the world, from the dozen machines and, then, distributing the parcels to the wire editor.

If the communiqué was preceded with the word *BULLETIN,* then it meant someone on the other end of the wire considered they were sending an important piece of news. It could be the start of a major story, or an update on one previously sent.

It was late Sunday afternoon, the 25th of June, 1950.

"What's going on, Mr. Webb?" Carty asked as he stopped at the doorway of the partially glassed-in enclosure. Paul Webb was chief of the copy desk, a brilliant man of very few words, possibly because of his small hair lip. He was tall, somewhat handsome, with a well-groomed crop of snow-white hair. More than anything, he was a good teacher to young men aspiring to be newspapermen.

"Korea," he said matter-of-factly.

"What the hell is Korea?" Carty quizzed.

After a look of disgust seasoned editors often fix on young reporters who ask stupid questions, Webb briefly explained that it was a small country in the Far East, near China.

"Looks like there's going to be another war," he added quietly.

A couple of hundred miles down the east coast at Camp Lejeune in North Carolina, Len Martin was getting his first taste of the real Marine Corps that Sunday afternoon when the word *Korea* began coming up in bull sessions. Martin, a lean seventeen-year-old from Forest Park, Illinois, had been enticed by a couple of classmates to enlist and join them in the Reserves during his senior year in high school. This was his first summer camp at the legendary Marine Corps advanced training center.

Martin had graduated from Proviso High School in Maywood only a couple of weeks earlier. That he might end up in a war was not what he had in mind the day he looked at pictures of his friends taken at a previous summer camp and thought it looked like a good idea.

"They were dressed in combat gear, rifles, helmets, and all that stuff," Martin said. "They looked pretty good and talked me into joining their outfit. At first my mother did not want to sign for me, but my father talked her into it." On 10 October 1949, he attended preliminary training at the Navy Pier in Chicago and eventually joined Able Company of the 9th Infantry Battalion in Cicero, Illinois. Once-a-week meetings and drill were okay. Then came his first summer camp and that historic day.

"It wasn't long before the regulars stationed at Lejeune were taunting the Reserves," Martin said. "They were saying that we would be back in thirty days. They didn't know how close to right they were." And little did many of those old salts realize they would be long gone from North Carolina ahead of the young reserves. Active duty Marines from all over the world would be converging on Camp Pendleton in Oceanside, California, as part of the "Modern Minuteman" force. They would be the backbone of First Marine Division that was hurriedly being brought up to combat-ready strength, destined for Korea, and one of the most epic campaigns in Marine Corps history.

Not too much to PFC Martin's surprise, once he realized the gravity of the situation unraveling on the other side of the world, he too was to become more than just a weekend Marine. He would be among many Reserves and young recruits to fill the much-needed Replacement Drafts that would steadily supplement the needs of the Fleet Marine Force's newly committed division.

Early in November, eighteen-year-old Len Martin arrived in Korea with the First Replacement Draft and was assigned to the First Tank Battalion. Just after Thanksgiving Day 1950, Chinese Communist Forces came storming through the Taebek Mountain range after deftly sneaking across the Yalu River. Martin and the First Tank Battalion, along with the rest of the trapped First Marine Division, would be involved in one of the most historic chapters in Marine Corps history.

Meanwhile, Jack Carty was biding his time. He loved sports and thought he was living a dream, getting paid $32.50 a week to write about them. More important, he had met Pat, the girl of his dreams, and they were about to become engaged. He was in no hurry to leave all of this because some Communists wanted to start another war.

Carty would wait for his draft notice to arrive before putting the black cover on his worn Underwood typewriter for the next three years. He was following his preconceived plan to enlist in the Marine Corps only after he got the postcard summoning him to the draft board. Early that October, while Martin was on his way to Korea with the First Replacement Draft for Korea, Carty was on a train heading to Parris Island. He would reach Korea the following summer and would learn the intricacies of flame tanks from his new tank commander, Cpl. Len Martin.

But there was an awful lot being changed in the world before the two strangers would meet and become good friends. It was a whole new thing for both of the young men all because that one word—*Korea*—had spun its influence on the world, but mostly in the United States. Not many men, or women, who were to become involved in the Korean War ever heard the word before 25 June 1950. When they found out what it was, there was a quizzical reaction:

"Where the hell is this place?"

Hundreds of thousands of guys would find out a lot sooner than they ever dreamed. For many, it would be a bad dream come true. For more than 36,000 Americans, it was a deadly nightmare.

Most of those called to fight the Korean War were Great Depression babies, born around the time the country plunged into a financial abyss from which it could not start digging out until Franklin D. Roosevelt got things rolling in the mid-1930s. FDR did his thing in the first of his historic four terms as president of the United States. But it took time, and most of the kids only knew parents and neighbors struggling to keep food on the table and clothes on their backs. Those kids thrived on peanut butter and jelly sandwiches. Steak was a strange delicacy seldom tasted. Cardboard cereal boxes often were cut to the shape of their feet, slipped inside hand-me-down shoes to cover holes in the soles. They didn't know that was tough times. They just thought it was the way things should be, and went about growing up.

Then, a lunatic named Hitler began stirring things up in Europe, eventually pushing nearly the entire world into a hideous war. Kids of the '30s weren't concerned with much more than playing cowboys and Indians and learning times-tables before that happened. Then came Pearl Harbor, and the sneak attack by Japan sent America hurtling into World War II. The Depression Kids were by that time ten, eleven, twelve, and thirteen years old, mowing lawns and shoveling snow, trying to earn a dime or two to get them into the Saturday afternoon matinee at the local movie house

But they watched and prayed as their dads, big brothers, and older guys on the block went off to strange places like Guadalcanal, North Africa, Sicily, Normandy, Bastogne, and the Solomon Islands for two, three, or more years at a time.

That's when the kids at home got an education in patriotism that would last a lifetime. There was a "war effort." They collected papers and scrap metal and saved pennies to buy ten-cent war stamps one at a time, then paste them in a book until they got $18.75 to buy a War Bond.

Everything was rationed. There were ration stamps for food and gasoline. There were air-raid warnings. Depression Kids listened with their parents to the nightly news about the war, as Lowell Thomas, Edward R. Murrow, H. B. Caltenborn, and Walter Winchell relayed history in the making through the old Philco and GE tabletop radios. Kids watched snippets of the real war in the newsreels at Saturday matinees in the town movie-house.

It was that patriotism that fueled the unquestionable response they gave when Korea called.

In high school, they really began to recognize girls and slow-danced to the crooning of Sinatra, Crosby, and Vaughn Monroe. They traded knickers and crazy designs on knee-high socks for peg pants with baggy knees and tight cuffs. It was the zoot-suit era, and they learned to perfect the jitterbug to the swinging music of Miller, Dorsey, Basie. They were growing into manhood, ever mindful they might be called to follow their brothers into the service.

Then, the atomic bomb brought World War II to a scorching halt, and everyone figured no one would be nutty enough to start another disaster like it.

Times became good. The Depression Kids were finding their way in the outside world: jobs, a few in college, possible careers, thinking about getting married, and starting families. There still was Selective Service for guys shedding their teens, and Reserves for a lot of veterans coming home from Europe and the Pacific. Little did those Reserves know how important a role they would play a few years down the road. That's when they took bewildered draftees and young enlistees under wing, in a not-so-tranquil place known as the Land of the Morning Calm.

Like Len Martin, still feeling very patriotic and impressed by the heroics of the guys coming out of the service in his hometown of Forest Park, Illinois, many followed them into the Reserves. Others, like Jack Carty, decided to just wait until the "Draft Notice" came in the mail. Then they'd decide what to do about a military commitment.

But when that strange word—*Korea*—jumped into their lives, their decisions became priority. It was their turn to step up and be counted by their country.

And, thank God, enough of those Vets from World War II were still around—however reluctantly—to provide help along the way until the Depression Kids got their feet wet, frozen, blistered, and often mangled. They were taking on Communism, front and center, in the first hot battle of the Cold War: Korea.

As a nation, or the world, nobody was ready for it. But it didn't take long before this newer generation of military got its ass in gear.

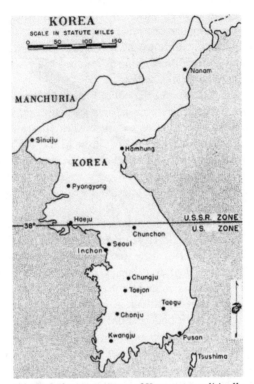

The little-known country of Korea was politically divided at the 38th Parallel when troops from the Communist North stormed into the democratic South on 25 June 1950, starting a bloody war that would last three years. (Map Copy Courtesy of Marine Corps Operations in Korea [MCOinK])

Bitter Fighting in Korea

When the North Korean People's Army stormed over the 38th Parallel during the rainy early morning hours of 25 June 1950, the western world was in a peaceful slumber, never dreaming anything like this could happen.

But it did, and we paid dearly for it, particularly here in the United States.

There was utter chaos on this 550-mile-long Korean peninsula, which stretched from the Manchurian border down to the Yellow Sea.

The North Koreans ran right over the Republic of Korea army in the south, and small U.S. Army units that were rushed there from Japan a few days later were ill-prepared to face such well-trained and experienced solders as the NKPA. The only thing Gen. Douglas MacArthur, the Far East Commander, had to throw in the way of the Communist juggernaut were scrounged-up draftees, many of them malcontents, who had been on post–World War II garrison duty with very little, if any, combat training. When those Army troops were pulled together in Japan and sent to Korea, they were so ill-prepared and poorly equipped, it was pathetic.

That version of the U.S. Army was not able to acquit itself very proudly.

Young kids in Marine Corps boot camps at Parris Island and San Diego were hearing horror stories about the Army in Korea. There were accounts of how the Doggies (Marine Corps terminology of the Army's Dogfaces) "bugged out [ran away] during combat, leaving their weapons and dying buddies to fend for themselves."

Boots who were being saturated with talk of esprit de corps and the legacy of the United States Marine Corps couldn't understand this. It was drilled into Marine recruits that no matter what the situation, Marines never left their wounded or dead, or operable weapons. They always tried to bring out their dead and wounded, even if it meant more casualties might be taken. That may be irrational thinking to someone never experiencing military life, but it sure was comforting to a Marine knowing that if he was in trouble, some other Marine was going to do his damnedest to try to get him out of it.

Marines in training for Korea had only the word of drill instructors, and later, hardened combat-tested NCOs at Camp Pendleton, passing along the skinny on what was happening in the war. Some of the new fuzzheads, with natural skepticism, thought it may only be part of the bull that D.I.'s were required to spread. However, after talking to the first vets returning from Korea and starting to fill the ranks of instructors, the young Marines were convinced it was common knowledge that the Army had nothing near the combat discipline and esprit de corps that was the backbone of the Marine Corps.

Soldiers caught in the initial surge by the North Koreans couldn't really be held responsible for what seemed like cowardice, because they dropped their weapons and ran, leaving their wounded to fall in the hands of the North Koreans. They just had no training for this sort of thing. Compounding the infamy was the fact the bodies of many dead Americans in the early part of the war were never recovered and brought back home to proper resting places.

Following World War II, the military was cut back considerably. Training, at least in the Army, became anything but what it took to be combat-ready. The Marine Corps manpower also was trimmed drastically, but as was custom, there was no relaxing of training procedures. Most Marines who remained active were kept combat-ready.

Donald Knox, who wrote *The Korean War: Pusan to Chosin: An Oral History*, made this observation:

> The United Nations force was comprised of four understrength, ill-equipped American Divisions stationed in Japan. Its World War II equipment was old and worn. The men who served in it, although enlistees, enjoyed the good life provided by a rapidly recovering Japanese economy. Occupation Duty consisted of troop formation and very little military training. With most enlistees, there were disciplinary problems.
>
> Meanwhile, the North Korean People's Army (NKPA) was trained and equipped by the Russians. Soon the NKPA was a large, vigorously trained, aggressive military force well supplied with Russian small arms, artillery, armor and propeller-driven fighter aircraft. Nearly all of its commissioned and non-commissioned officers were combat veterans of the Chinese Civil War.

It was no wonder U.N. forces were nearly pushed off the Korean peninsula. By the end of July, 1950, they were backed into the Pusan Perimeter, a small corner on the southern tip of Korea—a pocket of merely ninety miles north to south and sixty miles east to west from the Sea of Japan to the Yellow Sea.

> There were no Marine units of any size in the Far East at the time. On 2 July, seven days after the NKPA crossed the 38th Parallel, Gen. Douglas MacArthur, Commander in Chief of the Far East, requested the immediate dispatch of a Marine Regimental Combat Team [RCT] with supporting air to the Far East. It was built around two main West Coast Units at Camp Pendleton—the 5th Marines [Regiment] and the Marine Aircraft Group 33. They became the 1st Provisional Marine Brigade. On 14 July they were on their way to Korea. (Marine Corps Operations in Korea [MCOinK], Volume I)

By August 2, the Brigade was debarking at Pusan, its waterfront a scene of bedlam as the Marines offloaded under searchlights. The first combat unit shipped from the United States was about to put its collective finger into the leaking dike of U.N. forces holding the Pusan Perimeter. Two days later, segments of the Brigade were sent into the lines at Changwon, west of Pusan. The North Koreans had met their match, their advance had reached its extremity once the Brigade got into action. The 5th Marines would be a major part of the first offensive launched against the NKPA.

It was infantry, good fighting Marine Corps infantry, that MacArthur wanted in Korea because he knew it would be much better trained than the current forces he had in his command at the time. But the Brigade was only the leading edge of the Marine force he needed. It was a full division that he demanded from the Joint Chiefs of Staff so that he could launch his historic Inchon Landing.

And that's what he got less than two months after the 5th Marines landed in Korea. The task was monumental, but the Marine Corps pulled it off, and that's where the Flame Platoon, First Tank Battalion, First Marine Division made its debut.

Andrew Geer, in his book *New Breed: The Story of the U. S. Marines in Korea*, explained just how the 1st Marine Division was put into operation:

> Between the twenty-ninth of June and the twenty-eighth of July, General MacArthur sent six dispatches to the Joint Chiefs of Staff relative to the employment of Marines in Korea. As the military situation worsened, these dispatches became more urgent in tone until the final one demanded the use of commercial shipping to get the Marines to the Battle Area if government transportation were not available.
>
> For the second time in less than a decade, Marine reserves were hastily called back to

active duty. Fifteen per cent of the Marine landing force at Inchon was made up of civilian [reserve] Marines. This percentage grew to nearly fifty per cent in the battle of the Chosin Reservoir.

. . . Reservists in the twenty-four to thirty age group . . . men [who] had been in the previous war and had been released from active duty in 1946. . . .

At the outbreak of hostilities the strength of the regular Marine Corps was slightly more than seventy-four thousand. The Corps was ordered to send a division [to Korea] of twenty-three thousand and an air arm of nearly four thousand. In addition it had to continue to maintain Marine detachments [all over the world]. . . .

The Marine Corps fulfilled its obligations by organizing, training and sending to the Korean War a hard-hitting mixture of regulars and Reserves. . . .

After bringing the Brigade to strength, the 1st Marine Division had slightly more than three thousand officers and men remaining. In the next 27 days the division would have to form two war-strength rifle regiments, two battalions of artillery, a tank and motor transport battalion, a shore party and other supporting units.

Integrated into the First Tank Battalion was the newly conceived Flame Platoon, the first time in the history of the Marine Corps that such a unit would be made available to work in conjunction with gun company tanks and infantry battalions and companies. The tanks were rushed to Camp Pendleton by rail on flat cars from the Marine Corps Supply Depot in Barstow, California.

Geer further elaborated:

Between July 31 and August 10, the division joined 6,831 men from the 2nd Marine Division [stationed Camp Lejeune], 812 from the 1st Replacement Draft [mostly raw recruits who had completed infantry training], 3,630 regulars from posts and stations throughout the world and over 10,000 officers and men from the Organized Reserves.

Five days after the brigade had sailed, President Truman authorized the calling of Organized Reserve units. Ten days later, Reserve battalions . . . and companies [from California cities and Phoenix] reported at Camp Pendleton—the Minute Men of 1950. . . .

In the classification of Reserves pouring into Pendleton, two categories were set up: Combat-ready and Noncombat-ready. Combat-ready was defined as "Reservists who had been members of the Organized Reserve two years and had attended one summer camp and seventy-two drills," or "two summer camps and thirty-two drills," or who were veterans with more than ninety days service in the Marine Corps.' Noncombat-ready applied to all Reservists who did not meet these standards. This latter category was further divided into a Recruit Class for those who had been in the Organized Reserve less than one year or who had poor drill attendance records. . . .

PFC Leonard Martin, fresh from his first summer camp at Camp Lejeune, North Carolina, fell into the Recruit Class because he had only been in the Reserves 10 months and had never gone through boot camp.

Geer concluded:

The true nature of this accomplishment [organizing a combat-ready force], unprecedented in the annals of military history, becomes increasingly clear when it is realized the 1st Marine Division, with only three thousand as a cadre, reached a war strength in excess of twenty-three thousand officers and men and landed at Inchon in a period of fifty-three days [45 days since the initial Reservists arrived at Pendleton on 31 July].

Able Company of the 9th Infantry Battalion Reserve unit from Cicero, Illinois, had returned from its summer camp early in July. On 21 July, three days before his 18th birthday, PFC Leonard Martin, USMCR, received a "warning notice" that he would be activated.

"We were told that 'anyone who wanted out,' it was his last chance," Martin said. "Most of us were gung ho and never considered dropping out."

On 26 July, the Cicero Reserves were told officially that the unit would be activated on 8 August.

Meanwhile, Camp Pendleton was a twenty-four-hour-a-day, seven-day-a-week beehive of activity, and among all this organized confusion, the Flame Platoon, First Tank Battalion, grew to life.

As this was happening, political sparring was running rampant in Washington D.C. President Harry S. Truman was taking some heat for thinking about getting the United States involved in the Korean mess.

Truman became president of the United States when Franklin Delano Roosevelt died suddenly in May of 1945. The haberdasher from Independence, Missouri, was reelected over Thomas E. Dewey in an upset in 1948. Truman had been tested before, having sanctioned the use of the atomic bomb on Japan to end World War II. Now, he had the makings of another war on his hands.

Harry Truman was not very popular with the troops—Marines, at least. He was a World War I officer and once told a fellow officer that he thought Marines were a lot of publicity hounds. Things like that, Marines do not forget. Although many Gyrenes didn't think much of him at the time, the President did keep his wits about him when it came to handling the situation in Korea. Once committed to the task at hand, he was not about to let it escalate into World War III.

In the early stages of the war, when it was very difficult for anyone, including the experts, to decipher ramifications of North Korea's plunge across the 38th Parallel, Truman was attempting to decide how deep he wanted to take the United States into the conflict. What he was attempting to do was force the United Nations—then in its toddler years after coming to life following World War II—to take charge. He felt the U.N. should make some major decisions and become the world peacemaker, or enforcer of peace, that it was designed to be. This he managed to do, but it was the United States which wound up taking on the brunt of the *enforcing* in Korea.

What was at stake, at one extreme, was World War III. Just a little less significant was an armed confrontation with the Soviet Union, and that could have been set off in any number of ways during the decades of post–World War II Cold War.

While outlining plans for committing a sizable U.S. military force, Truman, on 29 June 1950 (four days after the invasion by the North Korean People's Army), committed a serious foot-in-mouth blunder which would follow him to his grave. It was the infamous *Police Action* statement attributed to him. And it would be a soiled label put on the Korean War for the next three years.

Police Action was not at all popular with Marines, or any other unit of the military. There was no mistaking, what was brewing in Korea was a full-scale war. But in the confusing days of late June 1950, when no one seemed to have good intelligence on what was transpiring, few outside of the simmering peninsula were taking the North Koreans very seriously. There was talk that it could be handled without too much trouble. Someone brought up the term *Police Action,* and it was Truman who got stuck with it, although there is a consensus that he was suckered into it.

In Richard Whelan's *Drawing the Line: The Korean War, 1950-1953:*

With politicians debating the pros and cons of major U.S. intervention in Korea on 28 June 1950, Senator William Knowland, who was known to be one of Truman's most critical adversaries, articulated on the floor of the Senate:

"The action the government is taking is a police action against a violation of the law of nation and the Charter of The United Nations."

Seizing on the key phrase that would come to haunt Truman, a reporter at the press conference [of 29 June 1950] asked the president "would it be correct to call this a police action under the United Nations?"

"Yes," answered Truman, "that was exactly what it amounted to."

This was not Truman, but a man (Knowland) who would again come to be one of his most virulent critics who first used—and in an approving sense—the term "police action" to characterize what would become the fifth most costly war in U.S. history.

This was the atmosphere in Washington while young men all over the country were being mobilized to fight a war in a place few of them had ever heard of.

Despite logistical problems that could have confounded the keenest of minds, the First Marine Division was ready to go in forty-five days.

1st Provisional Marine Brigade

". . . Most urgently request reconsideration of decision with reference to First Marine division. It is an absolutely vital development to accomplish a decisive stroke and if not made available will necessitate a much more costly and long operational effort both in blood and expense.

"It is essential the Marine Division arrive by 10 September 1950 as requested. While it would be unwise for me to attempt this message to give in detail the planned use of this unit I cannot emphasize too strongly my belief of the complete urgency of my request. There can be no demand for its potential use elsewhere that can equal the urgency of the immediate battle mission contemplated for It."

"Signed MacArthur"
Gen. Douglas Mac Arthur, Commander in Chief Far East
(Marine Corps Operations in Korea, Volume I)

It took one day after this message was received by the Joint Chiefs of Staff on 21 July 1950, to get the pace of the mobilization of the First Marine Division at Camp Pendleton quickly upgraded from rout step to double time. The United Nations supreme commander wanted the Marines at full battle strength for a 15 September landing at Inchon.

MacArthur already had the First Provisional Marine Brigade heading his way with all intentions of holding it in Japan, unless circumstances in Korea changed. Change they did. United Nation forces were about to become wedged in that ninety-by-sixty-mile perimeter north and west of Pusan, with a good chance they could be pushed into the Sea of Japan. Before the Brigade had a chance to get a glimpse of Mount Fugi, its convoy was diverted around Japan and sent directly to Korea.

By the time the USS *Pickaway* sailed into Pusan Harbor, the 5th Marine Regiment, under command of Lt. Col. Raymond L. Murray and the main element of the 1st Provisional Marine Brigade, had been informed that his troops should be ready to hit the ground running.

Brig. Gen. Edward A. Craig, the Brigade's commanding general who took the unit's advance party to Korea on 25 July, had been meeting with Lt. Gen. Walton H. Walker, commanding the U.S. Eighth Army, and the other United Nation forces which were being overrun by the North Korean People's Army.

The U.N.'s front was collapsing 60 miles west of Pusan as the Marines, including Able Company of the First Tank Battalion, began debarking late in the afternoon of 2 August. A day later, the Marines were plugged into the line west of Chingdon-ni, and it wasn't long before the lead element of the First Marine Division was doing what it was sent to do in the Land of the Morning Calm: help turn the tide of the war.

It was on 6 August, after the Brigade had been attached to the Army's 25th Infantry Division, that elements of the 5th Marines became engaged in combat.

Shortly after midnight, the 3d Battalion received an unexpected message which precipitated the first Marine infantry action of the war. Colonel (John H.) Michaelis (USA) radioed Taplett and passed on a directive from 25th Division, ordering the Marine battalion to commit immediately one reinforced platoon for the defense of Hill 342. He explained that this unit was to relieve a beleaguered Army company being slowly eaten away in a private war of attrition. Taplett informed the regimental commander that he could ill afford to spare 1 of his 6 rifle platoons, but was told in return that (Maj.) General (William B.) Kean (USA) had ordered 342 held at all costs.

Tagged with the ominous sounding name "Yaban-san" by Koreans, this hill resembles a huge molar whose roots rise from the MSR west of Chindong-ni and lead to a tremendous mass about 2,000 yards north of the road. There the ground climbs sharply, culminating in a peak 1,100 feet high. Beyond, a long saddle extends a few thousand yards northwest, connecting 342 with a height of almost 2,000 feet. The latter was a stronghold of NKPA 6th Division elements, making a determined bid to carry 342 and cut the MSR.

Assigned the mission of making the Brigade's first ground contact was young (2nd) Lieutenant (John H.) Cahill of Company G. His 1st Platoon was reinforced with a machinegun squad and SCR-300 operator before he led it from 3/5's perimeter.

Moving westward on the MSR, the platoon reached Michaelis' CP, located near the bridges south of Hill 99 . . . This headquarters was situated just north of the road, on the tip of 342's eastern "root," 1 of the 2 long ridges leading to the hill itself.

The Marine officer was told to relieve the Army company on the summit and hold the hill with his platoon . . . A few hundred yards along the way, the (Army) guide discovered that he had miscalculated in the darkness. More time was lost while the platoon descended to resume the correct route.

As the men threaded their way along the unseen trail, a few enemy artillery shells burst nearby. The column reached the end of the valley separating the two long spurs of 342, and a volley of rifle fire cracked in the darkness. Two of Cahill's Marines were painfully wounded.

Since the column was still in friendly territory, the guide advised Cahill not to climb 342 until dawn shed light on the mystery. It was then 0500, 7 August, and the Marine platoon had marched 3 miles from its original position.

Shortly after first light, it was discovered that soldiers of the 2d Battalion, 5th RCT, had fired on the Marines, not realizing that friendly units were moving within the area.

As the sun rose in a cloudless sky, Cahill took the lead . . .

The platoon made good progress at the outset, but the heat became stifling; and all the while the slopes of 342 stretched ahead like a continuous wall. Stumbling, gasping for breath, soaked with perspiration, every Marine reached the point at which he barely managed to drag himself up the steep incline. There were choked curses as men gained a few feet, only to slip and fall back even farther.

Water discipline collapsed as canteens were quickly emptied. Marines began to drop along the slope, some unconscious, others doubled over and retching. The tactical formation of the platoon became ragged, but Cahill and his NCO's urged the men upward. Accompanied by Sergeant Lee Buettner, Cahill set out to contact the Army company commander on the summit and reconnoiter the area. Seventy-five yards from the top, he was fired on from the eastern slopes. Since he was in sight of the Army troops on the crest, it was obvious that the North Korean People's Army had officially greeted the 1st Provisional Marine Brigade. (MCOinK, Volume I)

There were no flame tanks among the reinforced Able Company of the First Tank Battalion that was sent to Korea with the 5th Marines and the Brigade. But if there had been, the crews certainly would have had the upper hand on tankers in the gun company.

"There was not enough time in most instances for weapons familiarization training. Company A of the 1st Tank Battalion had been accustomed to the M4A3 Medium tank with either the 75-mm. gun or the 105-mm. howitzer. Activated on 7 July for service with the Brigade, the unit was equipped with M-26 'Pershing' tanks and 90-mm. guns. Captain Gearl M. English, the commanding officer, managed to snatch 1 day in which to take his men to the range with 2 of the new machines. Each gunner and loader was limited to 2 rounds, and the 90-mm. guns were never fired again until they were taken into combat in Korea. (MCOinK, Volume I)

Able Company did have two M4A3E8 Sherman tanks mounted with dozer blades under command of S/Sgt. Charles J. "Tiny" Rhoades, and he worked them well in concert with the gun tanks, not only as earth movers, but using their main armament of 105mm howitzers and their machine guns. He had the distinction of being among the first Marine tankers to take on the vaunted Russian T-34 tank.

The Third Platoon of Able Company Pershing M26s, along with Rhoades Sherman dozer, were attached to the Second Battalion, 5th Marines near Obong-ni Ridge and Observatory Hill. On 16 August, they were sitting behind the MLR refueling and taking on ammunition when word was passed that four T-34s were coming down the road in front of the 5th Marines after 2nd Bat jumped off to lend support to an assault on the Ridge.

The T-34 had been a major weapon used by the Russians in turning back the Germans when they invaded the Soviet Union early in World War II. It was mobile, fast with long range, and a powerful 85mm cannon. When North Korea fell under the Communist control, its army was not only trained by the Russians but equipped with the all kinds of Soviet material—including the T-34.

As the North Koreans ran rampant down through the south, the Russian-made tank was gaining quite a reputation. But before the First Tank Battalion arrived, the T-34 tank wasn't coming up against much competition. That changed when the Marines and Able Company, under the command of 2nd Lt. Granville "G.G." Sweet, came on the scene.

Sweet was in the turret of A-31, and Rhoades was standing in the left hatch of A-43, the lead Sherman dozer, when they received reports the four enemy tanks were on the main road leading to 5th Marines positions.

Before Sweet and his Pershings could get at them, however, Marine Corsairs dove into the fray and knocked out the fourth T-34 in line.

The first three tanks came on alone, passed Finger and Obong-ni Ridges, and approached the road bend at Hill 125.

Preparing a reception for the T-34's were the 1st 75-mm. Recoilless Gun Platoon on Observation Hill, and the rocket section of 1/5's antitank assault platoon on Hill 125. As the first enemy tank reached the bend, it took a hit in the right track from a 3.5" rocket. Shooting wildly, the black hulk continued until its left track and front armor were blasted by Second Lieutenant Paul R. Fields' 75's. The enemy vehicle burst into flame as it wobbled around the curve and came face to face with Technical Sergeant Cecil R. Fullerton's M–26.

Still aimlessly firing its 85-mm. rifle and machinegun, the T-34 took two quick hits from the Marine tank's 90-mm. gun and exploded. . . .

The second T-34 charged toward the bend, taking a 3.5 rocket hit from Company A's assault squad. Weaving crazily around the curve, with its right track damaged, the cripple was struck in the gas tank by a rocket from 1/5's assault section before meeting the fury of Field's recoilless rifles. It lurched to a stop off the road behind the first tank, and the 85-mm. gun fired across the valley into the blue yonder.

By this time a second M–26 had squeezed next to that of Fullerton on the narrow firing line, and the two Marine tanks blasted the T-34 with six 90-mm. Shells. (MCOinK, Volume I)

That was Sweet's A-31, which also got its licks in on the North Korean Tank. But those T-34s were tough, although they didn't seem to be handled well by the NKPA soldiers. Sweet, meanwhile, had radioed Rhoades to take his Sherman dozer to the top of a small hill overlooking the road.

Miraculously, the Communist vehicle kept on shooting, although its fire was directionless. Marine armor poured in seven more rounds, which ripped through the turret and exploded the hull. (MCOinK, Volume I)

Chalk up part of the kill to Tiny Rhoades and his old reliable Sherman M4A3E8 dozer, first cousin of the flame tank.

The third T-34 raced around the road bend to a stop behind the blazing hulks of the first two. Marine tanks, recoilless rifles, and rockets ripped into it with a thundering salvo. The enemy tank shuddered, then erupted in a violent explosion and died. (MCOinK, Volume I)

"That was a tremendous explosion," said Sweet.

Thus the Brigade shattered the myth of the T-34 in five flaming minutes. Not only Corsairs and M-26's, but also every antitank weapon organic to Marine infantry had scored an assist in defeating the Communist armor. (MCOinK, Volume I)

"We were pretty fresh out there when we had the first encounter with a T-34," Sweet said.

But if anyone knew what war was all about, it was G.G. Sweet. He had enlisted in the Marines after going through Conservation Corps Camp as a youth. He was one of the storied China Marines and survived the attack at Pearl Harbor. A gun captain on the USS *Nevada*, he was wounded and blown into the harbor when a Japanese plane dropped a bomb into the ship. He wound up in tanks when he recovered from his injuries and fought through the Pacific campaign in the older Shermans.

Able Company, however, would feel the sting of the T-34s early in September. Ironically, it was at the same road juncture near Obong-ni Ridge. One of the Able M26s rounded the bend and came face to face with a NKPA tank on the right. The Able tank had its turret toward the left, anticipating trouble from that direction. Before it could traverse the other way, the Pershing was hit by a series of 85mm shots. The Marine tank was destroyed, but the crew escaped.

Minutes later, another Able tank came on the scene to help, but in the tight confines passing the wounded M26 it had trouble maneuvering. It, too, took direct hits from the T-34. These North Koreans, unlike their first encounter with Marine armor, knew what they were doing and knocked out another Pershing.

But, in time, thanks to the Marines, the T-34s became virtually nonexistent after they were beaten up during the Gyrenes' run from Inchon through Seoul.

The Marines had landed!

Meanwhile, back in California at Camp Pendleton, the excruciating job of getting more Leathernecks and their equipment ready for a much bigger deal was going on around the clock.

Building the First Marine Division for the Korean War was a monumental, and historical, accomplishment in mobilization of a fighting force—considering the urgency and the little time in which it had to be done. But the Corps pulled it off and when it did, the newly minted Flame Platoon, Headquarters Company, First Tank Battalion, was right there with it.

Nine yet-to-be-battle-tested Sherman M4A3E8 flame tanks were rushed to Camp Pendleton from the Barstow Marine Supply Depot in California's Mohave Desert. They were unique because they had the CWS-POA-H5 (Chemical War Service- Pacific Ocean Area-Hawaii 5 [version 5]) flame guns mounted to the right of their 105-millimeter cannons on the coaxial shield.

The Marine Corps' newest fighting unit was on its way, but very little notice was taken of those pudgy Shermans with the two snouts, even as unusual looking as they were. In the confusion that was the mobilization, the Flame Platoon wasn't the only outfit that went virtually unnoticed. In reality, there wasn't that much time for anyone to stop and make an accurate check on anything.

MacArthur, with a newfound appreciation for the Corps, needed *his* Marines battle-ready for the invasion of Inchon. There was no way, under the time constraint between authorization of the Division on 19 July and what was to become a historic fall day, that the organization of the First Marine Division was going to be a lesson in exact science.

The First Tank Battalion, under the command of Lt. Col. Harry T. Milne, and with its new Flame Platoon, was a prime example of how the Division was reaching out for components.

Phillip C. Morrell, who within three months after the landing at Inchon would become Milne's executive officer, witnessed the confusion of the organization, and marveled at how it all came together.

With Able Company already in Korea attached to the Brigade, there were three other companies and the rest of the battalion to organize. But Baker Company was the only component at Pendleton until the Flame Platoon arrived from Barstow. "Dog Company was on maneuvers in the Mediterranean," Morrell said, "and Charlie Company was on the East Coast."

A reserve captain, Morrell took command of Charlie Company when it arrived in California from Camp Lejeune, North Carolina. "It wasn't until after we got into Seoul when we were called to a briefing that I was able to meet the other company commanders," Morrell said. Less than three months later, he was promoted to Major and became Milne's exec.

Compounding the situation was the fallout from normal standard operating procedure (S.O.P.) Marines typically encountered—the Corps usually got last dibs on equipment after the army had its fill. That meant the M26 Pershing, which was to be the staple armored tank of the battalion's line companies going into Korea, was a piece of equipment in which few of the crews had trained. The Pershing came along toward the end of World War II and, because of prescribed cutbacks following the Big One, Marines didn't get too many of them.

Most of the tankers in Baker, Charlie, and Dog companies would get their instruction on the more modern tank aboard ship en route to Korea. One thing in their favor, however, was that the Pershing was clutch-operated like the Sherman, therefore a little more familiar to drive.

But gunners and tank commanders who had to operate the 90-millimeter cannon required quite a bit of familiarization. Even new 1811s going through training at Camp Delmar (across Highway 101 from Pendleton) while the war was progressing, were being trained in M4A3 Shermans. Most of them would be assigned to the letter companies and wind up having to learn the nuances of the M26 on the run.

The Flame Platoon was the only unit familiar with its tank because it had been training in the Sherman at Barstow. And that was an oddity in itself, because most of the future Flame Tankers—replacements—would join the platoon without so much as ever having seen one of these rolling armor hybrids.

So what was going on at Camp Pendleton with the mobilization of the 1950 version of the Marine Corps Minutemen was nothing less than organized confusion—actually, something many Marines proudly addressed half-heartedly as S.O.P.

On 19 July 1950, the active duty roster of the Marine Corps was at 74,249 personnel.

The Fleet Marine force numbers 27,703 men, the security detachments included 11,087, and 1,574 were afloat. Of the 11,853 in FMFPac (Fleet Marine Force Pacific), 7,779 were in the 1st Marine Division, and 3,733 in the 1st Marine Aircraft Wing. The 15,803 Marines in FMFLant (Atlantic) included 8,973 in the 2nd Marine Division and 5,297 in the 2nd Marine Aircraft Wing. (MCOinK, Volume I)

The First Marine Division needed approximately 25,000 men in order to get up to combat strength, and it needed them in one hell of a hurry.

Behind every Marine regular, figuratively speaking, stood two reservists who were ready to step forward and fill the gaps in the ranks. Thus it was scarcely far-fetched when some inspired public information officer coined the phrase "Minute Men of 1950" for these recent civilians who made it possible for the 1st Marine Division to hit the beaches at Inchon. (MCOinK, Volume I)

That meant there were close to 129,000 Marine Reserves, not counting volunteer reserves on active duty, who were available to supplement the ranks of the Division, or move into billets where Gyrenes were being extracted for the buildup.

After the 1st Provisional Marine Brigade, with the 5th Marine Regiment, sailed for the Far East, the 1st Marine Division at Camp Pendleton could count only 3,459 officers and men. By 6 August they were bolstered by nearly 11,000 troops from the 2nd Marine Division at Camp Lejeune, and others from various posts and stations. On 7 August, more than 2,800 were selected as combat-ready from 10,000 reservists pouring into the Southern California encampment.

The first order of business in rebuilding the Division infantry strength was getting the 7th Marine Regiment ready to saddle up with the 1st Marines. With the 5th Marines already in Korea, that would bring the Division up to normal infantry combat strength of three regiments. The problem, however, was that the Third Battalion of the Seventh was on detached duty at sea with the 6th Marines, FMFLant, and dispersed on numerous naval ships throughout the Mediterranean. It wasn't until 16 August that 3rdBat7th Marines were fetched, brought together at Suda Bay, Crete, and sent on their way to Camp Pendleton.

It was the mobilization of the 7th Marines that brought the reality of his impending future to PFC Leonard Martin, a soon-to-be tanker and, later, a Flame Platoon driver and tank commander. However, it took the Illinois eighteen-year-old reservist a little time to realize that being a Marine and getting ready for something like a war was serious business.

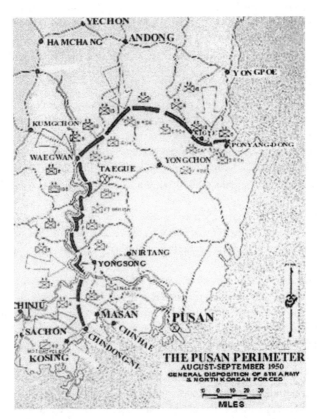

By the time the United States Marine Corps sent the 1st Provisional Marine Brigade to Korea, ill-prepared U.S. Army and Republic of Korea (ROK) units were pinched into the Pusan Perimeter. (Map Copy Courtesy of MCOinK)

Getting Ready for War

While President Truman was becoming more convinced that he had to take the bull by the horns and get the United States military in shape to handle the crisis escalating in Korea, young men all across the country were feeling the reverberations. Reservists like PFC Leonard Martin were being absorbed into the Minutemen of 1950 phase of the United States Marine Corps.

Martin's experiences were typical of what was going on with new and older Marines being called up for active duty. After turning eighteen on July 24th, he received notice that his unit would be activated on 8 August.

"Prior to leaving, we had a final physical and it was somewhat comical," Martin said. "I got the idea they were so hard up for warm bodies, that they were taking anyone with two arms and two legs."

It wouldn't be long before his warm body would shiver in the frigid mountains south of the infamous Chosin Reservoir in North Korea. It would be longer yet before he would become somewhat more comfortable driving and commanding an M4A3E8 Sherman flame tank.

When reality set in, Martin started to realize how the real Marine Corps worked— sometimes, not so efficiently. But that could be expected under the circumstances and the confusion involved with mobilizing a military force of the magnitude needed in this first hot episode of the Cold War.

"My family drove me to the armory on the 8th of August, and they were told that they could see me off at the train station," Martin said. "As I quickly learned, things often get fouled up, and this was the first of many I would experience. For some reason, my parents were not permitted to see me off at the train station, and my mother took it pretty hard."

It was four days before the Cicero Reserves reached Camp Pendleton in Southern California, where the First Marine Division, Fleet Marine Force, was being mobilized. When they arrived on 12 August, they were among trainload after trainload of Reserves and regulars streaming into the Oceanside encampment.

"There were troops all over the place," Martin said. They were being sorted out in an effort to determine those experienced enough to be sent right into the war. "Initially we were marched to a large staging area."

That's where anyone with prior active duty was assigned to the Seventh Marine Regiment, a basic infantry regiment. Most were veterans who had served in WWII and had remained in the active Reserves. They were not happy Marines. Who could blame them? The majority of them had settled into family life, newly married after coming home from the Big One, and had begun to raise young children. Now they headed for San Diego and loaded aboard ships with the rest of the First Marine Division. The only additional, or refreshment, training they would get would be those not-so-luxurious boats on their way across the Pacific, and that was not very much. Their experiences in World War II would have to suffice.

Because he was a Reserve with less than one year in the Marine Corps, PFC Leonard Martin was classified "Non-Combat-Ready" and assigned to the "Recruit Class" for further training. In that context, it meant he immediately was to pull a lot of working parties—loading gear needed by the 7th Marines who were being upgraded within the

First Marine Division for the landing at Inchon.

"The gear was brought to the regimental parade grounds at 24 Area in Camp Pendleton," Martin said. "We worked twelve hours on and twelve hours off. We were told to estimate size, weight, and volume. I understand that normally the loading of equipment aboard a ship is very precise and tightly controlled. So much for normality."

The 24 Area also was headquarters for the Commanding General of the Division. One day his command car cut in between Martin's platoon as young Reserves were marching across the street.

"There goes the General," someone commented, referring to Maj. General Oliver P. Smith, who would deftly guide First Marine Division through its historic first year of the war. He would distinguish himself as a tough, stubborn leader who stood up to Army superiors in order to get his trapped Marines successfully out of the Chosin Reservoir ordeal.

"Screw the General," said Martin that day, never realizing he would be one of those trapped Marines and be ever thankful that General Smith was in charge of his fate.

But in August of 1950, the young kid from Illinois was still to learn the meaning of Marine Corps respect and discipline. The next morning the entire working party was called out in formation. An officer said that someone had made derogatory remarks about the General and that this was not acceptable. "Fortunately, he did not ask who it was," Martin admitted, "because, being as naïve as I was, I probably would have stepped out." It was not how the young Reserve would have wanted to start his brief career in the United States Marine Corps.

After the feverish details with working parties ended and the Division was on its way to San Diego where it would be loaded on 19 Navy and commercial ships that would comprise the convoy to Korea, Martin and several buddies were given weekend liberty. They went to Los Angeles, but because of heavy traffic they got back to Camp Pendleton much later than the Sunday midnight deadline prescribed for liberty.

"Like a bunch of little kids, we got a written note from the bus driver explaining why we were late," Martin said. "Of course this was not acceptable and we were supposed to go up for Captains Mast (disciplinary action) on Monday."

However, the first thing that next morning, Martin, and several other new Marines, were told to report to Camp Delmar, on the coast just across Highway 101 from Pendleton. Delmar was about to become the training facility for tracked vehicles—tanks and amphibious tractors. Like many Marines being assigned to tank and amphib training, there was some bewilderment among Martin and his buddies. None of them ever applied for that kind of duty. They were just assigned to it.

Yours is not to reason why . . .

Len Martin and the rest of the Reserves in the *Recruit Class* had done their jobs helping get the 7th Marines ready and off to the war. Now it was their turn to prepare for the real thing.

"Before going on the working parties, I had gone through screening to see where they could assign me," Martin said. "Not knowing any better, I requested to be sent to the infantry. But since I had had two years of automechanics in high school, and since there was a shortage of tanker replacements, someone thought I would be a good candidate for tanks."

It wasn't unusual for Marines to look back and count their blessings for being pulled out of the infantry and draw duty in a tank outfit, and PFC Martin would be one of them. "All in all in was a good thing," Martin said. "Had I gone into the infantry there was a good chance that I may not have come back from Korea."

When they piled out of the six-bys after their short trip across Highway 101, the tank recruits began to wonder about Camp Delmar.

"It was a mess," was Martin's quick assessment of the comparatively small annex to Pendleton that was situated between the famous California highway and Pacific Ocean. "I think that we were the first troops assigned to Delmar since the Second World War. We had to clean out the barracks so that we had someplace to sleep. I remember cleaning up the second floor head (bathroom) and having a sergeant tell us to use plenty of water. We took buckets of water and poured it on the floor. Pretty soon someone started hollering that we were flooding the first floor."

Obviously, Delmar was not really prepared to handle the incoming tank novices. Classes consisted of films designed for infantry on how to knock out tanks. That was not encouraging to the fledgling tankers.

Eventually the new tank recruits began training at a remote area of Camp Pendleton called Los Flores Tank Park. It was a ride of about a half-an-hour or so in the backs of open six-bys from Delmar. At Los Flores, there were five or six World War II M4A3 Sherman tanks when the young Marines arrived the first day.

Before this, Len Martin had never seen a real tank. He climbed into the driver's compartment of one of the relics, and took quick mental notes as his mechanically oriented mind went to work. "On my left was a control panel, in front was a clutch pedal and gas pedal and two levers coming up from the floor," he noted. "These levers were used to steer the tank. Overhead and behind me were radio and intercom headsets, and I could see up into the turret."

Then he pulled the driver's hatch cover closed above his head. "I looked through the periscope and said to myself: 'This is no place for me.' I wanted no part of these things."

That night, when he returned to Delmar, Martin went to see the first sergeant. He asked to be transferred out of tanks.

"The Sgt. looked at me in a fatherly manner and said: 'Son, they need tankers in Korea. You're not going anywhere.'"

That ended that.

It wasn't long before the kid from Illinois had a change of heart about tanks.

"The next day or so we got around to driving them," he said. "We had a Reserve sergeant as an instructor and his favorite saying was, 'There are Gooks to the right of us, and Gooks to the left of us, and Gooks all around us. Let's get the hell out of here.' The object was to see how fast we could get up into the tank and get it operational.

"Once I started driving the tanks, I fell in love with them," PFC Martin admitted. Since the M4 had a clutch and gas pedal, it was somewhat like driving a car. But instead of a steering wheel, the tank had two levers for turning. Pulling back on either lever locked the corresponding track and allowed the tank to turn in that direction as the power of the opposite track pivoted the thirty-five-ton vehicle. The faster the tank was going, the easier it was to turn. At slow speeds, however, Martin discovered it took a bit of effort to pull the levers.

The tank had five speeds forward and one reverse gear, and normally was put in motion out of second gear. The secret was to double-clutch, and quickly shift into third gear before the 35-ton machine stalled. Once in third gear, it was easy to get into fourth and normal cruising gear. Very seldom was it wise to shift up to fifth gear. Unless there was fairly level ground, or an area of gently rolling hills, the engines were unable to pull such a load in that high gear. Top speed for the Sherman M4A3 was about twenty-five miles per hour, but with all that weight wrapped around the crew, it felt like the thing was flying. "Lots of fun," Martin said. "Imagine driving thirty-five tons of metal at twenty-five miles an hour!"

The tanks at Flores Park, however, were so old and worn out, they were very prone to breakdowns. "One day I broke a drive shaft on one," the Illinois Marine recalled. "Driving a tank is really not like driving a car. In a car you rely on the brakes to stop. But since the tank is so heavy, it takes a long time to slow down just using the braking levers. This is where knowing the machine becomes important. The gear mechanism is so much a part of the braking routine.

"Normally, the driver would gear down to the lowest speed, double clutching to ease from a higher gear to a lower range. This effectively winds down the engine to where the brake levers become more manageable. It takes some time to react to this without too much thought.

"Since I was inexperienced," Martin said, "I didn't realize that you were not supposed to suddenly take your foot off the gas, particularly when coming down a hill, since this puts a heck of a strain on the engine and drive shaft. The drive shaft, which ran from the engine compartment in the rear of the tank to the transmission up front, was so old and crystallized that it broke in two.

"When it broke, it went clanging around inside the tank, scaring the daylights out of us. The tank had to be towed back to the tank park to be repaired. I took a lot of ribbing," he admitted, "but nothing official came of it."

When their training was just about complete, the lieutenant who was in charge of this first class of Korean War tank trainees told them he didn't want to scare them, but that once they finished at Los Flores Park, they would be shipped overseas.

"You might finish on a Friday and ship out on Saturday," he warned them. As it worked out, PFC Martin and his new buddies wrapped up their training on Saturday and shipped out the next day—Sunday, October 1, 1950.

Going overseas has a prescribed ritual: shots—all kinds of needles for immunization! "Everyone was stripped to the waist and lined up in single file," Martin said. "Your records were checked to see which shots you needed. Each shot had a number, and as you stood there the numbers were written on your chest. Some guys got as many as five shots. As you moved forward, you got whatever shot you needed in either arm or both arms at once.

"There really wasn't much to it. Our arms were sore for several days, but some guys actually passed out. Tough Marines?"

The night before boarding ship, Len Martin called home. "I talked to my Dad, who had served in the Army before and during WWI. He had told me at one time that the Marines must really be hard up when they start taking punks like me. In his day, in order to be a Marine, you had to have had served in another branch of the military before the Corps would accept you.

"I knew he wasn't serious when he called me a 'punk.' He was very proud of me."

In less than two months after being called to active duty, and with fewer than four weeks of tank training, Len Martin was on his way to Korea. By the time he would get there, and eventually be assigned to the Flame Platoon, the *kid brothers* of the First Tank Battalion had earned their spurs.

Smith vs. Almond, Round 1

Tedious would be a gross understatement if applied to what was happening within the preparations of the First Marine Division for the Landing at Inchon.

It wasn't enough that plans had to be worked around the Inchon Harbor tide that rose and fell thirty-some feet in its normal cycle. Maj. Gen. Oliver P. Smith, commanding general of the First Marine Division, who had arrived in Tokyo on 22 August, was experiencing his first in a series of conflicts he would have over the next several months with Gen. Douglas MacArthur's chief of staff, Maj. Gen Edward M. (Ned) Almond.

It was Almond who was taking command of the newly designated X Corps, which was to be responsible for the landing. And history shows the Army General, sometimes, was not one to think out consequences of rash decisions he occasionally reached when ordering troops into battle.

Smith, to the contrary, did not go off half-cocked. He weighed consequences very heavily in his decisions. If he thought a plan was not sound, he said so—even to Almond and MacArthur.

Many a Marine has Smith to thank for getting out of Korea alive because the veteran of two previous wars stood up to Almond when the X Corps commander ordered the First Marine Division to be stretched too thinly as the problem at the Chosin Reservoir developed.

A graduate of the University of California '16, Smith was in France in the First World War and a regimental commander when the Marines were chasing the Japanese up the island chains in the Pacific during World War II. He was assistant commandant of the Marine Corps before he took over the First Marine Division.

So, Maj. Gen. Oliver P. Smith knew his stuff and was not about to get pushed around by the Army without firmly stating his case.

What he was up against in August 1950 was a logistics problem getting his troops organized for the Inchon Landing. Staging was being done at Kobe, Japan, but it wasn't until a week later that the main body of the First Marine Division began arriving there —and it took until 3 September before all troops were on hand. Some equipment and supplies still were on the high seas coming from the States.

At this point, only two of Smith's three infantry regiments—the 1st Marines and 5th Marines—were up to strength. And the Fifth was already committed in Korea as the First Provisional Marine Brigade. As of mid-August, elements of the 7th Marine Regiment were on maneuvers, spread out on ships in the Mediterranean Sea. The main body of the Seventh had been organized at Camp Pendleton around personnel from the 6th Marines, brought in from Camp Lejeune, and the priority draw of combat-ready reservists pouring into the California encampment. It wasn't until 14 August that the rest of the 7th Marines in the Med got the call, and they wouldn't catch up to the main force until after the invasion.

Then, during the staging at Kobe, the First Marine Division commander was informed by the Secretary of the Navy, Francis P. Matthews, that he would not be able to use 500 troops he had counted on because they had not yet turned eighteen years of age. These young Marines subsequently were transferred to the 1st Armored Amphibian Tractor Battalion, which had been stripped of personnel to bring the First Tank Battalion up to strength. The reasoning was that tanks would be used in all phases of the landing and push inland while the amphibs would not be required much beyond the beaches.

When landing plans were finalized, it was decided the 5th Marine Regiment would lead the assault on the small island of Wolmi-do, and then Inchon because of the First Provisional Marine Brigade's experience in the Pusan Perimeter.

This was another pending headache for Smith. It meant the Division had to pick up the 5th Marines at Pusan on its way to Inchon. The Third Battalion 5th was assigned to lead the preliminary landing on Wolmi-do. With it would be the First Tank Battalion's Able Company M26s, which also had the experience of fighting within the Pusan Perimeter, and three Flame Platoon Sherman M4A3E8s fresh from Camp Pendleton.

Then, General Almond stepped in and threw up a roadblock to this plan.

On 23 August, the Corps commander informed Smith that he could have the 5th Marines and the Able's tanks, only dependent on what was going on around the fragile Pusan Perimeter. Toward the end of August, however, he did agree to release the Fifth on 4 September—only eleven days before D-Day.

However, that was before the North Koreans mounted a major offensive and broke through the Perimeter on the first of September after the Fifth had been pulled out of the lines and sent south to Pusan. The NKPA, thirteen divisions strong, was threatening to break through to the port city. The release order was rescinded. With the Marine infantry and tanks at the Pusan docks, ready for debarkation, they were ordered back to the front as a mobile reserve.

Smith balked, even though he was offered the use of the Army's 32nd Infantry Division as a substitute for the Marine regiment. After a summit of the landing's top commanders in General Almond's office, the X Corps commander relented. He released the 5th Marines at midnight 5 September. The hole would be plugged by a regiment of the Army's 7th Infantry Division which would be sent to Korean waters as a "floating reserve" to be landed at Pusan if an emergency developed.

Finally, General Smith had the 5th Marines and enough of his division to work with. He and his staff could get down solidifying plans for the Inchon Landing.

Still, there were problems.

Much of the equipment was in its original containers and had never been checked or identified. Large quantities of Class I (rations, water), III (tank, jeeps, other vehicles) and V (units of fire, flame fuel, etc.) supplies, distributed throughout the incoming shipping, had to be reassembled and reassigned for the out-loading. In the lack of suitable storage areas near the piers, Classes III and V were off-loaded into Japanese barges and held in floating storage until they could be reloaded into assault shipping. (MCOinK, Volume II)

Meanwhile, Typhoon Jane struck Kobe on 3 September with seventy-four-mile-an-hour winds battering the port. The major loss was twenty-four hours of time. But Marine experience, gained through the numerous landings in World War II, prevailed. The landing would remain on schedule for 15 September.

Now it was up to the Navy to get the First Marine Division and the rest of General Almond's X Corps into the Inchon Harbor.

To transport, protect, and put ashore a force of this size calls for a considerable investment in shipping and in personnel, and "Chromite (Operation Chromite was the code name for the Inchon Landing)," despite the expected absence of air and sea opposition, placed a heavy load upon the Navy. (U.S. Naval Operations in Korea)

It would be Joint Task Force 7 commanded by Vice Admiral A.D. Struble, and bulked up by Rear Admiral James H. Doyle's Task Force 90, an attack force of an estimated 180 ships. Within JTF7, also would be Task Force 99, patrol and reconnaissance; Task Force 77, fast carriers; Task Force 79, a service squadron, and, naturally, Task Force 92, which was X Corps.

The total strength of Joint Task Force 7 amounted to some 230 ships of all shapes and sizes, from APDs of 2,100 tons full load displacement to transports of ten times that size. Except for a few gunnery ships held back to support the flanks of the perimeter, it included all combatant units available in the Far East. Fifty-two ships were assigned to the Fast Carrier, Patrol and Reconnaissance, and Logistic Task Forces; the remainder went to make up the Attack Force, Task Force 90, under Admiral Doyle. Of these, more than 120 were required to lift X Corps, while the rest were involved in gunfire and air support, screening, minesweeping, and miscellaneous other duties.

That so sizable an amphibious lift could be so rapidly assembled was remarkable, more so in view of the preexisting policies of economy and of down-grading the amphibious function. In 1945 the assembly of such a force would have seemed simple enough; by 1952 it would have become quite feasible; but 1950, the year that it was needed, was the year of the drought. Inevitably, therefore, the armada that eventuated was a somewhat heterogeneous one, and of the 120-odd units assigned to lift X Corps less than half were commissioned vessels of the U.S. Navy. Thirty of the LSTs assigned the operation were Scajap ships, manned by the hardworking and loyal enemy aliens, and, of the vessels collected by MSTS WestPac, 13 were MSTS-owned, 26 were American cargo ships on time charter, and four were chartered Japanese Marus. (U.S. Naval Operations in Korea)

It was time!

After five days of softening up Wolmi-do and Inchon with thunderous and devastating Naval gunfire, and bombing by Marine and Navy planes, the landing was on. But it was not without another glitch.

While the USS *Mount McKinley*, the flag ship of the attack force, arrived in the narrows of Flying Fish Channel on 14 September, an LST carrying the Second Battalion, 1st Marine Regiment, was slowed by engine trouble. Thanks to an ocean-going tug, it was slowly towed to the landing assembly point to fall in line—in time for its appointed assault of Blue Beach late on D-Day.

The landing would be launched in two phases in respect to the enormous tides that controlled any traffic coming into Inchon Harbor. A morning landing would be made on the north side of Wolmi-do Island at high tide. After the 5th Marines, supported by Able Company, 1st Tank Battalion, and the three flame tanks, secured the island, it would have to sit tight until later in the day while the tide receded, and again worked its way back up the four-story Inchon seawall.

Maximum tide of thirty-one feet was expected shortly after 1900 on 15 September, just around evening twilight of D-Day. Twenty-three feet of water was needed for LCVPs (landing craft, vehicle, personnel) and LVTs (landing vehicle, tracked) to clear the mud flats, and the LSTs (landing ship, tank) would need at least three more feet. Those parameters dictated the landing should be launched at 1700.

If the 5th Marines couldn't neutralize Wolmi-do, then things would get more than a little hairy when the rest of the regiment, and the 1st Marines sandwiched the island with their late afternoon assaults on the mainland. They were to strike on Red Beach, to the north at the Inchon seawall, and Blue Beach below the salt pan, south of the city.

So, it was not a cut-and-dried battle plan.

The final impact of the Inchon tides appeared in the planning for logistic support. Only small craft could negotiate Blue Beach at the southern edge of the city; only at Red Beach in the north and at Green Beach on Wolmi Do could LSTs be brought in, and there only during the high tides between D-Day and D plus 2. At low tide nothing could be landed, and behind its ramparts of yielding ooze the city lay secure. To supply the assault forces during the night of D-Day, it was decided to run LSTs ashore at Red Beach and leave them through the inter-tidal interval, accepting the possible loss of these vessels in the interests of adequate troop support. For the LSTs, high and dry and with cargoes composed largely of explosive and inflammable materials, the prospect was not enviable, but a scheme of maneuver was worked out which emphasized the fastest possible clearing of Red Beach in order to ensure, so far as possible, the survival of these ungainly vehicles and of their priceless contents. (U.S. Naval Operations in Korea)

But there was no turning back now. It was up to the Third Platoon of the 5th Marines, with support of the First Tank Battalion—Third Platoon of Able Company, second section of the Flame Platoon, and three dozers and a retriever of Service Company—to get the show on the road.

Flame Platoon's First Action

Wolmi-do Island was shaped like a bird modeled after Mae West—full-breasted—with its beak pointing north and its long skinny legs trailing behind on a southerly plain. It's jugular was Green Beach, where the Third Battalion of the 5th Marine Regiment landed at 0633 on 15 September 1950, and within minutes would have the support of nine tanks, including three flame-throwing M4A3E8 Shermans, from the First Tank Battalion.

Within five minutes after the seven LCVPs (landing craft, vehicle, personnel) eased into the sand and disgorged three platoons from How Company, and one platoon from George Company of 3rdBat5th, the second wave came ashore with the rest of the Regiment's companies.

By 0645, three LSUs (landing ship, utility) from the *Fort Marion* in the third wave dropped their ramps to cut loose the throttled-up armor of the First Tank Battalion. Six M26 Pershings of Able Company, the Sherman flame tank from the first section of the Flame Platoon, Headquarters Company, two dozer-bladed M4 Shermans and an M4 retriever were grinding down the ramps and into the pocked-marked beach. They were under the command of 2nd Lt. Granville G. (G.G.) Sweet, who was also leader of Able's third platoon. Two more flame tanks from the first section hit the beach in a subsequent wave, and all were under 1st Lt. Charles M. Blythe, the Flame Platoon Leader. The other six flame tanks would come ashore on Green Beach and lend their support to the main landing on Inchon later that day.

When Cpl. Robert Rosenthal sprinted out of his LCVP as the first wave settled into Green Beach, he saw utter devastation of Wolmi-do, which South Korean vacationers had been using as a summer resort.

"It was reduced to an ugly ashen piece of nothing," Rosenthal said.

PFC William (Bill) Kuykendall, who came ashore later in the day with the rest of the Flame Platoon, had a similar feeling when he drove F21 onto the pulverized beach.

"The naval bombardment tore the place apart," Kuykendall said. "At first look, there seemed to be little or nothing there to burn with our flame guns."

For five days, Wolmi-do had been under intense fire from Navy cruisers, and air strikes mounted by Joint Task Force 7. But the beach-turned-wasteland did not fool Rosenthal and the rest of Lt. Col. William Taplett's 5th Marines. He and other veterans of the Pacific invasions of World War II knew "some enemy forces were untouchable, manning their strongholds below ground.

"This is where flame tanks became important in the past, and we were counting on them here in the present," Rosenthal said. "We'd needed them to flush out enemy troops from their fortifications."

The United States Marine Corps fledgling fighting unit—Flame Platoon, Headquarters and Service Company, First Tank Battalion—was about to get its combat baptism of fire. The three flame tanks from the first section of the platoon would not be called on to use their primary weapon right away, but they would immediately become engaged on Wolmi-do with supporting fire from the 105mm cannons and machine guns.

Joint Task Force 7 was a massive display of military might, and Rosenthal remembers vividly the 230 warships, aircraft carriers, and 25,000 combat-ready troops—nearly

19,500 of them Marines—who were sitting in the Yellow Sea outside the Inchon Harbor waiting for H-hour. Along with the not-quite full-strength First Marine Division were the Army's 7th Division and a regiment from the ROK (Republic of Korea) army.

The first couple of waves of the 5th Marines had met little resistance. Within ten minutes they had the beach secured and quickly pushed inland with Lt. Sweet's Third Platoon of Able Company tanks and Lt. Blythe's flame tank right with them waiting for firing assignments from the infantry.

Rosenthal sure appreciated seeing the flame tanks roll out of the LSUs. Of course, they stood out as relatively "new"—well, at least clean—compared to the Able's dirt-covered Pershings, which had lost their luster in combat along the Pusan Perimeter. The contrast struck the young corporal.

"The three new Sherman flame tanks were the only armor that was not a hand-me-down from the Army," he said. They were popular with some Marine infantry because of what they could do to dug-in enemy troops—once they turned on their flame guns. "Whenever we called on them, they were right there for us. I saw them blasting into the caves with their machine guns, and the NK (North Korean defenders) coming out with their hands up, wanting no part of those flamethrowers. Any place, like clumps and possible machine-gun emplacements," Rosenthal said, "were hit by direct fire from the Flamers."

What the flame tanks, dozers, and Able Company's M26s were facing with the 5th Marines were about 400 North Korean People's Army troops garrisoned on Wolmi-do. There would be another estimated 2,000 enemy defending Inchon.

With 3rdBat5th making good use of the armor, half of Wolmi-do was in control of the landing force within an hour after hitting the beach. And there were several skirmishes that required the use of tanks.

From one of the many caves drifted noises indicating the presence of several occupants, hitherto unnoticed. While riflemen covered the entrance, a Marine tank drove forward and fired two rounds into the interior.

Muffled explosions shook the area, and billows of black smoke streaked with flame rolled out of the cave. Wide-eyed, as though watching ghosts emerge, the Marines of Company I saw the enemy soldiers stagger out of the blazing recess and throw up their hands. (MCOinK, Volume II)

The flame tanks had been expected to scorch pockets of resistance on Radio Hill, which dominated the island, and they were doing just that. Meanwhile, the Able's M26s, with their powerful 90mm rifles, blasted apart some of the holes. Often, an enterprising Sherman dozer, under the command of S/Sgt. Charles J. "Tiny" Rhoades, just rolled up and pushed earth into the entrances to seal the North Koreans into suffocating demise.

To complete the initial phase of the invasion, the Marines had to venture along a skinny 12-yard-wide, 750-yard-long causeway—the extended leg of this "big-busted bird" island—and secure the small lighthouse station on the islet called Sowolmi-do at the southern tip.

An islet of about 500 square yards, Sowolmi-do was topped by a low hill with the navigational beacon on the summit. (MCOinK, Volume II)

It was not a mop-up. The 3rd Platoon of the Fifth's George Company and a flame tank would run into a stubborn enemy.

It was about 1000 when Lt. Col. Taplett ordered 2nd Lt. John D. Counselman to take his third platoon and follow a flame tank down the gray rock causeway to the point and clear it out. "A severe firefight broke out," Rosenthall said, "and three Marines were seriously wounded."

The North Koreans, although in a hopeless situation, decided they were not going to make it easy on the Marines. Heavy machine-gun and rifle fire stalled the tank-infantry team. After an air strike by Marine Corsairs scorched the hill with napalm, a mine-clearing team of engineers led the tank along the rocky seaward edge of the causeway toward the nub.

Meanwhile, a mortar barrage from Three-Five blasted the small hill, pinning down the North Koreans and significantly reducing their firepower. As the flame tank reverted to its heavy armament and poured round after round of 105 ordnance into position, the infantry fought up the hill. Shortly after 1100, it was secured.

The two other flame tanks were called forward and the three roamin' candles spent another hour firing searing rods of burning napalm into the caves, sending many of the remainder of the determined, but foolish, North Koreans to fiery deaths.

> Covered by tank fire, the Marine infantry quickly fanned out and closed with the defenders. There was a sharp outburst of small-arms racket, interspersed with the clatter of machine guns; then a few scattered volleys and the main fight was over at 1115. Mopping up with grenades and a flame thrower continued for almost another hour, owing to the number of caves and the determination of a few Red soldiers.
>
> Nineteen North Koreans surrendered and 17 were killed, including some hapless warriors who tried to swim to the mainland. Despite the size of the islet, eight Reds succeeded in hiding out from the attackers; and General Craig (Brig. Gen. Edward A Craig, Assistant Commander, First Marine Division), after landing on Wolmi-do with the ADC group in the evening, observed the fugitives escape to the mainland. (MCOinK, Volume II)

In the early going, particularly on Wolmi-do and the smaller villages along the way toward Seoul, the twin-barreled Shermans were called on to torch the mud-brick and stick native homes. By noon, the entire island was secured, and the initial landing force spent the rest of the day waiting for Inchon's famous tide to expose the treacherous mud flats and return to the sea wall so the second phase of the landing could be launched.

> Gradually the phenomenal tide rolled back from its morning high of more than 30 feet. By 1300, the waters had receded, leaving 3/5 perched on an island in a sea of mud. For the next several hours Taplett and his men were on their own, speculating whether an enemy force might suddenly rush out of Inchon's dead streets in an attempt to cross the mudflats, or whether a Red tank column would abruptly streak from the city and make for the causeway.
>
> Nothing happened. The air of unreality, created by the stillness of the Oriental seaport, weighed down on the nerves of the entire attack force. As the afternoon wore on, the Marines detected movement here and there, but distant figures were identified as civilians more often than not. . . .
>
> Thus, the 3rd Battalion enjoyed an almost uneventful interlude during its isolation. An occasional mortar round or long-range machine gun burst was the feeble reminder that Inchon still remained in enemy hands. (MCOinK, Volume II)

The major activity stirring on Wolmi-do during the "interlude" was the establishment of supply dumps as LSUs unloaded their wares at Green Beach and artillery officers from the 11th Marines roamed the island staking out positions for their batteries to support the evening landing on Inchon.

When the rest of Flame Platoon's six tanks came ashore on Green Beach later in the day, they were ready to join the fray that evening in support of the main landing at Inchon. Neither Red Beach, to the north—with its seawall—or Blue Beach—with its treacherous mud flats—were thought to be very good for discharging tanks from landing craft. For that reason, all the armor came in on Wolmi's Green Beach.

Cpl. Maurice (Mo) Sims, driving F23, had been right behind his buddy, PFC Kuykendall, as the Platoon's second and third sections ground into Wolmi's powdery beach. Sims, who enlisted in the Marine Corps Reserve after earning his spurs as a Seabee in World War II, was called up for the mobilization at Camp Pendleton. Because of his experience as with the Seabees, he was quickly assigned to tanks and became the driver of F23. Though Wolmi was secured, he and the rest of the tankers had no idea what the scoop was. Were they going right into action?

"I was scared shitless when we hit the water and headed toward Wolmi-do," said Sims. He had thought things were bad enough on the stinking LSU, but the unknown of going into a landing is always fear-provoking. "Still, we couldn't wait to get the hell off them LSUs."

After World War II, part of the demobilization of military left some of the landing ships to the Japanese, and they used them as fishing trawlers. They were not very clean when the Navy rushed them back into service for Korea. "Boy, did they stink," Sims said.

Guys like Sims, reserves with experience and an age advantage coming out of World War II, often had to fill in as instructors on the way to Korea. "I was older," Sims said, "but most of the tankers were green kids, and not too many knew anything about a tank, let alone a flame tank."

Even with his experience in the Seabees, Sims had to learn the intricacy of the Sherman tank and practiced the shifting of the five-speed-forward-and-reverse transmission on the LSU en route from Kobe, Japan, to Inchon. He picked it up quickly and then taught the younger Marines.

Fortunately for Sims, his tank commander, Sgt. Alfred Betti, had trained in the specialized Sherman at Barstow and knew the workings of the primary weapon—the flame gun. "When we arrived at Kobe," Sims said, "we took one of the tanks out and had a demonstration shooting the flame gun."

That was it, a demonstration. The rest was left up to the few NCOs who had worked with the flame gun to teach others how to operate it—a pattern to be followed the rest of the war.

When the LSU dropped its ramp on Wolmi-do, and Cpl. Sims eased F23 onto the beach, things were not too bad. That part of the show was over, but later, he would see plenty going through Inchon and into Seoul.

Surprisingly, only seventeen wounded Marines were on the casualty list for the Wolmi-do Operation, "an incredibly small price for a critical terrain feature commanding the approaches to Korea's major west coast port" (MCOinK, Volume II).

On the other side of the ledger, 108 North Koreans were known dead, and another 136 were taken captive. Interrogation of the prisoners established on the island was defended by approximately 400 troops, which means that approximately 150 of them became entombed when the Sherman dozer tanks sealed caves, or they were scorched in their underground positions by the flame tanks and Marine infantry humping portable flame throwers.

The three double-barreled Shermans significantly struck the colors of the Flame Platoon, 1st Tank Battalion, First Marine Division, on Wolmi-do Island. What Marines would find as the main force of the invasion hit Inchon at Red and Blue beaches, was a more tenacious enemy defending its holdings in South Korea.

If the five-hour mission by the Fifth Marines and their buddies from the First Tank Battalion was a comparative stroll on the beach, what would follow that evening inland would be anything but. The assault of Inchon and the drive to Seoul, the capital city of South Korea, would exact its toll on the Marines, and the Flame Platoon would not escape paying its share of the fee.

The Task of Forming the First Tank Battalion

"I watched them flame tanks going all the way up and into Seoul after the Inchon Invasion. When they entered the streets in that place, it was like a firestorm, shooting napalm into the tops and lower parts of buildings where NK forces were holed up shooting down into our approach."
—Cpl. Robert Rosenthal, 3rd Battalion 5th Marine Regiment

As landings go, the high command aboard the USS *Mount McKinley* was in a bit of a quandary over what might happen with main assault on Inchon. Should it anticipate something as relatively bland as the operation on Wolmi-do, or another Tarawa, which was one of the most harrowing beach assaults experienced by the United States Marine Corps in World War II? It was at Tarawa that Marines got hung up behind bulkheads and shoreline rocks, and suffered tremendous losses.

At Inchon, they would be facing quick and fickle tides that rose and fell against a thirty-foot seawall. If the timing wasn't on the money, there could be all kinds of problems. Marine infantry had planned on using ladders to reach the top of the seawall from the landing craft. Nudging against the wall on a short tide would mean the ladders also would be short and Marines may not be able to scale. And there was always the question of just how much of a fight the North Korean People's Army would be putting up.

The plan for the evening of 15 September 1950 was to put ashore the remainder of the 5th Marine Regiment—its 1st and 2nd battalions—on Red Beach directly north of the 900-yard Wolmi-do causeway, which linked the island to Inchon. The objectives along that 3,000 arcing yards of the mainland were Cemetery Hill to the north and Observatory Hill at the midway point.

Meanwhile, three miles south, Col. Lewis B. "Chesty" Puller's 1st Marines would go ashore at Blue Beach in front of Inchon's suburban industrial center.

There could be a problem, however, if there was a dire need for rolling armor at Blue Beach. Tanks—the rest of Able Company and the Flame Platoon—were being dispatched ashore only at Green Beach on Wolmi-do because the other two beaches were far from tailor-made for bringing in the forty-five-ton Pershings and thirty-five-ton Shermans.

So tanks were going to be a scarce commodity, other than in support of some of the Fifth Marines units.

With Green Beach secured, Able Company was brought up to strength with its remaining two platoons of M26s, and the Flame Platoon's other six Shermans also came down the ramps at Wolmi-Do in time for the major assault on Inchon's seaport.

The consequences of the hasty embarkment from Camp Pendleton had borne down heavily upon the 1st Tank Battalion, commanded by Lieutenant Colonel Harry T. Milne. Crews trained with the M4A3 (Sherman) and 105mm howitzer were suddenly equipped with the M-26 (Pershing) and its 90mm gun. With the exception of company A, which was in action with the Brigade, few of the men had had any experience either at driving or firing the new tanks. The Flame tank platoon of Headquarters Company had received some training at Barstow, but most of the personnel of Baker, Charlie and Dog Companies were limited to shipboard instruction. (MCOinK, Volume II)

And that wasn't all. The logistics of pulling together the First Tank Battalion was a prime example of the amazing accomplishment by the First Marine Division to commit such an effort to the Inchon Landing.

Capt. Phillip C. Morrell, commanding officer of Service Company when its two M4A3 dozer tanks and the retriever went into Wolmi-do, knew the anxiety surrounding the pre-landing buildup when the First Tank Battalion was being organized.

"Able's tanks were down in the Pusan Perimeter while Baker and Charlie Company, at Camp Pendleton, were having problems with track bearings," Morrell said. "We worked day and night to get them [B and C tanks] ready, to put aboard ships for South Korea while the crews went aboard another ship."

Of course, this was after Charlie Company had been summoned from the East Coast. Forget about Dog Company. It was on the high seas coming from the Mediterranean with the 7th Marine Regiment.

Morrell marveled when he considered how elements of the battalion were scattered hither and yon. "And this was for the Wolmi-do and Inchon Landings," he said, more than a hint of wonderment in his voice. A reserve captain at the time, Morrell would be handed additional responsibility when he was promoted to Major in December and became Lt. Col. Milne's executive officer.

Baker Company's Pershings wouldn't roll out of their LSTs on Green Beach until the day after the main invasion was launched. And it was 18 September, when Yellow Beach was established in the inner harbor, that Charlie Company tanks made it into Inchon. Dog Company wasn't even brought into the equation right away because its M26s could not be counted on until they arrived with the 7th Marines on 21 September.

The first order of business—to get what tanks were available into the fight for Inchon—was left up to Marine engineers. They had to make sure the nearly 600-yard-long Wolmi-Inchon Causeway was clear of mines. That accomplished, the road was safe for tanks to get to the mainland where they could immediately provide closer support for the infantry working its way south.

Even before they crossed the causeway early in the evening of 15 September, the tanks got involved with their machine guns laying down covering fire for the foot Marines hitting Red Beach. There was a great deal of enemy fire coming from Cemetery Hill, overlooking the landing area, and Observatory Hill sitting inland about 1,000 yards. Pershings and Shermans laced NKPA positions with fire from their 50- and 30-caliber machine guns, the M26s also rifling 90mm ordnance into the two enemy hills.

With the First and Second Battalions of 5th Marines clamoring up and over the seawall, they not only were harassed by fire from the two hills; they were trying to beat the fast-moving tide.

> *Although the tide was racing in fast, the wall still projected about four feet above the ramps of the landing craft. The Marines readied their scaling ladders. On the right the boats of Company E touched the revetment at 1731. Up went the ladders as the assault troops hurled grenades over the wall. Following the explosions, the Marines from the four boats scrambled to the top of the barrier one by one. The ladders slipped and swayed as the LCVPs bobbed next to the wall. But they served their purpose. (MCOinK, Volume II)*

The 5th Marines quickly secured Red Beach, but there still was work to do to neutralize Cemetery Hill, and then take care of Observatory Hill.

By that time, Able Company's Pershings and the Flame Platoon had rumbled over the causeway and raced north to support the 5th Marines. It took less than fifteen minutes for the Fifth to secure Cemetery Hill. It was a tougher fight to take Observatory Hill, complicated early by a mixup of waves of LSTs and elements of two infantry companies being deposited on the wrong beach.

The LSTs themselves were taking mortar and machine-gun fire from Observatory and were forced to return fire. However, once all the troops were on land, the two battalions were reorganized and pressed the attack on Observatory Hill. Well after 2200, the Hill was in Marine hands, and by midnight, the Gyrenes settled in on the outskirts of the port city for the night.

Down at Blue Beach, things were not going as well. One of the major problems was a mustard-colored overcast caused by intermittent rain and smoke from fires set by the intense pounding of naval gunfire. Restricted vision was compounded by strong currents, which were taking landing craft off course from assigned wall and beach destinations. Waves of landing ships were becoming enmeshed, and there were problems at the line of departure, acerbated by the inability of Navy officers on the control ships to see what was going on near shore. The haze was a demon.

> Since current and smoke fought relentlessly against tractors seaward of the line of departure, not all of the vehicles could find the control ship. If they did, it was next to impossible to come in close enough to get instructions shouted from the bridge. Thus many wave commanders, amtrac officers, and infantry leaders gave orders to head shoreward on their own initiative. They went in with waves and fragments of waves, displaying the kind of leadership that made the operation an overwhelming success in spite of the obstacles. This was the case with the three waves of 2/1 that failed to arrive at BLUE One. They found their way ashore, some of the LVTs landing on BLUE Two, others diverted to BLUE Three; but the important thing was that they got there. (MCOinK, Volume II)

The 1st Marines made the best of it, and, like their counterparts from the Fifth to the north, they had their objectives in hand by midnight.

Although all nine of the flame tanks were on Wolmi-do before the Inchon phase of the landing began, they would spend little time together as a group. With the second section going across the causeway with Able's lead platoon, the other two sections were held back until Baker Company, hopefully having shaken its problems with track bearings, came ashore on D+1.

"After we took our three flame tanks from the second section across the Causeway into Inchon and were heading toward Seoul," said F21 driver PFC Bill Kuykendall, "the rest of the Platoon later was split up with three tanks attached to each of the letter companies."

It wasn't until Dog Company arrived with the 7th Marines in 21 September that the entire First Tank Battalion was in Korea. However, by that time, the Flame Platoon was getting the feel for the war, making use of its primary weapon to torch suspected enemy hiding in villages along the way to Seoul. "We learned early," said PFC Kuykendall, "that the gooks would come out of those small buildings and try to satchel charge us, or move mines under our tracks. So, hell, when we came across a village, we just burned the places down."

It was not wanton destruction. "You just could not tell who the enemy was," the F21 driver said. "They would put on peasant clothing and mix in with the people of the village. We found some covering their uniforms with white sheets so they would blend in."

Korean villagers basically dressed in native long white oriental garb—even the men.

When the NKPA soldiers disguised themselves among them, it was difficult to know the *goodies* from the *badies*. "Hell, they all looked alike," Kuykendall said, "but we watched them closely because we knew the enemy might be among them."

However, when they found the NKPA, they took care of him.

"We fired those flame guns quite a bit once we got over the causeway," said Cpl. Maurice (Mo) Sims, who was driving F23. "Mostly we burned huts and any place we suspected the enemy would be hiding. But we had to try to make sure no kids or innocent civilians were in those places."

After they backed up the infantry securing Cemetery and Observatory hills, the tanks roamed further south and inland to help seize other key objectives—Ascom City, Kimpo Airport, Sosa-Ri, and Yondungpo, which was a key to crossing the Han River and the direct approach to Seoul.

Once again, as it did at Obong-ni Ridge along the Pusan Perimeter, Lt. Granville G. Sweet's Third Platoon of Able Company M26 Pershings got into it with three unsuspecting NKPA T-34 tanks on D+1.

> Moving into Kansong-ni, the vanguard of 2/5 and its tank escort approached a sharp bend where the road veered northward for about a mile to avoid two large hills. Around the curve were the enemy tanks believed to have been knocked out by VMF-214 earlier in the day.
>
> A section of Marine armor turned left off the pavement just short of the bend . . . two M-26s crawled to the top of a knoll from which they could cover the infantry, as the latter advanced around the corner. Looking down from their vantage point, the tank crews saw three intact T-34s parked in column on the highway, about 300 yards beyond the turn. Hatches on the Communist vehicles were buttoned, with the 85mm guns leveled at the road bend.
>
> The M-26s opened up immediately. Twenty rounds of 90mm armor-piercing (AP) ammunition crashed into the enemy armor. There was no return fire, probably because the Red crews had not time to elevate and traverse their manually-operated guns. In the space of a few minutes, each of the T-34s exploded and burst into flame. The crews did not escape.
>
> The Marine attack rolled past the blazing hulks. Nearby were two other wrecked T-34s, obviously the victims of the air attack. . . .
>
> Lt. Sweet's five M-26s, which had supported the day-long advance from RED Beach, were relieved at dusk by the 1st Platoon of Able Company tanks. In addition to their score of three T-34s, Sweet's veterans of the Pusan Perimeter had captured an impressive tally of enemy materiel: three NKPA trucks, two 76mm AT guns, two 122mm mortars, and a pair of Russian-manufactured jeeps. (MCOinK, Volume II)

Able Company now was under command of Capt. Gearl M. English, and he ordered Sweet's veteran platoon relieved—following the destruction of the three North Korean tanks—by the First Platoon, under 1st Lt. William D. Pomeroy.

By now, the First Tank Battalion's Baker Company was in the war, and on 24 September, it felt the sting of combat—losing two of its Pershings, one to a mine and the other by direct mortar hit—in support of the Fifth's Second Battalion near Hill 56. Eventually, Baker would move south to finally provide much-needed support for the First Marines working their way toward Seoul.

But there were a lot of skirmishes along the way before the capital city could be assaulted.

Enemy Gets Dose of "Tanker's Fear"

Without a doubt, the one thing that will strike fear into any tanker's heart, forcing beads of sweat to quickly seep from under his helmet, is the sight—out of the corner of his eye while peering through a periscope—of the enemy leveling a shoulder-mounted rocket at his tank.

It's difficult to suppress panic. You know the shooter already has a bead on his target, and you're it! You know he is ready to squeeze off the armor-piercing round. Usually this menace is off to the side, and all of your weapons are pointing straight ahead. Chances are, the range of your bow gunner's 30-caliber machine gun is restricted, and the weapon can't be swung fully in that direction to drill him. Nor can the turret be traversed quickly enough into position for the tank commander to use his weapons.

It is raw fear! Nothing else. And Flame Tankers have their stories to tell about this nerve-racking experience, later, at a little Korean hill called Kum gok.

That kind of fear, however, works two ways. Infantrymen experience a relative terror when the clanking of tank tracks and rumbling engines penetrate the air, signaling possible impending havoc.

Five days into the invasion of Inchon, during the First Marine Division's drive toward South Korea's capital city of Seoul, units of the 1st Marine Regiment were facing such a tank menace. But the infantrymen's predicament soon was changed into a gory nightmare for enemy tankers, thanks to an act of bold heroism by PFC Walter C. Monegan, Jr.

A twenty-year-old regular from Seattle, Washington, Monegan was a rocket man with the 1st Marines Fox Company when he took on three Russian-made T-34 tanks at a bend in the road of the Inchon-Seoul Highway near hills 80 and 85. It was the second time in three days he faced off against enemy tanks, and he was a sure shot.

But Monegan's marksmanship was not the only noted success against the vaunted NKPA-manned Russian armor. Yet his heroics became one of the legends of the drive to the capital city.

It all started after the First Marines had worked their way out of Ascom City and along the Inchon-Seoul Highway. They were dug in just west of Mahang-ri in the predawn of 17 September, when six Russian T-34s passed below their positions. The tanks were leading a column of unsuspecting NKPA intent on stunting the Marines' progress toward the Han River.

It was obvious that the Communist soldiers had little or no knowledge of the situation ahead. For as they neared Ascom City at the crack of dawn, some were still sitting comfortably on the tanks and eating breakfast. Others laughed and jabbered as they trailed along the road. (2nd) Lieutenant (Lee R.) Howard saw them approaching his Dog Company (2nd Platoon, D/2nd/Bat5th) outpost on the knoll. He reported . . . first one tank, then three, and finally six . . . (his superior took) the information with the proverbial grain of salt, supposing it to be a delusion of youth and inexperience. Just as quickly . . . that impression . . . was shattered by the first reverberations of the battle.

The attitude of the enemy soldiers as they neared his outpost convinced Howard that they were unaware of the proximity of Marine lines. He let the head of the column slip by on the road below, therefore, until the tanks began to round the bend leading to Dog Company's MLR. Then the platoon leader shouted the order, and his men opened up with machine guns, rifles, and BARs.

The Red infantry went down under the hail of lead like wheat under the sickle. Soldiers on the tanks were knocked to the road, where many were ground under as the big vehicles lurched and roared crazily in reaction to the surprise.

Corporal Okey J. Douglas moved part way down the knoll and closed on the lead T–34 with his 2.36-inch rocket launcher. A few well-placed rounds, fired calmly at a range of 75 yards, killed the armored vehicle on the spot. Continuing the single-handed assault, Douglas damaged tank number 2 just as the main Marine position exploded into action.

Under attack by the outpost, the cripple and the four unharmed T–34s had continued around the road bend, some of them spilling off the curve in an attempt to deploy in the adjacent rice paddy. All five were taken under fire by First Lieutenant William D. Pomeroy's M–26s, about 600 yards away. Within five minutes, the Marine 90mm guns threw 45 rounds of AP at the enemy armor.

Recoilless rifles of Second Lieutenant Charles M. Jones' platoon (5th Marines AT Co) added their hot metal at a range of 500 yards, and the 75s with the 1st Marines across the road also erupted. Simultaneously, Second Lieutenant James E. Harrell ordered the 3.5-inch rocket launchers of 2/5's assault platoon into action.

The T–34's didn't have a chance. All of them exploded under the heavy fusilade; and when the smoke cleared, they were heaps of burning wreckage. Scattered around the dead tanks and along the road were the bodies of 200 Red infantrymen. So rapid and complete was the enemy's destruction that only one Marine casualty—slightly wounded—resulted from the fight.

It was only natural that conflicting claims would arise among the participants in the short, violent clash. To Pomeroy's tank crews, it appeared that the M–26s accounted for the five T–34s with little or no assistance from infantry arms. This was a reasonable conclusion on their part, owing to the limited visibility from the buttoned vehicles and the fact that their 90mm guns unquestionably wrought the greatest destruction on the NKPA machines. Since so many weapons were firing simultaneously from various other positions, however, and since the T–34s were wrecked so completely, kills and partial kills were also claimed by the recoilless rifles of both regiments. Moreover, the 3.5-inch rocket gunners of 2/5 and 2/1 believed that some of their rounds found the mark in the midst of the furor. It is known, for instance, that Private First Class Walter C. Monegan, Jr., rocket man in the assault squad of Fox Company, 1st Marines, closed on the enemy vehicles after they had rounded the bend and fired his weapon at point-blank ranges. (MCOinK, Volume II)

Officially, PFC Monegan was credited with taking on the lead T-34 and destroying it with a direct hit, and then turning his carbine on the lone surviving crewman and killing him as the NKPA tanker tried to escape from under the tank. Then, he picked up his rocket gun and sent two more rounds into the tank column to help compound the confusion the enemy was experiencing.

But it was at Sosa-ri, a few miles up the road, that Monegan went to work again and paid the ultimate price a few days later.

Midway between Mahang-ri and the phase line was the town of Sosa, and it was from this locale that North Korean soldiers were pouring westward to delay the Marine advance on the highway.

Since the 5th Marines had veered to the northeast to attack Kimpo, its boundary with the 1st had moved well to the left of the highway. Henceforth, (Col. Chesty) Puller's regiment would have to go it alone on the main road. This was the case as the 2d and 3d Battalions butted against enemy delaying forces between Ascom City and Mahang-ri, and the isolation became more pronounced as they attacked toward Sosa late on the 17th.

The 2d Battalion drove to the top of the high ground on the left of the road, and the Marines enjoyed a small-scale "turkey shoot" as the North Koreans pulled out and pelted toward Sosa. While the assault units consolidated their holdings, the remainder of the 2d and 3d Battalions moved into the area around the defile and dug in for the night.

The 1st Marines' attack along the highway had netted 4,800 yards. Despite repeated clashes in the course of the day, 2/1 lost only one killed and 28 wounded, and Company G of the 3d Battalion suffered six WIA. Enemy losses included 250 killed and wounded, 70 prisoners, one T–34 tank, several AT guns, and large quantities of small arms and ammunition. (MCOinK, Volume II)

By 18 September the First Marine Division had received orders to cross the Han River to the north of the 2nd Battalion, but there was a lot of work before that could be accomplished. Sosa-ri remained a trouble spot facing the Battalion as it dug in the night of 19 September in a three-mile perimeter along the Inchon-Seoul Highway. The key targets of Yongdongpo and the Han River were about five-to-six miles to the west. Early the next morning, the NKPA marshalled a column of tanks and infantry out of Yongdongpo.

In the van of the Red column were five T–34 tanks preceded, oddly enough, by a truck loaded with ammunition. Other vehicles, laden with less sensitive supplies, were safely interspersed among the infantry in the long file.
. . . Companies D and F, the latter in the fore, occupied high ground positions parallel to and south of the highway . . . The troops of Fox Company, tense with anticipation in their advance deployment, heard the first distant sounds of clanking armor and racing engines sometime before 0400. The noise grew steadily louder until, at 0430, the shadows of the ammunition truck and T–34s passed beneath the Marine defenses and continued along the road toward Easy Company's lines. At the latter, Private Oliver O'Neil, Jr., rose from behind his machine gun and shouted a challenge to the truck, which by this time was well out in front of the enemy tanks. O'Neil was cut down by automatic fire in answer, and pandemonium broke out on the highway.
Obviously the North Koreans had stumbled into it again, just as they had done at Ascom City. Two T–34s stopped . . . and opened up wildly. Companies D and F in turn exploded with machine guns, small arms, grenades, and mortars against the flank of the enemy column . . . Under the hail of fire from above, the Red soldiers milled about in panic and were slaughtered . . .
The T–34s began to lurch back and forth like trapped animals. Owing either to mines laid by Marine engineers or a grenade thrown from above, the ammunition truck exploded in a brilliant spectacle of pyrotechnics. In the midst of the furor, Private First Class Monegan moved across the hillside from Company F's front with his rocket launcher. Observing his progress against the backdrop of flames from the truck, his comrades either held or shifted their fire to protect him. . . .
Monegan closed on the lead tank and wrecked it with one 3.5-inch projectile. Approaching the second T–34 under intense fire, he paused and took aim with imperturbability. Again his rocket connected with a roar, and the black hulk on the road turned into a blazing furnace. Silhouetted against the hillside, the Marine leveled his weapon at a third armored vehicle just as it was pivoting around to retreat. But at this moment an enemy machine gun found the mark, and Monegan—killer of tanks—fell dead. (MCOinK, Volume II)

The costly heroism of PFC Monegan had started to turn the tide of the First Marines push into Yongdongpo and onward to cross the Han. It was a little after daylight when that portion of the battle was over, and in addition to the two tanks destroyed by the rocket man, the third T–34 was captured. The highway and its adjoining ditches were strewn with more than 300 North Korean bodies.

The smoldering tanks, victims of a shoulder-mounted rocket launcher, was testimony that all that iron and steel can be laid waste by the bravery of a soldier—be he friend or foe. North Korean tankers would not be the only ones on the deadly end of enemy rockets. First Tank Battalion Marines, including the Flame Platoon, were not immune to this horror.

But in the confrontation at Sosa-Ri, it was PFC Walter. C. Monegan who prevailed, and his heroism would be duly recorded:

Medal of Honor

Monegan, Walter C. Jr.
Private First Class, U.S. Marine Corps,
Company F, 2d Battalion, First Marines
1st Marine Division (Reinforced)

Citation

For conspicuous gallantry and intrepidity at the risk of his own life above and beyond the call of duty while serving as a rocket gunner attached to Company F, and in action against the enemy aggressor forces. Dug in on a hill overlooking the main Seoul Highway when 6 enemy tanks threatened to break through the battalion position during a predawn attack on 17 September, Pfc. Monegan promptly moved forward with his bazooka, under heavy hostile automatic weapons fire and engaged the lead tank at a range of less than 50 yards. After scoring a direct hit and killing the sole surviving tankman with his carbine as he came through the escape hatch, he boldly fired 2 more rounds of ammunition at the oncoming tanks, disorganizing the attack and enabling our tank crews to continue blasting with their 90-mm guns. With his own and adjacent company's position threatened by the annihilation when an overwhelming enemy tank-infantry force bypassed the area and proceeded toward the battalion command post during the early morning of September 20, he seized his rocket launcher and, in total darkness, charged down the slope of the hill where the tanks had broken through. Quick to act when an illuminating shell lit the area, he scored a direct hit on one of the tanks as hostile rifle and automatic-weapons fire raked the area at close range. Again exposing himself, he fired another round to destroy a second tank and, as the rear tank turned to retreat, stood upright to fire and was fatally struck down by hostile machine gun fire when another illuminating shell silhouetted him against the sky. Pfc. Monegan's daring initiative, gallant fighting spirit and courageous devotion to duty were contributing factors in the success of his company in repelling the enemy, and his self-sacrificing efforts throughout sustain and enhance the highest traditions of the U.S. Naval Service. He gallantly gave his life for his country.

The Fear of Flame Tanks

"Dawn of 20 September revealed a scene of utter ruin across the Marine front. The highway was littered with burnt NKPA trucks, tanks and equipment. Heaped on the road, in ditches and along hillsides were 300 enemy dead."

Thanks in large part to the bravery of PFC Walter C. Monegan, Jr., the North Korean People's Army venture into the teeth of the 1st Marines at Soso-Ri proved disastrous. This opened the door to capture hills 80 and 85, which eventually led to the assault and securing Yondungpo, a major acquisition needed to cross the Han River, which flowed west of Seoul and then curved east under the capital city's southern perimeter.

There was bitter fighting for two nights and two days, but the triangular-shaped objective with its apex at the juncture of the Han and Kalcon rivers was finally taken. By 23 September the 1st Marines were on the banks of the Han, poised to cross the river and hit the outskirts of Seoul.

Once across the Han, where engineers eventually had to replace blown bridges in order to give tanks and trucks accessibility to the east bank of the river, the NKPA defenders stiffened, and the Marines found things nothing like the walk on the beach at Wolmi-do.

One of the major bottlenecks was a range of three peaks, all given the number *105,* but dignified by the military as 105N, 105C, and 105S. Overlooking a rail line, the NKPA stronghold ran approximately 4,000 yards northeasterly from the Han River toward the capital building. It was here that the North Koreans put up one of their most stubborn defenses. But it was also where the Reds, making their final stand on 25 September, met the wrath of scorching doses of napalm from a flame tank and decided the Marines could have Hill 105.

After two days of give-and-take fighting for 105, Easy Company of 2ndBat5th Marines and George Company 3rdBat5th finally controlled 105N. How Company 3rdBat5th, despite paying a severe price in casualties, took 105C.

That left 105's southern nob. It was a job assigned to the 3rd Battalion, 1st Marines, supported by two platoons of M26 Pershing tanks from Baker Company and a section of fire-spitting Shermans from the Flame Platoon.

With engineers clearing the way, the small tank-infantry force came under heavy fire from the hill, where the company-strength NKPA was dug into a line of trenches. Captain Bruce F. Williams was commanding the supporting tanks and became so concerned for the platoon of 1st Marines infantry that he thought about "pulling them inside the tanks and withdrawing."

Then it occurred to him to send a flame thrower tank escorted by Staff Sergeant Altaire's M26, around the enemy's left flank by way of a primitive trail leading southward from the railway tracks.

This maneuver had a spectacular success. The flame tank moved into position enabling it to sear the length of the NKPA trenches with burst of napalm. When the terrified Red Koreans fled down the slope, they became targets for the machine guns of Lieutenant (Bryan J.) Cummings' platoon of tanks. (MCOinK, Volume II)

"Resistance had become increasingly heavy until the flame tank drove close enough to the enemy-held trench lines and bunkers," said Cpl. Robert Rosenthal, who had fought his way through Wolmi-Do, Kimpo, Ascom City, Sosa-ri, and Yongdung-Po with Fox Company of 2ndBat5th. "In that position, the tank unloaded a sweeping burst of napalm fire as the bow gunner and loader raked the hill with machine-gun fire. Out of the trenches, pot holes, and bunkers came NKPA troops."

Moments later, Lt. Cummings began to level the 90mm cannon of his M26 on the hill. He had spotted a cave and was about to throw a round into the opening.

> But before Cummings could fire into the cave, eight or ten NKPA soldiers come out with upraised hands. When they were allowed to surrender unharmed, the example had an amazing effect as the seemingly endless fire of enemy troops poured out of the cave. Altogether, 131 prisoners were taken, in addition to an estimated 150 killed, on a hill first reported secured two days before. Apparently the undiscovered cave had provided a refuge for nearly 330 Red Koreans. (MCOinK, Volume II)

Obviously, the enemy soldiers, holed up in the cave, wanted nothing to do with the terror rained on their comrades in the trenches by the flame tank.

PFC Bill Kuykendall was driving F21, one of the two flame tanks, which scorched the hill with napalm. "When the Gooks came out of those holes," he said, "they were ordered to take off their clothes."

Marine veterans of World War II had learned an expensive lesson with Japanese carrying weapons concealed under their uniforms, and they were taking no chances with the North Koreans. But this instance caught the Marines by surprise. "There were five women among enemy who were stripping," Kuykendall said.

Of course it didn't bother the Marines, but there was a news photographer tagging along with infantry and he snapped a shot of the prisoners. When the photo appeared in papers back in the States, there was some criticism. But the Marines were fighting a war, and as far as they were concerned, it just happened to be one of those things that sometimes happen.

Despite the controversy, the flame tanks were earning their keep.

Capt. Phillip C. Morrell, who went ashore at Wolmi-do with three of his Service Company Shermans, was well aware what flame tanks could accomplish, and when reviewing the incident at Hills 105, he knew full well what could be accomplished by "squirting their stuff."

Morrell had pulled off a pretty nifty caper of his own when he was on Okinawa in World War II. While commanding a platoon of Sherman gun tanks, he had the support of five Army flame-throwing M4A3s, and he used them wisely.

The Japanese were in a thicket the size of three football fields on the reverse slope of a hill. Their position was surrounded by heavy green grass. Morrell ordered the flame tanks to encircle the grass and saturate it with raw napalm—no ignition. After the film of napalm was laid down, the Marine officer ordered one of the flame tanks to fire a hot load.

There was a tremendous explosion as the entire Jap position went up in flame and black smoke. Not one of the enemy survived, most of them dead from loss of oxygen.

The concept, which fostered the creation of the Flame Platoon, grew out of the such successful use of early versions of this unique piece of equipment in the island-hopping warfare throughout the Pacific theater during World War II.

Now, early in the Korean War, the Flame Platoon was proving that the simultaneous—yet independent—foresight of two veteran tank battalion commanding officers was beginning to pay dividends. The torching of Hill 105S, which brought the ultimate surrender of the horde of North Korean soldiers, finally opened the door for the major assault on Seoul. This was to be launched with the three Marine Regiments—the 7th Marines finally had arrived on 21 September and were about to be committed to their first action. Support elements would include the Korean Marine Corps, the Army's 32nd Infantry Division, and the Republic of Korea 17th Regiment.

The Marines were in an arc, pinching toward Seoul's capital building. Lt. Col. Homer L. Litzenburg's 7th Marines were to come into the outskirts of the city from hills to the north, Lt. Col. Robert D. Tapplett's 5th Regiment in the middle, and the 1st Marines of Col. Lewis B. (Chesty) Puller going in from the southwest. To Puller's right and south of the city were the army and ROK forces.

Enter X Corps commander, Maj. Gen. Edward M. (Ned) Almond on the night of 25 September, eve of the planned assault on Seoul, and another order was issued that didn't sit well with Maj. Gen. Oliver P. Smith, the First Marine Division's commanding general. Based on intelligence information:

The enemy was fleeing the city of Seoul on the road north of Uijongbu . . . the X Corps commander messaged Smith: "You will push attack now to the limit of your objectives in order to insure maximum destruction of enemy forces." (MCOinK, Volume II)

As would be proven throughout the first year of the war, intelligence gathering by those advising both Far East Commander, Gen. Douglas MacArthur, and General Almond was far from accurate.

Smith was suspect of the report that the North Korean troops were fleeing Seoul and didn't like sending his troops into a city about which he, or any of the United Nations military, knew very little. When he questioned X Corps, Smith was told that he was expected to start his attack immediately. Smith then asked to speak with Almond, but could not get to the Corps commander. He was told "the order to attack was to be executed without delay" *(MCOinK, Volume II)*.

Reluctantly, Smith followed his orders. Late the night of 25 September, the Division commander issued subsequent orders to his regimental commanders, advising that they use only "avenues of advance which could be identified at night."

In the early hours of 26 September, the attack on City of Seoul was on its way. What would transpire in the next few days was a totally new ball game for the United States Marine Corps. And it was not lost on General Smith that some very bad scoop had been passed along by General Almond's staff, and the results would open a new era of fighting for the United States Marine Corps.

Weaned and polished in beachhead landings, routing enemy in hills, villages, and small towns through their proud 175-year history, Leathernecks were about to get their first lesson in street fighting through a major city. And that street fighting was also where the Shermans from the First Tank Battalion's Flame Platoon would play a major role.

The Maze That Was Seoul

More than one Gyrene looked down from the hills surrounding the capital city of South Korea and wondered what the hell they were getting into. Even for seasoned Marine Corps officers and NCOs who had been through the island campaigns of the Pacific in World War II, their next challenge in the Land of the Morning Calm was a whole new ball game.

This place was big. Seoul's city limits stretched about six-and-a-half miles northeastward from the Han River and it was approximately two-and-a-half miles wide in some sections.

There were clusters of one-story homes. Looking down on them, the tile roofs meshed with shingle-covered houses and presented a mosaic of overlapping lines and patches that concealed many of the small streets and alleys running within them. In other sections, there were larger buildings—some of them could have been five stories high—possibly small factories or warehouses. Above them all in the distance reigned the ancient capital building downtown and the surrounding, more citified multi-storied consulates, the university, and schools.

Not too obvious in the maze that was Seoul were systems of barricades blocking many of those streets. They were difficult to see from outside the city.

Seoul was no bean patch by any stretch of the imagination. There were people down there who wanted nothing to do with war, but who had no way out of the city's confines as long as the North Koreans were in control.

Marine Corps historian Col. Joseph Alexander, writing "Recapture of Seoul, Korea" for *Leatherneck Magazine*'s October 2000 issue, put it this way:

> Street fighting was not a strong suit for Leathernecks before 1950. In truth, the Marines spent most of their first 175 years fighting in the boondocks. Longago, Chaputlepec, Peking or Vera Cruz had been exceptions. The Marines fought two of their bloodiest battles, Tarawa and Pelelieu, in the total absence of civilians.
>
> Seoul was enormous—home to nearly a million-and-a-half people in 1950. While many fled from the North Korean invaders, nearly a million remained.

What this presented, Alexander noted, was

> the largest rural objective the Marines ever assailed. The battle for Hue City (Vietnam) in 1968 lasted longer and was equally as violent, but Seoul had twice the civilian population and three times as many defenders.

What the Marines would also learn very quickly as they entered the strange streets of the capital city was that the North Korean People's Army was ready for them—and the Reds had a very good idea of how to defend themselves. The First Marine Division was about to become entangled in the "Battle of the Barricades" and the Flame Platoon tanks that would play a major roll—and somewhat of a price—helping to blast and burn a path through the city.

Instead of bunker-busting, which tankers perfected in the Pacific and would refine again when Marines got back into the hills of Korea, the chore in front of them going into Seoul could be called home-wrecking and road-reconstruction.

The flame tanks would be right in the middle of it with their rods of darting orange-hot napalm torching buildings, turning structures into pyres of flame and acrid black smoke. Direct jolts of 105mm ordnance pummeled into junk-entangled road blocks and NKPA-infested factories, office buildings, homes, and shacks.

But the flame tanks did the job of clearing them out. The pudgy smaller Sherman M4A3E8 fire-shooters seemed perfectly suited for the street-fighting and once again would prove their mettle going through the capital city.

"When they entered the streets in that place, it was like a firestorm, shooting napalm into those buildings," said Cpl. Robert Rosenthal of the 5th Marines. "The North Korean forces were holed up in all kinds of places and shooting down into our approach."

If Maj.Gen Oliver P. Smith, the First Marine Division commander, really had the time to lay out plans to his liking for the attack on the Seoul, his mind might have been eased if he visualized what the specialized Shermans could do grinding through those streets and alleys.

But before he could do the planning he wanted, his nemesis and direct superior in the field once again caused him some concern.

Smith was not being apprehensive on 25 September when he got hurry-up orders from Maj. Gen. Edward M. Ned Almond, the X Corps commander, to "begin at once" the assault on Seoul. Smith was just cautious. He didn't like the idea of sending his Marines into a city he knew nothing about—particularly at night—and with so-called intelligence in hand that was suspect at best.

But his fruitless attempts to get through to Almond and have the attack on Seoul changed until he could get a better handle on the situation forced Smith to plan the jump-off for 0145 on the morning of 26 September.

Intelligence reports forwarded to Smith informed the Marines commander that NKPA troops were fleeing the capital city and there would be little opposition. Smith was suspect, and his fears proved to be on the money when the First Marines ran smack into a tank-supported attack by the North Koreans shortly after midnight. That scrubbed the original H-hour. Subsequent encounters with the enemy on other fronts kept pushing back the Marines' planned assault. It wasn't until hours later that they were able to jump off.

It had been Gen. Douglas MacArthur's goal to secure Seoul by 25 September, exactly three months from the day North Korean troops stormed across the 38th Parallel. The Far East Commander had planned elaborate ceremonies, replete with the Marine Corps Band with instruments rushed from Japan, to return the capital to South Korean president, Syngman Rhee.

Almond, who had become impatient with Smith's reluctance to barge hell-bent-for election into the NKPA stronghold, issued an announcement on 25 September that Seoul had been captured. Marines wondered about that news release as they were poised for the attack on the outskirts of the city. It wasn't until late afternoon of the 27th—and a lot of bloodshed later—that enemy resistance petered out and Seoul was under the Stars and Stripes, the Republic of Korea national banner, and the royal-blue ensign of the United Nations.

But before all of that could take place, the Flame Platoon would take its first casualty, losing one of its Sherman M4A3E8's while it was supporting the 1st Marines coming into the city from southwest where gravel-crunching Marines were becoming street-Marines and running afoul of the NKPA barricades.

Aiding the Communists behind the barricades were other North Koreans who fired their rifles and submachine guns from roof tops, windows and side streets. (MCOinK, Volume II)

So much for the intelligence reports that told General Smith the NKPA was fleeing the city a few days earlier.

The Marine infantry, therefore, had to defend in every direction as it attacked to the front. Intense heat from burning buildings (set afire by flame tanks) added to the handicaps, and the constant discovery of South Korean civilians, including women and children, huddled in the rubble further strained the taught nerves of men who looked for trouble from every quarter.

It was a dirty, frustrating fight every yard of the way, perhaps best described by Puller (Lt.Col. Chesty Puller, Commanding Officer, 1st Marine Regiment) himself who reported that "progress was agonizingly slow." A principal deterrent to speed was the fact that all supporting tanks simultaneously expended their ammunition and fuel, so that all had to await their return rather than pay heavily in casualties by assaulting barricades with small arms alone. (MCOinK, Volume II)

When the tanks rejoined the fray, Fox 22, the No. 2 double-barreled Sherman in the second section of the Flame Platoon, was among them.

At one point in the street battle, an enemy soldier darted from behind a building and charged a flame tank (F22) advancing behind two lead M26s. Ignoring the Marine infantrymen, who gaped in disbelief, the North Korean hurled a huge satchel charge over the engine compartment of the armored vehicle, then escaped unharmed as the explosion rocked the area. The flame tank was wrecked, but the crew escaped serious injury with the assistance of supporting infantry. Apparently a suicide squad of NKPA demolition men had been assigned the mission of destroying Marine armor in this fashion, for several other Red soldiers tried single-handed assaults shortly afterwards. The riflemen of 2/1 (2nd Battalion, 1st Marines) were alert for the later attempts, however, and the enemy fanatics were cut down before inflicting further damage. (MCOinK, Volume II)

Before that day—26 September—was over, the Flame Platoon would exact some payment for the loss of its first tank.

Late in the afternoon, while elements of the 1st Marines were raising the Stars and Stripes over the American and Russian embassies, flame tanks again were among the armor supporting Charlie Company of the regiment's 2nd Battalion near the railroad station between Hill 82 and the slopes of South Mountain, about 1,500 yards south of the U.S. Consulate. It was one of the last bastions of the final NKPA stand.

The flame tanks, which had been roaming the streets with a couple of M26 Pershings, came to the rescue.

Charlie Company had been held up at the outset in the neighborhood of the railroad station, but supporting tanks, including flame throwers, had paved the way burning a formidable nest of NKPA automatic weapons and AT Guns. (MCOinK, Volume II)

PFC William (Bill) Gobert of Tarentum, Pennsylvania, and PFC Glenn A. Kasdorf, of Milwaukee, Wisconsin, were in the Recon Company of Headquarters Company near the railroad station when all hell was breaking loose in the First Marines sector.

"The whole city was ablaze," said Gobert, referring to the devastation the flame tanks had unleashed. "Buildings were on fire, telephone wires, strung out all over the place, were burning. The railroad station was the last to get torched (by the flame tanks)."

Gobert and Kasdorf both said word was out that the First Marines believed "approximately two thousand NKPA were making a last stand there." That's when the flame tanks were called in.

"When the flame tanks started pouring napalm into the station," Kasdorf said, "there was nothing but devastation, and panic . . . the NKPA were on fire, running out of the building."

Some of the Reds had managed to escape the flames but only met a different kind of death. "The First Marines and machine guns from the flame tanks and other tanks just mowed them down," Kasdorf said. It was one of many favors that had endeared the Flame Platoon to Marine infantry throughout the campaign.

Cpl. Dean Servais, a nineteen-year-old Marine from Kinosha, Wisconsin, who came into Inchon driving D12, one of Dog Company's Pershings, formed an early respect for the flame tanks, particularly after he saw what they could do to buildings and road blocks. The smaller buildings on the fringes of the city and on into the area of the capital, were old and not too difficult to bring down with a shot of 90mm. But Servais watched many times when his tank's powerful ordnance couldn't do the job.

"We would hit that building and keep on hitting it, but it wouldn't fall down. That's when we'd call in the flame tanks. They would just burn 'em out. They'd put their flames into the bottom floors, and pretty soon that whole building was ablaze all the way to the top floor. You could shoot out a building, you could machine-gun it, and the Reds would just go deeper into it."

When the tanks stopped firing, a little later, the Reds started oozing from the building looking to exact their own revenge. Servais more than once saw the answer to that. "When the building was torched by a flame tank, the North Koreans didn't come out later. That intense fire just took all the oxygen out of the building." The Reds either got the hell out of there in a hurry, or paid the ultimate price.

The flame tanks were not shy about using their 105mm cannon on buildings. "There was one large building," PFC Bill Kuykendall, driver of F21, said, "that we blew a big hole in the top of it."

Another charge to the flame tanks was saturating utility poles with burning naplam. "That scorched attached wires and cut NKPA communications," said Cpl. Maurice (Mo) Sims, who was driving F23. But their major targets were where the NKPA was holed up. "We burned out a lot of buildings," he said.

Barricades were a nuisance the entire campaign through the streets of Seoul.

"The North Koreans seemed very apt at putting a lot of old vehicles, and destroying blown-up buildings so that they fell across the road," Servais said.

With the barricades full of wooden debris from the shacks the NKPA toppled into the streets and reinforced by rice bags, the rod of napalm searing through them from a flame gun would make short order of the obstruction.

Machine-gun nests were often set up behind the roadblocks. Once that torch pierced the barricade and created an inferno, the North Koreans found it very prudent to seek shelter elsewhere—if they could. Often they were unable to move fast enough. They were cooked.

"Those flame tanks did a big job in Seoul," Servais said. "They were very active, moving, on call, from one spot to another."

Credit for helping win the Battle of the Barricades in Seoul had to be shared by the Flame Tankers with another version of the M4A3 Sherman—the "dozer tanks," spread out among letter companies, Service Company, and the infantry regiments' anti-tank units. They often worked in tandem with the flame tanks, using their sturdy blades to plow through the roadblocks. "They would just bust open those barricades," Servais said of the bladed pigirons.

PFC Ben Gabijan, a native Californian who was B33's gunner in Baker Company's Third Platoon, saw the flame tanks come to the rescue of the Korean Marines who were pinned down in a Seoul Street. "They were called in to clear enemy positions," Gabijan said. "They hosed down both sides of the street with those flame guns."

Of course, the Pershings did their bit if the Shermans weren't around, sending their high-powered 90mm ordnance into mounds. But Seoul became a perfect place for the flame tanks and dozers tanks to do their stuff.

With such supporting efforts helping the First Marine Division's three vaunted infantry Regiments, General MacArthur was finally able to conduct his liberation ceremonies on 29 September. Even then, it was only after the NKPA had made three different attacks on the fringe of the city that morning.

Owing to the still-tenuous surroundings, the Far East Commander in Chief decided against the planned opulent ceremonies and left the Marines to guarding the city instead of ordering them to post an honor guard and strike up the band.

In the four-day siege of the capital city, 104 Marines were killed or died of wounds, and 300 more were wounded in action. They are significant numbers in light of the intelligence reports that triggered General Smith's skepticism when he was informed of "the enemy fleeing the city of Seoul on road north to Uijongbu."

By 1 October, the Reds truly were on a northeast run to Uijongbu with the 7th Marines hot on their tails. The 5th Marines took off to the northwest, shagging after NKPA elements headed for Suyuhyon, while the 1st Marines remained on the outskirts of Seoul to enforce the division's right and southern flank.

It was a total rout of the North Korean People's Army, which was not only folding under pressure of X Corps but also backpedaling ahead of the Eighth Army and ROK troops who were barreling north after breaking out of the Pusan Perimeter.

The NKPA retreat was so bad, it presented another serious problem for United Nation troops. The demoralized Reds were scattering, throwing away their weapons and uniforms, and dressing as civilians to mix with refugees in an effort to sneak back to North Korea.

Sections of flame tanks still were dispersed among the lettered gun tanks, tied in with Able Company's Pershings going toward Suyuhyon and with Dog Company, which was attached to the 7th Marines when they secured Uijongbu.

Officially, the Inchon-Seoul operation came to its conclusion on 7 October 1950, and the First Marine Division was pulled off the line. General Smith's city-fighters were headed back to Inchon, where they came ashore only 22 days earlier. There, they prepared for another mission—another landing on the other side of Korea.

Though it was believed the North Koreans were a beaten army and incapable of reorganizing to present any further serious problems to the United Nations constabulary, plans had been formalized for the Marines to go in at Wonson on the east coast. It was a smaller port city on a northeastly line across the peninsula from Pyonyang, the capital city of North Korea.

The respite and planning for the new invasion was somewhat of a break for the 1st-MarDiv. It was a chance to make and renew acquaintances. The helter-skelter organization of the Division was so fragmented, it was amazing, in a sense, that the left hand knew what the right hand was doing.

"It wasn't until we got into Seoul that I was able to meet the other company commanders," said Captain Phillip C. Morrell, who landed at Wolmi-do with three of his Service Company's Shermans. A few months later, Morrell was promoted to major and became First Tank Battalion executive officer under Lt. Col. Harry T. Milne.

Lt. Col. Raymond L. Murray, commanding officer of the Fifth Marine Regiment, never met his counterpart from the 1st Marines, Col. Lewis B. Chesty Puller, until they were in the thick of the fighting around Seoul.

There's something to be said for command abilities of General Smith, who managed to coordinate such a successful operation under circumstances like that—circumstances that were more typical than not in the First Marine Division's early days of the war. Smith would be tested more seriously a couple of months later, but his leadership from Inchon to Uijongbu set the precedent.

Looking back on the Division's first 22 days in Korea, and what it took to get there, reflection only conjures up a sense of amazement at the accomplishment. It was duly recorded in *Marine Corps Operations in Korea, Volume II:*

> *Expansion from a reduced peace strength (less the 1st Provisional Marine Brigade) to a reinforced war strength, less one RCT . . . in 15 days . . .*
>
> *Administrative sea lift and movement of over 15,000 personnel . . . equipment, and partial resupply from San Diego to the Far East Command commenced in less than three weeks after expansion was ordered. . . .*
>
> *Debarkation and unloading . . . and embarkation and reloading at Kobe, Japan, for the assault landing at Inchon . . . in a period averaging about seven days per unit, two days of which were lost due to a heavy typhoon in the Kobe area. . . .*
>
> *Operation order for the amphibious landing at Inchon . . . accomplished 17 days after the receipt of the initial directive . . .*
>
> *The 1st Provisional Marine Brigade was disengaged from active combat with the enemy on the South Korean front at midnight on 5 September, moved to Pusan, and outloaded in combat shipping in less than 7 days. . . .*
>
> *A successful assault landing was executed at Inchon . . . on 15 September under some of the most adverse landing conditions in the history of amphibious operations. . . .*
>
> *The Force Beachhead Line approximately six miles from Landing beaches was seized within 24 hours after main landing on Beaches RED and BLUE. . . .*
>
> *Kimpo Airfield, a primary objective . . . captured 50 hours and 35 minutes after H-Hour, D-Day . . .*
>
> *The first assault crossing of the Han River (400 yards wide at the crossing site) executed by RCT-5 employing LVTs, DUKWs, and pontoon ferries, less than five days after the landing at Inchon . . .*
>
> *The effectiveness of Marine air-ground team and close air support . . . were reaffirmed with outstanding success.*

The modern "Minute Men" of the United States Marine Corps, with a significant contribution from its newest unit—the Flame Platoon of the First Tank Battalion—had made their initial entry into history. What they would do before 1950 came to an end, however, would become one of the most grueling and proudest episodes in the 175 years of the Corps.

Recruit's Teammate Dies a Hero

With two of the First Marine Division's three infantry regiments still on the line outside of the capital city of Seoul, orders came from Gen. Douglas MacArthur to prepare the Division for another beachhead landing on the other side of the Korean peninsula.

The target was Wonsan, a small east-coast port approximately eighty miles above the 38th Parallel, a little north on an easterly line across the peninsula from Pyonyang, the capital of North Korea. The idea was to cut off the retreating North Korean People's Army backpedaling in disarray ahead of the rejuvenated Eighth Army and elements of the Republic of Korea army.

MacArthur had asked the North Koreans to surrender, but his suggestion did not interest Communist officials in Pyongyang. He had the okay from the Joint Chiefs of Staff in Washington to push ahead into North Korea, but he wanted to cut off the retreating remnants of the NKPA. To do this, he planned to use the landing at Wonsan to slam the door on what he suspected was the Reds' routed army.

Once again, it presented another logistical headache for Maj. Gen. Oliver P. Smith, commander of the First Marine Division. He had ten days, after the order was passed, to get his Marines off the line, back to Inchon, into a convoy, and then loop around the southern tip of the peninsula and send them into Wonsan by 15 October.

His protests to Maj. Gen. "Ned" Almond, commanding officer of X Corps, that the time element was impractical—particularly since the Marines still were engaged at Uibongju and Suyuhyon—once again fell on deaf ears. Almond was under orders from MacArthur to get it done, and he was not inclined to face up to the Far East Commander. As late as 2 October, the 7th Marines were still tangling with the Reds at Uijongbu and suffered most of the Division's sixteen killed in action that day.

Two days later, orders came from Almond to begin the move to Wonsan. On 5 October, the weary 5th Marines with supporting tank and artillery units, ended their twenty days on the front lines. The next day, the 1st Marines were pulled off, and the 7th Regiment was extracted on 7 October.

Warily, General Smith's staff had begun drawing up plans for the new landing, despite lack of formidable intelligence or updated maps of the area. Of course, the original landing date of 15 October had gone by the boards. Actually, the canceled D-Day was when the First Marine Division began loading at Inchon. It would be two days later before the entire task force was under way.

By that time, the situation had changed—and it would change again, and again, and again while the Marines were on the high seas. When the Division finally got around to Wonsan, the ROK 3rd and Capital Divisions already had taken the port city.

Then, there was the matter of mines in Wonsan Harbor. The Navy cautiously took two weeks to sweep the waters, much to the chagrin of MacArthur and Almond, who seemed to have a penchant for throwing caution to the wind. Had not Rear Adm. James H. Doyle, Task Force 90 commander, questioned the safety of the operation—and 7th Fleet commander Vice Adm. Arthur D. Struble flat-out said no to taking ships into Wonsan without sweeping for mines—the results could have been catastrophic.

A helicopter doing an aerial sweep over the waters early in October reported sighting more than sixty mines. There were so many mines discovered on a subsequent sweep a day later, they were too numerous to count.

Compounding the problem, the Navy was having trouble rounding up enough mine-sweepers and getting them into the area. It took ten days before the Navy would allow the task force to enter the harbor. By then, the always resourceful Marines had put a label on their strungout odyssey—"Operation Yo-Yo."

For the First Marine Division, it would be an "administrative landing" at Kojo a little south of Wonsan. By this time, MacArthur had decreed that United Nations forces would push on to Manchuria.

> On 22 October, General Smith issued a new plan based on the proposed X Corps deployment as far north as the Chongsanjangsi-Songjin line. The 1st Marine Division would now occupy the southern part of the extended corps zone, with each regiment responsible for the security of its assigned sector. But again planning went for naught when, two days laer, General Almond received MacArthur's order to disregard the re-straining line and use whatever forces necessary to drive rapidly to the Manchurian and Soviet borders. On 25 October, therefore, X Corps directed the 1st Marine Division to concentrate one RCT in the Hamhung area and to relieve elements of the I ROK Corps at the Chosin and Fusen reservoirs. South Korean troops had already begun their advance on these vital power centers, some 50 to 60 air miles north of Hamhung. (MCOinK, Volume III)

So, it wasn't until 26 October 1950, that D-Day came to Wonsan. General Almond, possibly miffed at the delay enforced by the Navy, called it "Doyle Day." The landing at Wonsan was on.

> LSU's began disgorging armor of the 1st Tank Battalion at 0730, and the big machines fit-ted with deep-water fording adapters, thrashed through the surf and onto the loose sand. Simultaneously, swarms of vehicles of the 1st Amphibian Tractor Battalion crawled ashore shuttling troops and cargo. (MCOinK, Volume III)

Less than two hours later, Col. Chesty Puller's 1st Marines came ashore in LSTs and were immediately dispatched by train to the railhead at Kojo, almost forty miles south of Wonsan. Although Marine infantry went into Kojo without any opposition, the small coastal town was about to prove costly. Puller, that day, learned he had been promoted to brigadier general, but the event would become stained with unexpected bloodshed by some of his troops in the next forty-eight hours.

Contrary to information passed along to them by ROK officers who were being relieved by Puller's men, Kojo was not what it appeared to be—a seaport of sun-glistened blue water lapping at its white sandy beaches. The Marines had been assured, by the ROK army they relieved, that the NKPA was long gone from approximately 5,000 yards of coastal plain they were being entrusted.

Marines were aware of hoards of refugees stretching almost into infinity during the afternoon of 27 October as they watched from Hill 117, west of Kojo. Estimated at 2,000 to 3,000, it was not possible to examine the all transients, and senior officers ordered the horde isolated on a peninsula north of the town that night.

As reported earlier, NKPA soldiers were shedding their equipment and uniforms, and mixing with legitimate refugees while attempting to escape north. When they got into the hills, they were forming as guerrillas, and it wasn't known until later—after POWs were interrogated—that there were more than a thousand enemy soldiers among them. They extracted a heavy price, especially from Baker Company, 1st Bat 1st Marines, on Hill 109 during the night of 27–28 October.

Infiltrating, the NKPA surprised the Marines. The infiltration turned into an all-night major assault that had the 1st Marines tied up through the next night and into 29 October. Baker Company had been cut off and at least one squad overrun. Other elements of the 1st Battalion ran into similar trouble. By the time the Marines beat back the Reds and had the situation under control on the afternoon of the 29th, the fate of one Baker Company platoon still was unknown.

Captain Wesley B. Noren, Baker's C.O., went back over his unit's fighting withdrawal from Hill 109 in an attempt to find his lost platoon. What he discovered when he got there were the bodies of twelve of his Marines. Ultimately, it was determined that twenty-three Marines had died in the attack, forty-seven were wounded, and four were missing in action. Seven were killed in their sleeping bags.

Halfway around the world, the fate of Baker Company, and a news clipping about one of its heroic men, became a sobering jolt to an unsuspecting, if not naïve, recruit at Parris Island, the Marine Corps Recruit Training Depot, in South Carolina: war is a serious and fatal business.

Jack Carty, a twenty-one-year-old sportswriter from Runnemede, New Jersey, had pulled the plug on his newspaper career at the *Courier-Post* in nearby Camden and was halfway through boot camp and the ten-week retooling of his attitude, discipline, principles, and commitment. Carty was about to learn that the rigid physical and mental reshaping of his life was nothing compared to the sacrifice made by a former high school football teammate at Kojo.

Carty's date with his own fate would come later when he was driving a flame tank on a ridge in the mountains of East Central Korea. But in early November 1950, there was no way he could, in his wildest imagination, ever foresee anything like that in his future. What he was about to realize for the first time, however, was that a fragment of the Korean War had entered his world.

Platoon 222 had fallen out for mail call between two rows of pyramid tents in the dusk of that November day. The "Boots" were still "Boots," but halfway through their recruit training, they were getting into the "routine," and most of them were now determined to hack "this Marine Corps stuff."

"Carty!" shouted Cpl. Skaugin, Platoon 222's drill instructor who had fought with the First Marine Division on Guadalcanal.

The twenty-one-year-old Pvt. Carty stepped out of ranks and immediately began his sprint between the two columns of fellow Boots. Jack Carty always got a lot of extra exercise at mail call, with letters from home and from his fiancée, Pat Bateman. At least two sets of sprints were normal for him. It did seem, however, that the D.I. liked to separate a guy's letters so it would mean more double-time trips up and down the platoon walk.

Despite all that added exercise, mail call always was a welcomed relief to the mental and physical routine of the day. But this would be tarnished—one he would not soon forget. Carty had received a letter from his dad, and with it came a clipping from the *Courier-Post*, the newspaper where he formerly worked. Before even reading the letter, the small headline on the clipping caught his attention.

Carty knew his father would not have sent the news article unless the story was something affecting him personally. The reality of war was about to get a little personal.

Camden Marine Killed in Korea

A Camden Marine has been killed . . . in Korea, according to word received by the family from the Department of Defense. . . .

PFC Kenneth O. Evans USMC, 20, was killed in action Oct. 27. . . . Evans was a member of the First Regiment, First Marine Division. . . .

In a letter to his parents received Oct. 21, PFC Evans had written 'we probably will make another landing.' In a previous letter, he told them he had been in the amphibious assault at Inchon. . . .

The news item was dated 11-4-50. Evans' parents had received the official telegram the previous Wednesday, 1 November. What was not known then was their son had died a hero.

Kenny Evans was a football teammate of Carty's at Camden (NJ) Catholic High School. A year behind Carty, the big tackle with a dark mop of curly hair and a freckled face, had quit school after his junior year and enlisted in the Marines. They were not close friends, but the Marine "Boot" knew his former teammate had gone into Inchon. The other landing PFC Evans had written about to his parents was Wonsan. It did not match up to turmoil at Inchon, but its aftermath proved just as deadly.

Less than a week after Evans' parents received the last letter from their son, the Camden Marine was with Baker Company, 1st Bat, 1st Marines assigned to that placid-looking little seaport town called Kojo. Although it appeared unscathed by the war, its tranquility soon would be violently disturbed, and all hell would break loose when Baker Company was overrun late on 27 October into the early morning of the 28th.

Co. B zone . . . was Hill 109. . . .

It was located about two miles south of the Kojo railhead and below Sonchon-ni. Hill 109 and Baker company came under a surprise attack and was overrun by "well-trained and led troops who threw grenades into the Marine foxholes about 2200 on the 27th." [It was estimated by MCOinK the 1,000 North Koreans had swarmed over the hill.] Two days later, a Marine officer led a patrol along the railway track south of Kojo. And retraced the route of his fighting withdrawal in the darkness. In the vicinity of Hill 109 . . . he found 12 Marine bodies. (MCOinK, Volume III)

PFC Kenneth O. Evans' name came up in the final count of twenty-three KIA. He was also listed as one of the battle's heroes. He had survived long enough to be cited for "conspicuous gallantry and intrepidity in action." His parents later would receive his Silver Star, awarded posthumously.

When Pvt. Carty got the news of Evans' death, he had no idea what the future held for him. All he realized then was the war in Korea was no John Wayne movie. It was real, and he knew he probably was heading into harm's way.

Little more than a year later, he would come to the conclusion that when his brush with destiny was charged to the books, he was very fortunate to have been sitting in the driver's seat of one of those the virtually unknown Sherman tanks from the First Tank Battalion's Flame Platoon.

First Replacement Draft

While "Operation Yo-Yo" was creating nothing less than frustration from the lowest private to the highest general of the First Marine Division in Korea early in October 1950, the Corps was in the process of getting the First Replacement Draft underway to the Fleet Marine Force.

It was the beginning of a punctuated route to the Flame Platoon of the First Tank Battalion for an unsuspecting young Marine from Forest Park, Illinois, whose experiences along the way would be just one of hundreds of mysterious paths taken by replacements to the little-known combat unit.

It was 1 October 1950 when PFC Len Martin, an eighteen-year-old reservist, boarded one of the Marine Corps's infamous "busses" at Camp Delmar, California. He was about to join a convoy with hundreds of other Marines, most of whom were remnants of the Reserve call-up that constituted the "Minute Men of 1950." In late June and early July, they lacked the training or experience to be part of the First Provisional Marine Brigade. Neither were they ready to fill the ranks of the First Marine Division for the landing at Inchon.

Now, three months later, they had had their training—however brief—and their combat experience would probably come a lot sooner than they could have imagined. As troops in the First Replacement Draft, they were part of the initial phase of a monthly replenishing system that sustained the First Marine Division throughout the three years of the Korean War.

It would be safe to say that very few, if any, Marine Corps tankers, who were assigned to the Flame Platoon during the Korean War, had ever experienced aspirations to be a Flame Tanker. The same would hold true for infantry, artillerymen, truck drivers, landing craft operators, office pinkies, or a myriad other non-1811 MOS (military occupational specialty) Gyrenes who were "conscripted" for the Platoon.

Asked for a choice of duty, Marines just didn't say: "I want to be in flame tanks."

First, since this was a relatively new combat unit, specifically brought into the First Marine Division T.O. (table of organization) for Korea, not many Marines ever heard of the Flame Platoon. Even going through tank training, there was very little talk, if any, about flame tanks. And few ever saw one outside of the newsreels or the war movies. Most of Flame Tankers were arbitrarily assigned to the Flame Platoon when they arrived in Korea. Often, those orders brought nothing but bewilderment to the men sent to the Platoon.

More than one Flamer took an unusual path to the outfit. But for Len Martin, his journey to the Flame Platoon had more detours and took longer than most of the replacements who would come along after him.

Martin, who wanted out of tanks immediately after he first climbed into an old M4 Sherman at the Los Flores Tank Park at Camp Pendleton, had formed a solid love affair with pigirons while going through the accelerated training preparing him for Korea. He had been told there was a shortage of tankers in the Land of the Morning Calm, and he would be ever-thankful that some tech sergeant refused to accept his request for transfer from tank training to the infantry. On the high seas, he felt quite confident that he would be heading for a tank outfit. Little did he know that before he ever got into his first pigiron, he would get a belated wish—something akin to being in the infantry.

It was 10 November, the 175th birthday anniversary of the Marine Corps, that PFC Len Martin jumped out of a six-by truck at the First Tank Battalion CP in the lower regions of the rugged Taebaek Mountains of North Korea.

Martin's road to the Flame Platoon had been a circuitous venture before he caught up to the Fleet Marine Force after it made its second landing at Wonsan. "It took us eleven days to cross the Pacific," Martin said. "You get the feeling of insignificance when all you can see to the horizon is open water."

Before the *Walker* docked in Yokohoma, Japan, on 13 October 1950, Martin's memory would have a permanent marker of his first seagoing voyage. "Every day on the shipboard radio, piped through the P.A. system, over and over they played the songs "Goodnight Irene" and "My Heart Cries for You," Martin said. "Every time I hear either of those songs, immediately, I'm reminded of going overseas."

For others, it could have been "Blueberry Hill," "The Tennessee Waltz," and later, Tony Bennett's "I Left My Heart in San Francisco." They became lingering markers of the times.

What the Marines of the First Replacement Draft were not aware of when they crowded the rails of the *General Walker* in Yokohoma Harbor, was the First Marine Division was packed aboard similar ships sitting outside Wonsan waiting for the Navy to clear eastern Korea's coastal waters of mines.

So the First Marine Division wasn't ready for the First Replacement Draft, and that meant Len Martin and his fellow Jarheads would debark in Japan and remain there for a couple of weeks. That got them more training, mostly infantry-oriented. It wasn't until 3 November that Martin and a couple hundred other Marines loaded aboard the Aiken Victory in Kobe and headed for Korea.

Just before they left, Lt. Col. John M. Bathum, who had been Martin's reserve battalion commander back in Illinois, gathered the troops to inform them they would be shipping out shortly.

"I really had mixed emotions," Martin said. Like most of the Marines, he had no idea what it was like in Korea, or what was in store for him. "I did not know if we would be in combat the minute we landed or what. I did a lot of praying that night."

Martin's reaction was not unlike those of thousands of other Marines, or soldiers, heading into the unknown of real war.

The colonel, who became Special Services Officer of the First Marine Division, had told the troops that if they ever crossed paths in Korea to stop and say hello. "I did eventually see him and we had a nice conversation," Martin said. "For a lowly PFC like me, it felt strange talking directly to a lieutenant colonel."

The pitching and rolling of the smaller transport in the rough waters of the Sea of Japan introduced most of the Marines to seasickness. "The ship first pitched fore and aft," Martin said, "and then rolled from side to side. Putting the two motions together, you ended up with the ship doing a figure eight. It was pitching so much fore and aft, that, when you went up a gangway with the ship rising, you felt that you were climbing a steep ladder. When it was dropping, you had to hang on to the rails to keep from falling off."

Martin was able to handle it until the third day out. That's when he was in the chow line and prepared food ran out. The wait for food made him queasy and he decided to go below to his bunk. It didn't work. He went topside and he felt worse. "My buddies were making fun of me and finally I had to throw up. "When they saw my vomit, several of them also got sick. That made me feel better."

Martin's experience aboard ship was just part of the initiation of most Marines, whether they were tankers, infantry, or artillery. Troop ships were not fun, especially on high seas. Of course, the Navy's Swabbies thoroughly enjoyed seeing the Gung Ho "20 per cent" of their service brought to such ignominy.

"We finally reached the port of Wonsan on 7 November," Martin said. The Aiken Victory was too large to go into the docks, so the Marines off-loaded over the side into LSTs, which took them to the beach. Formed up on a Marine Corps major carrying a briefcase, the replacements with their full field packs straining against their shoulders, were marched at rout step off the beach and through what was left of a bombed-out town. "I don't know how far it was," Martin said, "but it seemed like several miles. I almost passed out and marched with my head down watching the ground sink under the footsteps of the guy in front of me."

Finally, they reached the outskirts of the town, where what formerly were small houses were nothing but walls without roofs. "Korean air-conditioning," Martin cracked as his eyes moved from the ruins to the scattered live ammunition lying around them. It struck him that here were all these 30-caliber and 50-caliber shells all over the place. "Back in Japan, it was a court martial offense to have a single round of live ammunition, and here it was lying all over the place."

Welcome to Wonsan, Korea, PFC Martin!

"A whole different world," he thought, but the exhaustion of the day brought on a sound sleep that night.

It would be three more days before Martin and a few of his buddies would be taken to the First Tank Battalion. In the meantime, he learned quickly—war zone, or no war zone, Marines still had work parties. After his good night's sleep, Martin and other replacements were taken back out to the ships in Wonsan Harbor. His group wound up unloading fifty-gallon drums of fuel from a Greek liberty ship, the *Stagus J. Unagus*.

It was an extended stay in the harbor. The Marines were not told to bring their sleeping bags, but they remained aboard the ship for two nights. They had no place to sleep and nothing to keep them warm. The November nights had became very cold. In desperation, they wangled their way deep into the ship's rudder room, where a small amount of heat was being generated. But there was little sleep to be gained.

Not yet in combat, the eighteen-year-old Marine would encounter his first brush with death. Part of the unloading routine require men to go over the side on cargo nets to manhandle the barrels being hoisted below to a waiting, bobbing LSU (landing ship utility). The lack of sleep those couple of nights were beginning to take a toll on PFC Martin and his buddies.

"I was tired," said Martin, a lean six-foot-one, now-weakened 140-pounder. "While leaving an LSU to go back up the cargo net, I was standing on one of its gun ports. I grabbed the bottom of the net, but I did not have the strength to pull myself up and get my feet into the first row of the unstable net. I was hanging there when one of my buddies put both his hands under my butt and gave me a boost so I could get my feet into the net. I hate to think what would have happened had I lost my grip on the net. Both ships were rising and falling at different heights. Had I fallen into the water I would probably have been history," Martin said.

The work party finally got off the Greek ship and headed back to the outskirts of Wonsan, where the Marines picked up their gear and were told to prepare to move out to assigned outfits. Martin still wasn't sure where he was headed.

"It was typical Marine Corps—hurry up and wait," he lamented. They were told trucks would pick them up at 1100 the following morning. Hours later three six-bys finally arrived. Martin got the first hint that he was in a war zone after he climbed aboard the middle truck and saw two Marines with rifles sitting inside near the cab.

"They were from Headquarters Company, of the First Tank Battalion, and they were riding shotgun," Martin said. It didn't phase the eighteen-year-old replacement much at the moment, but along the road the truck stopped and the driver offered a ride to a couple of Marines who were walking along the road.

"We heard some shots a while ago," one of the Gyrenes mentioned after he climbed aboard. "Were they firing at you guys?"

"Nah," replied one of the guards.

Still, Martin had been startled that he may be getting close to the real thing.

"We had heard some scuttlebutt that an army outfit, that had left the day before us by train, had been ambushed and took many casualties," he said.

Then it happened! The short conversation had hardly ended when they heard gunfire coming from one of the hills that lined the road. The truck driver was so shook up, he stalled the engine. "He couldn't get it started," Martin said, "and the only thing I could think of was I didn't have a helmet." The night before, he had been heating water in his helmet over an open fire. The straps ignited and burned off. "I kept badgering the sergeant for another helmet, but he told me there weren't any extras."

The replacements, the guards, and driver didn't waste too much time getting out of that six-by. "I landed in a ditch next to the road," a shaking Martin said. "Some of the guys started shooting at a hill, and I fired off a couple of rounds, not really knowing what I was shooting at. It's surprising that we didn't shoot each other."

Finally, a sergeant who was in the group, came to the conclusion that the replacements had no idea what they were doing and got them to stop shooting. Warily, they climbed back aboard the six-by, but the driver still couldn't get it started. One of the other two trucks had to push it until it kicked over.

It was dark on the night of 10 November, 1950, when the small convoy finally reached Headquarters Company of the First Tank Battalion. PFC Martin and the rest of the replacements were a little surprised to find a piece of birthday cake waiting for them at the end of the chow line. Marines, no matter where they are, always seem to find a way to celebrate the anniversary of the birth of the Corps—and this was No. 175 since the those two battalions of colonial enlistees formed in Tun Tavern on the Philadelphia waterfront.

The next morning, PFC Martin got another lesson on when to keep his mouth shut. When the new tankers fell out for the daily head count, the staff sergeant taking roll asked if any of them knew how to fire a machine gun. Martin, figuring it would be a ticket to joining a tank crew as a gunner, quickly shouted: "Here!"

It was not what he thought.

"You soon learn in the military not to volunteer anything," he lamented.

Instead of being assigned to a tank, Martin pulled duty standing guard with a machine-gun crew at an outpost. It didn't take long to come to the conclusion that the stuff about "every Marine is an infantryman" was straight poop.

Martin was assigned to a machine-gun outpost about 300 yards from the CP. Some fifty feet in front of the outpost, there was another Marine, armed with his Garand M-1 rifle and a stash of illuminating and fragmentation grenades. The outpost was ringed by barbed wire, attached with dangling empty C-ration cans, with a few rocks in them.

"The slightest breeze would make the cans rattle," Martin said of his first night on the line. "Scary business in the middle of the night where one could not see ten yards in front of him."

It was up to the Marine in the listening post to be aware of any movement in front of him. Once detected, he heaved a grenade and scurried back to the machine-gun outpost. Martin never got the listening post duty. Still, he was cognizant of the fear of being dug in along the MLR (main line of resistance). "Sitting out there in the dark, one can imagine hearing all kinds of sounds," he said.

One night, one of the guys out on the listening post was particularly scared. "Suddenly," Martin said, "the guys in the machine-gun nest heard the sound of a grenade canister being opened. They assumed the guy was going to throw a grenade, but hoped he would throw in front of him and not at them."

Without warning, they heard someone running towards them. "Halt!"

The runner kept coming at them. It was the scared Marine from the listening post. "Instead of stopping, he ran all the way back to the CP," Martin said. "Apparently he thought he had heard a noise and threw an illuminating grenade that landed in some water and did not go off."

That episode got the Marine permanent KP (kitchen police, mess duty). "He was happy to get off outpost duty," Martin said, "but later during the Chosin Reservoir campaign, there was a shortage of messmen up the line and he was sent forward. Eventually, he was wounded."

Although he was in the First Tank Battalion, First Marine Division, PFC Leonard Martin was learning how the infantry does things. And he wouldn't be the only tanker—"boot" or "salt"—who would pull his share of snoopin' and poopin' in the hairy episode that would envelop all of the Division in the next few weeks.

Hung Out on a Frozen Limb

While the Eighth Army, under Lt. Gen. Walton S. Walker, was barreling up the western side of North Korea, Lt. Gen. Edward M. Ned Almond's X Corps—with the First Marine Division on the point—was on the other side of treacherous Taebaek Mountains.

The Marines were pushing toward the Changin Reservoir, which soon would become the infamous anglicized Chosin Reservoir. There, they were to relieve the ROKs, establish a perimeter at Yudam-ni west of the reservoir on the left limb of the Y that split at the bottom of the basin. From the small village within a restricted valley running north to south, the Marines were ordered to cut forty miles west across the Taebaeks to relieve ROK troops and take over the right flank protecting of the Eighth Army.

Lt. Gen. Oliver P. Smith, commander of the First Marine Division, never did like the plan because he didn't cotton to the idea of his Gyrenes being thinly strung out over the 78-mile mountainous primitive MSR (main supply route) and very prone to being cut off. As it was, he knew they were out on a very long, spindly, icy limb. Adding another forty miles to it forecast disaster.

The 7th Marine Regiment had already encountered a Chinese Communist Forces Division in the Sudong Valley in the first week of November when it relieved a ROK regiment, which had been briefly engaged with the CCF. The Marines became involved in a pitched battle involving Hill 891 and Hill 987 along the MSR about twenty miles north of Hamhung, just a few miles southwest of Chinhung-ni. After four days, during which elements of the Seventh had been cut off at one point, the Chinese disappeared.

The CCF regiment was known to have taken heavy losses, but that didn't give General Smith any reason to think they were not lurking around somewhere the craggy hills of the Taebaeks. Sudong Valley was only a small preview of what was to unfold as November passed into December.

However, generals MacArthur and Almond thought differently. Their plan continued to be one of going hell-bent-for-election to the Yalu River and the Manchurian border. The Marines commander thought this was foolish and knew his men could be hung out to dry—*freeze* was the more appropriate way of putting it—if they were forced to go west across the Taebaeks.

Smith flat-out refused to extend the point of his Division any further than Yudam-ni. He was deeply concerned even that was too far, and that his 7th Marines and the rest of the Division were in imminent trouble.

Sure enough, his worst fears came to pass when Communist Chinese barged into the war late in November of 1950.

The Taebaeks, which dominated most of the extreme northern part of Korea, were the most unlikely place to maneuver a tank. Although the Flame Platoon, as well the Shermans from Service Company, would be scattered up and down the MSR working with the four gun companies, its pudgy double-barrelled M4A3E8s were used extensively as security and on blocking missions.

The Taebaeks were not Wolmi-do—or Kimpo, or Yongdungpo, or Seoul—where the flame tanks and the rest of the Marine armor had relatively flat terrain in which to maneuver. The MSR wasn't wide enough in many places for two tanks to go abreast. When tanks were needed, they went single file most of the time to get into position for direct firing of their 90mm rifles or 105 cannons. The flame tanks had the added advantage of being able to lob their 105 ordnance indirectly over the hills into enemy concentrations.

It just wasn't real tank country on the road to the Yalu River, and only the gun companies, Pershings ventured to the near extremes of the Division's forward units.

"We used flame tanks as protection of our CPs with their 30- and 50-caliber machine guns," said Lt. Col. Harry T. Milne, commanding officer of the First Tank Battalion at the time. "The Flames were ideal for battalion security."

They also turned out be excellent rear guard when they were detailed to protect the Division when it was on its final leg south after fighting its way out of Yudam-ni, Hagaru-ri, and Koto-ri.

Had the high command listened to General Smith, the First Marine Division might not have been put in that predicament.

Smith was very wary and more than once made his objections known to General Almond, who seemed to have little grasp of the situation's gravity. Finally, when his Division had been cut in three unconnected pieces along the harrowing, winding MSR with Chinese surrounding each of the units, Smith bluntly told Almond he was not going risk stranding any of them because the high command wanted to press further toward the Manchurian border. Many a Marine had Smith to thank for getting them out of the very precarious situation that was the long fight back from the Chosin Reservoir.

After the 7th Marines had dispatched the Chinese at Sudong, the People's Liberation Army seemed to disappear. There was no further contact with Chinese Communist Forces for a couple of weeks, and General Smith reluctantly, and ever cautiously, allowed his Marines to continue north to Yudam-ni.

The fact that the Chinese appeared to drop off the face of Korea's big mountains only increased the euphoria in the high command of a quick victory. Now, General MacArthur was predicting "the boys will be home by Christmas."

But, as General Smith suspected, the Chinese did not go back across the Yalu. They pulled back deeper in the North Korean mountains and were preparing a major offensive across the entire front.

Part of the heady feeling by the Far East Command was due to the fact that the United Nations had built a sizeable force of its own by mid-November 1950. B. L. Kortegaard outlined it in his *Battle of the Chosin Reservoir:*

> Eighth Army consisted of: I Corps with the 24th Division, the British 27th Brigade, and the ROK 1st Division; IX Corps, with the 2nd and 25th Divisions and the Turkish Brigade; and ROK II Corps, with their 6th, 7th and 8th Divisions. First Cav was in reserve . . . (totaling) about 135,00 troops.
> In the east, X Corps had about 100,000 men: the 1st Marine Division (22,000), and the Army's 7th Division with the under-strength 3rd Division in reserve at Wonsan; and the Rock I Corps, consisting of the 3rd and Captial Divisions, operation along the east coast.

What Far East Command was not privy to, however, was that the Chinese had sneaked three armies across the Yalu. They had lined up 180,000 well-trained guerillas with a refurbished North Korean People's Army in the West. And, the CCF was poised to throw seven divisions against the Marines at the Chosin Reservoir.

By the time PFC Leonard Martin and the rest of the replacements for the First Tank Battalion had gotten their first glimpse of the unit's CP, Marines already had dispatched a division of Chinese Communist Forces in the bitter four-day battle at Sudong.

The MSR to the Yalu River, which flowed between Manchuria and the northern border of Korea, had been mapped out. It was a climbing seventy-eight-mile serpentine excuse for a road, meandering ever upwards from the port of Hungnam through narrow valleys crammed between the treacherous imposing crags of the Taebaek Mountains. One look at the map of the MSR should have warned even the lowliest boot private that Almond, under orders from MacArthur, was testing fate by stringing out the Marines on what officially was described as the

> *winding 78-mile stretch of dirt and gravel road leading from the supply port of Hungnam to the forlorn village of Yudam-ni at the western tip of the Chosin Reservoir. . . .*
>
> *The first half of the distance—the 43 miles from Hungnam to Chinhung-ni—is traversed by a two-lane road passing through comparatively level terrain. Rolling country is encountered north of Majon-dong, but it is at Chinhung-ni that the road makes its abrupt climb into a tumbled region of mile-high peaks. There are few straight or level stretches all the rest of the 35 miles to Yudam-ni, but the route from Chinhung-ni to Koto-ri is the most difficult.*
>
> *Funchilin Pass, comprising eight of these ten miles, represents an ascent of 2,500 feet for a straining jeep or truck. The road is merely a twisting, one-way shelf, with a cliff on one side and a chasm on the other. . . .*
>
> *The road from Hagaru to Yudam-ni climbs from the table and at the foot of the Chosin Reservoir and winds its way up to 4,000-foot Toktong Pass. Descending through gloomy gorges, it finally reaches a broad valley leading to Yudam-ni, where roads branch off to the north, west and south from a western arm of the Reservoir.*
>
> *This was the 78-mile supply route that would soon be claiming its page in history. In a few weeks it would be known to thousands of Marines as the MSR as if there never had been another. (MCOinK, Volume III)*

At best, the MSR that twisted along the mountainsides was wide enough for two six-by trucks to pass abreast in some places. On one side was the wall of the mountain. On the other, it was a perilous drop into a valley. The First Marine Division would pay a bloody toll up and down the seventy-eight miles of that road while attempting to carry out the wishes of General MacArthur. The Far East Commander saw no reason to fear a threat of Chinese intervention if he sent U.N. troops to set up across the Yalu from their southern Manchurian border.

It was the night of 14 November when nine flame tanks, the Y51 porcupine (communications) tank, command tank, and recovery vehicle—the advance echelon of Headquarters Company and Service Company of the First Tank Battalion boarded LSTs at Wonsan and sailed for the port of Hamhung.

For PFC Len Martin, and the rest of the "infantry" tankers, it was about a ninety-mile trip over a primitive mountain road. "I was assigned to ride up on the top of a load of crates of 90mm tank ammo," Martin said. "It was stacked so high that we were up above the cab of the six-by."

November nights in North Korea were becoming increasingly colder. That night, the mercury was hovering somewhere between zero and ten above. It was mild compared to what lay ahead.

"I was never so cold in my life," Martin said of the bumpy ride that took several hours. "There just was no place to get out of the wind, and it was blowing hard into our faces." In order to try to stay warm, the exposed Marines climbed into their sleeping bags but could not lie down in them. Along with the chilling cold came frequent urging to answer nature's call.

"My feet were so numb from the cold," Martin moaned, "that I had no feeling in them. Jumping off the truck I didn't know when I hit the ground."

Although the tankers carried loaded rifles in anticipation of enemy contact, no North Koreans were encountered during the ninety-mile trip. But there was plenty of evidence of him having been in the area. Several pieces of self-propelled NK artillery were strewn down the sides of mountains—apparently knocked out by Marine Corsairs.

The new tankers finally reached Hamhung, where they would spend the night sleeping on a concrete floor. Three days later, the First Tank Battalion CP was moved north to Soyang-ni, the site of a former agricultural college about eight miles to the northeast above Hamhung. Soyang-ni was in a flat valley between high ridges. "We were set up next to a narrow gauge railroad that came through from Hamhung and extended north," said Martin. "There was only one dirt road coming out of Hamhung and going north. This was the MSR. It could have been the OSR (only supply route) because it was the only passable road going north to Koto-ri, Hagaru, and Yudam-ni. The road went right by us through the town."

At Soyang-ni, the First Tank Battalion with its nine flame tanks was about fifty air miles from Yudam-ni and what was to become the storied Chosin Reservoir.

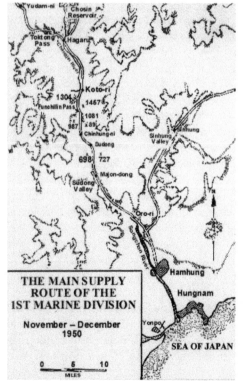

Brutal winter conditions and more than seven divisions of the Chinese Communist Forces could not keep the trapped First Marine Division from breaking out of North Korea west of the Chosin Reservoir over a harrowing seventy-eight miles down the rugged Taebaek Mountains. (Map Copy Courtesy of MCOinK)

Provisional Tank Platoon

As the First Marine Division pressed northward along the main supply route toward Yudam-ni and a possible, but controversial, jumpoff toward the west to facilitate the X Corps linkup with the Eighth Army, the road was becoming extremely more primitive. Not at all uncommon when Marine units are on the point, it was a fix-as-you-go operation—and this was one MSR that needed plenty of fixin.'

The road was so bad that the M26 Pershings of the First Tank Battalion's four gun companies had to be held back. They were too wide for the unimproved road between Chinhung-ni and Koto-ri, which the 7th Marines had taken on 10 November. Five days later, with the Seventh staged in Hagaru, it wouldn't be long before they began the push toward Yudam-ni.

It was on 18 November that Lt. Col. Harry T. Milne, commander of the First Tank Battalion, very much aware the advanced infantry needed tank support, devised a way to get armor forward from his CP at Soyang-ni. He formed a provisional gun platoon of seven old reliables—the smaller and narrower Sherman M4A3s—two Baker Company dozers, and three more like it from Dog Company. The Shermans were accompanied by a six-by truck with an SCR radio and operator, a corpsman, and a 2-1/2-ton cargo truck, ordnance technician, and tank mechanic from Service Company.

At 1300 on 18 November, the Provisional Tank Platoon, under the command of Capt. R. M. Krippner, left battalion CP at Soyang-ni and made it to the railhead at Chinhung-ni. The following morning, the road between Chinhung-ni and Koto-ri was closed to allow the provisional platoon to complete its drive to base of the Chosin Reservoir. It reached Hagaru without any enemy contact, or problems navigating the yet-unimproved MSR. There, the makeshift platoon was attached to the 5th Marines.

Meanwhile, the Flame Platoon, along with the rest of the First Tank Battalion—less Able and Charlie companies, which still were stranded at Wonsan because of lack of shipping—continued patrols along the lower portions of the MSR. There was particular attention being paid to the western sector.

While infantrymen of the First Marine Division were shivering in the winds of sub-freezing—and often subzero—weather, Headquarters Company and the Flame Platoon of the First Tank Battalion was set up in relative luxury for the time being. "We lived in pyramidal tents and had little diesel-oil-fired potbellied stoves," said PFC Len Martin, the future Flame Tanker who was getting his taste of infantry-like duty as part of security patrols around the battalion CP. He was very much aware how lucky he was. "Those poor guys in the infantry had to live out in the open."

Traditionally, the United States Marine Corps makes every attempt to provide for its troops. Unlike the troops in the Eighth Army, who still were wearing normal issue fatigue combat uniforms throughout the North Korea campaign, the Marine Corps had managed to get cold-weather gear to its fighting division. "We wore long underwear, a woolen shirt, sweater, field jacket, windproof trousers, and a twelve-pound fur-lined parka," Martin said. "The parkas were quite warm, but since they were relatively heavy, at the end of a guard duty shift, our shoulders ached from the weight."

But the Marines still felt the cold.

The one item of cold-weather gear that every Marine and soldier found totally inadequate was the "shoe-pac," the boot made of a leather top that came up to mid-calf, and with a rubber bottom. It had a felt liner. The shoe-pac was supposed to protect feet from the sub-freezing cold. It just didn't work. "The theory was," Martin noted, "that the rubber would be waterproof and allow you to walk in snow and water without getting your feet wet. In actuality, the rubber did not to keep out the cold."

Thousands upon thousands of U.N. troops suffered frostbite, and loss of toes and feet, after wearing that boot. "I would stamp my feet, going around in circles, for hours just to keep my them warm," Martin said. "We wore a regular pair of socks, two pair of ski socks, and had two felt liners in the boots. Still, our feet froze. I don't know how those guys in the infantry, out in the open, unable to move for fear of revealing their positions, were able to handle that cold. If you didn't keep moving, your feet froze."

Marines tried everything to keep their feet from freezing. Cpl. Dean Servais, a native of Kinosha, Wisconsin, and driver of D12 in the first platoon of Dog Company, was used to frigid winter weather, but he never experienced anything like the 1950 cold of Korea. He also kept two pairs of felt liners for his snow-pacs. "I'd insert one pair in the boots, and keep the other pair next against my chest to keep them warm and dry. Every day you had to change those liners—take the wet pair off and put them against your chest."

By mid-November, however, the grand scheme for the United Nations' attack north had been laid out, and Lt. Gen. Oliver P. Smith, commander of the First Marine Division, was not too happy about it. Although Gen. Douglas MacArthur had hedged a little and did reconsider that the Chinese could enter the conflict, he was not convinced they would be that much of a problem.

There was a known Chinese Communist Force buildup opposite the Eighth Army in the west. In fact, the Reds had stymied the Eighth's initial thrust toward the Yalu River. A modified plan to assist the Gen. Walton Walker's Dogfaces called for X Corps to attack west from the Chosin Reservoir and swing northwesterly to Manpojin on the Yalu.

On Wednesday, 15 November, . . . General Smith wrote a letter which foreshadowed future military events. Addressed to General Clifton B. Cates, Commandant of the Marine Corps, this communication made it plain that the 1st Marine Division commander and his staff did not share in the renewed optimism as to the course of the UN war effort. Not only did the Marines accept the possibility of imminent and formidable CCF intervention, but they were making preparations to meet it. (MCOinK, Volume III)

General Smith's letter:

So far our MSR north of Hamhung has not been molested, but there is evidence that his situation will not continue. . . .
  Someone in high authority will have to make up his mind as to what is our goal. My mission is still to advance to the border. Eighth Army, 80 miles to the southwest, will not attack until the 20th. Manifestly, we should not push on without regard to the Eighth Army. We would simply get forced out on a limb. If the Eighth Army push does not go, then the decision will have to be made as to what to do next. I believe a winter campaign in the mountains of North Korea is too much to ask of the American soldier or marine, and I doubt the feasibility of supplying troops in this area during the winter or providing for the evacuation of sick and wounded. (MCOinK, Volume III)

When the Marines occupied Hagaru-ri, they got a biting taste of what the North Korean winter was going to be doing to them for the next three weeks. Temperatures, intensified by winds, had plummeted to as low as four degrees below zero. And they would go much lower before the United Nations troops would extricate themselves from the horror that was to befall them in a few short days.

The original plan was for the First Marine Division to establish blocking positions west of the Chosin Reservoir at Yudam-ni and Huksu-ri, at the same time running a force north to the Yalu. Eventually, that operation was rescinded, but General Smith already had adopted an alternate plan until the rest of the Division could catch up with the 7th Marines and elements of the Fifth Regiment which was to share the blocking assignment.

Instead of sending his foot Marines beyond Yudam-ni, Smith issued an oral order for those lead elements to set up blocking positions along the Toktong Pass, at the midpoint of the MSR between Hagaru and Yudam-ni. He was very suspicious of a significant assault by the Chinese Communists and, unlike his Army superiors, he did not throw caution to the wind.

Still, the 7th Marines, and elements of the Fifth Regiment, remained out on a very spindly limb at Yudam-ni. The rest of the 5th Marines were in, or within the vicinity of, Hagaru, and the 1st Marines were still down at Koto-ri. What Smith was looking at—and unwilling to stretch his troops any further apart—was a fourteen-mile gap between Yudam-ni and Hagaru, which was eleven miles north of Koto-ri. The one-lane MSR back to the port of Hungnam wound fifty-five more miles south, partially through the treacherous Taebaek Mountains, which held all kinds of pockets where the enemy could—and would—cut into any effort to supply, or extract, troops.

And there were no tanks any further north than Hagaru on Thanksgiving Day, 23 November—and none would get beyond that point of the MSR before all hell broke loose on the 27th.

Hagaru, at the southern tip of the Chosin Reservoir, with highways branching off on both sides of that body of water, was an important communications center before the war. And even though many buildings had been flattened by bombing, the town was still impressive as compared to such wretched mountain hamlets as Koto-ri and Chinghung-ri. (MCOinK, Volume III)

Fortunately, General Smith had brought his CP and a division hospital to Hagaru, and had the foresight to have his engineers carve out a landing strip, which was a Godsend for resupplying his men and evacuating the most seriously wounded. Smith had taken Marines into the bitter landing and fighting at Pellileu in World War II, but in the storied history of the United States Marine Corps, there was nothing like the North Korean winter of 1950 and Chinese Communist Forces that were bearing down on his First Marine Division.

Bitter Cold!

With the First Tank Battalion taking responsibility of the main supply route above and below its CP in Soyang-ni, tank patrols and blocking assignments by the Flame Platoon and the M26 Pershings of the letter companies were not the only security missions. Headquarters Company also sent out its "infantry patrols" in another old reliable—the six-by truck.

"We went on frequent mechanized patrols into the surrounding mountains," said PFC Len Martin, who still had not been inside one of the battalion's combat tanks in his first two weeks in the Land of the Morning Calm. "We'd ride around most of the day in the back of the six-by. At the end of the day, every organ inside our bodies just ached from being bounced around."

The sturdy trucks—three-axle, six-wheel (four doubles in the rear) driven—were built to carry supplies and capable of hauling six tons. There was a provision, however, to transport troops because the sides of the bed of the truck was made of wooden slats. The center section of slats folded down to make seats. This truck, a staple of transportation and supply through World War II and now Korea, was not at all comfortable when almost empty. It was even more bone-rattling along the dirt and rock MSR and smaller, more primitive, mountain roads.

The six-bys heft, however, could be a problem.

"One day we came to a ditch that had a wooden bridge across it," Martin said of one of his patrols. "A jeep was driven over the bridge to see if it would support us, and the opinion was that it would. However, when our truck got halfway across, the bridge started to collapse, scaring hell out of me and the other guy sitting in the back with me. Fortunately, the truck just gently leaned and settled to one side and did not flip over."

The incident was near a small village, and the Marines had to get help from civilians to get the truck pushed out of the ditch.

Villages were part of the scrutiny conducted by tank battalion truck patrols. "When we went through small villages like that," Martin said, "we had to raid their police stations and take away their automatic weapons. You never knew who was on your side."

One day, going through a small village, they saw a young boy who looked like he was about fifteen years old. "He was standing on an intersection dressed in a Chinese uniform," Martin said. "We had to take him prisoner and turned him in when we got back to the CP."

The mechanized patrols were bad enough in the lingering cold, but outpost watches on the fringe of the battalion CP were brutal, making the shivering Martin ever more appreciative in later years of the twist of fate that made him a tanker-to-be. At least he could get back to a tent, heated by a potbellied stove, and climb fully clothed into his sleeping bag. "The poor infantry guys up at the Reservoir had nothing like that," he said with utmost respect of the exposed infantry. "How did they do it?"

The First Tank Battalion CP at Soyang-ni had two outposts. One was set up in an open field about 300–400 yards west of main area. The other was across the road, also in a field. The extreme outpost looked across a broad valley toward the western ridges, and the other faced north. "I helped gouge the westerly one out of some damn hard frozen ground," Martin said, "and I spent most of my guard duty in it. It was shaped somewhat like an inverted letter *U* with the bottom of the U facing west. There was a makeshift shelter behind it where we slept when not on watch."

Three or four men were assigned to the outpost, with one man standing three or four hours manning the machine gun while the others rested. The machine gun was set up in the middle of the U and gave the infantry-tankers 180 degrees of coverage. "Being down in the valley, it got so dark at night that you could not see your hands in front of your face," Martin said.

Despite all the clothing he would wear, Martin recalled never being warm as temperatures dipped to twenty below zero in the middle of that field. "There was no place to go," he said. "All you could do was freeze. At the end of my shift, I would crawl into the shelter and climb into my sleeping bag, clothes and all. Standing outpost was not one of the most enjoyable times of my tour."

It may have been that the frigid weather had numbed the senses of one of Martin's companions after coming off outpost duty early one morning. To fire a 30-caliber machine gun, it had to be cocked twice before the trigger could set it off. Marines learned a long time ago, in combat situations, to cock the gun once while standing by. That left only one motion when it had to be fired in a hurry.

"As we were coming back from the outpost," Martin said, "the guy carrying the machine gun had forgotten to clear it, obviously after having cocked it twice while on watch." As he set down the machine gun, he squeezed the trigger and a round went off. "Fortunately, no one was hit," recalled Martin, "but he had to walk around with the machine gun on his shoulder for the rest of the day."

As PFC Martin continued to pull more infantry-like duty, things were heating up at the Chosin Reservoir. The increased rumbling of artillery and the scuttlebutt seeping back from the North only made for a little more wear and tear on the nerves of the inexperienced young Marines from the First Replacement Draft.

An army 4.2 mortar outfit was set up next to the First Tank Battalion, and one night while Martin was on the outpost, the Marine detail got quite a scare from their neighbors.

"I had just crawled into my sleeping bag at the end of my watch," Martin said, "when the guy on watch started calling us. I pulled aside the flap to our shelter and there was a flare hanging in the sky, lighting the whole area."

Frantically, the Marine on watch cranked up the field phone connected to battalion to report. The sergeant answered, and when told excitedly that there was a flare overhead, he calmly asked what color.

"White," was the report.

"Don't worry," was the calm reply. "Theirs are green, ours are white.'"

The outpost crew then realized the army mortar squad had sent up the flare. But it took the inexperienced Marines a while to calm down. "Needless to say, this shook us up a little bit," Martin said.

As the situation worsened along the northern extreme of the MSR, security was stepped up everywhere along the line. Roving patrols within the First Tank Battalion CP were supplemented by a combination of tank and machine-gun emplacements around it. There were drills by novice tankers on guard duty to grab boxes of 30-caliber ammo and make "mad dashes" to the machine-guns nests. The two-man walking patrols fixed bayonets to their M-1 rifles.

"One night, I was walking post with a guy who had the sniffles," Martin said. "When the OD (Officer of the Day) was making his rounds, he told the guy to stop sniffling. 'Aye, Aye, Sir,' the guard replied. But he couldn't stop and went right on sniffling the rest of the watch," Martin said.

All of it was comparatively mundane compared to what Marines would experience when Chinese Communist Forces started swarming all over the northern hills in the final week of November.

Here Come the Chinese

Chinese Communist Forces came full bore into the Korean War on the night of 27-28 November 1950.

The sudden intrusion of a new enemy ultimately sent the Eighth U.S. Army into a reeling, total-rout retreat in the west. On the eastern flank, the CCF sealed off the point of the X Corps—the First Marine Division's three infantry regiments—in three separate pockets within a twenty-five-mile stretch at the northern extremity of the MSR.

The Marines were not only cut off from all other United Nation elements, they were without physical contact with many of their own units, one of which was seventy-eight miles from the safe harbor of Hungnam, up the now slippery, narrow, and enemy-encased main supply route.

On the morning of the 27 November, the 7th Marines and elements of the 5th Regiment had pushed north, tentatively following the ill-fated plan to work their way to Yalu River and west to the right flank of the Eighth Army. They were going without tank support, although four Shermans from the Provisional Tank Platoon tried to get to them from Hagaru. "Two of the tanks got up to Yudam-ni," said Phillip C. Morrell, then a Captain and C.O. of Service Company, but that was costly. "A tank commander was killed and some of the crew wounded."

Because of the icy conditions on that narrow stretch of MSR., the Shermans eventually were forced to back track to Hagaru. The subzero temperatures also were plaguing the M4s in the provisional platoon. Tank engines were freezing and seizing. "We had a helicopter bring in two (Service Company) crewman, who brought along fan belts," Morrell said. "They got the tanks running." (On 1 December, Morrell was promoted to major and took over as battalion executive officer to Lt. Col. Harry T. Milne.)

Although it was without the mobility of rolling firepower from tanks, the infantry regiments still had plenty of heavy support from the 11th Marines big guns when they jumped off for Yudam-ni on the 27th. They didn't quite accomplish all the objectives mapped out for the day, and this very well may have been a blessing in disguise as a quiet came over the front and they settled in for the night.

Sitting on the high ground above and around Yudam-ni were

10 understrength rifle companies of both regiments . . . two battalions of the 5th in the valley near the village; and two rifle companies, Charlie and Fox, of the 7th in isolated positions along the 14-mile route to Hagaru. (MCOinK, Volume III)

About to be encapsulated at Hagaru, along with the First Marine Division CP, was the Provisional Tank Platoon, the rest of the 5th Marines, the small airstrip, and the field hospital. Eleven miles down what soon would become the unprotected MSR, the 1st Marines at Koto-ri were chaffing at the bit to get north and join the fight pushing to the Yalu. It was not to be. They soon would become a surrounded bastion unto their own, and have enough on their hands maintaining the keystone that eventually would bring together the entire First Marine Division's three infantry regiments and assorted support units for the first time since Wonsan.

At 1830, two hours after the looming mass of Sakkat Mountain had blotted out the sun on 27 November, Yudam-ni was pitch black. The temperature dropped to 20 degrees below zero.

On Northwest Ridge, the infantrymen of 3/7 and 2/5 slowly grew numb from the penetrating cold. Trigger fingers, though heavily gloved, ached against the brittle steel of weapons, and parka hoods became encrusted with frozen moisture. In the cumbersome shoe-pacs, perspiration-soaked feet gradually became transformed into lumps of biting pain.

When men are immobilized for hours in such temperatures, no amount of clothing will keep them warm. Yet, even more disturbing to the Marines on the Yudam-ni perimeter was the effect of the weather on carbines and BARs. These weapons froze to such a degree that they became unreliable or, in some cases, completely unserviceable. . . .

While the Marines sat in their holes and cursed the frigid night, the quiet hills around them came alive with thousands of Red Chinese on the march. Unseen and unheard, the endless columns of quilted green wound through valleys and over mountain trails leading toward the southern pits of North and Northwest Ridges. These were the assault battalions of the 79th and 89th CCF Divisions. With seven other divisions, they comprised Red China's 9th Army Group . . . dispatched to Northeast Korea specifically to destroy the 1st Marine Division. The knockout blow, aimed at the northwest arc of the Yudam-ni perimeter, amounted to a massive frontal assault. Another CCF Division, the 59th, had completed a wide envelopment to the south, driving in toward South Ridge and Toktong Pass to cut the MSR between Hagaru and Yudam-ni.

This was . . . three divisions against two regiments of Marines. (MCOinK, Volume III)

The silent, undetected approach of the Chinese, amazingly surviving the bitter cold with their feet clad only in rubber sneakers, got them within a few hundred yards of some of the Marines. A little after 2100, amid the strange cacophony of whistles, bugles, the *pffft* of eerie green flares, machine-gun fire, and exploding mortars and grenades, Communist Chinese Forces burst headlong into the Korean War.

As they would for the next couple of weeks, while vainly trying to stop the determined Marines from extricating themselves from what would be considered at some points an impossible situation, the Reds paid a brutal price their first full night in the war. The cost on 27-28 November was "grotesque heaps (of Chinese bodies) up and down the front . . ." *(MCOinK, Volume III)* as they unleashed attack after attack in waves of human sacrifice. When Marine machine gunners set a native hut afire, the resulting background of light exposed enemy troops packed into a narrow opening. It was a "turkey shoot that ended with the virtual annihilation of the main enemy force" *(MCOinK, Volume III)*.

But this was only the beginning, and there would be many more nights like it before the First Marine Division, also paying dearly, would finish its epic fight in another direction. Grudgingly, it was only at this stage of the "game" that General Douglas MacArthur, in Japan, and Lt. General Ned Almond were finally coming to the conclusion that the Chinese were in this thing for the long haul.

That same night, however, when Task Force Drysdale, with elements of the First Tank Battalion deeply involved, got mauled in Hell Fire Valley, the two senior Army commanders still thought the CCF intrusion was merely making token attacks.

Headquarters Company was set up next to Service Company at the First Tank Battalion CP in Soyang-ni. PFC Len Martin, now in his third week of pulling infantry-like outpost, guard patrol, and battalion security details, was privy to some of what was going on when Task Force Drysdale was being pulled together to get relief up to Hagaru from Koto-ri.

Lt. Col. Douglas B. Drysdale, and his British 41st Commando Royal Marines, had been assigned to the First Marine Division. Although he didn't like the idea, General Smith, at the urging of General Almond, had ordered Lt. Col. Chesty Puller, the 1st Marines CO, to organize Task Force Drysdale. The situation at the bottom of the Chosin Reservoir where it met the Changjin River, was precarious, to say the least. Hagaru needed more infantry and tanks.

The activity going on in Service Company as it prepared to join the convoy at Koto-ri caught PFC Martin's attention. "We watched thirty-two trucks from Service Company leave and head north to Koto-ri," Martin said. When they got to the 1st Marines CP, they were joined by 24 Baker and Dog Company M26 Pershing tanks; five more from the 5th Marines anti-tank company; and 600 infantry reinforcements from the British Marines, 3rdBat1st Marines and the Army's 31st Infantry. Little time was wasted launching the convoy toward Hagaru, but the Chinese were waiting. On their way, a lot of men were killed, wounded, and missing, and Service Company lost thirty of its trucks."

Cpl. Dean Servais, who was driving D12 in Dog Company's second platoon, was right in the middle of it. "We were between Koto-ri and Hagaru," said the nineteen-year-old tanker from Kinosha, Wisconsin, "when we came under a lot of fire from the Chinese. The road ran down the valley and, naturally, there were hills on both sides. The Chinese controlled these hills most of the way. We got into a terrific firefight that night."

It was Hell Fire Valley, halfway up that eleven-mile stretch of the MSR. Drysdale's command was ambushed on 29 November.

The tanks couldn't go anywhere, so they were ordered to shut down their engines to save fuel. The crews started their generators so they could use their radios and traverse their turrets during the fight. "We were under fire for a good five or six hours," Servais said. "We had a hell of a fight on our hands." Finally, the Chinese were beaten off and the road was cleared, although the task force still remained under fire.

But there was trouble with D12 when the order came to restart the tanks, which now had been pulling power off their undercharged batteries for hours. "I cranked it over," said Servais, "but it wouldn't start. We didn't know what was wrong with it." The assistant driver climbed out of his hatch, running back and climbing up on the engine doors. He opened the doors to see if he could find anything obviously wrong. Nothing!

Servais continued to crank the starter. Still nothing. They tried the generator. Now that didn't work. Eventually, the battery went dead. "We were holding up the whole column," the exasperated driver said. It was decided to ditch the M26—strip and destroy it. Despite the magnitude of the Chinese ambush, it was the only tank Task Force Drysdale lost.

One of the Baker Company tanks suffered damage, but was able to make it back to Koto-ri. "We were hit in the rear sprocket," said PFC Ben Gabijan, the B33 gunner. "It was in Hellfire Valley while we were with the 41st Royal Commandos."

Even though the other Pershings and approximately 400 men, among whom were about 300 veteran infantrymen, reached the Division CP at Hagaru, the cost was high. The casualty list included 162 killed or missing in action. Five Service Company Marines were KIA or MIA. Forty-four men were captured—25 either escaped or were released from POW camps much later during prisoner exchanges. Among the 159 wounded was Lt. Col. Drysdale.

It was a steep price. But the tanks that got through became instrumental when the First Marine Division breakout began. Tanks were the last out, pulling up the rear of the slow-moving, southbound column after the last Marine infantry trudged into the convoy leaving Hagaru. Pigirons covered their backs all the way to Hungnam.

Without a tank, Servais and the rest of his crew had to hitch a ride north, and he wound up perched on the front fender of a six-by.

The Chinese used a lot of initiative in lieu of equipment. They rolled, or dynamited boulders into the road, forcing trucks or tanks to go around them. When the truck drivers would see one of these roadblocks, they would look for an opening and gun their engines to get around, or through it. Often the trucks would hit or scrape the boulders. The sturdy six-by would get jolted and roll over.

This happened to Servais' ride. "We got thrown over, and we broke through a creek. I got wet, and it was like twenty below zero." The tanker, otherwise, was not hurt and made it to Hagaru. When he got there, he was taken to an aid station. The corpsman took one look at the nineteen-year-old corporal and barked: "Get that man into a heating tent."

The tent was full of wounded; the gravity of the situation at Hagaru immediately came into focus for the shivering tanker. Still, he realized he had to get warm. "I had to stand about two inches from a potbelly stove that was glowing red hot." Servais did dry out, but the chill never passed, and he would soon find out firsthand what it takes to survive like the infantry.

About the same time Task Force Drysdale was getting into trouble, the three-battalion Task Force Faith from the Army's 7th Division was being pushed around and beaten up by the CCF while trying to get to the Yalu along the east side of the Chosin Reservoir.

General Almond arrived at Col. Don Faith's CP in a helicopter on 29 November and proceeded to try a little psychology on the troops:

> The enemy who is attacking you is nothing more than some remnants of Chinese divisions fleeing north. We're still attacking and we're going all the way to the Yalu. Don't let a bunch of Chinese laundrymen stop you. (Russell Spurr, *Enter the Dragon,* Newmarket Press)

This was the command mentality General Smith was up against, but he was having no part of it. He knew the Chinese presence was for real. He did not see the enemy as Almond's "remnants," or "laundrymen." The Division commander was not about to let his men be stretched any farther over a very suspect unknown trail to the Yalu.

Smith already had begun ordering his Marines to pull back, and on 30 November after Task Force Faith had been cut to pieces and Colonel Faith was killed in action, General Almond finally gave in to what really was going on. The X Corps commander, then, abandoned any thoughts of advancing beyond the Chosin and agreed that the Marines should start "falling back."

General Almond wanted General Smith to abandon and destroy everything—Army-like. The First Marine Division commander would have nothing to do with this. "My movement would be governed by my ability to evacuate the wounded, that I would have to fight my way back and could not afford to discard equipment," Smith replied. His division was going back to the port of Hungnam with everything his Marines could carry, and Almond was astonished to learn that meant weapons, equipment, wounded, and, yes, even as many dead Marines as they could handle.

It would be a fight in another direction, and what a fight it was.

First it would be the 7th Marines and fellow infantrymen from the 5th, along with three battalions and four other artillery batteries of the 11th Marines coming back from

Yudam-ni to Hagaru. Like many tankers, the big gunners of the 11th Marines quickly had to rely on their basic infantry training. Fragments of other units, some surviving from Task Force Faith, also were in tow.

Between 1-4 December, the courageous Marines from Yudam-ni were adding multitudes of heroic chapters to Corps history. Written with blood and unbelievably numbed bodies in snow and ice, never to be thawed by the heat of time, the breakout from the west side of the Chosin Reservoir literally defined the word *courageous.*

It was a litany of numbers and clichés reflecting pride of survival and death in combat—*1419, 1542, 1520,* hills ranging so tall above sea level to be climbed and conquered; *Fox Hill, Ridgerunners of Toktong Pass, Darkhorse.*

In and around the four-mile perimeter of the Hagaru base, it was *East Hill,* ultimately lost to the Reds, but symbolic of the gritty fight,

> . . . a bob-tailed battalion, two artillery batteries and an assortment of service troops had stood off a CCF division . . . reinforced with organic mortars and some horse-drawn artillery. Chinese prisoners reported . . . 90 per cent casualties. (MCOinK, Volume III)

After four days and nights over fourteen miles of narrow, winding, icy road and scrambling knee-deep in drifted snow on craggy mountain sides, the Marines didn't know what a couple of hours' good sleep was. It took nearly sixty hours for the first groups to make it back. By the time the trail units of the 7th and 5th Marines trudged into Hagaru, the breakout had consumed about seventy-nine hours. They had made the most of slim rations, munching on crackers, and occasionally gnawing at a canned ration, sometimes warmed, but not completely unfrozen, by body heat. Yet within sight of the Hagaru perimeter, some of the 5th Marines came to a halt, reformed into their best parade-ground column. With shoulders arched back, singing the Marine Corps Hymn, they marched into another enemy-surrounded oasis.

General Smith's grand plan was taking shape. He had about two-thirds of his depleted Division in one place, tenuous as it was. But like the temperature, his numbers were falling. Now crammed into the "safety" of the encircled Division CP were thousands of wounded and weather-related casualties, among them remnants of mauled Army units. More than 4,300 men were evacuated by air, but that still left hundreds of walking wounded. From 30 November to 4 December, the First Marine Division lost 154 killed due to combat; 55 were listed as missing; 921 wounded; and non-battle casualties, mostly frostbite, amounted to almost 1,200.

The sacrifice was not lost on the Division commander:

> Under the circumstances of its execution . . . the breakout was remarkably well conducted. Since centralized control of the widespread elements was a difficult task, particularly with the joint command, unit commanders were required to exercise a high degree of initiative . . . The spirit and discipline of the men under the most adverse conditions of weather and terrain was another highly important factor contributing to the success of the operation and also reflecting the quality of leadership being exercised. (MCOinK, Volume III)

Smith's steadfastness itself, in balking at the thinking of higher command, certainly reflected his own "quality of leadership being exercised."

But there was a long way to go, not so much in miles, but in face of relentless Chinese pressure from the hills and roadblocks, complicated by the severest winter weather in Korean history.

Flame Tanks Protect Battalion

The Flame Platoon of Headquarters Company, First Tank Battalion, had not been sitting by idly while things were popping all along the seventy-eight-mile stretch of the main supply route.

The use of tanks in the craggy Taebaek Mountains was very limited at best, and once the newer, more powerful M26 Pershings were able to navigate the narrow MSR and get forward to Hagaru, they became the primary rolling armor of choice with their devastating 90mm rifles. Meanwhile, Lt. Col. Harry T. Milne, commanding officer of the battalion, continued to keep the Flame Platoon within reaching distance of his CP at Soyang. "In the extremely fluid situation," Lt. Col. Milne said of the ever-worsening problems confronting the First Marine Division, "we found ourselves running up and down the Korean Peninsula. We had few suitable flame targets."

Where "fixed and dug-in targets" in Wolmi-do, Inchon, and Seoul presented ideal missions for flame tanks, the intervention of roving Chinese Communist Forces in the highly inaccessible hills of the Taebaeks confined the platoon to security of the battalion CP and setting roadblocks along the MSR. "Providing protection for our CPs with their 30s and 50s (caliber machine guns)," Milne noted, "flames were ideal for battalion security."

Meanwhile, it would be five Sherman dozers from the Provisional Tank Platoon helping the Pershings from the battalion's B and D companies, and the anti-tank platoon herding the convoy down the mountain. Often the tanks would be on the point leading the way. Always, they were the caboose guarding the rear.

Lt. General Oliver P. Smith, commander of the First Marine Division, had finalized plans for the "advance" south from Hagaru to Koto-Ri, and it would be the 7th Marines on the point. The order went out:

> (a) RCT-5 [5th Marine Regiment] (3/1[3rd Bn/1st Marines] attached) to relieve all elements on the perimeter defense in the Hagaru area by 1200, 5 December; to cover the movement of RCT-7 to the south on the Hagaru-ri-Koto-ri-Chinhung-ni axis; to protect the Division rear from Hagaru to Koto-ri; and to follow RCT-7 from Koto-ri to the Hamhung area as Division Reserve.
> (b) RCT-7 to advance south at first light on 6 December on the Hagaru-Koto-ri-Chinhung-ri axis to close the Hamhung area.
> (c) RCT-1(-[3/1]) to continue to hold Koto-ri and Chinhung-ni, protecting the approach and passage of the remainder of the Division through Koto-ri; and to protect the division rear from Koto-rui to the Hamhung area. (MCOinK, Volume III)

General Smith caught a break of sorts before leaving Hagaru. The Chinese had decided to back off. For five nights after the initial attack on Hagaru, it was calm, except when it was mistakenly bombed by our own Air Force. Otherwise, without harassment from the Chinese, Smith and his staff worked long hours to set up the next stage of the advance south. Figuring something was up, he wanted to get his Division on the road by 6 December, and that's just what he did.

It still was going to be a long and arduous trip, and there were going to be no free rides for the able-bodied.

All personnel except drivers, relief drivers, radio operators, casualties and men specially designated by RCT commanders, were to march on foot alongside motor serials to provide close in security. It was directed that vehicles breaking down should be pushed to the side of the road and destroyed if not operative by the time the column passed. During halts, a perimeter defense of motor serials was to be established.

Nine control points were designated by map references to be used for reporting progress of the advance or directing air-drops. Demolitions to clear obstacles from the front and to create them to the rear were planned by the Division Engineer Officer.

Helicopter evacuation was indicated for emergency cases. Other casualties were to be placed in sleeping bags and evacuated in vehicles in the column. (MCOinK, Volume III)

By this time, Cpl. Dean Servais, who had survived Hellfire Valley with Task Force Drysdale, but who had to leave his M26 tank sitting along the side of the MLR, was using his own ingenuity to join the breakout from Hagaru. He and the rest of the crew from the immobilized D12 Pershing were doing anything they could to help other crews in Dog Company prepare for the trip south. They also were helping beat off Chinese attacks, which were frequent along the perimeter of the First Marine Division CP.

"There was an old M4A3 Sherman up there," Servais said. "It was out of commission. The engine had burned out and could not be repaired. It was sittin' in the tank park, and it became our home while we were up there."

When the Chinese came down out of the hills at night to harass the Marine lines, the orphaned crew made use of the two machine guns on the relic. They couldn't use the 30-caliber bow gun because the tank was sitting too low to get any elevation on that weapon. But by traversing the turret by hand, they could make use of the co-ax 30 and the 50-caliber on the top of the turret. "We'd get the 30 goin' and then use the 50," said Servais. "We'd raise hell with them."

The young tanker was also learning something about the Chinese, who were desperately trying to keep the Marines in North Korea. The enemy was just as cold as he was, and not as prepared for the harsh winter as the Marines. The Chinese soldier was also hungry, very hungry.

Servais was on the inner line of defense around Hagaru, and he could see very clearly what was happening if the ChiComs managed to overrun a Marine emplacement. "The first thing they would do when they came to one of our fallen Marines, is bend down and strip off the wounded or dead man's shoes and his coat. They searched bodies for food." It was obvious to the displaced tanker that they were very cold, and very hungry. "That was more important to them than winning the battle."

Servais also saw the effects of the brutal cold on the feet of captured Chinese, who wore only tennis shoes or lightweight boots. Enemy or not, he could not help but feel somewhat sorry for the foe. "Their feet were black—frozen black. They couldn't walk. How could anyone send men into battle like that?"

Before the Marines left Hagaru, an army engineer outfit, which had been next to the tanks, had pulled out without a lot of its equipment. Servais, and the gunner from his crew, PFC Sherwood Miller, a South Carolina boy, went through the engineers' equipment to see what they could find to help them. "We picked out a nice-looking six-by truck and a beautiful trailer, painted out the Army numbers and put USMC on it. We drove that all the way back to Hungnam," Servais said. "We loaded it up with food and everything for the run out of there. By the time we got halfway back, we had used everything we loaded and were carrying wounded and dead. The trailer we used for the dead, and the truck was for the wounded."

When they got back to Hungnam, they parked the truck at an aid station.

"They took the wounded and we left the dead for the mortuary."

To facilitate the move from Hagaru, Lt. Col. Milne was given charge of one of two Division trains. Motor serials within each of the trains were to have available radio communication with the commander of the train.

A key to the breakout from Hagaru was retaking East Hill, which dominated the MSR where the Division would be opening its back door. The 5th Marines got the job and they did their job, but not before the Chinese expended waves of human life, particularly late on the night of 6 December, long after the battle first had been joined.

> Although the Chinese endured frightful casualties, they returned again and again to the attack until midnight. It was evident that they considered this a fight to the finish for East Hill, and at 0205 they renewed the assault against all three companies of the 2nd Battalion as well as Charlie Company of the 1st Battalion.
>
> The struggle during the next three hours was considered the most spectacular if not the most fiercely contested battle of the entire Reservoir campaign even by veterans of the Yudam-ni actions. Never before had they seen the Chinese come on in such numbers or return to the attack with such persistence. The darkness was crisscrossed with a fiery pattern of tracer bullets at one moment, and next the uncanny radiance of an illumination shell would reveal Chinese columns shuffling in at a trot, only to go down in heaps as they deployed. Marine tanks, artillery, mortars, rockets and machine guns reaped a deadly harvest, and still the enemy kept on coming with a dogged fatalism which commanded the respect of the Marines. Looking like round little gnomes in their padded cotton uniforms, groups of Chinese contrived at times to approach within grenade-throwing distance before being cut down.
>
> The fight was not entirely one-sided. The Marines took a pounding from CCF mortars and machine guns, and by 0300 Dog Company was hard pressed in its three extended positions pointed like a pistol at the heart of the enemy's assembly areas. (MCOinK, Volume III)

Dog tanks led the 7th Regiment vanguard out of Hagaru. Not far down the MSR, the lead Sherman dozer tank had to clear a roadblock, and once it broke through, it was rocked by three 3.5 rockets. It took a combined infantry-tank team to break up the attack. Not too much further down the road, Dog tanks again got into it with the Reds. Some fine shooting by tank gunners dispersed the ChiComs. It was like that most of the way, but late on 6 December the lead elements of the train entered Koto-ri. By 1700, the next afternoon, RCT-7 was all here.

However, the Chinese quickly closed parts of the MSR once the 7th left it, and Lt. Col. Milne's Division Train 2, which had not left Hagaru until 1600 on 6 December, was still making its way to the rendezvous at Koto-ri. It was a walking series of fire-fights all the way. The line of Marines and their equipment stretched the full eleven miles between the two towns, and it wasn't until after midnight of 6-7 December that the last of the rearguard tanks were pulling into line outside vacated Hagaru.

The tankers had one parting shot for the Chinese. After teams of Marine Corps engineers had wired all supplies that could not be transported out, small fires of unknown origin broke out, eventually screening the dumps with smoke. But the engineers, the last troops in Hagaru, finally set their fuses and within twenty minutes, "the entire base seemed to be erupting like a volcano" (MCOinK, Volume III).

Chinese troops braved the holocaust, despite presenting open targets when pockets of smoke cleared in the midday-like light. Tankers, as they waited for the engineers to join the end of the column, got in their last licks with some deadly machine-gun fire.

It was midnight when the tanks followed the tail of the column into the perimeter of Koto-ri, a short stop before the next excruciating leg of the fight to the sea. The initial phase of breakout took nearly forty hours to get approximately 10,000 Marines and assorted men from other U.N. units, along with an estimated 1,000 trucks, tanks, and other rolling stock to the next jump-off point. It was expensive—103 killed or dead of wounds, 7 missing in action, and 506 wounded.

But there was little rest for the weary, still wary, and far from warm combatants. Before the caboose of Lt. Col. Milne's Division Train 2 was sealed within the "terminal" that Koto-ri had become, orders were issued to resume the march south at first light on 8 December. In fact, General Smith had ordered a "station" set up on high ground a little south, but within the protection of the 1st Marines at Koto, to handle the influx of weary troops.

The responsibility for Koto-ri had been in the hands of Col. Lewis B. Chesty Puller, C.O. of the 1st Marine Regiment. Again, wounded and severely frost-bitten men were flown out. That was made possible by the expansion of a small airstrip ordered by Colonel Puller as he prepared for the arrival of the two Division Trains and their subsequent quick departure en mass.

Puller was ready for them. At the station just below his own encampment, Puller had local troops set up warming tents, and he also made sure all the new arrivals would have a hot meal sometime between the time they came into Koto-ri and when they would continue their advance south the next day. All told, Puller had more than 14,000 troops on his hands, the bulk of which were 9,000-plus Marines coming in from Hagaru and another 2,600 of his own 1st Marines. Added to the mix were more than 800 Army survivors from Hagaru, another 150 of Colonel Drysdale's British Royal Marines, and not quite 40 ROK police. So, it was the almost-full First Marine Division, with assorted tag-alongs, that began to make its exit from Koto-ri on 8 December.

Easing out of Koto-ri, their objective was Chinhung-ni, a valley village at the terminus of the a MSR's steep drop. Between the two points was a ten-mile stretch of unlevel, rarely straight road weaving through peaks poking a mile high into the winter sky.

Adding to the monumental task, about three miles south of Koto-ri, a bridge over a deep gorge had been destroyed by the Chinese. A gap of twenty-four feet over the gorge had to be re-spanned, but Marine and Army engineers figured it out. On 7 December, they got an airdrop of eight 2,500-pound bridge sections and plywood center sections at Koto-ri. Six of the bridge sections were recovered. Essential equipment, among which were two U.S. Army treadway bridge trucks, was gathered within the perimeter.

The plan called for the crucial pieces of the Division's lifeline—the Treadway Bridge Train—follow the 7th Marines, the vanguard of the push down the Taebaeks from Koto-ri. They had broken camp at 0800 on 8 December in a swirling snowstorm that at times reduced visibility to less than 100 feet. Several hours earlier, in the same snowstorm, a battalion of 1st Marines, detached at Chinhung-ni, began clearing the MSR of Chinese from the other end.

It wasn't until early afternoon—because of the weather, and infantry being forced to remove CCF troops from the surrounding hills—that the Treadway Bridge Train was able to fall in line behind the point regiment and plod its way out of Koto-ri. That delay put off assembling the span until the next day.

When the bridge was opened late in the afternoon of 9 December, it was not without more anxious moments.

> Only a few vehicles had reached the other side when a disastrous accident threatened to undo everything that had been accomplished. A tractor towing an earth-moving pan broke through the plywood center panel rendering it useless. And with the treadways spaced as they were, the way was closed to wheeled vehicles.
>
> A first ray of hope glimmered when an expert tractor driver, Technical Sergeant Wilfred H. Prosser, managed to back the machine off the wrecked bridge. Then Partridge [Lt.Col. John Partridge, CO, 1st Engineer Battalion in command of the construction] . . . came up with the answer that a total width of 135 inches would result if the treadways were placed as far apart as possible. This would allow a very slight margin at both extremes—two inches to spare for the M-26s [tanks] on the treadways; and barely half an inch for the jeeps using the 45-inch interval between the metal lips on the inboard edges of the treadways.
>
> Thanks to skillful handling of the bulldozers the treadways were soon respaced. And in early darkness Partridge's solution paid off when the first jeep crossed, its tires scraping both edges. Thus the convoy got underway again as an engineer detachment guided vehicles across with flashlights while . . . troops kept the enemy at a distance. (MCOinK, Volume III)

That was an amazing feat of engineering, construction, and bravery, under conditions that could not have been worse. Tanks had to pass slowly and very cautiously on the metal outer spans. Drivers of trucks and narrower rolling stock had to line up wheels of one side of the vehicle within an outer span while the opposite side had to find traction on the plywood center section.

It was a constant file of troops and vehicles, with North Korean refugees mixed in through the night of 9-10 December—military trudging in a column on one side of the machines, and natives with their families, belongings, and scattered animals on the other side. As the column snailed along, Chinese prisoners, beaten by the cold, were taken and brought into the column.

It was hairy, but it was far from being the only treachery the Marines faced.

Like the attacks south from Yudam-ni and Hagaru, again there were series of enemy strong-points and intrusions that had to be overcome. Hills 1328, 1457, 1081, 1304, 891—those numbers alone, meters above sea level, speak for themselves. Funchillan Pass was a key part of the artery that had to be kept open below those peaks. Fierce firefights and grenade attacks from both sides cost dearly, particularly to the Chinese, who left more than 500 bodies scattered around Funchillan Pass.

Trouble erupted at Sudong, but the Chinese, some of them hidden among lines of refugees, were killed or routed.

There were forty tanks, an assortment of the First Tank Battalion's Dog and Baker companies and platoons from the regimental anti-tank companies, at the end of the column. They were ordered there by General Smith, not only to make the Chinese think twice about trying to overtake the back of the column, but also to safeguard against possible clogging of the road if any of the monsters became disabled within the trains or ahead of them. Slowly, agonizingly, they rumbled their way over the icy, twisting, narrow, uneven MSR with a protective screen of infantry from the 1st Marines walking closely behind them part of the way. But not all of them made it to Chinhung-ni.

"We lost five tanks coming down that Hill," said Maj. Phillip C. Morrell, newly promoted from captain when he was assigned as executive officer of the First Tank Battalion on 1 December. Despite recon and infantry patrols in the hills flanking the winding column, the Chinese found ways to make things difficult.

The 1st Marines were called away from the protection and as the column of pigirons came down the hill toward the Treadway Bridge, a Recon Company took over a screen on the flanks, with a platoon of them assigned to the last ten tanks.

When the ninth tank from the end of the column had to grind its way to a stop because its brakeline froze, it blocked the MSR, just what General Smith feared might happen. But because of Smith's foresight, there weren't long lines of troops and other rolling equipment behind them—only refugees who had not been permitted within the column. Mixed with them were Chinese infiltraters. While the rest of the column continued, the nine orphaned pigirons were held up for almost an hour.

"The fifth tank in line experienced a steering problem," Morrell said, "and its track was hanging over the edge of the road. The crew had to get out, but pulled the gun mechanism before they destroyed the tank."

The hordes of Korean civilians, who had not been permitted within the column, were tagging along in the distance behind the tanks. With that part of the column halted, they began edging closer. For the most part the tankers—guns constantly trained on the pitiful looking civilians—had not let anyone, no matter how impoverished they appeared, near the back end of that column. This was the costly exception as Marines refrained from firing at the civilians.

Chinese, mingling among refugees, managed to attack the rear of the column. During the firefight, crews were forced to abandon seven of the tanks. Men manning the last two M26s in line were reported either killed or missing.

The First Tank Battalion counted four missing in action. The Recon Company lost two to mortal wounds, another unaccounted for, and twelve wounded. Only two of the nine orphaned tanks made it to Chinhung-ni, and the toll paid by the First Tank Battalion was five M26 Pershings.

Once the column had gotten to the railhead at Sudong, four flame tanks were brought up to bolster the rear guard to protect the flanks. "They set up two of them on each side of the road," Cpl. Servais said. "They had their turrets swung right and left facing the hills. They didn't use their flame guns but fired their 105s and machine guns into the hills, keeping the ridges clear and keeping the Chinese heads down. Further down the road, there were two more flame tanks, and they were traversing their turrets from one side of the road to the other looking for targets."

This was one time the Flame Platoon was not looked on like the kid brothers tagging along after their Pershing siblings. "They were there and we were damn glad to see them," the Wisconsin Marine said, relief and gratitude in his tone. "It was like seeing your big brother coming to protect you after you had been in a fight with a bunch of big bullies."

PFC Bill Kuykendall, driving F21, and Cpl. Mo Sims, the F23 driver, were with the flame tanks rear guard and had plenty of targets when the Chinese braved the Marines perimeter. "We could see them," PFC Kuykendall said when the enemy attempted to attack. We used the 105 with canister shot when the gooks got close to us." Canister is like buckshot, only with a much larger pellet, range, and coverage. For the blocking duty they were pulling, the flame tanks carried three rounds of canister in the restricted confines of their turrets.

"It did the trick for us," Kuykendall said. "The gooks were all over us, and we had to use the canister to blow them off."

However, the Shermans' machine guns were the flame tank's key weapons necessity for protecting the rear of the column.

"We used the 30s mostly," said Cpl. Sims of his bow gun and the coax which was operated in the turret. "But on occasion, the guys in the turret would have to pop the hatches and man the 50-caliber."

Seventy-five Marines died at the hands of Chinese coming down the hill from Koto-ri. There were 16 missing and more than 250 wounded. On 11 December, the First Marine Division and its assorted comrades cleared Chinhung-ni, passed through Majon-dong without incident, and began arriving in Hamhung.

There still was the matter of getting everybody down to the waiting ships, but the breakout from the Chosin Reservoir, for all intents and purposes, had been accomplished.

General Smith Thinking Ahead

Once again Lt. Gen. Oliver P. Smith had been thinking ahead, confident his First Marine Division would fight its way out of the heights of the Taebaek Mountains. He had ordered preparations made to accommodate his warriors and other United Nations units when they got to Hamhung. As at the station in Koto-ri, there would be hot food and warm-up tents.

Little did PFC Len Martin, who had been tanker-trained but assigned like an infantryman since he arrived in Korea a month earlier, realize the significant role he was playing in the historical breakout.

Although Martin was miles away from most of the action when attached to the First Tank Battalion CP in Soyang, he had been involved in countless patrols and outpost assignments—like the flame tanks he would later join—protecting the lower end of the MSR. Now, he and his newly made friends in Headquarters Company were about to pull up stakes. "We knew the outfits up north were fighting their way back from Yudam-ni, Hagaru, and Koto-ri towards Hamhung and us," Martin said. "As they neared, we broke camp and moved someplace else. I had no idea where it was."

It was in the Chigyong-Yonpo Airport area where the First Amphibian Tractor Battalion had been assigned as early as 8 December to set up tents, install stoves, erect heads, and equip galleys in preparation to facilitate wary heroes of the amazing breakout.

What Martin would learn shortly, he was about to provide a lot of miserable, numb Marines with just a *scoshi* bit of relief from that misery and numbness.

"We were put to work setting up pyramid tents for them," Martin said, finding it hard to believe how Gyrenes coming his way had survived frigid wind, snow, and ice for days—maybe weeks—on end without even so much as the flimsy protection of canvas. "It was so cold that we worked about twenty minutes and then had to come in and warm up. I kept thinking that we had a warm place to sleep, but those poor guys in the infantry were constantly out in the open in the freezing cold."

Now, arriving in Hamhung, just as they had at Koto-ri, the once-beleagured Marines would get a few hours of relief before going down to the staging areas of the Hungnam beach for evacuation by the Navy. What they would suddenly realize—a little surprised, at that—was they no longer would be harassed by the CCF.

Chinese Communist Forces that attacked the eastern front along the Yalu had one objective in mind—wipe out the First Marine Division. Instead, its own armies were left in shambles, heaps of wasted humanity, grotesque shapes of lifeless figures, frosted white where they stood, crouched, kneeled, lay—numbed in place unable even to wretch in death. They were nothing but surreal snowmen.

Enemy losses . . . were estimated at a total of 37,500 – 15,000 killed and 7,500 wounded by Marine grounds forces, plus 10,000 killed and 5,000 wounded by Marine Air. (MCOinK, Volume III)

As for the Marines, "We lost more people to frostbite than anything," said Maj. Phillip Morrell, executive officer of the First Tank Battalion. The Battalion's after-action reports of the Breakout were fraught daily with repetitive references: "Ten (10) non-battle frost bite casualties . . . fourteen (14) non-battle casualties, frost bite," etc. They mirrored numbers from the Division's other units. Of the more than 7,300 non-battle casualties from late October through the November-December ordeal, minor frostbite cases were the most prevalent.

At Hamhung, the final stage of the "advance" south was complete, and, although the Marines didn't know it right away, the worst was over. There were no more intrusions by the Chinese for now. The CCF was left in the Taebaeks, beaten and disorganized, too frozen to be frustrated. They were incapable of sustaining pressure on the First Marine Division.

More than seven CCF divisions had confronted and tried to annihilate the Marines. Now they sat, muted, in the hills around the two cities as a giant Navy task force began to extricate one of the Marine Corps most gallant band of fighters, their equipment, and the assortment of army units and refugees they pulled along with them. By its own count, the Red incursion left at least 25,000 of its own brave troops dead, another 12,000 wounded. It was not a winter carnival for the Marines, either—718 KIA, 192 MIA, 3,508 WIA, thousands suffering various degrees of frostbite.

PFC Martin got some firsthand details on what had been going just a few days earlier. "One day while I was waiting in chow line," he said, "I saw a bunch of trucks coming in. Many had flat tires and were loaded with men sitting on the fenders. These were some of the Marines who had fought their way back from the Reservoir. They brought back their wounded and many of their dead. I talked to several of the tankers and they said that the Chinese just kept coming, and coming, and coming in waves."

Haggard, grimy, shivering Marines who withstood the most grueling demands of the breakout were the first to be loaded aboard ships after they got some hot food and maybe a little rest.

It was 11 December when Lt. Col. Milne came off the hill at Chinhung-ni with the Baker and Dog companies' tanks and continued south through Majon-Dong and Hamhung to the beach at Hungnam where LSTs were waiting. But it would be awhile before the Battalion was completely ready to debark.

Because Able Company tanks had been providing covering support while the Division Trains were clearing Hamhung, it wasn't until early the next morning that its M26s showed up at the beach, followed closely by Charlie Company.

Those who finally had gotten to Hungnam now dared think that they were going to make it. They could see the ships, hundreds of them sitting in the harbor and offshore. The First Marine Division would be loaded on an APA (assault transport), an AKA (assault cargo ship), APs (transports), LSTs (landings ship tanks), LSDs (landing ship dock), and commercial cargo ships. The Navy came through big.

"Since we knew we also were to be evacuated and we couldn't take all of our gear with us," PFC Martin said, "we started to destroy what we could not take. We buried boxes of 50-caliber machine-gun ammunition. We made piles of clothes, doused them with gasoline, and burned them."

The destruction of supplies by Martin and his tanker-infantry buddies was nothing compared to the pyrotechnics that would be set off by engineers as they rendered the Hamhung-Hungnam area a pile of rubble.

"We eventually moved to the seaport of Hungnam," PFC Martin said. That was 12 December, and the "tent working party" from Soyang had rejoined Headquarters Company, complete with the Flame Platoon, which had arrived after doing its bit as part of the rear guard covering the final leg of the "advance" south. "The port was loaded with men and equipment," Martin said, but the freezing weather still was a problem. "In order to keep warm, someone started a fire, and a cook started throwing large chunks of baking grease on it."

That was a hot fire.

Before loading on the LST, Martin and a few of the infantry-tankers had some time on their hands. "Several of us roamed around the port, and we could see a large group of civilians. We learned, later, there were almost 100,000 of them." Talking to some South Korean soldiers who spoke English, they were told that the refugees were North Koreans who were fleeing the Chinese and Communism.

"They were leaving everything behind—their homes, places where they had lived all their lives, and the graves of their ancestors. If the Chinese had caught them, they would probably all have been executed. I felt sorry for them," the young Marine said. "I knew I would be getting out, but they might have to stay. Fortunately for them, they all were evacuated and relocated in South Korea."

The problem of Korean refugees threatened to disrupt the schedule [of embarkation of the last Army units]. But CTF-90 [Commander Task Force-90] contrived somehow to find the shipping, and the homeless Koreans were willing to put up with any hardships to escape from Communist domination. It became standard practice to embark at least 5,000 on an LST, not counting children in arms, and no less than 12,000 human sardines found standing room on one commercial cargo ship. (MCOinK, Volume III)

When Service Company of the First Tank Battalion began staging at Hungnam, five two-and-one-half-ton trucks were borrowed from the Army to handle its equipment. Although the Division had fought down the MSR with its wounded and most of its equipment, there still were needs at the end of the line.

"Since there was so much Army equipment on the beach, and since the Marine Corps had lost a lot of theirs," Martin said, "the Marines borrowed—well, maybe stole—a lot of the Army gear. It got to be somewhat of a joke. Marines were crossing out Army serial numbers on jeeps and trucks, and painting on their personal serial numbers. Later, the Army finally asked that they change the markings from Army to Marines, but that they leave the original serial numbers on the vehicles so that they could account for them."

It was 12 December when PFC Len Martin, along with the Flame Platoon, the rest of Headquarters Company, and the 7th Marines anti-tank company loaded aboard LST Q009 and into the safe harbor of Hungnam. Two days later they were in the Sea of Japan with the rest of the First Marine Division, heading south for the Masan.

In their wake was the devastation of Hungnam and Hamhung. Since there was no Chinese interference in the evacuation, all of the military equipment and stores could be loaded on shipping. All told, "105,000 military, 91,000 refugees, 17,500 vehicles, 350,000 tons of cargo loaded out in 193 shiploads by 108 ships" *(MCOinK, Volume III).*

Late afternoon of Christmas Eve 1950, Hungnam was a ghost town, and after the engineers got through with it, a ghost may have been all that could have survived. "The entire Hungnam waterfront seemed to be blown sky-high in one volcanic eruption of flame, smoke and rubble which left a huge black mushroom cloud hovering over the ruins" *(MCOinK, Volume III).*

It was the consensus that the intensity the Chinese Communist Forces expended against the First Marine Division, and the high cost paid for it, took the pressure off the Eighth Army in the west. Despite having retreated more than 250 miles in an undisciplined rout, the Eighth was able to get far enough south to outstumble the riddled Chinese.

Had not the Marines drawn so much CCF attention, the Reds may have had the wherewithal to cut off the other side of the peninsula and completely wipe out the Eighth Army, or force its evacuation. As it was, the Eighth, eventually absorbing X Corps and with it, the First Marine Division, would live to fight proudly another day as EUSAK—Eighth United States Army Korea.

Eighth U.S. Army Korea

Contrary to a prediction made by Gen. Douglas MacArthur, Commander in Chief Far East, American troops fighting the Korean War would not be home for Christmas in 1950.

Communist Chinese Forces had become a new equation in the problem confronting the United Nations command in the Land of the Morning Calm. But after the First Marine Division pulled off its incredible breakout from the Chosin Reservoir in the north, U.N. forces quickly began to reorganize under the mantle of Eighth U.S. Army in Korea (EUSAK).

Meanwhile, the Red regime orchestrating things from above the Yalu River also had to do some rethinking of its own. While the Chinese intrusion forced United Nations troops out of North Korea, the cost to the Reds was so steep they could not fully take advantage of their accomplishment. The North Korean People's Army had barged over the 38th Parallel almost to Pusan in the first stage of the war. U.S.-dominated United Nations troops recoiled 180 degrees and nearly made it to the Yalu River in mid-November, threatening to set up opposite Manchuria. It came back the other way during the December debacle, and that left the separation of the two adversaries just about where it all started—relatively along the 38th Parallel.

By the time the Marines fought their way from Yudam-ni and were evacuated from Hungnam, and the Eighth Army stopped backpedaling in the West in late December, Republic of Korea (ROK) units were able to tie in with their staggering American counterparts. By late December, this stabilized a main line of resistance (MLR) with the Eighth's I Corps and IX Corps in the west, the ROKS taking up positions stretching eastward from the middle of the peninsula. That strung the new MLR from Munsan just south of the 38th in the west, northeastward above Chunchon and sharply north across the Parallel to above the East Coast town of Yangyong.

As for the First Marine Division, its chilled and bone-weary survivors of the Chosin had completed their "cruise" down the Sea of Japan from Hamhung, and Lt. Gen. Oliver P. Smith set up his command post at Masan, a small port city northwest of Pusan. It was not strange land to Leathernecks from the 5th Marines who had labeled it "Bean Patch." They had spent some time there after engaging the North Koreans for the first time at the Naktong River the previous August. They were then known as the 1st Provisional Marine Brigade.

The nickname of the new Division CP was prompted by the expanse of farmed fields on the outskirts of the city. It may have been a bean patch in August. But in the third week of December, it was a frozen snow-covered flatland.

The Flame Platoon of the First Tank Battalion, along with the rest of Headquarters Company, arrived there 17 December by LST after an "entangled" stop at Pusan Harbor to cram some of the 5th Marines into the ship. Most of the Division was off loaded at Pusan because of the larger facilities and then taken overland about twenty miles to Masan.

LST Q009 already was packed with the First Tank's units, platoons of anti-tank company Pershings of the 7th Marines and some of the British 41st Commandos who escaped Hellfire Valley. For some reason, there were orders to pull into Pusan Harbor and pick up some of the 5th Marines before continuing on to Masan.

"On entering the harbor, the LST got its propeller tangled up in a submarine net," said PFC Len Martin, the young tanker who had yet to be assigned to one of the Tank Battalion's rolling units. "Divers had to come and cut us loose." Once the screw was freed of the cable, the ship went in to pick up the Gravel Crunchers. "We must have taken aboard around a thousand of those 5th Marines," Martin said with a bit of wonder on his mind. Where were they going to put these guys? An LST usually has sleeping accommodations for about 250.

"We had close to 300 Marines and British commandos already on board," Martin said. "When the Fifth came aboard, guys were sleeping everywhere. The crew couldn't feed all of us, so we ate C rations. It was hard to believe that many people could be crammed into an LST, what with all the equipment that was on it, too. But the Navy did it."

Last on, first off! That's the way it went when LST Q009 finally docked in the narrow port of Masan. Martin and his fellow tankers, of course, were last to debark, and they had mixed feelings about that.

"Those guys from the Fifth left a lot of gear behind—boxes of machine-gun ammo, mortar rounds, a big pile of weapons in the center of the deck," said the young Marine from Forest Park, Illinois. "That pile must have been five feet high—mostly M-1 (Garand) rifles and carbines they had recovered from their dead and wounded. We scrounged around and took whatever we wanted. I picked up an automatic carbine, and later I traded it to a ROK soldier for a Russian Rifle."

There was a down side to the tankers' windfall. "Since we were the last ones off the LST, we had to clean up what the Fifth left behind. We ended up throwing boxes of ammo and a lot of other stuff overboard."

Once off the ship, Headquarters Company and the Flame Platoon moved to the Division CP where the First Tank Battalion area was set up temporarily near some existing buildings, which would be used for mess halls and storage.

"We lived in pyramid tents again," Martin said. "This was nothing new to us in the First Tank Battalion, but it must have been a real luxury for guys in the infantry who had been out in the open for the last three weeks."

The Bean Patch was where the First Marine Division would rest, recover, regroup, replenish, and refit for the next couple of weeks. Hot meals were a must, as were hot showers, which quickly led to very hot bonfires. As Marines peeled off stinking clothes they had been wearing for nearly a month, the rags were thrown into a huge pile, saturated with gasoline, and incinerated. Gyrenes got everything new, from skivvies on out.

At the Bean Patch, the Marines were 200 miles behind the lines, an unusual position for them, but it wouldn't last long. Meanwhile, the Third Replacement Draft had arrived to begin filling the personnel shortage. Equipment was another story, and it might be safe to say the Marines were victims of their own discipline. Although they brought much of their equipment out of the Chosin Campaign, there still were major shortages, but the Marines would have to wait.

The Army got first priority on resupply—which was nothing new. This time, however, it was because retreating Eighth Army had left most of its gear up north when it dropped everything and ran in a panic bugout as the Chinese overran the overextended and ill-prepared Americans.

Among the Marines' needs were seven M4A3 Sherman dozer tanks and sixteen M26 Pershings lost by the AT companies and the First Tank Battalion. No new Shermans came in, and only four of the Pershings had been replaced by the end of 1950.

One major replacement in the whole scheme of the Korean War, however, was about evolve out of tragedy.

A jeep accident had claimed the life of Lt. Gen. Walton H. Walker, the highly regarded commander of the Eighth Army, although he had little success getting his Patton-like spirit through to his troops. That was 23 December and two days later—Christmas Day—Lt. Gen. Matthew B. Ridgway was in Tokyo, given command of the newly designated Eighth U.S. Army in Korea. He would take over all United Nations forces in the war-torn country.

Ridgway was a no-nonsense breath of fresh air as far as the U.N. troops go, particularly when it concerned the Army. He commanded airborne troops in World War II, and was immediately identified by the two hand grenades always attached to straps of his shoulder holster harness.

Ridgway did not like what he saw of the U.S. Army. He immediately dismissed a plan, put together by the Eighth Army staff before he arrived, for another withdrawal to Pusan amid rumors of a general exit from Korea.

Conversely, Ridgway wanted a workup for attacking the Communists.

The new commander may have had doubts as he toured the Army's troops now dug in close to the 38th Parallel the final week of December. He later commented in his memoirs *(MCOinK)*:

> *I must say in all frankness that the spirit of the Eighth Army as I found it on my arrival gave me deep concern. There was a definite air of nervousness, of gloomy foreboding, of uncertainty, a spirit of apprehension as to what the future held. There was much "looking over the shoulder" as the soldiers say.*
> *These criticisms were not applicable to the 1st Marine Division.*
> *"Our men were in high spirits and busily engaged in getting ready to fight again," commented Brigadier General Edward A. Craig, ADC. "In my travels around the various units of the Division, and in talking to the men, I never even once noticed any air of nervousness or apprehension. . . . When General Ridgway visited the Division at Masan he made a tour of the entire camp area and observed training and general arrangements. He stated that he was quite satisfied with the 1st Marine Division and its quick comeback after the Chosin fighting." (MCOinK, Volume IV)*

Once the First Tank Battalion got to Masan, there was plenty to do, but the emphasis, as it was throughout the Division, was also to wind down from the rigors of The Breakout—start getting back in shape. And, yes, troops were to relax a little. There was some touch football and, even in the cold of December, softball games. It was activity to shed the tensions of so many cold nights and days in combat.

"It seems everyone was feeling sorry for the Marines," Len Martin said, "so they sent us rations of turkeys. I think that we had turkey and trimmings at least three times between Christmas and New Year. We even pulled some liberty, but there wasn't much to do or see. Masan did have an open-air market that was somewhat interesting, raw fish, et cetera. One night some South Korean kids, who came from a Christian school, came around singing Christmas songs."

For Martin, still wondering when he was going to be assigned to a tank, there were the usual low points of a young Marine still feeling he had not quite fit in yet. "I got stuck on mess duty," he said. "One day, I was assigned to the garbage detail." Mess duty garbage detail also included going around camp and picking up all kinds of discarded items—

clothing, sleeping bags, and whatever else. The trash was loaded in the back of a metal bed six-by truck that had a metal tailgate hinged at the top.

"We took the truck outside the camp to a dumpsite on the top of a hill." Martin was about to get his first lesson on being up close to poverty and what the ravages war also do to those not carrying guns. "When we reached the dumpsite, we were surrounded by a large group of civilian men, women, and kids. Before we even started to dump the garbage down the side of the hill they swarmed all over the truck to scavenge whatever they could. One young kid got his leg caught in the tailgate as it was raised. The crowd was packed in so tight, I had to use a shovel to move them back so that I could get the kid free and dump the garbage."

As the garbage cascaded down the hillside, it was followed by the civilians trying to grab what they could. "It was quite a sobering experience for an eighteen-year-old and made me appreciate what I had back home," Martin admitted. He still was a long way from home, and the Korean War was a long way from over. It was about to heat up again.

Here They Come Again

It didn't take the Chinese Communist Forces long to lick their wounds. As 1950 was coming to a close, the Reds began pushing against the U.N. lines, which forced Lt. Gen. Matthew Ridgway—much against his grain—to allow his Eighth U.S. Army in Korea to bend a little in an effort to not have it break.

By 1 January, the ChiComs were threatening Seoul. The threat became a reality, and two days later the Reds once again were roaming the ruins and streets of South Korea's capital. By 8 January the MLR had taken about a forty-mile adjustment south from below Pyongtaek in the west, Yoju and Wonju in the middle—with a deep thirty-mile dip south to Tanyong before it rose sharply to the east coast town of Samchok.

The Flame Platoon of Headquarters Company, First Tank Battalion, had not been sitting idly by. Precautions were being taken. The Battalion had been assigned to road blocks around Masan and on 3 January, the nine flame tanks took over two positions in relief of a platoon of Able Company M-26 Pershings.

However, three of the Sherman fire-spitters—the first section—were relieved at a roadblock on 10 January and sent back to Masan where the crews learned they and their tanks were to join with Able Company and the anti-tank platoon of the 1st Marines to board an LST.

Again, it was time for the First Marine Division to come to the rescue, so to speak. Ridgway summoned Lt. Col. Oliver P. Smith, the division commander, to EUSAK headquarters in Taegu. After the conference, a revised plan called for the Marines to take over the MSR between Andong and Kyongju to prevent North Koreans and Chinese from penetrating as deep as Pohang and Yongchon.

The entire First Marine Division was about to be relocated to Pohang. It would be the Marines' first step toward going deep into the northern reaches of the East-Central front. For the next fifteen months, they once again would confront the North Korean People's Army and Chinese Communist Forces in the rugged mountainous terrain that the 38th Parallel cut through to the Sea of Japan.

LST 914 was waiting for the section of Flames and the rest of the tracked convoy when it arrived at Masan early in the evening of 10 January. Two more flame tanks went aboard LST 742. Another LST picked up other units, and within a few hours, the small convoy was on its way around the southern tip of Korea and going north in the Sea of Japan.

Lt. Col. Harry C. Milne, who had continued to use the Flames for overall Division security in his capacity as Southern Defense Section coordinator, was relieved of that task that day to oversee the movement of his battalion. The rest of the Flame Platoon, which had been working with Baker Company tanks, was taken off roadblock assignment the following day and went to Masan for shipment north.

The first section of Flames arrived in Pohang-dong mid morning of 12 January. LST 742 with two other Flamers beached at Kuryongpo-ri about an hour later. When all the LSTs carrying the First Tank Battalion made land by early afternoon, the tanks moved to what would become the Battalion CP about fifteen miles inland between Sinhung to the north and Kyongju to the southwest.

The immediate mission for the 1st Tanks was to guard an airfield yet to be activated, and the road from Pohang to Kyonju, which bordered the western edge of 1stMarDiv's E section—some 300 square miles stretching inland from the Sea of Japan. The Division as a whole was responsible for an area fifty miles across from the sea, and twice as long from Kyongju north to above Andong.

It wasn't until 16 January that the First Tank Battalion CP came aboard the LST014 from Masan along with the final troops from Headquarters Company, including PFC Leonard Martin and his tanker-infantry friends.

"That night aboard the LST, we slept on top of communication trucks," Martin said. The next day, they landed at Pohang and immediately started inland. "When we got to the CP, we were set up next to the airfield," said Martin, who was about to pull more mess duty and began wondering if he was ever going to see the inside of any kind of tank. "This did little to make me happy," he groused. Normal mess ran thirty days and in that time, Martin, who was not above letting people know how he felt, and the mess sergeant managed to foster a mutual dislike. "He told me that if I did not get a good recommendation from the cooks that he would put me on another thirty days. I told the cooks that they had better give me a good recommendation or they would be stuck with me for another month. I got a good recommendation."

Meanwhile, the airfield was about to be activated and, one day, a pair of Air Force F80 Shooting Stars were making touch-and-go landings to try it out. The strip was set up on a small plateau, and at the far end it dropped off about thirty or forty feet. There were several ridges beyond the end of it.

"One of the F80s must have lost power as he was trying to get back up," Martin said. "He went off the end of the runway and piled into one of the ridges. The pilot never had a chance. I can imagine what his buddy in the other plane must have been thinking."

Once off mess duty, it was back to "the infantry" for tanker Martin. Foot patrols were the norm. It wasn't long before the always-glib Marines called them "Rice-Paddy Patrols," according to Maj. Allan C. Bevilacqua, writing *"Pohang – the Guerilla Hunt"* for *Leatherneck Magazine,* January 2001.

> *". . . elements no larger than a fire team . . . combing back-country foot paths and trails while larger patrols, some of them motorized and with tank and artillery support, maintained constant presence along main roads . . ."*

The First Marine Division's primary job was to rout out Chinese and North Korean guerillas threatening the seventy-five-mile arc of MSR from Pohang west to Yongchon, north through Uihung, Uisong and Chongja-dong to Andong.

> *Captured documents indicated that enemy forces in unknown numbers had already infiltrated through gaps in the eastern sectors of the Eighth Army's Line . . . Guerrilla activity was reported as far west as Tanyang, on the MSR of IX Corps, and as far south as Taejon, threatening the supply line of I Corps. Train ambushes occurred on 13 January in the Namchang area and to the south of Wonju. Other attacks took place on the rail line about 60 miles north of Taegu. (MCOinK, Volume IV)*

All of this was in the west and central areas above the 1stMarDiv concentration.

> *The tactical problem of the Marines was quite simple—on paper. About 1,600 square miles, most of them standing on end in mountainous terrain, were included in the new zone of operations. The experience of World War II had demonstrated how effective guerrilla warfare could be as an adjunct to large-scale military operations. Officers of the 1st*

Marine Division had no illusions about their mission, therefore, when they received un-confirmed reports of NKPA guerrilla infiltrations behind the EUSAK lines toward Andong.

All uncertainty vanished on 18 January . . . when a patrol of the 3d Battalion, 1st Ma-rines, flushed out an undetermined number of North Korean troops east of Andong. They took to their heels so earnestly that the Marines barely managed to catch three of them after a long chase.

Following the Inchon-Seoul operation, the remnants of the badly mauled NKPA 10th Infantry Division had straggled back across the 38th Parallel to the Hwachon area. There they were reorganized by the Chinese for guerrilla operations . . .

Late in December the rebuilt division, still short of arms and equipment, departed Hwa-chon with a mission of infiltrating through the UN lines to cut communications and harass rear installations of the Andong-Taegu area . . . Stealthily moving southward, marching by night and hiding by day, they were soon in a position to heckle the rear of the X Corps sector. This advantage did not last long. Before they could strike a blow, the element of surprise was lost along with the three prisoners taken by the Marines.

As the Marine units moved into their assigned zones . . . The purpose was to block a possible southward advance of the three CCF armies that had operated in Northeast Korea during the Chosin Reservoir campaign.

The east coast littoral was considered the most likely route of approach. (MCOinK, Volume IV)

This was the situation when PFC Len Martin got off mess duty in the First Tank Battalion and once again became a tanker turned infantryman. The gravel crunchers from the infantry regiments had done a pretty good job of ferreting out the infiltrators, but caution was not thrown to the wind by General Ridgway, the U.N. nor Smith. Ridgway was not taking the enemy lightly, and Smith knew from experience that the Chinese were a crafty lot.

"From time to time we would go out on foot patrols looking for remnants of North Koreans," Martin said. "This usually meant hiking with helmets, rifles, cartridge belts (with ammo), canteens, and sometimes field packs. We were looking for infiltrators or anything unusual, but we never did find any on our patrols."

That's not to say there weren't any Reds around.

"On at least one occasion," the tanker said, "a patrol covering the same area we had gone through came back with several prisoners. Mostly, these patrols served as condition-ing hikes," he said facetiously, adding, "I sometimes thought that I covered more miles hiking than I did when I finally got in tanks."

The patrols Martin and most of the Division's hikers were assigned usually started on flat land, valleys in between the mountains (or hills), and ended up with the tanker-infantrymen and regular infantry climbing the hills.

"We would climb up looking at what we thought was the top of the ridge," Martin said, "but as we neared it, we would find that there were more ridges. After the first fifteen minutes or so we were completely pooped, but had to keep going. All we could do was put one foot in front of the other and hope you would make it."

At times, he found it a bit comical. "When we did stop for a break and took off our packs, our arms would automatically rise up when the weight was off. We didn't dare lie down because it was too much of an effort to get up again. I never did get used to climbing mountains. Glad I wasn't in the real infantry."

Because of the relative inactivity at Masan, the tanker-infantrymen had become pretty soft. "I remember the first patrol," Martin said. "It was a long, grueling hike of about twenty miles up and over the mountains." As luck would have it, Martin drew guard duty that night after they got back. Someone had been stealing eggs from the mess tent, so it had to be guarded, and Martin drew the post.

"I was so tired that after walking the post for a while I went into the mess tent and sat down with my head between my legs. After a while I saw a pair of boots at my feet; it was the Sergeant of the guard." (Sleeping on guard is a court martial offense.) "This sergeant had a reputation for being strict," Martin said. "I was so tired that I didn't care."

"Martin, are you on guard duty?" he was asked.

"Yes," came the reply of the exhausted Marine.

"Were you on the patrol earlier?"

"Yes."

There was a slight pause, and Martin fully expected to be run up.

"I think that you should get back to your post," the sergeant ordered.

"Yes, Sir!"

Martin managed to stay awake the rest of his watch.

By the time he had a few patrols under his belt, the young Marine, like the rest of his buddies waiting for tank assignment, was in pretty good shape. "I could have walked from New York to California without getting tired."

PFC Martin once again had occasion to experience the other side of the war. On one of the patrols, his squad came upon a small village. In the village square, civilians were conducting a funeral. "The officer in charge of our detail told us that we could observe but not to interfere," he said. "There were about four mourners, I assumed they were women, whose heads were covered with sackcloth. The front of the sackcloth bags were wet from their tears."

The casket was placed on top of a structure of logs that were spaced apart and joined by ropes. There were posts on either end of the casket and a string was strung between the posts. Hanging from the string was the man's smoking pipes.

"There were about a dozen or so pallbearers who were drinking something out of saucers and proceeding to get drunk," Martin observed. "They were also singing (moaning) some kind of funeral chant."

After some time, the pallbearers hoisted the platform onto their shoulders and proceeded out of the square into the road outside the village. They went out of town towards the surrounding hills, swaying from side to side of the road and bumping into the houses that lined the road.

In the Korean countryside, it was customary to bury the dead in the hills in order to leave the flatter ground available for farming. The body was interred in a standing position facing the rising sun in the east.

Although Martin's patrols had come across quite a few burial mounds in their travels, this was the first native funeral they had encountered. Martin came away with one firm conclusion: "We figured that the reason that the pallbearers got drunk was so that they could make it up the hills with the platform, which must have been pretty heavy."

By the first week of February, General Smith felt a little more at ease with regards to the guerrillas and informed EUSAK:

> The original 10th NKPA Div forces in the 1st Marine Division area have been dispersed into many groups, reduced to an effective strength of 40 per cent, and are no longer capable of a major effort while dispersed . . . . It is considered that the situation in the Division (1stMarDiv) area is sufficiently in hand to permit the withdrawal of the Division and the

assignment of another mission at any time a new force to be assigned the responsibility for the area assumes such responsibility and the 1st Marine Division can be reassembled. (MCOinK, Volume IV)

Mission accomplished, and it wouldn't be long before Smith's Marines would be leaving Pohang and moving further north because organized Chinese units were spearheading another serious offensive.

But before the First Tank Battalion departed Pohang, PFC Leonard Martin finally became a *real* tanker. He was assigned as loader on Y51, the M26 Pershing of battalion commanding officer, Lt. Col. Harry T. Milne.

"Most Powerful Division In Korea"

Chinese Communist Forces began knocking on the door again in the second week of February 1951, when they launched a counterattack above Wonju, which was about sixty miles north and a little to the west of Andong.

Lt. General Matthew Ridgway put in a call for what he considered "the most powerful Division in Korea." He wanted the First Marine Division to pull up stakes from the Pohang area and move lock-stock-and-barrel to Chunju. The ChiComs were reacting to the Eighth U.S. Army in Korea's push north in the west. Inchon and Kimpo Airfield had been retaken and Seoul was the next objective, but on 11 February, the enemy counterattacked all along the line.

In the East-Central area, Wonju was a key to the U.N. situation, and it was the task of the 1stMarDiv to evict the Reds between that point to a series of comparatively low (536-201-meter range) hills about sixteen miles due north, above Hoengsong. By 15 February, the Reds controlled Hoengsong and were dangerously near Wonju.

That same day, the First Marine Division began moving from its positions in the Pohang-Andong sector. Finally, PFC Leonard Martin was starting to feel like a true tanker as he climbed into the turret of Y-51, the M26 Pershing assigned to the First Tank Battalion's commanding officer, Lt. Col. Harry T. Milne. However, the C.O. was rarely aboard the tank, but it was assigned to him if he needed to direct missions personally.

The experience for PFC Martin would not be without its moments. "We loaded the tanks aboard railroad flatcars," Martin said, wondering whether the wide-bodied Pershings would fit on the flatbeds.

This railroad, like most of the tracks in Korea, was narrow gauge, which meant the rails were not as wide apart as he was used to seeing back in Illinois. It was a testy maneuver to run the tanks up a ramp onto the flatcars because the tracks of the pigirons' stuck out over the edges of the cars. "We had just enough clearance between the tank tracks and the station platform when we went through train stations."

With the tanks crammed on sixty-seven flat cars, the crews began relating to the days of the hobos who crisscrossed the United States during the Depression era. The tankers slept in boxcars, emulating the free-traveling wanderers of another era. But the rail travel also took Martin's thoughts much further back in history. "Reminded me of reading about the 40&8s of WWI."

Martin's father had served in the Army prior to and during to the First World War, arriving in France three days before the armistice. With his father relating stories about that war, Martin often made it a point to read the history of it.

One night the tankers' train with its long string of flatbeds and box cars stopped in the Taegue railyard. "Across from us were some brand-new Army M4A3 tanks," Martin said. "We stripped them of their pioneer tools (picks, shovels and tanks bars—long crowbars) that were on the outsides of the tanks."

Good old Marine Corps "Midnight Requisitions."

After several days, they offloaded in Andong. Time for the tankers to hit the road, after they warily eased their pigirons off the flatcars. Headquarters and Service Company and Baker Company of the First Tank Battalion would finish the march north to a place called Chunchon the hard way—120 miles over a narrow mountain road that Colonel

Milne claimed then was "the all-time Marine Corps distance record for Armor."

It didn't take long for Martin and the rest of the tankers to see they were in for some tedious travel. "The roads in the town were definitely not made for large tanks. We tore down the corners of buildings when we turned into one street from another. Most of the buildings were made of mud and straw, so there was no damage to the tanks. Can't say the same for the buildings."

The Y51 Patton would not always be as cozy and safe as Martin had anticipated. Early in the long arduous trip, the right brake failed as the tank came to a curve, and the forty-ton M26 slid off the road and into a rice paddy. "Fortunately, the paddy was frozen, and we didn't sink in," Martin said with relief.

But the problem was about to be compounded. The driver of the tank behind Y51 was new, and at the beginning of the march, was told to "follow the tank ahead of you." Unaware of the problem the Pershing in front of him was having, he followed Y51 into the paddy. Fortunately, the crews managed to get both tanks back on the road without too much trouble.

By that time, the convoy had come to a stop for the night, and most of the crews were getting a little rest. Not Martin. "While everyone else was crapping out, we had to take everything out of the turret and try to find out why the brake locked up."

They really didn't solve the problem—they could get the brake working sometimes, and other times it didn't perform. Still, Y51 was ordered to rejoin the convoy the next morning.

While climbing up a long mountain pass, the right brake once again became finicky. It was not working all the time. This was not a place to be operating with only one brake. The road was dirt and rocky with one hairpin turn after another—and it dropped off sharply on the right. Close to the left side of the tank was the mountain wall. Standing in the loader's hatch of the turret, Martin was not exactly overwhelmed with confidence that the driver could continue to control the balky bulk of steel.

"When that right brake didn't work, the left track kept the tank going straight, and we were taking pieces off the side of the mountain. It was kind of interesting, if not scary. I could look down and see all kinds of tanks on the road below us."

Since the brakes worked independently of each other, pulling back on the right or left brake levers to lock the tracks turned the tank in the direction of the locked track. Without the right brake, it meant the tank could not make a right turn. On a winding hill, driving a forty-five-ton monster like an M26 was somewhat precarious. If the driver pulled back on the right brake stick and it did not work, the tank continued straight. If the narrow road had a drop-off to the left and the right brake failed, the tank could go off the side of the hill. If there was a mountainside on the left, it would run into the wall of the hill.

The problem began to get worse as the tank was climbing a hill. "Since we were climbing," PFC Martin said, "the tank was going slow. However, when we reached the top of the mountain pass, the drop-off was on the left side. If that right brake didn't grab, the tank could go straight off the edge and down the hillside. The driver eased very slowly into the first turn."

Everyone, except the driver, was out of the tank in a hurry, and standing on the engine doors. The tank entered the turn and the driver pulled on both brake levers. The left track grabbed, the right didn't. The right brake failed, but the driver managed to bring

Y51 to a slow, straight stop. The left track was hanging over the edge.

"It was a drop of several hundred feet," Martin said. For Martin and the rest of the crew, discretion outweighed valor. "We all jumped off the tank."

The young loader took a quick look at the driver. "He was white with fear, but he didn't panic," Martin said. "He backed the tank up and managed to maneuver it over to the side of the mountain. He refused to go any further."

Orders came for the crew to move the tank. "We told them to go to hell," Martin said. "If they wanted it moved they could move it themselves."

When on a road march, a convoy cannot hold up if a vehicle breaks down. So the convoy just cautiously rolled around the disabled tank on what was left of the narrow road.

Y51's crew decided to make the most of the idle time waiting for a mechanic. "We set up our stove, made ourselves some hot chow and coffee, and watched the world go by," Martin said.

Sometime later a jeep with an Army officer stopped to find out what was wrong. He was the security officer in charge of the pass and warned the crew there were about 1,500 guerillas roaming around in the mountains. He said he would come back to check on them later. If they were still there, then, he would take them down to his camp for the night. "He told us to strip off as much of the armament that we could."

Ditching the tank wasn't necessary. Eventually a mechanic from Service Company of the First Tank Battalion arrived. He found that the linkage was jammed and was able to repair it. Neither the tank commander nor the driver were totally convinced Y51 was safe to take down that mountain. PFC Martin, although he had no vote in the matter, agreed.

"To play it safe, we let the mechanic drive the tank the rest of the way down to the valley floor." Martin watched as the mechanic showed his own apprehension. "He scraped the side of the mountain all the way down. As soon as we hit level ground he took off."

By this time, the convoy was long gone, and the Y51 crew had no idea where they were going. They just followed the road. "We figured we would run into the rest of the tanks sooner or later," was Martin's somewhat guarded assessment. Trying to play catch-up, the driver revved up the M26 to its maximum speed of forty miles an hour when he could. Standing in the turret, Martin could feel the February winter biting into his face.

"We were breezing along, but suddenly the tank slowed down and went off the road." No, it wasn't the brake, again. "We had run out of gas!"

The tank commander wasted little time climbing from the turret to the road, quickly flagging down a passing jeep. Without saying anything to the rest of the crew, he hopped in the jeep and was gone. PFC Martin figured he was going to try to scrounge up some gas. "We sat there for a while and made a sign that we hung on the tank: "For Sale Cheap.""

When the T.C. didn't return, the crew started to flag down passing jeeps and trucks, asking if they could spare any gas from the G.I. cans they were carrying.

"Where's your tank commander," asked one Army captain who stopped.

Of, course they couldn't tell him because they didn't know where he was.

"Where are you going?" They sure as hell didn't know.

"Where did you come from?" They weren't sure about that, either.

Martin noticed the Captain wasn't too happy about the responses he was getting to his questions. "At this point he blew his stack and started swearing. Hell, we told him that we couldn't help it."

At that, the Army Captain sped off. "I think that he left with a very low opinion of Marines," Martin said.

However, not all the passersby were as uncooperative. The Marine tankers finally scrounged enough gas from various good Samaritans to get the tank moving again. They made Wonju, a comparatively large town, and PFC Martin was well aware the tank had not slowed appreciably. The driver had begun to believe that his brakes were okay.

"We went flying through an intersection and standing there, talking to an Army MP, was our tank commander. It took a full block before the driver got the tank to stop."

Without saying too much, the tank commander climbed aboard and took his place in the turret, but Y51 wasn't more than a 100 yards down the street when it sputtered to a stop—out of fuel. This time, however, the Tank Gods were smiling on Y51. A truck from the First Tank Battalion passed by, and the driver provided enough gas to get the M26 a short distance up the road to the battalion CP.

The First Tank Battalion was set up on the northern outskirts of Wonju, an area where scuttlebutt had the Army taking and losing several times. Scuttlebutt—in lieu of official word—maybe half the time, is somewhat truth. PFC Martin figured it was more truth than fiction this time. "There was little still standing, mostly just foundations," he said of the town.

A few days later, the young Marine tanker would get his first real look at what the horror of war was all about. Y51 was tagging along with a "large number of tanks" approaching Hoengsong. Martin was awed by what he saw. "We came into the town and there was an intersection where the road broke of into a T. To the left, on the corner, was a building that had no walls, just posts and a roof. Lying on the floor were the bodies of about a half a dozen soldiers—our Army." His memory was about to be seared.

"There was one in particular. He was lying parallel to the road, dressed in Army wool khaki, had small tech-sergeant stripes. He had no shoes. He seemed to be lying there so peacefully. I wondered how his family would feel when they found out he was dead."

Martin saw Hoengsong "as nothing but a sea of metal corrugated roofs." It also was the scene of a massacre. Two Army infantry divisions and a regimental combat team took more than 2,000 casualties between 11-13 February. The worst of the Battle of Hoengsong was inflicted on the Army's 503rd and 15th field artillery battalions, which were ambushed and wiped out—530 men killed in action.

The aftermath of that battle was staring up at PFC Leonard Martin and the other tankers. Bodies and equipment were strewn everywhere. "Following the other tanks through a turn, we drove over half of a jeep that was abandoned in the road."

Y51 eventually rolled left over some small rises and joined the other tanks on a hill. Martin couldn't see too much now, since he was buttoned up under the loader's hatch. "There was quite a bit of machine-gun fire, and the tank next to us let go with a couple of rounds of 90 millimeter. We eventually moved out and circled around the town. I happened to look into a nearby field and saw the body of a soldier. He had been stripped of his clothing."

Additional scuttlebutt was that the Chinese apparently chased any survivors of the ambush into the hills and killed them. Martin had good reason to believe it as fact. There was a stretch of road outside of Hoengsong that was littered with burned out trucks, jeeps, tanks, and artillery "three deep on both sides of the road."

Marine infantry are not always enamored with tanks. Often, the big machines draw too much heavy incoming fire. Where tankers can button up, gravel crunchers usually don't have much protection from that kind of stuff. But once in a while, tankers will come in handy for infantrymen.

This was one of those rare occasions. The foot Marines had to dig in, but the ground was still frozen, and it took a great deal of work with a utility shovel to gouge into the concrete-like turf. "While we were there, the infantry borrowed our picks and shovels so that they could dig foxholes," Martin said. "Even at that, the 0300s were not above using a grenade or two to get a hole started."

There was still a little hazardous duty left for some of the tankers.

On 23 February, two flame tanks attached to the third platoon of Able Company were in support of the 1st Battalion, 1st Marines going into Hoengsong. Entering the ruins of the town, they ran into mortar and machine gun fire from the hills to their left. The antennae were shot off two of the tanks. At that point, the C.O. of Charlie Company, 1st Marines, got the M26s to level their 90s at the hills to fire directly at Red positions. That took care of the harassing fire coming from the West.

That night, Martin talked to some of the guys who took part in that operation. "They said they had caught the Chinese in a draw and killed quite a few of them."

The mission of 1stBat 1stMarines, Able Company tanks, and the two flame-throwing Shermans could have courted disaster if it had not been for an alert aerial observer who reported the patrol was headed for a Chinese ambush. The patrol was rerouted.

An air strike was directed on them while Wray (Capt. Robert P. Wray, Charlie Company commanding officer) rescued several survivors of "Massacre Valley," northwest of Ho-engsong . . . The patrol returned before the ground had completely thawed. Only a few hours later a jeep passing over the same road, was blown up by a land mine which killed the driver. This was one of the first object lessons illustrating the danger of enemy mines which were harmless until the midday sun thawed out the ground. . . . (MCOinK, Volume IV)

The following day, Lt. Col. Milne, C.O. of the First Tank Battalion, was designated Defense commander, Wonju Area, another key assignment handed to him by Lt. Gen. Oliver P. Smith, 1stMarDiv's commanding officer. It was also the day the second and third sections of the Flame Platoon left the CP at Pohang for the city's railhead to be shipped north to Andong. One day later, General Smith himself would be elevated temporarily to higher command.

On 24 February 1951 came the news that General Moore (Maj. Gen. Bryant E. Moore) had suddenly died as the indirect result of a helicopter accident. The aircraft had plunged into the Han River, after hitting a telephone wire, and the IX Corps commander was res-cued unhurt only to die of a heart attack half an hour afterwards. . . .

As his successor, pending a permanent appointment, General Ridgway named Gen-eral Smith to the command of IX Corps. When announcing this decision, the Eighth Army commander said, "General Smith is to be taken into their hearts in IX Corps, and, by definite action, made to feel that he belongs there."

. . . [There were] only two similar occasions when Marines commanded major U.S. Army units. Major General John A. Lejeune had headed the 2d Infantry Division in World War I, and Major General Roy S. Geiger led the U.S. Tenth Army to victory during the closing days of the Okinawa operation after a Japanese shell killed Lieutenant General Simon Bolivar Buckner, Jr., USA.

. . . with General Puller (Maj. Gen. Lewis B. Chesty Puller) taking command of the 1st Marine Division, General Smith flew to Yoju by helicopter to begin his new duties . . . The

following day General Ridgway arrived for a conference . . . He also asked for a recommendation as to future operations of the Marines, and General Smith replied that he knew of no better employment for his division than to continue attacking along the Hoengsong-Hongchon axis. (MCOinK, Volume IV)

On 5 March, General Smith handed over the reins of IX Corps to Maj. Gen. William H. Hoge, USA. A color guard turned out to pay tribute to the First Marine Division commander as he left by helicopter to resume command of of the First Marine Division.

Operation Killer had become Operation Ripper, which was in full swing and accomplishing its objective: to drive the Communists back to the 38th Parallel. By 11 March, the ChiComs had abandoned Seoul, the fourth and final time the South Korean capital city had changed hands. The First Marine Division continued moving up the East Central Region, clearing out a path north of Hoengsong from Hongchon to Chunchon.

It also was a busy time for the Flame Platoon of the First Tank Batallion as small groups of two or three twin-barreled Shermans pulled a lot of duty working with platoons, or companies of the larger gun companies.

On 11 March, two flame tanks, under the watchful eye of First Tank Battalion executive officer Maj. Phillip C. Morell, were sent forward with a platoon of Charlie Company M26s in direct support of the 7th Marines as they pressed through Oumsan toward Hongchon.

The Flamers tied in with 3rd Battalion infantry and supplied direct fire support during the advance, burning out houses and emplacements after ten Chinese were sighted in a small village. One tanker was wounded, but the results of the overall effort sent seven of the Chinese to join their ancestors.

Flame tanks continued support of the Seventh, this time with Dog Company, the following day. Another Sherman Flamer provided security for engineers as they constructed a bypass needed for the push toward Hongchon where the 1stMarDiv linked with the Army's 1st Cavalry.

The Flame Platoon, rolling with Able Company on 13 March, took up with the 1st Marines, but there was little action as the Chinese were becoming more scarce while pulling back into North Korea. It was more of the same the following day when a section of flame tanks again went with Charlie Company in direct support of another 7th Marines mission. The tanks and two battalions of infantry closed on the objectives and took them without opposition.

The Chinese were on the move, helter-skelter so to speak, with the Marines in hot pursuit. Positions were changing so fast, it was hard for the guys to keep track of where they were. Korea was not known for road signs, and it was not uncommon for troops to spend weeks, or months, or maybe an entire tour in the Land of the Morning Calm and not know exactly where they were. If they were privy to a map that might put a name on an area, okay. But good maps, even for high-echelon military, were hard to come by in this war.

It really didn't matter at the time, but some, like PFC Martin, were a little perplexed at not knowing where they were, or where they were going. Martin did know Y51 had taken him north to Hoengsong through Chunchon and that Chunchon was close enough to the coast that it had been targeted by the sixteen-inch guns of the battleship *Missouri*.

"The town was pretty much devastated. I saw a casket sitting in a destroyed building and further on, the bodies of a man, woman and a baby—maybe a year-old—lying alongside the road." Innocent victims of a cruel war!

"After that, we moved so often, so fast following behind the infantry, I lost track of the days and the months. We finally ended up about fifteen miles behind the front lines." This was in the vicinity of the Soyang-gang (river) above Chunchon.

By this time, the First Marine Division was tied in with the Army's First Cavalry and was pressing toward Line Kansas, which ran northeasterly from Uijongbu (above Seoul) through the 38th Parallel to Hwachon. There, it leveled almost directly east to the Sea of Japan, about sixteen miles north of the 38th Parallel.

The Flame Platoon pulled a lot of night roadblock duty through the latter part of March 1951, again, mostly with two or three of its tanks attached to a platoon of M26s from the letter companies. Although the Chinese were on the run, there were pockets of problems, and the Flamers paid a little bit for them.

Mines were beginning to become a major problem to tracked vehicles, as well as jeeps and trucks, now that the weather was easing and the ground thawing. Frozen ground often provided an unforgiving shield over the buried explosives. Now, the softened road-bed was yielding to the pressure of heavy vehicles, and the weight often penetrated deep enough to trigger the mines.

The Chinese and North Koreans made extensive use of mines, some of which were not very sophisticated. But they were used craftily and continually cost the Marines.

One very simple item was a water jar filled with TNT—American-made TNT, at that. It had a potato-masher-type hand grenade attached to detonate it. It caused severe damage to tank tracks and suspension systems.

Another was the box-type mine, which also did major damage to tracks and suspension. This type was deceptive because it was encased in wood and difficult for mine-detectors to pick up. If the buried load contained two or three box mines, it was much more effective, not only on the track mechanism, but it was capable of blowing escape hatches into the tank, causing serious injury to the driver or assistant driver.

Russian-type mines were encountered, but the damage to our tanks was comparatively light. However, some of our own technology came back to haunt us because the Reds got their hands on M-6 mines made in the USA. Not only were they used singularly, but often in tandem with box mines. That combination totaled an M4A3 Sherman dozer tank, one of thirteen lost to the plantings of the North Koreans and Chinese in the first four months the First Tank Battalion was in Korea.

The Reds were smart enough not to always pack the covering dirt too firmly. Rule of thumb in suspected mined areas was to stay in the same track as the tank, vehicle, or man in front of you. Usually that indicated a safe path. However, with a softly covered mine, it would take several impressions before there was enough weight bearing down to trigger the explosion—wreaking havoc within the column instead of just the lead element.

On 27 March when Maj. Morell was searching out a new CP in an area near the Soyang River for the First Tank Battalion, he took along a section of flame tanks and the Battalion S-3 who was in an M26. The S-3's tank hit a mine, and a short time later, one of the Sherman flame tanks was also disabled by a similar contraption. There were no serious injuries this time, but the same couldn't be said for Charlie Company off on another mission that day. Both C44 and C45 hit mines. Charlie 45 was a total loss, and three of its crew were seriously wounded.

The flame tank and the Pershing, which were damaged in the early incident, were eventually repaired and put back in service.

It was about this time that PFC Martin was transferred into flame tanks, and the First Marine Division was getting higher into the rugged mountains of East Central Korea. "Since our range of the flame gun was only a little over 100 yards, and since this part of Korea is mostly mountains, we didn't have much to do," Martin said.

However, this would soon change!

MacArthur Fired!

The Chinese continued to pull back early in April 1951, and Marine units once again crossed the 38th Parallel into North Korea while the First Marine Division command post was sitting at Sapyong-ni just south of the invisible line that split the peninsula in half.

The Gyrenes were in a position with orders to be ready to drive further north to the projected Line Quantico, which swung west to east above Hwachon, rising from four miles above the 38th Parallel on the left to approximately twenty miles into North Korea on the right.

The front was relatively quiet early in April. To the contrary, things were popping in Washington, courtesy of Gen. Douglas MacArthur, and the fallout would be worldwide.

The Commander in Chief Far East had one too many public wars of words with the White House, and ignored more than his share of orders and guidelines set down by the Joint Chiefs of Staff. More flagrantly, he had shown very little regard for President Harry S. Truman. On 11 April 1951, MacArthur was recalled from Japan.

To that point, MacArthur still was held in fairly high esteem by his troops. He remained a hero and very much respected as one of the great generals of World War II.

"What the hell is Truman doing?" was a common refrain coming from Marines, soldiers, sailors, the Air Force—U.S. servicemen all over the world. Harry S. Truman was not a very popular president among the troops when that news reached them.

What the troops in Korea—much more concerned with carrying out Mac's orders and trying to save their own asses in the process while engaged with the Chinese and North Koreans—didn't realize was the General's ego was getting the best of him. His stubborn disregard for policies that were safeguarding against bringing Russia formally into the conflict—and possibly triggering World War III—were his undoing. Had Truman not made his decision, God only knows what could have happened—not only in Korea, but globally.

The clincher came when a MacArthur-authorized communique was released from Tokyo.

> Despite his formal bookish phrasing, it was another bombshell. MacArthur defied direct orders from his president by mixing military with foreign policy. . . ."
>
> The communiqué was received in Washington at ten P.M., March 23. An hour later a group of senior government officials met in the living room of Acheson's (Dean Acheson, Secretary of State). Everyone agreed MacArthur had to go. His message was a direct attempt to intimidate Peking. It mocked the Volunteer soldiers and intimated that the enemy would be wiped out unless they surrendered . . . Someone suggested they phone Truman, but the secretary of state said they would break up and sleep on the problem.
>
> Next morning Truman was stunned and irate at MacArthur's open defiance of his orders as president and as commander in chief under the constitution. The general's communiqué not only was a challenge to the president, but it also flouted the policy of the United Nations. By this act MacArthur left Truman no choice: "I could no longer tolerate his insubordination. . . ." (John Toland, In Mortal Combat Korea, 1950-1953)

It became official on 11 April when President Truman called a press conference at one o'clock that Monday morning:

With deep regret I have concluded that General of the Army Douglas MacArthur is unable to give his wholehearted support to the policies of the United States Government and of the United Nations in matters pertaining to his official duties. In view of the specific responsibilities imposed upon me by the Constitution of the United States and the added responsibilities entrusted to me by the United Nations, I have decided that I must make a change of command in the Far East. I have, therefore, relieved General MacArthur of his commands and have designated Lieutenant General Matthew B. Ridgway as his successor. (MCOinK, Volume IV)

General Ridgway took over the U.N. Forces on 14 April, and Lt. Gen. James A. Van Fleet became the new Eighth Army commander in charge of the war in Korea. Van Fleet was another well-respected field officer out of World War II. Like General Ridgeway, he was known for his penchant keep his troops on the offense.

That concept would soon be put to a severe test.

Plugging the Hole

"Martin! Martin! Get up!"

PFC Leonard Martin, one of the newest members of the Flame Platoon, Headquarters Company, First Tank Battalion, had been sound asleep on his cot in the pyramid tent that was the home of the crew of Fox 22. After months of pulling infantry-like duty while waiting to be assigned to a tank, he had joined the crew of the No. 2 Sherman in the second section of the Flame Platoon a couple of weeks before.

Martin was scheduled to take over the watch at 0400 this particular morning, but he was sure he had not been in the sack that long and was startled by the abrupt shaking that was rolling him from side to side in the flimsy rack. Half awake, and looking into the excited face of his crewmate who had the watch before him, his senses finally responded enough to clearly hear, "We're surrounded on all sides and have orders to stop anyone coming down the road. . . ."

Martin rose bolt upright as the excited guard rattled on, ". . . take them prisoner and wake up our relief man to guard them."

It was 22 April, and somewhat reminiscent of what happened almost six months ago. The Chinese had licked their wounds, stealthily reorganized, and were swarming all over the United Nations lines. The CCF Spring Offensive had broken loose.

MacArthur was gone, savoring a hero's welcome back in the States. Ridgway, the new Far East CIC, was in Tokyo, and it was up to Lt. Gen. James A. Van Fleet to marshal the Eighth U.S. Army Korea against the newest onslaught.

Ridgway and Van Fleet were ready. Unlike their predecessors, who ignored warning signs about the Chinese the previous fall, intelligence gatherers listened as prisoners talked freely of plans being drawn up by the CCF. G-2s knew who, what, where, and when.

Convinced by POW interviews and aerial observation that the Chinese were on the way, the U.N. high command told Lt. Gen. Oliver P. Smith to beat them to the punch and get his First Marine Division on the move. The 7th and 5th Marines, along with the Korean Marine Corps Regiment, a highly respected unit modeled after the USMC, jumped off at 0700 on 21 April and moved forward toward Line Quantico. The advance, covering up to 9,000 yards, was met with little resistance. Marines were not too comfortable with the relative quiet along the front.

What caused the stir in the First Tank Battalion the next night resulted from a 2,500-yard gap in the lines, created when the ROK (Republic of Korea) army division lost contact to the left of the Marines. Before the ROKs could close east to the Marines sector, the Chinese came boring through the opening. Fortunately, the KMCs had picked up a ChiCom prisoner who told them the attack was imminent. Marine infantry along the line had two hours to dig in and set up.

Still, when it came, the CCF Spring Offensive was massive. The ROK division collapsed, its poorly disciplined troops dispersed, discarding their equipment. At some points, they relinquished up to fourteen miles of terrain to the Chinese. The 1stMarDiv's left flank was fully exposed. Fortunately, the 1st Marine Regiment was in reserve and available to lock in with the Seventh and begin shoring up the west flank—though it would be coiled more to the south toward the Pukhan River, which came out of the confluence of the Hwachon and Soyang gangs.

Welcome to Korea, Lt. Col. Holly H. Evans!

On 22 April, Colonel Evans had taken over as First Tank Battalion C.O., relieving Lt. Col. Harry T. Milne, who was heading back to the States after completing his tour. Evans hardly had time to unpack his gear when he was thrust into the war. Immediately, he had to dispatch Able and Baker Companies' tanks to support the 1st and 7th Marines on the left flank. They filled the bill and were given much of the credit for keeping the ChiComs from breaching the gap because the Pershings leveled their 90mm ordnance directly into the enemy's paths, discouraging any thoughts of testing the tankers' lethal marksmanship.

Meanwhile, with the threat of Reds reaching the First Tank Battalion CP, PFC Martin, after being rudely awakened, had joined a detail guarding the only road coming down from the front. What they discovered coming their way, however, were stragglers from the ROK army that had been overrun and stampeded south. Still, the tankers were wary of any oriental coming their way.

"I ended up standing guard over two South Koreans," Martin said, before he was relieved and moved up to the roadblock where the stragglers were intercepted. "The first thing that we did was unload their weapons so that they didn't shoot somebody." Just to protect against the possibility that the stragglers were not ChiComs infiltrating, the tankers herded them into a large field. "There was some talk of taking their weapons away and sending them back up to the front." That, however, did not materialize right away.

That roadblock intercepted hundreds of ROKs while also passing through supply trucks racing back and forth on the road—taking ammo forward and returning with dead Marines.

Eventually, the Flame Platoon was set up next to the Soyang River, and it was back to some infantry-like necessities for Martin and the rest of the Flamers. The first order of business was digging foxholes in the dry riverbed. "It was all rocks and took us hours to dig them."

A day or so later, Fox 22 was part of a tank-infantry patrol sent up the road to look into a potential problem. "We were told that a tank roadblock ahead of us had been engaged the night before," Martin said. The F22 crew temporarily found themselves right up there with the lead infantry. "We went out several miles into no man's land and found nothing. Where two days ago we were fourteen miles behind the front lines, we were now on the front lines. There were a couple of ridgelines in front of us, and the infantry had set up their mortars alongside us. They kept those ridgelines lit up all night long with flares."

Because of Chinese pressure all along the line, General Van Fleet ordered an overall pullback on 24 April. Much like Ridgway before him, Van Fleet was of the school to give a little ground to draw in the enemy where he could be more easily handled, if not destroyed. Thus, the First Marine Division pulled up stakes and reverted to Line Kansas.

Consequently, the Flame Platoon was moved back in a blocking position at the juncture of the Hwachon-Soyang rivers feeding into the Pukhan. "We got there early in the morning and sat around most of the day, watching a steady line of infantry pass by. It seemed like the Division's entire three regiments of infantry came down that road. After the infantry passed we moved out again, crossing the Pukhan River."

The Flame Tankers were riding unbuttoned in their turrets. Looking back over their engine doors, they could see the rear guard gun tanks firing their 90s into the Chinks coming over a ridge to the north. "We eventually ended up driving at night without lights," PFC Martin said.

Later in the night, the flame tanks rolled up to an old log bridge. It was neither very sturdy nor wide, Martin was soon to find out. "They were guiding us by flashlight over that thing."

Although the situation wasn't chaotic, it was hectic. There was a shortage of trucks to transport all the infantry, which meant there was a lot of shuttling back and forth by motor transport units. It wasn't long before Martin's F22 and the rest of the Flame Platoon were carrying their share of passengers. "Eventually we took a bunch of the infantry on board the tanks."

As F22 was passing an Army eight-inch self-propelled howitzer, the artillery piece let loose. "Although we were some distance away," Martin said, "the muzzle blast was so strong that it almost blew those guys off the tank. A sheet of flame extended out at least six feet from the end of that baby's barrel."

For the next couple of weeks, the Flame Platoon, as well as other units of the Division, were moving quite a bit. It was hard for Martin to keep track of time or movement. "We moved around every day, usually stopping at night on ground that the infantry had taken that day. We crisscrossed the 38th Parallel about five or six times."

The luxury of sacking out at night on racks, in tents, was gone for the time being. The tankers were in the boondocks getting a taste of what the infantry goes through all the time. "Even with all the moving we were doing," Martin said, "I saw very few towns or civilians."

Meanwhile, there was another changing of the guard, and this was very significant for Marines. Lt. Gen. Oliver P. Smith, the man whose firm convictions had kept the First Marine Division from total disaster during the Chosin Reservoir campaign and consequently saved the lives of hundreds of his men in the process, had completed his commendable tour. On 24 April he turned over 1stMarDiv to Maj. Gen. Gerald C. Thomas, a decorated veteran of Belleau Wood in World War I, and later Guadalcanal and Bougainville in the Second World War.

> General Smith had won an enduring place in the hearts of all Marines for his magnificent leadership as well as resourceful generalship during the Inchon-Seoul and Chosin Reservoir campaigns. Speaking of the Marines of April 1951, he paid them this tribute in retrospect:
>
> "The unit commanders and staff of the Division deserve great credit for the manner in which they planned and conducted the operations which resulted in blunting the Chinese counteroffensive in our area. In my opinion, it was the most professional job performed by the Division while it was under my command." (MCOinK, Volume IV)

By the latter part of April, the Eighth Army was ordered to pull back again, this time to No Name Line, stretching northwesterly about five miles above Hongchong where General Van Fleet ordered

> . . . to inflict maximum personal casualties by an active defense utilizing artillery and sharp armored counter attacks. Withdrawal south of this line will be initiated only on personal direction of Corps commander.
>
> It would, in time, be referred to as the "April Retrograde," and there would be no reason to carry it any further south.
>
> UN estimates of enemy casualties ranged from 70,000 to 100,000. The Fifth Phase Offensive was an unmitigated defeat for the Communists so far, but EUSAK G-2 officers warned that this was only the first round. Seventeen fresh CCF divisions were available for the second. (MCOinK, Volume IV)

In anticipation of the second round, General Van Fleet reorganized the entire Eighth Army, bringing the First Marine Division back into X Corps under Lt. Gen. Edward M. Ned Almond. It was Almond, who had not endeared himself to Leatherneck commanders during the march into, and through, Seoul, and the debacle that was the Chosin Reservoir. Would this constitute a problem for General Thomas as it did General Smith? Maybe not!

MacArthur was gone, and generals Ridgway and Van Fleet had a firmer grip on the situation. Almond did become more conciliatory to the Marines, which did bode well as the Division remained in the East Central Zone—with the Army's 2nd Infantry Division and the 5th and 7th ROK divisions on the right. The Marines would be the element to tie in with IX Corps to the West. The rest of the MLR belonged to US I Corps, ROK III Corps, and ROK I Corps.

> From the foxhole to the command post a confident new offensive spirit animated an Eight Army which only four months previously had been recuperating from two major reverses within two months. The Eighth Army, in short, had been welded by fire into one of the finest military instruments of American military history; and the foreign units attached to it proved on the battlefield that they were picked troops.
> "I don't want to lose a company—certainly not a battalion," Van Fleet told the corps commanders. "Keep units intact. Small units must be kept within supporting distance. . . . Give every consideration to the use of armor and infantry teams for a limited objective counterthrust. For greater distances, have ready and use when appropriate, regiments of infantry protected by artillery and tanks." (MCOinK, Volume IV)

About this time, PFC Leonard Martin became CPL Leonard Martin and also had been promoted to driver of F22. Eventually, he would become 22's tank commander and figure prominently in some of the action as the second round—the Chinese Communist Forces' Fifth Phase of the Spring Offensive—got underway in mid-May.

Flame Tanks Shoot up Hills

By mid-May 1951, the Fifth Phase Offensive of the Chinese Communist Forces was sputtering and just about to peter out. Still, there was some serious, and deadly, work remaining for the First Tank Battalion and the Flame Platoon before EUSAK flipped the coin and went on the offensive to cut off the retreating Reds.

It was early in the morning of 17 May that the First Tank Battalion's Dog Company, reinforced with a couple of flame tanks and anti-tank Pershings from the 7th Marines, were attacked by a battalion of CCF. At the time, they were in direct support of 3rdBat7th at a roadblock along the Chunchon-Hongchon Highway.

It all started around 0245, and before the Marines turned back the attack at dawn, one of the AT Pershings was rocked with a satchel charge, killing two of its crewmen. Throughout the night, the Chinese, dressed in captured U.S. uniforms, were climbing on the tanks, beating on the hatches and shouting in English: "Hey, tank. Let me in!"

Tankers didn't fall for the ruse, and the ChiComs paid dearly for the tactic. There were more than a 100 enemy soldiers found dead in the area and almost as many waiting to be taken prisoner. The infuriating part about those attacks is that each one of those *friendly* U.S. uniforms worn by the Chinese must have been taken off a dead or wounded American.

That afternoon, another Communist patrol ventured unsuspecting into a roadblock of tanks and infantry and was cut to pieces, leaving 100 Chinks dead on the road.

> . . . the UN counterstroke of May and June 1951 . . . was more than a CCF withdrawal; it was a flight of beaten troops under very little control in some instances. They were scourged with bullets, rockets, and napalm as planes swooped down upon them like hawks scattering chickens. And where it had been rare for a single Chinese soldier to surrender voluntarily, remnants of platoons, companies, and even battalions were now giving up after throwing down their arms.
>
> There had been nothing like it before, and its like would never be seen in Korea again. The enemy was on the run! . . .
>
> Communist casualties from 15 to 31 May were estimated by the Eighth Army at 105,000. This figure included 17,000 counted dead and the unprecedented total of some 10,000 prisoners, most of them Chinese Reds taken during the last week of the month in frantic efforts to escape. Such results were a vast departure from past occasions when Mao Tse-tung's troops had preferred death to surrender. . . .
>
> General Almond congratulated the Division for its accomplishment of "a most arduous battle task. You have denied [the enemy] the opportunity of regrouping his forces and forced him into a hasty retreat; the destruction of enemy forces and materiel has been tremendous and many times greater than our own losses." (MCOinK, Volume IV)

With the tables turned, EUSAK once again had spun 180 degrees and started north, pushing toward the Punchbowl, a five-mile circle of craggy ridgelines, some poking 600 meters or more into the sky but dropping sharply into the surrounded valley below. To the north, higher mountains overlooked the bowl. Line Kansas skirted its southern base ten miles northeast of the Hwachon Reservoir. Line Hayes with hills 930, 1026, and 924 ran about a mile north of it.

The First Marine Division fought doggedly through the month of June, driving a mixture of Chinese Communist Forces and the North Korean People's Army out of

Hwachon Reservoir and Punchbowl areas until they were pushed up to the Kanmunbong Ridge above the Hayes Line.

The Flame Platoon was heavily involved with the letter companies in support missions, despite the mountain warfare becoming more foreboding to tanks the further the Division climbed north into the rugged hills.

Cpl. Len Martin was riding as the loader in Fox 22 when the second section of the Flame Platoon went along with a platoon of Able Company M26s into the Hwachon reservoir area early in the morning of 6 June. "We were on the road about 0200," Martin said, as the tank convoy headed in direct support of two battalions of the 1st Marines on the west flank of the Division sector, where they were working to drive elements of the NKPA off a ridge north of the Hwachon Reservoir.

Eventually the convoy of tanks reached the valley that ran between several ridges, which were at right angles to the flat land. Four of the Able Pershings turned off into the valley while the fifth M26 and the three Sherman flame tanks continued further up the road before veering off the road and setting up in a field. There, flame tanks were ordered to pivot and face the road. The two units of tanks were not visible to each other. The Flame Tankers were about to take in a pretty good show.

"We sat there with our hatches open, doing nothing all morning," Martin said, although the infantry was trying to take the hill, and the now-out-of-sight M26s were working their 90mm rifles along the ridges above them. "It was almost like watching a demonstration of firepower."

But it was working both ways. The four gun tanks in the valley between the ridges were taking a lot of incoming while they were working over the hills with their 90s. "From where we were, it was hard to tell whether the commotion behind us in the valley where the other tanks were, was incoming or outgoing," Cpl. Martin said. Later, the Flame crews definitely were aware of mortars and artillery going over the hills behind into the area where the rest of the Able tanks were.

Cpl. Martin was also beginning to get somewhat of a blow-by-blow account over the radio. "We could hear the infantry requesting more fire from the tanks, in the valley behind our positions." But there was a problem. "T.C.s in the Able tanks were reporting they were under enemy mortar fire and, because they were buttoned up, their loaders were passing out from the fumes of their own guns."

While the letter tanks were in a little distress, the guys in the flame tanks, under orders to sit tight, were pretty much relaxed until they heard the problems coming over the radios.

It was close to noon when one of the guys from another tank approached F22, hoping to exchange his brand of C rations for lunch. The North Koreans obviously sighted the exposed tankers and started to lay in several mortar rounds.

"The guy made a mad dash for his tank," Martin said, "jumped up on the turret and through his hatch, which he immediately closed." Martin didn't waste any time doing the same. The shelling continued for a while, but with the tanks now buttoned, the North Koreans eventually stopped firing on them.

Orders came to move the four tanks up the road, but the M26 in the lead got only about twenty feet when it hit a land mine. The powerful explosion broke the right track and tore off one of the road wheels. "It was quite a blast to do that much damage," Martin said. "I had just put my head down into the turret when the mine went off. I stuck my head up, and there was dirt flying all over. Fortunately, no one was hurt, although the M26 tank crew was shook up."

Don Chaney, a buddy of Martin's, was the assistant driver, and the blast went off underneath him. "He was a pretty lucky guy that day."

The Pershing had been driving in the tracks of previous tanks when it hit the mine. This was one of the many ways the Reds had of duping U.N. troops, who advanced under the theory that since other tanks had gone safely over this path, it was considered okay to follow the leader.

Chinese and NKPA mines weren't very sophisticated, but the Reds, nonetheless, were when it came to the way they used them.

Although engineers had gone over that road prior to the mission, this must have been one of those deeply buried box mines, which are difficult to pick up on a mine detector since that tool is geared to set off impulses from metal.

Fox 22 was third in line when all of this happened. That meant the flame tank in front of it now had to create a new path around the disabled M26. This was scary since the M4A3E8 Sherman flame tank had a thinner hull than the more fortified M26.

Martin had seen the effects of a mine on a Sherman dozer tank earlier in the spring. It was heavily damaged and its crew seriously injured when it tried to avoid a jeep and went off the side of the road, hitting a mine. The thinner, lighter M4 hull lifted and jolted the crew wildly within the tight confines of the compartments when that blast went off.

The knowledge of that wounded tank passed through Martin's mind as the three double-barreled Shermans cautiously moved around the disabled Pershing, up the road, and around a bend before ordered to stop. This brought them parallel to a ridge the infantry was trying to clear of NKPA.

"We got the word to fire at will," Martin said, but he figured he'd just be watching again. However, the flame tank gunners were ordered to spread covering fire into the hills with their 50- and 30-caliber machine guns. The "50" is mounted on top of the turret between the tank commander's hatch and the gunner's hatch. Normally, if it is to be fired, it has to be done by standing in the turret with the upper part of the body protruding out of the tank commander's hatch, or the loader's hatch. It also was common for a crewman to leave the turret and stand behind it to man the gun.

Martin was a little surprised when his tank commander became "somewhat chicken" and didn't want to stick his head out of his hatch. He gave the T.C. the benefit of the doubt, however. He didn't know him that well, and maybe he was a "short-timer" and was scheduled to be rotated out of Korea within a couple of weeks. Guys who have experienced combat, and know their ticket home has been punched, are not too eager to put themselves in harm's way. Martin could understand that.

Although he was sitting on the right side of the turret in the loader's seat, Martin was given the option of handling the guns. "I had no qualms," the lean Illinois corporal said.

He started with the 30-caliber coax machine gun. Then he began loading and firing the 105 cannon mounted next to the flame gun. Flame tanks, because napalm is stored in tanks beneath the decks where ordnance usually is kept in a Sherman, carry only about half a dozen rounds of the artillery ammo. Still, that gave this version of the M4A3 more lethal weapons than any other tracked vehicle in the war.

With cannon ammo expended, Martin opted for the 50-caliber machine gun.

Since the tank was parallel to the ridge and the turret was facing it, in order to fire the 50-caliber machine gun that was mounted forward the T.C.'s hatch, Martin had to lean out of the turret to "hang my butt over the edge of the tank. I walked my fire across the top of the ridgeline with both the 30- and 50-caliber machine guns. Frankly, I was having a ball."

What Martin didn't know at the time was the area he peppered with both the machine guns, and pounded with the 105, was a concentration of NKPA heavy mortars that had been harassing the Platoon of M26s supporting the infantry from down in the valley.

At least one Able Company tanker was glad Martin was having his ball. Harry Davis, who was with the platoon of Able Company Pershings that had been pinned down and surrounded by NKPA, had reason to believe Martin and the other Flamers had saved their day. The Able tanks had been taking a lot of incoming and were threatened with being overrun until the pressure was taken off them by Flame Platoon pulverizing the hills around them. "A couple of our tanks became trapped and surrounded," Davis said. "If it wasn't for flame tanks and their 105s, we wouldn't have made it out."

Word was finally passed to the flame tank commanders to cease fire. The crews sat back while the gravel crunchers did their stuff. "We watched as the infantry moved out across the valley in front of us and started up the ridgeline," Martin said. "Later, a flight of Corsairs came over, strafing the ridge, and dropping bombs and napalm. We were close enough that I could see the smoke from the Corsairs' 50-caliber machine guns."

After the show, Martin and his buddies were lying out on the engine doors of their tanks taking advantage of the warm June sun—working on their tans—when a corpsman came walking by. He looked at Martin.

"How 'r' things?"

"From what I can tell from here, it looks good," the tanker replied.

The corpsman told the crew he was coming back from the aid station. He had caught a piece of shrapnel in his rear end.

"You the guy who was firing the 50-caliber machine gun?"

"Yeh!"

"Too dangerous for me," he told the Marine.

Martin was struck by the fact he was having a ball with the machine guns and the big cannon, and this guy had been wounded. "He had gotten hit, and he thought what I was doing was too dangerous."

The tankers, however, felt pretty good when they learned the 1st Marines had taken both their objectives on the ridge that day, and the infantry were passing back the word that the supporting arms contributed a lot. "I guess they meant us," Martin figures. "They said there were a lot of dead gooks lying around when they got up there."

For the rest of the month of June, the Flame Platoon sent out sections, pairs, or singles running with platoons or full companies of letter tanks.

As the Korean War approached 25 June 1951, its first anniversary, the Communists did not boast a very good report card. Most of the MLR was above the 38th Parallel, and the Reds had 2,100 square miles less of North Korea than they had when they started the whole mess. Its industrial base was a shambles, left practically useless by bombing and artillery.

Seoul was back in the hands of Sigmun Rhee and the South Korean government. I Corps broke through Chorwan and Kumhwa at the base of the Iron Triangle—Pyongyang, the capital of North Korea, was the apex. X Corps, with the Marines leading the way, penetrated the East-Central mountain range along with IX Corps.

The Kansas line now swung northeast from Munsan-ni (twenty miles above Seoul) on a west-east line above Chorwan and Kumhwa, around the southern base of the Punchbowl and twenty miles north to the east coast town of Chodo-ri.

The Communists were reeling and were now asking that both sides discuss a truce. Replacement drafts from the States were unloading with regularity every month, and most of the veterans of the severe fighting of the previous winter were either on their way back home or about to leave the Land of the Morning Calm.

A Father's Rage, a Son's Rebellion

While Cpl. Len Martin was just getting acquainted with flame tanks in the spring of 1951 and becoming deeply involved with the First Marine Division's part in repulsing the Chinese Communist Forces' spring offensive, the Army's Starburst 40th Division had its hands full a little further to the northwest.

Formed out of the California National Guard, the Starburst was an amalgamation of many units, including the 140th AAA (Anti-Aircraft Artillery), which was setting up in the Kumhwa Valley, on the southeastern corner of the Iron Triangle. The Iron Triangle was a pyramidal area pointing directly north with Pyongyang at its apex, Chorwon to the southwest directly opposite Kumhwa, which was about ten miles to the east. It sat in the middle of North Korea with Pyonggang about sixteen miles above Kumhwa and some thirty miles north of the 38th Parallel. Activity there would have an uncanny tie to the Flame Platoon more than a year later.

As Battery B of the 140ths AW SP was setting up in the Kumhwa Valley on 2 May 1952, S/Sgt. Joseph Ravino, was manning a quad-50-caliber machine gun on his half track. A demolition team was blowing out a slot in the side of a small hill to position a powerful 155mm howitzer. When the blast went off, rock and debris were hurled everywhere.

Though the quad-50 was some distance away, a small boulder came hurtling at the unsuspecting Ravino. He couldn't get out of the way and it struck him, full force, in the left arm. The arm was shattered. S/Sgt. Ravino was med-evaced to nearby Mobile Army Surgical Hospital. Eventually, he was flown to Japan for more advanced treatment, which required the insertion of two plates in his arm.

During World War II, Joe's older brother, George Angelo Ravino, Jr., had enlisted in the Navy when he was seventeen years old. A gunner on the USS *Colorado,* he took part in the shelling of Okinawa and later was aboard the battleship when it went into Tokyo Bay for the Japanese surrender.

In the Boston suburb of Roxbury, George Angelo Ravino, Sr., a combat-wounded veteran of World War I, was extremely proud of his two oldest sons. The same pride was not reflected on son Gerald, who was twenty-one and the third in line of eight Ravino siblings. Gerald was on his own, living in Groton, Connecticut, where he had a good job with Pfizer Chemical Company.

The Ravino Boys called their father Par, and their mother, Catherine, Mar. Par Ravino was a tough, patriotic veteran, a machine gunner and bugler, who knew 105 calls. "He could still do them perfect," Gerald Ravino said. He was wounded in action, hit in the left arm by a sniper in the Argonne Forrest. For more reasons than one, Gerald "Jerry" Ravino was in awe of his father's feeling for his country. "I never knew a more patriotic person. If we were watching television and the National Anthem was being played, you had better stand up at attention if Par was in the room." It was very important to Par Ravino that his sons have a strong feeling for their country and enter the service when in time of war.

After the official telegram arrived informing the Ravinos that Joseph had been seriously injured, his father's first concern was how bad it was. When the senior Ravino received word from Joseph that he was going to be okay, the father's mind started to become occupied with young Gerald. He was deeply troubled why the boy hadn't signed up to serve in the Korean War. Since he did not see Gerald that often, the anger began to fester as the summer of 1951 passed into fall, then winter.

One Sunday, late the following January, Gerald Ravino came home to visit his parents and was immediately confronted by his father. Par called his third son into the living room. "Gerald," was the stern summons, "when are you going to get off your ass and join the service?"

"For what?" Gerald replied quickly.

"For the war in Korea where your brother Joseph has been wounded by them Chongos."

"Well, sorry to hear that, Par," his son replied, his tone bordering on flip, "but Korea is of no interest to me."

"Are you a coward?" the elder Ravino shot back.

The insinuation stung the son. He had been an amateur boxer and was on the same Golden Gloves card with a young Brockton fighter named Rocky Marciano, who later became heavyweight champion of the world.

"You know better than throwing that shit at me, Par!"

Young Ravino, his temper rising, reminded his father he had a good job and was saving his money to marry Dotty Daly, his girlfriend of six years. "I don't give a good shit about Korea and never even heard of the place before the war started."

His father went into a verbal rage. It was nothing new to the son, who many times had been through this kind of outrage. Often, it was accompanied by getting a couple of backhanders across the head. Pissed off, Gerald yelled, "I'll show you what the hell I'm made of!" He stormed out of the living room and didn't talk to his father again that Sunday.

He did not return to Groton. Early the next morning, Gerald Ravino showed up at the first recruiting station he could find in Boston. He was looking around for the toughest outfit he could join when he spotted a poster of paratroopers. "This'll show him," he said angrily to himself. He signed up, took the physical, which he assumed he'd passed because the recruiter was completing the paperwork and about to apply the red stamp—PARATROOPER—to it. That's when one of the doctors came out.

"We can't take Ravino," the doctor said, "he has two teeth missing."

"Great!" Ravino snarled, his frustration showing. "Screw it."

He looked around and saw a Marine in dress blues. "Taking anybody today?" he asked, noting how sharp the Marine looked.

"You're lucking out son. You came to the right place. We're making up a platoon called the Mayor John B. Hynes Marines and we can use you."

"Sign me up!"

Jerry Ravino went right home and told his father he joined the Marines. Par Ravino didn't say a word.

Gerald became more insensed. "I'll show you, and when I get out of that boot camp, off to Korea I'll go—even if I have to see the general. Now don't that make you happy?" he snapped at his father.

There was no reply and that's the way it ended before Gerald P. Ravino went off to Parris Island with the Mayor John B. Hynes Platoon.

If Par Ravino didn't show any emotion, Dottie Daly did. "What's the matter with that man?" she questioned through her tears. Then she confronted Par Ravino. "Did you ever see my brother when he came back from Guadalcanal?" she snapped at her fiance's father. "He was a mess. And now my Jerry is going away because of you."

As Jerry Ravino headed for Parris Island, like most of the young recruits making that trip in the early 1950s, little could he visualize what the future held for him.

Almost a year to the day he enlisted in the United States Marine Corps, he would be involved with the Flame Platoon in the most harrowing experience of his life. As his brother before him, and his stern patriotic father decades ago, he would receive the Purple Heart—wounded in action.

A Look of War

The thousand-yard stare . . .

It's made its way through centuries of wars. And it will be around as long as people continue to think that the only way to settle their differences is to mutilate other people with knives, and spears, and arrows, and bullets, and cannonballs, and mortars, and artillery, and napalm, and rockets, and atom bombs.

See too much of that stuff . . . *the thousand-yard stare.*

In mid-summer of 1951, the Korean War had marked its first full year of violent battles yo-yoing from one end of the peninsula to the other.

The 10th Replacement Draft, headed for the First Marine Division in the mountains of East Central Korea, was debarking from the *Gen. William Weigel* at the port of Pusan on the last day of June.

Jack Carty, a twenty-two-year-old PFC, who had put his newspaper career on hold ten months earlier when he preempted his draft summons by enlisting in the United States Marine Corps, wasn't too surprised at what he saw. That is, before he walked into a little Red Cross canteen not too far from the waterfront, where ships still were disgorging men and supplies.

Pusan was not what you'd call the garden spot of the world. Only eleven months earlier it was within the only United Nations–held bastion—a sixty-by-ninety-mile perimeter pressured by the freewheeling North Korean People's Army. That communist juggernaut was trying to push ragged remnants of the Republic of Korea army and the beleaguered survivors of the U.S. Army's ill-prepared, quick-fix United Nations defenders, into the Sea of Japan.

But this hot summer day in 1951, after the tide of war had shifted and was beginning to stabilize, Pusan was the major port in which troops and supplies from all over the world—but mostly from the United States—were arriving into Korea. Going the other way—a Rotation Draft about to ship out—were the haggard veterans of the first year of what earlier had been dismissed as a "police action."

Fighting had settled down somewhat. Inchon, Chosin Reservoir, and the Punch Bowl were on their way into the history books. The savage spring fighting had subsided, and the front lines became virtually stationary, mostly stretched just north of the infamous 38th Parallel, where it all started a little more than twelve months ago.

Pusan now was a bustling port city of small, ramshackle buildings, clogged with soldiers, Marines, and war-weary native Koreans trying their best to wangle anything they could from gullible servicemen new to a ravaged land.

Seabags, stuffed with dress uniforms and anything else incoming Marines weren't going to need in a combat zone, were being left in Pusan and later shipped up to Ascom City, outside of Seoul. No need for stateside dress uniforms and spit shines here, where the pungent stench of "honey pots" mixed with the strange odor of Korean food being cooked over open fires and filtering through clay chimneys and mud-straw roofs. The more fortunate Marines and soldiers would be reunited with their seabags a year or so later when they were rotating home. Many would not have that opportunity. Their gear would be shipped back to the States to surviving families.

Pusan wasn't filthy, maybe because there was so much military activity going on. But it wasn't what anyone could call clean.

As PFC Carty and a few of his buddies were hanging around the docks while the offloading continued, word had spread that there were coffee and donuts a couple of blocks away. For some unknown reason, the Marines were not ordered to remain dockside. There was time, before departure northward and unit assignment, to grab a quick snack.

Before heading for the Red Cross canteen, PFC Carty and his good friend PFC Dan O'Sullivan arranged with a couple of buddies to watch their 782 gear—a haversack with bare essentials to survive in the field, mess gear, and a blanket roll wrapped within half of a poncho. Naturally, the Marines carried their M-1 rifles.

"So, this is Korea," Carty said to O'Sullivan as they made their way from the dock area through a narrow street they were told would take them to the canteen.

"What'd ya expect?" O'Sullivan cracked in an unmistakable accent that was New York Bronx-Irish. "You didn't think these people were living in mansions, did you?"

That Dan O'Sullivan was in the Marine Corps, let alone in Korea, was a little ironic. He was a kid from 129th Street in the Bronx and had not yet reached his seventeenth birthday, so he had told his new friend not long after they met at Camp Delmar, the tank training facility adjacent to Camp Pendleton in California. "Ah, I got gung-ho last year," he cracked. "I liked the idea of wearing those dress blues, so I joined the reserves." He gave a half-assed explanation about his birth certificate, and convinced the recruiter he indeed was old enough to enlist. "Hell, I only wanted the uniform so I could pick up girls."

Like most New Yorkers, especially those from the Bronx, Dan O'Sullivan was wise far beyond his years. That he and PFC Carty, almost five years his senior, hit it off so well never seemed relevant to either of them.

Although both had been through Parris Island in the fall of 1950 and made the same long troop train excursion through the southern states to Pendleton where they went through advanced infantry training, they never crossed paths before Delmar. They had been in separate infantry-training units when they were closing out cold weather training in Big Bear Mountain near Lake Arrowhead. That's where they were getting their tickets punched for the Eighth Replacement Draft to Korea when fate began taking an unexpected turn for both of them.

"Hell, I was trying to shave with ice-cold water on the banks of a mountain stream one morning," Carty said. "I heard the first sergeant call my name, and holler for a couple of other guys."

"Up here on the double," he ordered, hands on his hips like the lord of the hill above where the troops were splashing their faces with the frigid mountain stream water.

"Wonder what kind of a shit detail this is going to be," one of the guys cracked.

It wasn't a shit detail. "Get your gear and get on those trucks," the first sergeant ordered. "You're going back to mainside." That meant Camp Pendleton, where the Korea-bound trainees had spent almost three months learning how to be infantrymen.

No explanation—the Marine Corps doesn't provide detail if it thinks it's unnecessary, and not very often when it might be necessary. It didn't take most recruits long during boot camp to learn Marines are trained to just follow orders. No questions asked. In boot camp, you didn't dare ask many questions, anyhow. *Yours is not to wonder why . . .* that kind of stuff.

All the way back to Pendleton, a ride of more than two hours, the dozen or so young

Marines, packed into the canvas covered six-by truck, worked the rumor factory to the limit.

"Hey, maybe we're going to get a fifteen-day leave before we ship out," one guy said with a laugh.

"Sure," scoffed another. "We won the prize for climbing those hills better than the other Jarheads."

Once off the truck at headquarters, they got the scoop. "Get back to your barracks and get all your gear," the lieutenant said. "You're going over to Delmar. Some of you will get tank training, the others will be in LVTs (Landing Vehicle Track)."

Since they were at ease, heads began going from side to side. The expressions were obvious: *"Me, driving a tank?" "How the hell did I get picked for this?"*

Carty also wondered, though he was relieved. On the way back to mainside, he had been concerned, once again, that he was going to wind up as an "office pinky." That's what Gyrenes called guys who worked behind desks and shuffled papers. His fears were prompted by his newspaper background, and the fact he could type. No way did he want any of that crap. Pushing paper was not his idea of being a Marine.

But driving a tank? Little did he realize the twist that fate was taking for him.

When they got to Camp Delmar, just across US 101 from Pendleton, Carty and O'Sullivan happened to land in adjoining bunks.

"Dan O'Sullivan, Sully," the lean, almost-skinny kid said, offering his hand.

He didn't need the name to prove he was Irish, and one word out of his mouth, there was no mistaking he came from somewhere in New York City.

"Jack, Jack Carty."

PFC O'Sullivan, who seemed to always wear a mischievous broad grin and never gave the impression he was shy, quickly inquired, "Where ya from?"

"New Jersey . . . Runnemede."

"Running Weed?" Sully asked as his grin broadened to a big smile, almost breaking into laughter.

"No. Runn-a-meed," Carty shot back quickly, emphasizing the phonetic pronouncement. "It's a little town in South Jersey, outside Camden, across the Delaware River from Philadelphia."

"Oh. I'm from 129th Street in the Bronx."

A friendship had been born.

PFCs O'Sullivan and Carty found the Red Cross canteen—donuts, hot coffee, and milk from the powdered concentration for those, like the New Jersey Marine, who not yet had been addicted to the black liquid called "Joe."

The canteen was not a very big place, and it was packed with milling servicemen, a mixture of replacements' clean, new-like dungarees—Marine utility and battle uniform—and the not-so-clean combat-faded utilities worn by the others. They weren't there very long when PFC Carty nudged his friend. "Dan," Carty said quietly, nodding his head forward, "over there."

The thousand-yard stare.

The expression they saw jolted the two newcomers from naive curiosity to stark reality. The Marine across the room, motionless, expressionless, and standing alone, obviously was not one of the replacements. His dungarees had seen their day. The stenciled "U.S. Marines" on the left breast of his utility jacket was just about visible. His unkempt blond hair was anything but Marine Corps regulation. It obviously hadn't known a comb, or barber's clippers, for some time. His face was gaunt. And the eyes, deep in their sockets, were riveted on something far beyond the confines of this little building.

The thousand-yard stare.

This mixture of troops, coming and going, included Marines rotating back to the states. They were veterans of bitter fighting at Inchon, Yudam-Ni, Koto-Ri, Chosin, Hagaru, Hamhung, Hwachon, and Chunchon, the Chinese spring offensive.

His face—*their* faces—reflected untold stories of what the horror of war was all about.

Welcome to Korea, PFCs Carty and O'Sullivan.

This was the place its natives call Land of the Morning Calm, but which had not been so tranquil the last twelve months. Realization set in. It was not a gung-ho John Wayne scene. This was the real thing. Marines had died. More Marines were going to die.

The thousand-yard stare . . . it spoke a thousand words.

Tankers, or Infantry; Truce, or War?

If nothing else was on the minds of the PFCs Jack Carty and Dan O'Sullivan as they left the Red Cross canteen in Pusan, it was a fact drilled into recruits from day one by D.I.'s at Parris Island and San Diego: All Marines are infantrymen!

It mattered not that O'Sullivan and Carty had subsequently picked their "1811–tractor operator—MOS." That did mean they could drive a tank—and the infantryman's 0300 was now their secondary *military operational specialty*. But they were Marines. If any of the First Marine Division's three infantry regiments were short of men, that's where they would go—1811 MOS or not.

After getting a dose of the "thousand-yard stare," it was a sobering possibility—if not probability—that they very well could end up in an infantry regiment. They were experiencing some apprehension. Two months ago, it wouldn't have mattered. They hadn't had their first fling with tanks yet. Now, after learning how to control thirty-some tons of rolling pigiron, it was a different story. Both definitely had become infatuated with tanks.

What Carty and O'Sullivan, and most of the guys in the 10th Replacement Draft didn't know, was the lull after the CCF Spring Offensive and the EUSAK [Eighth U.S. Army Korea] counterpunch had allowed First Marine Division units to heal fairly well. In fact, the Division was pulled off the line for the first time since the amazing march back from the Chosin Reservoir. That meant most of the new "1811s" were going to tank outfits, not to the trenches and bunkers up in the mountains of East-Central Korea.

But after the experience in the Red Cross canteen, Carty and O'Sullivan had gotten a good idea of what war can do to the mind of a combat soldier.

By the time they had left the states on 15 June 1951, the fighting in Korea was winding down after a bitter spring in which Chinese Communist Forces had launched a determined, but ill-fated, drive southward. U.N. units, after yielding several miles across the entire front, had turned back the Chinese and the North Koreans, and retaken all, and a little more, of what had been lost for a few weeks.

EUSAK, which commanded all U.N. forces in Korea, had faced up to the massive CCF offensive, stopped it cold, and had rebounded to Kansas Line. Most of the MLRs were given names like Kansas, Brown, Hays, James, et cetera. These lines stretched eastward from the comparative lowlands of the Inchon-Seoul sector across a series of mountain ranges and hills, to heights of East-Central Korea. In First Marine Division areas, the Corps naturally preferred to use its own designations of lines—Quantico, Pendleton, et cetera.

Division responsibility at the start of the CCF offensive was Quantico Line, just above the Hwachon Reservoir, which was more than five miles north of the 38th Parallel. Although the CCF had forced U.N. lines as far back as twenty to thirty miles south of the Parallel midway through May, it was only temporary.

By the middle of June, EUSAK had rebounded and stabilized the MLR along Line Kansas, which ran north and slightly east from Munsan-ni to Chorwon and Kumhwa at the base of the Iron Triangle. Then, it almost straight-lined east until it passed just south of the Punch Bowl to Sohwa, where it swung northeast to the coast above Chodo-ri. At the Punch Bowl, it was about twenty-five miles north of the 38th Parallel.

The Punch Bowl was a dead volcanic crater, sort of egg-shaped, about 6,000 yards south to north and 4,000 yards east to west, surrounded by high mountains and located northeast of the Hwachon Reservoir and east of Inge. It was the scene of some bitter fighting involving both the Marines and Army during the summer of 1951 before it finally was taken out of Communist hands.

The First Marine Division was responsible for an area roughly ten miles wide between Soyang-Gang and Sochon rivers before it was pulled off the line in mid-July.

The cost of the spring offensive to the Communists was astronomical. After that episode, CCF and NKPA troops, since the start of hostilities on 25 June 1950, were estimated at more than a million killed, wounded, and missing. The U.N., by comparison, suffered about 250,000 killed, wounded, and missing. Exactly one year later—25 June 1951—the Communists held less territory by 2,100 square miles than they occupied when they first crossed the 38th Parallel.

North Korea, which was considered an industrial center of the entire peninsula, was in ruins. Cities, factories, and power plants had been reduced to rubble. They had gained nothing and lost much. The CCF and NKPA had been rendered inoperable as a serious fighting force after their spring offensive, thus, a call by the Communists for truce talks and a toning down of action as the 10th Replacement Draft arrived in Korea.

The new replacements had heard scuttlebutt about the overtures of the North Koreans made about a truce. In fact, on 23 June while the 10th Draft was on the high seas, there was a suggestion in New York by the Soviet delegate to the United Nations that a truce in Korea be explored. Unofficially, it was endorsed by the Chinese Communists. The outcome was an agreement that representatives of both sides would meet on 7 July at Kaesong, then located between the opposing lines in west Korea. However, the initial truce talks seemed to be a ploy by the Communists to stall the advantage United Nations forces were gaining in the war.

The tempo of the war was much reduced during the initial negotiations, and all three infantry regiments (First, Fifth, and Seventh) of the First Marine Division were in defensive positions along the MLR—Kansas Line. When the 10th Replacement Draft joined the Division at Tripoli around 1 July, there still were units on line. But by 17 July, all segments of the 1stMarDiv were on their way back to assembly areas in X Corps' rear.

When the First Marine Division was ordered into reserve, it was only the second time since the landing of the 1st Provisional Marine Brigade on 2 August 1950. That was a little more than a month after the Korean War erupted, and Marines had not been away from the front for more than a few weeks until the Summer of '52. The one big exception was when they got hung up for several days in Wonsan Harbor in Operation Yo-Yo.

From 23 July to 20 August 1951, it was prescribed that the "division maintain a stiff daily schedule of general and specialist military training." All of this was taking place along the Honghon-Hangyi Road in the vicinity of Tangdong-ni. That's what PFCs Carty and O'Sullivan got caught up in when we were assigned to the First Tank Battalion.

Meanwhile, the Truce Talks finally had gotten underway. But the Chinese were doing their best to make a mockery of them. The initial negotiations were anything but congenial, rendered antagonistic by Communist tactics.

UN Delegation, headed by Admiral Turner Joy, held a first meeting on 10 July 1951 with his opposite number, NKPA Major General Nam Il, and the Communist truce team. This was the first of the talks that were to drag on for two dreary years. (MCOinK, Volume IV)

Right off the bat, there was an indication that things were not going to go smoothly. Even in the preliminary stages, before Admiral Joy and General Nam Il ever sat down with their respective negotiating teams, most of the concessions were gained by the Communists.

Nam Il appeared to generate an aura of obstinacy that constantly frustrated the negotiations. He had been educated in Russia, serving with the Soviet army during World War II, rising to the rank of captain. When he returned to Korea in 1945, he was credited with playing a major role in setting up the Soviet-like puppet government in North Korea.

With the talks being held above the 38th Parallel, the environment was clouded with North Korean demeanor. United Nation delegates at Kaesong were met by a Chinese Communist Forces guard who wore a large medal he proudly made known he received for killing many Americans. U.N. messengers, on orders from Admiral Joy to report to EU-SAK commander General Matthew Ridgeway, constantly were turned back or detained by communist guards. Often they were threatened by burp guns, the staple communist weapon. Admiral Joy finally raised enough protest that the communists backed off.

But tactics to delay or extend—even suspend—the talks appeared to be all part of the Communist plan. It was buying them time to heal their wounds. They had suffered tremendous losses and setbacks in the first year of the war and needed time to rebuild their emaciated armies.

With the start of talks, they knew the United Nations would not be aggressive with its forces. And that's just what happened. There were to be no more major offensive pushes North by the U.N. Peace was the objective of the American-led team. Time to rebuild was the theme in North Korea.

Even the site of Kaesong for the talks was a Communist setup. It was in the path of the U.S. Eighth Army juggernaut that was pushing the Communists back into the north. With the Truce Talks there, an area of neutrality would have to be avoided if the U.N. wanted to continue an offensive.

Political pressure also was coming from the United States to get things settled and get American troops back home. So U.N. negotiators continued to put up with a lot of crap from the Communists. Little could they imagine that things would drag on for another two years.

So this is what was going on when the 10th Replacement Draft from Camp Pendleton arrived in the Land of the Morning Calm, and two tank trainees had no clue what lie ahead of them. Would there be a truce? Would the war heat up? Would they go to tanks? Would they be infantry?

It was nothing that every other Replacement in the 10th Draft—and drafts before and after—was not experiencing.

Introduction to Korean Honey

Jack Carty and Dan O'Sullivan had expected Pusan to be just about what it was, but the episode in the Red Cross canteen really had a sobering affect on them.

Eventually, the two "1811s" were loaded on six-bys with infantry, artillery, and an assortment of other replacements, but because of the alphabetical polarization, they were not on the same truck. The small convoy headed north and west out of the port city, along a dusty primitive road. The young Marines didn't have the slightest idea where they were going. Once again, Marine Corps discipline took over—orders were orders, and it was no use asking questions.

While riding out of Pusan, the Marines got their first whiff of Korean "honey." What a jolt to the nostrils that was.

Most Koreans, before the war, and more so after it started, lived in very basic homes, or huts. In the villages, the huts were a concoction of native-made mud brick, scrounged timber, even cardboard, and often thatched roofs. If inhabited, they always seemed to have acrid smoke coming from their chimneys, which were also made out of mud brick. The Koreans heated their homes and cooked their meals over the same open hearth. Many American servicemen never did get used to the aroma of their food.

But less appealing were the "honey pots" and "honey ditches," in which many a Marine sought cover—stinking or not—if surprised by the enemy while patrolling along a road. Indoor plumbing was not a staple of Korean households. Koreans did their business in pots, which they kept inside their homes. "I never did see an outhouse there," Carty said.

By the time Korean families filled their pots to capacity, there usually was a very acrid-sweet odor emanating from them. "Honey pots" smelled anything but like the tasty nectar produced by bees.

Some sarcastic, imaginative, American G.I. probably came up with that one, Carty thought.

When the pots were full of human waste, Papasan, the head of the household, or sometimes, Mamasan, would have the job of emptying them. Koreans transported much of their wares manually—on an A-frame rig strapped to their backs, at the ends of a yoke balanced across their shoulders, or in pots or baskets atop their heads. When it was time for Papasan to empty the "honey pots," he usually would do it two at a time, attaching the rope handles at the ends of a yoke. He'd squat, place the yoke across his shoulders behind his head, and stand up.

He'd start walking down the road a ways with these two "aromatic" pots balancing on the yoke. Koreans did not have a central sewage system for the villages, but almost every road had a drainage ditch running along it, sometimes on both sides. Papasan would find a ditch and dump his "honey." Often the humus would find its way into the plentiful rice paddies as fertilizer. The selection of where to make the deposit was probably based on which way the wind mostly blew away from their homes. "On a very hot summer day," Carty noted, "it smelled like the whole damn peninsula was coated with 'honey.'"

That July day turned out to be full of a series of "firsts" for a lot of the guys from the 10th Replacement Draft. Some experienced their first flight in an airplane, ferried from a small field outside of Pusan, up to the First Marine Division command post.

The 1stMarDiv, when on line, was responsible for a large combat zone in East-Central Korea, above the 38th Parallel, a couple of hundred miles north and east of Pusan. It was easier, and a lot quicker, to fly in replacements than transport them all that way by six-by. PFC Carty had no idea where he was when the load of replacements jumped down from truck at the primitive airstrip. "It was nothing more than a large flat area with a dirt runway, and a few tents and shacks which housed military personnel," Carty said.

There were about twenty or thirty guys on the plane, a two-engine cargo R4D, or C-47 as they also were known. "The flight was less than an hour and wasn't bad," Carty said. "I thought I might get airsick, but I didn't. We really got a great look at the Korean countryside, which was very mountainous. I could picture myself trying to hump those hills if I got into the infantry."

The R4D landed on a small airfield at Chunchon. "We saw our taxis," Carty said, and the six-bys took their "fares" seventy bumpy miles to Camp Tripoli, the First Marine Division CP. Tripoli was approximately ten to fifteen miles from the MLR. It was located slightly west of the Soyang-Gang (or River) within ten miles northeast of the town of Yanggu, and about two to three miles directly west of the village of Wontong-Ni. Yanggu sat at the southeast tip of the Hwachon Reservoir.

Division forward command was about two-and-a-half to three miles from the southern rim of the Punch Bowl, dead center between the Sochon River and the Soyang-Gang. The nearest village to the forward command was Sohwa-Ri, about seven miles to the northeast.

It was then that the replacements learned Division had been pulled off the line and had been in "reserve" for a couple of weeks. What that meant was Marines were behind the lines and in the process of retooling, resting, and training. *I don't see any tanks,* PFC Carty thought with continued apprehension.

It wasn't long after Carty arrived in Tripoli that PFC Dan O'Sullivan jumped out of a six-by. "You reserve me a rack in the hotel?" O'Sullivan asked when he saw Carty standing near a squad tent. Both were surprised that tents were available for peons this far forward, especially if they were going infantry—which still was a question in their minds.

The two friends managed to get racks under the same canvas and both continued to wonder about that decree—*all Marines are infantrymen.* But scuttlebutt was passed that all the 1811s were headed for the First Tank Battalion. That was the first time either of them had heard mention of the outfit. "We were told it was several miles away from Tripoli," Carty said. There seemed to be no urgency to get them there.

They hung around Tripoli for two days before they were trucked over to the First Tank Battalion and assembled in front of the Headquarters Company first sergeant.

"Think we have a chance to get in the same tank?" O'Sullivan asked his friend. Carty had hoped so, but the chance of two "cherries" in one tank seemed unlikely. Maybe the same Company, but probably not the same tank.

The idea was quickly quashed. "Carty," the first sergeant hollered. "Headquarters Company. You stay here. . . . "

"Shit," he muttered, *Headquarters Company* quickly dominating his thoughts and oblivious to the rest of the sergeant's order. What didn't sink in right away was the rest of the sergeant's order: ". . . Flame Platoon."

"Damn it," he mumbled to himself without absorbing the sergeant's last two words, "that means I'm probably going to get a desk job—Office Pinky!" He figured his ability to type finally caught up with him. Then, it registered: *Flame Platoon*.

What the hell is that? he wondered. He had no idea there was a platoon of nine Sherman M4A3E8s not too far away.

"O'Sullivan!"

When Carty heard his buddy's name, he retreated from his selfish concern.

"Over there." Dan was ordered to join a small group going up to Dog Company. He looked at Carty with that broad Irish grin as much to say: *Hey, I'm going to a real tank outfit, and you're staying here with a desk.*

PFC Carty only muttered, "You lucky Irish Mick."

PFC Carty still wasn't sure what he had drawn, and his mood didn't change until a buck sergeant took him in tow and led him to a group of small pyramid tents. That's when the Runnemede, New Jersey, Marine saw them—the familiar Shermans, like the ones he trained in. But these had two muzzles protruding from their coaxal gun shields. A cautious smile began to form on his face.

Flame tanks! Then he remembered the movie *Halls of Montezuma*. There was a flame tank in it, shooting napalm into a Japanese bunker. And there was a brief mention of flame tanks during training at Camp Delmar. His mood quickly changed.

Man, are they beautiful, he savored inwardly. Especially when he realized he probably wasn't going to be driving a desk and shifting keys of a typewriter.

"Little did I know how lucky I was," said Carty.

First Drive, Wrong Way

The First Tank Battalion CP moved twice in the first two months PFC Jack Carty was in Korea, but he still had not been permanently assigned to one of the flame tank crews. He was a floater, hopping rides as loader whenever there was room in one of the tanks.

It was during the first move north that he did not endear himself to one of the veteran Flame Platoon crews. This was compliments of a young second lieutenant who had gone through training with the 10th Replacement Draft tankers at Camp Delmar. "We were in a convoy of tanks driving from reserve toward our new C.P., God only knows where," Carty said. "We were going forward because the First Marine Division had been put back in the line."

When Division moved, every unit attached to it also followed.

The rookie tanker was assigned as a temporary assistant driver on one of the flame tanks, only because they had to find a place for him during the move. "I really thought I was there just for the ride," Carty said. "Being a raw rookie, I never expected to get a chance to drive, particularly since most of the move was being made at night."

Tagging along in the turret was the Second Lieutenant, who had not been very popular with the tank trainees at Camp Delmar. "We didn't know much about him," Carty said. "But he gave us the impression he thought his gold bars shined bright just so PFCs could see he was boss. He didn't know anything more about tanks than we did, but he was an officer and he made sure we knew it."

When he arrived in Korea, the lieutenant was attached to Headquarters Company while waiting assignment to a line company. In the infantry, Second Johns were very high on the casualty lists because of their closeness with the riflemen in firefights. They were always in demand by infantry regiments because their casualty rate was extremely high.

Tank officers, because of the specialty training and the Corps siphoning so many junior officers for infantry, had to be among the more rare species. Most of the officers brought into the Korean War were reserves who had been activated. Many were like the youthful-looking, probably inexperienced, Second John up in the turret. He more than likely enlisted near or at the end of World War II, served his compulsory two or three years, and then went home to a reserve outfit—one meeting a month and two weeks training during the summer. When Korea exploded, he was among the thousands of reserve officers and enlisted personnel called up.

Anyway, not too many peons had much time for *this* lieutenant at Delmar. "He came off as sort of prissy, probably a little miffed that he was yanked out of civilian life and was being trained as a tank officer," Carty said was the common feeling among the tank trainees. "Pissed off or not, he gave the impression, particularly around the NCOs, and us PFCs, that he was something special—being a lieutenant in the United States Marine Corps. We respected the gold bars, but we were not as impressed with them as he seemed to be. I don't know what he was thinking this night."

All of the sudden, the lieutenant was on the intercom: "Why don't we give PFC Carty a chance to drive?" It was more an order than a request. "I know he remembered my face from Delmar, but I didn't think he took the time to get my name," the rookie tanker thought. Carty wondered if the lieutenant was trying to make points, figuring he was in a war zone and had better start looking at enlisted men a little differently than he did in the States.

When the driver heard the "suggestion," he quickly glanced at the wary PFC sitting across from him. "I could see he didn't like the idea one bit," Carty said. "Of course, we were in a line of tanks in a convoy, and it was dark as hell. We could hear the rumble of the engines and grinding of track from the tanks ahead of us, but we lagged behind as far as we could to avoid the dust while still trying to keep visual contact."

When the lieutenant insisted that Carty drive, it meant the flame tank had to pull out of line to make the switch. By the time the rookie got into the driver's compartment and nervously jerked the Sherman into motion, no one could see, or hear, the tank in front of them.

The Shermans have five forward gears and reverse. Not having driven much since leaving Delmar, Carty managed to grind the gears getting out of second—the usual starting gear into third, and finally into fourth, the common gear for cruising on level ground. The fifth forward gear was used when there was wide-open level terrain, but in the dark— even though moving only around twenty miles an hour—the speed gear was not a wise choice for controlling more than thirty tons of rumbling steel.

However, the tank was making up some ground, but none of the crew could have picked up the tank in front of them as Carty saw the Sherman was coming to a fork in the road.

The lieutenant told the "driver" to slow down. "I think we bear to the right, here," he said meekly over the intercom.

Carty recalled enough of his training to know he had to double-clutch to shift down in the gear ratio, and surprisingly, smoothly got the pigiron into third gear while pulling back on the right brake lever.

"We didn't get more than fifty yards into the turn," Carty said, "and, all of the sudden, we were going down a small embankment into a ditch. I yanked back on both brake levers, when I felt the tank tilt downward, but it was too late. Half of the tank was down an incline, and the ass end of it was sticking up in the air."

Fortunately, the next tank in line was far enough back—when the *wrong turn* was made—that it didn't plow right into the wayward Sherman in the ditch. It was also fortunate that the little ravine was where it was—only a short way off the fork—and not a semblance of a road that Carty would have followed. "Every tank and truck behind us would have been going with us to Lord only knows where."

At that point, the tank commander yelled down at the regular driver. "Get us the hell out of this damn hole!"

In the precarious bow-down position in the ditch, the driver knew better than to try to switch seats now. He just told Carty to put it into reverse and ease it back, which the now-embarrassed rookie managed to do without too much trouble.

That was the end of the New Jersey PFC's first venture as a tank driver in Korea.

After switching seats, the expertise of the experienced driver meshed those forward gears like it was fluid drive. Not too long later, they were tooling down the *left fork* and eventually caught up to the rest of the column.

The convoy got to the new battalion C.P. early the following morning and Carty never saw the lieutenant again. "I figured he had been assigned to line tank company," Carty said.

Dan O'Sullivan, Carty's good friend who had been sent up to Dog Company, later told his buddy he heard the lieutenant turned out to be a pretty damn good tank officer. "Maybe he learned something that night, too," Carty said.

The Flame Platoon spent only a few weeks at that C.P. before the First Tank Battalion moved again in mid-September and finally settled in for the rest of the fall and winter somewhere near the Soyang-Gang, forward of Camp Tripoli.

It was there that Carty really started to feel he was part of the outfit and was learning about the flame tank. "I was assigned to Corporal Len Martin's crew as loader in the turret of F22 (Fox 22), one of three tanks in the second section of the Flame Platoon," Carty said. The loader is lowest on the totem pole in the four-man crew. It is where the novice starts learning all about that special brand of 35-ton pigiron.

The war, at this juncture, had slowed down somewhat. That might be a tough sell to the guys on line. There was still plenty of give-and-take along the MLR, and a lot of Marines weren't going to go home. Many more would suffer lifelong scars to remind them of the "slowdown."

As for flame tanks, there seemed to be very little use for them in the rugged highlands of East-Central Korea. Had the First Division still been fighting in the west, as it was early in the war in Seoul, or just above the 38th Parallel in the western sector where the terrain was not quite as mountainous, there may have been more use for flame tanks. It would come later, after Operation Mixmaster, but for most of the next five months, the Flamers were rear echelon.

That meant *cherries,* like the guys who came over in the 10th Replacement Draft and those who would follow the next couple of months, had plenty of time to learn about this unique creation called a flame tank. "It was advanced training, allowing a lot of time with the sticks in our hands, gradually getting the confidence to handle thirty-five tons of iron and steel on the move," Carty said. "It also meant we traded in our four-man pyramid tents for thirteen-man squad tents, slept in comparative comfort, and had three hots a day in a mess tent."

Line company tankers, like Carty's friend Dan O'Sullivan, were quick to rag Flamers as "pogey-bait" Marines. But the newest guy in the F22 crew, as well those who had been through the Spring Offensive, figured the good life wouldn't last. They expected to be called up to do something, sooner or later. It was later more than sooner.

At this point, however, they couldn't really refute that the Flame Platoon had it pretty good in Korea as the war was well into its second year—what with tents, cots, and three sit-down meals most of the time, it was about as good as you could get in a war zone.

The Flame Platoon continued to train, and Carty thought being part of the F22 crew was great. Cpl. Len Martin proved to be a knowledgeable and fine tank commander. Don Hurst, who was from Deer Lodge, Montana, was the driver, and Dick Greenwood, a native of Syracuse, New York, was the assistant driver/bow gunner. As the loader up in the turret with Cpl. Martin, it didn't take long before the former sportswriter felt he was fortunate to have been assigned to that crew. He was not treated as a rookie—just one of the guys.

There was a lot of cross-training, and tank commanders made sure their crews knew all four positions in the pigiron, even taking over the No. 1 spot in the turret. The training was priceless.

Cpl. Martin, who was introduced to Flames after mushing his way through the

December breakout from the Chosin Reservoir, most of it as a quasi-infantryman with Headquarters Company, knew his tank. He was very aware that his entire crew should be as versed with it as he was. Of course, Hurst and Greenwood did most of the clutch work. But the tank commander made sure the new guy got ample opportunity with his hands on the sticks. Even the T.C. got down there quite a bit.

Such was the luxury of being in the rear, a luxury that also cemented a lasting bond with this particular version of the Sherman M4A3E8.

For a while it never really bothered most of the guys in the Flame Platoon that they weren't seeing any action. The veterans of the Spring Offensive had their fill, and the newcomers were too intent on learning the ropes as summer turned to fall in 1951. "We all thought that our turn would come," Carty said. "However, sitting it out began to bother us as October passed into November, and November into December. We were feeling a little guilty that we had yet to put our two cents into the war."

Their time was coming, however.

Hiatus for Flame Tanks

During the late summer and early fall of 1951, there wasn't much call for the Flame Platoon in Korea, even after the First Marine Division came out of reserve and went back into the line on 27 August.

There was plenty going on forward with the three infantry regiments taking over the Kansas Line, which wrapped around the bottom of the Punch Bowl and halfway up its eastern base before angling due east. But it was so mountainous up there, it was difficult territory for tanks.

The First Tank Battalion's letter companies were brought up to small cleared positions, gouged out of the reverse slopes of hills by anti-tank Sherman dozers, so they could be used as mobile artillery. Often they navigated narrow dozed-out roads around the edges of infantry positions, edge forward of the MLR to fire their 90mm rifles point-blank into enemy trenches and bunkers across wide canyons.

But as far as maneuvering for basic tank warfare, the East Central Mountains ranging up to the Kanmubong Ridge—some at heights more than 1,000 meters above sea level—just weren't the place for it. And it was less favorable for flame tanks, whose priority use was to burn out the enemy at close range, although their 105s could have helped in a pinch if the Shermans were able to carry more than just a few rounds of heavy ordnance.

That shortcoming—restricted room for 105mm ordnance due to the napalm tanks taking up room in the hull where shells normally were stored—would be remedied somewhat later in the war when the Division returned to the Western front. But in the East Central Zone, flame tanks just weren't part of the equation most of the time.

There would be one exception when Flames would get a crack at working in those hills. But it wouldn't be until after the war had settled into a hunt-'n'-peck mode, and Marine infantry was getting fed up with guys they called Luke the Gook, who was doing too much pecking at friendly positions from a granite knob along the Kanmubong Ridge.

For the time being, however, the Flame Platoon crews remained in what Marines referred to "pogey bait" duty—miles away from hostilities, feeling pangs of occasional guilt as fall became winter. They knew there still was a war going on. They could hear it almost every night. Tanker friends from the Able, Baker, Charlie, and Dog companies, coming back from firing missions, rubbed it in when they could, letting the extinguished Flamers know how good they had it.

Flame Tankers were chaffing at the bit, yearning to get a crack at the Gooks. In this kind of war, they just had to wait their turn. It would come in time, and once it did, they would be kept plenty busy.

Meanwhile, they made the best of it—learning the M4A3E8 Sherman flame tank inside and out. Like most of the Flamers, Cpl. Len Martin had a passion for driving the Sherman tank, and for that reason he was very good at teaching others how to handle the 35-ton monster. PFC Jack Carty was an appreciative recipient of his expertise.

"Handling a tank in a place like Korea was a lot different than where we trained at Camp Delmar," Carty said. The terrain in Korea was completely different, and no one in the Flame Platoon in late summer of 1951 was more aware of that than Martin, now tank commander of Fox 22. Martin had earned his spurs a tanker-infantryman during the breakout from the Chosin Reservoir, then as a driver and loader on a flame tank during the previous spring's ruckus around the Punch Bowl and the Hwachon Reservoir.

"We spent a lot of time training and teaching the new guys how to drive the tanks and how to fire the weapons," Martin said, thankful for the opportunity to work with rookies before they had to take one of the tanks into a combat situation. "We had a chance to really work on the finer arts of driving by constantly taking the tanks up and down embankments and revetments that the artillery had used to protect them from incoming fire." The technique of deftly taking a thirty-five-ton tank over that kind of obstacle was not wasted on PFC Carty, who had a habit of cresting on a hill and slamming the thirty-five-ton tank into the ground at the bottom of it.

"Len Martin taught me how to keep from popping him out of the turret," Carty said appreciatively. "He drilled into us that there are a few seconds at the crown of the hill when the tank is coming off its peak vertical position and the bow starts to drop. That's when the foot pressure relaxes on the accelerator to let the tank settle, leaving its weight to bring it down more gently. In the meantime, it was smart to double-clutch and drop down a gear to pick up a more powerful drive train before hitting the gas and continuing on, once the entire track surfaced on flat ground. It made a very smooth transition coming up and over those ditches or inclines. It was such a good feeling to master something like that."

As new replacements started coming into the Flame Platoon, Martin for all of his nineteen years was surprised many of them even lacked experience driving cars. He wondered, sometimes, how many of them got through tank training.

"I remember starting with one group by asking who had driven a stick-shift car. Since most of us drove stick shifts at home, I thought that at least I would not have to teach them the art of using the clutch and gas pedal. Surprisingly, I found that several had never driven a car before. I had to sit down and explain from scratch how to shift gears. And when I mentioned double-clutching, they didn't know what I was talking about."

Although shifting gears in a tank was similar to that of a car, there were some differences when working with five forward speeds of the M4A3E8, compared to three in a 1940 Chevy. Shifting up the gear chain was relatively the same, but because driving a tank required changing speeds so often, a lot of down-shifting was necessary, particularly when trying to bring the tank to a stop. "Due to the weight of the tank, it was difficult to stop its motion, particularly with the brake levers," Martin said. "We had to use the power of the engine to assist the braking."

That's when double-clutching was needed. When shifting down from a higher gear to the next lower range, the driver released the accelerator and depressed the clutch pedal to bring the shifter into neutral. Once in neutral, he might wobble the gear-shift a little in the free position to make sure it was fully disengaged before he released the clutch pedal. Then, the driver revved the engine slightly in order to ease the meshing of the gears before depressing the clutch pedal a second time to bring the shifter into the lower range.

Slowly releasing the clutch pedal, and simultaneously depressing the accelerator, he began matching the speed of the engine to the speed of the tank. As the speeds synchronized, he then was able to let up on the gas pedal and use the engine to slow the tank to the point of near stall. At that point, he depressed the clutch and pulled back on the brake handles to bring the monster to a complete stop.

In time, it became just a matter of *feel* to tank drivers, most of whom could make the transition up or down the gear chain with little or no disruption in smoothness of the ride.

But Martin also warned his drivers about going up the gear range: "It often is difficult, even with double-clutching, to get into third from second, and it requires pulling back as hard as you can, sometimes grinding into the higher range." There were times, because the tank was so heavy, or it was lumbering on an incline, that not enough speed was there to pick up the third gear. "The tank would almost come to a complete stop before the gear would grab."

Once in third gear, the tank could move relatively fast, and it was no problem to get it into fourth. Very seldom would the terrain in Korea allow enough speed to shift up to fifth gear. The road had to be relatively flat—and long—for the luxury of "speeding" in fifth gear. "But," Martin said with a smile, "there is nothing like rolling down a road in fifth gear in a thirty-five-ton Sherman tank. You become very aware of the sound of the tracks and the dirt flying off in front from them. You're only going 25, maybe 26, 27, miles an hour, but in that tank, it feels like you're at the wheel of a Caddy doing 50 on a dusty back road at home. It is a tank driver's heaven. I loved it!"

The Flame Platoon got a new platoon leader that summer—M/Sgt. Grady Turnage, a by-the-book veteran of World War II. Normally in a small unit like the Flame Platoon, there is a lot of camaraderie, particularly among the enlisted men, and even with senior NCOs. M/Sgt. Turnage was not one who seemed to think that way. He was a good tanker, but he had his rank, and it was not to be taken lightly by those under his command. This did not sit too well with some of the veterans who had come through combat in the mean winter months before he got there.

Cpl. Len Martin had a lot of respect for M/Sgt. Turnage, but he admitted not getting along with him. "He liked to go by the book," Martin said, "and some of us resented the fact that we had more experience here than he did, or that our time in Korea was due a little respect from him. He may have had it, but didn't show it, as far as I was concerned."

Well, maybe he did sometimes. "One thing I did like about him," Cpl. Martin admitted, "was every time he ran across a situation where he wanted to see if a tank could do something, such as climbing steep hills, or going over ditches, he would call on me." Cpl. Martin's F22 was the newest tank in the platoon, having replaced its predecessor that was destroyed by a satchel charge in the Seoul street fighting.

"Do you think your tank can make it?" Turnage would ask Martin, pointing to a challenging obstacle.

"There's only one way to find out," a slightly bit cocky Martin replied. "Let's try it."

Martin would trade places with his driver and put the tank through its paces. "One time," the tank commander said, "I inched '22' up a steep artillery embankment until I reached the tank's balance point. I had it rocking back and forth at the top. Fun and games!"

It was not fun and games the day tanks were out in the fields and the T.C.s were teaching new guys how to fire the 105mm howitzer. The 105 had a horizontal breach that slides open to allow the shell to be inserted into the chamber. It was opened by a handle on top of the breach. After a round is inserted and the breach block closed, the gun is automatically cocked and ready for firing.

At this point the loader says "UP," letting the gunner (tank commander in a flame tank) know that the gun is ready to fire. The T.C. says, "On the way," and squeezes the trigger. If everything goes right, the gun fires and the loader opens the breach block, allowing the casing to eject.

The 105's ordnance on the Sherman flame tanks were called semi-fixed rounds, meaning the projectile was not crimped to the casing, which contained powder bags that propelled the warhead. Some of these bags could be removed to control the range. The later tanks with rifles, rather than howitzer, used fixed ammo.

Since flame tanks did not do much firing with their 105s, and since their meager allotment of rounds were carried in the turret, the shells were subject to getting water inside the casings. There were problems with some rounds not going off, causing a misfire. With a misfire there was always the danger that the fuse would be burning slowly and would go off at any time. When this happened, the normal procedure was for the loader to reach up on top of the breach block and activate a cocking lever. If it still didn't fire, it was S.O.P. (standard operating procedure) to wait five minutes, open the breach, remove the round—and pray that it did not go off. Normally, a lieutenant was responsible to unload the gun. "Not a nice job," Cpl. Martin admitted.

One day, Martin was teaching some new guys how to fire the 105. He was standing outside behind the loader's hatch, when one of the rounds did not fire. "After waiting awhile, I told the loader to recock the gun."

Instead of reaching up and recocking it, the loader opened the breach block and then closed it. If the round had gone off, it would have severely injured, or killed, the entire crew.

Martin reached down into the turret, grabbed the guy by his shoulders, and pulled him up. "You stupid son-of-a-bitch, you could have killed all of us!" At that, the gun was recocked, but it still did not fire. "We got out of the tank and had the lieutenant clear it."

F22 began flying a pair of Irish flags from its two antennae after PFC Carty had a visit from his friend PFC Dan O'Sullivan, his Bronx-Irish buddy who had been seeing plenty of time on the line as a gunner in an M26 Pershing with Dog Company. O'Sullivan had given Carty the flags, about 10x14 inches each. One was the green, white, and orange Irish national ensign, and the other was Kelly green with a yellow leprechaun and *Erin Go Bragh* [Ireland Forever] printed on it.

"Here," Dan said, "put these on your antenna so I can see you coming if you 'pogey bait Marines' ever make it up our way." When O'Sullivan's tank was not on the lines, he also flew a similar pair on the M26.

By now, most of the "Old Breed" Marines were rotating out as replacements, coming in monthly, and began to fit in and take more responsibility in the tanks. Loaders were becoming assistant drivers/bow gunners, who in turn were becoming drivers when the stick handlers moved up into the turrets as tank commanders.

Cpl. Martin's crew was changing as the experienced Dick Greenwood and Don Hurst took over other tanks. That also afforded PFC Carty the chance to move in as driver of F22. Now feeling confident of his role in the Flame Platoon, he suggested to his T.C. that their tank have a more definitive title.

The Marine Corps frowned on that kind of stuff, but Carty had noticed someone, before his time, had lettered "Fire Box" in small letters on the port-side hull below the driver's hatch of F21. And F23 had "Fire Bug" on its hull. Sportswriters are notorious for cliches, and he had been mulling one over for a few weeks. He suggested the name to Martin.

His T.C. didn't seem very enthused, but relented, "Yeh, why not."

Carty scrounged some white paint and a small brush, and labeled the bow of the tank right below his driver's hatch in three-inch letters:

The
Roamin'
Candle

It didn't impress anybody other than the crew. The other tank commanders sort of ignored it, and the three second-section Shermans remained the only flamethrowers with titles other than their "F" designation.

The good life in the rear was enhanced by the monthly rations of goodies like toiletries, soda, cigarettes, candy, 3.2 beer—cans of Schlitz, Pabst, Budweiser, and once in a while a couple of 12-ounce bottles of Asahi beer, which was a very weak brew made in Japan. Of course, 3.2 wasn't what Marines would call a kick in the ass. However, they took care of the more powerful stuff on their own.

Marines in Korea weren't the first in the services of their country to concoct their own private little distilleries. Many a G.I. in WWII got a buzz on from creative brewmasters who could do wonders with a five-gallon jerry can, some sugar, leftover fruit, and a little fire and time.

In the rear tank outfits of Korea, it was not unusual to have a little cheer brewing next to the kerosene stoves, which heated the squad tents. It came in several brands —apple jack, raisin jack, potato jack, cherry jack, or whatever garden-variety fruit or vegetable could be weaseled out of the galley to make a base for homemade booze.

Some serious buzzes and hangovers came along with that stuff.

All that was needed was the five-gallon jerry can to start with. Scrounged apple peels, or potato peels, or boxes of raisins, or canned peaches, or pears, any fruit—usually "requisitioned" from the galley—was basic. It didn't matter, just something to add flavor and help the fermentation.

The exact—even approximated—mixtures varied, but fruit in large quantities would be poured into the jerry can, over which would go several pounds of sugar and a block of yeast. Water was added. The can and its contents would be set on top of, or very close to, the kerosene heaters, to force fermentation. Depending on the mix and the *master mixer*, it took about a week or ten days before the "jack" was ready—if it didn't blow up in the meantime. Of course, the longer it fermented, the stronger the concoction and the merrier the jack "busts."

Being in the rear, like the Flame Platoon was, allowed for more mundane things.

It was in the fall of 1951 that singer Tony Bennett had come out with his newest hit, "I Left My Heart in San Francisco." The Flame Platoon was on a training run one day and had stopped for a break. One of the guys had a portable radio and he climbed up a small hill to get better reception. Fiddling with the dial, trying to clear the static, he finally picked up a station in Japan that played American music.

He heard Bennett crooning the new song, which eventually would leave an indelible mark in the minds of Marines in Korea, who received a great boost from those kinds of programs. Of course the guys on the lines couldn't take advantage of it, but if someone in the rear had a portable radio, it often was dialed into the stations in Kyoto and Kiushu, Japan, which geared their programs, mostly music, to Americans in Korea.

For outfits in the rear, like the Flame Platoon, nights were fairly free, maybe a two-hour guard duty, but nothing like the 50 percent watches needed in the bunkers and trenches a few miles north. That left a lot of time to play cards, write letters, and bull sessions.

Like most outfits well behind the lines, there were always Korean civilians hanging around outside the restricted areas—looking for food, even more than willing to work for handouts. There was a young Korean kid who used to hang around the Headquarters Company and the Flame Platoon. A lot of the guys got him to do their wash for them. This was quite common in rear areas. They were sometimes called Washy-Washy Boys.

Somewhere this kid got the name "Murphy," and each of guys would give him a buck or two of script a week to do their wash. He'd pick up the dirty clothes in the morning and have the laundry back that night, if the weather was such that the clothes could be dried in the sun during the day.

Murphy was one of the fortunate Korean natives. He made a living by being allowed around the company area, and because of his resourcefulness, he was able to support a few other Koreans. He had a deal going with people outside the Battalion area. He gave the clothes to the women in the nearby village and they would take them down to the river, or stream, and do the wash.

When the flame tankers took their Shermans out for a run, they'd see the women doing the wash in the river. They'd soak them in the shallow water, dip them in a bucket of soapy water, then pound them on a rock to beat the dirt out of them. Murphy gave them a cut of his take from the Marines, spreading the wealth, so to speak, among the villagers.

But it was pathetic to see how most of the natives had to try to survive during the war. They just hounded the Americans for food, or anything that could be bartered for food. It was not uncommon to see families waiting for trucks coming from the mess tents to dump trash and garbage outside the military confines. The Koreans would dig all through that slop and salvage every edible thing they could find. It was sobering to think how spoiled Americans really didn't know how good they had it.

Murphy knew enough English that he could hold a basic conversation with the Marines. He probably had plenty of other guys around the Battalion for whom he worked. He made out pretty well, and his associates were better for his enterprising ambition.

Such was another phase of the being in the rear during the Second Year of the Korean War.

Despite the good life in the Flame Platoon, guys who came to the outfit in the summer and fall on 1951 were getting itchy to be included in the actual war. The ones who finally did get their flame tanks into combat shortly after the calendar flipped over into 1952 would have a story to tell. And it would not be the last to be written in the short history of the Flame Platoon, Headquarters Company, First Tank Battalion, First Marine Division in Korea.

Different Approach to War

With the possibility that negotiations, now shifted to Panmunjom, would be the forerunner to ending the Korean War in the not too distant future, there was dramatic change in tactics by the U.N. command. It probably had a lot to do with why the Flame Platoon, although not quite suited to mountain warfare, had not been reinserted in the conflict since late spring.

Officially, it was noted:

> The Division continued to organize, construct and defend positions along a 13-1/2-mile front; patrol forward of the MLR and screen rear areas; and maintain one U.S. Marine regiment which could not be committed without authority from X Corps in a reserve area 17 miles behind the lines.
>   . . . the opening paragraph of the report of the 1st Marine Division for October 1951, sums up in a nutshell the new trend of operations since 10 September. It is significant that for the first time in 1951 the Division Historical Diary departs from a daily account of events and divides the month into two equal parts for the chronicle of operations. Not enough had happened to justify day-by-day summary. (MCOinK, Volume IV)

In mid-September, General James A. Van Fleet, EUSAK commanding general, dropped in on the Marines in the middle of the X Corps front. There was a good reason for the visit after nearly three weeks of hard fighting, which had been costly to the 1st-MarDiv. Van Fleet ordered X Corps, which included the First Marine Division, to solidify its lines and not to undertake any offensive stature. It was a turning point in the war, which was to become one of position rather than one of movement. "There are few dates as important in the entire history of the war" *(MCOinK, Volume IV)*.

This did not mean that the Marines neglected any opportunity to do the enemy serious hurt. It meant only that the opportunities offered in defensive warfare were limited as compared to the preceding six months of offensive operations.

Late in November, the following was part of instructions EUSAK relayed to all corps commanders and sent by X Corps to the 1st Marine Division:

> PART III. While negotiations [at Panmunjom] continue, X Corps: (1) Demonstrate its willingness to reach an agreement by reducing operations to those which are essential to insure maintenance of present positions. Counterattacks to regain key terrain lost to enemy assault are authorized, but other clearly offensive actions will be taken only by direction of this Headquarters: patrolling only to that line beyond which contact has been repeatedly established; limiting supporting fires, including air strikes, to destruction of those targets which appear to constitute a major threat, or to improve the enemy's offensive capability. (2) Prepare for offensive action by: Conserving ammunition; maintaining combat effectiveness through intensified training; preparation for and rehearsal of limited-objective attacks, to be launched near the end of the 30-day period in order to improve the MLR. PART IV: Every effort will be made to prevent unnecessary casualties. (MCOinK, Volume IV)

This was the atmosphere of war which kept the Flame Platoon out of combat and, just maybe, got a lot of its tankers back home in one piece before things heated up again in the summer of 1952.

Still, some Marines were not so lucky. The MLR was Line Minnesota and while the so-called truce talks were going on in November and December of 1951, patrols, probing attacks, hit-and-run defensive warfare continued. Nitty-gritty stuff and Marines still died. Those "foot patrols" and all of that "snoopin' 'n' poopin'" were responsible for a lot of KIAs. There were 24 Marines killed and 139 wounded in "patrol actions" during the month of December.

It's hard to think "small" in terms of those numbers, particularly for families suffering one of the losses. But those numbers were small compared to what were recorded during full-scale offensive operations the previous spring and summer—and what they would have been if this was not a defensive phase of the Korean War.

The defensive war in late 1951 even got to the point where ammunition was "rationed"—not because of shortages, but because EUSAK just wanted to control, very tightly, the kind of fighting in which U.N. forces would become involved. It got down to making daily reports on how many rounds of ammunition were utilized.

It went to the extreme the following summer. Some rear echelon types wanted Marine tankers involved in missions in front of the MLR on the West Coast to collect and turn in all their "brass"—brass being shell casings. In firing areas, such as ranges, and even in combat artillery units behind the lines, there's always an order following a mission: "Police All Brass," which means clean up the shell casings.

Because of the tightness of quarters in the tank turret, when 105mm or 90mm guns are fired the "brass" is ejected back into the turret. If buttoned up, the gunner, loader, or tank commander would throw the casing out of the turret through a little hatch on the side—the pistol port.

To send a man outside of the tank, in clear view of enemy snipers to police the area of brass, was ludicrous. Of course, First Tank Battalion commanders let X Corps desk jockeys know where they could put that order. They were not about to risk Marines' lives so some paper shuffler twenty or forty miles behind the lines could make his ledger balance.

Helicopters had become a very important vehicle for extricating wounded from the highly inaccessible hills and narrow valleys of Korea very early in the war. But the First Marine Division went one better in the fall of 1951 when it launched Operation BUMBLEBEE—a revolutionary mode of warfare—transporting of troops and supplies by helicopter. It was 11 October 1951 when:

"Twelve helicopters (HRS-1s [Sikorsky]) were employed in 156 flights" to transport the 7th Marines from reserve "to a landing site . . . just behind the 5th Marines MLR, northeast of Hill 702. A flight path of 15 miles took advantage of the concealment afforded by valleys and defiladed areas.

"Ten to 12 minutes were required for the flight . . . A total weight of 229,920 pounds included 985 combat-equipped troops, averaging 240 pounds. . . .

"These statistics of Operation BUMBLEBEE made it certain that Stateside headlines would proclaim another Marine 'first.' Only four days later, HMR-161 demonstrated its ability to carry out on short notice an emergency resupply and evacuation operation in a combat zone." (MCOinK, Volume IV)

Len Martin, shortly after being promoted to sergeant, rotated out in November and arrived home in Forest Park, Illinois, on Christmas Eve, 1951.

One of the constants of war is attrition. In Korea, casualties were the primary cause of depletion early in hostilities. But rotation had as much to do with the need to replenish troops as anything after war had settled down a little midway through 1951. During the second year of the war, as the momentum of it stabilized, guys were rotated back to the states after having spent twelve months—a little more, a little less—in the Land of the Morning Calm.

This attrition also had an effect on keeping the table of organization in line, and that meant when a noncommissioned officer was rotated out, the T.O. called for another NCO to take his place. Because of shortages, up and down the ranks, promotions, although not always warranted, came a lot quicker.

Gaining rank in the Corps used to be quite hard. Peacetime Gyrenes might well be PFCs their entire first four-year enlistment. But now, demands dictated by the war made it necessary to initiate promotions much more frequently. They were called All-Mars (All-Marine)—Marine Corps wide.

The "Old Breed" Marines—those who didn't make PFC until they re-upped for their second four-year hitch, or didn't get a Corporal's stripe until they were well on the way to their second hash mark—had a few choice words about how promotions were coming in Korea.

When Flame Platoon promotions came through that November, it really didn't mean much in the way of assuming more responsibility. While PFCs were picking up another stripe, so were the NCOs above them. But those were the times, and career Marines from World War II—some of whom re-enlisted two or three times and never got that many stripes—just shook their heads. Of course, by this time those "Old Salts" were also moving up to staff, technical, or master sergeant. So rank still had its privileges.

The one major difference was a minor increase in pay. PFCs getting $92.50 a month, now would get the corporal's $104.55. Most of guys in the First Tank Battalion who arrived in Korea as PFCs, left with three stripes on their sleeves and were able, if prudent, to send most of their pay home to have it banked by a parent or wife.

The guys from the 8th, 9th, 10th, 11th, 12th Replacement Drafts—now were the Flame Platoon.

Sergeants Chuck Wager and Emery Prine; and corporals Jim Waltz, Roger Davis, George "Corky" Manfull, Patrick "Packy" Wassell, Red Smith, and Bob Haase were among the newly assigned Flame Platoon tank commanders as the second winter settled on the Korean War. When rotation began thinning their ranks in the spring, that left T.C. openings for corporals Pat McDermott, Chuck Lasche, and Leonard L. Kleczewski.

It was Cpl. Wassell, a tall, lean Southern Californian from the Ninth Draft, who took over F22 from Sgt. Martin and Cpl. Jack Carty, who became a competent driver under Martin's tutelage, remained in charge of *The Roamin' Candle*'s sticks. PFC Alvin Chalk, a chunky, easy-going kid from Baltimore, now was in the assistant driver/bow gunner's seat, and newcomer PFC Jack MacGregor, from Montana, was the loader.

Although it would not be as harsh as what the Chosin Reservoir Marines experienced twelve months before, the second winter still was colder than most of the Flame Tankers were used to. However, Marines now had pretty good cold weather gear—insulated parkas, insulated half coveralls (vest-like top). Most important were the new "Mickey Mouse" thermo boots, developed by the Marine Corps after the disastrous experience with the crappy shoepacs Gyrenes, and soldiers, wore during the push to and from the Chosin.

The new thermo boots, which resembled the shoes worn by Walt Disney character Mickey Mouse, were rubber on the outside and insulated between the rubber and interior lining. With only one pair of wool socks, feet were always warm. Even if ice or snow got inside them, it didn't take long to dissipate from heat within the boot. Even when the

Marine was not active (walking) these things did not lose their warmth.

Frostbite and frozen feet were a tremendous problem during the first winter's fighting in Korea. The shoepac was just plain lousy. Feet would sweat, and when guys would stop walking—or even while they were walking—in the near-zero or subzero climate, the lack of proper insulation allowed the cold air to penetrate. Sweat would become ice inside the boot. Those shoepacs took a tremendous toll on Marines coming back from the Chosin in snow and bitter cold.

Most of the Marines in Korea during the second winter were spending their second Christmases away from home—the first was in boot camp at Parris Island or San Diego. But for some Catholic Marines, there was a chance to attend Christmas Day Mass celebrated by Francis Cardinal Spellman, the well-known vicar from New York City, who was touring Korea for the holidays. Flame Tankers of Catholic persuasion had an advantage being in the rear. It was possible for them to get to mass almost every week at Camp Tripoli, the division CP at Mago-ri, which was a little more than seven miles down the MSR (main supply route) from the First Tank Battalion C.P.

The Marine Corps always did its best to make the holidays special for the troops—even if they were on line. For Christmas, there was dinner with all the fixings, just like Thanksgiving, and the Marine Corps Birthday (10 November)—turkey with mashed potatoes and cranberry sauce. This also went for the infantry on the lines. They'd be relieved and pulled out of the bunkers and trenches for an hour or so to enjoy the holiday meal in a warmed mess tent behind the MLR. Once the war went static and front lines were fairly stable, the infantry also got hot meals regularly, coming down from their bunkers to areas on the reverse slopes to eat trucked-in hots.

Yet it was hard to beat the duty the Flame Platoon had been pulling since midsummer. But with the new year coming in, that was all about to change.

Hill 1052—The Rock, Luke the Gook's Castle

"Hill 1052" was an enigma to the Marines—and Army—long before, and long after, the Flame Platoon of Headquarters Company, First Tank Battalion, First Marine Division had its brief but chilling experience with it.

Terrain in military parlance, and maps, is a series of rises and depressions. Hills and mountains, on military maps, are identified by their highest point above sea level. Thus, Hill 1052 is 1,052 meters—that's on the plus side of 3,450 feet—above sea level. Nearby peaks in the mountains of East-Central Korea topped off on Hill 980, Hill 812, Hill 1000, Hill 758, and Hill 800—all considered prime positions for combat units, until compared with 1052, which was crawling with North Korean People's Army looking down on Marines.

Hill 1052 never was taken by U.N. troops after the "slow down" late in 1951. Had the war not been one of defensive positions when that granite knob became an issue, it could have been secured by Marines. It would have been at greater cost of lives than what was paid in the cat-and-mouse maneuvering while the Marines were up there during the second year of the war. If United Nations forces had been in an aggressive mode, Hill 1052 could have been stormed and taken, or encircled and isolated, by advancing troops.

But that was not the situation when Marines first encountered Hill 1052 in September of 1951 during the last real offensive by the United Nations forces. The war then, because of the Truce Talks, was beginning to phase into probing patrols and relatively status quo MLRs. Marines and soldiers died, but not nearly as many as North Koreans and Chinese who were killed. Yet there was no appreciable land exchange from mid-summer 1951 until the truce was settled in the summer of 1953.

> *Marine operations were still limited by the EUSAK [Eighth United States Army in Korea, which commanded U.N. military units] "cease fire" directive which went into effect for a month on 27 November 1951 in accordance with a decision reached during the armistice negotiations at Panmunjon. . . .*
>
> *When the agreement expired on 27 December, it was renewed indefinitely. Actually, it brought about few changes in the warfare of position which had replaced a warfare of movement on 20 September. Each Marine infantry regiment on the MLR continued to send out several squad-size patrols nightly for such purposes as ambush, reconnaissance, and taking prisoners. . . . (MCOinK, Volume IV)*

The First Marine Division was responsible for a thirteen-and-one-half-mile section of Line Minnesota, with Hill 812 the centerpiece. From there it stretched northeast to beyond Hill 884, where a ROK [Republic of Korea] army unit was responsible. To the southwest from 812, Marines were charged with a meandering line extending through Hill 758 to Hill 800 above the northwest corner of the Punch Bowl.

Hill 1052 was near the eastern extremity of the NKPA-held Kanmubong Ridge, a seven-to-eight-mile-long crag of mountains. Kanmubong Ridge extended on a southeasterly line toward Hwanggi, a small town at the apex of Line Minnesota, which in September of 1951 was EUSAK's MLR. Hill 1052 was about five miles directly above the northeastern rim of the Punch Bowl.

When Marines first took on 1052—which was topped by a granite knob about twelve feet high—in the fall of 1951, NKPA troops were dug in through a series of tunnels. The

Gyrenes were calling it "the Rock." By the time five flame tanks got up there in late January 1952, after North Korean snipers had become very adept at picking off Marines, it was not-so-affectionately known as "Luke the Gook's Castle."

From the time the first elements of the Fifth Marines encountered fire from Hill 1052 early in the morning of 18 September 1951, until the area was turned over to the Army—when the First Marine Division was disengaged from East Central Korea and sent to the west coast—"the Rock" was every bit a deadly piece of mountaintop. It was a menace to any troops opposing it.

The night of 18-19 September (1951) passed in comparative quiet, but at daylight the enemy on Hills 980 and 1052 was still looking down the throats of the 2/5 (2nd Battalion, 5th Marine Regiment). None of the participants will ever forget a landmark known simply as "the Rock"—a huge granite knob athwart the ridgeline [Kanmubong Ridge] approximately 700 yards west of Hill 812. Only 12 feet high [the knob above the rest of the ridge], its location made it visible from afar. The Marines outposted the top and eastern side [of the ridge], while the enemy held tenaciously to the western side. Along the northern slope of the ridge leading west to The Rock were the only positions affording protection to the dug-in forward elements of the battalion. . . .

Again, on 19 September, 2/5 incurred most of the casualties reported by the Division. . . .

NKPA action was confined to incessant long-range fire during the daylight hours of the 19th, but at 0315 the following morning the enemy made a desperate effort to retake Hill 812. After a brief, but intense mortar and artillery barrage, North Koreans in at least company strength came pouring around the north side of the Rock to attack with grenades and burp guns at close range. [The burp gun was the staple weapon of the NKPA. It was something like Thompson submachine gun, but Russian-made, and was called Burp Gun by U.S. troops because of the burp-like sound it made when it was fired. It was deadly]. The left platoon of Easy Company counterattacked, but was pushed back by superior numbers to positions on the left flank of the hill.

The enemy immediately took possession of evacuated ground which enabled him to fire into the front lines of Easy Company. At 0500, another Marine counterattack began . . . . The surprise was too much for enemy troops who hastened back to their own side of the Rock, leaving 60 counted dead behind.

This was the last action of a battle that had occupied all three Marine regiments from 11 to 20 September . . . Three of the four Division objectives had been secured after savage fights, but Objective CHARLIE, the ridgeline [Kanmubong] northwest of Hill 1052 . . . had yet to be attacked when Division OpnO [Operations Order] 26-51 put an abrupt stop to offensive movement.

Not only was the fight west of Hill 812 the last action of the 1st Marine Division's nine-day battle; it was the last action of mobility for Marines in Korea. As time went on, it would become more and more apparent that 20 September 1951 dated a turning point in the Korean conflict. On that day the warfare of movement came to an end, and warfare of position began. (MCOinK, Volume IV)

Thirty-five Marines were killed and 235 wounded during those three days mentioned above. But most of the casualties were incurred by 2ndBat5th, which was exposed to the Rock.

So, "warfare of movement came to an end, and warfare of position began," but despite toning down of action, Marines still were going to die.

Marines, for the most part in the winter of 1952, were dug into a series of trenches and bunkers along Line Minnesota, the forward-most nub of which was Hill 812. It stuck out, thumb-like, at the eastern end of the Kanmubong Ridge and looked west right at 1052. The two strongholds were less than a thousand yards apart—peak to peak. A couple of hundred yards to the southwest of 812, was Hill 758, another thumblike extension which was also face-to-face with Luke's Castle. The North Koreans also held Hill 980, northeast of 812 about 500 yards out, but that mound was not nearly so menacing a problem to the Marines as "the Rock."

What had been going on between the end of September 1951 and late in January of 1952 when Flame Tankers got their first look at Luke the Gook's Castle was consistent harassing, and deadly, sniper fire from Hill 1052. It appeared Division was going to try anything, short of a full-scale infantry assault, to get those Gooks out of there.

> . . . Its base was a maze of trenches and bunkers, and the . . . granite knob could have been taken only at an excessive cost in casualties. Although this bastion was hit repeatedly by almost every type of supporting ordnance, it was never completely destroyed nor denied to the enemy. (MCOinK, Volume IV)

Then why not try flame tanks with their searing spurts of flaming napalm to torch the NKPA and convince Luke to vacate the Castle? That type of warfare had worked in the islands of the Pacific during World War II, when the Japanese were so difficult to extract from caves. Why not try here in Korea? Everything else had been thrown at Luke the Gook, including a relentless barrage of artillery, naval gunfire, and air attacks on "the Rock" in honor of the Marine Corps birthday on 10 November 1951.

> A note of grim humor crept into proceedings on 9 November. Division OpnO 50-51 directed that all supporting arms and weapons commemorate the Marine Corps Birthday the next day by firing a TOT [Time on Target—an artillery order calling for all guns to time their fire so that projectiles will hit the target simultaneously] on Hill 1052, the key enemy observation point overlooking the friendly sector. While the cruiser USS Los Angeles contributed naval gunfire, the Commanding General of 1st MAW [Marine Air Wing] . . . led an air strike of 83 Marine planes [mostly gull-winged Corsairs] to blast this enemy strong point.
>
> The performance was embellished on the 10th when Marine tanks, mortars, and machine guns added their fire to the grand crescendo of exploding shells and bombs. The Communists were also bombarded with 50,000 leaflets inviting them to the Marine birthday dinner that evening. (MCOinK, Volume IV)

All that ordnance on 10 November couldn't roust the North Koreans from Hill 1052. For the next four months, Gook snipers continued to cut down Marines, who dared venture from the safe confines of the bunkers and trenches on the perimeter of Hill 812.

January 1952 had been cold and bitter much of the time, temperatures in the teens and below, and a lot of snow had fallen. M/Sgt. Grady Turnage, who became platoon leader of the nine flame tanks the previous fall, had been pushing the brass to get his platoon involved in the war. Like most of the other tankers in the Flame Platoon, M/Sgt. Turnage was getting weary of sitting around battalion doing nothing more than training and taking a lot of guff from senior NCOs in the gun companies about being a pogey bait Marine.

When the continuing problem with Luke's Castle finally got Division brass frustrated enough, Turnage's steady badgering of his superiors to activate the Flame Platoon evidently got up the ladder and struck a chord. On 17 January 1952, Turnage was told by Maj. Walter "Mu Mu" Moore, First Tank Battalion executive officer, to get two sections of flame tanks up to the battalion forward C.P. to join Charlie Company for planned operation to support the 2nd Battalion of the 1st Marine Regiment.

Cpl. Patrick "Packy" Wassell, the tall, lanky tank commander of F22, came barging into the second section's squad tent. "Five of our flame tanks are going to be sent forward for some kind of a mission," he said with a broad smile on his face. Wassell was doing his best to keep the satisfaction he was feeling from overflowing. Like most of the other Flamers, he was more than happy he finally was going to get to do something in Korea other than training runs and testing the equipment.

This was not going to be a training mission. "The real thing!" he said, looking at Jack Carty, his driver. "And we're taking '22' up there."

Wassell hadn't the slightest idea what was going on, only that *The Roamin' Candle* would be one of the flame tanks. When the official word came down from M/Sgt. Turnage, the group would be led by Sgt. Chuck Wager, the platoon sergeant in F32. Also going along were Cpl. George "Corky" Manfull's F33, Cpl. Roger Davis' F21, and Cpl. Jim Waltz' F13.

Finally!

They'd all been looking forward to this, and most of the guys were genuinely glad to get the chance. But once the excitement of the news settled down, reality set in. There was a ripple of trepidation that comes with knowing you're about to go into combat, particularly the first time. These guys had been in Korea long enough to know what was going on up there. This war was no game. They had no illusions about any gung-ho crap, yet they had their fill of sitting around behind the lines. There was enough naïveté among them, however, that the chance to get their two cents' worth into this war was overriding their qualms. The guilt complex of having been sitting out the war in the rear was about to go away.

Bright and early on 18 January, the five of flame tanks were on their way up the MSR to the Charlie Company C.P., accompanied by two Service Company Shermans equipped with dozer blades. There was an unspoken air of satisfaction in *The Roamin' Candle* that morning. With the sun glistening off the snow, Cpl. Jack Carty pulled F22 into the line of flame tanks, and they rolled out of the platoon tank park at the First Tank Battalion C.P. in Pyongchong to join the small convoy on the MSR.

Cpl. Packy Wassell was in the turret with PFC Jack MacGregor, the loader. Assistant driver PFC Alvin Chalk was across from Carty in his usual spot where he also would man the bow machine gun.

Wassell and Carty had made corporal the same time the previous November. They weren't tight friends, but they were friends. Wassell had a little more time in Korea than his driver, and when Sgt. Len Martin rotated out and the T.C. job opened, the Californian's seniority in land put him in the No. 1 hatch. Although he was the tank commander and had to take responsibility for the machine and everybody in it, Wassell never pushed his "command" rank. Wassell-Carty-Chalk-MacGregor made a pretty good crew.

After about a four-mile drive to the forward C.P. at Sugong-ri, two of the Charlie M46 Pattons pulled ahead of the small convoy and began leading the way further north. It had snowed heavily a few days prior, and the sub-freezing temperatures had kept most of it where it fell. But as flame tanks left C.P. and ground their way up the MSR, the roadway was beginning to take on a brownish hue.

There were no paved highways in that part of Korea. MSRs, which had to be kept operable because of the importance of running supplies to forward units, were maintained dirt or gravel roads, mostly just wide enough for two six-by trucks to pass in opposite directions in rear areas. Put a tank on one of those roads and it could get a little hairy for a six-by coming the other way, particularly if one of the vehicles is running on the outside of a mountain pass.

Of course, the tracks from the tanks were churning up the snow. And the more the thirty- and forty-ton pigirons that passed over the road, the deeper their tracks clawed into the packed snow, eventually getting down to the frozen roadbed and pulling up its remnants to turn the residue a dirty brown.

For a few minutes, Carty's mind wandered a little bit. "From the time we left Pusan to join our units the previous July, and the more I saw of East-Central Korea, the more impressed I was with its beauty," he said. "Step back and look past the ugliness of war and what it was doing to these poor Orientals—and our guys—and you would see beautiful green mountains and rolling streams in the summer. Once, while we were swimming in the Soyang-Gang late that first summer, I looked across the water into a gorgeous rising mountain and thought: This really would make a beautiful vacation spot some day."

As the tanks were moving forward in the lowlands between the hills toward the front lines, Carty glanced into the scenic snow-covered mountains and briefly pictured the Land of the Morning Calm fit for a postcard. "What a ski resort this place would make," he thought. "Then, I looked at the rear end of the F-21 and down at the brown fluff it was churning up, and I was back to reality. Korea was not such a nice place to be this particular morning."

About an hour and a half into the drive, Wassell came over the intercom: "Hey, you Irish jerk! The lieutenant just called back and told me to get the damn flags down."

Carty had forgotten all about the pennants he had attached to each radio antennae. Dan "Sully" O'Sullivan, the young Bronx Irishman who had become one of his best friends after they met during tank training at Camp Delmar, had given 22's driver two flags about 10x14 inches each. One was the green, white, and orange Irish national flag, and the other was Kelly green with a yellow leprechaun and *Erin Go Bragh* (Ireland Forever) printed on it.

"What the hell you trying to do," Wassell cracked, "make it real easy for the Gooks to zero in their mortars?"

While most of the early journey was in defilade among the hills, the antennae would get above the natural concealment of the terrain sometimes. Although the rods were very thin and very difficult to see from a distance, a couple of rags waving from them could make a Gook's eyes light up. Then, he might light up the area pinpointed by the flags.

Wassell knew very well he had forgotten them, too, although they were whipping in the wind on bowed fiberglass rods behind the T.C. in the turret. Finally, he and MacGregor just turned in their hatches, bent the flexible antennae toward them, and untied the two pennants.

Where possible, tankers always traveled head and shoulders out of the hatches, rather than close the "lids" and use the periscopes. Visibility was much better, and so was the air because fumes from the engines usually crept into the hull. Although on a morning like this, the icy wind bit pretty hard into the exposed faces, but it was worth it not to be buttoned.

The small convoy finally made it up to Hill 758, which was under bright sun, about mid-morning. At the time, the Flame Tankers didn't know the number of the hill. In fact, they didn't know anything. They never had heard of "the Rock," "Luke the Gook's Castle," or "Hill 1052." They didn't even know what the "planned operation" was until they got there. Then, they were told that the flame tanks would be sent out on a ridge to try to throw some napalm on a hill where the Gooks were dug in.

The granite knob of Luke's Castle was to the west of the Easy Company, 2ndBat-1stMar position about a couple of hundred yards. From Hill 758, where Fox Company infantry were dug in, the knob was more northwest. However, where the North Koreans were holed up on the slopes, was only a couple of hundred yards out.

There was only one approach to the Gook positions. It was a narrow ridge that was just about wide enough in most places to span the tracks of a tank. The ridge went out for about 100 yards and then turned left, northwest, toward the Castle on Hill 1052. The sides of the ridge dropped off about 200, 300 feet in spots. A less severe slope was at the end of it—in front of the NKPA position. The end of that part of the ridge was about 100 yards across a small valley from the slopes of the Castle.

The brass had a plan, but it never developed the way it was supposed to. It was time for some old Marine Corps S.O.P.—*hurry up and wait!*

Snow, and what appeared to be some upper-level procrastination, put the operation on hold for a couple of days. And while they were waiting, nobody ever bothered to warn the Flame crews that there were snipers on that hill who were crack shots and just delighted using Marines as targets.

"We walked around behind the hill like we were still back in Battalion C.P.," Cpl. Carty said. "It didn't occur to us right then that there were very few guys from Fox Company, manning 758, exposing themselves like us 'cherry' tankers. We were below the reverse slope of the MLR, but never took into consideration there were areas where a sniper might have found an open shot."

Luke the Gook, however, would welcome the new tankers when the time came. It was 23 January—a Wednesday—when the show finally got on the road.

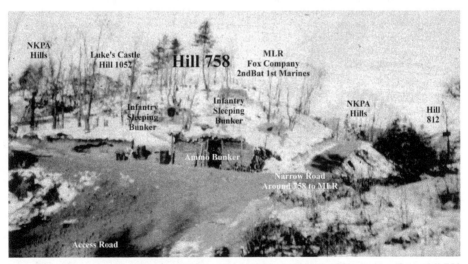

Five flame tanks spent the better part of two weeks in late January 1952 working from Hill 758 when they were tasked to "warm" Luke the Gook's Castle with shots of napalm. (Photo Jack Carty)

One Marine's Description

Cpl. C. S. "Cautious" Crawford, like a lot of the Marines looking across the valley at the enemy fortress, got to know Luke the Gook fairly well. Crawford was a forward observer with a 4.2 mortar company working with Easy Company of the 2nd Battalion 1st Marines on Hill 812, a few hundred yards northeast of Hill 758, during the winter of 1952.

The 4.2s were the big daddies of the Marine mortar arsenal. They actually were 106 millimeters in diameter, which equates to 4.2 inches across the base. The four-point-two was easier to say than 106mm. But Jarheads, being what they are, called it a "Four Deuce," and it was better known by that name. It had a range of more than 7,000 yards.

In his capacity for calling in havoc on the North Koreans, Crawford spent a lot of time on those hills facing Luke the Gook. The FO witnessed so much of Luke's lethal shenanigans and the constant pressure and futility Hill 1052 put on Marines, it lodged in his mind. He knew their frustration, and the ever-present danger he and the infantry faced from the Rock's snipers. C. S. Crawford would become an author and write *The Four Deuces*, a chronicle of his experiences in Korea.

This is how Crawford introduced the nemesis of Luke the Gook:

It took the first dead grunt to make believers out of the rest of Easy Company. We had been told about Luke and Luke-the-Gook's Castle first thing that late December morning, some four hours before the first man became a casualty. . . . It was almost as if Luke the Gook had waited for the pink of dawn's early light to shoot out the lights of a red-eyed grunt. The Easy Company rifleman died with a large-caliber bullet entering just below his helmet and directly above his nose. A perfect shot . . .

When we relieved grunts of the 7th Marines . . . they tried to give us the word . . . we didn't want to screw around with Luke the Gook when he was in his castle . . .

"He's got you bore-sighted [adjusting the sights of a weapon more accurately by looking down its bore, rather than through the apertures atop it] with a Russian-made 61-millimeter antipersonnel and antitank rifle. You better move fast in the trench line on the eastern side of the hill, and you better keep your ass way down because he shoots through sandbags," was the word that had been passed on to us. . . .

Crawford described Luke the Gook's Castle:

In a great outcropping of granite halfway up the slope . . . a mountain area to our front owned and operated by the North Korean People's Army, an area of unyielding firmness and endurance, the gooks had enhanced natural characteristics of the terrain with man-made entrenchments. Their sniping holes were constructed of logs and sandbags impregnably positioned in and around the hard igneous rock. They had constructed killing spots on the living mountain. The name Luke-the-Gook's castle would come to signify to us a keep for killing, a tower of terror. . . .

Fortunately, our fighting holes were protected, covered over with planks and sandbags. Unfortunately, the slug from the 61mm sniper gun could pass through one sandbag and still kill. Getting to the fighting holes during the daylight hours was a real man-killing proposition. . . .

Snipers usually are well-concealed marksmen who shoot from a range of 250 to 300 yards. Generally, the sniper is used as a harassing element, shooting a single, sometimes a second aimed and directed shot at a selected target from a hidden position. The sniper, after firing, normally moves quickly to another preselected position and perhaps fires again. . . .

Luke the Gook, it was a different story. He used three well-protected holes, and no amount of rifle, machine gun, mortar, or artillery rounds was going to hurt him. Like a turtle, Luke the Gook would pull back into his protective shell and wait out return fire. All we were really doing with the return fire was giving relief to our frustrations while diminishing our ammunition supply. . . ."

Would a hot shot of sizzling napalm from one of the Flame Platoon tanks do what riflemen, mortars, artillery, even those monster shots from the USS *Los Angeles,* and later the USS *New Jersey,* could not do? It was worth a try—or was it?

Naturally, the closer the convoy of flame tanks, Charlie Companies M46s, and the Service Company dozers got to the lines that mid-January day in 1952, the narrower, more primitive, and steeper the roads became. When they reached the Fox Company sector, there was a comparatively leveled-out area on the backside of Hill 758. The Flame Tankers figured engineers, or dozer tanks, had carved it out after the hill had been secured by Marines for the final time. There was an ammunition bunker dug into the corner of it. The uppermost part of Hill 758 was about thirty or forty feet above the flat area.

The clearing on the right (east) was larger, and there was a mess bunker shielded by another small hill. That's where the infantry could come off the line if hot meals were sent forward, as they occasionally were after the war became more positional. However, there were a lot of C Rations consumed on the line, or in three sleeping bunkers—heated by kerosene stoves—which were built along the back of 758 above an ammo cave dug into the reverse slope.

That was a sobering thought—sleeping above a storage hole filled with ammo.

The forward nub of Hill 758 stuck out like the end of a thumb, jutting northwest near the eastern end of the Kanmubong Ridge. Actually, it was a bunkered and trenchline area on the Hayes Line. Fox Company occupied the trenchline and bunkers on the forward slope of the hill. They were dug in about ten feet below its highest point and wrapped around what could be imagined as the edge of the thumb's fingernail. The trenchline was topped with sandbags and logs that had shooting holes (or slits), like the ones Crawford talked about.

The road up the eastern side of 758 to the MLR, was a gradual serpentine gravel and dirt path gouged from the side of the hill. About 100 yards, in Cpl. Jack Carty's rough estimation, it angled a little northwest and was just wide enough for a tank. There were two lees cut in it, the forward-most one at the base of the "thumbnail" just before it swung around the tip to the MLR. All along the right side of the road was a sharp drop into a valley.

At the base of 758 along the MLR, there was a clearing where it met the ridge extending north and west to Luke the Gook's Castle. There was room for only one tank to navigate a tight, guided turnaround—or for two tanks to sit closely side by side. "Thank God that turnaround was there," Carty admitted, although the clearing and most of the road were exposed to Luke's Castle, or to the NKPA on Hill 980, just west of Hill 812. "That road had to be cut just for tanks—the wider M46s—to access a firing line from clearing," Cpl. Carty thought. "It was not prudent to risk taking a truck up that road."

Soon enough, it would be the avenue forward for the flame tanks.

Jutting out from the turnaround was *the* ridge, just about wide enough in most places to support the tracks of a tank. "We were told engineers cleared trees from the path our tanks were supposed to follow," Carty said. "But that was wide-open no man's land, and from the way the logs were splintered and strewn around, we kinda figured the Pattons with those 90s did the demolition."

The ridge dropped off sharply on both sides. It stretched north about 75 to 100 yards before it turned more westerly heading directly at Luke the Gook's Castle. The westerly extension was maybe another 200 yards or so.

But before any of the flame tankers got a good look at the situation, four days would pass, and all they could do was wonder what the hell was going on. The crews would shuffle back and forth from their tanks sitting behind 758 to the Fox Company C.P., a few hundred yards down the access road. "Any night we remained with the tanks," Carty said, "the crews pulled two-hour watches in the turrets of the Shermans. *The Roamin' Candle* was parked astride the mess and warm-up bunker and shielded from the northern and western hills."

There were no hot meals then, different for the tankers, but S.O.P. for the infantry. "It was an eerie feeling that first night," 22's driver said. "Bitter cold. Had to be down in single digits, or below zero. But I didn't dare let myself complain. Hell, the guys in the trenches were going through this crap every night, months on end. We were just up there a couple of nights."

Flame Tankers always stood watch at battalion, but this first night on the line was a hell of a lot different. Carty would wonder, "You'd see someone coming down that road from the top of the hill, and at first, you couldn't be sure it was a Marine. But I figured if this guy was walking out in the open and some other Jarhead hadn't dropped him, he had to be friendly.

"There was a moon, and it was bright enough that we could avoid the embarrassment of challenging anyone. We figured the infantry would rather we not be there—because of the potential for incoming we could draw—and would just as well tell us to go to hell as answer a password. Fortunately, on my watch, only one guy from Fox Company came by the tank, and I could see him well enough to know that he wasn't a Gook. He needn't be challenged. He just glared up at me as he walked by with a roll of toilet paper in his hand."

A plan finally had been drawn up for the big burn, and the skinny on why the platoon was there finally trickled down to the Flame Tankers. One tank was to go out, dump a load of napalm and return—backing out. Another flame tank would follow it up the path and sit in that last lee to be ready if it was needed to help protect the lead tank. At best, it was risky because once out there, the tank charged with giving Luke the hotfoot had to come in ass backwards. That meant some very tricky driving and guidance by the tank commander from the turret.

From the start, things had been screwed up. It took four days to get it into operation because of some snow and hell knows what else, which was never made clear to any of the crews other than the one that went out on the ridge.

When the order came down for the flame tank to light up Luke's Castle, the Gooks were waiting.

Going After Luke

Charles P. "Chuck" Wager was the senior buck sergeant in the Flame Platoon. Like most of the young Marines in Korea during the second year of the war, he was relatively new to the Corps.

Yet Chuck Wager rocketed up the promotion ladder. Three months after he came out of boot camp, he made corporal. Before he was in the Corps a year, he had his third stripe. He came to the Flame Platoon, Headquarters Company of the First Tank Battalion, from the 10th Replacement Draft in July 1951. It wasn't long before he was tank commander of F32, one of the three twin-barreled Sherman M4A3E8s in the platoon's third section.

Because the Flame Platoon hibernated in the battalion C.P. most of the fall and winter, there was a general camaraderie among the crews. But Sgt. Wager kept pretty much to his own section and the friends he had among fellow sergeants, staff NCOs, and tank commanders from the other six tanks. The rest of the platoon did not get to know him very well.

His competency as a T.C., and his standing as the senior three-striper, was the reason the staff NCOs and officers of Headquarters Company put a lot of trust in him. After the Flame Platoon reached Hill 758 and plans were being developed for the strike against Luke the Gook, Wager was brought into the discussions when M/Sgt. Grady Turnage, the platoon leader, met with officers in the Fox Company command bunker on 758.

When the Flame Platoon was ordered to crank 'em up for its first combat mission since the Hwachon Reservoir and Punch Bowl skirmishes the previous spring, it was Sgt. Chuck Wager who was given command of the tank that would be used on the mission. As the plan was drawn up, Wager would hand-pick his crew and take a tank out on the ridge in no man's land. When he got to within a range of 100-to-125 yards of the trenches and bunkers on the lower slopes of Hill 1052, he was to splash a full load of 290 gallons of napalm all over the midsection of Luke the Gook's Castle. "There was a lot of confusion about who was going to get the first crack with a flame tank," he said. "I had been lobbying hard with Master Sergeant Turnage and Captain Clark." Capt. John Clark was C.O. of Charlie Company and the officer in charge of the tank missions in that area of the MLR. "Since I was the senior sergeant in the platoon, Turnage assured me that if and when a flame tank went out, I would go and I could pick the crew."

It was Wednesday, 23 January, when the word came down to send a flame tank along the ridge forward of Hill 758, and T/Sgt. Turnage kept his word. He told Wager to pick his crew and take F21 to do the job.

Like any mechanism, particularly one rigged like the POH5 flame gun, not all of them had the same range or consistency. One that had proven to be among the most reliable—getting its load delivered to maximum distance ranging more than 100 yards—was the Fire Box, Cpl. Roger Davis' F21. That was the tank M/Sgt. Turnage wanted out on the ridge, and he wanted Wager in the turret, despite the fact he was T.C. of F32.

At the time the decision was made to put the mission in motion mid-morning of the 23rd, many of the Flame crews had not yet arrived at their tanks behind Hill 758. They had spent night in one of the Charlie Company squad tents down the trail below the hill. When the word finally came down that everyone was to report to their tanks, Roger Davis was one of the guys sprinting up the access road to where the pigirons were parked.

By the time they got there, Sgt. Wager had picked his crew and F21 was revved up and slowly grinding up the narrow road on the east side of Hill 758. Cpl. George "Corky" Manfull, a fun-loving veteran of the spring offensive and T.C. of F33, was driving. Manfull's normal driver, Cpl. Ernie Whitcher, who also had been around the platoon longer than many of the other tankers, was next to him in the bow-gunner's compartment. In the turret with Sgt. Wager was Cpl. Jim Waltz, Davis' good friend and T.C. of F13. It was a crew of very competent flame tankers.

Cpl. Davis was a little surprised to see 21 already moving with Sgt. Wager standing in the tank commander's hatch. "When we finally made it up to the hill, and got to our tanks," Cpl. Jack Carty said, "the rest of us wondered what the hell was going on." Carty was the driver of Cpl. Patrick "Packy" Wassell's F22. "We figured the decision to get the mission started had been made with some urgency, and Turnage and Capt. Clark decided to go with men they had on hand," Carty said.

Davis, quiet-spoken and reserved as he was, obviously was more surprised than most of the late arrivals that his tank was moving without him—especially since it was the first combat mission for most of these tankers. But he had little choice.

Cpl. Davis did feel a little better when he saw Waltz standing in the loader's hatch. Davis, Waltz, and Carty had formed a fairly solid friendship in the six months they had been in Korea. So, seeing the Pittsburgh native in 21 helped ease what little chagrin Davis had allowed to show through his normal calm exterior.

As Manfull was slowly urging 21 up the serpentine path to the clearing, which would take them to the ridge, a Charlie Company M46 Patton pulled in behind the flame tank to provide protection. By now, the rest of the crews had arrived at the clearing behind Hill 758.

"Wassell! Get 22 ready to follow them," M/Sgt. Turnage barked. Cpl. Wassell didn't have to urge *The Roamin' Candle*'s crew to get their asses in gear. Carty thought the single-digit temperatures of the previous night would have made the F22 a little balky, but she cranked right over, and it wasn't long before he was able rev the 500 horses of the powerful engine. Alvin Chalk had jumped in the bow-gunner's compartment, and Jack MacGregor climbed into the turret with Wassell.

Slowly, Carty eased 22 up the road behind the gun tank. But before they reached the clearing out in front of Hill 758, Wassell received orders on the radio to wait in the second cutout on the east side of snow-covered mound until F21 came back off the ridge.

The guys in F22 had thought that after Wager brought 21 home, *The Roamin' Candle* would go out and dump its load of napalm on Luke the Gook. That, however, was not the plan laid out that morning. *The Roamin' Candle* was sent forward to provide added protection or help if something went wrong.

The whole idea of F21's mission was to scorch the Rock—which it had been commonly called earlier in the war—with so much napalm that Luke and his fellow Gooks would either be fried, suffocated, or sent scurrying out the back door of their fortress. The theory was to make them think seriously about ever returning to the fortress.

January 1952 had not been kind to higher elevations of East-Central Korea, particularly the Kanmubong mountain range. There had been plenty of snow and the temperature hovered near, or below zero, much of the time. On the best of days, that particular portion of the ridge itself was a nightmare. In most places it was just wide enough for a tank to creep along and keep its two tracks on something resembling level ground. It was strewn with logs jutting in every direction, remnants of lumber chopped apart by artillery, or mangled by the charges of engineers.

What little snow had managed to melt under brilliant sun when temperatures occasionally edged near twenty or thirty degrees above, had coated almost everything with a crust of ice. Cpl. Manfull had to navigate F21 about a hundred yards northwest before the ridge took a sharp left turn and meandered another couple of hundred yards west in order to get the tank within the 100-to-125-yard range of the flame gun.

"We had no problem going out on the ridge," Sgt. Wager said. "It was no roadway, that's for sure—with the trees poking every which way out of a foot of snow covering the crest. Corky did a hell of a job handling the tank. When we finally turned toward the Castle, we could see a slow dropoff through the periscopes. It was a gentle slope, not like the steep drop.

"Lt. Barry (John A. Barry, Fox Company C.O.), who knew the ridge better than any of us tankers, was watching us closely from the bunker back on Hill 758. He came on the radio and warned us not to go any further. He was concerned about being able to protect us with covering fire from the MLR."

With the downward slope of the ridge at that point, there was also the chance the tank would lose traction because of the foot-deep snow and ice that was packed under it. The combination could present a problem backing up. Wager was satisfied with the decision to start working from there and told Manfull to stop the tank. "That was fine. We were about a hundred yards from the Gooks' bunkers and we could see the Castle good from where we were." He knew he was well within range of the flame gun.

Wager was a cool customer. While Manfull was slowly guiding F21 toward the enemy hill, the tank commander had cracked open his hatch a couple of times. He had brought along a small camera and managed to snap some pictures of his target. His coolness under fire would also be a big factor over the next several hours.

Gradually, Manfull brought the Sherman to a stop. Wager and Waltz had set up the flame gun, and the tank commander started firing. Slightly arced lines of scorching fire— the size of a baseball—darted from the gun's muzzle, expanding into stream of softball proportions as it reached out to the Gook positions. The bright-orange rods of searing napalm splashed into the slopes of Luke's Castle, flaring out like a huge belch from a refinery stack.

Much faster than molten lava, it was running into the trenches and bunkers. Horrified enemy soldiers, those not yet caught in the surge of flame, bolted out of the positions that had been impregnable to artillery and mortars.

Wager traversed the turret to spread the lethal dose left to right across the NKPA trenchline and into enemy bunkers. Looking through their periscopes, the crew watched the havoc on the other side of the small valley. "We could see it go into their trenches, and the Gooks started to come out of their holes," Wager said. He continued to fire bursts of flame into the Castle, traversing from side to side and cranking the coaxial shield slightly up and down to get more coverage. After about ten minutes, the 290-gallon load of napalm was expended.

The tank commander radioed to the brass back on Hill 758 and told them he had shot his load. He was ordered to bring the tank back in.

"Let's get the hell out of here," he shouted to Manfull, who gladly revved the idling engine, double clutched, and put the tank into reverse. The shoot, so far, was a great success. It came off perfectly. Now came the tricky part.

Since there was no room to turn F21 around, Manfull was driving blind, depending on his tank commander to guide him from the turret. This wasn't quite a piece of cake for Wager, either. He kept the turret forward so he could use the 105mm cannon and the coaxial machine gun on Luke's Castle in case any surviving Gooks decided to come out of their tunnels and attack his tank.

The T.C. swiveled his periscope 180 degrees, looking out over the engine doors to the ridge behind him. Slowly, Manfull eased the Fire Box backwards. "I don't think we backed up any more than thirty or forty feet," the tank commander said. They actually made it nearly 100 yards before things suddenly went sour.

There was an explosion. The port side of F21 lifted slightly, and quickly settled hard on the ridge. Its left track had rolled on a mine, although Wager was reasonably sure he was tracing the path Manfull had used coming onto the ridge. What probably happened was the result of Gook ingenuity. The Communists would conceal a box mine deep enough to allow one or two vehicles to pass over it without detonation. When the earth had packed enough, a second, or third, vehicle's weight would be enough to eventually trigger the mine. In this case, the frozen ground could have softened enough under the warm sun, and the pressure of thirty-some tons on the-now less-firm ridge, set off the mine.

The concussion knocked the crew around, but other than being a little bruised, they were none the worse for wear. The same couldn't be said for the Fire Box. It had "thrown a shoe," its left track split apart and laid wasted in the snow. "We still have the engine," Wager quickly thought, then realized when Manfull attempted to keep it rolling that they were going nowhere with only one track.

The tank commander, after checking his crew on the intercom to see if they all were okay, radioed the command post on 758 of his situation. "I wanted to know what the plan was to get us out of there," Wager said.

There was none—at least at that stage of the situation. Time would begin to drag very slowly for the crew. "It seemed like an hour or so that we were receiving conflicting messages what to do," Wager said.

Meanwhile, Luke's Gooks, who had survived the scorching flame on Hill 1052, saw their chance to take a measure of revenge for the hot foot they had just received. They began emerging from the Castle, although the infantry on Hills 758 and 812 continued to keep up a base of small-arms fire covering the stranded tank. Still, a couple of North Korean soldiers managed to try their luck. Peering through their periscopes, the F21 crew knew things were about to get dicey. "We could see grenades being thrown at us," Wager said. Grenades weren't going to hurt them as long as the Marines were buttoned up in the tank, so they were not about to venture outside the pigiron in the near future. It was a long way back to the safety of the MLR bunkers.

Two hours after hitting the mine, they still were sitting more than a couple of hundred yards out in no man's land, without recourse to better their situation.

Cpl. Whitcher began firing the 30-machine gun from the bow. Wager thought his assistant driver was getting a little "unnerved," but Whitcher's steady raking of the Castle's bunker-line was keeping the Gooks from coming at 21 from the front. However, the hot brass, expelled from the machine gun, was beginning to pile up around the assistant driver's feet. Some of the casings bounced up his pantlegs, and he was getting burns on his legs.

When Wager saw two other North Koreans again venture toward the tank and start throwing grenades, he quickly radioed for permission to fire the 105. "We got the okay," he said, "but Captain Clark instructed us not expend over 50 percent of our marbles."

Fifty percent isn't much in a situation like that if there's only about six or seven rounds of 105 ordnance on board—the maximum a Sherman flame tank carried because the area under the turret deck where ammo normally was kept was taken up by the napalm storage tanks. But Wager made the most of it, bracketing the area with a couple of shots over and under, then sending a few rounds of HE directly into the apertures of Luke's bunkers. Wager liked the results. "We blew some logs sky high." And probably some Gooks, too.

It also looked good from the command bunker. "I guess Captain Clark could see the logs flying because he congratulated us on the firing mission."

Then, things began to get a little tense. There was some problem getting clearance on what to do with the tank. Maj. Walter MuMu Moore, the First Tank Battalion Exec, and Capt. Clark had agreed that 21 should be abandoned and then destroyed. It was to be blown to pieces by the big 90mm rifles of the Charlie Company Pattons.

The order was passed to Wager to take the crystals out of the radio, remove the firing pin from the 105, and detach the back plates from the machine guns. What the tank commander didn't know was, for some reason, the plan had to be run up the ladder—sent back to battalion for approval. That took time. Battalion sent it up to Division. More time.

From what Wager was told, Division turned it down. The tank was not to be destroyed if at all possible.

Lt. Col. Holly H. Evans, commanding officer of the First Tank Battalion, radioed his exec that an attempt must be made to recover the tank. By then, it had been more than three hours since F21 had hit the mine. Once the decision was made not to abandon the Fire Box, Major Moore and Captain Clark quickly put another plan into operation.

Sitting in the upper lee along the east side of 758, wondering what the hell was taking so long to come up with a rescue plan, the crew of *The Roamin' Candle* had long since gotten fidgety about their fellow tankers. They had been monitoring some of the activity over their headsets. They heard the big explosion earlier and immediately became more concerned when Wager told the command post that something had rocked the tank.

"It was hard to imagine what was going on out there," Carty said. Still, it really hadn't registered on the crew of F22 that they were right on the edge of it. "We hadn't grasped the gravity of danger we were in. It never occurred to us sitting there—all of us shoulder-high out of our hatches—that the Gooks very well could drop some pretty heavy ordnance on our position." Surely, the NKPA had Hill 758 and every square yard around it preregistered with its mortars and artillery.

"We could hear the rifle and machine gun fire, but until then, there was no heavy incoming," Carty said. "Maybe it was because we felt safely tucked in that lee. We just didn't realize at the time that we could be hit." It wouldn't be long before they would be jarred to reality.

It was somewhere around 1500 when Maj. Moore and Captain Clark got the ball rolling. Cpl. Packy Wassell received orders to move F22 out of the lea and get it up to the clearing in front of the Hill 758. *The Roamin' Candle* would be used with a Service Company Sherman retriever as a tandem to attempt towing the wounded F21 and its crew off the ridge. Charlie Company already had sent out one of its Pattons to cover the operation. On the way out, the Charlie tank hit a mine. However, that blast just beat up two road wheels, and the Patton continued toward the disabled flame tank.

Meanwhile, Wager still didn't know what the hell was going on. He, Manfull, Whitcher, and Waltz had been sitting out there for more than four hours. Through the periscope of the tank commander's hatch, Wager could finally see the Patton easing its way out on the ridge. It got a few yards from 21 and stopped. Since the radio in the flame tank had been shut down, there was no way to make contact with the gun tank.

But nothing was happening on the Patton. It just sat there. No one got out of the M46, and there was no signal of any kind coming from it. Wager decided he had to take a chance. He opened his hatch and climbed out of 21, making a beeline for the rescue tank to see what the plan was. He wouldn't get much help.

He made it safely to the Charlie tank and got up on the engine compartment, crouching behind the turret, hoping it would keep him out of view of the Gooks in the Castle. "I pounded on the hatch," he said, anger building in his voice. "The tank commander, a warrant officer, wouldn't open the lid."

Wager jumped off the gun tank and clamored back to the 21. A half-hour later, still fuming over the Patton's T.C., he decided to go back to the gun tank. His frustration would grow. "I got up on the back of that tank about six times," Wager said. "Finally, he cracked open his hatch. That's when I finally learned we weren't going to abandon our tank. They were going to try to tow us back in."

With that plan in the works, the 21 crew was told to put the crystals back in the radio and reactivate its weapons. Fortunately, the tank's battery was still strong, and Wager was able to renew communication with the command post on Hill 758.

Wager had thought the Patton was there to hook a cable to F21 as well as deliver the message of the impending rescue. "No one would get out of the gun tank to hook up a cable," Wager said angrily.

It was about 1600 when a Service Company Sherman retriever finally backed out to do the tow, and the Charlie gun tank remained there to provide cover. Sgt. Wager came out of his turret, and Cpl. Manfull opened his driver's hatch and climbed out to help the Service Company guys hook up the cables.

The North Koreans, naturally, were waiting for the Marines to bring more equipment into harm's way, and started laying in mortars and artillery from Hill 1052 and Hill 1161, which was west of Luke's Castle. Somehow, the tankers completed the cabling before running like hell to get back in their hatches and button up as incoming mortar and artillery became more intense.

Meanwhile, as Cpl. Carty drove *The Roamin Candle* up the final fifty or sixty-so yards around the hill to the clearing in front of the MLR, the sound of heavy incoming couldn't be ignored. By the time Wassell's tank had reached the clearing, Major Moore had ordered the retriever out. Wassell was told to keep F22 in the clearing until the Sherman retriever hooked up to the stricken F21.

"Maybe it was because we had never been under fire before," Carty said, "but we still had not lowered our seats and pulled down the lids of our hatches. For some reason, the imminence of the danger we were in hadn't taken hold. When a couple of Service

Company guys jumped out of the retriever and started hooking the cables to 21, we just thought it was part of their job. We were going to do the same thing if 22 was needed out there. So, what the hell!"

Then the Gooks started laying in more mortars. Real war finally made its impression on *The Roman' Candle*'s crew.

The retriever roared in first gear, and slowly 21 began to move. The retriever's powerful engine moaned as the tank dragged the wounded F21 more than a hundred yards on the ridge's straightaway. All the while the Gooks were dropping 82mm mortars on the two tanks without causing any serious damage.

But when the retriever made the turn to where the ridge went toward the clearing in front of Hill 758, the Fire Box was sliding sideways, and all of the sudden, it skidded to the left. It was near impossible to control the disabled hulk, either from inside of it, or with the tow cables. With more than thirty tons of dead weight, and only one track, there was no way it was going to stay on the narrow crown of that ridge.

That damn thing's on it's way down into the valley, Carty thought, suddenly gripped with the horror. All he could think of was those four guys being tumbled like chunks of rocks inside a cement mixer as that pigiron went ass over head 200, 300 feet down the side of the mountain. Fortunately, some pines, just off the crest of the hill, stopped the hulk, it's bottom hung up on the edge of the ridge.

By this time, Carty had begun backing F22 onto the ridge toward the now immobile sister tank. That was when Wager decided it was time to leave, and he, Manfull, Waltz, and Whitcher opened their hatches and got out of F21 as fast as they could. They weren't taking any chances going down that mountainside in an iron coffin. "We had to come out of our hatches," Cpl. Manfull said. The driver and Whitcher couldn't use the escape hatch on the floor under Whitcher's seat because it was frozen shut.

"We had passed through some streams coming up the first day," Manfull added. "We never gave it a thought then, but the water froze around the escape hatch." It was sealed tight. "There was no way we were going to get it open out there."

The four Flame Tankers clamored out of their compartments and onto the ridge and began sprinting toward *The Roamin' Candle*. How they got through some of that open ground without getting hit by snipers, stepping on a mine, or being blown away by an 82 is one of those mysteries. "They were running the races of their lives," Carty said.

Packy Wassell, the F22 tank commander, climbed out of his turret and moved down the engine doors to the back of his tank as his four friends came running toward him. He reached down to help each one of them aboard F-22. "It was pretty hard getting up on that tank in a hurry," Wager said. "The snow on our Mickey Mouse boots (thermo boots) made it slippery as hell on that cold steel. I'm sure glad Packy was there to help hand us up on the back of that pigiron."

Finally, they were all up on the back of the tank, and Wassell got back in the turret. "Man, we were glad to hear from Packy that those guys were aboard," Carty said.

The F22 driver wasted little time getting *The Roamin' Candle* on its way toward the MLR. Fortunately, none of the tankers, exposed as they were, got hit by incoming, and it wasn't long before the four nomads were scampering up the side of Hill 758 to the safety of Fox Company bunkers.

Once back to the clearing, Wassell got orders to get 22 down the serpentine road to the safer haven behind the hill. They had unbuttoned to help get the guys off the ridge and stayed that way when the word came to get back behind the hill.

"As we were rounding the front of 758, we had begun to get more incoming from Gook mortars," Carty said. One thudded into the side of the hill above the tank. Wassell yelled, "I've been hit!"

Shit! Carty thought. *How the hell were we going to get a corpsman to him?*

The tank commander was shoulder- and head-out of the turret when a mortar crashed on the embankment. A piece of shrapnel ricocheted off the hill and nicked him below the hairline in the back of the left side of his neck. Fortunately, he wasn't hurt badly and he yelled on the intercom, "I'm okay. Just a scratch. Damn thing burns like hell."

Two Service Company tankers also took some shrapnel, but like Wassell, no serious wounds.

With a little light still left on the horizon, and the retriever still cabled to the wounded tank, there was one more attempt to tug F21 loose. But it was no use. Wedged in the trees and dug into the side of the hill, it wasn't going to budge on the power of just one other tank.

As late afternoon light faded behind Hill 1052 and the Kanmubong Ridge, Major Moore decided to secure the retrieval for the night and come back the next day to try to get the wounded tank off the ridge.

The day's unit diary would record that 200 rounds of 82mm and 120mm mortar fire had rained down on the vicinity of the recovery operation. A price was exacted. Wassell and nine others were wounded. One of them was Major Moore, a veteran of the Pacific campaigns in World War II. He would receive his second Purple Heart after taking some shrapnel from incoming up on Hill 758.

The Flame Platoon "cherries" had tasted combat for the first time, and it was a scary education—once they came to the realization of what was going on out there. "Not having ever been exposed to anything like that," Carty reasoned, "I wouldn't say we were cocky before we got up to Hill 758—naive, maybe, but not cocky. There had been no rifle or machine-gun fire, or mortars that we were aware of when we first got there a couple of days before. We knew we had arrived on the line, but without any of the sounds of war, we may have been lulled into a false sense of safety."

The Flame Tankers had been walking around—some of time exposed to the dominating Gook hills within several hundred yards of the MLR—without much regard to the reality of the situation that surrounded them. "We didn't have the slightest idea how bad this place was," Carty said. "Before things started to pop, there seemed to be no noticeable fear among us. It never entered my mind that some North Korean might be lining up my noggin in his sights."

That all changed as events unfolded on 23 January. "That afternoon was very sobering," Carty admitted. "Some of us were pretty damn stupid, but very fortunate!"

And the worst was yet to come.

"Dear John" and a First Cup of Coffee

Once again, Flame Tankers who did not have to pull guard duty around the Shermans behind Hill 758 were sent back to the Charlie Company C.P. behind the MLR to spend the night. It was left up to infantry from the First Marines Fox Company to baby-sit the disabled F21 and keep the Gooks away from it. It was made a little easier because of searchlights, which the infantry employed. They'd aim the lights into the sky—to avoid, as much as possible, giving the Gooks a direct shot into the lens—and bounce the light off the clouds.

"It lit that tank up like it was in broad daylight," said Sgt. Chuck Wager, who had taken F21 out on the ridge the day before.

Baby-sitting that tank probably wasn't very popular with the infantry that night because of the target it made for the North Koreans. However, probably because it was illuminated all night, they didn't bother it. "I'll bet the infantry really loved that detail," cracked Cpl. Jack Carty, F22's driver when the crew got the word the host Marines would have to keep an eye on the pigiron. "I'm sure we had not endeared ourselves to those guys."

It puzzled Carty why he and his crew didn't stay up there that night. "We knew we had to take *The Roamin' Candle* back up to the ridge the next day to try to get 21 out of there. I just thought it would have been better for us to stay near our tank."

But they were sent down below, and spent the night in a heated tent.

There were about six or eight of the Flame Tankers assigned to the thirteen-man squad tent, like the ones that were home to them at Battalion. Not too long after they had picked out their racks, their mail had caught up to them, and that cut into the chatter among them because they started reading letters.

Suddenly, one of the guys started hollering. He had jumped up on one of the cots and began bounding from cot to cot, cussing like mad. He was crunching a letter in his hand. Finally, he shouted angrily, "She dumped me! She dumped me!"

He had gotten a "Dear John" letter from his girlfriend. He cussed and stomped around the tent for about five minutes. The rest of the guys just kept quiet. When he finally calmed down after about ten minutes, he just went to the other end of the tent by himself. He didn't want to talk to anybody.

"I drank the first cup of coffee I ever had in my life that night," Carty admitted. "I don't know whether it was finally realizing that I had survived my first day in combat, the guy's 'Dear John,' or everything combined. After he settled down, I just walked over to the kerosene stove where one of the guys was brewing coffee and held out my canteen cup."

The next morning, all the flame crews reported to their tanks, a bit more apprehensive than they were the day before. They knew there was going to be another attempt to get F21 off that ridge, and they were well aware that Luke the Gook and his friends were not going to make it easy for them.

Wassell's *Roamin' Candle* again was ordered to go up to the clearing in front of 758 along with two Service Company Sherman retrievers and one of Charlie Company's M46 Pattons. Sgt. Chuck Wager, who had taken F21 on the flame mission the day before, hitched a ride on one of the retrievers.

Some of the Flame Tankers, not knowing Wager that well, wondered why in the hell he would want to go back out there after what he and his hand-picked crew went through the day before. But there was no way anything, outside of a direct order from one of the officers, was going make him sit out this one.

Just as determined to get in on the recovery was Cpl. Roger Davis, F21's T.C., who had waited out the previous day's drama of his tank behind the hill. He wanted in on whatever was to be done getting F21 off the ridge. Davis talked Wassell into letting him go along in the *Roamin' Candle,* so Packy told him to jump into the bow gunner's compartment. That sent PFC Alvin Chalk up in the turret with the tank commander and left PFC Jack MacGregor, 22's regular loader, odd man out.

The idea was for one of the retrievers to back out to F21, and its crew once again to cross hook cables on the disabled tank. The second retriever would do the same and hook up to the other Service Company tank. F22 was to stand by in case more help, or protection, was needed. The power of the two Sherman retrievers should have been enough to dislodge the Fire Box from the trees, drag it onto the crest, then completely off the ridge.

One of the Service Company retrievers, for some reason, got behind *The Roamin' Candle.* Unfortunately, it could not get around the flame tank, which meant F22 had to back out of the way, and then maneuver toward the access road along side of Hill 758 to make room for the passing retriever.

With 22 and the retriever sitting in that small clearing just in front of the face of 758, it was necessary for someone to arm-signal the flame tank so that Cpl. Carty could be guided while backing and turning in such a tight area. When tanks are pinched in a condensed maneuvering area, it is S.O.P. (standard operating procedure) for another tanker to stand in front and use pumping motions with his arms to guide the driver. The guide holds his arms L-shaped, forearms vertical and fists knotted at the top. He pumps the arm like a piston on the side he wants the tank to be turned. This tells the driver which brake lever to pull back and lock the selected track.

When it appeared the Gooks had stopped their mortars, Sgt. Fred Castle climbed out of the retriever waiting off to the side of F22 and started to guide Carty. They had never met, but Carty knew Castle from seeing him around Battalion.

With his arm signals, Castle had guided Carty and gotten him turned. "I was about to start 22 down the hill," Carty said after Sgt. Castle had stepped from in front of his tank, about five or six feet off to the left. "He was standing on the edge of the narrow road just opposite our left sprocket."

Jack Carty heard it coming. "There wasn't a thing I could do."

The Gooks had started lobbing in mortars—82s—and some 76mm artillery, a whoosh, and a thud—a millisecond before a tremendous explosion. This particular one hit right on the road, near *The Roamin' Candle*'s left track, a little forward of the turret. The concussion was powerful.

Carty wasn't sure what happened in those next few seconds. "Before I knew it, I was down in the tank." The drivers' spring-loaded seats had a lever on the right side which, when released, allowed the seat to rise when the body weight was taken off it—or go down if the driver remained seated, full weight, on it. It could be locked at several heights. Carty's was locked up at the time because he was driving unbuttoned. Actually, he was just about standing in the compartment to have a better view of where he was going.

When the mortar hit, the seat went down. "When I hit bottom, my hand was on the lever," Carty said, "and I was about to pop right back up to see what was going on when I realized the hatch had slammed closed above me. Whether I instinctively hit the lever when the shell hit, or it was the concussion of the blast, I don't know. But that seat went down and I went with it. It had released and dropped as low as it could."

Instinctively, the driver yanked back on the two brake levers, bringing the tank to a stop. He pushed open the hatch and quickly grabbed the seat lever, popping up through the opening above him.

"As I did, I saw Sgt. Castle," Carty said, and thought, *"My God, that poor guy."* He finally realized Castle had been wide-open to the blast of that shell.

"Roger!" Carty quickly looked right for Cpl. Davis, about to tell him to get out and help Castle. But the words weren't all out of his mouth before Davis, oblivious to his own safety, had started climbing over 22's bow.

"I could see that Castle's face was full of blood," the shaken driver said. "The entire left side of his parka and cold weather trousers were shredded."

Davis ran around the front of the tank, took one look at Castle, then at Carty, and shook his head from side to side. They both hollered "Corpsman!" about the same time. It was in vain. Sgt. Castle never knew what hit him.

The mortar had impacted the road, blasted against the tank, and threw most of its shrapnel right into the mechanic. He took a full load of the ricocheting chunks and splinters of metal, rock and dirt. It didn't take two corpsmen long to get to Sgt. Castle, but all they could do was carry him off the road and into the shelter of that lee in the side of Hill 758, which shielded them from Gook snipers.

Davis and Carty, although shaken, were unscathed. So was Wassell, who was standing in his compartment, much of the upper half of his body out of the turret and also exposed on that side of the tank.

Carty didn't realize it at first—everything happened so fast—but that open hatch lid obviously saved him from being a casualty himself. When the oval-shaped lid was open, it was hinged on the corner of the hull behind the driver's left shoulder. At that position, it was a perfect shield for his head extending out of the tank. At the angle the shrapnel took after bouncing off the side of the tank, some of it glanced off the hatch cover and rocketed up and over the driver. That same blast had hit one of the other retriever crewmen and had broken his jaw.

Meanwhile, Sgt. Wager, who had performed so bravely during the unsuccessful attempts at recovery the first day, had gotten out of the other retriever just before the shelling started.

"I was behind the dead tank," he said. "I heard that round coming in and I knew when it hit between the two tanks, it was bad because I had seen the maintenance sergeant get out of his tank."

Carty knew he was one lucky Marine. Had that thing hit *The Roamin' Candle*, or been a few feet more forward of it . . . then he thought, *The Man Upstairs was on my side that instant.*

About that time he heard someone yelling at Packy: "Get that damn tank down the road!" The engine still was running, but evidently, when Carty pulled back on the brake levers, he had yanked a little too much on the right one. *The Roamin' Candle* had banged into the side of the hill. He had to put it in reverse a little to back up before he was able to start down the road.

The death of Sgt. Castle and the serious injury to the other mechanic quickly brought the recovery attempt to a halt. Luke the Gook had exacted some measure of revenge for the scorching he had received the previous day. From his castle on Hill 1052, with some help from NKPA on 1161 further up the Kanmubong Ridge, he peppered the operation around the Marines MLR with 120 rounds of deadly 82 and 120mm mortar rounds and artillery from 76s throughout that Thursday.

The loss of the sergeant—a tanker, one of "our guys"—not only shook up the crews but had an impact on the brass. F21 sat out there on the ridge like a derelict for almost a week.

The First Marines reported two days later that they saw some Gooks near the disabled tank, and they heard two explosions. The Fox Company infantry called in some friendly mortar to chase them off.

The following Tuesday, 29 January '52, Service Company officers came up to Hill 758 and started to work on a plan to get the wounded flame tank. It was strictly their operation. They had the experience with this kind of stuff, and there was no need for outside help, so the Flame Tankers were not involved. Battalion wanted as few people out there in the open as possible.

What they did was take two of the Sherman winch-rigged retrievers up there to slowly wind that baby back in off the ridge, into the clearing in front of the MLR.

The word coming back to the anxious Flame Tankers was one of the retriever tanks went out on the ridge without incident. It got close enough to 21 for some gutsy tankers to get out and hook a cable to the back of the hulk. Then, the other retriever cross-cabled to the first one. They just used the raw power of the two Sherman's 500-horse engines to drag that unconscious giant off the ridge. It was a great demonstration of the brute strength of the M4A3 Sherman tank, because 21 was nothing but thirty-some tons of dead weight with the mangled, trackless left side bottomed out and digging into the uneven ridge the whole time it was being yanked backwards toward the MLR.

When the retrievers got F21 back to the clearing in front of the Fox Company bunkers, they stopped. Crews got out again, unhooked the cables, and the rescue tanks turned around so they could use the more powerful forward lower gears. Recabled, they just dragged the derelict down that winding road along the side of Hill 758.

Incoming during the recovery operation was neutralized somewhat because Charlie Company, the First Anti-Tank Platoon, and artillery were busy keeping the Gooks pinned down. Still, there was enough stuff impacting around the tanks to make the situation anything but ideal. Once the Service Company guys got the towlines hooked up and returned to their tanks, they buttoned up, and it was a matter of the Shermans' bull strength doing the rest.

It took awhile, but the Fire Box was slowly dragged back to the clearing that day. Later, when the Flame Tankers finally saw it being tugged down the serpentine access road and into the clearing behind 758, there was a new height of respect for those Service Company Marines. They were just doing their job, but their bravery is a story unto itself.

They do this kind of stuff all the time, Cpl. Carty realized, and nothing made it clearer than his vivid memory of Sgt. Castle. Sobering as the thought was, it made the recovery of F21 all the more important. No way could that tank have been left out there when one Marine had paid the ultimate price to get it back. "We sure were all glad to see F21 back among the rest of our tanks," Carty said. "It didn't look pretty, but the damage wasn't as bad as I had thought."

Naturally, the left track was gone—still somewhere out on the ridge. The port-side road wheels were caked with snow and mud, and it was hard to see some of the damage. The third top roller, which holds the track in place as it is being pulled forward by the sprocket, was cut in half. Oddly, the three sets of road wheels were intact. Their rubber casings were chewed up, but that could have been as much from dragging the tank as the explosion.

It seemed to some of the tankers, looking at the severe damage to the upper rollers, that it could have been a cannon shot—some 76mm artillery—that hit the tank. Maybe it hadn't backed over a mine. But Sgt. Wager was sure it was a mine. Wager should know—he was there. And that was the consensus from the command bunker the day it happened. Capt. John Clark, the Charlie Company C.O., and Lt. Barry, Fox Company C.O., had their binoculars on the F21 the whole time.

The next job was to load the hulk onto one of Service Company's flatbed trailers, which had been bought up from battalion. It took most of the rest of the day for the mechanics to winch it onto the flatbed and get it secured. The flatbed was hooked up to a good ol' six-by and hauled down off the mountain and back to Battalion.

In a couple of weeks, Cpl. Roger Davis and his 21 crew, working along with Service Company mechanics, had his tank back, and it ran as well as any of the others in the platoon.

The North Koreans laid enough mortar, artillery, and machine-gun fire on that ridge while the flame tanks were there to make it very hard for the Fox Company Marines to have any love for guys in fire-spitting pigirons.

The Flame Platoon's primary mission was a success. F21's crew had done its job, and a little more owing to the fact they got the 105 into action. The immediate aftermath, however, became a costly botched-up mess, thanks to a series of unanticipated circumstances. Overall, the truncated mission really hadn't done anything for the infantry other than draw more incoming on them.

Infantry, unless they are getting a free ride, or using tanks as shields while advancing on a target, really don't like being around them. Often they look on tanks with much disdain. They know damn well that the flame tanks were just going to put a gleam in Gook eyes. If the enemy spots a tank, the first thing he wants to do is try to pulverize it. He throws anything from artillery to rifle fire against it. If infantry is anywhere near a tank when artillery, mortar, or rifle fire is laid on a pigiron, he has very little cover.

The Flame Tankers could not have been very popular with Fox Company, particularly after they failed to completely burn out Luke the Gook. They did cause a lot of commotion for nearly two weeks, but there was a stiff price paid for it.

The tragedy was that a good Marine was lost.

Sgt. Fred Castle, a native of Dayton, Ohio, was a well-respected technician in Service Company, and quite popular with tankers from other companies. "Fred was a regular visitor to A-T5," said Sgt. John Cronin, tank commander of one of the 5th Marines anti-tank Pattons. Castle was a good friend of Sgt. Don Dennany, the AT-5 mechanic, which is part of the reason the 5th's tankers saw him a lot. They were so close, Dennany was helping Sgt. Castle study for conversion to becoming a Catholic.

"When we had problems and needed a retriever or expertise on repairing our tanks, it usually was Fred Castle who showed up," Cronin said. "He had designed a tool for pulling track end connectors. The Marine Corps liked it so much, it was going to adapt it to their maintenance program."

It could have been named the Fred Castle Tool.

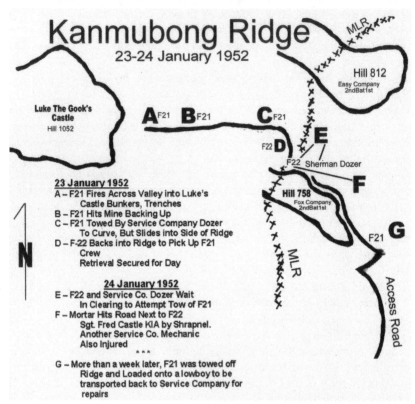

Kanmubong Ridge
23-24 January 1952

MLR

Hill 812
Easy Company
2ndBat1st

Luke The Gook's
Castle
Hill 1052

A F21   B F21   C F21

F22 D   E

F22 Sherman Dozer

F

Hill 758
Fox Company
2ndBat1st

F21 G

MLR

Access Road

N

23 January 1952
A – F21 Fires Across Valley into Luke's
      Castle Bunkers, Trenches
B – F21 Hits Mine Backing Up
C – F21 Towed By Service Company Dozer
      To Curve, But Slides into Side of Ridge
D – F-22 Backs into Ridge to Pick Up F21
      Crew
      Retrieval Secured for Day

24 January 1952
E – F22 and Service Co. Dozer Wait
      In Clearing to Attempt Tow of F21
F – Mortar Hits Road Next to F22
      Sgt. Fred Castle KIA by Shrapnel.
      Another Service Co. Mechanic
      Also Injured
              * * *
G – More than a week later, F21 was towed off
      Ridge and Loaded onto a lowboy to be
      transported back to Service Company for
      repairs

Based on a rough sketch made by Cpl. Jack Carty a few days after the Flame Platoon's burn mission at Luke the Gook's Castle, recent interviews with fellow Flame Tankers, and information gleaned from declassified First Tank Battalion diaries, Carty reconstructed the graphic of 23-24 January 1952 activity.

Anti-Tank Platoons

If flame tanks were briefly considered kid brothers in the First Tank Battalion gun companies in Korea, the A-Ts probably would have to fall into the category of stepbrothers.

Hell, they didn't even have the dignity of a letter or number identification on their turrets. Unlike the Flame Platoon's Shermans, which bore a designation F11, F12, et cetera, or the gun companies' letters (A, B, C, D followed by two numerals), the A-Ts had nothing until late in the winter of 1951. That's when one tank commander in the Fifth Marines decided his platoon needed some I.D. and numbered the tanks from one to five on each side of their turrets.

Each of the three infantry regiments had their own tank platoon, comprised of five fluid drive M46 Pattons after the Pershings had been surveyed. What better way to fend off an enemy tank coming against infantry than have a friendly pigiron monster at hand? While the First Tank Battalion gun companies always were on call to work in support of the 1st, 5th, and 7th Infantry Regiments, the A-T platoons were with their gravel-crunching fellow Marines all the time.

The A-Ts regularly worked in concert with the First Tank Battalion lettered tanks and the Flame Platoon, but their constant lot was to stick closely by their infantry units. Often they could be found dispersed among their regiment's positions as a stationary big gun on call around the clock.

It was after the Flame Platoon came off the Kanmubong Ridge in early February 1952—and the 5th Marine Regiment took over that section of the Line Minnesota from the 1st Marines—that the 5th A-Ts, under their new platoon leader, took on Luke the Gook.

There is a special breed of officers in the United States Marine Corps—former PFCs, and NCOs who come up through the ranks, showing such outstanding leadership qualities that they are recommended and later commissioned second lieutenants. "Mustang" is their proud fraternity.

Pete Clapper was a Mustang, and he frolicked with a small herd of M46 Patton tanks in the wilds along the Kanmubong Ridge shortly after the F21 left its charred calling card on Luke the Gook's Castle. It was early February 1952 when the Fifth Marine Regiment took over that part of the Minnesota Line from the 1st Marines.

That's when 2nd Lt. Pete Clapper showed up around Hill 812 commanding the 5th Anti-Tank Platoon of M46s. Like the guys who found their way in the Flame Platoon of Headquarters Company, First Tank Battalion, Lt. Clapper and a lot of his men took a similar circuitous route to the anti-tank platoons.

Clapper enlisted in the Marines in January 1945, eight months before the end of World War II. He made it through boot camp at Parris Island and then went to Camp Pendleton. There he applied for OCS and was shipped back east to Quantico. Before he could complete training for his commission, the war ended and he was discharged. "I came out a buck private, but re-upped in the Reserves."

When the Korean War broke out, Clapper was activated at Camp Lejeune in September 1950. He was a corporal by then and got into the screening course for officers at Quantico, finally earning his commission the following June. Three months later, Lt. Clapper was flown directly to Korea, where he was assigned to Able Company, 1stBat5th Marines.

While the flame tanks were becoming involved with Luke the Gook, Lt. Clapper was offered command of the five Patton tanks in the Fifth's A-T Platoon. "I jumped at the chance," he said. "Here was major firepower—and protected by beaucoup armor, too. No more hiking."

As a gold-bar infantry lieutenant, Clapper was nothing more than a high-grade gravel-cruncher, and he put in his share of snoopin' and poopin' in front of the MLR up in the rugged mountains of East-Central Korea. Suddenly at his disposal would be five 90mm rifles whose flat trajectory, high velocity, and long range made them fearsome weapons indeed. *The Communists had nothing to compare with those guns,* he thought. *Awesome!*

Of course, he soon learned that as an A-T platoon leader, it was up to him to find out where to have his tanks fire, and often that meant more snoopin' and poopin' out in no man's land boondocks.

Pete Clapper was no dummy. He knew a good enlisted man was worth his weight in gold. Two of them were a bonus. Clapper naturally had his first sergeant, S/Sgt. Gerald Ford, but he also latched on to Sgt. John Cronin, the tank commander of the No. 2 Patton in the platoon. Cronin, a native of East Los Angeles, California, had been in Korea since the previous September, and like many A-T Marines, he had not arrived as a tanker. He was an 0300—infantry—by default.

Fresh out of boot camp he was sent to Camp Delmar for training as an Amtrac—amphibious tractor, or LVT (Landing Vehicle Tractor)—mechanic. The weekend before he was to start training, he was clipped by a car while hitchhiking on California's infamous Highway 101.

When PFC Cronin got out of the hospital, he was sent back to Pendleton, took infantry training, and headed for Korea with the 12th Replacement Draft. In the web that only the Marine Corps can weave, he was told he was going to A/T5. "What's A/T5?" he muttered to himself, completely befuddled by the lingo often crafted in a war zone.

"We arrived at the A/T5 C.P., and for the first time in my life I saw a tank—five of them," Cronin said. He became the loader, low man on the totem pole, in Tank No. 2, eventually worked his way down to the bow as driver, picking up his corporal stripe along the way, and then became T.C. as well as Sergeant. By the time Lt. Clapper arrived on the scene, Sgt. Cronin was a veteran tanker. He was also the proud anti-tank sergeant who wanted to identify his unit. "I personally painted the numbers, one through five, on our 46s."

Later that year the numeral "5" preceded each of the single digits which identified the platoon as being attached to the 5th Marines. He expected the A-Ts from the 1st and 7th Regiments would follow suit. "We heard Clapper was a stickler for details and we might have to change our ways a little," Sgt. Cronin admitted. "A year or two older than the rest of us, we knew he had done a short stint with the infantry."

When he arrived at the tank platoon, the lieutenant had a bandage on his cheek. "We didn't think it was necessary, although we heard he had been nicked by a burp gun," Cronin said. "He was a little guy with red hair and a handlebar mustache. Banty Rooster was the nickname we settled on."

The guys in the tank platoon had heard the lieutenant's father was a well-known war correspondent during World War I, and the new platoon leader's prized possession was a German Lueger pistol his dad had brought back from Europe. Tankers were issued the standard Colt 45-caliber pistol.

"We weren't supposed to carry personal weapons, but this was one rule Clapper was not going to abide by," Cronin said. "Otherwise, he did keep us on our toes." And his platoon soon decided he was an "all-right guy."

Cronin described Hill 812 somewhat like the Flame Tankers saw the terrain around Hill 758 a few weeks earlier: "There was plenty of snow on the ground, and if we humans weren't up there disturbing things, it would have been a solid blanket. The entire reverse slope of 812 and the forward slopes of the hills behind it were covered with black craters—like a moonscape. Not a tree was standing, only stumps."

When AT/5 first arrived at 812, Lt. Clapper looked at the sergeant, who felt his C.O. already knew the answer to the question he was asking. "Do you think we can get our tanks up here, Cronin?"

"Oh, sure," Cronin replied blandly. It was a steep climb to the small cleared area behind the hill, and Cronin would discover his answer was not quite on the ball.

The next day, two of AT/5's tanks started to climb to 812, and Tank-1 was struggling. It became a little embarrassing, but not a complete surprise for the tankers when that particular Pershing couldn't complete the climb.

AT/5 had picked up their new M46s back in November. They were Cadillacs of rolling armor in Korea. Cronin, a car buff from the time he was a teenager, was wide-eyed with the replacement for the M26 Pershing. The Patton had 810 horses, more than 300 in excess of the Pershing. It had a dual-use wobble stick to shift the two-speed hydromatic transmission, in addition to power-assist steering. The braking system also was power-assisted. It was a hefty forty-five tons when fully loaded. But like some automobile manufacturers back in the States, once in a while a "lemon" came off the production lines. AT/5 got its "lemon" in Tank-1.

"Tank number one gave us problems from Day One," Cronin said. "I say 'us' because everybody would pitch in when No. 1 broke down. One day when I was helping with one of the problems, my cigarette lighter fell out of my breast pocket and deep down into the engine compartment." Cronin told the guys not to worry about it. "I'll get it back the next time we pull the engine."

Two days later he had his lighter back.

So it was no surprise when No. 1 balked at taking the incline to Hill 812. The other tank made it easily. Fortunately, only one tank was needed up there because there was only one firing station. Had two gone up, the other would have been on standby behind the firing slot. "The embarrassing part," Cronin said, "was a six-by-six truck made the climb."

One of Lt. Clapper's first assignments was to see what his tanks could do with the sniper who continued to be causing some grief to the Marines on Hill 812 and their buddies down on 758. Of course, that was Luke the Gook who was getting his jollies at the expense of the Gyrenes from Hill 1052.

Lt. Clapper wanted to make sure he had the best shooting position. He jeeped up to 812 with S/Sgt. Ford and Sgt. Cronin and found out quickly that Hill 812 pushed the MLR much further out than the rest of the Minnesota Line, and the extreme protrusion of the trenchline was to the left, facing Hill 1052—Luke's Castle.

The lieutenant decided to reconnoiter on his own, with the help of a guide from the

Fifth's more experienced infantry, leaving his two NCOs in the safety of the bunkers. "Scuttling like a crab," Clapper said, "I was escorted through a shallow winding trench to a very exposed outpost with a sandbagged parapet."

The lieutenant's guide would poke his head up, take a quick look, and duck down behind a sandbag. He would pick out something like "a big rock by a pine stump about 400 yards straight ahead." Clapper would stick his head up and look for it, then duck down. "Yeah, I see it. There's a hole about ten yards to the left of the stump," the infantryman said.

Clapper would pop his head up again. This went on several times—first the Marine rifleman would look, then the lieutenant. "All that head bobbing must have really attracted the attention of the sniper," Clapper figured. "I was crouching with my hand on a sandbag when there was a sharp report and a thud." Sand trickled over his hand. "Right where my head had been," the lieutenant cringed. "I didn't get a shot at the sniper that day, but fortunately, the shot he had at me missed—barely."

Lt. Clapper, however, would get in his licks when the AT/5 tank engaged in a fire mission targeted at Luke the Gook's Castle. That day, the platoon commander was shooting up the trench line along the Castle's forward slope with the 90mm rifle. He wasn't satisfied and wanted to get a higher explosive into the chamber. To do this, he had to rotate the turret in order to access the storage racks under the turret deck.

The Gooks saw the huge gun swinging away from them and must have figured that it was a signal to come out of their holes. Clapper, however, had swiveled his periscope counter to the turret and still had his eye on the Castle. "I saw an enemy soldier, dressed in one of those white snow suits, appear in the blackened area we had just clobbered. He had binoculars, and although he didn't realize it, we were eyeball-to-eyeball."

Lt. Clapper ordered his gunner to load a round of high explosive, rotate on the target and shoot. "He did, and the poor soul on Luke's Castle was blown out of the trench. He did a remarkable swan dive up, out, and down. His body remained spread-eagled— pinned by a stump—on that forward slope for days."

Two things struck Pete Clapper. He calculated that a round of 90mm high explosive cost around $100, and he spent a lot of the government's money killing one man. He knew, however, from his six months with Able Company, both as a line infantry officer and in charge of the A-T platoon, that killing enemy soldiers was a matter of self-preservation.

"But there is something memorable about looking so closely at a man as I ordered him killed, about viewing the body for days afterward, about comparing it to the cost of the shell, about not feeling bad about the whole thing. I was that man's executioner." It is not the only time he thought about the quirky fates that work on the minds of men in combat.

On one sojourn in front of the lines to reconnoiter a target, Lt. Clapper and Platoon Sergeant Ford were losing daylight. "We were humping over hill and dale as dusk began to overtake us," he said. "I chose a shortcut back to our positions on the MLR." After a few minutes, the lieutenant tripped. He didn't think much about it until, after a couple of steps, he fell again.

"That got my attention." His infantry experience in those same hills kicked in. He told S/Sgt. Ford to stop in his tracks. They were trip wires to mines the lieutenant had stumbled over—not once, but twice. The two Marines quickly surveyed the area. They were in the middle of a field of very deadly "bouncing Betty" anti-personnel mines.

"Trip wires were all over the place," Clapper saw. "We backed out of there with exquisite care." They did make it back to the lines safely. The lieutenant, in retrospect, figured the mines had rusted, or froze, or were badly laid. "Was that good luck, or what?" he wondered.

Luck also could be applied to the persistent North Korean soldier near Luke's Castle who had a habit of repairing his bunker. He was lucky the Fifth's A-Ts weren't on line that day. It was when Lt. Clapper and some of his crews were peering out of the infantry bunkers that they noticed the shovel.

"We couldn't see this digger," Clapper said, "because his excavation already was deeper than he was tall." However, each time he pitched dirt, his shovel briefly appeared above to rim of the hole. "We took turns with our M1s. Rules allowed only one Marine to fire each time the shovel appeared. I know we hit the shovel repeatedly because we could see more and more daylight through it. But that character never gave up. He shoveled all day. Home improvement was as important to him as target practice was to us."

Not too long after that, the tables turned the other way when the platoon commander and his sergeant were out in the boonies figuring another tank shoot. "We were scrunching back and forth in a shallow trench with a sizeable contingent of curious Marines in tow," Clapper said. Suddenly, there was rifle fire zinging over the top of the trench. "We were in defilade—out of sight—and just hunkered down a little more. I took a peek behind us to see if they might have targets back there—nothing. They fired and fired. Must have been some kind of harmless practice for the Gooks. Funny, I felt exactly like I was back in the butts on the rifle range at Parris Island: 'Ready on the Right! Ready on the Left! Already-on-the-firing-line! Watch your targets!'

"Ding went the bell. Up went the targets, *pop* went the bullets. Then another ding, followed by a moment of reverent silence . . . and finally the command: 'Mark your targets!'

"Oops, Maggie's drawers again, you feather merchants."

Lt. Pete Clapper had his moments at Luke the Gook's Castle, some provoking, some light, but all a part of war. And he would see much more of it when the First Marine Division moved to the West Coast of Korea.

Too-Young Friend Wounded, Sent Home

After the Flame Platoon returned to Headquarters Company at the First Tank Battalion following the encounter with Luke the Gook, things again settled into the same sort of training routine that occupied the outfit the previous six-and-a-half months.

Fox 21, the Fire Box rescued from the ridge in front of Hill 758 by Service Company's very brave mechanics, was back, running just fine, and the Platoon once again was up to snuff with its full complement of nine tanks. With nothing more than a training routine on the agenda, things were relatively uneventful for most of the guys. Flame tanks didn't have anything to do with the war until after Operation MIXMASTER shipped the entire First Marine Division to the western sector of Korea.

However, a couple of weeks after *The Roamin' Candle* came back off the line, the F22 driver, Cpl. Jack Carty, received some disturbing news.

"We heard scuttlebutt that Dog Company's tanks ran into some trouble when they were up along the MLR," Carty said. Then he got word that Cpl. Dan O'Sullivan, his good friend from the Bronx and a gunner on one of the M46s, had been wounded. That was all he heard.

"Nobody could tell me how bad he was," the concerned Flame Tanker said. "All they said was that he was still in a MASH unit down the road from us." That brought a little bit of relief, because if O'Sullivan had not been sent to one of the hospital ships off the coast of Korea—or, worse, Stateside—then his wounds probably weren't real serious. As soon as Carty could find a ride, he went to the field hospital.

He got a little bit of a jolt when the corpsman was taking him to find his buddy. At first, he thought the worse.

"We had to go through the morgue," the Flame Tanker said, "and here was a row of four or five tables, about chest high, with Marine KIAs on them. They were covered only with ponchos, their thermo boots sticking out over the ends of the tables."

Carty felt a surge of panic. *Was this guy bringing me in here to see Dan? What the hell happened, did he die?* No, it was just a worried Marine jumping to conclusions.

"This way Corporal," the corpsman said, " he's over here in the ward."

The somber walk through the morgue, however, was a bitter reminder of Hill 1052 and Sgt. Castle, and Marines were still being killed up in those mountains.

When Carty finally saw his friend, there was immediate relief. O'Sullivan was wearing a sling on his right arm but had his usual wide mischievous Irish grin. Just by looking at him, Carty knew he was okay. Sarcastically, his friend cracked: "I zigged when I should have zagged."

Ironically, O'Sullivan's tank went forward of Hill 758 on the same ridge that spelled trouble to the Flame Platoon tank a month earlier. While working over Luke the Gook's Castle with its 90mm rifle, the Dog Company Patton took a direct hit from a round of 76mm, which broke one of the tracks mid-morning of 23 February.

As the crew tried to evacuate the disabled M46, more incoming rained on them, and an assortment of 82mm and 120mm mortars. Dan O'Sullivan and another tanker were wounded, O'Sullivan taking enough shrapnel in the shoulder that he had to be evacuated to the MASH unit.

"Ah, I'll be outta here in no time and back to my pigiron," he assured his concerned friend.

But he never did return to Dog Company. What Dan O'Sullivan didn't know was that because of that wound, the Corps somehow found out he shouldn't have been in Korea in the first place—because of his age. He had just turned seventeen, and technically, he never should have been in the Marines, let alone sent to Korea.

He was sent home to be separated from the Marine Corps. When he arrived in the Bronx, he was wearing a Purple Heart, a Presidential Unit Citation the First Tank Battalion had earned, and three battle stars on his bright blue Korean Service ribbon.

O'Sullivan often mentioned to Carty that when he got out of the Marines, he was going to join the New York City police force. When his shoulder fully healed, he filled out the application and listed his actual age. He was shocked when told he was too young to carry a gun—despite his combat record.

When Carty received a letter from O'Sullivan detailing his frustration with the New York City Police Department, he thought it ironic. Here was a guy who carried a 45-caliber pistol on his hip for seven months in Korea, was a qualified marksman with an M-1 rifle, and, as a gunner on an M46 Patton tank, controlled and fired one of the most powerful weapons in the Korean War. But when he got back to New York, he was too young to carry a gun and walk a beat in Manhattan or the Bronx. Somehow, that didn't add up for Carty.

Meanwhile, the Flame Platoon was going about its uneventful, behind-the-lines routine, but it was going to be a little more interesting for guys like Cpl. Patrick "Packy" Wassell, the F22 tank commander.

When the First Marine Division arrived in Korea, it had been S.O.P. to work closely with the Korean Marine Corps, much like the Army had been doing with ROK units. Early in February of 1951, the KMCs began organizing their own tank company, and the training of their tankers fell on the guys from the First Tank Battalion.

Wassell, the lean Southern Californian, became one of the instructors and would spend a couple of weeks TAD (temporary attached duty) with the fledgling tank outfit. While Wassell was down the road with the KMCs, Cpl. Jack Carty took over as temporary tank commander of 22—*The Roamin' Candle*. PFC Alvin Chalk moved into the driver's job, PFC Jack MacGregor moved down as the bow gunner/assistant driver, and PFC Dick "Ruf" Ruffner joined the crew as the loader in the turret.

It was pretty good duty for Wassell, who was a very sharp T.C. Working with the KMC, he had a chance to see if the scoop on the Korean Marines was as good as it sounded. It was. The KMC, because it was trying very hard to mirror the USMC, was earning quite a bit of respect from Gyrenes. They were nothing like the undisciplined ROK army. Like U.S. Marines, the KMCs had quite a bit of pride in their outfit. Wassell now was seeing it firsthand.

There also was a change in attitude around the Flame Platoon after it got back from Luke's Castle. M/Sgt. Grady Turnage, the by-the-book platoon sergeant who usually seemed to have little regard, or time, for many of the men in the outfit, had mellowed a little. He was not all peaches and cream with the guys he previously just about ignored, but he did become a little more apt to treat them like fellow Marines and not raw recruits he seemed to think they were when he first came to the platoon. He did, however, maintain enough of his old self to dispense the usual ration of horseshit to cherries from each new draft.

Still, flame tanks once again were relegated to nothing more than training for the crews. Maj. Walter E. Reynolds, Jr., who had been Major Phil Morrell's replacement as Battalion Exec, took over as battalion commander in February, replacing Lt. Col. Holly H. Evans. While Evans, at Turnage's urging, had gotten the flame tanks some action at Luke's Castle, Reynolds would hold them back until there were more favorable conditions for their unique firepower.

And that wouldn't be until the entire Division was sent back to western Korea.

Go West, Marines, Go West!

Operation MIXMASTER—flip-flopping the First Marine Division from X Corps in the East Central Mountains to I Corps on the flank of the Eighth U.S. Army to the west in order to cover the Inchon-Seoul-Kimpo-Uijongbu-Yongdungpo sector—was about to come to life.

Mixmaster was a complicated rearrangement of UN divisions across the entire Korean front during March, and involved the shuffling of about 200,000 men and their equipment over distances from 25 to 180 miles. It was a severe test of Eighth Army mobility.

General Van Fleet visited the 1st Marine Division CP on 12 March 1952, and announced an important command decision. After six months of defensive warfare in the same sector along Line Minnesota (20 September 1951 to 16 March 1952) the Division was to move across the peninsula to West Korea.

The Marines had orders to relieve the 1st ROK Division and take over a sector at the extreme left of the Eighth Army line under the operational control of I Corps. There they would have the responsibility for blocking Korea's historic invasion route to Seoul. The reasons behind this EUSAK decision were summarized in the 1st Marine Division report as follows:

"(1) The abandonment of plans to carry out an amphibious envelopment somewhere on the east coast;

"(2) Concern over weaknesses in the Kimpo area defenses;

"(3) The overall situation would not permit loss of ground on the EUSAK left (South Korea) as this would endanger the capital at Seoul; that if retraction of lines was necessary, territory could better be sacrificed on the right (North Korea) where the country was mountainous and had little economic or strategic value."

Up to this time the four corps of the Eighth Army had defended a 125-mile front across the peninsula with the following units in line from left to right on 15 March 1952.

I CORPS—ROK 1st Division; British Commonwealth Division; U.S. 3d Infantry Division (–); U.S. 45th Infantry Division (Oklahoma National Guard); ROK 9th Division. In reserve were the ROK 8th Division and RCT–65 of the U.S. 3d Infantry Division.

IX CORPS—U.S. 2d Infantry Division; ROK 2d Division; U.S. 40th Infantry Division (California National Guard); ROK 3d Division. In reserve were the U.S. 7th Infantry Division (–), RCT–17 of that Division, and the ROK Capitol Division.

X CORPS—ROK 7th Division; U.S. 25th Infantry Division; U.S. 1st Marine Division (including 1st KMC Regiment). In reserve was the ROK 6th Division (–).

I ROK CORPS—ROK 5th Division (–). In reserve was the ROK 11th Division (–).

Allowing for a few changes, these were the positions held by major EUSAK units through the winter of 1951–1952.

The Marine move was launched . . . and provided that the 1st Marine Division would be relieved by the 8th ROK Division as a preliminary to movement overland and by sea to the relief of the 1st ROK Division and defense of Line Jamestown in the I Corps sector in the west . . . transportation by truck and ship was specified, and the move was to be completed prior to 1 April.

Obviously such a transplacement—moving entire divisions great distances from one sector of the MLR to another—necessitated careful timing and close coordination, but the planners involved were equal to the task . . . "the move from east to west was a masterpiece of logistical efficiency with no unnecessary paper work and no undue harassment."

In addition to transporting the Division, the arrival of replacements and departure of personnel to be rotated to the United States were smoothly coordinated into the over-all plan. (MCOinK, Volume IV)

Of course, when all of this was getting under way, there was very little information about what was going on reaching down into the ranks. Tankers in the Flame Platoon, Headquarters Company, First Tank Battalion were told only to strike their tents, stow as much gear in or on their tanks, and be ready to move out.

Scuttlebutt was running rampant, but eventually the solid skinny was passed—the Division was shipping out to the west coast.

"We had no idea how we were going to get there," said Sgt. Jack Carty, who had picked up his third stripe along with several other former corporals when the AllMar promotion list came out on 1 March. AllMars (All Marine) were blanket upgrades throughout the Corps for guys who had kept their noses relatively clean. PFCs became corporals. Corporals were upgraded to buck sergeants. Three stripers got their rocker and now they were staff/sergeants. The Flame Platoon bulged with buck sergeants.

"Hell, we'd only been corporals for less than six months," Sgt. Carty mused, "and most of us didn't have two years in the Corps."

"Just like mail call," cracked one new corporal. But no way were any of them going to offer to give back the new stripes.

Still, nobody happened to mention to the crews of the Flame Platoon what the hell was going on and how the hell they were going to get to the west coast. Operation MIXMASTER very well could describe the mixed-up events that were about to involve members of the Flame Platoon.

When the orders came down to make the move, the tankers still didn't know where they were going, or the enormity of the thing—even though, for a couple of days, they were busy making preparations. Straight poop was the entire First Marine Division moving west. But there was no word at the platoon level how it was going to get there.

"Once we got the word we were moving," Sgt.Carty said, "we figured we'd be driving it. Eventually, the skinny came through that we would take the tanks down to a port on the east coast, load into LSTs, and be part of a convoy of the Division's heavy equipment."

It was 3 March when things started to get under way. The First Tank Battalion struck its tents at Pyongchong and moved a few miles south down the MSR to a temporary CP at Chirychon, which officially became operational on 7 March. Two of the Flame sections were in that move. The other section had been attached to Charlie Company in a temporary C.P. at Nadang across the Pukchon River from Mago-ri where Camp Tripoli, the First Marine Division C.P., was located.

This was in preparation for the drive to the coast—the port of Sokcho-ri. But nobody in the Flame Platoon knew the destination at the time. The two sections remained at Headquarters Company for two days before rolling into the Charlie CP with the anti-tank platoon from First Marines on 16 March.

It was late afternoon 17 March—St. Patrick's Day—when the Flame Platoon pulled out of Nadang in line with the gun tanks and all the support vehicles. "We had to come down out of the mountains before we could head east to the embarkation port at Sokcho-ri," Carty said. "The port was situated a couple of miles above the 38th Parallel."

Right before the move, Sgt. Packy Wassell had returned from TAD as an instructor to KMC tankers and took over the turret of *The Roamin' Candle*. Sgt. Carty went back to driving. "It sure felt good to get the sticks in my hands again," Carty said.

There were signs of spring—sunny and fairly nice—when the nine flame tanks ground out of the CP behind the Charlie tanks and the Pattons from AT/1 and AT/7.

"We knew we would be on the road most of the night," Carty said. What they didn't anticipate—because of the spring-like day that preceded it—was lousy weather.

Sometime after dark, it started to snow, with a little rain mixed in. Alternately, it would be all snow, then mixed. It really loused up the roads and visibility. The next two days were fraught with nature's soggy mixture, several inches of snow in some places, extremely narrow roads, and all kinds of bypasses.

"We were driving unbuttoned," the F22 driver said, "and I was having one hell of a time trying to follow the road and the tank in front of us. We were wet, we were cold, and we were miserable. And we were getting tired. "I didn't think much of St. Patty the next couple of days. What the hell kind of a way was this to treat an Irishman—especially a guy who flew two Ol' Sod flags from the antennae of his tank?"

The weather slowed the convoy quite a bit, but it stayed on the move most of the first night.

The Division's heavy equipment was not the only thing moving in caravan. The infantry regiments and the 11th Marines artillery also were bouncing out of the East Central Mountains. They would make the entire trip overland.

It was still miserable when daylight finally appeared gray through the soggy sky on 18 March. The snow had turned to rain as the tanks, six-bys, and a few jeeps were getting to lower areas of the mountains. There were occasional stops for hot chow brought in by mess trucks, and a little rest. But the drive continued most of the following day. It still was cloudy, cold, damp, and miserable.

By then, the string of vehicles began passing through villages periodically, and if the convoy stopped at all, there were kids running up to the tanks with their hands out. They knew Americans were soft touches. "We got rid of all our pogey bait (candy) and some C rations," Carty said.

Finally, the weather broke. The following day was sunny and a little more pleasant. The tankers had pulled off the road for a fairly long rest the previous night and had a chance to dry out and change clothes.

A few hours into the drive that morning, the flame tanks still were playing follow-the-leader as they came into the lowlands, where there were only some smaller hills to navigate. Going up one hill, Sgt. Carty—a little refreshed and once again enjoying the feel of thirty-some tons and 500 *horses* in his grasp—lost sight of the tank in front of him when it had disappeared over the crest. When *The Roamin' Candle* reached the top of the hill, Carty still couldn't see any tanks ahead of him.

As he started down the hill, the road below was level and straight as an arrow. He shifted 22 up to fourth gear, then fifth to get maximum speed out of it.

"We were going down that hill full bore, at probably somewhere around twenty-five miles an hour or more," he said. It was just about top speed for the Sherman tank. That doesn't seem very fast—if it were a car. But put one of these M4A3E8s in that kind of a run down a hill, and it's like the odometer needle bobbing past seventy in Sgt. Carty's old blue '40 four-door Chevy.

Carty saw the village at the bottom of the hill. What he didn't see, because of an embankment, was the road on the left where the other tanks had turned. Standing higher in the turret, Sgt. Packy Wassell had a perfect view of the whole area—the road on the left, the tank in front of us that had made the turn, and the mud-brick homes that lined the edge of that little road. He also knew the way *The Roamin' Candle* was barreling down the hill that his driver didn't see the other road. If Carty didn't soon start grabbing some stick and slow down the tank, he would never be able to brake that left track in time to make the turn. *"JACK!"* he shouted into Carty's headset, *"LEFT, TURN LEFT!"*

As Wassell was hollering, his driver saw where the road T'd. "I don't know how far away from it I was," Carty said, "but I pulled on both brake levers, let go of the right stick momentarily, double clutching to shift down to fourth gear, another double-clutch, and down to third."

The tank began grinding slower, coming around to the left. Carty's right hand, after shifting, automatically came back to the starboard lever, but his grasp was tender. He only yanked back harder on the left while leaving just about all pressure off the right one. "If I do say so myself," Carty cracked, "we made a beautiful pivot and cut right into the road, with not too much room to spare between the right side of the tank and those mud huts. I was pretty proud of myself until I saw the impending problem."

One of those Koreans had built a chimney on the front of his house. There was nothing Carty could do. "I didn't have enough time to brake or turn. The right track just gobbled up the lower two or three feet of the stack, and the tank itself sheared the rest of it right off the front of the house—as clean as a whistle."

Mud brick, dust, and soot showered Cpl. Alvin Chalk, sitting across from the driver on the right side of the tank. "He probably thought he was about to meet his Maker when he saw that chimney coming right at him," the very disturbed driver thought. Some of the flying debris even hit Jack MacGregor, the loader, who was chest high out of the right-side turret hatch.

But Sgt. Carty had another grave concern. Just before F22 de-chimneyed that house, out of the corner of his eye the driver saw the Papasan standing in a doorway, which was a couple of feet from the chimney. He turned to look back but couldn't see anything because he was on the opposite side of the tank. He started to slow down, worried. "I wanted to see if I hurt anybody."

But Wassell came on the intercom, hardly able to talk, he was laughing so hard. "Keep going," he finally said. "You didn't hit anybody, but you sure did a job on that chimney. You ought to see the look on Papasan's face!"

He burst out laughing again.

Carty felt guilty as hell, but relieved that he didn't put more than thirty tons of pigiron in that poor Korean's living room. He worried about it the rest of the day and night. And if he wasn't thinking about it, the crew—and even some of his good buddies from other tanks—were not about to let him forget it. Every time he saw a jeep, he imagined it was MPs coming for the jerk who destroyed a chimney. If he didn't see a jeep coming, every once in a while he'd be told: "Hey, Jack, I think there's an MP coming."

All Carty could think of was a court martial, losing his new sergeant stripe and maybe brig-time.

The village he managed to rip through was about five miles away from Sokcho-ri.

It was around 1600 on 20 March when Charlie Company led the Flame Platoon—along with the anti-tank platoons from the First and Seventh Marines, and a company of KMC M4A3 older Shermans armed with 76mm guns, into Sokcho-ri.

Four hours later, the nine flame tanks began easing up the ramp into the bowels of LST No. 1138 which also would be carrying the KMC company, a Sherman communications tank, and three dozer tanks. The tankers helped the Swabbies and some Shore Party

Marines lash them down with huge chains—four to a tank, one on each corner. Shore Party Marines concentrated in shipping, landing maneuvers, and supplies. Like all specially trained Marines, they were good at their jobs.

It took several hours to get everything aboard and battened down. In addition to the tanks, the deck of the LST was crammed with six-bys. After loading, the Marine tankers were able to get a fairly good night's sleep in the cramped living quarters of the ship. The ramp went up at 0700 the following morning, and the LST moved into the Sea of Japan to rendezvous with the convoy.

"I didn't feel relieved," the still-worried Carty said, "until that LST got out of port the next morning. Had I known how I was going to feel a few days later, I might have preferred the brig."

The LSTs were pretty nice ships—when the seas were calm. Above the cargo area were sleeping, mess, and recreation quarters. Not elaborate, but much better than Marines, even tankers, get in a war zone. And, like all chow aboard Navy ships, the food was very good—that is, if the Marines could keep it on their trays, and in their stomachs.

The route of the convoy, which had ships as far as the Marines could see to the horizon off the stern, was south from Sokcho-ri for roughly 300 or 400 miles in the Sea of Japan, around the southern tip of Korea. Then it went north through the Yellow Sea about 300 miles to Inchon.

"We shipped out on a nice calm day," Sgt. Carty said. "But that second day was absolutely awful. I don't know just where we were, but we hit one hell of a storm. That damn LST bobbed like a cork." LSTs are basically flat-bottomed, displacing only about 10 feet of water, the tankers were told.

"That's a pretty damn shallow draught," Carty and his queasy fellow tankers soon found out. "That thing pitched and rolled like it was going to flip over.

"Before I got sick, I went down for chow and I couldn't keep anything on the metal tray. As soon as the messman would spoon something onto the tray, the ship would roll, the damn tray would fly out my hands, and I'd be sliding down the deck after it—not always on my feet. Food became slop all over the decks.

"That about did it. We were getting sick as hell. I began wondering if some MP might not have done me a favor if he put me in the brig at Sokcho-ri."

They weren't the only tankers puking out their guts. Lt. Pete Clapper and his Fifth Marine anti-tankers were on the last LSTs to leave Sokcho-ri since they were held back at the Kanmubong Ridge to help protect the exchange of the MLR from the Marines to the ROKs. And the Gooks sensed something was going on because they were giving the Marines a big sendoff.

"The morning we were scheduled to pull off the hill for the west coast," said PFC Chuck Batherson who was loader on AT/5's No.1 tank, "there was so much incoming that we couldn't get to our tank."

That was compliments of the Luke the Gook on the Castle and some of his buddies from the other hills manned by the North Korean People's Army overlooking the Marines on Hills 812 and 758.

"Watching from the door of our bunker," Batherson said, "All you could see was shrapnel, dirt, and rocks flying all over the place. "Finally, we just decided to make a run for it. Surprisingly, nobody got hit."

The anti-tankers from the 5th Marines also ran afoul of the bad roads going down to

Sokcho-ri. By the time they pulled onto that MSR, the roads had been thoroughly chewed up and extremely compromised by the bad weather.

"The road was in poor condition for all the heavy traffic it had carried the previous three days," said Sgt. John Cronin, T.C. of AT/5's No. 2 tank. "Temperatures were above freezing during the day, and the road got slushy. Several times we found our tanks in mud up to their bellies." But when they came into the valleys, it was a chance to let the Pattons fly. AT/5 had moved so well that they were passing disabled tanks of some of the gun companies and other A-T outfits.

"We were determined to make this road march without having to get help from the Tank Battalion," Cronin admitted. They were having some problems with Tank No. 5, but they made it intact to Sokcho-ri and were the last tanks loaded on LSTs.

"The beach was filled with tanks," Cronin said. "A lot of special equipment like cranes, bulldozers, and the like was also ready to go."

They could see the armada of LSTs, which had been loaded earlier, sitting off the coast waiting for the rest to complete the convoy. The loading of the M46s took longer because there was room for only fourteen of them on the bowels of LSTs, which were designed in World War II to house twenty-one of the lighter M4A3 Shermans.

Lt. Pete Clapper's No. 1 tank and Sgt. Cronin's No. 2 Patton of A/T5 were on the last LST out of Sokcho-ri. It was while they were waiting to board the ship that Sgt. Don Dennany, AT/5's mechanic, heard the bad news of his friend, Fred Castle, being killed in action when the flame tanks were at Luke the Gook's Castle.

So, Flame Tankers were not the only ones wondering whether they would ever get through that storm and around to Inchon.

"It was fairly choppy out there," Lt. Clapper understated. "I was feeling woozy and wondered how the poor tankers down below were faring." Their concerned C.O. opened the hatchway to their crowded quarters to look in on them.

"Took one whiff and decided they'd just have to get along without me."

Sgt. Cronin, however, found a way to beat the seasickness. He ate as much as he could. "Some guys had it so bad," he said, they only left their bunks to go to the head. A few ate little more than crackers and some sips of water. My theory about keeping a full stomach worked, though at times it was a struggle."

At times, he was the only Marine in the galley, where even the Swabbies were admitting that this was one rough ride. On Day 3 of the storm, Cronin managed to get topside and looked back over the convoy.

"No two ships were parallel," he said. "At times some of the ships were sideways to the direction of the fleet."

When he asked one of the sailors what he thought about the storm, the reply surprised him: "This is the worst I've ever seen."

But the seas quieted down, and it wasn't bad at all as the convoy began to enter Inchon Harbor.

If anything sets off a United States Marine Corps officer, particularly one who has had combat experience with the infantry, it is the lack of care for weapons. Lt. Clapper got very riled when he discovered an M1 rifle was left exposed to the weather on the seat of a tank battalion truck. He called all the Marines aboard to formation on the deck.

"He had fire in his eyes," Cronin said. "He went into a tirade about Marines and their rifles."

There was another issue he addressed at the same time, but not so vehemently. A ship's captain came to Lt. Clapper and informed him about some missing Thompson sub machine guns. Marines are notorious for their "Midnight Requisitions," but Lt. Clapper was unaware his tankers were involved.

"They denied complicity," the lieutenant said with a straight face. The captain ordered the Marine officer to take appropriate action, which he did by assembling his tankers on the deck. However, he allowed a salty sergeant to take over.

"He lectured them at length about the virtues of honesty and the evils of theft," Lt. Clapper claimed, "but the weapons never turned up."

That storm in the Yellow Sea lasted a couple of days, but the rough seas didn't settle down for another few days—and neither did the stomachs of the Flame Platoon crews. By the time they got to Inchon, however, most of them were beginning to think about eating again.

It was 26 March, late in the afternoon, when four LSTs arrived at Inchon and began debarkation of the tanks. Inchon was an amazing sight to the Marines who had not been there before. They had heard stories about the giant seawall that protected the port against thirty-foot tides. It was low, or near low, tide when the fleet of LSTs got there and the tankers could see this huge wall protruding from the water and what was left of the port's facilities high above the water. They had a new appreciation for what the Marines accomplished at the Inchon Landing a year and one-half before.

The Flame Platoon was off-loaded south of the main port, in the area of the Landing's Blue Beach, well below the Kimpo Peninsula airfield. "A lot of us were pretty happy to feel land under our tanks as we drove off the ramp," Sgt. Carty said. "Those Swabbies can have the nice comfortable shipboard life, and the roller-coaster rides that go with it."

The unloading began at 1600 and the tanks made their way to the railhead, where they carefully eased up ramps and onto the narrow gauge flatbed cars. The railcars, much narrower than the standard trains the tankers were used to seeing back in the states, were just wide enough to hold the tanks – although a couple of inches of their tracks hung over the both sides of the cars. The much-wider tracks of the M46s extended much further beyond the sides of the rail cars.

It would be a slow all-night trip from Inchon to Munsan-ni with the crews unable to do more than sit in, or on, their tightly stored equipment. It would not be until early the following afternoon when the train reached the Munsan-ni railhead and the tanks began their tedious debarkation from the flatcars.

Oh, the Thompson machine guns missing from the LST which carried the Fifth Marines AT Platoon? "When we disembarked," Clapper discovered, "the tankers proudly broke out their new Tommy guns."

Renewing Old Acquaintances:
CCF (Chinese Communist Forces)

Operation MIXMASTER, the transfer of the 1st Marine Division began on 17 March . . . in the motor march to West Korea, Marine units traveled approximately 140 miles over narrow, mountainous, and frequently mud-clogged primitive roads. Day and night . . . (it) rolled through rain, snow, sleet, and occasional good weather . . . The MIXMASTER move was made primarily by truck and by ship [tanks were shipped around the southern tip of Korea and off-loaded at Inchon] or rail for units with heavy vehicles.

Upon its arrival in West Korea, the 1st Marine Division was under orders to relieve the 1st ROK Division and take over a sector at the extreme left of the Eighth Army line under I Corps control, where the weakness of the Kimpo Peninsula defenses had been of considerable concern to EUSAK . . .

Within the Marine boundaries ran the route that invaders through the ages had used in their drive south to Seoul. It was the 1st Marine Division's mission to block any such future attempts . . . at the end of March 1952, the division main line of resistance [Jamestown Line] stretched across difficult terrain for more than 30 miles from Kimpo [Peninsula] to the British Commonwealth sector on the east, a frontage far in excess of the textbook concept.

. . . Panmunjom was less than 5 miles away [to the north] and within the area of Marine forward outpost security . . . the area to which the Marines had moved as situated in the western coastal lowlands and highlands area of northwestern South Korea. . . . (MCOinK, Volume IV)

After debarking from the LSTs on 26 March 1952, the Flame Platoon tanks loaded on flat cars at the Inchon rail yards and trained up to Munsan-Ni with the crews riding along with them. It wasn't until the following day that the drivers eased their Shermans off the narrow flat cars and left the railhead for the new Battalion and Company CP, which was about fifteen miles south and slightly east of Panmunjom, site of ongoing Truce Talks.

The First Marine Division now was opposite some of the more elite Chinese Communist Forces (CCF). It would be a whole new ball game after the cat-and-mouse games with the North Korean People's Army in the mountains of East-Central Korea.

The western zone of the United Nations charge was much less mountainous around the 38th Parallel. There were hills, but the meter-numbers identifying them generally were in the low to mid one-hundreds, not hovering in high three figures and often four digits that dominated the East Central front.

Steep-sided hills and mountains, which sloped abruptly into narrow valleys pierced by many of the rivers and larger streams, predominated the terrain in the I Corps sector where the Marines located. The most rugged terrain was to the rear of the Jamestown Line . . . Ground cover in the division sector consisted of grass, scrub brush, and, occasionally, small trees. Rice fields crowded the valley floors. Mud flats were prevalent in many areas immediately adjacent to the larger rivers which intersected the division territory or virtually paralleled the east and western boundaries of the Marine sector.

The transfer from the Punchbowl in the east to western Korea thus resulted in a distinct change of scene for the Marines, who went from a rugged mountainous area to comparatively level terrain. Instead of facing a line held by predominantly North Korean forces the division was now confronted by the Chinese Communists. The Marines also went from a front that had been characterized by lively patrol action to one that in March 1952 was relatively dormant. With the arrival of the 1st Marine Division, this critical I Corps sector would witness sharply renewed activity and become a focal point of action in the UNC line. (MCOinK, Volume IV)

What this meant—unbeknown to the Flame Tankers at first—was that there was much more area available for pigiorns to clank around, and the Flame Platoon soon would be deeply involved in the war once again.

The change of scenery impressed most of the tankers. "There was no snow on the ground here," remarked Sgt. John Cronin, the T.C. of Tank 1 in the 5th Marines Anti-Tank Platoon. "We were a good seventy miles south (in latitude) from the positions we left in the East, and we were essentially at sea level. The hills rolled gently, there only a few isolated trees, and the weather was mild but damp."

Heading north on the MSR to the 5th Marines position, Cronin couldn't help but compare the road as his group of tanks sped along. "The road was like a super highway, compared to what we left in the Eastern mountains. It was still dirt, but wide with good drainage."

Since it was nearing the end of March, going home was becoming a major part of the thought process to guys who had been in the Flame Platoon nearly a year. Sgt. Packy Wassell was a true "short-timer"—a Marine who had about a month to go before scheduled rotation. Sgt. Jack Carty was getting close. Unless all hell broke loose, Wassell would be gone by the end of April, and Carty a month later after the May replacement draft arrived.

In the first year and one-half of the war, Marines—particularly the surviving gravel-grunchers with infantry units—were spending at least twelve, sometimes thirteen, fourteen months, in the Land of the Morning Calm. By the time the 10th Replacement had arrived in the summer of '51, the duration of the normal tour was not more than twelve months. When the war quieted down a little because of the peace negotiations, and there were fewer casualties, it was down to about eleven months.

Sgt. Packy Wassell did leave for home shortly after the Division arrived in the west, and Sgt. Carty moved back into Fox 22's turret—tank commander of *The Roamin' Candle* for the rest of his tour. He thought it was no big deal. Yet ask any Marine, and if fact is told—when the Corps decides he is worthy of command—it does nudge the pride a little.

At this juncture, however, the attitude of being the kid brothers of the First Tank Battalion returned as a cloud hovering over the Flame Platoon because of the relative inactivity of the uniquely specialized Shermans since coming back from Luke's Castle. But that was about to change—subtly at first, but eventually, it would be very emphatic. In a few very short months, the flame tanks would be pulling their share of the First Tank Battalion's load.

The use of tanks—and that meant the Flame Platoon, too—would be a integral part of the First Marine Division's system of carrying out its responsibility of protecting a very crucial sector of the United Nations MLR.

One of the reasons for moving the Marines to the west was that the terrain there had to be held at all costs; land in the east, mountainous and less valuable, could better be sacrificed if a partial withdrawal in Korea became necessary. At the end of March 1952, the division main line of resistance stretched across difficult terrain for more than 30 miles, from Kimpo to the British Commonwealth sector on the east, a frontage far in excess of the textbook concept. . . .

Although Seoul was not actually within the area of Marine Corps responsibility, the capital city was only 33 air miles south. . . . The port of Inchon lay but 19 air miles south of the western end of the division sector. Kaesong, the original site of the truce negotiations, was 13 miles northwest of the nearest part of the 1st Marine Division frontline while Panmunjom was less than 5 miles away and within the area of Marine forward outpost security. From the far northeastern end of the Jamestown Line, which roughly paralleled the Imjin River, distances were correspondingly lengthened: Inchon, thus being 39 miles southwest and Kaesong, about 17 miles west.

The area to which the Marines had moved was situated in the western coastal lowlands and highlands area of northwestern South Korea. On the left flank, the division MLR hooked around the northwest tip of the Kimpo Peninsula, moved east across the high ground overlooking the Han River, and bent around the northeast cap of the peninsula. At a point opposite the mouth of the Kongnung River, the MLR traversed the Han to the mainland, proceeding north alongside that river to its confluence with the Imjin. Crossing north over the Imjin, Jamestown followed the high ground on the east bank of the Sachon River for nearly two miles to where the river valley widened. There the MLR turned abruptly to the northeast and generally pursued that direction to the end of the Marine sector, meandering frequently, however, to take advantage of key terrain. Approximately 2 miles west of the 1st Commonwealth Division boundary, the Jamestown Line intersected the 38th Parallel near the tiny village of Madam-ni.

Within the Marine division sector to the north of Seoul lay the junction of two major rivers, the Imjin and the Han, and a portion of the broad fertile valley fed by the latter. Flowing into the division area from the east, the Imjin River snaked its way southwestward to the rear of Jamestown. At the northeastern tip of the Kimpo Peninsula, the Imjin joined the Han. The latter there changed its course from south to west, flowed past Kimpo and neighboring Kanghwa-do Island, and emptied eventually into the Yellow Sea. At the far western end of the division sector the Yom River formed a natural boundary, separating Kanghwa and Kimpo, as it ran into the Han River and south to the Yellow Sea. To the east, the Sachon River streamed into the Imjin, while the Kongnung emptied into the Han where the MLR crossed from the mainland to Kimpo. (MCOinK, Volume V)

To most of the tankers, they were aware only of their own little niche in the scheme of things. But those niches would be spread out and overlap as the summer of 1952 heated up.

Throughout Korea in March and April there had been a general stagnation of offensive action on both sides because of fog, rain, and mud. In May, however, the Chinese launched no less than 30 probing attacks against the ROK 1st Division in the I Corps sector, without gaining any significant advantage. (MCOinK, Volume V)

Headquarters Company, and its Flame Platoon, was located near the Panmunjom Corridor. The "Corridor" was a J-shaped road 500 yards wide breaking out of the northwestern edge of the Munsan three-mile no-fire zone. It extended northeast for about three miles after it crossed the Imjin River, and then went northwest for six miles to Panmunjom, and through the key city another two miles or so to Kaesong. Like Munsan-ni, Panmunjom and Kaesong also were encircled by three-mile no-fire zones. And there was a 200-meter no-fire fringe on either side of the Corridor.

The Flame Platoon was involved in a lot of training near the Corridor, and the Freedom Gate Bridge which crossed the Imjin. The crews weren't privy to what was going on, but there was a grand plan in the works.

Munsan-ni was a small town in South Korea about five miles below the northern extremity of Jamestown Line and ten to eleven miles from Panmunjom. Admiral Joy, the chief negotiator for the U.N. Truce Talk party, and his people were headquartered in Munsan-ni. Later, the town would house Freedom Village where returning prisoners of war were brought when first released by the Reds.

The First Tank Battalion CP was a mile, or so, east of the Panmunjom Corridor, about four or five miles south of the MLR in the 5th Marines sector near the Imjin. The Flame Tankers became very active in a training routine around the Corridor, but the reason for it—once again—never was passed down to the guys manning the Shermans.

Not long after the Platoon settled into its new "home," three flame tanks—31, 22, 13—went forward as security for an S-3 Liaison C.P.

> *A unique rescue and recover operation also came into existence about this time. On 19 April the division ordered the 5th Marines, occupying the center regimental sector, to organize a tank-infantry force for rescue of the United Nations Truce Team, should such action become necessary. The regimental plan, published 22 April, utilized a reinforced rifle company-tank company organization . . . The Everready Rescue Force, from the regimental reserve, occupied the high ground (OP 2) [Outpost 2] east of and dominating Panmunjom.*
>
> *. . . Taking advantage of the Truce corridor in the western end of the center sector, a Forward Covering Force would speed tank-riding infantry to the high ground one-half mile behind the objective, Panmunjom. Following would be the Pick-Up Force, from the 1st Tank Battalion Headquarters Platoon [Flame Tanks], which would retrieve the principal UN delegates and take them quickly to the assembly area two miles to the rear of the MLR. (MCOinK, Volume IV)*

So there *was* somebody who thought the Flame Platoon could begin to pull its share of the load again.

Then there was the preparation for extracting U.N. truce negotiators if push ever came to shove at Panmunjom.

"Our Pattons were often assigned blocking positions just south of Panmunjom," Lt. Pete Clapper said, "in case the Communists decided to end the peace talks there with an offensive through that supposedly neutral corridor—or in case they tried to kidnap our negotiators."

Along with the Flame Platoon, the Fifth Marines anti-tank platoon also was involved in training for Operation Pick Up! "Marines to the rescue," Sgt. John Cronin, tank commander of the No. 2 Patton in the AT/5 Platoon, commented about forming with the rolling armor of the First Tank Battalion.

"Along the way we would pick up a company of infantry armed with automatic weapons and hand grenades," the Sergeant said. "The first platoon of tanks would go to the far side of the neutral circle to hold off the enemy. The second platoon, with only the drivers and tank commanders on board, would act as taxis to pick up the delegates. The rest of the tanks would cover the rescue and withdrawal while the infantry would stand by for support, and possible intervention if needed.

"The first time we rehearsed, it took us a half hour to arrive at the south edge of the neutral circle," Cronin said. That was from the time they got the call without warning. Eventually, they got it down to eight minutes.

Cronin, however, had a technical, if not amusing, question about it. "I wondered if anyone had briefed the Navy Admiral and his delegates how to board and enter a tank."

Fortunately, the operation never was needed, and plans eventually were altered if it was necessary. "At some point," Cronin said, "the 'taxi platoon' was replaced with six armored personnel carriers borrowed from the Army."

But had something popped, the Flamers surely would have been involved.

Since the Chinese didn't pull any shenanigans with the delegation, activity for the Flame Tankers returned to normal—not quite normal because the routine, for a while, took on a little bit of chicken-shit routine.

The tank battalion C.P. was only a mile from the U.N. delegates base camp (Admiral Turner Joy and his entourage), so it was considered a neutral zone. The place was strictly "stateside"—a spit-and-polish post—and the Flame Platoon, which was providing battalion security, was expected to be spic-and-span.

Otherwise, the flame tanks went about the daily routine as usual—take the Shermans out to make sure they were in good mechanical condition. There was very little testing of the flame guns in the first two months in the new sector. This was odd because the lowlands of the western sector were more conducive for the use of the flame guns—the specialized Sherman's primary weapon. Soon, that would be recognized.

Meanwhile, with the weather becoming spring-like, the Flame Tankers liked the idea of being able to get their pigirons in the upper two gears and go rumbling over the countryside with the hatches open without having snow, or subfreezing wind, chilling their bones.

Early in April, there was a little bit of excitement down the road from the Flame Platoon. The commotion was coming from Service Company. The flame crews stopped everything they were doing when they looked up and saw thick black smoke. Most of them made a beeline toward Service Company.

One of the Sherman dozer tanks had caught fire. By the time the Flame guys got there, smoke and fire were pouring from the engulfed tank. Then there was a big explosion. The tank probably had some 105mm ammo in the hull, and the fire had set off the rounds in unison, or quick succession. The force of the blasts was so powerful, the turret was lifted off the hull and flipped it on its side before it came back down in the recess of its mounting.

The fire finally was controlled and extinguished, but that Sherman dozer was one sorry-looking pigiron. The scuttlebutt was that a crew was working on the engine when something shorted out and a spark hit an open gas line. No one was hurt badly, but the tank sure took a beating.

As usual, the Service Company guys went about their business of retrieving it. They got their boon-rigged tank, lifted the turret, reset it properly on the hull, and unhooked the dozer blade. Before long, they were winching the hulk onto one of their flatbeds—just like they did with F21 up at Luke's Castle a couple of months before—and eventually trucked it off to their "repair shop," to be refitted, or surveyed.

Word finally came that the 10th Drafters would be going home by the end of May, that is, unless the Chinese decided they wanted to foul up the Truce negotiations and start playing games. It was common knowledge that the ChiComs had been taking advantage of the talks and rebuilding their armies. There was the possibility, born out by their sleazy tactics since the talks started, that they'd get up from the table and walk out of the negotiations, precipitating a heat-up of hostilities.

EUSAK was very wary of this, and was not relaxing preparations for the resumption of all-out war. Fortunately, it didn't come—although, after the 10th Drafters left, there was a little more action when both sides began to "work out" more vigorously.

Toward the end of April, the Flame Platoon did get a chance to put its two cents' worth into the war. It was the start of a routine that flame tanks would be assigned to carry out for the rest of the war. Word came down one day that the nine flame tanks were going to do some indirect firing into CCF lines that night. The news had all the crews buzzing—finally, they were going to do something more in the damn war.

But there was a little trepidation among some of the flamers—the few short-timers. Every Marine who knows he is going home soon wants to stay as far away from trouble as he can.

Just how far forward were we going that night? Sgt. Jack Carty thought. He was one of the 10th Replacement Drafters scheduled to go home in a couple of weeks. As it turned out, they just crunched the Shermans up the road to an area with some small earth ramps—the special work of dozer tanks. There, they ran the tanks up the embankments and parked them at an elevated angle. This gave them more trajectory to loft 105mm ordnance into enemy targets.

The reason for the scheduled shoot was concern in the First Marine Division over the CCF buildup.

> Division intelligence estimated that the Chinese could muster up to '57 infantry battalions supported by 12 artillery battalions and 40 tanks . . . for a thrust into the Marine sector.
> . . . But before the month [April] ended, Marines, in conjunction with other I Corps [First Corps] divisions, had deluged the enemy with artillery and tank fire in Operation CLOBBER. The purpose of this shoot was to inflict maximum casualties and damage by employment of the element of tactical surprise. (MCOinK, Volume V)

Sgt. Carty had a slight problem on *The Roamin' Candle* that night because the elevation estimates were a little off. After F22 fired for register, on recommendations from the forward observer, there was a panicked radio message from the F.O. that something was wrong. The first two shots out of *Candle's* 105 didn't reach the Gooks, and the third round just about cleared the MLR, shaking the hell out of the infantry in the trenchline.

"I went over the numbers again with our platoon leader," the worried Carty said, "and we found the problem. Once the adjustment was made, we did all right. We fired all 10 of our rounds before Operation CLOBBER was secured."

Unfortunately, the platoon never did find out how well it did on that mission:

> The reinforced 11th Marines [artillery regiment], augmented for this occasion by Company D, 1st Tank Battalion and nine of the battalion's 105mm howitzer and flame tanks, blasted Chinese CPs, bivouac areas, artillery and mortar positions, and observation posts. Since most of the firing took place at night when results were unobserved, no estimate could be made as to the effect of the operation on the enemy. (MCOinK, Volume V)

Carty had about two more weeks of actual work with the tanks before turning *The Roamin' Candle* over to Cpl. Al Chalk, who had been F22's driver.

Now, twenty-three-year-old former sportswriter from New Jersey was a real short-timer, but there was a hint of "Old Salt" showing in him when he wrote a letter to his first tank commander, Len Martin, who had rotated home to Illinois the previous November.

"Speaking of replacements, every draft that comes in gets saltier. Boy, these guys come over and expect to have things handed to them on a platter. We got a selective service (draftees who didn't enlist in the Corps, but were assigned to be Marines) bunch last batch and what a crew. Salts! Ye Gods, you'd think they were on the islands the last war."

The same thing was happening in other units. "The character of AT/5 was changing," Sgt. John Cronin noticed. "Reserves were being sent home and replacements were now a mix of new regulars, draftees and career Marines with rank.

"The career Marines were being plucked from various duty stations throughout the Corps. Until now, we were mostly guys who had a duty to perform and just wanted to do it and get home and get out of the Corps."

But the newcomers were coming in with their own ideas and a little more salt sprinkled among them than previous drafts.

"It took some, let's say, *adjusting* on both sides to get along," admitted Sgt. Cronin. The tank commander was not used to ordering someone to do something and having a more junior NCO suggest: "At Camp Lejeune, we did it this way."

"This was not the thing to say to one of us who has been in Korea for a while," Cronin would admonish the subordinate.

Sgt. Carty needn't have worried about his beloved Flame Platoon, however. It would get along just fine without him, but under much more duress than it had experienced in the last eleven months.

Several of the veterans of Luke's Castle confrontation would take over in the turrets. Cpl. Chuck Lasche, who was F13's driver, replaced Sgt. Jim Waltz as T.C. and also become first-section leader. Cpl. Werner Litzman was his driver. When Sgt. Chuck Wager left in May with Carty, Cpl. Leonard Klewzewski took over the third section, and Cpl. Pat McDermott moved into the command hatch on F31. The second section was being led by Sgt. Bob Rawlins, the new T.C. of F21, when Cpl. Roger Davis rotated out.

The war had changed, and so had the attitude toward employment of nine elite double-barreled Sherman tanks. They were going to be very, very busy.

AT/5s Not Too Busy, Either

Meanwhile, Lt. Pete Clapper, commanding officer of the 5th Marine Regiment anti-tank platoon—AT/5—and Sgt. John Cronin, who was tank commander of the No. 2 Patton in the platoon, were also running out their time in Korea.

Contrary to the Flame Platoon taking on more responsibility in the war, the step-brothers in the 5th A-Ts were not quite as busy as they had been in the mountains of East-Central Korea.

"We weren't going on as many firing missions as we did on the East Coast," Cronin noted. "And I can't recall going to the same place twice during April. Any firing we did was just a one-day thing, with no overnight stays."

What Cronin and the rest of the AT/5 tankers also were discovering, was initial difficulty estimating the range of their 90mm rifles because of the lower, rolling hills. "Our range estimating was a good 50 percent off," Sgt. Cronin remarked. "The replacements just coming in from Pendleton were better at it than us veterans."

After referring to hills with numbers as high as 812, 884, 1052, and the like in the East-Central mountains, it seemed unusual to the Fifth Marines anti-tankers to be sighting in comparative humps like 67, 84, 86, and the rest of the two-digit mounds they encountered. But once they got the knack of reading the smaller hills, their 90s were just as destructive as they were in the mountains. "The 90 was deadly accurate as far as 5,000 yards," Cronin bragged.

It was a whole new way of working with the 5th Marines infantry, however. They were used in the open escorting infantry patrols, much different from the stationary positions they had to hold in the eastern mountains. Roadblocks and recovering wounded also were regular missions for AT/5.

Lt. Clapper was doing a lot of roaming over the new landscape looking for possible firing sites for his 90s, most of the search taking place in no man's land.

"One day the lieutenant took me, another guy, and a jeep driver to a hill a couple of miles from our camp," Cronin said. "We drove to the top of a small hill which was covered with dry grass."

The Sergeant was puzzled that there was only a pup tent open at the front facing north with two Army guys in charge of a 30-caliber light machine gun. They did have a field phone. It was his first shocking glimpse of outpost warfare.

"There was not another person in sight," the bemused Cronin said. "there was no trench, foxhole, or any other signs that this was a war zone. I was dumbfounded!" More so, the Doggies ignored the four Marines.

Lt. Clapper was nonplused. He had a map and a ruler and was trying to estimate ranges and trying to identify terrain features. "I was a little nervous," the Sergeant admitted, "standing on top of that hill in broad daylight." He had trouble paying attention to what the lieutenant was saying. Finally, it dawned on him that he was being asked a question by his commanding officer.

"What do you think, Sergeant Cronin? Will this ground support a tank?"

"Oh, sure, Lieutenant," he replied warily.

Why the Chinese Communists didn't fire on the small group is one of those weird mysteries of war that sometimes is unexplainable.

As Cronin said earlier, the character of the AT/5s was beginning to change, and this was never more apparent than one day when Lt. Clapper thought he had a text-book firing mission for his five tanks underway from a ridge in no man's land. Many of the crews had new replacements—52 in the March Replacement Draft, nearly half of the platoon's strength—and the platoon leader figured it would be great training for the cherries.

"The ridge paralleled the enemy hill," Clapper said. "Each of the five tanks would then pivot to the north and shoot up the trenches."

The lieutenant's tank fired willy-peter (white phosphorus) rounds at the extreme left and right to mark the shoot. The other tanks were to fire on his order. "We executed the column move onto the ridge with the kind of dash that would have pleased even old Georgie Patton," Lt. Clapper bragged. "Then each tank snapped a smart left-face that Rommel would have loved."

The Platoon Leader's gunner was on target—one WP on the left boundary and down the line with three more smoking shells to complete marking the entire field of fire. "It was textbook, better than a training film," the Platoon Leader said proudly. "I sure was hoping the powers-that-be were watching from the safe heights far to the rear."

But Lt. Clapper's careful instructions came back to haunt him. He had given strict orders to his tank commanders not to fire until he gave the word. He instructed his gunner to commence firing up a storm. However, the other four Pattons were not following suit.

Meanwhile, Sgt. John Cronin, who had not received the order to fire, was hunched in turret of Tank 2 wondering when the word to fire was going to be passed down over the radio. Eventually, the other tanks sporadically began rifling shots into the Gook hill, but not Tank-2.

"I was determined to hold my fire until we were given the word," Cronin said. But he said he never received the official order to fire. "Before long, every tank but us was firing." He was wondering why Clapper had not radioed all the tanks to commence firing.

Finally, Sgt. Cronin gave in and told his gunner, PFC James Fisher, to rip a round into the top of the hill where some fresh digging was apparent. "He hit within a few feet of it," the tank commander said proudly.

By then, Lt. Clapper gave the ceasefire, puzzled why the other tanks had been so reluctant to disperse their ordnance. "I radioed the rest of the tanks, asking why," Clapper said.

One response made him chuckle: "Well, lieutenant, you said we should train the new guys. We're showing them where the ammo is."

The fact that Tank-2 only got off one round did not escape the lieutenant. Without mentioning names when he critiqued the mission, Clapper pointed out, according to Sgt. Cronin: "one tank got off only one round."

Cronin had his own assessment. "I think he knew, in his own mind, that he screwed up in the communications. I was actually sorry we had fired that one round. If we hadn't, we wouldn't have had to clean the 90."

A/T5 continued to firing missions from the MLR and the outpost areas, much like the Flame Platoon. Unlike the gun tanks' ability to see their targets because their 90mm rifles were designed for that type of direct shooting, the flame tanks 105s were perfect for the longer-range obscured enemy positions designated by forward observers.

For all, however, it was maneuvering among the outposts, some near the MLR and others as much as a mile or more into no man's land. "Some outposts were manned by only a few Marines, some by a full company," Sgt. Cronin pointed out. "The size of the force depended not only on the distance from the MLR, but also its elevation with respect to the MLR."

High ground was considered an extension of the MLR. "I got a chance to check out one that had been held by the Goonies," Cronin said, "and was amazed at the size of the living quarters and tunnel work of the those Gooks."

That was not much different than what had been the norm of enemy-held hills in the East Central Zone. But in the West, the access to those positions was much easier, yet a bit more vulnerable because of the lack of cover.

Tanks were prime targets when they were roaming around the hinterlands. For sure, infantry didn't want to be anywhere near those monsters when they were churning up the landscape—out in the open—between the MLR and those outposts.

Changes Benefit Flame Platoon

Three major changes fell into place to significantly affect the future of the Flame Platoon as the second year of the Korean War subtly began to pass into the final thirteen months of the conflict that, during its tumultuous birth, had been christened a "police action."

President Harry S. Truman's infamous characterization of the Korean War after he was suckered with a comment from a reporter when few people could fathom what the hell was happening in the Land of the Morning Calm late in June 1950, was a blatant miscalculation. The "police action" had quickly escalated into a full-blown, few-holds-barred war.

Now, the First Marine Division was back in the western zone, responsible for real estate in an area where it had so doggedly expelled the North Korean People's Army more than eighteen months earlier.

That shift of the FMF (Fleet Marine Force) troops from the treacherous mountains of East-Central Korea to the smaller-hill-and-valley terrain along the Jamestown Line, made the use of tanks—all tanks, including the nine uniquely armed Shermans of the Flame Platoon—much more compatible.

That was followed by the arrival, late in May 1952, of Lt. Col. John I. Williamson, a reluctant newcomer to the war, who assumed command of the First Tank Battalion. Williamson had seen his share of combat in World War II and tried a number of ways to get around leaving his comfortable billet of writing manuals in the Marine Corps Development Center back in the States when the Korean War beckoned. All of the Colonel's maneuvering did little to change his new assignment. Reluctant or not to be in another war, Williamson didn't take long to conclude that keeping flame tanks around battalion was a waste of good material, a unique tactical weapon, and some outstanding Marines.

Not long after the new battalion commander grasped the reins of First Tanks, a young, high-spirited, not-so-by-the-book second lieutenant named Clement S. Buckley was transferred out of Baker Company of the First Tank Battalion, where he commanded a platoon of M46 Pattons to take charge of the Flame Platoon. Lt. Buckley would not only be a firm and imaginative platoon commander both in and out of combat, but his leadership and loyalty to his men would endear him to those who served under him.

The more gentle countryside of West Korea opened a whole new ball game for the use of tanks. With the turnover in personnel in the First Tank Battalion came a fresh look at the Flame Platoon and a decision to use its lethal firepower against the enemy rather than to leave it in hibernation as it had been for most of the last year.

Thus, the flame tanks, once again, were about to join the fray in earnest. And, by duking it out with the Chinese Communists—bloodying more noses than the jabs it would take, just like the big gun tanks—Flamers put the exclamation point on a statement that their versatile Sherman was one hell of a valuable weapon.

About the same time, there were changes up and down the United Nation's command. General Mark W. Clark took command of the United Nations forces when Gen. Matthew Ridgway was reassigned to head allied troops in Europe. I Corps, under which the First Marine Division fell, now was commanded by Maj. Gen. Paul W. Kendall, USA. Vice Adm. Turner C. Joy, who—from Day One—steadfastly stood up to the Chinese in truce negotiations, turned over the U.S. Naval Forces Far East to Vice Adm. Robert P. Briscoe.

With the change in the Division's sector of responsibility, and the political influence emanating from the ongoing truce talks, came a different type of war to be fought. It was becoming an "outpost war," and it was stretching the responsibility of the First Marine Division dangerously thin.

This was much to the chagrin and deep concern of Maj. Gen. John T. Seldon, who had replaced General Thomas as commander of the First Marine Division in January. As an outpost war, MLRs were being advanced to OPLRs—outpost lines of resistance.

> A heavy drain on the limited manpower of Marine infantry regiments defending James-town (Line) was caused by the need to occupy an additional position, an outpost line of resistance (OPLR). This defensive line to the front of the Marine MLR provided additional security against the enemy, but decreased the strength of the regimental reserve battal-ion, which furnished the OPLR troops. The outposts manned by the Marines consisted of a series of strongpoints built largely around commanding terrain features that screened the 1st Marine Division area. The OPLR across the division front was, on the average, about 2,500 yards forward of the MLR.
>
> To the rear of the main line were two secondary defensive lines, Wyoming and Kansas. Both had been established before the Marines arrived. . . .
>
> Rear and frontline units alike found that new regulations affected combat operations with the enemy in West Korea. These restrictions were a result of the truce talks that had taken place first at Kaesong and, later, at Panmunjom. In line with agreements reached in October 1951:
>
> "Panmunjom was designated as the center of a circular neutral zone of a 1,000 yard radius, and a three mile radius around Munsan and Kaesong was also neutralized, as well as two hundred meters on either side of the Kaesong-Munsan road." (MCOinK, Volume V)

As early as the first week of April,

> guns of the First Tank Battalion began to render valuable support to Marine frontline regi-ments . . . Tank companies were used almost daily in the forward sectors for destruction by direct fire of the Chinese MLR fortifications. (MCOinK, Volume V)

When Lt. Col. Williamson took over from Lt. Col. Walter Reynolds, the First Tank Battalion already was proving its value as a bonafide support unit to the infantry. Wil-liamson, however unhappy he was to be in Korea, was not shy about assigning his tankers as much action as he thought they could handle.

John I. Williamson earned his spurs as a tank battalion commander in the Pacific and he was willing to let that experience speak for itself as he went up the ranks. He also had a journalistic background, and later chronicled his command in Korea, based on a series of letters he wrote to his wife, Buckie. He prefaced those tales in *Dearest Buckie* with a glib personal assessment in reaction to orders sending him to Korea.

> I was the original war protestor, at least I objected to going to war long before the Vietnam war popularized the idea . . . Physically I have always been a devout coward. Only two years married, I was happily enjoying marital bliss. (JIW, Dearest Buckie)

He boldly told his commanding officer he didn't want to go to Korea. His superior replied that he, himself, would like to be taking over command the tank battalion. Wil-liamson seized the opportunity and offered to let his C.O. go to Korea in his place. He would gladly remain in the States. That suggestion, he thinks, probably hastened the new battalion commander's trip to Land of the Morning Calm.

This was Williamson's style. He never seemed to back off saying his piece.

Although he was a tough commander in World War II, he admittedly attempted to mellow his approach to his tankers in Korea. However, he stood for no foolishness and rarely thought twice about proper Marine Corps discipline to foul-ups and goof-offs.

It was later in the summer when Clem Buckley, newly promoted to first lieutenant, was given the Flame Platoon by Williamson, and he immediately started looking for ways to better utilize its nine twin-barreled Shermans. Buckley seemed to be Williamson's idea of how a commander of a unit of tanks should perform. He was aggressive, a good leader, looked out for his men, and had a certain way of rankling his superior without letting it get out of hand.

Cpl. Hank Amos, the Flame Platoon mechanic from Clementon, New Jersey, also doubled as Buckley's driver when he arrived in Korea early in the summer of 1952. He got to know the lieutenant as well as any NCO. "Lt. Buckley was quite an officer," Amos said, "and, he was the *Colonel's boy*. Lt. Col. Williamson liked the way Buckley operated."

By the time Lt. Buckley came aboard, Williamson had been giving the flame tanks increasingly more assignments, using their 105 cannons on both direct and indirect firing missions. Once in a while Buckley would be ordered to take them forward to rake enemy positions with their flame guns. "We did quite a bit of indirect firing, usually taking three or four tanks out a time," Buckley said.

Prior to Lt. Buckley's arrival, Colonel Williamson had the flame tanks involved in several missions, including the big Fourth of July shoot.

In honor of Independence Day, I Corps issued orders for massive firing at specific times for one-minute periods on 4 July. That was a TOT—Time on Targets—designated Operation Firecracker, and the Flame Platoon would get in its two cents' worth of the 3,200 rounds launched from First Marine Division muzzles. "All day on the Fourth of July we lusty Americans celebrated by firing without restraint at every possible target on our front" (JIW, *Dearest Buckie*).

The Division officially claimed 21 ChiCom kills, several injured, and destruction or serious damage to CCF artillery and mortar positions, bunkers, and trenches.

The flame tanks also were used in diversionary tactics, and a few days later, they would be involved in a big one that was not too popular with Division command.

As General O.P. Smith had his differences with X Corps commander General Ned Almond during the first year of the war, General Sheldon was not always in agreement with directives coming out of I Corps from General Kendall. And it was so noted:

> *More casualties, however, resulted from the issuing of another I Corps directive, this one dealing with the conduct of raids to seize prisoners, obtain information about the enemy, and to destroy his positions, supplies, and equipment. Back in June, the EUSAK commander (General James Van Fleet) had first stressed to his corps commanders the increased importance of combat raids to obtain additional intelligence during this period of stabilized conflict.*
>
> *Although General Selden had submitted two division plans, he strongly believed that smaller patrols could accomplish the objective with fewer casualties and loss of life. In particular, the division commander pointed out to I Corps that adequate defense of the 35-mile-long Marine division front did not permit the withdrawal of a sizable force for patrol missions without endangering the security of the entire Corps sector. The attack order was issued, however, on 3 July for the first large-scale raid to be conducted prior to 7 July. The code name BUCKSHOT 2B was assigned for this particular raid. As soon as he*

received the date of execution for the proposed operation, the Marine division command-er advised I Corps that designation of 7 July as the cut-off date for the raid precluded proper rehearsal of attack plans. The operation would also conflict with rotation to the States of 2,651 Marines, whose replacements would not be available until 11 July. Corps turned a deaf ear; division then ordered a battalion-size attack for the night of 6–7 July.

Before dusk on 6 July, . . . reinforced 1st Battalion, 7th Marines moved into position—on the left, a tank-infantry force, A/1/7 . . . to create a diversion; in the center, the main assault force, Company C . . . and on the right, a reinforced platoon from Company B . . . to sup-port the attack by fire from positions close to the objective, Yoke. Earlier, three reinforced squads . . . had occupied combat outposts in the area of operations to deny the use of key terrain to the enemy and to provide additional fire support in the attack. At 2200 . . . Company C crossed the line of departure and set its course for Yoke, three-quarters of a mile northeast. Five minutes later the Company B support unit moved out to occupy the intermediate objective, COP (Combat Outpost) Green, one-half mile southeast of Yoke. As it took up positions on COP Green . . . the Company B platoon discovered that no Chinese were in its vicinity; in fact, the platoon was not to encounter any enemy forces during buckshot.

Even though Company B failed to engage any Chinese, the remainder of the bat-talion encountered more than its share. About 450 yards southwest of the objective the Company C attack force was hit by an enemy ambush, which cut off the lead element. Although the Chinese directed strong efforts at halting the Marine advance, they were unsuccessful in this attempt. The Marines pressed the attack and seized Yoke 20 minutes after midnight. (MCOinK, Volume V)

A section of flame tanks was involved, but en route to the rendezvous where it joined a platoon of Able Company M46s, one of the twin-barreled Shermans ran off the road and overturned. The tank commander and loader were injured and had to be evacuated. "The two uninjured crewmen were quite shaken. They were sent to the rear for a shot of brandy and bed, which is what they needed" (JIW, *Dearest Buckie*).

The other two flame tanks continued forward with the Pattons. But Williamson wasn't happy with the results, particularly with the overall operation of his unit, although after-action reports were complimentary.

On the left, the diversionary attack unit, Company A supported by the five tanks of the 2d Platoon, Company D, 1st Tank Battalion, and by a section of flame tanks from the armored battalion headquarters, began its mission at 2355. In three-quarters of an hour, the tank-infantry unit reached its objective, the first high ground southwest of Yoke. Tanks turned their 90mm guns on known Chinese positions on the hill to the north. During the next hour, the big guns of the M–46 medium tanks sent 49 rounds into enemy emplace-ments. The Marine tanks ceased fire at 0113. (MCOinK, Volume V)

Williamson saw it this way: "The flame tanks . . . did not fire as ordered because of mechanical difficulties, and a marked lack of initiative of their lieutenant" (JIW, *Dearest Buckie*).

This was before Lieutenant Buckley came on board, and the battalion commander, then, would have no cause to worry about this junior officer's "lack of initiative." Mean-while:

Over on the high ground to the north and east, the attack force was under heavy fire from Communist mortars and artillery and was also receiving a number of enemy small-unit probes. At 0200, Company A made contact with Company C . . . . the main force (was) somewhat disorganized as a result of the wounding of the company commander . . . the loss of several key officers and NCOs, and the effects of the lead element of Company C being ambushed and cut off . . . At 0310 the two companies at Yoke began to disengage, returning to the MLR by 0636 on the 7th, without further casualties.

The one platoon of Company A and seven tanks of the diversion unit were still in their forward positions on the left and had prepared to resume firing. At dawn the M46s relaid their guns on targets that had become visible. Tank gunners destroyed two observation posts and three machine gun positions and damaged many feet of trenchlines. . . .

With the return at 0645 of the tank-infantry diversion force, the special operation for obtaining prisoners and information ended. No Chinese had been captured and no data gleaned from Communist casualties, listed as the 19 reported by the tankers and an estimated 20 more wounded or killed. Marine casualties from the operation were out of proportion to the results achieved—12 dead, 85 wounded, and 5 missing. It had been a high price to pay for a venture of this type, particularly when the primary objectives went unaccomplished.

During the entire 4–7 July period, 22 Marines had lost their lives in combat operations. Division reported that 268 Marines had been wounded during the long Fourth of July. These figures were the highest since September 1951 when large scale attacks by UN forces had first been abolished in line with the new tactic of positional warfare that would be waged until the truce talks resulted in an armistice. (MCOinK, Volume V)

Williamson's assessment after he watched one of his tanks throw a shoe and another get stuck coming down off the hill: "the whole operation became a bitched-up melange of disabled tanks and others trying to assist them" (JIW, *Dearest Buckie*).

But he still mustered some satisfaction for the way his men responded to their adversity. "The tankers got out to work on the disabled vehicles, established their own ground defense, and performed heroic and yoeman service throughout the day" *(Dearest Buckie).*

Nonetheless, three of the disabled tanks had to be left in no man's land and Williamson figured they'd probably have to be destroyed. However, the crews went back the following day, and although exposed to enemy fire, worked diligently to prepare for their possible extraction. The effort was not lost on the battalion commander. "They stayed out there all day, exposed to fire which caused about ten slight casualties, and behaved in a fine courageous fashion" *(Dearest Buckie).*

For the second straight day, the crews returned and finally recovered one tank that was deemed savable, and the hulk of another. They weren't finished. A day later, they went back and attempted to recover the third tank, but when they got to it, it was in four pieces and half buried. "I ordered them to leave it there, and withdraw" *(Dearest Buckie).*

As a result of that scenario, the battalion commander, faced a problem with Division. Williamson received word that General Seldon was going to reprimand a lieutenant he deemed responsible for the loss of a tank. It would be a report to be inserted in the lieutenant's personnel file.

Williamson—never a real fan of the Division C.O.—went out on a limb and wrote his own letter to the commanding general defending the lieutenant. He suggested that if anyone be held responsible, it should be the battalion commander. General Sheldon eventually relented and ordered Williamson to handle the situation. No letter of reprimand was to go into the lieutenant's file.

With all that was going on, the Flame Platoon had been quite busy during the month of July. Indirect firing and diversionary missions were common. Then there were a couple of rescue missions after Lt. Buckley took over the Platoon. One of them occurred on the west flank of the Division, somewhere outside the no-fire zone around Panmunjom. "It was at night," Lt. Buckley said. "We went down there and could see the area, at least what we could see in the dark, and then we gave them harassing fire with the machine guns and the 105s."

Although the flame tanks did not incur any damage, one of the Pattons got in trouble that night. The next day, at first light, Lt. Buckley took four flame tanks out in attempt to bring the forty-five-ton M46 back to the to forward C.P. "It had thrown a shoe," he said. "We had to hook up four tanks in front of it to get it out of there."

It was a harness, or serial, operation and took that many tanks to move one 45-ton gun tank without a track. "We just crossed our cables," Buckley said, describing the left-to-right, right-to-left connections from the back of one tank to front of the next tank, "and just hooked 'em up two-three-four tanks together, whatever it took to move 'em."

On something like this, they could use the Shermans or Pattons. "Whatever was around," Buckley said. "We had to get the wounded tank out of there." They did!

On 9 and 10 August, flame tanks got into some action in the Korean Marine Corps zone on the left flank of the Division's sector. Three of the Shermans, positioned slightly north of Munsan-ni just above the Neutral Corridor in the Korean Marine Corps sector, unloaded more than 100 rounds of 105 ordnance on Chinese positions west of the Sachon River, well below Panmunjom.

While the 76mm cannons on the KMC Shermans could never reach those Communist targets more than five miles out, the Flame Platoon's 105s easily found the range. Decimated were two trenches, nine bunkers, and seven mortar positions. At least one ChiCom was known KIA, another twenty-eight estimated killed, and nearly a dozen others possibly wounded.

The next night, flame tanks went along with Able Company Pattons further southwest to set up for a shoot on CCF hot spots about four miles west of the Sachon. The barrage consisted of nearly 150 rounds from the 105s. Combined with the 90mm rifles of the M46s, they destroyed six houses in the area and as many bunkers along the enemy MLR. At least one Red soldier was confirmed KIA.

It was typical of the extremely effective fire the flame tanks could provide with their howitzers, which far outdistanced the 75mm guns of the KMC older Shermans. While working out of the KMC zone, the indirect fire of flame tanks dropped much ordnance on Hill 288, a Chinese O.P. opposite the KMCs which the Korean Marine tanks could not reach. Intelligence reports coming back after several of those missions noted the severe destruction to the reverse slopes of enemy positions.

Pounding the reverse slopes was a valuable asset the flame tanks 105s could provide that the more powerful 90mm, or the smaller 75mm could not manage. It was the mobile artillery, as well as an in-close purveyor of scorched death, that made the Sherman flame tank so valuable.

It wouldn't be long, however, when their flame guns would be the weapon of choice. On 11 August, four of the Shermans under the command of Lieutenant Buckley left the Battalion forward CP at Changdan Road with four Charlie Company gun tanks for a much bigger, and crucial, mission.

Scorching Feint by Flame Tanks Helps Bunker Hill

Bunker Hill was the 122-meter-high pinnacle on a stretch of Bunker Ridge about 750 yards in front of the First Marine Division's center sector of the Jamestown Line, the main line of resistance (MLR).

It was the pillar of the Division's outpost line of resistance. It got its name from Marine ingenuity of felling timber well behind the lines, trucking it forward, and employing infantry under the supervision of engineers and shore party experts to build a miniature outpost fortress.

Division saw the Bunker Ridge—an axis running about 1,000 yards from Hill 124 to the pinnacle of 122—protecting the slightly higher positions west of the Jamestown Line.

On Jamestown, the dominating height was Hill 201, 660 feet high, and immediately to the rear of the MLR in the left battalion sector. Southwest of this elevation was the Marine stronghold, Hill 229, just 23 feet lower than Taedok . . . Directly north of Hill 201 was Hill 122, adjacent to the enemy OPLR, and called Bunker Hill by the Marines. It was shortly to become the scene of bitter fighting. The crest of Hill 122 was about 350 yards long. At a distance of about 700 yards, it generally paralleled the northeast-southwest direction of Jamestown in the left of the 2/1 sector and adjoining 3/1 sector.

Southwest of Bunker and a little more than 200 yards from the Marine MLR was Hill 124. This Hill 124–122 axis, for tactical purposes, was known as the Bunker Ridge. The ridgeline, roughly "cashew" in shape almost anchored back into the MLR on the forward slopes of Hill 229. To the northeast of Bunker Hill and separated from it by a wide saddle was another enemy position, Hill 120.

Approximately one mile east of Hill 124 was Hill 56A, or Samoa, the right flank limit of the immediate battlefield. It guarded the best avenue of approach into the Bunker Hill area, the Changdan Road. Another Marine position west of Samoa was Hill 58A, or Siberia, a sentinel overlooking a long draw running down the east sides of Hills 122 and 120. Both Samoa and Siberia were outposted by squads. Another 1st Marines squad occupied Hill 52, on the other side of Changdan Road and not quite a half-mile east of Samoa. The entire battlefield was cut up by numerous gullies and draws, most of which paralleled Bunker Hill. (MCOinK, Volume V)

All of them were OPLR (Outpost Line of Resistance) positions coveted by Marines, as well as the Chinese. They were high spots in a landscape of gullies and draws in the vicinity of Bunker Hill. But Siberia and Samoa were key positions protecting against what could be the ChiComs' best route to Bunker Hill.

"Siberia was one of the big ones, for the flame tanks," remarked Lieutenant Clem Buckley, the Flame Platoon commander. Buckley wasn't privy to the entire operation. All he knew was "it was to be a diversion on the right flank of the people that were taking Bunker Hill."

At dusk of 11 August, four flame tanks followed a quartet of Charlie Company Pattons and sat in an assembly area about a mile behind the MLR waiting for the word to move out. They would be in support of the 1st Marines Second Battalion for a diversionary assault on the squad-sized outpost Siberia. It had been in Marine hands until 9 August, when a company-sized assault by the Chinese forced the 1st Marines back to the

MLR. There were futile attempts to retake the hill. Three times the Marines reclaimed it, three times they were pushed off.

Hill 122—Bunker Hill—also had fallen into the hands of the Chinese. Because the Bunker ridge was key to the strength of the 1st Marines sector—and its higher vantage point could neutralize Siberia (58A)—Bunker Hill was the main objective. However, attention had to be drawn away from the ridgeline, and the plan of the attack was to renew an assault on 58A, a feint to occupy the Chinese while the main attack would be launched on the primary target.

It was up to the mix of gun tanks and flame tanks, along with a reinforced rifle platoon, to create the commotion on Siberia. For a while, however, there was a question whether the flame tanks were going to be available to use their primary weapon, which was a key to the mission. There was a shortage of CO_2 gas for the flame propellant, and normal channels were unable to get supplies. The glitch surfaced on 10 August, but later that day, Division was able to get EUSAK to release canisters of the gas, and they arrived in time for the next night's mission.

Although the M46s were equipped with eighteen-inch fighting lights—a searchlight with a shutter to conceal it when not in use—to help with night missions, the flame tanks were rolling blind. However, Lt. Buckley's imagination and ingenuity would solve the darkness problem.

It was shortly after 2100 that dark night when the flame tanks and their cohorts from Charlie Company were in position for the diversionary assault. The twin-barreled Shermans swung north off the Changdan Road, and the Pattons continued further east to approach Siberia from the other side.

The M-46 gun tanks . . . their powerful 90s opened up on the objective . . . the first section of flames (two tanks) made its way along the stream bed between the MLR and Hill 56A (Samoa). (MCOinK, Volume V)

Lt. Buckley, with M46s on the east side of the hill and unable to help with their fighting lights, was hampered by the poor visibility until he solved the problem on his own. "When we got to Siberia itself," the platoon commander said, "we couldn't see very well. So we ignited the flame guns and shot little spurts to give us enough light to see where we had to go."

They had approached Siberia from the southeast.

There the vehicles paused momentarily, then began to move up the near slope, using longer spurts of flame to sear the ground and sparse vegetation to the crest of the position. The gun tanks, in the meantime, had shifted their fire from Siberia northeast to neutralize Hill 110. When the flame vehicles reached the top of Siberia, they lumbered down the far slope, firing then in shorter bursts and sweeping the area with machine guns to discourage any enemy infantry interference.

With some fuel reserved to light their way on the return trip, the flame section reversed its course from the far side of the objective, mounted the crest, and clanked back to the Changdan Road. (MCOinK, Volume V)

Still sitting on the front slope of Siberia, Buckley's two tanks had more to throw at the Chinese. We shot the flame out as far as we could," Buckley said, "and then we laid back and waited for whatever we could see in the way of enemy fire. Whenever we picked up something like their tracers, then we would throw some 105 rounds at them—direct fire."

Their howitzer routine occasionally was supplemented by machine-gun fire. "We knew the enemy was out there, so we just tried to keep them off balance."

However, the flame tanks were about to realize they were a little victimized by their own scourge. "Coming back," Buckley discovered, "we couldn't see very well." Between the darkness and the smoke from the incinerated hill, they had trouble picking up the road.

"So we had to hang over the fronts of the tanks, just a foot or two off the ground to see the trail," Buckley said. One of the crew would belly out over the bow of the tank while another held on to his feet.

When the first two flame tanks got back to the jump-off area, Buckley turned the mission over to the second pair of fire-throwing Shermans under command of 2nd Lt. Henry F. Barry, in the lead, and Cpl. James Nelson in trace. Like the initial thrust by Buckley's team, Barry and Nelson took their Shermans to the top of Siberia and saturated the forward slope. As they backed their tanks down the reverse slope, they continued lacing rods of scorching napalm into Gook positions.

Siberia was far from the ice-cold mound of its namesake. It was a sizzling hill of orange flame and black smoke.

The flame tanks did experience more intense incoming than the big Pattons on the other side of Siberia. But fortunately, there were no injuries or damage to the vehicles.

PFC Ronald D. McKinney had a ringside seat to what was going on at Siberia and Bunker Hill. He was with the third fire team in the third squad, third platoon of Item Company, 3rd Battalion, 1st Marine Regiment which was manning the military crest of Hill 209-211 along the Jamestown Line that night.

McKinney and PFC Robert Lee Fowler were the designated sniper team for Item Company, and Siberia was directly in front of them.

"We had both our 20-power spotting scope and the 6-power scope on our sniper rifle," McKinney said, "and we had a good view of the two flame tanks as they fired the napalm on Outpost Siberia. "The two tanks made a coordinated advance up the slope of Siberia to about the eighty-meter contour level."

McKinney and Fowler watched through their scopes. From their point of view, one tank drove to the right flank of Siberia, and the other remained on the left. "Then, they simultaneously squirted their napalm across the crest from opposite directions," he said. "Both tanks traversed and fired again, creating an arc of fire along the slope facing us. They continued to traverse and fire until it seemed like the hill had been contour plowed and the furrows filled with flaming napalm."

McKinney and Fowler were enjoying the show, and it wasn't over, yet. As the tanks began to withdraw, they expended the remainder of their napalm, setting the entire forward slope of the hill afire.

Of course, in a few minutes, this did not bode well for the sniper team and the rest of the dug in Marines along the MLR—one of the reasons infantry aren't always happy to have tanks around. "Needless to say," McKinney cracked, "the Flame Tankers got the attention of ChiCom observers." It wasn't long before Siberia and the MLR behind it was bombarded with heavy mortars and artillery. "In spite of it," McKinney smiled, "we continued to watch the spectacular fireworks."

When the flame tanks had done their job, McKinney and Fowler watched their fellow infantrymen from Baker and Easy companies assault and take Bunker Hill.

Lt. Col. John I. Williamson, the First Tank Battalion commander, was another watchdog of the Flame Platoon and Charlie Company work that night and had nothing but praise for his "boys" and their first night's operation:

> *We made a splendid plan, and it was brilliantly executed . . . It was a night attack, which is difficult at best, and almost impossible for tanks, but my boys carried it off in magnificent style. It was the nearest thing to a perfect small-scale action I've seen. (JIW, Dearest Buckie)*

Watching the whole operation from another hill, Williamson commented

> *. . . it was beautiful. As darkness closed in and I heard the tanks moving out, I was filled with dread, for the tanks couldn't see a thing, comparatively speaking. It was pitch black. They had to leave their hatches open in order to see, which is quite dangerous. It takes great courage for those lads to plunge off into the dark unknown of the battle field like that. (Dearest Buckie)*

The next night brought the tanks back for more. There was a fierce battle as the Chinese attempted to recapture Siberia. Again, Williamson was watching. "Some gun and flame tanks moved out in front on the right to get a better crack at the attackers. One burst of flame caught six or eight Chinks" *(Dearest Buckie).*

That same night, PFCs McKinney and Fowler had their own problems when Item Company was alerted to relieve Baker Company on Bunker Hill. Fowler and McKinney were on Item's point leaving the MLR and heading toward Bunker Hill. "We advanced as though we were going to assault the summit of Hill 122," McKinney said, and then with wry humor, admitted: "Being the 10-percenters who never got the word, Bob and I went out about fifty yards beyond the finger where the rest of our platoon was ordered to 'dig in.'"

When the two pointmen discovered nobody was following them any longer, they decided something was wrong and hit the dirt, planning to dig in. The problem was, they didn't have their entrenching tools to gouge out a foxhole. "I used my combat knife and Bob used his canteen." It was hardly adequate for what was in the offing.

"Neither of us owned a wristwatch," McKinney soon realized, "we could only guess at the time and we figured it was about 2100 hours when the ChiComs began to counterattack."

It looked like a company of Reds coming down the slope on the east flank of Bunker Hill. McKinney and Fowler were fearing the worst.

"Then we heard Sgt. Jimmie Howard to our rear," McKinney said. "He was talking very loud on his radio requesting a 'spotter' round from his 4.2 mortars."

A white phosphorous round exploded just forward of the two advanced Marines. "Both Bob and I were showered with burning particles." Then, Howard bellowed: "Drop twenty-five and fire for effect!" That brought a mortar barrage into the charging Chinese. But that wasn't all the Reds were getting thrown at them. One of the Charlie Company Pattons turned on spotlights after pulling its nose up in a draw and began firing its machine gun into the Reds.

"Seemed like their tracer rounds were passing only a few feet in front of us," a very nervous McKinney said.

The two infantryman weren't just sitting by idly. They went into action with the BAR (Browning Automatic Rifle) and their hand grenades. Before they were ordered to withdraw from their shallow hole, which had been reinforced by the bodies of mortally wounded Chinese falling near their position, they expended most of their ammo and grenades. McKinney emptied a dozen 20-round magazines with his BAR, and Fowler used up four doubled, 30-round magazines with his M-2 Carbine.

McKinney admitted he and his buddy weren't quite calm as cucumbers. "We had been hunkered down in our little fox hole," McKinney said, "and chain-smoked a pack of cigarettes."

He had one other observation: "We thanked our lucky stars that the tank which had effectively covered us had not been one of those flame tanks." The infantryman didn't want anything to do with a scorching orange stream of napalm if it was being sent in his direction—even if it was aimed at oncoming ChiComs.

It wasn't the only activity undertaken by flame tanks those two nights. A little further northeast, a couple of the Shermans joined a platoon of Baker Company Pattons to work over Stromboli and Harlow in the Kum gok area in concert with what was going on around Bunker. It was a 105 mission for those flame tanks, which lowered their howitzers and lined nearly 40 rounds of HE and WP directly into the sides of those hills. Baker rifled another 150 rounds of 90mm at the Gooks, and the combined firepower ripped apart several bunkers and trenches.

The first two nights were merely the beginning of the battle for Bunker Hill. It would take four more days of give-and-take fighting along the line of outposts before Bunker ridge was permanently in Marines hands. Siberia was lost and retaken three more times before it was secured. All the while, Flame Platoon tanks were involved in support of the gun tanks and infantry.

> It was quite natural that the flurry of ground activity during the battle of Bunker Hill created a need for increased participation from Marine supporting arms. The magnitude of infantry action during the contest for Hill 122 resulted in a monthly record to date in 1952 for the amount of air support received as well as the volume of both artillery and tank fires supporting the division. . . . medium tanks (Flame Platoon) fired day and night missions during most of the infantry action. (MCOinK, Volume V)

Considering the amount of incoming that was thrown against the tank operations over the four days, it was considered fortunate there were no serious injuries or damage to the flame tanks. One night alone—13-14 August—when four of the twin-barreled Shermans went along with three Charlie Company platoons of M46s and a platoon of the First Marines anti-tank Pattons, the ChiComs saturated the mission with nearly 400 rounds of 60mm and 82mm mortars, and 122mm and 76mm artillery.

Colonel Williamson's pride in his tankers was augmented by General Seldon.

> The Commanding General, as well as the Regimental Commander, called me on the phone and personally commended the battalion for their splendid performance in the first night's battle. We were further complimented for subsequent performance. (Dearest Buckie)

In retrospect:

> During the early part of the August fighting, tanks of the division were able to get the first real test of a technique of night support, and at the same time experiment with a towing device to permit retrieval of disabled vehicles under fire without getting outside the tank. The use of the lights to support both the diversionary force and the defense of Hill 122

showed the value of these instruments. Lieutenant Colonel Williamson recommended that tanks be employed in pairs, one to spot and adjust fire and the other to fire. With respect to the towing device, he considered the new piece of equipment an improvement over the manual hook-up method, but noted that the device limited tank maneuverability and had a tendency when bouncing up and down over rough terrain to dig into the ground, impeding the forward progress of the vehicle. . . .

One measure of the results of the Bunker Hill fighting is seen in the price paid. Chinese losses were estimated by the 1st Marine Division at approximately 3,200, including more than 400 known dead. Marine casualties in the action were 48 killed and 313 seriously wounded. Several hundred additional wounded were treated at 1st Marines medical facilities and returned to duty shortly thereafter.

The battle of Bunker Hill resulted in the first major Marine action and victory in West Korea. It ushered in two straight months of hard fighting, the most difficult ones yet for Marines on the western front. (MCOinK, Volume V)

The Western Front! The term would not be lost on historians. "On both sides, the lines entrenched and solidified into something horribly reminiscent of the Western Front of World War I. Big offensives gave way to localized actions, bruising for those who fought them but with little effect on the grease-penciled lines on the big picture situation maps. (The Marines, Marine Corps Heritage Foundation)

The extensive use of flame tanks in no man's land, and the initiative of their crews, once and for all solidified their standing as an integral element of the First Tank Battalion. What infantry and fellow gun company tankers saw flame tanks accomplish in those mid-August battles earned a new and wiser respect for the twin-barreled Shermans—a respect that would be steadily reinforced as the war ground on for nearly another year.

New Forward Home for Flame Platoon

Following the Siberia-Bunker Hill action, the remainder of August 1952 still was fairly active for the Flame Platoon, which continued to be involved in direct and indirect firing missions.

As Marines and Chinese kept exchanging vantage points in front of the midsection of the Jamestown Line, the pummeling of Bunker Ridge by artillery and tanks—with some help from enemy incoming—amounted to severe refining of its soil. Lt. Col. John I. Williamson, the First Tank Battalion commanding officer, recorded it succinctly:

> *I went up to look at Bunker Hill to see if there is anything we can do to help out with the tanks. The place is completely pulverized from all the firing. As one correspondent said: "It looks like a box of talcum powder that had been dumped out of a dresser." (Dearest Buckie)*

It was after the Bunker Hill episode that 1st Lt. Clement Buckley, the Flame Platoon commanding officer, decided that all the running back and forth from the battalion C.P. to firing assignments was a waste of time, energy, and fuel, not to mention wear and tear on the tanks. Their 105mm cannons already had become quite effective as rolling artillery, but the tanks were constantly on the road getting to and from firing positions. The platoon commander went to Colonel Williamson and pleaded his case.

"Headquarters Company is located so far in the rear," Buckley emphasized to Williamson, "that it's taking too long to get forward for any kind of mission. We should find a suitable forward site for the Platoon."

As the crow flies it was a good seven miles, minimum, from the C.P. east of the Imjin River. Skirting hills, rice paddies over less than adequate roads, depending in what direction the Platoon's tanks were needed, added many more miles. And, in bad weather, getting across the Imjin could be a problem if the Spoonbill Bridge went out.

The battalion commander agreed and set out with his enterprising young lieutenant to locate an area for a small tank park in the proximity of the MLR. They found it within a stone's throw of the forward C.P. used by the battalion's gun companies. It was up the Changdan Road outside of Line Kansas less than a mile east of the MLR and a short distance north of the Panmunjom-Munsan-ni neutral corridor. It was at a point east of Panmunjom, where Jamestown sort of mirrored the Imjin River two miles to its south. "It is a natural setting," Buckley observed, "horseshoe shaped, surrounded by a natural slope about forty feet high."

Tanks entered the horseshoe off Changdan Road from the northeast. Dozer tanks from Service Company dug revetments into the west (facing the MLR), south, and east interior walls of the horseshoe. The revetments garaged the nine flame tanks—Fox 11-12-13-21-22-23-31-32-33 and the Thumper. They called the specially rigged flair tank Thumper because of the thudding sound its whirling chains, mounted on the front of an M4A3 Sherman, made when they beat into the ground—hopefully finding and detonating mines.

The crews stretched camouflage netting on poles made from felled trees to disguise the revetments.

Coming off the Changdan Road, tankers entered the horseshoe, where the tank revetments were dug into the side of the U-shaped hill.

Over a small knoll, about thirty feet high, in the back of the horseshoe was fuel and ammo dump. Between two of the revetments on the left bank of the horseshoe was a path going up the fifty-foot-high hill. On the crest were two squad tents for the flame tank crews, and pyramid tent for the Platoon Commander and the platoon sergeant, as well as the communications tent, which housed two Marines manning the radios, and the Navy corpsman. Between the two Flame crew tents, dug into the opposite side of the hill, were steps made of ammo-box wood and descending to a broad flat area where the mess tent was.

About 100 yards from the stairway, the tank battalion's gun companies kept a command post and tankers tents. Running along the perimeter of the lower area was a stream. On the other side of the water, partially hidden by bushes, was the infantry regiments' reserve area where they regrouped and trained after coming off the line. Portable showers were set up along the stream for the infantry, but the tankers were welcomed to use them once a week.

Once in the forward platoon tank park, the crews could quickly crank up their Shermans and move them into position for quick-ordered indirect fire, or take them further forward for direct fire missions at enemy positions across the front. "With Buckley," said one Flame Tanker, "you best have your vehicle always at the ready . . . or else!"

The forward platoon position was akin to a small CP with mechanics and cooks. "We had about fifty or sixty people up there," Lt. Buckley said. And because there was a company of gun tanks in the area, that meant there would be a mess staff and hot meals in a mess tent.

The new Flame Platoon C.P. was ideal for maintaining quick access to its missions, which were becoming quite plentiful in the outpost war. However, sometimes there weren't too many calls for flame-throwing missions, but the 105s were quite popular in complementing the Patton 90s support infantry.

One of the advantages of the flame tank's howitzer was that it was a relatively short canon, which didn't quite extend over the bow of the Sherman. The 90mm of the M46 reached several feet beyond the Patton's front. The stubbiness of the 105 tube allowed it a loftier arc at the maximum elevation of 60 degrees for dropping mayhem on reverse slopes of close targets. That same arc on the longer 90mm rifle would not allow its projectiles such minimal distance.

When on indirect firing missions, the flame tanks would be run up small mounds. Occasionally, dozer tanks would be brought in to manufacture small firing ramps. The idea was to increase the elevation of the 105s, in turn giving more loft or arc and the ability to fire on targets closer to Marine lines.

Because the napalm storage tanks consumed all the space in the hull below the turret, flame tanks could not carry more than six to ten rounds of 105 ordnance, which had to be secured along the back wall of the turret by specially made straps. M4A3E8 Shermans without the flamethrower would be able to store almost seventy rounds under the turret deck.

On missions specifically written for indirect firing, the Flame Platoon Shermans each rolled with a jeep-pulled trailer of fifty rounds of 105 ordnance, usually a mixture of HE (high explosive) and WP (Willy Peter, technically known as white phosphorus). While the advantage of the stubby tube was great for closer targets, the 105 also had some umpf. The conventional thirty-three-pound of HE had a range of 11,270 meters—that's better than 12,000 yards, nearly seven miles.

Indirect firing missions were safer for crewmen than taking the tank up on the lines for direct fire, or beyond when flame missions were called for. Direct support of infantry, or making a charge at a Chicom bunker for a flame shoot, brought the pigiron out into the open and naturally more susceptible to incoming or enemy infantry carrying rocket launchers. Yet there was some misgiving about indirect fire.

"It was most frustrating," noted one Flame Tanker, "that we were shooting the canons at called-in targets of opportunity, but never knowing what we hit."

The count, however, did come up in after-action reports, which rarely trickled down to the crews from battalion, unless it was particularly spectacular—or off the mark. There were occasions, though, when the Flame Tankers were made aware of their marksmanship—notably when they were extraordinarily successful in knocking out troop movements, pulverizing yard after yard of enemy trench lines, or destroying mortar or artillery positions.

This was all done with the precise recommendations of forward observers called in directly from within a few hundred yards of the target, or with intelligence grid locations of strongholds further away. Those F.O.s were pretty sharp, and once a round or two was fired for registration, it usually was sufficient enough for them to adjust the gunner's numbers and have succeeding volleys right on target.

Colonel Williamson also alluded to the "blind" shooting: "Most of the time we can't see what we hit, because of the range, and we make very low estimates, for fear of exaggerating. I'm sure we've killed over twice as many as we have claimed" (JIW, *Dearest Buckie*).

In the instance the battalion commander was referring to on 19 August, the Chinese KIA count was 22, which Williamson claimed was the highest for his tanks since he took over. That was when an indirect firing mission lobbed 95 rounds of 105 ordnance on outpost Irene in direct support of the 2nd Battalion, 5th Marines.

Williamson was told the foot Marines were in quite a pinch, and when the tankers had eased their situation, a wounded infantryman proclaimed: "You great big pigiron bastard, if I could, I'd kiss your ass!"

It wasn't unusual for the battalion's letter tanks to ask for some 105 support and they would work much the same as the infantry forward observer. Once in a while, aerial photographs would be scanned for selected targets, but because they were over a hill or two, tankers once again had to rely on the sharp calculations of an F.O.

When flame tanks were sent forward for direct support, often it was to do a lot of bunker busting, which meant sending well-aimed rounds of HE into the log-and-sandbag strongholds anchoring the Chicom trenchlines.

There was such a mission on 17 August when several of the Sherman 105s unleashed more than 200 rounds blasting Gook positions on outposts Elmer, Hilda, Ronson, and Bruce to the left of the Hook. At least three bunkers were eliminated with 150 yards of enemy trenchline.

There was a Flame Platoon torch mission on 22 August against Outpost Irene where the twin-barreled Shermans joined Baker Company Pattons, again in support of the 2ndBat5th. It didn't come off as planned and the Battalion Commander didn't think much of it. "It went okay, but didn't accomplish much" *(Dearest Buckie)*.

The 5th Marines were attempting to regain possession of Outpost Irene, which was an integral part of the perimeter in front of the Hook, in the northern sector of the Jamestown Line. There would be more heated confrontations with the Chinese later in the fall of 1952. Irene, Hilda, and Elmer were three outposts in a northeast-to-southwest line—smaller hills to the left of Jill—which Marines occupied only during daylight hours early in August.

Midway through the month, the Reds decided to stay on the hills around the clock, and Marine infantry ran into trouble trying to dislodge them. Early on the evening of 22 August, two Marine ambushes, supported by tanks, surprised the ChiComs.

Flame tanks went into the fray with Baker Company's gun tanks, which were mounted with the fighting lights that had proved so successful around Bunker Hill. With Baker's tanks trying to lure the Chinese out in the open, it was up to the flame tanks to purge rods of blistering napalm at the enemy intruders. However, the Reds smelled out the ruse and kept their distance from the lethal firestorm.

The infantry—on both sides—however, took heavy casualties in fire-fights around Irene.

The next day it began raining, and between 23-25 August, nine inches were dumped along the Jamestown line. That not only washed out roads but put a damper on any thought of serious combat. That was one of the occasions when tanks stayed on station, not willing to risk being caught too far behind the MLR and unable access muddy, or washed-out, roads to supply support to the infantry.

That storm was the edge of a typhoon that came racing over the Far East. Fortunately the main force passed south of the First Marine Division.

Although the flooding conditions in the division sector were not so extensive as the July rains, they curtailed ground activity considerably and air action to a lesser degree. Division roads were badly damaged but not trenches and bunkers, strengthened as a result of the experience with the July floods . . . the Imjin (river) crested to 42.5 feet. If the sudden flash floods wreaked havoc with some of the Marine division installations, the Chinese were the recipients of similar disfavors; intelligence indicated that damage to the CCF frontline positions was even more severe than to the Jamestown defenses. (MCOinK, Volume V)

When the weather cleared, however, flame tanks turned off their burners and elevated their 105s to loft ordnance on the reverse slopes of enemy-held positions for three days.

With the Pattons and their 90s on station, and F.O.s guiding their gunners, Baker Company was also doing a job concentrating on CCF troop movements, wreaking devastating consequences on bunkers and gun emplacements. The accuracy of the Patton gunners prompted one Flame Tanker to comment, "As quick as the speed of sound, it appeared the 90mm rounds exploded with direct accuracy on enemy positions, and it reminded me of a guard in a prison tower honing in on prisoners trying to escape."

On the morning of 30 August, two flame tanks sitting more than two miles behind the lines in the KMC Sector, dropped ninety rounds from just beyond the Peace Corridor on enemy positions west of the Sachon River. They took out two Chinese outposts, a machine-gun position, five bunkers, 200 yards of trenchline, and a house. That was a good shoot, and since it was blind, it had a lot to do with the ability of the F.O. to bring that havoc right on the button.

The day before, there was a changing of the guard when the First Marine Division welcomed its sixth commanding officer since hitting Inchon nearly two years earlier. General Seldon turned the task over to Major General Edwin A. Pollock on 29 August.

> *A brief ceremony at division headquarters, attended by senior officers of EUSAK and KMC, marked the event. . . .*
>
> *The new division commander . . . had commanded the 2d Marine Division at Camp Lejeune, North Carolina . . . He had more than 30 years of military experience. During World War II, he had participated in no fewer than five major campaigns in the Pacific, including the first at Guadalcanal, where he earned a Navy Cross, and one of the war's most costly battles, Iwo Jima. (MCOinK, Volume V)*

Going into September, the outpost fighting would escalate, but Marines in their ability to find the flip side of almost anything, continued to make the best of it with a little imagination of their own.

Names of towns and areas were hard to come by in Korea, particularly when Marines got away from the larger villages and what few cities were located near the hills indigenous to combat areas on the Western Sector. Few Marines knew more than map coordinates—if that much—of where they were in Korea. Unless there was a pitched battle, or area, which they were occupied long enough for its location to become well known, it just was not S.O.P. for it to be labeled. Some villages had names, but most Marines didn't know them—and couldn't care less. It wasn't anywhere near home, so who gave a crap?

It was about the time the Korean War entered its third year that Marine creativity started to blossom in the infantry's day-to-day grind. Marines being what they are, it is not surprising how their imagination worked. A hardened combat Marine, asked where he fought during the final year of the war, would not stumble over an oriental location. He'd likely reply: "Russell, Dagmar, and oh, yeh, Hedy."

Marines are very quick to cut through government-issue terms to simplify things. Tired of calling hills by the numbers representing their heights in meters, Marine infantry had a better idea. The probability that the smaller hills, some of them comparative bumps, stretched the infantrymen's imagination to remind them of the finer things of life—*GIRLS!*

Some of the most ferocious fighting in the Marines zone of responsibility outside the Jamestown Line was identified by anything but government issue nomenclature. *Nice set of boobs right out there—those two hills.*

A voluptuous movie starlet and one of many shapely pinups of the day probably came to mind. Thus, the "set of boobs" were christened Dagmar. And Russell may have honored sex symbol Jane Russell of the movie *Outlaw* fame. Not many ladies of Korean War time were as popular as Marilyn Monroe. Naturally, a hill had to be named Marilyn. And Hedy? One of the real striking actresses was Hedy Lamar. Irene? A deviation probably—no Marine passing through Camp Pendleton, Camp Delmar or Oceanside California, could forget one of the most popular ballads of the day—"Good Night Irene, Good Night."

Esther (Williams, the sturdily put-together famous actress-swimmer), Ginger (Rogers, who looked better and danced as well as Fred Astaire), Ava (Gardner, what she could do to a Marine's imagination). So hills in the outpost war in Western Korea provoked a bevy of stimulating names.

Not that the Marines could have run out of sexy pinups for their hills, but there were a couple of guys in there—Elmer, Donald, Felix, Gary, Clarence, Bruce, some possibly influenced by Walt Disney's characters—Elmer Fudd, Donald Duck, Felix the Cat.

Actually, all but Elmer were among a string of hills running south to north in front of the 5th Marines MLR and identified alphabetically—Allen, Bruce, Clarence, Donald, Felix, Gary. The guys, however, were jilted for cities when the 7th Marines took over the area and found the Chinese were too familiar with the nomenclature. There must have been gamblers among those Gyrenes because outposts became known as the Nevada hills.

The 7th Marines put their bets on Carson (which had been Allen), Reno (Bruce), Vegas (Clarence). When they rolled the dice for the others, up came Berlin (Donald), Detroit (Felix), Frisco (Gary). A little further north, opposite the Hook, Jill became Seattle, which was near Warsaw—in Korea, that is. Hard to figure? Not for Marines! *Yours is not to reason why.*

Miserable Rain "Welcomes" Replacements

The outposts continued to catch hell early in September. But periodically, the weather, once again, was also creating problems for the First Tank Battalion—particularly early in the month.

Although not quite the magnitude of typhoons, there were rainstorms so intense they completely negated tank warfare. It made roads and bridges, normally used by the First Tank Battalion, impassable—completely sidelining pigirons because their weight reduced their traction to wallowing in the mud. A byproduct of the inclement weather was the cost of material damage to the in-place armor by enemy firepower. This became a factor because normal tank firing missions could not be carried out S.O.P.

Tank firing missions, both direct and indirect, normally were initiated from forward C.P.s, and when complete, the rolling armor would retrace to the forward tank park. When the rain made roads and bridges non-negotiable, it was necessary to leave some of the armor forward to help protect the infantry, and be on site to carry out future firing missions.

Sitting in their firing positions, the behemoths could easily be seen from across no man's land, and the targets were not lost on the Chinese. They took the occasions to pummel the areas with all kinds of ordnance, and it produced a measure of destruction on the tanks. It also cost one tanker his life when the First Platoon of Able Company came under artillery fire on 27 September and a round scored a direct hit on a turret periscope mount.

Rain in Korea, as in any war zone, was not a very pleasant experience. In the fall when the atmosphere was beginning to chill at night, life could be downright miserable—particularly if Marines had little more than canvas, or ponchos, for protection from the elements.

Debarking from ships to begin their tours of unknown consequences in a war zone was bad enough for young Marines and soldiers arriving in the replacement drafts. When the trepidation is compounded by intolerable weather, the feeling has to be experienced to know its depth of despair. The coincidence was not lost on Lt. Col. John I. Williamson, commanding officer of the First Tank Battalion, writing to wife, Buckie, on 2 September 1952.

> *Our new draft is coming in tonight. We get a large chunk of men. Of course, it is raining. It seems like all replacements must come in when it is dark and rainy, so that they must be even more miserable and confused than they would be anyhow. (Dearest Buckie)*

Neither was it lost on PFCs Jerry Ravino and Jimmy Olivieri, who were in the 24th Replacement Draft when it debarked from the USS *General Walker* at Inchon. They had been dispatched to 1st Tanks, their trip somewhat enveloped by mystery.

The rain and misery to which the Battalion Commander alluded was not making a very good impression on the two buddies who had enlisted together with the Mayor John B. Hynes Platoon in Boston a little less than a year before. They had managed to remain together through boot camp at Parris Island, infantry training at Camp Pendleton, LVT training at Camp Delmar, and the "cruise" to Korea aboard the *General Walker*. They were about to be assigned to the same outfit in Korea. The problem was, they had no idea what kind of an outfit it was.

The rain became the ultimate damper for Ravino and Olivieri. They had been trained in landing vehicles, tracked, which both relished and were looking forward to operating in Korea. However, before they had set foot in the Land of the Morning Calm, they had been called out of formation on the *General Walker* in Inchon Harbor and handed small cards on which were four numbers: 1-8-1-1.

The cards were their tickets to the First Tank Battalion—the Flame Platoon—and it was another one of those Marine Corps S.O.P. mysteries: *Yours is not to reason why.*

It was not *reasoning*, but deep concern, which had been going on in Division command for several months and now was having its effect on the two replacements from Boston. As far back as July, it had become apparent that there were some imbalances in the First Marine Division, particularly with personnel shortages in tank and artillery units. That's when Maj. Gen. John T. Selden, commander 1stMarDiv, requested Lt. Gen. Franklin A. Hart (Commanding General, Fleet Marine Force) to assure qualified tankers would be made available to the First Tank Battalion, citing:

> The other major shortage in the division was that of qualified crewmen—both drivers and gunners—for the M–46 tanks. Neither tank driving nor gunnery for the M–46 was taught in the tank crewmen's course conducted at Camp Pendleton, California . . . "that tank crewmen be thoroughly trained prior to leaving the U.S."
> Fundamental to the tank problem was a shortage of the M–46 itself. At the training facility, Training and Replacement Command, Camp Pendleton, M–46 engines had been available for maintenance instruction but no tanks for the training of gunners and drivers. On 13 August the Commandant (General Lemuel C. Shepherd, Jr.) directed the transfer of five tanks to the training installation from the 7th Tank Battalion, also located at Camp Pendleton. At the same time General Shepherd ordered an increase in the school quota for tank crewmen. The first graduates would not reach the division in Korea, however, until the November draft. (MCOinK, Volume V)

Jerry Ravino and Jimmy Olivieri had no idea what was going on with Division tables of order, but they fell into the gap where tanker replacements remained a priority. They got their "1811" designations handed them because in Marine Corps *reasoning*, if they could crew LVTs, they could crew its tracked cousin, the tank.

They had been dispatched to the First Tank Battalion. But the irony of the Marine Corps' often-mysterious ways of working out problems, Ravino and Olivieri were not going to be M46 Patton tank crewmen in gun companies. Standing in formation with the rest of the tanker newcomers, they were about to get another jolt to their already disillusioned senses, which had been literally dampened as much by a driving rain that escorted them most of their trip from replacement staging at Munsan-ni to the battalion C.P.

A gunny sergeant had told them to get on another truck. "You two are going to Flames." Now they were really upset. All they could picture was humping cans of lethal napalm, strapped to their backs, up some hill and trying to squirt fire into bunkers. In that picture is a hot round of rifle or machine-gun fire, or a grenade, setting off an inferno in their package. The word "flames" only reinforced their fears they were being sent to the infantry.

All kinds of wild, and not very pleasant, ideas raced through their minds as the six-by bounced them around for nearly an hour before they finally realized the truck had stopped in front of a squad tent alongside an embankment. The canvas was sagging beneath the relentless downpour. It was a forward outpost of the First Tank Battalion—Changdan Road tank park.

In the soggy darkness, the two replacements wearily lifted their butts off the hard, wooden slated seats of the six-by and dropped off the back of the truck into the mud.

By this time, PFC Jerry Ravino and PFC Jimmy Olivieri just didn't give a shit. They were too miserable to care where they were, even if it was the infantry, even if they were going to be carrying napalm on their backs, and waving a wand that was expelling flame from its nozzle.

First Lieutenant Clement Buckley sensed their consternation as he got his first look at the two newest members of his Flame Platoon. He was standing in the doorway of the canvas canopy that was the Platoon mess tent when he called them by name and told them to come inside. *At least he knows who we are,* Ravino thought.

Knowing they were wet and weary, the lieutenant's voice eased. The new tankers realized he sounded less irritated than he looked as he offered them hot coffee. Both declined. They just weren't in the mood.

By this time, the Bostonians still weren't sure what the hell was going on. They thought the "1811" cards they received were going to get them to a tank outfit, but this seemed to be their destination, and there were no signs of tanks in the soggy gloom. All they saw outside was this hill next to the tent. It must have been thirty, forty feet high.

"Fill you in with all the scoop in the morning," Lt. Buckley said, and motioned to the corner of the tent, where there were some folded cots. "Grab a rack."

Only slightly relieved that they could finally dry out, and rack out, the newcomers were willing to wait for the scoop. But they still wondered what the hell was going on. They headed out the door of the mess tent, up roughly made steps carved into the side of the slope where the lieutenant had pointed. Straining their eyes in the dark and rain, they finally made it to another squad tent on top of the hill. They still did not see any tanks.

The two replacements were a little startled when greeted at the entrance of their new home by a bleached human skull, mounted on a pole—another subtle welcome to the war.

The inside of the tent was dark, except for a dim glow peaking through the top of a potbellied stove. The warmth felt good to the damp Marines, and they found their way to an open spot where they could open their cots.

Olivieri hit the rack immediately. But as fate would have it, Ravino discovered there was a hole in the tent just above where he set up his rack. It was still raining, and he felt the water dripping on him. "The hell with it," he muttered and flopped on the rack, pulling his damp poncho over his weary body.

Although the incumbent tankers had made a rough wooden floor out of ammo crates, it was not the Ritz Carlton. "I would have been better off in my pup tent without all this bullshit," whispered Olivieri, starting to doze off, only to be jolted wide awake. "Where ya'll from?" It was the deepest southern drawl the two Bostonians had ever heard.

"Baaston," they replied softly in their unmistakable broad New England accent.

"Boston!" the Rebel yelled. "Damn Yankees!"

Laughter filled the tent. "What the hell outfit we in?" Ravino asked.

"Ya'll will probably become crew members of F21."

"So what the hell is F21?" Ravino snapped.

The Southerner giggled like a little kid. "Ya'ller the newest members of the flame tanks. Ya'ller in the Flame Platoon, Headquarters Company, First Tank Battalion."

"Oh, wow, Jim," Jerry Ravino said half seriously, "We saw one in the movies, remember?" recalling the *Halls of Montezuma*. "The one with Richard Widmark. The tank was shooting flames."

"Great! Thanks a lot, pal," he said with a hint of relief in his voice.

Finally, PFCs Jerry Ravino and Jimmy Olivieri knew they were in a tank outfit and were feeling a little better about the cards they had been dealt. The "1811" cards weren't exactly a straight flush, but they would be a good pair in this high-stakes game called the Korean War. The apprehensions about going to the infantry were quelled.

The two replacements had been sent directly to the Flame Platoon's forward C.P. Their arrival, although shrouded in somewhat more mystery than usual, was not unlike the unknown other Flamers—before and after them—experienced when they were dumped at Headquarters Company to be assigned to this specialized unit with a hybrid Sherman tank. Few, if any, had ever heard of the Flame Platoon, or saw a real live flame tank.

It wouldn't be long, however, before PFCs Ravino and Olivieri would become very attached to these unusual machines, and get their baptism of fire with them. They were about to experience Korea's outpost war in front of the Jamestown Line, which the First Marine Division was protecting in the center of the United Nations western front.

Boston Buddies in F21 Crew

As miserable and confused as PFC Jerry Ravino was when he finally hit the rack that first night in the Flame Platoon forward C.P., his mind was starting to go a mile-a-minute.

What's a flame tank really like? How close are we to the action? What the hell am I going to be doing in a flame tank? Will we get a chance to go over the tank before they send us up? What's this outfit really like?

There was a little more conversation among the newcomers and their hosts before the Southern boy piped up: "Ya'll get some sleep. Meet you in the chow line in the morning. We eat good in this outfit. The big tank outfits down below, they serve mess."

Ravino's mind still was whirling all over the place, but fatigue eventually took over, and he dozed off.

He came awake, groggily, when he heard the muffled sound of voices, and stirring within the tent as the other tankers sluggishly reacted to the casual chow call. Maybe he had grabbed four hours of shuteye. Slowly, Ravino eased himself up to sit on the edge of his rack, still not quite fully awake, which may have retained the confusion in his system. Then, the realization hit him: "Finally, we're here! We've got our outfit."

Olivieri, his attitude a little brighter than the night before, felt the same relief. "Well, Vinnie, we made it!"

Pulling on their utilities and boondockers, Ravino and Olivieri were center stage as other tankers, naturally curious about their new buddies, who began to introduce themselves. There were gentle reminders that the new guys now were the "long-timers" in the outfit.

"Glad to have you aboard," somebody said, ". . . means the rest of us are closer to rotating outta here."

The light banter made Ravino and Olivieri a little more comfortable.

"There's an old saying," chided one tanker, "that when you head out of the tank park on a flame mission, we'll pack your seabag and ship it home if you don't come back."

Laughter broke the ice, and the two newcomers begin to feel like they were welcomed—in more ways than one. *This seems like a pretty good outfit,* Ravino thought.

But his mind once again began to rev as they walked outside the tent into a clear, fall morning and he looked down the scene below.

The mental weariness was gone, and their attitudes began to match the hint of sun that reminded both the Boston natives of their beloved New England. Then, Ravino and Olivieri got their first quick glimpses of the twin-barreled Sherman tanks. They were parked in revetments dug into a horseshoe-shaped hill, ringing a small field below where crews' tents were perched on a slightly higher plateau. All kinds of questions were running through Ravino's head.

Where is the MLR? Who is my tank commander? Will Jimmy and me be on the same crew? Hell, we've always been together. Why break us up now? On and on it went. *Who is the C.O.? Hope it's the lieutenant we met last night. How many combat veterans in the Flame Platoon? I need to talk to them—experience is the best teacher. How often are the missions? How are they lined up? Do we get a whiskey ration?*

On the latter—sorry, Jerry—only weak 3.2 beer: Pabst, Schmidt's, Budweiser, maybe

Asahi from Japan.

PFC Ravino thought a lot but said little as he walked with his new buddies to the mess tent in the gun tank C.P. at the bottom of the hill. He watched and was beginning to feel this outfit was like most Marine units. There is a subtle air of pride. He never would have the pogeybait, or kid brother feeling some of his flame tank predecessors had when the outfit was battalion-bound in the east central mountains most of the previous year. The Flame Platoon—despite its youth, he would quickly find out—had proven its mettle and was an integral fighting element of a fighting tank battalion.

He also would find, later, that some of the guys in the letter companies looked at the Flame Platoon as a suicide outfit because the smaller Shermans get up close—within 100 or so yards—of enemy positions to fire their loads of sizzling mayhem. His curiosity gave way to hunger as the group finally entered the mess tent.

"How many ya want?" barked the cook, cracking fresh eggs on the sizzling griddle. "How ya like 'em?"

Any trepidation Ravino and Olivieri had left over from the night before began to dissipate as they wolfed down their chow, and tanker after tanker came over to their table.

"Where ya from?" That's always the first thing asked when replacements showed up. Guys were looking for anyone who would know where their own hometowns were, or who they knew back in Pendleton, Delmar, Lejeune, or other Marine billets.

"What's going on back in the States?"

Ravino and Olivieri, more and more, were beginning to feel less like strangers.

"Hey, Reeevino, you here, too?"

Jerry turned and smiled as he saw Standing Bear, a Native-American Indian who was ahead of him in LVT training at Camp Delmar. He was the grandson of the great chief Standing Bear and one tough Indian. During grabass sessions at Delmar it would take five Marines to pull him down. Ravino thought Standing Bear had a head almost as big as the opening of a tank hatch. He was bow gunner, now, on a Patton M46.

Ravino was much more at ease in his new outfit, but as he left the chow tent, the burning questions resurfaced. Most were quickly dispersed once the tankers got back to their hooch at the top of the hill.

The two new tankers met Cpl. Thomas Clawson, a tall Marine with the gait of a farm boy. He was from Munsie, New York, and was tank commander of F21, the first tank in the second section of the Flame Platoon.

Clawson wasn't a man of many words, but he welcomed Ravino and Olivieri to the F21 crew, introducing them to Cpl. John Corsi, another New Yorker who hailed from Elmira and was the tank's driver. Neither of the veteran tankers had enlisted in the Marines. Both were drafted and then fed into the Marine Corps. Anyone around them bitching about assignments or work details, got a quick reminder. "You volunteered for this outfit," Clawson said many times. The meaning was: *You were gung-ho enough to enlist in the Marines, so you're getting what you asked for.*

Draftees or not, Ravino and Olivieri soon came to the conclusion that their new tank commander and his driver were top-notch Gyrenes. Clawson didn't start ordering them around. He was more interested in their training and background. After he learned a little more about the New Englanders, the tank commander gave them the option of deciding which of the two open jobs in F21 they preferred—loader or bow gunner.

Yeh, Ravino thought, *but when do we get to see the tank so we can make up our minds?*

Maybe the corporal was reading the replacement's mind, or it was just a matter of routine. He told the new crewmen to follow him and Corsi as they left the tent. They filed along a trail where they could see hills and mountains to the north and west. By this time, the rookie tankers knew they weren't very far from the MLR.

Gradually, PFC Ravino began to take in the surroundings. Along the top of the hill, some forty feet above the mess tent and the letter company C.P., were the two squad tents where they had slept the previous night. They were set against another hill. There was a small pyramid tent for the Weasel Switch's two men who control communications for the tank battalion. They shared space with the Platoon's Navy corpsman.

There was another squad tent where tank parts were stored. All the tents were surrounded by sandbags, stacked three feet high. Across the lower compound is the well-reenforced fuel and ammo bunker.

Ravino was quite impressed with the layout, out of harm's way just off what he would come to know as the Changdan Road, a few short miles from the MLR. Soon he learned the road provided quick access for gun tanks assigned to direct fire missions, and flame tanks, which now were doing mostly indirect fire.

He also would marvel at the versatility of the flame tanks—designed primarily to dispense their lethal napalm, but also very capable of lofting 105mm high explosives indirectly on reverse slopes of enemy strongholds, or fire their cannons directly into Chinese positions to bust bunkers and chew up trench lines.

Looking down from the top of the trail, Ravino this time studied the large horseshoe-shaped tank park with all the twin-barreled tanks backed into deep revetments and covered with camouflage netting. It was his first good look at all the M4A3E8 flame tanks. He noticed they were in order of their numbered turrets, section by section: F-11, F-12, F-13; F-21, F-22, F-23; F-31, F-32, F-33.

Now we're talking, thought Ravino, who had begun to warm more to this task of becoming a Flame Tanker.

Cpl. Clawson, followed closely by his driver, led Olivieri and Ravino to the revetment where F21's two muzzles were poking from under the camouflage. The tank commander gave them a quick review about the tank, and that prompted the two replacements to start considering their options.

The friends agreed: Jimmy Olivieri would be the bow gunner, and Jerry Ravino would go up in the turret with the T.C. and be the loader.

"When can we wind it up?" Ravino asked Clawson. "Can we open the engine doors so I can get an idea of what makes this thing go?" The loader's mind, again, started going a mile a minute, but Clawson slowed him down. Ravino grasped the tank commander's intention: *I guess we'll learn as we go along.*

But the newest Flame Tanker, who had left a good job in the production department of Pfizer Chemical in Groton, Connecticut, was not willing to wait around. With Pfizer, he had some experience in heat exchangers, coil heating/cooling systems, pressure cylinders, and operating regulators. He couldn't let go. His analytical mind kept pressing his curiosity.

When Jerry Ravino set his mind to something, he usually went full-bore to satisfy it. Into the fourth week of boot camp at Parris Island, Sgt. R.H. (Zimbo) Zimmerman, a veteran of the fighting in the Pacific during World War II, assigned the former amateur boxer from Boston as the recruit platoon's first section leader. Zimbo, after that, regularly addressed him in typical D.I. lingo: "Private Goddamn Ravino, you gung-ho bastard."

Maybe he was a little gung-ho when he finally began settling into the Flame Platoon, but Jerry Ravino was not going to be caught short when it came to his job if this tank was going to be doing anything serious here in Korea. He didn't waste any time, opting for a lot of self-education. While the rest of the crew went to chow, Ravino gave up lunch to scour F21. By the time Olivieri came back, his buddy called him over to the tank.

"Jimmy, follow me over this monster so we know what's up. I have a strong feeling this Cpl. Clawson—he's a good man—but I think he might not be so good at training us. I think we should learn what we can."

At the time, Ravino wondered—his gung-ho philosophy kicking in—that because Clawson and Corsi were draftees, they might not have the same attitude as boot-camp-trained Marines. That false reading would be quickly dispelled the first time the new F21 crew went into combat.

While Ravino and Olivieri were going over the their pigiron, Corsi arrived with his close buddy, Charles Craig.

"I hear you guys are from Boston," the stocky, good-looking Craig smiled. "Well, I'm from South Weymouth Landing."

"Yeh," Ravino quickly replied. "I know where that is, outside of Boston heading down the Cape."

The three New Englanders shot the bull and exchanged pictures as another new friendship began to meld.

Getting to Know a Flame Tank

PFCs Jerry Ravino and Jimmy Olivieri were all over F21 in their first few days as the newest crewmen in the Flame Platoon. They were fascinated with the Sherman M4A3E8 tank and all of its intricate facets.

"Man, what a piece of equipment," marveled Ravino, slowly discarding his love affair with LVTs for the not-so-ugly duckling of the First Tank Battalion.

"To me, being in this tank is equal to being part of a fighter plane crew, submariner, amtrak, or any fighting outfit," he tried to impress on Olivieri. "Jimmy, the crews have to work together."

And that they did. Even though there were no manuals on the tank itself, or the flame gun—its strange new primary weapon—the two Bostonians began learning the machine inside-out. What they were discovering was one hell of a piece of weaponry.

Poking around the flame tank innards, Ravino and Olivieri got their first look at mechanism of the POA-CWS-H5 flame gun, which was mounted to the right of 105mm howitzer. To the left of the cannon was a 30-caliber machine gun in a fixed position coaxially in line with the cannon. Another 30-caliber machine gun was in the hands of the bow gunner in the lower right compartment opposite the driver.

Atop the turret were two mounts for the 50-caliber machine gun. One was between the two hatches, the other to the rear and right of the tank commander's opening. It had 360 degrees capability, as did the turret, which could be traversed full circle. Each of the four-man crew carried a .45-caliber pistol, and the tank commander also had a Thompson sub machine gun with him in the turret, as well as a satchel of hand grenades.

They liked the idea of being Flame Tankers!

The operation of the flame gun mechanism and its lethal payload intrigued Ravino, and with his background in Pfizer's plant, he was quick to analyze it and find exactly how it worked.

That flame gun, along with the main armament of the 105, he would soon be convinced, *without a question, marked that tank as one of the most dangerous lethal close-combat tanks that ever rolled out of Detroit.*

The Sherman M4A3E8 flame-throwing tank was an extremely lethal weapon. Although the flamethrower was its primary weapon, it was designed so that its crew had enough other armament to adequately defend it, or unleash another form of mayhem at the enemy—particularly with the 105mm howitzer—and the supplementary machines guns.

PFCs Ravino and Olivieri would not be deprived of the exhilaration of crewing their tank in a number of missions using all these weapons. Neither would they escape the harrowing fear that strikes when one of the behemoths became disabled in no man's land, and the Chinese began hovering and swarming like vultures attacking the carcass of a wounded rhinoceros.

But the two Bostonians were too new to the war to have such premonitions. At this point, they were just trying to learn what made this monster tick.

Meanwhile, activity along the Jamestown Line had grown a little more intense in the early part of September with the Chinese on the initiative.

These sharply increased offensive measures resulted, in part, from the Communist inter-est, as evinced during the summer truce negotiations, in certain forward positions held by UNC units. On 7 September, the CG, I Corps had alerted his division commanders to the fact that the enemy "may attempt to seize and hold certain key terrain features . . . over which there was extensive disagreement during [the 1952 summer truce] negotiations for the present line of demarcation." Since much of the critical land was in his sector, Major General Kendall (I Corps commander) further warned his division commanders "to take the necessary action within your means to hold all terrain now occupied by your divisions." Critical terrain features in the 1st Marine Division area of responsibility were Bunker Hill and the height on which COP Bruce had been established (Hill 148), in the center and right regimental sectors respectively.

Two days later, General Pollock (Commanding General of the First Marine Division) amplified this directive by underscoring the necessity for holding these two positions, plus eight more he considered vital for sound tactical defense. These additional positions, from west to east, were Hills 86 and 37 in the KMC sector; Hills 56 and 48A in the center sec-tor; and the outposts then known as Allen, Clarence, Felix, and Jill, all the responsibility of the right regiment.

Although the eastern part of the division main line thus contained at this time more key hills than any other Marine sector, much of the increase in Marine patrol and ambush activity took place in No Man's-Land forward of the middle frontline regiment. Of the two Jamestown sectors manned by U.S. Marines, the one in the center of the division area offered better ground for infantry operations. (MCOinK, Volume V)

There would be tank activity in the Marine infantry's many skirmishes with the Chi-nese, and at least one flame tank would be called out on a minor burn mission, but it wasn't until midway through September that the Platoon would be getting more involved up on the Jamestown.

However, the aftermath of that one flame shoot was about to make a lasting impres-sion on PFCs Ravino and Olivieri, who would see for the first time just how vulnerable a tank can be when a little carelessness enters the equation.

Flame Tank Lost, but Not to Enemy

The first couple of days in the Flame Platoon, as it was for most replacements, was like going back to training camp for PFCs Jerry Ravino and Jimmy Olivieri. Well-schooled in the operation of LVTs, they just about had to start all over again—learning about this unique machine called the Sherman M4A3E8 flame-throwing tank.

The education, however unexpectedly and unplanned, would be expanded to the perils of being a crewman in one of these pigirons.

It was close to dusk on 9 September when Fox 23 rolled into the Flame Platoon horseshoe tank park. S/Sgt. Emery L. Prine and his crew had just topped if off with gasoline at the fuel and ammo dump just over the hill in the adjacent Able Company CP. The dusty Sherman was returning from a flame mission forward of the MLR.

As Cpl. Eugene J. DiPretoro drove toward F23's assigned revetment, the serious and haggard expressions on dirt-covered faces of the crew made a lasting impression on PFC Ravino.

As the tank slowed and began pivoting to back into the revetment, Ravino, with some other Marines, moved toward the pigiron, eager to get the skinny on where Prine's tank had been and what happened.

"Holy shit," Ravino realized. DiPretoro, a short-timer due to rotate out in a couple of weeks, looked like he had blood caked near his eyes. It was not blood, but the deep red dust and dirt being churned up from a tank in front of F23 that had given the appearance of caked blood on the driver's face. However, the loader in F23 had the real thing, a slash under his chin. Standing in the turret, the weary tanker hadn't seen a strand of communication wire as F23 tank was rumbling down a road. The wire caught his chin a second before he saw it. He could not snap his head completely out of the way in time.

The lesson: *Keep your arm out in front of you if you're standing in the turret while the tanks are in a rolling column.* There were hundreds of miles of communications wire strung to the MLR from numerous command posts in the rear, and they could be hanging anywhere.

The injury to the F23 loader was not serious but enough to remind Jerry Ravino that he was far from playing grabass in Camp Pendleton.

Cpl. DiPretoro began backing the tank up a small slope, the powerful engine whining against nearly thirty-five tons of pigiron as it rolled grudgingly under the camouflage netting. The uneven slope of the ramp canted F23 a little left, just enough to send a trickle of the gasoline from the fill pipe into the hot engine compartment. When the raw gas hit the flame-fuel copper heat exchangers wrapped around the manifolds, it ignited. Fire shot through the louvers of the engine compartment doors. *That damn thing could blow,* Ravino thought after a few seconds. His knowledge of solvents and their reaction to fire quickly drew a second conclusion: *have to get that thing out, now, or it will be too late.*

The other tankers, some running from their own revetments, didn't have to know about chemicals, but they came to the same conclusion. Dozens of hands began scooping dirt off the ground and throwing it on the engine doors. S/Sgt. Prine, leaning out of his turret hatch, was hollering: "Get more dirt up here."

Maybe he thought we had a pile of sand right here waiting for this, Ravino thought. *What the hell did he think we were trying to do?* It didn't take them long to realize they were fighting a losing battle.

"All of you, get the fuck out of there and up on the hill!" It was 1st Lt. Clem Buckley, C.O. of the Flame Platoon, who had just come in off Changdan Road in his jeep. "We saw the smoke coming up the road," said his driver, Sgt. Hank Amos. "We weren't sure what it was until we pulled into the tank park. Then we saw them trying to put out the fire by throwing dirt on it."

He heard Prine holler: "I burned my hands." The tank commander had tried to lift open the sizzling hot engine doors.

Buckley hadn't thought much of the smoke when he saw it from the road. Now, at the park, he knew it was a serious fire. That's when he ordered everybody away from the tank. *"Prine,"* he shouted again! *"Get the hell off that tank! That's an order!"*

The tankers got the message. They began retreating to their platoon commander about fifty yards away from what was now a fully-engulfed Sherman flame tank.

This baby's going to blow, thought Ravino. And blow it did, mostly internally, fueled by the napalm residue and some 105mm ordnance. The pyrotechnics were reminiscent of a little Fourth of July celebration. It burned for hours. "The turret was glowing red hot," Ravino said.

Every so often, there was an explosion. "Yeh. Glowing and blowing," the rookie tanker said.

Finally, as it cooled, the turret took on an ashen-white hue. In a couple of days it was a burned-out hulk, dragged up on a flatbed trailer to by a Service Company retriever and taken to the battalion C.P. in the rear where it would be surveyed. Eventually, a new Sherman flame tank would arrive to replace F23.

Prine suffered burns on his hands and received a Purple Heart. Lt. Buckley thought of putting him in for an award. That didn't sit too well with the troops.

"Hell, it was his own dumb fault that tank caught fire," Ravino said, repeating what many of the other tankers had thought. "It was overflowing with gas. It had to spill out when the tank backed up that ramp."

The Powerful 105 Howitzer

For the next week-and-a-half, the two newest crewman of F21 continued to learn the ropes of their new jobs. On 18 September, sixteen days after their arrival in Korea, things would change.

Four of the flame crews were ordered to report to the tank park after morning chow. Among them were Cpl. Tom Clawson, Cpl. John Corsi, and PFCs Jimmy Olivieri and Jerry Ravino gathering around F21. The day before, they were making preparations by loading their ammunition trailers with a full 50-round assortment of 105mm ordnance.

Ravino saw a new side of his tank commander. Cpl. Clawson showed a sense of urgency, but kept a very keen eye on his crew, making sure each Marine had grasped the importance of the job at hand. Like all of the flame tank commanders, Clawson emphasized the need for teamwork.

Once Corsi had the tank warmed up, he pulled 21 into line with F11, F12, and F22 at the entrance to the tank park.

"Finally," Ravino murmured to himself. Despite the short time he and Olivieri were with their new outfit, they were tiring of the preventative maintenance routine. Like any gung-ho Marine, they were getting anxious to do something more meaningful in the war. Frustration was starting to set in. When word of a mission was planned, activity around the tank park took on a measure of excitement for the two cherries. And, because of the unknown, there was a little apprehension there, too.

"Well Vinnie, you gung-ho bastard," Olivieri yelled up to his friend in the turret, "here we go."

"Our first day out, some action, Jimmy," Ravino shouted.

"Yeh, you gung-ho bastard," Olivieri repeated, "now it starts for us."

The mood was not the same with Clawson and Corsi, and the others who had experienced enough combat to know better. Their somberness was not lost on Ravino, despite the inner exhilaration he felt. But he was thinking he was ready for this.

He and Olivieri were feeling they now were part of something important. It had been building with a casual learning process and maintenance sessions with the veterans.

Ravino didn't say it, but in his mind: *Here I am with new friends in a specialized unit of the United States Marine Corps; to me this is being a Marine at his fullest. I'm in a flame tank with all this destructive power.*

Then, his mind flashed back to the awful Sunday in Boston and the argument that propelled him into the Corps. *Par may have blasted me into the service, but I wish he could see me now.*

"Go face the colors," his father, the World War I veteran, often had said so proudly. *Well, Par, I'm about to face the colors!*

PFC Ravino snapped back to now. He realized F21 and the other three flame tanks were in line, ready to pull out of the tank park and onto the Changdan Road leading to the MLR. In tow behind each tank was a small trailer holding 50 rounds of 105mm ordnance. Since the napalm storage tanks in the hull of the Shermans took up the space where ammunition normally was housed, these hybrid pigirons had to haul most of their artillery in trailers when they were going on a 105 shoot.

A jeep pulled ahead of the lead tank. It was Lt. Henry F. Barry, a cool grin on his round face. Although Lt. Clement Buckley was the Platoon Commander, Lt. Barry was attached to Headquarters Company to fill in when other officers were needed elsewhere. There wasn't any word where Lt. Buckley was, but there seemed to be no problem among the Flamers with Lt. Barry in the lead.

Sgt. Hank Amos, driving for Lt. Barry, had fixed a large sign on the front of the jeep. It read:

TANK CONVOY

That meant the road was theirs. Other vehicles had to pull off to the side if there was room for only one-way traffic. Lt. Barry's right arm went up and then quickly extended forward. There's no order shouted, just the signal, and all the drivers instinctively accelerate their tanks.

"Move out!" Cpl. Corsi responded to Cpl. Clawson's calm voice on the intercom, and revved the engine while depressing the clutch pedal and shifting into second gear, which was the gear of preference to put the tank in motion. First gear was used only if severe strength was needed. The tank normally started to roll very easily in second gear.

As F21 approached Changdan Road, Corsi had the monster still in second gear, but gave it more gas while pulling back on the left break lever to pivot the Sherman out of the tank park and north on the MSR.

The transition through the series of gears was smooth, a knack veteran drivers like Corsi mastered to make the sleek transition up the power train. As third gear engaged, Corsi slightly relaxed pressure on the accelerator while his left foot allowed the clutch pedal to gradually rise. Once the gear was fully engaged—the clutch pedal at its height—he began applying pressure to the accelerator building up the speed of the tank.

As Corsi smoothly glided into fourth gear, and the tank felt like it was cruising on a highway, PFC Ravino smiled at the driver's ability to control this thirty-some-ton monster so confidently. It was only going around twenty miles an hour, but when thirty-five tons rumbled along at twenty miles an hour, it was like a speeding Greyhound bus.

Standing shoulder high out of the loader's hatch in the turret, PFC Ravino realized the noise of the four rumbling tanks was like no other sound he had ever heard. It was part of the exhilaration he felt. Suddenly, he was full of Marine pride going into his first action, a pride that momentarily overcame the fear of the unknown. This one wasn't going to be that exciting, but there would come a time when he felt differently about engaging in combat.

F21 was only cruising at about nineteen to twenty miles an hour, but to the new loader, remembering the squinting bloodshot eyes peering out Cpl. DiPretoro's dust-caked face when F23 pulled into the tank park a couple of weeks before, became concerned for the driver. "John," Ravino called to Corsi over the intercom, "don't you think you should pull your goggles down?"

Sgt. Clawson just looked at his new loader. Corsi came on the radio: "Can't do it, Jerry, unless you want me to run this monster off the road."

Ravino realized then that the dust would only cover the lenses and cut the driver's vision. He'd rather squint through the dust.

"Keep your eyes open, Ravino," barked Clawson. He was motioning to the strands of comm wire flying by the tank, sometimes head high. "When we're coming back in the dark," the T.C. warned, "you won't be able to see that stuff. Get an idea now where it is."

Ravino nodded, recalling the gash under the chin that F23's loader got from comm wire.

"Vinnie!" That can only be Olivieri on the intercom to his friend. "What d'ya think, Vinnie?"

"Love it, Jim! What a ride! Corsi is some kind of good at this."

Clawson made it a three-way conversation: "He's the best driver in this outfit," the T.C. said with a little pride and a lot of respect in his voice.

In the little time Ravino had known Corsi, he would concur—as much because he saw that the Corporal was a good mechanic and looked after his engine, as well as being very smooth with the clutch and accelerator.

Rumbling up the Changdan Road between columns of infantry, the dust-spewing Shermans got all kinds of looks through the haze. Some of the gravel-crunchers even managed to wave. Ravino had not yet learned infantry often did not like tanks hanging around them. The big machines were known for drawing too much incoming—mortars, artillery.

Walking Marines will tell tankers their pigirons are okay when they are ripping into the ChiComs and keeping enemy heads down. But when the big crap starts coming back, *take those damn monsters somewhere else.*

Still, Ravino savored his first ride through the ranks of the infantry. Only a tanker knows how it feels to be riding high in the turret and how proud he can feel. *Right now, I could not feel any better if I was a flying a Corsair.*

Then he thought, *Hey, we have some of that same firepower—machine guns, a bigger cannon, and our napalm! Yeh, this is okay!*

Ravino felt F21 drop into a lower gear as he saw the hill in front of the column. At the crest, the gears begin going up again.

"Watch this, Jerry," Corsi called on the radio, "this is what a tank driver lives for. So pay attention. Someday, you'll be down here."

"You'll think you're on the top of a roller coaster," Clawson warned his new loader. "Kick it in the ass, John!"

Corsi already had gone from fourth to fifth gear, the highest forward in the box and one the drivers rarely got to use.

"This is what Buckley likes, Jerry," the tank commander said of his platoon leader. Ravino was hearing stories about Lt. Buckley—that he was sort of a maverick officer and was not beyond having his driver barrel down a dusty road and run a command car into a ditch. One such incident got him called into Lt. Col. John I Williamson's office for a little dressing down by the battalion C.O.

Buckley admitted that one. "I ran a colonel, one of the regimental commanders off the road," the lieutenant said. "He got all ticked off, caught up to our tank, and stopped me. He threatened me with his big stick and told me: 'Put yourself on report.'"

When the Flame Platoon commander got back to battalion, he wrote out a report and presented it to Williamson, who went through the routine of admonishing his young lieutenant. "I guess he had a check or two next to my name," Buckley said with a smile.

Buckley was, however, Williamson's kind of an officer, and the C.O. never came down too hard on him.

"Floor-boarding it," Buckley said, "is the most fun we had going down a road, hell-bent for election." The lieutenant's theory: "You get a good road, you got to get there!"

That also mimicked the Platoon Commander's philosophy of command: "If you're going to do a job, do it," he often told his tankers. "Be aggressive, be forceful."

As F21 continued racing down the hill, Ravino knew Corsi had floored the accelerator, and like Sherman in front of him, this monster was flying. All thirty-five tons of it now going over the *book* maximum speed of twenty-four to twenty-five mph. On a grade like that, he had to have it close to thirty.

To Ravino, the thrill was wild. It felt like the tank was hitting twice that speed. That's the sensation when thirty-some tons goes thirty-some miles an hour. "Wow, what a ride!" Ravino shouted.

"How'd you like that, Jim?"

"Great, Vinnie! But I ate a lot of dust."

At the bottom of the hill, the ride was more pedestrian, but Ravino became further convinced of Corsi's adept handling of this creature as he pulled one brake lever or the other, double-clutching, shifting down with precision, time and again. *He's a master driving this thing*, the rookie loader conceded. "Great job, John."

Clawson laughed. "This is nothing," the T.C. said. "You should have been up north on the big hills, Ravino. You would have needed your toilet paper." It was a reference to the rugged terrain of the Korea's East Central Mountains.

"Right, John?"

The intercom erupted in laughter.

They had been driving about forty-five minutes when the column finally rolled to a stop at an outpost to the right of the Munsan-ni-Panmunjom-Kaesong Highway, slightly south of where the Truce Talks were being held. Lt. Barry directed the drivers to pull the tanks to a small hill, then nudge their noses up the incline, lining up side by side about twelve feet apart. That angled the four 105 canons skyward. It was an indirect fire mission where HE (high explosive) was lobbed over hills and into enemy positions the tankers were unable to see.

Their eyes were the F.O.s (forward observers) who called the shots—setting the numbers—for the tank commanders to calibrate the 105s degree of loft. Once the tanks were set and braked, the crews gather behind them, stretching tarpaulins on the ground to start making up the rounds of 105mm ordnance.

The trailers full of 50 rounds of ordnance had been emptied, and the projectiles were lined up in front of brass casings—row after row—ready for the powder bags to be cut. The number of bags per round depended on how much propellant was needed for the required distance of the shoot. Each round was made up separately.

Cpl. Clawson brought F-21's crew into a huddle, going over each man's assignment once the firing started. "Ravino," Clawson ordered, "you stand behind the turret and help hand up the shells."

The cherry loader expected this. Although his job was supposed to be in the turret to load the ammunition into the breach for the T.C. gunner, he knew he had not been trained enough for Clawson to feel comfortable having him handle ammo in such close quarters.

"John, get up there," Clawson barked to his driver. Cpl. Corsi already was walking around the side of the turret to the loader's hatch. He knew the routine. He had worked with the tank commander many, many times on missions like this.

"Watch what he does, Ravino," Clawson told his new loader, just before he settled into his seat to begin setting up the gun. "You'll be in here soon enough, and you have to know how to handle this stuff."

Behind each tank, the remainder of the crews took the shells out of their transport tubes and made up the shot. Usually, the driver and the bow gunner work behind the tank. This day, with Ravino up top observing, Sgt. Amos was schooling PFC Olivieri in the job of fixing the ammo.

Once it was determined what the range of the mission would be, the shells were packed with a specific number of powder bags to control the distance. As they were made up this day, the two-foot-long pieces of ammo were handed to Ravino near the turret.

Inside, Corsi, wearing asbestos gloves to handle the hot brass after it was ejected from the cannon, was seated facing the breach block. He kept two rounds, each weighing about thirty-three pounds, on his lap, and one upright against his chest ready to slide it into the breach once Clawson opened the block. The first round was already in breach and the block closed.

"You don't ever want to get behind that breach block, Jerry," Corsi warned the new loader. "The recoil will knock your head off!" The force of the cannon, depending on the shot, can send a projectile more than 11,000 meters (in excess of 12,000 yards).

The order came from Lt. Barry to fire for registration. He had received distance coordinates from the F.O. Rounds of HE, cut to four bags in the casing, were ready in each tank. Clawson stepped on the firing switch. There was a tremendous noise. Ravino was startled, even though he was anticipating it. The mighty Sherman, all 35 tons of it, rocked back on her locked tracks, then settled.

Ravino and the startled Olivieri, standing behind the tank helping fix the ammo, had experienced their first shot fired at the enemy. Their ears were ringing as all hell broke loose. It was not just F21 firing. All four of the Shermans had let loose.

"That was the registration round, Jerry," Corsi yelled.

Not far enough came word from the F.O. The crews were told to cut six bags. "One more ready to go."

Ravino and Olivieri were not quite as startled by the second shot, but they had become aware of the odor of gunpowder—cordite—and the turret began to look like a chimney spewing clouds of smoke through the hatches. *What the hell is it going to be like when I fire that gun with the hatches buttoned down?* Ravino wondered. *Sure hope those exhaust blowers work.*

For a couple of hours, the four flame tanks pummeled the Gook positions on the reverse slopes of their MLR, tearing into hills the Marines called Boot and Claw. They also swung their cannons southwest and battered Chinese positions near the Imjin River. By the time the shoot was over, Ravino and Olivieri had become somewhat accustomed to the noise, smoke, and the smell of cordite. Between 0940 and 1130 that morning, the four flame tanks lofted 245 rounds into the Chinese lines and were credited with destroying 17 bunkers and damaging at least 16 others.

The tankers wouldn't know about those numbers and how much enemy real estate they were pulverizing at the time—maybe they never would. They couldn't see the damage, and it's not likely that anyone in Division thought to pass down the word that low in the chain of command.

For the crew of F21 and the other Flame Tankers—Sgt. Bob Rawlins, Sgt. Elmer Betts, Cpl. Gerald DeCoursie, PFC Charles Craig, Cpl. Marvin Dennis, PFC Billy Baker, PFC Daniel Calabaza, Sgt. Donald DeWolf, PFC Andrew Pittmon, Jr., PFC James F. Doyle, PFC Eugene J. DiPretoro, or Sgt. Henry D. Amos, Jr.—it was the usual: *Yours is not to reason why.*

When the four Shermans returned to the tank park, Lieutenant Barry made a point of seeking out Ravino and Olivieri. "What did you guys think of indirect fire?"

"Great, sir," Ravino responded, and quickly asked: "But when do we head out on a flame mission?"

The Lieutenant looked firmly at the rookie tanker. "It will come before you know it, Ravino."

Olivieri looked at the officer. "He's a gung-ho bastard, sir!"

Lt. Barry smiled: "I've already heard about his nickname. And that may change when we get up there close to the Chinese—firing napalm at them. The shit hits the fan then!"

The two PFCs exchanged quick glances as the lieutenant turned and walked away. They said nothing, but both began to wonder just what they might be getting into later.

Possibly, the magnitude of the 18 September shoot had something to do with the presence of Commandant of the Marine Corps, Gen. Lemuel C. Shephard, who was watching the whole show. As Lt. Col. John I. Williamson put it, "We did a lot of shooting today, mainly to let Lem know we were here. I hear he was impressed" (JIW, *Dearest Buckie).*

General Shepherd, a hero in both World War I and World War II, hadn't lost any of his feel for combat. He did not sit back in some secure C.P. miles behind the lines when he was there to inspect the First Marine Division.

"He walked out in front of us a little bit," said 1st Lt. Clement Buckley, the Flame Platoon commanding officer, "and we ended up firing over his head on one mission. Good thing we didn't have any short rounds."

PFC Ravino, and the rest of the Flame Platoon, were unaware the Commandant had been in the area. He couldn't care less. He was too impressed with the 105, particularly they way it recoiled. *What power?* he marveled. And he was beginning to see the importance and versatility of the Sherman M4A3E8 flame tank. *This is a real mobile artillery battery,* he thought. *We can move out on a moment's notice and go right where we're needed most . . . and we can keep on going. If we run low on gas, or out of ammo, Motor Transport can get it to us.*

He still had a lot to learn and would be more impressed when he saw the devastation the flame gun could cause.

His days of regret about not going to LVTs were quickly fading.

Flames' 105s Big Help to KMCs

The left flank of the First Marine Division zone along the Jamestown Line was the Korean Marine Corps sector. This was in the vicinity of Hill 155 to the west of the Munsan-ni-Panmunjom-Kaesong corridor. In front of the MLR were outposts 31, 33, 36, 37, and 39 in an arc ranging from a thousand to a couple of thousand yards out.

The Korean Marine Corps, modeled after the USMC, was a fine fighting outfit and quite proud to be under command of the First Marine Division. That meant both Division infantry and specialized units like tanks and artillery trained KMCs and maintained a close working relationship with them.

The Korean Marine Corps tank company was a small fleet of older M4A3 Shermans whose main armament was the less-potent 75mm cannon. When the KMCs needed some pinpoint indirect fire—or some bunker torching—the Flame Platoon was called in.

It was long before the sun rose on 24 September when Sgt. Tom Clawson, Cpl. John Corsi, and PFCs Jimmy Olivieri and Jerry Ravino, still shaking the cobwebs of a very short night's sleep, climbed aboard F21. This day, they were going in support of Capt. Clyde Hunter's Able Company Pattons in the far western sector to work over a couple of the outposts manned by Chinese Communists. More recently, Captain Hunter and his gun company crews had been handling much of the training of the KMC tankers.

Four days earlier, six of the flame tanks were dispatched to the KMC sector to pound Hill 36 before the Korean Marines launched an assault to retake the outpost. The original mission was to burn off the OP, but the ChiComs had hightailed it before the flame tanks could go into action. Instead, they peppered the hill with more than 50 rounds of HE (high explosive) to help take out seven bunkers, a couple of gun emplacements, and some trenches.

That 20 September shoot was not all one-sided. Flame tanks and supporting Able Company were exposed to more than 100 rounds of incoming heavy mortar and artillery fire. F31 took a direct hit from artillery, and the 122mm round destroyed the final drive, sprocket, and cannon. Fortunately, there were no injuries to tankers. The tank was recovered and trailered on a low-boy back to Service Company, where the mechanics worked their magic and returned her fit as a fiddle to the Flame Platoon.

Although it was early morning of 24 September, it was still dark, which meant this was the first night road drive for PFCs Ravino and Olivieri. They had been warned it would be much more tedious. Poor visibility, complicated by the ever-present dust, and what could be lethal communications wire were the main culprits.

Actually, it was like driving through a smoke screen with all the dust. "And you never know when a strand of that comm wire is going to pop up in front of you," Ravino and Olivieri were told ahead of time. Still, the two rookies were looking forward to meeting the KMC tankers, if for no other reason than the curiosity to see how much like Marines they were.

The KMC tank park was on the other side of the restricted (no-fire zone) Munsan-ni-Panmunjom Corridor. Combat-bound military equipment was forbidden to use this road. In order to get to the other side of it, tank convoy must dip south into the Munsan-ni United Nations no-fire zone, go west, and come out on the other side of the Corridor.

By the time Lt. Buckley's jeep led the four flame tanks into the KMC tank park, dawn was just breaking over the horizon behind them. Ravino saw some of the KMC's older Shermans camouflaged with pine boughs and started laughing. "They look like big green bushes," he cracked.

Clawson glanced sternly his way. "Jerry, don't laugh. They're good, dependable tankers. You'll find that out today." The F21 loader also would note that the South Korean Marines were good mechanics and, during the day, would envy their diminutive size because of the way they could maneuver around, and even in, the engine compartments of their tanks.

Clawson told his new crew members that the KMCs had a thing about checking fan belts in their tanks. "Funny thing is," the T.C. said, "they'll come over and want to check the belts on our tanks. So we let them."

First Lt. Clement Buckley, the Flame Platoon Commander, had arrived in another jeep. He and Lt. Henry F. Barry were heading for morning chow with a KMC major, who was the tank company commander. The enlisted Marines followed the officers and began meeting their opposite number Koreans. Ravino was a little surprised that some could speak fairly good broken English. *I guess they had to pick up some of our lingo after working with our tankers all this time,* he thought. Always eager to learn, Ravino went off on his own after chow and checked out the KMC outfit. He was very impressed with the South Koreans' sleeping quarters. Shallow bunkers were dug out of the side of a hill. The KMCs slept on some kind of a slab, the American noticed. Under the slab was a full open fire pit of small burning twigs. The pit had a stack at one end to vent smoke and some of the heat. *That's something worth having a patent on,* Ravino thought.

Two of the Korean tankers left the mess tent laughing about something on their way back to their bunkers. A Korean major walking behind them suddenly began screaming orders at them. The two enlisted Koreans did an immediate about face and snapped to attention. The major's harangue became louder and louder until he dismissed them in a few minutes. *Just like boots at Parris Island,* the American thought.

A few minutes later, two more South Korean Marines, infantry by their appearance, walked by Ravino carrying a small squealing pig. They walked into a bunker, the pig's high-pitched protest still going strong. All of the sudden, it stopped. The two KMCs came out of the bunker, each holding half of the pig, which had been slit perfectly down the middle.

It wasn't very long when Ravino heard engines winding up and two of the "bushy" tanks moving out of the KMC Park. The Flamers waved, hoping their counterparts understood enough English that they were wishing them luck.

Around 0830, the four flame tanks, positioned almost two miles below the Corridor just behind the MLR, began sending round after round of 105mm into the sky toward the reverse slopes of several Commie outposts southwest of Panmunjom on the other side of the Sachon River. Over the next three hours, they supported a KMC Regiment with 234 rounds of high explosive. The official tally was a gun emplacement, a bunker, two observation posts, a house, a cave, and damaging 650 yards of trenchline.

That seemed like a lot of ordnance for the results, but the KMCs appreciated it because it had to cause some ChiCom casualties, and the continuous firing kept the enemy pinned down and off the KMC backs for most of the morning.

Three days earlier, Lt. Buckley took four other flame tanks on a torch mission, which dumped four full loads of napalm on Outpost Hedy (Hill 124) at the southern extreme of the Bunker Hill Range. While sitting out in no man's land, those tanks came under fire, counting twenty rounds of 82mm mortars and 122mm artillery. But they escaped unharmed.

On 27 September, however, the First Tank Battalion experienced a black day. One of Captain Clyde Hunter's Able Company tanks, sitting about a mile south of the Hook at the eastern extreme of Jamestown, was working over Commie positions on Pheasant, Warsaw, and an area further north in the Samichon River area. The Patton took a direct hit in the turret gunner's scope, killing the Marine. The projectile drove through the scope recess into the interior of the turret. The explosion buckled the top of the turret, and a three-inch gap opened in the front of the tank commander's cupola. Damage was so severe, the tank could not be repaired when it was trucked back to Service Company.

On the last day of September, the Flame Platoon helped Able Company exact a measure of revenge in two separate missions.

Rolling out with Able Company, and again working from below the Corridor in the KMC sector to target positions on the other side of the Sachon, three flame tanks unleashed nearly 300 rounds over a three-hour span. They took out five bunkers, disheveled six others, knocked out a house, and filled in about 300 yards of ChiCom trenches. On another 105 shoot the same day, flame tanks expended 108 rounds of HE with similar devastation on enemy bunkers and trenches.

The Flame Platoon was recognized significantly in the summary of the First Tank Battalion's September accomplishments:

> This company (Korean Marine Corps Tank Company) was occasionally reinforced by flame tanks mounting the 105mm howitzer for indirect fire missions against Hill 288. Intelligence revealed that this fire conducted beyond the range of KMC organic artillery, was extremely effective against enemy reverse slope positions. During operations of the 1st KMC regiment to regain lost positions on Hill 36, on 20 September, tanks of this company proved very effective in inflicting many casualties on the enemy. The counter-attacking forces were reinforced by six (6) flame tanks. However, the objective was secured before these tanks could bring their primary weapons (flame) on a suitable target and assisted only in their possible shock effect upon the enemy.

It was becoming more and more evident that the Sherman flame tanks were not only extremely valuable for their ability to utilize the primary weapon in-close to torch enemy bunkers and trenches, but there was a new appreciation for the very mobile and deadly 105mm howitzer. It could be called on to readily move up and down the MLR—in front of it to bunker-bust with direct fire, or behind it to exact large numbers of enemy casualties miles in the distance with appreciable accuracy of indirect fire.

Continuing to take on more and more assignments, appreciation grew from fellow gun-tankers for the Flame Platoon's unique assortment of firepower as this outpost war headed into another Korean winter. Still wary of retaliatory incoming, infantry also was willing to give a nod of approval to the Flamers—as long as they did their dirty work far away from friendly positions.

Fig. 1. Sgt. Jack Carty, Korea, 1951-52.   Fig. 2. Cpl. Jerry Ravino, Korea, 1952-53.

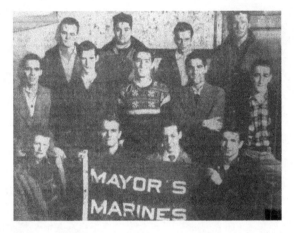

Fig. 3. An aged newspaper clipping from the Boston Traveler *shows Jerry Ravino (middle row, center) with some of the recruits in the Mayor John B. Hynes Platoon before they left Boston for boot camp at Parris Island in February 1952. (Jerry Ravino Scrapbook)*

Fig. 4. Sherman M4A3E8 flame tanks from the Flame Platoon, Headquarters Company, First Tank Battalion, First Marine Division, idle in a valley of mountainous East-Central Korea early in January 1952. (Photo Courtesy Jack Carty)

Fig. 5. PFCs Jerry Ravino (left) and Jimmy Olivieri, buddies since they enlisted in the Boston Mayor's Platoon in early 1952, were assigned to F21 of the Flame Platoon, Headquarters Company following a confusing scenario that landed them in the First Tank Battalion, First Marine Division in the fall of that year. (Photo Courtesy Jerry Ravino)

Fig. 6. PFC Len Martin, an eighteen-year-old Marine Corps Reservist (left), was getting his first taste of tanks at Camp Delmar in Oceanside, California. (Photo Courtesy Len Martin)

Fig. 7. Some of the original crewmembers of the Flame Platoon, Headquarters Company, First Tank Battalion, First Marine Division, gather on deck of their ship on the way to Korea early in the fall of 1950. Identified are T/Sgt. Adam "Gunny" Iler (back row left), PFC Chris Christenson (back row, second from right), PFC Bill Kuykendall (kneeling left), and Cpl. Maurice "Mo" Sims (kneeling right). (Photo Courtesy Mo Sims)

Fig. 8. Cpl. Maurice "Mo" Sims (left), driver of F23, and PFC Chris Christenson take a break against the Fire Box (F21) following the Inchon Landing. (Photo Courtesy Mo Sims)

Fig. 9. A tanker peering through the pistol port of an M26 Pershing catches a fiery scene of buildings in Seoul after flame tanks unloaded their napalm during the street fighting in the capital city. (Photo Courtesy Len Martin)

Fig. 10. The Flame Platoon's F22 is stopped outside Seoul in late September 1950, before entering the capital city. During the battle of the barricades in the street fighting a few days later, F22 was destroyed by a satchel charge. The crew escaped serious injury. The replacement F22 also was lost in no man's land in the winter of 1953. (Photo Courtesy Mo Sims)

Fig. 11. Original crews of the Second Section, Flame Platoon, which were the first Sherman flame tanks to land on Wolmi-do, pause for a historic picture. Identified are: (front row) Cpl. Mo Sims (left), driver of F23, and Sgt. Alfred Betti, F23 tank commander; (middle row) Sgt. Grady Love (left), TC of F22; (back row) T/Sgt. Adam "Gunny" Iler (left), S/Sgt. Tom O'Neal (left), TC of F23, and PFC Bill Kuykendall (second from right), driver of F21. (Photo Courtesy Mo Sims)

Fig. 13. Flame Tankers set up a checkpoint in a quickly made foxhole in Seoul. (Photo Courtesy Mo Sims)

Fig. 12. Top commanders (from left) Maj. Gen. Oliver P. Smith, First Marine Division; General of the Army Douglas MacArthur; and Navy Vice Adm. A. D. Struble, who was in charge of Joint Task Force 7, meet after the historic landing at Inchon. (Photo Courtesy U.S. Navy/Marine Korean War Photo Essay)

Fig. 14. S/Sgt. Tom O'Neal, the Flame Platoon's F21 tank commander, was extremely popular with Korean children as he entertained them with his guitar when there was a break in the fighting during the Inchon-Seoul campaign. (Photo Courtesy Mo Sims)

Fig. 15. Shortly before the First Marine Division was strung out over the Taebaek Mountains, Flame Tankers began bundling up in layers of standard issue gear when November of 1950 ushered in the first signs of a miserably cold winter. (Photo Courtesy Mo Sims)

Fig. 16. It's any port in a storm for crews from D Company, First Tank Battalion, who take advantage of a small stream near Seoul on a warm Korean day in September 1950 to bathe and wash clothing. The four letter companies in the First Tank Battalion had complements of Sherman M4A3E8 tanks for "bull work" among their Pershing M26s. (Photo Courtesy Mo Sims)

Fig. 17. PFC Len Martin (standing, second from left) and fellow First Replacement Draft buddies who were fresh from tank training at Camp Delmar in Oceanside, California, were issued M-1 Garand rifles when they reached Hamhung in November 1950. Most of them would pull infantry-like duty for the First Tank Battalion during the First Marine Division's breakout from the Chosin Reservoir before they were assigned to tanks. Standing (from left): Bob Dotterer, Martin, Carmen Armanetti, Milbon Bonet; kneeling: Jim Hansen, Bob Shurte, and John DeNyse. (Photo Courtesy Len Martin)

Fig. 18. As bitter as the weather was at Koto-ri, Marine Corps infantry managed a few smiles while resting during the final leg of the drive south to Hamhung. (Photo Courtesy MCOinK)

Fig. 19. An M26 Pershing from the First Tank Battalion paves the way for Marine Corps infantry during the breakout from the Chosin Reservoir in December 1950. (Photo Courtesy U.S. Navy/Marine Korean War Photo Essay)

Fig. 21. Packing their gear at Camp Delmar, Oceanside, California, PFC Dan O'Sullivan (left) and PFC Jack Carty, who became good friends during tank training, are headed to Korea in the 10th Replacement Draft. (Photo Courtesy Jack Carty)

Fig. 20. By the early summer of 1951, Cpl. Len Martin became tank commander of F22 after serving his time as loader and then driver during the spring campaigns, in which the Flame Platoon was quite active with the 105mm cannons in support of infantry. Flame tanks also pulled a lot of roadblock duty. (Photo Courtesy Len Martin)

Fig. 22 & Fig. 23. (Below) Flame Tankers from the 9th and 10th Replacement Drafts, which arrived in Korea in June and July 1951, got in their final two cents' worth of action prior to rotating home the following spring when they handled some indirect firing missions after reaching the West Coast. Among the short-timers (left) were (from left) sergeants Roger O. Davis, Jim Waltz, and Red Smith. (Photo Courtesy Jack Carty)

Fig. 24. Lt. Pete Clapper (fourth from left), commanding officer of the 5th Anti-Tank Platoon, gathers some of the unit's crews. From left: Sgt. John Cronin, Cpl. George Crowley, Cpl. Chuck Batherson, Cpl. John Wolf, S/ Sgt. Jerry Ford (back to camera), Cpl. Richard Bennett, Cpl. Fugay, and Cpl. Howard Broadwater. (Photo Courtesy Frank Curnow)

Fig. 25. Enjoying bull sessions and card games at night are (left to right) Dick Stone, Al Chalk, Lou Lirette, and Bob Haase. (Photo Courtesy Jack Carty)

Fig. 26. Sgt. Chuck Wager, cracking the tank commander's hatch of F21, took a picture of the log-strewn ridge. Cpl. George Manfull (left) was driving the Flame.

Fig. 27. Training runs in the snowy valleys of the East-Central mountains were routine for the Flame Platoon in the early 1951-52 winter. During a break, Cpl. Howie Cramer (left) joins Cpl. Patrick "Packy" Wassell (center), F22 tank commander, and Cpl. Roger O. Davis, TC of F21, for a snapshot. (Photo Courtesy Jack Carty)

Fig. 28. When Lt. Col. John I. Williamson became commanding officer of the First Tank Battalion in late spring 1952, he immediately saw the dual potential of flame tanks and wasted little time getting them into action. (Photo Defense Department (Marine Corps)

Fig. 29. Sgt. Jack MacGregor (foreground) relaxes with Cpl. Kennie Jones, PFC Lucien Mercier, Cpl. John Corsi, Cpl. Charles Craig, and PFCs Jerry Ravino and Jim Olivieri on a warm autumn day in 1952 near the Changdan tank park. (Photo Courtesy Jerry Ravino)

Fig. 30. PFC George Fish (left), driver of F13, with his buddy Irvin Kelly, before he rotated out of Korea late in the summer of 1952. (Photo Courtesy George Fish)

Fig. 31. Lt. Clement Buckley (right) took over the Flame Platoon early in the summer of 1952 and vigorously lobbied to have the unique Shermans take a more active part in the war. (Photo Courtesy Clement Buckley)

Fig. 32. PFC Servart Standing Bear (kneeling) was an old friend of PFC Jerry Ravino (second from right) during LVT training days and greeted the new Flame Platoon crewman in September 1952. Standing Bear drove the M46 Patton D34 (background) of Dog Company and later was wounded in action. From left: Standing Bear, unidentified, Hank DeStefano, Ravino, and Wil Watkins. (Photo Courtesy Jerry Ravino)

Fig. 33. Sgt. Chuck Lasche (left) and his crew are set up for an indirect firing mission with Cpl. Tom Clawson (right), the F21 TC looking on. (Photo Courtesy Pat McDermott)

Fig. 34. Sgt. Hank Amos, a tank mechanic, was also the Flame Platoon C.O.'s driver and helped stake out indirect firing missions when the Shermans brought their 105mm howitzers into action. (Photo Courtesy Hank Amos)

Fig. 35. PFC Bob Atkinson worked several body-recovery missions in no man's land with the newly formed Recon Company. (Photo Courtesy Bill Giguere)

Fig. 36. 1st Lt. Michael McAdams, a "Mustang" in the Marine Corps tradition of becoming an officer after serving in the enlisted ranks, took over the Flame Platoon in January 1953. (Photo Courtesy McAdams Family)

Fig. 37. Following a mission in Western Korea in late 1952, the crew of a flame tank purges napalm from storage tanks to prepare for a fresh load of the jellied mixture of naptha, palmetic acids, and gasoline. (Photo Courtesy Chuck Batherson)

Fig. 38. F21 crew with the help of Sgt. Hank Amos (standing center) begins preparing ammo while setting up for an indirect fire mission. (Photo Jerry Ravino)

Fig. 39. After months of MP patrols in Japan, Cpl. Joe Discher volunteered to go to Korea and wound up being thrust into the battle of the Hook as a squad leader with Baker Company of 1stBat7th Marines. (Photo Courtesy Joe Discher)

Fig. 40. A tank commander standing in his hatch has this view of a scorching bead of napalm being laid on a target during practice shoot. (Photo Courtesy Jerry Ravino)

Fig. 41. Napalm is pumped into a flame tank after being mixed on the spot by a specially-designed apparatus, which stirs the naptha, palmetic acids, and gasoline. (Photo Courtesy Clement Buckley)

Fig. 42. Cpl. Bill Giguere experienced many patrols into no man's land after joining the Recon Company. (Photo Courtesy Bill Giguere)

Fig. 43. Sgt. Jim Putnam, Weapons Company, 2ndBat7th Marines, pulled a lot of Recon duty despite being a leader of a machine-gun section. (Photo Courtesy Jim Putnam)

Now They're "Flame Dragons"

By the beginning of October 1952, the First Tank Battalion table of organization was coming up to snuff. Lt. Col. John I. Williamson had more than 800 men in his command—nearly 60 Marine officers and in excess of 760 enlisted men, along with a Navy medical complement of 2 doctors and 15 corpsmen.

The Flame Platoon was only a small part of the T.O.—forty to forty-five men—but tanker-for-tanker, they were kept as busy as any. The two major weapons the Shermans offered were a diverse, mobile arsenal, on call only a few miles behind the MLR. No other tank outfit in Korea could make that weaponry available.

Naturally, the flamethrower was its primary weapon. But when Colonel Williamson came aboard, he appreciated—and so did his infantry counterparts—how effective that snub-nosed 105 could be at lobbing devastation on unseen targets, or be used as direct fire for bunker busting.

The flame tanks had acquired a new respect. They became quite popular as support weapons for infantry and gun tanks because they had the ability to hit targets like artillery. More so, they had the added advantage of moving into position faster than any battery of cannons that had to be towed by truck.

Like the two previous months, October 1952 would be equally busy—and sometimes dangerous—for what now some members of the Platoon were calling the Flame Dragons.

"A lot of us are getting fed up with being called Ronson Raiders, Zippos, and double-barreled shotguns," said PFC Jerry Ravino when several of the Flamers were shooting the shit one day. Ravino, the LVT-trained replacement who came into the Platoon about a month earlier, was warming to his job as loader on F21. He also was beginning to feel quite comfortable around the rest of the guys in the platoon and, never one to hold back an opinion, he would speak his peace if he thought it needed to be spoken. "We don't like those names. We should do something about it."

Ravino knew some of the descriptions dated back to World War II. In fact, one of the original flame guns was called the Ronson after the cigarette lighter company that designed it. Zippo, naturally, was a popular butt lighter of the day. He respected the history, but he didn't like the tone of the gun tankers when they used the terms.

One day, PFC Al Carter had watched Ravino put a new coat of Marine Corps green on F21 and finish it off with a gold Marine Corps emblem on the slope plate. PFC Richard Courchaine was a gifted artist from California and had brought his oil paints to Korea. A few days later, he showed Ravino a painting of F21 with a dragon—belching a plume of flame—stretched over the top of the tank.

Flame Dragons!

The fiesty PFC from Boston had yet to fire his first flame mission in combat, but he had been training with the gun, and the time would come when he would take his Flame Dragon against the Chinese. However, before he would become embroiled in anything like that, Jerry Ravino would be earning his spurs as the F21 loader, and it wouldn't be long before he personally felt the power of the tank's other weapon—the 105mm howitzer.

On the second day of October, five tanks were firing indirect at targets forward of the Corridor on the right side of Panmunjom. "I made a mistake," Ravino admitted, "and my wrist got hit by the block on the recoil." The loader received a cut and a bruise, but it wasn't much. He was taken to the field hospital and was back on duty within three hours. However, he was told word would be sent back to the states informing his family that he was hurt.

"You better write them right away," the corpsman advised Ravino, "so they don't worry. They'll only tell your family you were hurt, but no details."

That night, Ravino wrote his girlfriend and future wife, Dotty Daly: "You may hear from my family that I was hurt, but nothing serious. So, don't worry, dear."

Continuing to work closely with the Korean Marine Corps, the Flame Platoon and gun companies from the First Tank Battalion were kept quite busy in the KMC zone on the west side of the Munsan-ni-Panmunjom-Kaesong Corridor. On 5 October, Lt. Clement Buckley, the Flame Platoon commanding officer, took four of his tanks to revisit Hill 37, one of the outposts forward of the KMC sector of the Jamestown Line.

Hill 37 was the middle outpost in an 4,000-yard slightly-arced group that included Hill 36 to the southwest and Hill 39 to the east. The targeted hill was a key position taken from the KMCs a week earlier and highly coveted by the Chinese. If the truce talks failed, Hill 37 could influence the corridor between Panmunjom and Munsan-ni. Flame Platoon tanks had pounded all three of the outposts regularly with indirect fire; now they were going to burn the hell out of 37.

The four twin-barreled Shermans—F12, S/Sgt. Emery Prine's new F23 , Sgt. Robert Rawlins' refitted F31, and F32, the command tank with Lt. Buckley—eased into no man's land, all the while strafing the peak and base of the hill with their machine guns. Buckley kept the tanks staggered and ordered them slightly up the base of the hill in order to get maximum range with their napalm.

The tank commanders sparked their shrouds, brought up the pressure in the lines, and commenced lacing the hill with bright-orange bursts, traversing their turrets left and right, creating crossing fire, until the entire crest was sizzling. They began elevating the coax to make sure plenty of the napalm went over the top of the hill and down the reverse slope.

Lt. Col. John I. Williamson, commanding officer of the First Tank Battalion, was impressed enough to write his wife, Buckie, about it.

We were rather vigorously engaged yesterday. As you know, we lost some of our outposts last week and still haven't taken them back, although we have been fighting bitterly since. We made a successful counterattack yesterday, spearheaded by some of my flame and gun tanks. The flame tanks, led by Lt. Buckley, together with some of my Korean Marine tanks, actually got up on the hill and helped clobber the Chinese. The Chinese counter attacked in battalion strength later, and retook the hill. They show great courage and determination in the attack. One tank shot up a group of about 50 until there was only one left, but he still came charging on . . . The Korean (KMC) tankers killed over 300. (Dearest Buckie)

"We really pissed them off," Buckley said as the incoming from adjoining Gook hills and beyond began to fall on the four tanks when they started backing off 37. Any Marine knows the Chinese are extremely good with their mortars and artillery, particularly where they have the grids preregistered.

Still in reverse, the flame tanks once again began spitting machine-gun fire in all directions, in case any more brave, or foolish, Chinamen decided they wanted to come out in the open. As the Shermans turned to start back to the KMC lines, F31 was hit by artillery—one of an estimated 500 rounds of 76mm, 105mm, and 122mm the ChiComs threw onto the operation around Hill 37 that afternoon.

Sgt. Rawlins felt the jolt and the tank ground to a halt. "The right track must be off," he heard his driver yell over the intercom. "I can't turn the tank."

Both tankers thought they had taken a direct hit in the suspension system and the track was blown off.

Rawlins, disregarding the incoming barrage—and a standing order from his C.O.—opened his hatch and climbed out of the turret to see how much damage there was. The track was still intact. However, the explosion had blown loose one of the tow cables which was attached to the hull. It had gotten caught in the rear drive wheel. That was enough to knock the track off alignment.

Rawlins jumped off the side of the tank and began trying to work the stiff one-inch wound-steel loose. All the while, he was yelling to his driver, who had unbuttoned, to try get the tank in motion—hoping movement, and his pulling the cable, might work it free.

When Lt. Buckley saw what was happening, he came out of F32's hatch, hollering at Rawlins to get back in his turret. Buckley was adamant about tankers unbuttoning hatches while under fire. The Platoon Commander had emphasized this several times in briefings he held before missions. "You better call me first," he warned, "before you take it on your own to unbutton and expose your crew."

Sgt. Rawlins, who had acted on instinct, not thinking about the oft-given warning, immediately retreated to his turret. But before he made it into the hatch, a chunk of shrapnel from incoming grazed his face. Fortunately, he was not seriously wounded.

Meanwhile, Buckley had dismounted the command tank and ran to F31. He grabbed the entangled cable and began yanking on it, loudly shouting instructions to the driver.

It worked. The power of the engine finally forced the sprockets to drag the track forward far enough that Buckley was able to free the cable. The Platoon Commander was somewhat surprised when the track had somehow shifted back into alignment and began tracing over the idler wheels like it never had been out of line.

There was still a lot of metal flying around. The ChiComs seemed to intensify their fire when the two tankers were exposed, and they would get a measure of satisfaction. As Buckley did a broken-field run back to his tank, a round of incoming exploded behind him, spraying shards of shrapnel into the backs of his legs. He staggered but managed to limp back to F32. He had a hell of a time pulling himself up on the tank, but he made it and painfully got into the open hatch of the turret. The other tankers, heeding his earlier warnings, did not come out to help him because they saw he was making it on his own.

"Had he gone down," Ravino said, "and could not get up on that tank, any number of us would have defied his order and gone to get him."

F32 raced back to the staging area with the severely wounded Platoon Commander who lost consciousness on the way. An AH-13 helicopter was waiting. The tank's crew, with the help of corpsmen, gently got the lieutenant out of the turret and onto a stretcher, quickly lowering it to waiting hands. In minutes, the lieutenant was strapped to one of the chopper's bubble-capped skids.

Lt. Buckley was flown to a MASH (Mobile Auxiliary Surgical Hospital) unit and then med-evaced to the USS *Consolation,* a Navy hospital ship sitting in Inchon Harbor.

Three days later he was transferred to the USS *Repose*.

The Flame Platoon—and the Batallion—had just lost one of its most effective and popular commanding officers—an officer who had as much respect for his men as they showed for him. Lt. Buckley remained on the *Repose* for three weeks before he was returned to active duty, but his tour as Flame Platoon commanding officer was over. Lt. Henry F. Barry was assigned to take his place by Colonel Williamson. By the time Buckley came back to Headquarters Company, he was a short-timer and spent the remainder of his tour in battalion until he rotated back to the States.

As much as his "boys" admired Buckley, there was no less feeling toward him from his commanding officer, Colonel Williamson.

I got down to the hospital just before he was flown out in a helicopter to the hospital ship. I talked to him as he lay on a stretcher in the ambulance. He was in good spirits and suffered little pain. I think he'll be all right, but sure hated to lose him. He has handled the flame platoon with great courage and aggressiveness. I intend to recommend him for a couple of medals . . . A splendid young officer. (Dearest Buckie)

Williamson did recommend Buckley, as well as Sgt. Clawson, for citations. Both were awarded Silver Stars for their bravery, and their wounds merited Purple Hearts.

Williamson hated to lose Buckley as a platoon leader, and the lieutenant also had some misgivings about not returning to Flames. "I had a real good bunch of boys in the Platoon," he was quick to tell anyone.

One of his favorites was Gunnery Sergeant Badge Myers, his maintenance chief whom he also made platoon sergeant. They were good friends, despite rank differences, while in the platoon.

"We had an old jeep," Buckley said, "kind of beat up, no windshield in it. Badge and I would get in, take a couple of shotguns and a fifth of whiskey with us, and get supplies for the troops—whatever else we could scrounge. Maintenance people loved to see us coming. We'd barter and trade."

Buckley was good at it because, on the ship coming to Korea, he made a lot of friends—particularly mess officers and senior mess sergeants. At one point, he was in charge of the ship's mess deck. That paid big dividends when he took over the Flame Platoon, and he and Gunny Myers went off on foraging details. "When we got to Korea, I knew the NCO in charge of the bakery and ice cream plant, and a couple of others around the Division. It made our scrounging pretty good."

He took care of his boys—and his C.O. "John I. Williamson used to love my exploits."

Williamson couldn't have appreciated Buckley running a regimental commander off the road with his tank, but he sure liked his aggressiveness. Yet the battalion commander may have reserved comment on his maverick lieutenant's way of signing off on an indirect-fire mission. "When we finished firing, I'd take one of our tanks so it had maximum elevation with the 105 and let it fly!"

It was Buckley's way of having one for the road!

105 Firing Missions on COP2

The ongoing battles for possession of the outposts between the Main Lines of Resistance rarely seemed to settle down. It was a constant exchange—give up one, take it back, give up another, take it back, take one, give it back.

If nothing, the give-and-take of the outposts along the Jamestown Line expended a lot of ammunition and equipment. More costly, however, were the hundreds of lives—more so to the Chinese—that were being sacrificed. Yet both sides, forced by each other, had their reasons, and for the First Marine Division, it was the early warning network that would alert any kind of serious pressure headed for Jamestown.

There was another factor coming into play the closer those outposts were to Panmunjom, site of the sometimes-volatile Truce Talks. The United Nations needed to control a couple of those key OPs—the larger of which were called COPs (combat outposts) because they could be heavily fortified around the clock. Their importance was based on the threat of the Chinese shutting down negotiations and taking U.N. representatives captive. There had to be a sight line into Panmunjom, and there had to be a forward jump-off point if Marines needed to go in there and get U.N. delegates.

The singular primary outpost was COP2 near Panumjom, a little more than two miles east of truce-talk hub and aligned about a half-mile to the right where the Munsan-ni-Panmunjom Corridor entered the no-fire bubble around the truce-talk site. COP2 also looked south, about two-and-a-half miles, to the Jamestown Line.

It was in Marine hands, and it was set up as a staging point if a U.N. rescue mission was necessary. An armored personnel carrier, two late-model M46 Patton tanks, and a contingent of Marine recon infantry were at the ready just behind the MLR to be rushed forward for launch from COP2. There also was a flame tank always sitting in one of its revetments. It was hardly secret what was going on there.

"The enemy possibly knew the Marines were always ready if the talks failed," says Sgt. John L. Camara, a veteran of many night patrols in the no man's land around COP2. Sgt. Camara was with a recon company from Division Headquarters Company, which did nothing but snoop' 'n' poop around those OPs to gather intelligence.

Because of its juxtaposition to the no-fire zone around Panmunjom and the Corridor, COP2 was without a doubt one of the most sensitive little pieces of real estate forward of the entire First Marine Division MLR. The Chinese often turned the truce talks into heated confrontations, which at any time could erupt into a very hostile situation for U.N. negotiators.

This was the political jockeying of the Korean War—the Chinese bent on buying time to rebuild their forces, the United Nations trying to put an end to the bloodshed and death that was staining the Korean soil. There also was the matter of prisoners of war. We wanted our guys back. It was a very tedious area, particularly for those charged with operating near the demilitarized zone.

COP2 was defended strongly. Marine infantry had rocket launchers, machine guns, mortars, and anti-tank weapons out there. It was a base for direct and indirect fire missions of flame tanks—their 105s so much in demand, that one of the specialized Shermans remained there constantly, manned by rotating crews from the Flame Platoon.

As each new crew went up to COP2, they had to undergo intensive instruction about what they could do and what they couldn't do. They had to sign off on their orders, and any infraction could be a court martial offense.

F21's crew—Cpl. Tom Clawson, the tank commander; Cpl. John Corsi, driver; PFC Jimmy Olivieri, bow gunner; and PFC Jerry Ravino, loader—were in the Flame Platoon forward tank park when they received orders to pack their gear and load a jeep trailer with fifty of 105 ammo. The following morning they were going up to COP2 to relieve the crew of F11. They knew the routine, although this was the first trip for Olivieri and Ravino. They would leave F21 in the tank park—no reason for another pigiron to go up there as long as the one on line still was serviceable. F11 was staying put for this tour. The crews changed monthly.

It was the 5th Marines sector now, and before the new crew could go near the tank, there was a meeting with one of the Fifth's infantry company commanders—a captain. Ravino was impressed with the officer, who emphasized the delicacy of keeping the war out of the demilitarized Corridor and Panmunjom. *He's very stern,* Ravino thought as he listened to the Captain dwell on the consequences the tankers faced if they dropped a round into one of those restricted zones.

The infantry officer laid a map out on a table and outlined the positions that were off limits. When the indoctrination was over, the four tankers each were given a form to sign. "I will never forget this," Ravino said. "In so many words, this stated that if our crew made a mistake and we fired into a no-go area, we could be fully responsible for a possible restart of a full-scale war. And that could have resulted in each of us being court-martialed. There was no doubt about it!"

Each of the Flame Tankers signed their forms—in red ink. They were asked if they fully understood what they were signing. "Yes, sir," they replied almost in chorus as they left the command bunker—highly pissed off!

"What a screwed-up war," Ravino cracked sarcastically. His sentiments echoed many times when he started talking to some of the guys in the 5th Marines. He wondered what would have blurted out of grizzled ol' Chesty Puller, the famed World War II hero who brought his 1st Marines through Inchon and Seoul before they anchored the breakout from the Chosin Reservoir. *Political bullshit,* Ravino imagined Puller's reaction to this crap.

At the time F21's crew was ordered up to COP2, Division also was quite concerned with an unidentified armored regiment intelligence reports had indicated was poised somewhere in the vicinity of Kaesong. In fact, some of the Russian-made T-34s were seen at times roaming below the reverse slopes all along the Chinese MLR.

There had not been too much enemy tank activity along Jamestown, outside of a foray in the middle of September when the Commies were trying to take Hill 36 away from the KMCs. However, with the threat of enemy armor coming out of hiding and into an assault around COP2, there was something else for the Marines to be concerned about.

"There's been a great number of enemy armored vehicle sightings," the 5th Marines captain told Cpl. Clawson's crew. "They've been firing in support of the their infantry to the left of us in the KMC sector." However, the captain admitted the difficulty of finding the CCF's well-covered forward tank revetments. "We've had problems locating their positions," he said, emphasizing he'd be calling in an air strike on them when he could find them, "or take them on one-on-one with our own tanks."

So the Flame Platoon crew was put on alert to watch for any movement of armor coming from the north, or west through or near the Kaesong-Panmunjom-Munsan-ni Corridor. The other major approach would have been down through the Samichon River valley, far to the northeast area of the Marine sector.

There was a bit of excitement on COP2 that first night, but it had nothing to do with the Chinese. The four tankers were told to go up to the two-man bunkers near the revetment in which F12 was tucked. Clawson and Corsi knew the way. The corporals racked together, and the two rookies took the other sand-bagged bunker. Ritz-Carlton accommodations, these weren't!

Ravino and Olivieri soon learned what Clawson and Corsi already knew—most of the bunkers were inhabited by rats, foraging for food. Sand falling on sleeping bags was a byproduct of the rodents clawing their way into the bunkers.

That night, a candle tipped over and ignited some matting in the Corporals' bunker. "The whole bunker's going up!" Corsi was yelling as he ran out of it, and sprinted to the Ravino-Olivieri hole.

Shit, what a great start for us this is, thought Ravino. Flames were pouring out of the bunker when the two new tankers got to it.

"Close it up with sandbags," the more experienced 5th Marines were shouting.

"There's a bag of grenades, and 50 and 30 cal ammo boxes in there," Ravino hollered back. "Our Tommy gun's in there, too!"

No matter! "Suffocate it!" The infantry helped the tankers toss sandbags on the bunker, but it wasn't long before the noise of "war" began. With the grenades exploding and the live ammo popping, it sounded like an intense muffled firefight.

While all of this was going on, the Captain came down from the top of COP2, screaming at the top of his lungs. *"Do you people know where the fuck you're at?"* His reference, Ravino guessed, was that they were lighting up the entire OP for the Gooks to see.

As serious as this was, Ravino could just about hold back laughter. The Captain was standing there screaming, regaled in his bathrobe.

When the excitement died down, Clawson and Corsi squeezed into the same bunker with the two PFCs.

The next morning, it was back to the real war. With Clawson and Ravino in the turret and Olivieri down in the right bow seat, Corsi began easing F12 out of its revetment and up to the side of COP2—it was second gear all the way. At the crest, Corsi turned right, then made a sharp left to the center of the skyline slot that had a mound as high as the drive sprocket.

The tank mounted the small hill and stopped. That gave the crew an open view of no man's land and the intimidating mountains off in the distant background.

Cpl. Clawson dismounted, and his driver joined him as the tank commander ran bustle-phone extension down the hill to the command bunker. That's where the firing orders would be issued to the tank. Meanwhile, Ravino and Olivieri were up in their unbuttoned hatches enjoying the view.

But not for long. There was a *whoosh* and then a *thud*. Sand flew all over the tank. Incoming! In seconds, the bow-gunner and loader were down in their compartments, the hatch lids quickly closed above them.

Clawson and Corsi soon returned, quickly climbing aboard and buttoning up. Once the tankers were out of sight, the incoming ceased. The Gooks were watching.

It would be PFC Jerry Ravino's first day on the job as a loader. The firing mission had been relayed to Clawson, and he began adjusting the elevation of the cannon. They were going to unload on the reverse slopes of different hills where F.O.s had seen movement the night before. Ravino—two rounds of 105 shells in his lap, another in his arms cradled to his chest—at first, found the operation awkward. But he was being watched, and guided, closely by his tank commander. After a while, it was getting easier to load that round into the breach.

"Good job Jerry," the T.C. commented later. "It's going to work out—you and me."

The shoot was a good one that day, with the F21 crew in F11 credited with knocking out several enemy positions in addition to disrupting Gook troop movements.

It continued to be a busy month of October for flame tanks, mostly utilized to spread havoc with their cannons.

In the early evening of 19 October, two flame tanks working with Able Company Pattons about a mile behind the MLR lofted nearly 150 rounds directly north into Felix. They also hit Hilda north of the Hook. They destroyed bunkers and caves in addition to tearing up more trenchline on ChiCom reverse slopes. The next three days, it was more of the same. The count included one confirmed enemy KIA on 21 October when a pair of Shermans lobbed 158 rounds in a late-night shoot on Hilda and the Chinese MLR.

Late in the afternoon a day later, three enemy were known not to have survived a 90-round barrage which once again targeted the caves and trenches of Felix.

This is the way it was for the time-being in the give-and-take of outpost war. If Marine infantry got pushed off a hill in no man's land, flame tanks and gun tanks did their best to disrupt the comfort of the new inhabitants. If the Chinese continued to hold outposts, they could bank on continued harassment by incoming, compliments of the tanks.

However, Maj. Gen. Edwin A. Pollock, the First Marine Division commanding officer, was working on a plan to alter the system a little.

> In all, during the first week in October, the 1st Marine Division gave up six outposts, or forward positions, that had been sited on some of the commanding ground in the Marine area. On the division left, COPs 37, 36, and 86 were the ones most removed from the Korean (Marines) MLR and thus easily susceptible to being overrun by the enemy at will and to his early reinforcement. The division theorized that near winter and the subsequent freezing of the Sachon (River) would facilitate the movement of Chinese troops and supplies across the river to new positions. The enemy was now able to operate patrols east of the river without interference. At the opposite side of the division MLR, on its right flank, Detroit, Frisco, and Seattle had been lost. By gaining this string of outposts, the enemy was better able to exert pressure against other Marine positions forward of the line and the critical ground on Jamestown.
>
> To counter this threat, General Pollock strengthened the outposts close to the MLR and increased his patrolling requirements. It was decided that in some cases the mission of the COP—that of providing early warning of impending attack and slowing it down—could be accomplished as effectively by using patrols and listening posts at night. . . .
>
> The serious situation on the outposts was compounded by existing political considerations, which prevented the Marines from initiating any real offensive campaigns. Moreover, any hill taken was invariably backed up by a still higher one, controlled by the enemy. The key factor was not so much holding an individual outpost as it was to insure that the enemy was unable to penetrate the Jamestown line. (MCOinK, Volume V)

This was not a problem that was going to go away. As long as the outposts were objects of major contention, there was going to be conflict, and it was not lost on Division that Chinese success in October would breed contempt in November and beyond.

Before the month ended a different type of critical situation was to confront the division. It appeared that the enemy's success in seizing a half-dozen outposts earlier in October had only whetted his appetite for more. Chinese eyes were turned towards positions that held still more potential value than the stepping-stones just acquired. The extreme right battalion in the division front held by the 7th Marines was the focal point of the new effort. (MCOinK, Volume V)

As winter began to show its face toward the end of October, the Chinese were dropping their calling cards more often on outposts Marines had dubbed Ronson, Seattle, Warsaw, Reno, Carson, Vegas. All of them were indigenous to the defense of the Hook, a nasty sore finger that jutted out of the 7th Marines section of the MLR.

By this time, PFC Jerry Ravino not only was becoming a proficient loader in F21 under the tutelage of Cpl. Clawson, but he took it upon himself to watch his tank commander as closely as he was being watched. His ability to grasp what went on and how to operate the full scope of the turret, would come in very handy—particularly months later when Clawson was wounded and Ravino would have to take over F21 right in the middle of a pitched battle.

Buddy in Infantry MIA on Patrol

The euphoria PFCs Jerry Ravino and Jimmy Olivieri experienced on that first run up to COP2 was shattered several days after the crew got back to the forward tank park near Changdon.

Ravino and Olivieri were well aware that Rocky DeRose—who started with them in the Mayor John B. Hynes Platoon 113 out of Boston and made up the other third of a tight friendship that was bonded during boot camp and LVT training—was also roaming around the Jamestown somewhere.

For another of those reasons known only to the Marine Corps, DeRose, despite his proficiency in LVTs, was sent to the 1st Marines as an infantryman when he arrived in Korea with Ravino and Olivieri. When the regiment went into the lines replacing the 5th Marines, DeRose was pulling duty on COP2 with How Company, 3rdBat1st.

Routinely the Flame Tankers gathered for morning briefings, and the Platoon Commander filled them in on what was going on along the Jamestown. It was one morning in early October 1952 that Lt. Henry Barry told his crews that the First Marines had a little problem around COP2 the previous night and that a patrol from the outpost ran into some Gooks and took losses. That immediately struck a nerve with PFC Ravino. He knew DeRose was up there.

"Any idea who they were?" Ravino asked.

"Did you know somebody up there?" Buckley inquired.

"Yeh, PFC DeRose . . . Rocky DeRose," Jerry said.

Barry hesitated and Ravino quickly looked at Olivieri.

"Sorry, Jerry," Barry said. "He's MIA."

A chill came over both of the Boston Marines. "It was like the feeling I had when we first came into Flames," Ravino recalled. "Helpless, not knowing why what was happening, was happening. I was no good that day."

PFC Rocky DeRose was reported missing 5 October 1952. Exactly a year later he was declared KIA.

It wasn't until F21 was on standby with the 1st Marines near Bunker Hill in March of '53 that Ravino found out what happened to his friend. He had asked some of the infantry guys if they heard of Rocky DeRose.

"Ya, I knew the Rock," replied a guy who had heard Ravino. Jerry became a little shaky. "The fool was told not to go out on this certain patrol I was on one night," the infantryman said. "He decided on his own to follow us."

The rest of the patrol was unaware DeRose was behind them. "Returning from the patrol," the Marine said, "we found his broken carbine and a pool of blood."

"Are you sure that was Rocky's carbine?" Ravino snapped.

"Ya, man. All the other guys on the patrol were accounted for when we got back to COP2. Sorry, man!"

Ravino couldn't help thinking back. Ironically, before he met Rocky in the Hynes Platoon as it headed for Parris Island, Jerry Ravino had worked for his father. "Mr. Rocco DeRose was my foreman on construction when we built Hoosak Dock #1 out of the Boston Navy Yard."

When the new recruits of Platoon 113 were about to leave Boston by train in the fall of 1951, Ravino was surprised to see Mr. DeRose, who came over to him at South Station and gave him a very firm handshake. "You take care of my boy," Mr. DeRose said to Ravino.

"Rocky's mother was there, too," Ravino said. "After we got to know her, we called her 'MaMa DeRose.' MaMa was very upset that her son 'was going to war.'"

Months later, after the recruits had returned home from boot camp as new Marines, she was more upset. Once again at South Station, the Marines from Boston were boarding trains and among the family and friends was Mrs. DeRose.

"Gino," she hollered after Jerry Ravino. For some reason, she had always called him Gino. She was shaking her fist at the two Marines, now fast buddies. "You take care of my Rocky."

Jerry Ravino had no idea how prophetic that plea would be. But a couple of months later, he would begin to wonder.

As Ravino, DeRose, and Olivieri progressed through training at Camp Pendleton and Camp Delmar, Rocky began telling Jerry he was not going to come back from Korea.

"We went round and round about this," Ravino recalled. But there was no way his friend could dissuade the troubled DeRose, who became more convinced of his fate as their training was coming to an end.

Rocky DeRose's uncle had been wounded at the Chosin Reservoir. Shortly before the 24th Replacement Draft left for Korea, Rocky asked Jerry to go with him to the hospital at Camp Pendleton to see his uncle. "I think Rocky joined the Marines because he wanted to be like his uncle—a Marine," Ravino said. "After seeing his uncle, he seemed more convinced he would not be coming back."

The buddies became separated on the *General Walker* on the way over, and it was difficult to see each other in the confines that are a troop ship. They didn't get together much until the replacements were getting their assignments at Inchon. And like the bewilderment beating down on Ravino and Olivieri in the confusion of being sent to "Flames," DeRose was having similar feelings when his orders came to join the infantry of the First Marine Regiment.

"Like us, he wanted to know why," Ravino said.

That was the last time Ravino and Olivieri saw Rocky DeRose.

More than a year later, Rocky's girlfriend, Dolly, wrote to tell Ravino that the official word of his friend being Killed In Action was delivered to the DeRose home by a Marine Corps captain, bearing the customary insurance check for $10,000.

Mrs. DeRose hollered at the officer, refused to accept the check, and chased him out of the house. "My Rocky is alive!" she cried.

She kept his room the way it was when he left and it remained that way until she herself passed away.

The Hook

All of the ordnance from tanks and artillery units expended on hills and the Chinese MLR above the extreme right section of the Jamestown Line seemed to be an effort to discourage the threat of an anticipated major attack on the Hook.

It didn't work.

Elements of the 7th Marine Regiment were sent out on a limb when an army general decided the First Marine Division should drive to the Yalu River beyond the Chosin Reservoir in December 1950. Now, nearly two years later, the 7th Marines were manning another United Nations extreme position called the Hook. Though the precarious perch would not produce the epic bit of history recorded at the Chosin, it nonetheless was another heroic and bloody battle experienced by the 7th Marines.

The Hook was the vantage point that protected the Samichon Valley through which ran the Samichon River and provided a natural thoroughfare if the Chinese decided to bring a major force from Northeast Korea to storm the South Korean capital of Seoul. For centuries, invaders from the north used that particular route as a throughway to that coveted jewel of the South. The Chinese were no different. The Samichon Valley was their best shot at getting at the capital city.

In their way stood the Hook, which overlooked the ancient approach, the valleys and lower hills north and west of it, as well as an expanse of smaller hills and the plains behind the Jamestown Line. But the Hook was the antithesis of where to enforce a proper defense. It was well-noted:

> Its susceptibility to capture derived both from violation of a defensive axiom that the "MLR should not have sharp angles and salients," and to the fact that the ridgeline on which the Hook was located continued northwest into Communist-held territory. (Outpost) Seattle, which the Chinese had seized on 2 October, lay only about 500 yards northwest of the Hook . . .
>
> The importance of this part of the MLR, in the extreme eastern sector, lay not in its strength but rather in its weakness . . .
>
> In spite of its vulnerability, the Hook could not be abandoned. There was no other terrain feature held by the Marines that could command the critical Samichon Valley . . . The salient also dominated the entire nearby area of the Imjin River to the south. Possession of the Hook and adjoining ridge would give the Communists observation of a substantial portion of the Marine rear areas beyond the Imjin, as well as the vital river crossings . . . had the salient been lost, a withdrawal of 4,000 yards would have been necessary. (MCOinK, Volume V)

It fell upon the 7th Marines to defend the vastly overextended six-mile regimental front of the MLR that wound northward from Toryom, a village which long since had been decimated, to the protrusion of the Hook and then southeast to the Samichon River.

> Jutting as it did towards the Communist lines, the salient formed a J-shaped bulge in the main line, which not only gave the Hook its nickname but also established the vulnerability of the position. (MCOinK, Volume V)

That "J" in the line started at the furthermost northwest tip of the salient, came slightly southwest about 1,000 yards before scooping gradually northwest.

Combat outposts varied greatly as to their distance from Jamestown. Farthest from the line were the three in the left (sector) . . . Carson, Reno, and Vegas, were approximately 1,000 yards forward of the MLR. Berlin and East Berlin (a new outpost established on 13 October) were the forward positions in the center line . . . To the right, Ronson, Warsaw, and Verdun . . .

Ronson was the outpost nearest to the Hook . . .

At the beginning of October, this vital area had been protected by COPs Seattle and Warsaw. When the former was overrun, it became necessary to establish a new position . . . Ronson was established 200 yards southeast of Seattle and 275 yards west of the Hook. About 600 yards northeast of the salient the remaining position, COP Warsaw, commanded the lowlands to the east and the narrow, east-west oriented valley of a Sami-chon tributary immediately to the front. (MCOinK, Volume V)

Seriously adding to the concerns of the First Marine Division as October started to fade was the rationing—because of shortages—of ammunition. This hit the artillery, mortar, and tank units hardest. It got so bad that only twenty rounds-a-day of 105mm were permitted for each howitzer, and the 11th Marines 155mm cannons were dropped to 4.3 rounds for each tube. Mortar companies had a shortage of 81mm ammo. Conversely, the Communists' stocks appeared to be plentiful. Case in point was a forty-eight-hour shelling of the Hook 24-25 October—laying the groundwork for an all-out assault with more than 2,800 rounds.

Why the disparity?

Defense of outposts and mainline positions along the EUSAK (Eighth U.S. Army Korea) front in early and mid-October 1952 consumed a great deal of this type ammunition. This heavy expenditure was brought to the attention of the corps commanders by Eighth Army. General Van Fleet pointed out that ammunition consumption rates for both the 105mm and 155 mm howitzers during these two critical weeks in October not only exceeded the expenditures of the massive spring offensive in 1951, but also the UN counterstroke that followed. (MCOinK, Volume V)

Thus, restrictions followed as Van Fleet prodded commanders to "insure maximum return for all ammunition expended." Eventually, the Marines paid a price at the Hook because defenders were restricted on the amount of artillery they could call in on known buildups of troops preparing to attack them.

However, restraints were eased somewhat, although not fully, a couple of days before the Chinese came rushing against the Hook. Gun tanks' 90s and the Flame Platoon's 105s were called to lay in barrages on the CCF front on 20 October, as well as the following day. Then, the 11th Marines got their howitzers blazing with more than 500 rounds the next day.

On 25 October, Capt. Clyde Hunter's Able Company tanks once again turned the 90s northward, firing more than 50 rounds. With the Chinese attack imminent on the 26th, the Able Pattons unleashed 175 more rounds. Meanwhile, the strings were loosened on the 11th Marines, and they put up more than 1,000 rounds of 105 and 155 mayhem the same two days.

But it must have been too little, too late. The Chinese were not immobilized.

After a heavy counter-barrage by the Communists on the morning of 26 October, the Reds swarmed at the outposts. Warsaw was overrun, Ronson was under heavy assault, and out of the skies came round after round pummeling the Hook. Six-feet-deep trenches were caving in, and Gooks were pressuring crests of the Hook from three sides.

Division decided the hell with it, and lifted all ammo restrictions on the 1stBat 7thMarines defending the Hook and all its supporting units. But the Chinese kept coming in force—hitting the northern tip of the Hook head on, driving into the middle of the west side of the hill about 400 yards below the tip, and striking a nub on the east side about 500 yards down.

It was a bitter two-day battle with the Chinese penetrating the MLR and taking over some of the forward trenchline. But after the enemy had controlled about a mile of Jamestown, a counterattack was mounted, supported lustily by the 11th Marines and Capt. Hunter's Able Company tanks unloading with their 90mms. Thirty-six hours after it started, the 7th Marines, spearheaded by Baker Company, chased the Gooks off the Hook:

> The going was extremely difficult, complicated by a moonless night and the many shell craters that pockmarked the terrain. But at 0019, 28 October, the platoons mounted their assault firing their rifles and machine guns, and hurling grenades to silence enemy automatic weapons and to reach dug-in Communist soldiers occupying the trenchline.
> The Marine charge was met by a burst of small arms fire and a shower of grenades. Weapons supporting the Chinese defense were still very active. After a standoff of 90 minutes the Marines pulled back, calling on their mortars and artillery to lay precise fire concentrations on the trouble spots. The weapons also fired on enemy approach routes through Ronson and Warsaw. After this preparation, Company B (1stBat7th) again made an assault against the enemy, at 0340. This advance was contested vigorously by the Chinese, but their resistance this time was not lasting. Quickly B/1/7 Marines deployed throughout the entire area, and by 0600 the Hook was again in Marines hands. (MCOinK, Volume V)

Cpl. Joe Discher, who had wearied of MP duty in Japan and volunteered for a tour in Korea, missed the big show on this infamous piece of real estate. But when the twenty-one-year-old NCO from Audubon, New Jersey, was assigned to take over a squad in Baker Company shortly after the summit was retaken, reality set in. He soon learned trying to keep Jarheads and Swabbies out of trouble in the sleazy streets and alleys of Yokosuka and Atusuki was a piece of cake compared to the Hook and its outposts.

When Discher was assigned to Baker Company, the situation on the Hook still was extremely tenuous. "It was really shaky the way they took it back," Discher said, describing the situation he walked into. "We didn't have too much of a foothold. Charlie Company only had about fifteen guys left. Baker also was down quite a few men, and that's when they pulled us out of reserve to fill in the gaps.

"The first night, they came and got me and said 'we got a gate here.' It was down the bottom of the reverse slope on the west side of the hill."

"Nobody in or out," Discher was told, "until you can identify them."

Gate was the term Marines used to designate re-entry to, or debarkation from, the MLR or the perimeter of an outpost. It wasn't a real gate, just a spot in the lines where friendly troops passed through.

"The first thing I saw when I got down there was a truck bouncing toward the gate— loaded with dead Marines, arms and legs hanging and extended every which way." Of course, once he was sure it was friendly, he let the truck pass.

The action was so hectic and Marines so harassed by the Chinese during recovery operations, they had little chance to be gentle with their fallen buddies. Marines always want to bring back their wounded and dead, but it can be very harrowing, and costly.

"They were bringing back the dead—Marines and Gooks. There was so much chaos up there, I guess they were just picking up bodies and tossing them on the trucks, just to make sure they got all the Marines. *Holy mackerel*, I thought, *why the hell did I ever leave Japan?*"

There still was a hell of a battle going on. "That first night, we got hit like you wouldn't believe. They just kept coming and coming," Discher said. "But you learn quickly, this is the way it is."

Baker Company was holding most of the Hook facing Ronson, the O.P. directly to the left of the western tip. It was the closest O.P. to the Hook, and it had been taken by the Chinese. But on 28 October, Marines regained it.

"Our guys had left some grenades out there when they were shoved off Ronson," Discher said. "When we went back, we were ordered not to try to use the grenades. The Gooks had short-fused them. The minute you pulled the pin, the damn thing would explode before you could get it out of your hand."

Discher had his own close call with a grenade a day or so later. "We were being overrun and I was running down a trench when I saw a Gook grenade," he said. "There was so much confusion, my first reaction was to jump over it. The damn thing went off and blew me out of the trench. Fortunately, it was a concussion grenade, but I had one hell of a headache."

There was a lot of give-and-take with those outposts before the month of October came to an end. "Mass chaos," Discher commented. "Often we had to call in VT (vertical trajectory) around us to try to chase the Gooks back. When VT started, we went into the bunkers hoping the Gooks, caught out in the open, would be killed or dispersed. It worked, but we did get hit again . . . but we held."

It was Baker Company that finally assaulted, and took over the Hook and spread out over the retaken real estate:

> The Hook was again in Marine hands . . . Most of the . . . area was held by Company B .
> . . The 1st Platoon . . . quickly searched the retaken area of the MLR (except the caved in
> parts of the trenchline and bunkers, which were investigated later), but found no enemy
> soldiers. During the day . . . Company B expanded its responsibility along the Marine
> main line. . . .
>   The company had to be reorganized. In addition to these missions, there were two others, regaining Ronson and Warsaw. As it turned out, the duties were discharged nearly
> at the same time. COPs Ronson and Warsaw were reoccupied by the 7th Marines (on
> 28 October). . . .
>   In organizing the recaptured position, the Marines were hampered to some extent
> by a dense ground fog. Nevertheless, work still went ahead on these necessary tasks.
> (MCOinK, Volume V)

"The smell of cordite was all over," Cpl. Discher said. "It just hung there."

Some of that cordite odor came from Captain Clyde Hunter's Able Company Pattons, whose 90s were on call. It was on the Hook that Hunter and his tankers came up with a novel idea that had to startle the Chinese. The Gooks must have thought they were facing a rolling pill box atop Hill 146, the Hook's dominant mound.

It took some "tricky maneuvering," Hunter said, but the Able tankers managed to get one of the M46s "perched on top of the mountain, and we stayed perched up there for four days."

The tank was driven over the top of a trenchline and stopped laterally above the slit.

That left the escape hatches over the trench. It was like a mechanic's pit in a service station where cars went for oil changes. "We dropped the escape hatches, and we could resupply the tank up through the openings. The crew also was able to drop out to take breaks and clean up."

The five-man crew could stay buttoned and didn't have to exit the tank from the exposed turret or hull hatches. Everything was accomplished from underneath. Sitting on top of the hill like that, there was 360-degree vision and firing capability from an extremely prime vantage point. "It was a sight that could be seen for miles around."

Of course, the incoming it drew didn't make the infantry too happy at times, but the advantages of having that sweep of heavy artillery at the ready outweighed the disadvantages.

On 29 October, the tank, from a range of about 2,000 yards, rammed nearly 100 rounds of 90mm HE into Frisco on the left flank of the Hook. The gun tank got some help from two flame tanks, sitting about three miles south and firing indirectly. The Shermans supplemented the Able crew with 90 rounds of 105mm HE on Frisco and were credited with three Chinese KIA when a couple of shots slammed into a cave.

Although restrictions on ammunition were lifted to provide much-needed support to the 7th Marines, Cpl. Joe Discher would have his own experience with the rationing after his outfit, relieved right after retaking the Hook, went back into the line further south, in the vicinity of COP2. "We were on one of the O.P.s when we saw some activity across the way," Discher said. "I called for mortars to be laid in on the Gooks, but was told I had spent my allotment."

"The hell with the allotment," Discher snapped, "we need this!"

"Is it an important target?" the corporal was asked.

"I wouldn't be calling for it, if it wasn't!" the squad leader angrily replied.

Minutes later, he was informed that he had to get an officer to make the request. That was a little hard to do since the squad leader was the senior Marine on the outpost. He never did get the mortar coverage, and some lucky Chinese soldiers lived to fight another day because of red tape wrapped around ammunition supplies.

Sgt. Jim Putnam of Fenton, Michigan, was another newcomer to the 7th Marines who got his baptism of fire in battle for the Hook, and later would have much more contentious and harrowing experiences operating out of COP2.

Like a lot of Marines who wound up in the Flame Platoon, Jim Putnam had no idea how the Corps came to the conclusion of what his niche would be in Korea. "I was an armorer, a 2111, at Camp Lejeune and Quantico," Putnam said. "With that MOS I figured the closest I would get to the front would be Division Headquarters. When I told the platoon sergeant that I had no experience in tactical machine-gun usage and none whatsoever as a squad leader, he just smiled." That old Marine Corps theory caught up with Putnam: *Every Marine is an infantryman.*

He was assigned squad leader in the first machine-gun section attached to Dog Company, in the 3rd Battalion, which was strung out left of the Hook where the MLR dipped sharply nearly 3,000 yards to the southwest.

It was during the Hook operation that Sgt. Putnam and his machine-gun crew was ordered to set up just to the right of 76 alley, where the 3rdBat7th was responsible for outposts Berlin and East Berlin. "We were right down on the floor of the rice paddy," Putnam said, "about 50 to 100 yards below the riflemen. We had no trenches and no fighting holes." There was a four-foot wall of 12x12 timbers on their flank. "But it was no place to be under any incoming."

The squad's job was to produce grazing fire 50 to 100 yards below the infantry positions up on the hill. "We were told just to hold what we had," Putnam said. That they did, despite a lot of incoming and frequent probes.

Marines were just about finished with the Hook, but the three-day battle exacted its cost—more so to the Chinese, who suffered 274 confirmed KIA and 73 wounded. Marines took 70 killed and nearly 400 wounded.

There were lessons learned:

> *Perhaps as significant as any result of the Hook fighting is the amount of supporting fires the Chinese provided their infantry. Calculations of total incoming ran from 15,500 to 34,000 rounds during the 36-hour engagement. The 1st Marine Division reported conservatively that the enemy expended between 15,500–16,000 artillery and mortar rounds; estimates by supporting arms units put the total at the higher level. In any event, the 12,500 rounds the 7th Marines received during the first 24 hours represented the heaviest bombardment any Marine regiment had been subjected to up to that time. Moreover, it had now become clearly evident that the enemy could stockpile a plentiful supply of ammunition, despite attempts of UN aircraft to interfere with the enemy's flow of supplies to the frontline.*
>
> *With regard to combat tactics, the attacks during 26–27 October confirmed earlier reports that extremely heavy use of preparatory barrages by the enemy signaled an imminent infantry attack on the area. Defensive concentrations of apparently unlimited quantity typified Communist artillery support for their attacking forces. (MCOinK, Volume V)*

Even though the war was entering its third winter, and activity once again would be slowing somewhat, there was no way United Nations forces could relax. Skirmishes would be plentiful. Marines and the rest of the U.N. troops were still going to be wounded and killed.

The Flame Platoon and other elements of the 1st Tank Battalion, 1st Marine Division, would experience this firsthand as hotspots of the war continued to flare up among the outposts in Western Korea.

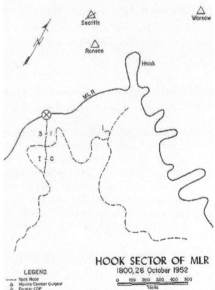

A bitter battle involving the 7th Marines, Able Company tanks, and eventually flame tanks, was about to erupt in early October 1952. (Map Copy Courtesy MCOinK)

HOOK SECTOR OF MLR
1800, 26 October 1952

LEGEND

Tank Road
Marine Combat Outpost
Former COP

0   100   200   300   400   500
Yards

Flames 105s Needed

The 7th Marines had sent the battered Chinese Communist Forces packing after the three days of bitter fighting on and around the Hook, but there still was work to be done to keep the enemy from trying another major assault.

It was up to artillery and tanks, with their heavy ordnance, to pound into the Gook lines in an effort to squelch any attempts the Reds might make to regroup and mount another charge south in the Samichon Valley area.

Flame tanks would be called on to help out here, setting up late in the afternoon of 30 October about 1,000 yards west of Hagorango, some 2,000 yards inside the Jamestown Line. From there two Shermans loaded up their 105s and went to work on Frisco, Hilda, and East Berlin, key outposts south and west of the Hook, lofting more than 100 rounds on the three hills.

About an hour later, the Able Company Patton M46 sitting astride that trench atop Hill 146 took over and fired its 90s until it expended close to another 100 rounds just before sunset.

October 1952 would close out as the most "intense combat" month in more than a year. But the onset of war's third winter came with a gearing down of activity on both sides of the open country in front of the Jamestown Line. "Neither side appeared eager to pursue the offensive. Chinese aggressiveness declined noticeably . . . small unit actions along the rest of the UNC (United Nations Command) frontline began to slacken" *(MCOinK, Volume V)*.

The Flame Platoon was not about to be given a holiday right away, however. One of those "small unit actions" brought them into play on the first day of November, when the Korean Marine Corps needed some help down near the Peace Corridor. The Chinese had shifted their attention to the Hills 31, 33 and 39, the arc of outposts in front of the KMC battalion holding Hill 155 inside the MLR. OP 51, about 1,500 yards directly south of Hill 31, was also among the outposts coveted by the Gooks.

The KMC position looked down on the Tongjang-ni Road, which swung south in front of Jamestown until it broke west above Hill 33 and crossed the Sachon River about 2,000 yards from the MLR. Like the Samichon River Valley, which the 7th Marines had just defended to the north, the Sachon River Valley was another key route south for the CCF. Those four outposts manned by the KMCs not only afforded a good view of the valley, they also were important warning stations for the defense of Hill 155.

Actually, the probability of a determined enemy attack against the four outposts had been anticipated since early October following CCF seizure of three positions (former COPs 37, 36, and 86) in their strike against the KMC regimental OPLR (Outpost Line of Resistance). The enemy had then proceeded to organize an OPLR of his own with the two northern outposts, COPs 37 and 36, and informally occupied another position to the south and one toward the north in the vicinity of COP 39. "With this OPLR once firmly organized, the enemy will have an excellent jump-off point towards our OPs 39 and 33, his next probable objectives," KMC officers reasoned. (MCOinK, Volume V)

There had been probes throughout October, and the Reds increased their heavy fire from tanks and artillery on the 30th. The attacks came shortly before midnight of 31 October.

Beginning at 2200, the enemy delivered an intensive eight-minute 76mm and 122mm artillery preparation against the four outposts. Chinese assault forces from four different infantry regiments then launched a simultaneous attack on the positions. Moving in from the north, west, and south, two CCF companies . . . virtually enveloped the northern outpost, COP 39. Two more CCF companies (unidentified) lunged against the two central outposts, COPs 33 and 31, a company at each position. The southern and most-heavily defended post, COP 51, where a company of Korean Marines was on duty, was assailed by four Chinese companies . . . Even though the enemy exerted his strongest pressure against COP 51, the position held and the Chinese broke off the attack there earlier than at the other outposts.

The enemy's efforts appeared to have been most successful, temporarily, at COP 39, the northern post and one nearest to Hill 155. Although the Chinese wrested some ground from the KMC platoon, artillery fires continued to punish the enemy and by 0410 had forced him to pull back. A small hostile force returned at 0600 but after a 15-minute exchange of small arms it left, this time for good. At about this same time the last of the Chinese had also withdrawn from the two central outposts, 33 and 31.

In terms of sheer numbers, the enemy's strongest effort was made against COP 51. This was the most isolated of the Korean positions and, at 2,625 yards, the one farthest from the MLR. . . . As it turned out the action here was the least intense of the outpost clashes. After initial heavy fighting the Chinese seemed reluctant to press the assault even though they vastly outnumbered the Korean company deployed at the outpost. In the early morning hours the enemy broke contact and by 0330 had withdrawn from COP 51.

During the night approximately 2,500 rounds of CCF artillery and mortar fire lashed the positions. Korean Marines, aided by friendly artillery, repelled the assault and inflicted heavy casualties on the enemy. Supporting fires included more than 1,200 rounds of HE shells from the KMC 4.2-inch Mortar Company. Chinese casualties were listed as 295 known killed, 461 estimated wounded, and 9 POWs. Korean Marine losses were 50 killed, 86 wounded . . . By first light the Korean outposts had thrown back the enemy's latest well-coordinated attack. This ended the last significant action of October in the 1st Marine Division sector. (MCOinK, Volume V)

Before the smoke had cleared on the morning of 1 November, however, a couple of flame tanks with a platoon of M46 Pattons from the First Tank Battalion were called up to help throw a counter-punch at Gook hills facing the outposts. Lt. Col. John I. Williamson, the battalion commander, watched from one of the O.P.s and wasn't a very happy camper.

The thing didn't go well at all. Three of my tanks got stuck and they were never able to get up on the objective, so it didn't please me much. I watched the infantry, KMCs, get up to the top of the hill, but they didn't run into much resistance, just barely crossed the crest and then came back . . . we had aimed to get over behind the hill and burn the goonies out with flame, but failed. (JIW, Dearest Buckie)

The Colonel may have been as much embarrassed as displeased. He was viewing the action with Brig.Gen. Robert O. Bare, the assistant division commander.

Up to the north, the 7th Marines were getting ready to turn over the First Marine Division's extreme right responsibilities to the 1st Commonwealth Division—with its famed Black Watch, Scotland's highly respected kilted 29th Infantry Brigade. It had been planned earlier, but when all hell broke loose at the Hook, the transfer was put on hold.

Now, early in November, with the 1stBat7th in firm control, it was time to constrict the overextended MLR responsibility of the First Marine Division and turn over the northernmost finger of the U.N. line to the British.

Cpl. Joe Discher, one of the 7th's new replacements who had taken over a Baker Company squad in the middle of the fracas on the Hook, had been hearing about the Black Watch. It was not just rumor, but fact, that the Scots had a reputation as brave and fearless fighters.

"We had a lot of respect for the Black Watch," Discher said. He'll never forget the first time he met one of them, a sergeant wearing one of the old World War I skimmer-type helmets. "He came into our bunker to look around," the corporal said. "We noticed after a few minutes he started to grimace, wrinkling his nose like a rabbit. Then we realized what was the matter. We hadn't been off the line for a couple of days. We stunk like hell."

On 10 November, the Marines invited the Scots to their birthday party. "We always wondered if they wore anything under those kilts," Discher said. "We had these artillery shells—piss tubes—plugged into the ground down at company. When one of the Scots came down to relieve himself, there must have been about 200 Marines around him—just to see what he was wearing under that kilt. *Nothing!*"

The Chinese, aware the Marines had vacated the Hook, decided to take another crack at the salient, but the tough Scots did as their predecessors did. They sent the Gooks back where they came from.

Despite other action initiated by the enemy, the I Corps sector remained the chief Communist target. On 19 November, the British 1st Commonwealth Division successfully withstood what was initially a company-size attempt to capture the Hook. In sharp fighting between 1900 and 0430, Black Watch and reinforcing Canadian units repulsed a determined battalion-strength CCF assault, killing more than 100 Chinese. Marine and I Corps artillery units fired almost continuously throughout the night in support of the Hook defenders. (MCOinK, Volume V)

It was one of the last major skirmishes before winter set in. But that didn't mean it was time for the Marines and the rest of the UNC to hunker down in their bunkers and hibernate for a couple of months. As in any lull in the action, there always was the feeling that something might be coming down the pike.

Korean winters just are not conducive to sending thousands of troops into major battles. Both sides wisely figured this out after the Chinese vainly tried to annihilate the First Marine Division in December of 1950. They had grandiose plans when they stormed through the snow at the Chosin Reservoir. But the Communists would lose thousands of troops in a futile pursuit of Marines seventy-eight miles down the Taebaek Mountains to the Port of Hungnam.

It was not easy on Gyrenes, either. But there was a lesson learned by the United Nations Command—and obviously by the Chinese: don't mess with Mother Nature when she turns on the deep freeze in the Land of the Morning Calm!

Like the two previous winters in Korea, the inevitability of icy Manchurian weather prompted the front to settle down somewhat—though not for a long winter's nap. There would be confrontation, killing hundreds on both sides, before the scent of honey pots once again wafted over warmer valleys of the troubled land.

The early months of the war's third winter brought with it a profusion of deadly sparring matches between Marines and Chinese—jabbing and poking at each other with no holds barred. It was like sub-cards of a big boxing show—not the main event, but hard-hitting preliminaries. It was war that did not take a holiday because the weather was getting cold. It was the war of position, platoon-sized patrols into the unknown, trying to find out what the other guy was cooking up. It was recon, and there was nothing easy or nice about it.

With Truce Talks still active in Panmunjom, the area in the vicinity of the North Korean city was such a tender powder keg that, at the very least, it could set off a major battle. Worse, it could blow the slow-moving negotiations sky high. Thus, an ignominious piece of real estate called COP2 (Combat Outpost 2) just north of the "Peace Corridor"— some 2,000 yards east of the Panmunjom center, but a good 4,000 yards in front of the Jamestown Line—was a centerpiece of all kinds of winter intrigue.

The Flame Platoon of the First Tank Battalion still stationed one of its tanks on COP2 for heavy support when needed. More so, however, the outpost was a launching pad for patrols into the unoccupied areas around it and into known outposts occupied by the Chinese.

This was the left flank of the First Marine Division sector of the Jamestown, the extreme point it protected was in the hands of the Korean Marine Corps, which came under 1stMarDiv command. After the 7th Marine Regiment had been pulled off the Hook and had a few weeks in the rear, it was assigned to tie in with the KMCs in late November.

That's when recon and patrol activity heightened.

"Seeing the Elephant"

It's very strange . . . difficult, if not impossible, to convey the adrenaline flow, fear (hopefully controlled), and trepidation one feels when he is out there in the dark, basically all by yourself, and knowing that you are going to meet the enemy.

"I always called it 'Seeing the Elephant.' You have a plan of action—however, things seldom, if ever, go as planned. And, you pray that you do not get ambushed, do not shoot up your own people, do the job holding off the Chinks, and yet, can get out before you get cut off by the inevitable counter attack.

"It's a roll of the dice every time."

Sgt. James Putnam
Section Leader, Heavy Machine Gun Platoon, Weapons Company
2nd Battalion, 7th Marine Regiment, First Marine Division

Recon! Reconnaissance – *the act of examining or spying on some area, as in war, in order to get information.* That's Webster's definition.

Flat out, it's one hell of a dirty, nasty, dangerous job in Marine parlance—or any combat outfit, for that matter. But recon is the battlefield lifeline to intelligence about the enemy. Knowing what your enemy is up to saves lives. Trying to find out what he's up to can cost lives.

Recon was a constant throughout the Korean War. But it was a heightened facet of conflict in the frigid winter months, which congealed big-unit combat like the blood that still managed to slowly ooze from those warriors whose fate determined they must continue this absurd rite of idiocy called war.

The First Tank Battalion, like many of the support units of the First Marine Division, had its own recon section, and it would bear its measure of grief early in 1953. But night in, night out, infantry was doing most of the snoopin' 'n' poopin' in and around Chinese positions—gathering intelligence for all to use—toward the end of 1952.

Sgt. Jim Putnam of Fenton, Michigan, and PFC Bob Atkinson of North Turner, Maine, learned all about recon in the fading, cold months of 1952 that turned downright frigid going into the new year. Both were attached to Dog Company of the 2nd Battalion, but their paths never crossed. Putnam was a section leader in a heavy machine gun platoon, arriving with the 25th Replacement Draft that October. Atkinson came aboard a month later and was an "ammo humper."

"I was fair game for patrols at night, along with humpers from 3/7 rockets, light 30s (machine guns), and 81mm mortars," Atkinson said. "We provided a little relief in alternation with infantry squads."

There was no mistaking in his mind that patrol and recon are synonymous. "Every patrol is a recon patrol, no matter how it is conducted," Atkinson said. "The end result is information about your enemy."

Sgt. Putnam elaborated: "Generally, a recon patrol is primarily to detect activity in enemy territory on trenchlines, bunkers, gun pits, fighting holes, concealment, and its orientation relative to the MLR for reasons of potential probes or attacks."

Putnam had been tested at the Hook but wouldn't get too involved in recon patrols until the Seventh moved a little further west to the area around COP2. Eventually, he would have a couple very hairy experiences early in 1953.

It was the routine of nightly patrols that played on the minds of Marines like Putnam and Atkinson. "You knew the Chinese were there. It was your sole purpose to engage them. You had to be tuned to the maximum. You did not want to get ambushed. It was very easy to see the elephants."

"Seeing the Elephants" was Sgt. Putnam's term for the huge aura of overwhelming pressure he felt when imminent danger of a suspected large enemy force was at hand.

"Scary, unpredictable, and always that everlasting fear of being captured," Putnam said. "My fear was not knowing how I would react if taken prisoner. I often thought I would rather die than be captured, especially after hearing of the atrocities and torture the Chinese laid on Marines."

The word was out in the Division: "You better not be taken prisoner, and do everything in your power to recover your wounded and dead."

That was another element of recon. Often the patrols were designed to recover dead comrades, which is nothing new to Marines who learn early in their first enlistment: "We bring back our wounded and dead."

The Chinese, however, seemed to know all about this and took advantage of it. Purposely they would take Marine dead, or kill the wounded, so they could use them as bait to draw other Marines out in the open for the chance to inflict more casualties.

It was not uncommon for infantry scanning areas of no man's land to see the body of a fellow Marine deliberately placed out in the open by the Gooks. The sight triggered an immediate anger, followed by determination to get the Marine back where he belonged, even though the outraged Gyrenes knew it was a dangerous mission.

The Chinks exercised a couple of options when they did this. They usually had the area where they left the corpse preregistered with mortars, booby-trapped the dead Marine, or both. Either way, it was a crapshoot for the patrol.

But Marines knew it had to be done. More often than not, they became costly missions. So many Marines sent out to retrieve the wounded or dead suffered the same fate as their fallen comrades that Maj. Gen. Edwin A. Pollock, commanding officer of the First Marine Division, decided that would not do. He wanted a specialized "volunteer platoon" specifically for retrieving wounded and dead Marines stranded in no man's land.

PFC Bob Atkinson would find himself a volunteer in what often was referred to as the "Raider Platoon." But there were plenty of guys throughout the Division who, on seeing the way the Chinese used bodies of Marines to bait a recovery, were often ready to take matters into their own hands.

It was not a good idea. But more than once, commanding officers, though admiring the initiative of their troops, had to discourage that kind of reaction. General Pollock would make these decisions.

Some wondered why it took so long for the order to come down to get those Marines back, which set off a new round of rumblings in the ranks.

Taking the Bait, Recovering a Dead Marine

The bodies were flung on the wire.

The Gooks had taken the three Marines—captured and killed, or whose lifeless forms had been dragged back to the enemy outpost—for just such an atrocity. They were draped over barbed wire purposely to be in view of Marines along the Jamestown Line.

The Chinese knew the Marines had a passion for coming after their wounded and dead. They had baited them before, but this was more bizarre—denigrating!.

The report was skipping through the First Marine Division unit-by-unit like a midsummer tornado ripping over the midwest plains. Only this was Korea, and it was the onset of winter 1952-53 and the Chinese once again had stirred up a hornet's nest among Gyrenes. Marines along the line, and off it, were starting to lose their cool.

When the word got back to the Flame Platoon in the tank park off the Changdan Road, Cpl. Tom Clawson, F21's tank commander, his driver PFC Jerry Ravino, and F33 Cpl. Elmer Betts were so angered they went to their commanding officer.

"We wanted to take three of our flame tanks out there," Ravino said, "and get those guys back where they belonged."

Troubled that there hadn't been any word of an effort to retrieve the bodies, Clawson, Betts, and Ravino feverishly worked out their own plan, which would include three flame tanks going out with a couple of the Pattons covering them. "We would torch the hill," Ravino said, "to chase off the Gooks. Then, while the gun tanks covered us, we'd send one or two of our guys out to pull the bodies off the wire."

They planned to either bring the corpses up through the escape hatches of the tank, or haul them up on the engine doors where they could be tied down.

Satisfied they had a good plan, the three tankers went to Lt. Henry Barry, the Flame Platoon commanding officer. Lt. Barry took it up the chain of command but didn't get very far.

In their haste to do something, the three angered tankers failed to take into consideration that the bodies very well could be booby-trapped and the area probably was preregistered by the Chinks so they could lay in a barrage of mortars or artillery—or both. That was the Gooks' grand plan. They knew their enemy's dedication: Marines bring back their wounded and dead.

"We were told: 'No Go!,'" Ravino said. "Division was working on it."

The three mutilated Marines eventually were brought back by the specialized unit set up by Maj. Gen. Edwin A. Pollock, First Marine Division Commanding Officer. It was a mission similar to many PFC Bob Atkinson would make after he joined Dog Company, 2nd Battalion, 7th Marine Regiment. He got to Dog Company when it was strung out on Hill 229 near Pookhan and rotating reinforced platoons to COP2 every three or four weeks. Low man on the company totem pole, he manhandled ammunition for a 60mm mortar squad.

He wound up in patrols coming off COP2 and running south and east of the outpost in the area of Three Fingers, which wasn't a hill of great height, just a series of small humps, giving the appearance of three fingers.

Little did Atkinson realize at the time, however, that these forays into the unknown during his comparatively brief stay on the line in November was on-the-job training for what he would eventually be *volunteered* to do the rest of his stay in Korea. He would spend only a few weeks humping ammo and filling in on patrols before the 7th Marines were sent back to reserve. But he was learning what recon work was like.

"This provided me with the familiarity I would need later for body retrievals in that area," Atkinson said. He hadn't run into any major problems in his "training" tour, but he saw firsthand what could happen when things did go wrong.

During Dog Company's last week on COP2, the Recon Company ran its First Platoon on a patrol between two of the Three Fingers facing the outpost and was ambushed. Atkinson had the gun pit watch on COP2 when all hell broke loose around three or four in the morning. "They must have expected something was going to happen," he said, noting there was a reinforcing platoon on standby. "The Second Platoon was in the trench line . . . in case of fireworks."

And fireworks there were.

"As it worked out," he said, "the First Platoon got wacked, and some of the Second Platoon got hit providing assistance. It was like a Fourth of July . . . with tracers and grenades flying all over the place."

Shortly after that action, the 1st Marines took over that area of the Jamestown, and the Seventh went into reserve for a couple of weeks of rest, retooling, absorbing replacements, and helping build the Kansas Line. Kansas was a mirror of the Jamestown and set up to provide and secondary MLR if the Chinese overran the front. It also was where Atkinson learned about *volunteering*.

"After two weeks of this comparatively sweet duty," he said, "we fell out for morning roll call one day, and the First Sergeant read off the notices for the day, in the process relaying orders to Atkinson and PFC Bill Giguere: 'Pack up all your worldly goods by 0900 and proceed via battalion motor pool truck to the Division Sergeant Major's office.'"

Puzzled, but following orders without any explanation of what was going on, the two infantrymen picked up their transportation and went down to Division, where they immediately met the Sergeant Major. "He introduced himself," Atkinson said, "and told us: 'You're *volunteers* for the Recon Company.'"

Atkinson thought a minute. "I don't ever remember *volunteering* for anything, least of all Recon Company." Somebody thought Atkinson would make a good recon Marine, and he found, in the way the Marine Corps does things sometimes, he *volunteered* to join the outfit. With him in this new assignment was a fellow from Fox Company who also could not, for the life of him, remember *volunteering*.

"Maybe there was something in the drinking water that caused this brief bit of amnesia," Atkinson wondered.

What the *volunteers* were getting into was a specialized Reconnaissance Company ordered by the commanding general of the First Marine Division, specifically for retrieving wounded and dead Marines stranded in no man's land. General Pollock wanted a unit specially trained for this extremely dangerous kind of mission.

General Pollock found the man he wanted to head this unit in 2nd Lt. William Livingston, who already had been put up for, and ultimately would received, the Navy Cross. The citation came after Lt. Livingston had brought back several wounded and dead following a battle with Communist Chinese Forces.

The *volunteers* for Lt. Livingston's new Raider Platoon were told they could go to the Recon Company for at least ten days and, at the end of the trial period, if they wanted to go back to the 7th Marines they could—no questions asked! They also were reminded recon was *strictly volunteer.*

Sometime later, Atkinson pondered his decision. "It stands to reason that the Commanding General has to have his own pool of dimwits to do crazy stuff that normal people would not think of doing."

After the ten days with the new company—which later became known along the line as the Raider Platoon—Atkinson decided to stay and was assigned to its First Platoon. "I was too lazy to pack up and leave, so we went to work to earn our pay," he said facetiously.

It wasn't long before the platoon became involved in missions to bring back bodies from places like Three Fingers, where a fallen Marine lay exposed on one of the sloping hills for several days. The body had to be retrieved, and although there were plenty of volunteers among Marines who were looking at one of their buddies from the MLR, the okay for something like that had to come down from the top.

Only CG himself—General Pollock—could approve the mission.

When the order came, Lt. Livingston's platoon, with Atkinson and PFCs Mark Brown and Billy Mills on the point, left the COP2 trenchline about 0330. The routine had been rehearsed many times.

"The whole platoon was on this caper," Atkinson said. Twenty Marines, including the lieutenant, were strung out at maybe ten-yard intervals. PFCs Giguere and James Coe were along on the patrol. "We were going after three bodies," Giguere said they had been told.

Atkinson noted the patrol moved with as much stealth as a group of twenty men could manage. Reaching the slope of the hill, Akinson ventured toward one of the bodies, trying to determine if it was tethered to a stake, or if he could see any signs of booby traps. The safety measure was to make sure that at least a ten-foot area around the body was clear of mines, potential booby traps, and trip wires. A tough order in the dark, but they lucked out on this one. "It appeared to be clean with no visible hookups," Atkinson said. He motioned to PFC Brown that it was okay to come up the slope.

As Atkinson backed down the hill about thirty yards, PFC Brown, armed with a handmade tool—a broomstick attached to a long length of rope with a couple of half-hitch loops at the end—closed on the body. When in position to reach the fallen Marine with the wooden probe, he started the routine—poking around the corpse with the stick, trying to make sure it was wasn't booby-trapped.

Meanwhile, Atkinson had fallen back to set up to cover a firing field in an arc from 12 to 9 o'clock while PFC Mills ranged the opposite direction to 3 o'clock. The rest of the platoon was in position to fan the rest of the small perimeter's circle.

PFC Brown, after probing with the stick, moved closer to the dead Marine. The routine was to slide the wooden probe under the remains, praying he would not trip a booby trap, or set off a land mine.

Once the Marine deftly slipped the stick under the body, he threw the loose end of the rope over corpse and jerked it into position to engage the other end of the stick with one of the loops. With the rope secured to the stick, the PFC Brown had to move back down the hill, sliding on his back feet first while letting out the rope.

Out of range of possible explosions of booby traps—he hoped—PFC Brown pulled on the rope, lifting the free end of the stick while the other end dug into the ground. As the rope lifted the stick, the body began to raise and roll along it toward the Marine.

Pulling harder, PFC Brown dislodged the entire body.

Nothing exploded. So far, so good.

Atkinson and Mills went forward to help slide the body down the hill. When Atkinson and his two buddies got the dead Marine to the bottom of the hill, they discovered he still had on utilities—trousers and dungaree jacket—but the body was swollen and tight against the clothing.

"Shoes, socks, flack jacket, web gear, helmet, and weapon," Atkinson said, "all of that was gone."

The body had been out there so long, most of the stench was reduced. "It was brittle," Atkinson said, "and there was a strong ammonia-like aroma."

The routine was repeated.

Once the two bodies were freed, Lt. Livingston motioned to PFCs Qiguere and Coe to grab a fold-up litter and transport one of the dead Marines. After carefully placing the brittle body on the stretcher, they covered it with a shelter-half. Quickly, they picked up the litter and fell in line with the patrol heading back to COP2. Somewhere along the way, Coe asked Giguere to stop and put down the litter.

"He told me an arm fell off the body," Giguere said. After setting down the stretcher, Coe picked up the limb and placed it under the poncho next to the lifeless Marine. They wasted no time taking the litter in hand again and getting back into line with the patrol.

There still had been no reaction from the Gooks. "I don't know why," Atkinson said, "and God only knows, but the Chinese must have been asleep."

PFC Giguere had similar reaction. "I cannot believe we were never detected," Giguere said. "I guess the good Lord did not want us—thank God!"

Giguere made one notation about that retrieval. "We came back with two of the three bodies that night. One was a redhead and the other had blond hair."

Although "body snatching" was not a frequent assignment for Sgt. Jim Putnam, sometimes it just happened to develop on a recon patrol in which the Fenton, Michigan, machine-gun section leader was involved.

The price paid for bringing back bodies of fellow Marines not only was exacted in the ever-present danger of possibly being wounded or killed but in the residue that was left in the mind after immediate contact with the mutilated remains of what once was a living, breathing person.

There were several such incidents seeing dead Marines laid out in the open by the Chinese that made indelible notations in Jim Putnam's mind. "After a few days of viewing bodies lying out there," he said, "it definitely gets to you. You think about it being you, or one of your buddies." That made Marines like Putnam more determined to bring back the mortally wounded. "After a while, you would definitely take the risk to get that body out of there."

But one retrieval in which he became involved was not planned. It happened on a platoon-sized patrol to the right of the restricted Peace Corridor in front of the Korean Marine Corps sector. It was about a quarter of a mile out, in the rice paddies near a formation called the Stadium, east of Panmunjom.

"This turned out to be an interesting caper," Putnam said. "Two of us were flankers on this safari, and we were ahead of the patrol, paralleling the main body."

They were in a dry stream bed about thirty yards out on the flank, in order to protect the platoon. The patrol moved without incident until it came upon a well-hidden bunker complex. The Chinese were using it to store propaganda literature and the stench indicated bodies were, or had been, hidden there to be used as bait.

It wasn't long before the investigating Marines found the body of one of their own. Since the patrol was recon, and not expecting retrieval, there were no body bags or stretchers brought along. "We carried him out in a poncho, rolled up liked a carpet," Sgt. Putnam said, ever aware of the odor, but mustering as much respect as he could for a fallen comrade. Putnam carried the partially decomposed body half the distance back down the trail before another Marine relieved him to finish the tedious trip back to the friendly outpost.

"The degree of decomposition was advanced to the point where the limbs were brittle and could snap off with any sudden movement," Putnam said. This was not a very pleasant mission, but it had to be done, either by design or happenstance. "Body retrieval was an unpleasant coincidence in designed recon patrol," Putnam said. "But as dirty as it was, it was beneficial to know the Marine would not be exploited any further by the enemy."

Bringing back dead Marines in the course of recon also eliminated the necessity of having to assign a platoon, or squad, to venture into harms way for the specific job of recovering that particular body.

Near the end of the war, up around Vegas and Boulder City and the rest of the Nevada outposts, there was an increase of Marines MIA. When their bodies were put out as bait by the Chinese, it got extremely costly for retrieval squads. Division finally decided, reluctantly, it was too costly and stopped most of these type patrols. "We took to destroying the bodies with artillery bombardments, or air strikes," Sgt. Putnam said sadly. "Not a pretty sight, either!"

On the Wire! In Front of the Wire!

Marine infantry called it being "on the Wire!" The reference was pulling a tour of duty on Line, peering over or through the rolls of barbed concertina that was the final inanimate deterrent to enemy coming at them along the MLR. It was the last line of defense in front of their trenches and bunkers.

When you were on the Wire, you were there, Marine, front row-center, waiting for the curtain to go up on what very well could be your last day on earth. Being on the Wire was almost a constant state of emotion. Being *in front of* the Wire is *the* constant state of emotion.

"No matter how many times you have been in front of the Wire," said Sgt. Jim Putnam, "the feeling is eerie at best. Most of the time on Line, one could not see the man in the next fighting hole. After an hour or so on watch, especially in the winter, shrubs seemed to be closer to you than they were the last time you looked in that direction. Trees, if there were any, sometimes appeared to move laterally. Rocks became prone Chinese soldiers sneaking up on you. Rats were raiding parties. In other words," Putnam said, "one had to keep a tight rein on his emotions so as not be spooked."

In infantryman's terms, *spooked* was synonymous with being *shook*. And when one guy gets *shook,* Marines around him become very wary.

"Men who were *shook* could not be counted on," Sgt. Putnam reasoned. "No one trusted a *shook* person on watch, and no one slept remotely well knowing they were there. Thus, they were mildly shunned."

The fear that erupted like this usually surfaced among short-timers—guys who had only a few days, or few weeks before they were scheduled to be rotated out, going home. When it happened, there always was a strong effort among their buddies to have them transferred off the Line—get them back to battalion, regiment, anywhere in the rear where their nervousness would not effect the stability of a watch on the Wire—or a patrol in front of it. Patrols had a myriad of their own problems.

"On patrol it was twice as bad, since you now were in front of the Wire in no man's land," Putnam said. "It was always dark, and the territory unfamiliar. Every noise is magnified to the point of being blaring."

Putnam felt fortunate, in his capacity as a Dog Company machine-gun section leader in 2ndBat7th, that he did not have to be in front of the Wire that often. His knowledge of what went on out there fostered a sincere admiration for riflemen who stomped that ground about every third night.

But he knew the routine, and it wasn't pretty, particularly one February night in 1953 during an ill-advised recon patrol heading toward Three Fingers, the triple-mound hill facing the east side of COP2. It became one of the Michigan NCO's most traumatic experiences.

Sgt. Putnam, and one of his men from the heavy machine-gun section, were backing up a rifle squad with one of their light 30-caliber machine guns. MG support on patrols like this—although the section's T.O. weapon was a water-cooled 30-caliber—never took the heavies away from their gun pits. "Their ranges of fire were carefully laid in," said Putnam of the heavy machine guns, "and they were seldom, if ever, moved. Even when a section moved on or off line, the tripods were never moved so as not to disrupt the firing scheme. We merely exchanged tripods with the relieving troops, or gave our tripods to the gunners we relieved."

So it was the air-cooled light-30, a much lighter and more transportable weapon, that machine gun support carried on the patrols.

"Our mission that night was to enter an area of Three Fingers where we knew the Gooks were, and take prisoners, " Putnam said. "A support force was set up on No Name Ridge just east of COP2 in order to protect our return."

The Dog Company commander, a captain, was in charge of the operation. "He was an inexperienced S.O.B. who had just taken over the company," the chagrined section leader snapped.

It was very cold that night, maybe 0 to 10 degrees above, with an inch of snow on the ground. The squad's first checkpoint was about 100 yards east of No Name Ridge. "Before we got out that far, there were all kinds of pyrotechnics going on north and east of the ridge," Putnam said. "Something was going to happen."

The patrol leader radioed back to the command post and requested to sit in (stay put) for a while because numerous flares were illuminating the whole area. "The good captain got on the radio," Putnam said angrily, "and called us a bunch of scared cowards. He ordered us to continue to the next checkpoint."

That checkpoint, a little blown-out bridge across a small stream, was two to three hundred yards further east—about two hundred yards from Three Fingers. The reinforced squad moved out, following the stream. "We could hear the sound of men and equipment on either side of us," Atkinson said. "Obviously, they were not ours."

Again the squad leader radioed back to command to ask if there were supposed to be any other friendlies out there. "The captain told us we were just getting spooked and to get on with the mission at hand," Putnam said.

They started out again, but became aware of shadows on both sides of them, going in the opposite direction towards COP2. The squad leader took it on his own to hold fast and halted the squad, waiting. "It seemed like forever under all that tension, but it was no more than fifteen minutes or a half hour," Putnam said. "We were between a rock and a hard place, and because we traveled light on a partrol like that, we were not wearing parkas. It was damned cold!

"Then, all Hell broke loose behind us in the general vicinity of COP2. We called in and were told that Grey Rock and No Name Ridge were under heavy attack. That's when we got orders to abort our mission and return to COP2. *Told you so, captain!*" Putnam snapped to himself.

The squad started making its way back, deciding to walk over the frozen stream. It wasn't frozen enough. Sgt. Putnam and two other Marines broke through the ice into the frigid water. "We were soaking wet and *cold!*" Putnam said. "Our thermo boots were full of freezing cold water."

They pulled themselves out of the shallow water and moved on, hoping the pace of the activity would lessen the chill. Finally, they reached the base of No Name Ridge. "I set up my machine gun there," Putnam said. "There was all kinds of noise coming from up on the ridge, mostly burp guns and grenades. We were getting some of it."

Slugs from the Chinese burp guns were cutting up tree branches all around them. Suddenly, the sergeant saw someone coming off the base of the hill to the road.

"I was just about to shoot, when he yelled, *'MARINE!'* He will never know how lucky he was," Putnam said with relief. "He told us that when our covering force reached the top of No Name Ridge, it was ambushed by a couple of platoons of Chinks that were laying in wait for them.

"He was shaken," Putnam said. "He said the Gooks opened up with everything—burp guns, grenades . . . then they were grabbing the wounded and dead, and trying to haul them off the hill."

Mortars and artillery—incoming—started pound into the Ridge. "It was obvious," the sergeant figured, "they were trying to box us off the hill."

It didn't take long for the Marines to regroup. Sgt. Putnam, his gunner, and what was left of the recon squad became part of the relief and rescue unit sweeping No Name to recover wounded and dead Marines.

"It was a real fiasco," Putnam said. "We were getting hit with our own 81s and 60s (mortars) in the confusion."

As the recovery group spread out, Putnam was on the extreme northern end of the line, and started up the hill. Small arms, grenades, mortars, artillery were going off all over the place. "We never did get to the top of the hill," the sergeant said, "but another Marine and I were able to pull three of our wounded guys out and get them down below."

More Marines were sent out from COP2 to help the recovery operation, but it was fruitless. "Incoming and small arms fire was so heavy," Putnam said. "We began taking so many casualties ourselves, we were ordered back to the outpost."

At one point during the recovery, Putnam thought he was about to meet his own fate. "I had a Chink not more than fifteen to twenty feet away shooting at me with a burp gun. I don't know how he missed me. I will never know."

By daybreak, the Chinks decided to go home. Putnam, like the rest of the able-body survivors, were bringing the wounded back into their bunkers to wait evacuation. "We had several KIA, and many missing that we never recovered—at least not that night," the Sergeant said. "But I'm sure somebody would be going back out to try to find them, no matter what the cost. It was a night I would never forget!"

It was not uncommon that once all hell starts breaking loose, all thought seems to stop. "You either perform, or you don't," Sgt. Putnam emphasized. "Fortunately, most of us performed—it is a controlled fear."

When Jim Putnam was on COP2, he had his first experience with flame tanks, not realizing then that their main armament was the 105mm cannon. When the Sherman would go to the top of the outpost for a firing mission, it meant the bunkers built into the sides of the hills were under the powerful tank. He learned quickly what it was like to be around them with their powerful cannons.

"We were always in bunkers below the tanks when they fired and they were loud," Putnam admitted. "We had headaches for a couple of days after they used their cannons. They were so loud and powerful, the sand from the bags over our bunkers was always falling on us."

He thought of tanks as a mixed blessing. Like most infantry, Putnam would rather not be around them, unless they were needed for close-in protection. "They usually drew incoming, but sometimes it was nice to have them around to keep the Chink artillery and mortars pinned down for a while."

He never saw their flame guns in action. "I never had the opportunity to be involved in action with flame tanks," Putnam said once. "Thank the Good Lord."

But after he spent some time patrolling the Nevada outposts, he wished he had. He eventually heard how lethal the flame gun could be when turned loose on an enemy hill, or the unfortunate Chinese who dared stay in the range of the scorching napalm. Then he reconsidered his missed opportunity. "Wish we could have had a couple on Vegas and Boulder City."

Putnam spent about ten months patrolling with the Dog, then Fox, recon companies 2/7th. The one problem was the constant change in personnel with monthly rotations out and replacements in. It was difficult to keep team-like cohesion.

Then again, the danger of such missions unfortunately meant casualties would be part of the job. This was not a requisite for forging good friendships. The constant turnover limited the knitting of tight bonds, and that reduced some of the emotional buildup when a Marine, not known well to another Marine, was killed or wounded.

Seeing a Marine go down was tough enough, but the closer the friendship, the harder that man's fate hit home.

New Commander in Chief

Thanks to the recon work of both the infantry and the First Tank Battalion's own patrols, there were enough Chinese targets—despite the general slowdown of action all along the front—to keep the Flame Platoon busy with indirect fire missions.

> *As the third Korean winter approached outpost clashes and small unit actions along the rest of the UNC (United Nations Command) began to slacken. During November and December, neither side appeared eager to pursue the offensive. Chinese aggressiveness declined noticeably. (MCOinK, Volume V)*

Nevertheless, the First Marine Division was not about to let the Chinese just crawl up in their holes and have a peaceful winter's nap. There was going to be plenty of thunder provided to disrupt their snoozes, and by the same token, the Gooks seemed to be thinking that way, too. Early in the month of November 1952, there was an increase of incoming on tank positions from the other side of the MLR, and it took its toll. Although flame tanks escaped damage, five gun-company M46 Pattons were badly beat up.

It seemed that nearly every firing mission by tanks was followed by retaliation on their positions by the Chinese. Obviously, there was some fairly good recon work also being done by the enemy.

Meanwhile, there was big news back home. Dwight D. Eisenhower—the famous Army general who engineered the Allied victory in Europe in World War II—had been elected president of the United States. President Harry S. Truman, who was not so popular with the troops at this point of the Korean War, had decided not to seek a second term, and General Eisenhower handily defeated democratic nominee Adlai E. Stevenson to replace HST.

During the campaign, Eisenhower had promised, if he was elected, to come to Korea to personally investigate the war's operation and get a good look at the troops. He fulfilled that promise with a four-day visit early in December. How many troops he was able to observe never was determined. Although he was the commanding general of one of the world's most powerful armies during WWII, he now was elected commander in chief of one of the world's two superpowers less than a decade later.

Korea seemed no place for the president-elect of the United States. However, by this stage of the conflict, the Korean War was wearing on everybody, even the citizenry back in the States.

> *The stalemated combat situation in Korea had become a depressing, no-win daily routine by the end of 1952. Back in the states, the Korean War was not only unpopular and ill-supported, but the slow progress of the conflict also dulled public interest . . .*
>
> *General Eisenhower's promise to visit Korea . . . to see the situation first-hand and his subsequent election had renewed American hopes for an early peace . . . negotiations. (MCOinK, Volume V)*

It didn't appear to do much good, because it took another eight months before an uneasy truce would be in hand. The truce talks recessed early in October when the United Nations negotiators became fed up with the Chinese balking and stalling over everything the U.N. put on the table. Three separate proposals dealing with the sensitive POW issues had been offered to the Reds. All were rejected.

When chief U.N. delegate Gen. William K. Harrison decided to call a recess, it took the Chinese by surprise. He stood fast by his decision: "We are not terminating the armistice negotiations, we are merely recessing them. We are willing to meet with you at any time that you are ready to accept one of our proposals or to make a constructive proposal of your own, in writing, which could lead to an honorable armistice . . . Since you have offered nothing constructive, we stand in recess."

> *After October, while the truce negotiations were in a period of indefinite recess, liaison officers at Panmunjom kept the channels of communication open between the Communist and UNC sides. Several developments along other diplomatic lines about this time were to prove more fruitful and lead the way to solution of the POW dispute and, in fact, to the end of the war. (MCOinK, Volume V)*

So it was that the Flame Dragons continued their ever-dependable roll as the 105 Boomers for the balance November 1952.

Usually, the elements of the Platoon were working attached to one of the letter companies. It was a hookup with Charlie Company when four of the Shermans went back into action on 5 November and unleashed their heaviest assault of the month with their 105s. They pounded the Hedy and Bunker Hill quadrants with more than 200 rounds and were credited with killing at least two Chinese while ripping into bunkers and trenches.

They were particularly busy in the middle of the month. Five straight days, two to four of the Shermans worked in concert with Charlie Company, sitting south of Munsan-ni-Panmunjom-Kaesong Peace Corridor. They pounded Chinese positions in the Sachon River Valley southwest of the bubble around the Truce Talks site.

Usually, there were more 90mm ordnance sent aloft than 105s, but the combined shoots did their jobs. The most telling was on 15 November. Flame tanks sent more than seventy rounds of 105 on target to supplement 200 shots from the Patton 90s. They clobbered Gooks in the Sachon area and counted twelve confirmed enemy dead.

Charlie Company went off line near the end of the month. So Flames then teamed with Able Company and started working further north for a couple of days, lofting their ordnance on outposts Berlin, Frisco, Detroit, Vegas, and Elmer up near the Hook. They also had one mission on targets further north, west of outpost Warsaw.

While Lt. Col. John I. Williamson, commanding officer of the First Tank Battalion, was somewhat pleased with what was going on in the Flame Platoon, he still felt those tanks could be better utilized.

Lt. Henry Barry had taken over the Flame Platoon when Lt. Clement Buckley was wounded early in October. Buckley, who had a little bit of maverick in him, appeared to rank fairly high in the esteem of Colonel Williamson. It seemed apparent, anyone following him in the Flame Platoon was going to be compared to his predecessor by the battalion commander. That comparison didn't always develop in Lt. Barry's favor.

The battalion commander was about to come down a bit firmly on the Flame Platoon's leader.

New C.O. Feels Heat in Flame Platoon

Filling the shoes of one of the commanding officer's favorite boys is not an easy thing to do. And that was the job laid at the feet of 1st Lt. Henry Barry when he was assigned to take over the Flame Platoon of the First Tank Battalion by Lt. Col. John I Williamson, its commanding officer.

Lt. Clement Buckley, a bit of a maverick, but a well-respected tank officer, had endeared himself to Colonel Williamson. He was respected for his aggressive approach to tanking, even though it was not beyond his personality to buck the trend and incur the ire of one or two staff officers in the First Marine Division.

When Lt. Buckley was taken out of action with a heroic performance while in front of the lines with a couple of his flame tanks, Williamson gave Lt. Barry, who had been filling in where needed in the Battalion, command of the nine specially equipped Shermans. By his nature, Barry was less the aggressor and more the let-things-come-as-they-may officer.

Even the tankers in the Flame Platoon noticed it right away and found it hard to fall in line with their new Platoon Commander after having followed Lt. Buckley through some exciting, if not hazardous, routines.

Williamson was never shy about letting his troops know what was on his mind. It was part of the makeup of a good commanding officer.

Despite the activity of the Flame Platoon in November of 1952, Lt. Col. Williamson maintained his dissatisfaction with the unit. Unfortunately, Lt. Barry, one day early in December, decided to see his commanding officer about something. He soon found it was a serious misjudgment.

"Lt. Barry, leader of my flame platoon, came down to see me this afternoon, and I bitched at him a bit about keeping his tanks running and doing a bit more shooting. He is a pretty good boy, but not as aggressive as Lieutenant (Clement) Buckley, the former platoon leader" (JIW, *Dearest Buckie*).

The final month of 1952 roared in like an angry mountain lion bringing brutal cold, which crept in rather delicately with drizzling rain on 2 December, but turned to snow and a more Korean-like ten degrees within the next twenty-four hours. More snow and a status-quo thermometer left no doubt in the minds of Marines guarding the Jamestown Line that winter was here.

Lt. Barry, however, continued to feel the heat, and it wasn't because he got too close to one of his tank's flame guns. A week after his first encounter with Williamson, his C.O. still was on his case. "Read off my flame platoon leader to parade rest this afternoon because of his foot-dragging on some of the things I want him to do" *(Dearest Buckie)*.

Maybe that did it for Barry. On 18 December, the Platoon Commander sent four of the Shermans with Charlie Company, and they unloaded with a vengeance into a ridgeline south of outpost Yoke and east of Ingrid. It was a Flame Platoon mission of its own, and more than 300 rounds dropped on the hills.

Colonel Williamson was on hand to watch that one, and Lt. Barry regained some points with his commanding officer. "Watched my flame platoon firing indirect fire, which they were doing very well" *(Dearest Buckie)*.

Two days earlier, he might not have been so inclined to let up on Barry. It was on

16 December when four flame tanks—F12, F13, F21, and F22—were staged in back of outpost Marilyn, 1,300 yards in front of the MLR just west of the Neutral Corridor to the connecting Munsan-ni to Panmunjom, where the Truce Talks were taking place. They were ready to roll with nine Dog Company tanks on a flame mission to scorch Three Fingers, from where the Chinese had been raising hell with the Marines on Combat Outpost 2 (COP2) since they returned to the Western Sector.

Three Fingers got its name, because Marines looking east to it from COP2 saw a hill with three side-by-side protrusions extending south. The appendages looked like three fingers, pointing right at Marine outposts Star and Marilyn.

Along for the mission was the Flail Tank—Y54, which also was a Sherman M4A3E8, but was set up as a minesweeper. It had two long arms extending in front of the tank's bow, which held a tank-wide steel shaft that rotated when engaged by a separate motor. Attached to the shaft in no particular array was a series of heavy chains with weights at the end of them. The concept was that when the shaft was rotating, the chains flailed in front of the tank, beating on the ground to set off buried mines.

Tankers called it "Thumper." When Lt. Buckley had convinced Colonel Williamson late the previous summer that the more active Flame Platoon should be set up closer to the MLR—instead of languishing in the Battalion CP—and moved into the Changdan tank park, Thumper moved forward with nine Flames. However, it had not been active at all. This was Thumper's first mission—clear the road toward Three Fingers for the four flame tanks.

It was not to be Thumper's day.

Just before noon, the nine Dog Company tanks, under the command of popular Capt. "Devil Dog" Walker, were sitting by firing at targets of opportunity from positions on friendly hills and down below in the valley. They called Capt. Walker "Devil Dog" because of his aggressiveness and penchant to show all who mattered that Marine tankers were second to none.

Two of the M46 Pattons were on a hill behind Thumper as it ventured from behind Marilyn in to open no man's land. Sgt. James A. Martin, a former welterweight boxing champion of the Pacific Fleet Marine Force, was Thumper's T.C. He was the first Colored tank commander in the First Tank Battalion. He came to the Platoon after six years in the Corps as a cook and would not be the last Negro to serve in the Flame Platoon. However, when Sgt. Martin took Thumper on its first mission, he was a relatively inexperienced tanker.

Sitting in the gunner's seat of D54 up on the hill behind where the flail tank was making its way toward Three Fingers, Cpl. Harry Regan of San Jacinto, California, had a perfect view of what was going on down below. "The Thumper had stopped on the road to start up the flail," Regan said.

When Y54 began moving forward again, it hadn't gotten more than ten yards. There was a tremendous explosion, and the dust and smoke made a cloud around most of the tank. Thumper had been ravaged by the very thing it was out to destroy—it had run over a double box mine.

Regan watched the tank through his powerful gunner's scope as its right side lifted off the road and quickly settle in the cloud. "The track was blown apart, and the road wheels appeared to be bent," Regan said. "It was not a good situation for them."

D24 began to traverse its turret, looking for any sign of enemy soldiers trying to storm the stricken pigiron. Cpl. Regan was very aware of the traffic on the radio. "Y54, Thumper, Thumper can you copy?" It was Captain Walker. There was no answer.

"Thumper, Thumper," Walker tried again. "If anyone inside is hurt, then traverse your turret to the left. If you can receive my transmission, traverse to the right."

Cpl. Regan was impressed with how cool and calm, relative to the situation, the captain sounded on the radio.

Regan then noticed the Y54 turret move ever so slightly to the right.

"Stand by," he heard Walker say. "The beetle doctor is on the way." The beetle doctor was Dog Company's retriever. That would be Sgt. Frederick MacKay Jr.'s specially rigged M46.

Immediately, Walker then called for a Willy Peter (white phosphorous) saturation from his 90s to smoke the area around the tank to protect it from the Chinks.

It wasn't long before MacKay had his rig, followed by two more Dog Company Pattons, moving toward Thumper. MacKay was a veteran tanker. He and his crew of mechanics had a lot of time in the line doing just what they were about to do with the flail tank.

MacKay, assured by the two other tanks protecting him, quickly climbed out of the retriever and went to the bustle phone on the back of Y54. He connected with Sgt. Martin and told him they were going to be pulled the hell out of there. MacKay and his crew were going to hook crossed cables to the back of the flail tank to the front of the retriever and do a reverse tow.

As the retriever began nudging backwards and tension built on the cables, the Thumper started to move. Regan heard his tank commander ask: "Harry! You ever see a cable snap on one of those?"

Before Cpl. Regan could answer, lo and behold, one of the cables broke. "We could see it in the air," Regan said. "We could hear it singing as it snapped and landed behind the retriever."

Whipping like that, it could have cut someone in half. Fortunately, none of the tankers were in its way. Making a bad situation worse, the Chinese finally had seen what was going on after some of the smoke had cleared. Immediately there was incoming, but the crew took their chances and stayed in the open while hooking up the wench system.

Lady Luck, and probably a more powerful Friend, was on their side this day.

Cpl. Regan watched from above as the retriever backed toward the protection of Marilyn, dragging the immobile Thumper with it. The retriever continued the struggle and hauled the wounded beetle through the gate and to the Dog Company C.P. behind the MLR. Sometime later, it was winched onto a lowboy by Service Company and taken back to the First Tank Battalion to be repaired.

But never again was Thumper used in the Korean War.

While all the tank rescue work was going on, the four flame tanks remained on standby to commit to their mission, but it was too late. The scheduled burn on Three Fingers was scratched.

The flail tank, its crew bounced around and bruised, was physically none the worse for wear.

However, the Flame Tankers did not get the full skinny until they got back to the Changdan park. They had no idea what really happened to the Thumper, other than it had hit a mine.

PFC Ravino was climbing the hill toward his tent when he heard someone calling him. It was Sgt. Martin. "Brother Ravino," the soft-spoken Thumper T.C. said uneasily. "We need to talk, okay?"

When Martin first arrived in the Flame Platoon and was given command of the flail tank, he and Ravino immediately hit it off. Both were former amateur boxers, both were devout Catholics, and they found they had many common interests. They became very good friends, and it was one of the reasons the Boston Italian never had a problem, like some other Marines, when Colored tankers were being assigned to the Flame Platoon. He mixed very well with fellow PFCs. James S. Doyle, Robert Clark, Andrew Pittmon, Jr., and Samuel Graham—all Negroes.

"What the hell is going on, James?" Ravino asked his friend, who was visibly shaken. "You look like hell!"

Martin just wanted to talk to someone to try and calm down. When he told Ravino what had happened out in front of Three Fingers, it was a process of calming down.

"That's what friends are for," Ravino said.

The scratched flame mission at Three Fingers, and the 105 assault on Yoke two days later, was it for the Platoon in 1952.

It was about this time—not surprisingly because winter had begun to settle in and slow the war somewhat—that all battalion commanders began feeling the itching of rear echelon types who every once in a while tended to get in their hair.

Despite the success the First Tank Battalion was having spreading havoc among the Chinese, non-combatants in EUSAK (Eighth U.S. Army Korea) apparently had nothing better to do than to start picking fly-shit out of pepper. And as it came sprinkling down the chain of command, it was doing more than sending Lt. Col. Williamson into a fit of sneezing.

Two days before the New Year shivered into Korea, Williamson's ire was near the boiling point, and he vented some of it in a letter to his wife, Buckie.

> I'm a rather bitter man tonight. We've been having quite a hassle the past few days. The Army has directed that we turn in the shell cases from our tank ammunition, and won't issue us more ammunition until we turn in what they consider a sufficient amount of brass. As a great deal of our firing takes place in front of the MLR, we have not been recovering much brass, because the crews throw it out of the tanks as soon as they shoot to keep the powder fumes from bothering them. Normally when they fire in rear of the MLR we send trucks up to haul the brass back. Much haggling, heckling, and harassing has flowed up and down the chain of command regarding this matter, with yours truly on the butt end of most of it. We are now trying to leave the stuff in the tanks, disregarding the comfort of the crews, so that we'll bring it back to turn in. To my mind this is the absolute end in asininity, capping the climax of a veritable torrent of administrative harassment that has burgeoned as activity to our front has decreased. When not assailed by the enemy from the front, we are eternally harassed by supposedly friendly echelons to the rear. In this regard it would be much better if we were slugging it out heavily with the foe, for then the bastards in the rear would perforce knock off this crap and concern themselves with the vital issue of fighting. (JIW, Dearest Buckie)

For the record, in the last month of 1952, the First Tank Battalion gun companies unleashed more than 15,000 rounds—assortments of 90mm HE (high explosive), WP (white phospherous), and APC (anti-personnel canisters). The Flame Platoon sent more than 800 rounds of 105mm from its tubes. Added to all that were approximately 3,500 rounds of 76mm from the very active KMC tanks.

Ironically, this compared with much lighter action the previous month, when the three units consumed less than 14,000 rounds among them.

Williamson just expressed the feeling of his men. When crap like that came down the line—which wasn't the first time—Marines could do little more than shrug it off with a few choice words, which, freely translated, would amount to: *"What a way to fight a war!"*

Flames Work over No Man's Island

While cat-and-mouse patrol and recon activity, along with the heavy use of tank and artillery long-range fire, permeated what subdued ground activity there was in mid-November through December of 1952, it didn't take too long before the new year began to heat up.

And what better place for the Flame Platoon of Headquarters Company, First Tank Battalion, to get started under its new commanding officer, Lt. Michael McAdams, than at Hill 134?

Marines called it "No Man's Island."

In the central lowlands below the mountain range that was the Chinese Communist mainline of resistance (MLR), there was a series of outposts, mostly controlled by the enemy east of the neutral bubble that protected Panmunjom Truce Talks site. Hill 134 was a little nub of a Gook outpost sitting about 1,000 yards east of Marine-held Combat Outpost 2 (COP2), and 500 yards west of ChiCom-controlled Three Fingers.

Hill 134 also was about 2,300 yards in front of the Jamestown Line, and was descriptively named "No Man's Island" because it was surrounded by rice paddies and small creeks.

Unlike any other hill out beyond the MLR, the island had no trench lines, bunkers, or stationary gun emplacements. However, it remained one of the most desired observation points because of the clear view it offered looking over all four points of the compass.

In broad daylight, it appeared a rather tranquil piece of real estate when Gooks remained off its surface, or were concealed on the reverse slope. It became a treacherous place once the sun went down. Hill 134 was a special target of Marine recon seek-and-destroy patrols because it was ideal for taking prisoners. Yet such patrols could be costly.

Ambushes by both the CCF and Marine units were very frequent, causing heavy casualties, depending who was laying in wait in the dark. That necessitated body retrievals if some Marines did not return—which produced more problems. It seemed a vicious cycle for Marine infantry. Maybe the Flame Platoon, with its primary weapon—the flame gun—was the solution.

No Man's Hill was well zeroed-in by the flame tank stationed on COP2, which regularly provided fire support with its 105mm howitzer. When things really got dicey for infantry patrols probing Hill 134, the Sherman was called on to "Box us in"—meaning the Recon guys were surrounded and wanted pinpoint incoming around their position.

Usually, one flame tank was left on COP2, and crews interchanged monthly to man the 105. After a time—depending on how much use the 105 got—another Sherman was pulled up on the hill to replace the resident so heavier maintenance would be performed on the overworked howitzer. Normally, it had fire missions day after day, sometimes month after month, while in place.

Hill 134 was a primary target during daytime shoots. Now it was time for the Flame Platoon to get up-close-and-personal with No Man's Hill.

On 7 January 1953, crews of F21 and F22 were called into the platoon commander's small pyramid tent to discuss the flame mission. Lt. Michael L. McAdams, a twenty-four-year-old Mustang who had come up through the ranks to earn his bars, had just taken over the platoon. He had been given the command by Lt. Col. John I. Williamson, the

First Tank Battalion C.O. after several months of snoopin' 'n' poopin' in front of the Jamestown with battalion recon.

What Williamson saw in McAdams was another version of Lt. Clement Buckley, the former Flame Platoon commander by whom the battalion C.O. was quick to measure future platoon leaders.

When Lt. McAdams first came to the Flame Platoon, the tankers manning the twin-barreled Shermans were a little wary. "He dressed everyday like he was ready for a G.I. (general's inspection)," said PFC Jerry Ravino, loader in the turret of F21. "We were afraid we were in for a lot of spit and polish." Commonly, when Marines are Stateside and constantly made aware of their appearance, the term "spit-and-polish" is used in reference to spit-shine polishing their shoes and generally being ready for inspection.

"We always looked like grease monkeys," Ravino said. Working in, around, and under tanks, is not a good way to keep uniforms clean.

Lt. McAdams, although he made it clear he generally operated by the book, did not impose uniform-of-the-day restrictions on his Flame Tankers. This critique for the new mission, as usual was casual—crews sitting where they could, with the smoking lamp lit as the lieutenant commenced describing the action plan for the next day.

"Gentlemen," he said—that greeting alone, something that right off the bat had triggered a deep respect for their new boss—"early tomorrow morning, we will be part of a raid on a hill called number 134. Our primary mission will be to napalm the hell out of this place in support of the assault force from elements of the Second Battalion, Seventh Marines."

It was going to be a major tank-infantry operation with the Flame Platoon right out in front of it.

McAdams explained that the operation would be under the command of Charlie Company tanks, which would support the operation with the second and third platoons of their M26 Pattons. Additional cover was coming from the second and third platoons of Baker Company tanks.

"The Seventh Marine infantry also will be supported by their own A-T platoon (five more Patton M46s)," Lt. McAdams added. "We are also going to deploy the Korean Marine Tanks with two platoons," he said. The KMC tankers, of course, were not strangers to the Flame Platoon. They had been trained by some of early Flame Tankers as well as NCOs from the gun companies. Marine tankers respected their Korean counterparts, whose older model M4A3 Shermans were armed with 75mm cannons.

"I have been up to speak with Sergeant Ellis and his crew on station at COP2," McAdams went on, "and told them their tank will be involved."

That meant Sgt. Jerry Ellis would have F13 sitting in the slot at the top of COP2 with a view of the entire operation, and he would be there to provide 105 fire if needed.

"So gentlemen, we will be using three flame tanks during this battle—two to burn and Ellis for direct fire support."

McAdams set up the crews, only because he was going out as T.C. of F22, which required a little shifting in the former *Roamin' Candle*. With McAdams in the turret, Cpl. Gerald "Joe" Decoursie, 22's regular tank commander, would drop into the bow gunner's hatch. Cpl. Daniel (Danny the Apache) Calabaza, as usual, would drive, and Lt. McAdams would have the added expertise of Sgt. Bob Rawlins, T.C. of F32, helping in the turret as loader.

F21's crew, commanded by Cpl. Tom Clawson, remained intact. Cpl. John Corsi would drive, PFC Jimmy Oliveri was bow gunner, and PFC Ravino remained in the turret with Clawson.

Up on the COP2, Sgt. Ellis F13 was crewed by driver PFC Pittmon, bow gunner PFC Bobby Doyle and loader PFC Richard Courchaine.

"As you know, with F13 looking it all over from the top of COP 2, Ellis will have the best seat in the house."

With that, the meeting was over, and the crews left the platoon commander's tent in somewhat relaxed moods. They knew they had a big job coming up, but the lieutenant's confidence and enthusiasm seemed to relieve the pressure a little.

Still, it was the first time out on a flame mission for Ravino and Olivieri. Clawson and Corsi had experienced a few missions in which their tank's flame gun scorched enemy positions. All of them did some tossing and turning in their racks that night—Clawson and Corsi because they knew the perils of such an assignment. Ravino and Olivieri were in mixed states of mind. The adrenaline was racing, but the apprehension pulled at them.

After early chow on 8 January, F22 and F21 were warmed up by their drivers. About 0630, the tanks were lined up at the entrance of the Flame Platoon tank park at Changdan. Weasel Switch, the two-man battalion communication team, had set up the crystals in the radios of the two tanks, and that completed the last-minute preparation. Crystals were plastic modules, encasing different wiring schemes that allowed radio signals to be transmitted on varied wave lengths. Changing crystals changed the wave length of radio messages. This was done to keep the enemy from locking on one or more stations to monitor transmissions.

While all of this was going on, Olivieri, still apprehensive, got a chance to talk to Cpl. Corsi. "What's it like, John?" Olivieri asked.

"Hey, Jim," the driver replied with a faint note of excitement in his voice, "now you'll get to see the fireworks. And as soon as we shoot napalm, we can expect incoming. That's why the infantry always bitches when we pull up near their positions. They know we're going to draw some heavy stuff."

Olivieri had discussed the conversation with Ravino, but by then, the F21 loader had such strong respect for his tank commander, his concerns were diminishing. Ravino had a habit of glancing over at Clawson every once in a while, and when the T.C. turned to acknowledge the quizzical look, Ravino always sensed the air of confidence in the veteran tanker's grin. It told him the T.C. was now very comfortable in the ability of his entire crew, which had been working together for nearly five months.

Ravino also felt confident—with the flame gun next to the 105, the 50-caliber machine gun on top of the turret, a 30 in Jimmy Olivieri's hands, and another one poking out of the turret—these Flame Dragons had more firepower than any other tank in Korea. "It's a damn good feeling," Ravino said.

Still, in the back of his mind, he was well aware of all the ammo, napalm, and fuel that made the Sherman flame tank so lethal. "That has a way of working on you," he said. "If an enemy shell ever found its mark on this thing . . . " He left the thought dangling.

Then, *The Roamin' Candle* came to mind. F22, the tank which Lt. McAdams would be in to lead the mission, once had *The Roamin' Candle* printed in three-inch letters on the bow under the driver's hatch.

Yeh, he thought, *we are Roamin' Candles. We can go almost anywhere and light up the place*. He knew it was a very versatile piece of equipment with the ability to spread fiery destruction—not be the victim of it.

At one time, F21 was called the Fire Box, inscribed on the port side of the hull near the driver's hatch. It had been beat up near Luke's Castle in the East Central Zone of Korea when it hit a mine. It didn't blow apart, it just lost a track and survived to fight another day—many other days. This day was one of them.

(Those nicknames had been ordered painted over with Marine green by some unimaginative young lieutenant before Ravino reached the Land of the Morning Calm.)

Finally, the platoon's beat-up, windowless jeep, with Sgt. Hank Amos, the popular Flame Platoon mechanic at the wheel, pulled up front to lead the small convoy.

Lt. McAdams, standing in the turret of 22, raised his right arm and then dropped it parallel to the top of his turret. Calabaza and Corsi slid their transmissions into second gear, the common start gear used by Sherman drivers, and the two thirty-five-ton pigirons were on their way.

It was a brutally cold forty-five-minute trip to the staging point behind the Jamestown Line. Ravino—many times warned by his tank commander and usually much aware of the dangers from comm wire—was a little lax that cold morning.

The F21 loader, waist-high out of the turret, despite the frigid near-zero-degree wind biting into his face, was lashed by a piece of comm wire he didn't see in the dark, and took and nice slice on his neck. "Fuckin' wire!" he yelled.

It was just before 0730 when the two flame tanks, broke from behind the MLR, negotiated the gate—a slot dozed out of a lower portion of Hill 229 where it dropped off near the east side of the Neutral Corridor—and entered no man's land. Rolling parallel to the Corridor, McAdams' F22 led F21 past Marilyn, the outpost nearest the MLR, and in behind Star.

Star was a small hill, shaped like a pointed celestial planet, about 2,000 yards in front of Jamestown and just about 300 yards from the edge of the restricted corridor. There was enough concealment on the backside of Star, especially since dawn had not quite broken yet, which allowed Lt. McAdams to halt the tanks and dismount most of his crews. (One man was left in each tank on radio watch.) The Platoon Commander just wanted to go over the mission with his men one last time.

He didn't get into all the details of other units. He just made certain his tankers were completely sure what they were doing, first reviewing the approach to Hill 134, with him leading the way. He emphasized heavy use of .30 cal. machine gunfire long before the climb up onto the hill.

"Then, we will split apart when we reach the top and lay a perfect burn on the reverse slope. Do we all understand, gentlemen?"

"Yes, sir," echoed in the air as the small group of tankers broke like they were coming out of a huddle in a football game!

Of course, one of them shouted: "Gung ho!"

It was 0745 and daybreak was slowly coming over the top of the Jamestown line when the crews clamored back into the tanks. A half-hour later, Lt. McAdams ordered the crews to button up, and told Cpl. Calabaza to swing F22 around to the left (the west) side of Star and into the open.

McAdams kept the tanks parallel to Neutral Corridor twisting and turning on the trails to stay away from the frozen rice paddies which separated them from the Corridor.

After several hundred yards, he ordered Calabaza to turn right. It would be a straight line approach to the base of No Man's, about 1,700 yards to the north.

As in all missions requiring these specialized tanks, they were out there all by themselves about to poke the fiery noses of these two Flame Dragons right into the midst of a bunch of bewildered, but very angry, Chinamen.

There are no Russian-made T-34 tanks hovering anywhere behind the enemy hills. Communist tankers, both Korean and Chinese, long since had learned, and respected the deadly accuracy of sharp-shooting Patton tank gunners, and their predecessors in the M26 Pershings.

The weather was clear and cold—and becoming very bright as two flame tanks pivoted right and moved toward Hill 134. The grinding of tracks into the frozen ground could be heard for miles in the crisp morning air. The 2nd Battalion 7th Marines infantry in full battle gear was assembled, waiting for the command to attack.

F22 began moving at a good pace, Calabaza getting the most out of third gear. F21 had lagged a little behind, but Corsi, noting the widening space in front of him, laid a heavier foot on the accelerator.

Tempting targets that they were, the flame crews were not surprised when they felt the rather bland concussions of mortars falling around their tanks. That was followed by machine-gun fire ricochetting off the turrets and slope plates. The shower of ordnance was coming from Three Fingers to the east of No Man's Hill.

The enemy fire was quickly countered and stopped. The 90mm rifles of the big gun tanks and the 76s of Korean Marine Corps Shermans opened fire, pounding the hell out of Three Fingers' Hills, and anything else they found trying to impede the approach of the two flame tanks.

As Cpl. Tom Clawson, peering through the tank commander's periscope of F21, saw that the two tanks were close to the base of Hill 134, ordered John Corsi to veer the tank left and split away from F22. The rice paddies, in the deep freeze of February, were like concrete and navigable.

"Fox 21," McAdams ordered just as the second tank was breaking into the clear and starting to climb the hill in tandem with the lead tank, "fire all .30 cal. machine guns!"

"Roger 22," Clawson acknowledged.

Through the slits in their periscopes, the tankers could see hand grenades coming from the reverse slope over the top of the hill toward the tanks. Nearing the crest of the hill, the two tank commanders set up the flame mechanism. The lines already had been pressurized, and it was time to ignite the electrodes in the flame gun nozzle.

Both tanks commenced lacing the reverse slope No Man's Island with bursts of orange, baseball-sized rods of molten napalm splashing down the hill.

Chinese in their tan-colored quilted suits frantically tried to outrace the scorching mayhem. They were only met with fury of 30-caliber machine-gun fire coming from the bows and turrets of the Shermans. They could not hide from the two Flame Dragons.

Several enemy made a break for Three Fingers but also were cut down by the 30s. There was no escape.

The hill was a scene of large billowing clouds of black smoke and orange flame as the two turrets traversed left to right saturating it with the napalm and machine-gun fire.

"Holy shit, Tom," Ravino yelled to his tank commander, "Nothing could ever live through that." Hill 134 virtually disappeared, enveloped by black smoke.

All the while, Lt. McAdams had been on the radio with instructions. Finally, the lieutenant reported F22 exhausted its load of napalm.

"Roger that, Fox 22," Clawson responded. "We're burned out, too!"

"Fox 21, have your driver back down off the hill and return," McAdams ordered. "Roger that 22."

Backing off Hill 134 was perfectly executed by both tanks, and as they pivoted 180 degrees, John Corsi wasted no time double-clutching, getting F21 into third gear, then fourth, quickly beating 22 into the return trip back to safe haven behind COP2. The Gooks couldn't dare fire anything heavy on the reverse slope of the combat outpost, because it was tucked so close to the joint where the Neutral Corridor broke into the Panmunjom bubble. An overshoot might possibly land where it shouldn't.

However, mortar fire, as expected, was tracing, and occasionally banging into, the two tanks making their hasty getaway.

PFC Ravino swiveled his scope toward COP2, wondering whether his friend Sgt. Jerry Ellis was having any fun up there.

"Hey, Tom," he hollered at his tank commander, "take a looksee at F13."

Ellis—with the best seat in the house—had just let go with a round of 105, sending it to Hill 134. It was one of the fifteen high-powered contributions his tank made to the operation.

"What a beautiful show you guys made," Ellis later told Ravino. "We could see the flame gun shoots for miles."

A Long Shoot

Fresh off the successful burn mission which scorched No Man's Hill two days earlier, the Flame Platoon of Headquarters Company, First Tank Battalion, was wrapped in the euphoria of pride and walking around with a heady attitude that reflected the Marine Corps mantra—Gung Ho!

They knew their show on Hill 134 was in full view of infantry on Combat Outpost 2 and many gun tankers. Marines along the western rim of the Jamestown Line also could see the orange of their napalm shoot igniting the Gook hill and pushing clouds of black smoke hundreds of feet in the air.

The crews of the Flame Platoon now had a good idea that working under their new C.O., Lt. Michael McAdams, was going to be a lot more interesting. And it wasn't long before he called four of his crews in for a critique of another mission.

It was late evening 9 January when the Platoon Leader summoned the crews of F11, F12, F31, and F32 to his tent. The shit had hit the fan at the extreme northeastern end of the Marine section of the Jamestown line and flame tanks were going to be needed the following morning to apply some pressure on positions deep into the Chinese lines.

This time, it was an indirect fire mission, and the tanks would not have to go very far from the forward C.P in Changdan. It was going to be a long shoot, but it was something the powerful 105mm cannons were very capable of accomplishing.

At 0700 the next morning, the low rumbling of the four flame tanks dominated the crisp air as drivers idled the engines before moving out of the camouflaged revetments.

Sgt. Hank Amos, the Platoon's mechanic who was doubling as Lt. McAdams' driver, pulled the beat-up old jeep in front of F11 and waited for his commanding officer. McAdams, now quite popular and well-respected among his Flamers, had walked to each of the four Shermans, giving his tankers thumbs-up.

When he got into the jeep, his right arm, as usual, went up then dropped forward. That set the four Flame Dragons in motion. This day, each of the Shermans was pulling a trailer loaded with 50 rounds of 105mm ammunition.

It was cold, somewhere between ten and twenty degrees above zero. The movement of the tanks created a breeze, mixed with the chunks of snow and ice kicked up by tracks in the pigiron ahead, that put a bitter bite on the faces of the tankers who prefer to ride unbuttoned. It was a frigid one-hour drive more than a mile north to firing positions near Changhwa-dong.

The four tanks finally reached their destination, about a mile inside the MLR. They would be firing directly north over the Nevadas outposts and also working over targets a little northwest. All were about three miles out from the Jamestown Line.

When the command jeep pulled into the firing area, Sergeant Amos drove to a series of small mounds, natural ramps for the tanks, and parked. Amos ran forward where all the drivers could see him. He began signaling the individual tanks, positioning each Sherman until it was able to mount the ramp that raised the front of the pigiron to give maximum elevation of the 105 cannon if needed.

All the flame crews, with the exception of the tank commanders, were busy setting up red and white firings stakes at prescribed positions in front of their tanks. The tank commanders opened their breaches and lined their 105s on the stakes, adjusting their height and lateral position as Lt. McAdams, consulting a book, relayed combinations of numbers to them for the adjustments.

With the firing stakes set, the crews got busy behind their tanks. They had laid tarpaulins and carefully took the ammunition out of the thick, cardboard-lined steel cases in the little trailer. The driver and the bow gunner lined the projectiles in one line and the brass casings in another. Small bags of gunpowder were unloaded.

Communications had been tested, and Lt. McAdams was hooked into the forward observers, who were concealed in outposts several miles away marking the targets.

Depending on the distance, so many bags of powder were dropped into the brass casing before the projectile was inserted into the top and crimped with a special tool. Either the driver or the bow gunner would set up the ammo, and the other tanker would climb on the back of the tank behind the turret to receive the round from down below, then hand it to the loader inside the turret.

On command of Lt. McAdams, each of the tanks fired a round for effect. The forward observer, watching the impact, relayed the results. If the round was short, the elevation could be changed and/or more powder added to the next shot. The Platoon Commander determined the adjustments in elevation and powder, and passed them on to crews.

Once all the tanks were zeroed in on their targets, Lt. McAdams specified the number of rounds to be fired and told the T.C.s when to commence firing.

It was an awkward way to run an artillery battery, but this was a "mobile battery" operation that Marine Flame Tankers—thanks to forward observers—made state-of-the-art perfection through experience.

It was going to be a noisy day but a welcome sound for the Marines, manning the MLR and outposts, who would be under the flights of the powerful ordnance. They would appreciate that it was going the other way, and not coming in on them. It was one of the most extensive long-range indirect fire missions the Flame Dragons ever had been involved in during the Korean War. With a good F.O., it would be a piece of cake.

Hopefully, the failure of a round to fire would be nil, or few and far between. If one did get hung up, even after a second attempt to fire, the breach was opened ever so slowly. From the outside, the cleaning rod, with a cone-shaped adapter on the end of it, was pushed down the tube to force the ordnance out of the breach. Sometimes it had to be gently tapped to free it from the chamber. It was not a favorite job of any tanker.

Once Lt. McAdams gave the word to the crews to stand by to fire for register, they did not have much time to rest. Turrets were traversed left and right, the coaxial mount raised and lowered as new targets were selected, and ranges passed along to McAdams by the F.O. The Flame Tankers, just by the variety elevations, depressions, and direction the turret was being moved, knew they were pounding into a broad expanse of the Chinese MLR.

The daylong shoot, they learned later, was targeted into CCF positions around Manghoe san, Chichoe dong, Hyanggyo gol, Mung hoe san, Sangbyon, Hosokchuawon north of hill Elmer, and Songsohubuwon. Working over CCF bunkers, trench lines, and hill fortifications and disrupting troop movements was what it was all about, and it was a perfect assignment for the Shermans because of the 105's ability to loft heavy ordnance into targets that no other tank could reach with such accuracy.

They had started firing shortly before one o'clock that afternoon, and before the cease-fire order was received five hours later, 277 rounds of high explosives had left the tubes of the 105s. The ammo in the four trailers, and what the tanks were able to carry in their turrets, had to be supplemented by additional rounds from an ammo truck.

But the workday was not over when the cease fire came. *Fire a weapon, Marine, and you have to clean the weapon.* It was back to the Changdan Road Tank Park and at least another hour's work swabbing out the 105s' barrels with a wire brush and cleaning fluid. This required ramming a six-foot-long rod, with the round brush attached to one end, in and out of the barrel. All of the carbon residue had to be removed. When the inside of the tube was shining like freshly polished silver, a rag was wrapped around the wire brush and dipped into gun lubricating oil to coat the barrel. This protected it from rusting and pitting—a no-no with any weapon.

The Flame Tankers slept well that night.

Putting a Torch to Hedy

"Go get 'em!"

Maj. Gen. Edwin A. Pollock,
Commanding General, First Marine Division

More profound statements have been delivered by more famous commanding generals in time of war. But those three words were as good as any historic charge to battle for the crew of F21 as the twin-barreled Sherman tank from the Flame Platoon of the First Tank Battalion idled in readiness for a burn mission against troublesome Chinese snipers.

It's not often PFCs and NCOs in the United States Marine Corps come face to face with a general—let alone the one who's running the whole show—and then get a direct order from him. But that's what happened to Cpl. Tom Clawson and his crew when they were standing by, just below the command post on the Bunker Hill Ridgeline, which was a contested part of the MLR along the Jamestown Line.

Cpl. Clawson and his driver, Cpl. John Corsi, had experienced a few missions in which their tank's flame gun scorched enemy positions. But this was only the second time out for PFCs Jerry Ravino, the F21 loader, and his buddy from Boston, Jimmy Olivieri, the bow machine gunner. They were quite intrigued with their first flame mission at No Man's Island (Hill 134) and were eager to go again when this one came up, simply because their Flame Dragon was the only one from the platoon to get the call.

On 17 January, the day before, PFC Ravino was asked to tag along with Cpl. Clawson and Lt. Henry Barry, who was still attached to the Flame Platoon, even though Lt. Michael McAdams had been given command. Lt. Barry and Clawson had been called up to the Jamestown Line to help finalize plans for an upcoming mission.

There was an outpost called Hedy, a 124-meter-high hump at the southern end of the Bunker Hill ridge. Some enterprising Marine must have had the seductive Hedy Lamar, a popular beautiful movie star, in mind when he christened this mound atop the ridge.

What the Chinese—using the base of the hill—were doing, however, was far from attractive. They were giving infantry from How Company of the 3rdBat, 7th Marines a lot of trouble. Snipers, entrenched at the bottom of the western slope of Hedy, had been taking pot shots at anything moving above them in the trenchlines and bunkers on the ridgeline.

No matter what manner of ordnance was laid on Hedy's lower extremities, the Gook snipers, taking refuge in crab holes, would wait out the shelling. When it was all clear, they'd manage to get back into their sniper slots, eventually picking off another Marine—and another, and another. All of How's victims had shown just enough of themselves on the horizon for an instant that would be their last on earth.

A plan was conceived to run one of the Flame Platoon's tanks to the top of Hedy, angle the pigiron slightly down her cleavage, scorch her belly, suck the oxygen from under her skirts, and maybe incinerate some Chinese hiding in her petticoat.

While Lt. Barry and Cpl. Clawson were up on the hill in the How Company command bunker going over the mission, and Ravino was down below minding the jeep, the snipers became active. Once again, they were reacting to some bad judgment by a Marine.

It wouldn't be long after Ravino heard the gunshots that he would see the results.

Somewhere up the trenchline from the command bunker, one of the How infantry-men, a tall guy typically clad in his helmet and flack jacket, was walking along the ditch. Not quite so typical for enlisted infantry, he was holding a 45-caliber pistol in his right hand, nonchalantly reaching over the parapet and firing indiscriminately toward the bottom of the hill. What he expected to hit with such a short-ranged weapon as a .45 was a good question.

Wisely, at first, he kept his head below the top of the trench. But to the puzzlement of his buddies, he decided to walk about ten more feet further down the trench, where his head momentarily went above the protection of the parapet. One shot rang out—right into his forehead. By the time his buddies rushed to his fallen body, he was dead.

As they carried the Marine down the hill past the tankers' jeep, Ravino had realized what happened. *So senseless,* the Boston Marine thought. "At first, I was surprised at how fast it all happened," he said.

Irreverently, again he thought: *Here today, gone tomorrow.*

Then, a little anger surfaced. Unlike infantry on the line, who often see carnage like that day-in and day-out and force themselves to build walls around their feelings, Ravino found it very disturbing.

The bastards, he muttered to himself, *they'll pay for that, big time.* He was thinking of what his job would be the next day.

Then, he thought of the dead Marine's family. What will it be like when the word officially gets back home? He recalled growing up in the Boston suburb of Roxbury during World War II. He thought of the service flags parents and loved ones displayed in windows—eight-by-ten inches with a wide red border surrounding a white field in which there was a blue star for each family member in the service.

He remembered the shock that went through his neighborhood when that blue star was changed to gold. That Gold Star told everyone—a son, a father, a brother had been killed in action. Silver meant a loved one had been wounded.

PFC Ravino's melancholy lasted until Lt. Barry and Cpl. Clawson came down the hill to the jeep. They had seen what happened, but they weren't talking about it. They just told the loader that the flame mission was on for the next day.

Ravino's anger began to ease. Anxiety, and a little pride of being part of a flame mission, were starting to take over. "I was feeling prouder than hell that our crew had been chosen to take our tank on such a crucial assignment," he said.

It was early afternoon the following day when John Corsi eased F21 out of the revetment in the Flame Platoon tank park off the Changdan Road. He brought it in behind Lt. Barry's jeep and when the lieutenant—driving alone—raised his arm and stiffly motioned forward, the tank's intercom came alive.

"Kick it in the ass, John," Cpl. Clawson ordered his driver. "Move out!"

There was a new sensation running through Ravino and Olivieri—one of apprehension. This drive to the front was different than the previous where three or four of the Platoon's Shermans would be in trace up a dusty road heading for an indirect firing mission. F21 was not in a line of tanks this time. It was spewing dust all by itself behind the platoon command jeep. "There's a certain loneliness, this way," Ravino admitted. "It's hard to describe."

As F21 followed the lieutenant's jeep up the Changdan Road, PFC Ravino was distracted a little from his excitement—and the gravity of the impending mission. The raw beauty of the country had a habit of occasionally poking its nose through the bleak savagery of war. This feeling rarely surfaced with Marines on the line. But tankers, roaming valleys and looking into the hills or across terraced rice paddies, occasionally became aware of the softer, more pleasant character of the countryside.

Ravino, this day, was not oblivious to the gentle cascades of the rice paddies, oddly showing green since one snow storm had worn away and another had not yet arrived with its new blanket of white. He noticed small clusters of trees. It all took the Boston Marine back to winters in his native New England.

A quick flight of a pheasant disturbed by the vibration and noise of the 35-ton Sherman tank triggered a more current response. *Wouldn't the Colonel love to see that bird,* Ravino thought.

Lt. Col. John I. Williamson, commanding officer of the First Tank Battalion, was an avid hunter. He had a reputation throughout his command of "enlisting" junior officers to join him for a little pheasant hunt, supplying them with shotguns he had brought along from home. It was his way of easing the incessant pressures of command in a war zone.

Of course there always were the pitiful looks of Korean civilians along the sides of roads—papasans squatting, out of the way of the military traffic. Their A-frames, lashed to their backs and full of branches for tinder—or their worldly possessions—protruding three feet above their heads. Often a mamasan had her child strapped to another A-frame.

The small villages emitted the undeniable strange odor of native food being cooked in hearths of flimsy homes, basically made of straw and mud, as smoke puffed from clay chimneys above thatched roofs. *These poor people,* Ravino thought, *they're doing everything they can just to survive.*

The tanker was quickly jarred back to reality as a flight of Air Force Sabre jets cleared the mountain before them, heading back to their base. Then, coming from the South, nosing toward the lines, choppers darted in and out of the hills with supplies—maybe troops—for Marines along the Jamestown.

They also might be returning with wounded.

PFC Ravino heard F21's engine race, then idle down, as Cpl. Corsi began double-clutching to shift down gears. The Sherman was laboring to climb the access road that would take them near the top of Bunker Hill Ridgeline.

Up there, an Able Company M46 Patton, mounted with a dozer blade, had cut a slot into the top of the ridge. The excavated dirt and rock had been pushed out on the forward slope in front of the trench line to provide a ramp, slightly pitched down, which would allow the flame gun enough depression for a good line to the target below.

It presented a precarious position. The ramp and slot were only wide enough for the tank. The angle of the ramp's decline also could be trouble if the tracks didn't lock. The sharp drop-off was a good 100 feet to the bottom.

The plan was twofold. First, it was designed to burn, or rout, the Chinese out of their firing holes, bunkers, and trenches on Hedy's bottom. Second, infantry needed a better view of the enemy's paths of approach to his crab holes around the bottom of the hill. Burning off scrub and trees in the lowland would accomplish this.

F21 finally made it up the back slope of the ridge and pulled into a small clearing, just below the How Company command bunker.

All of the sudden, a jeep came barreling down the hill, just about fitting into the limited space along the port side of F21. The driver braked a little too hard, and the jeep skidded before it came to a stop along side the flame tank.

"What the hell is this nut doing?" Ravino said, and looked at his tank commander. Cpl. Clawson's expression showed similar surprise.

There was an elderly Marine, obviously an officer—although the tankers could not see his insignia—sitting next to the driver. He had a crop in his right hand and turned toward the tank. He called to the two tankers in the turret, his voice firm, commanding: "Go get 'em!"

"Yes, sir," Ravino automatically responded as the jeep began to pull away.

Then, the twenty-one-year-old loader looked at Clawson. The tank commander pressed the button on the side of the mike in his hand. "Hey, in the bunker," he called up to the command post. "Who the hell was the officer with the stick who just pulled up to our tank?"

The response jolted the crew. "That was General Pollock!"

Almost in chorus, their reaction blurted over F21's intercom.

"Holy shit!"

The four young tankers had just received a direct order from the commanding general of the First Marine Division. Not many guys in the ranks get that honor from the Division commander. That really put them in a gung-ho state of mind. But they had little time to savor their feeling.

It was close to dusk when Cpl. Clawson, monitoring the radio in the turret of F21, received the order to take his tank out on the protected part of the Jamestown hill about fifty feet. Once there, Cpl. Corsi brought the left brake lever back to him, and the tank pivoted in that direction. Then, a tug on the right stick brought the flame tank to the approach to the slot.

"Are you ready?" Clawson heard in his headset.

"Fox 21," he replied. "Set to go."

"Move out!" was the order from the CP.

"Button up," Clawson told his crew, all them aware of orders and commentary coming through their headsets from the command bunker.

Corsi, peering through the two-by-eight-inch lens of the periscope that gives him a restricted view of the slot ahead of him, cautiously, but confidently, lined up F21 with the opening. After passing through the narrow slot onto the improvised short ramp, he was seeing more sky than dirt, but enough of the roadway that his driving expertise enabled him to make subtle adjustments with the break levers and accelerator. The Flame Dragon, its belly full of jellied napalm, gradually crawled in front of the ridge that was *the* main line of resistance.

Ever so gently, Corsi gradually nosed F21 slightly down, before firmly setting the brakes.

PFC Ravino peered through his periscope, looking out over no man's land. "The whole damn Chinese army can see us," he said excitedly.

Almost immediately, Ravino and Olivieri heard the sledgehammer-like pounding of incoming mortars on the turret and hull. They must have been heavier than the ones that hit their tank at No Man's Island. The concussion was more vibrant, the noise louder. Pinging of small arms fire blended another tone to the cacophony of this feel of war.

Clawson reacted to the order from the command bunker and began to traverse the turret left to about nine o'clock. Then he ignited the flame gun and started firing. Slowly, the tank commander brought the turret to the right. All the while the rod of yellow-or-ange flame, purged from the muzzle of the gun, was beating against the bottom of Hedy's slopes, where it flared and spread fiery havoc.

When the turret got to about three o'clock, Clawson reversed the sweep.

The whole lower portion of Hedy's slope was on fire. On the other side of no man's land, the Chinese reaction was fierce as they pounded the ridge around the tank with increased mortar and artillery fire. That's why infantry has mixed feeling about tanks.

Ravino and Olivieri were experiencing something any tanker has a hard time forgetting. The tank was vibrating from incoming, rocks loosened by the explosions added, again, another strange sound inside the turret. Still, they were straining their eyes into their periscopes to see what was going on down below.

To the left, Ravino caught frantic movement. "They just came out of the ground," he shouted. Some Chinese were hit with napalm and were on fire. Taking advantage of the panic being spread around Hedy's bottom, How's riflemen began to open up with their M1s and machine guns, cutting down other fleeing Chinese. Olivieri got into the act and raked the expanse below with his machine gun.

It was not lost on PFC Ravino that his tank commander was doing a masterful job with the flame gun, working the turret while listening to orders from the command bunker. And the four sets of eyes in the tank were suggesting a few targets of their own.

"Burn, you bastards!" Ravino shouted, as the previous day's experience of seeing the mortally wounded infantryman being brought down the hill flashed in his mind.

"We shot our load, sir," Cpl. Clawson informed the command bunker. Quickly he ordered Corsi to back F21 out of the slot.

The driver had to be extremely careful maneuvering the tank back. There was no room to turn around. He had to put the monster in reverse and back up to the approach. One overexaggerated pull on a brake lever out on that ramp, and that pigiron, with its crew encased, could go tumbling down the forward slope right into the Gook positions it just torched.

Ravino suppressed a moment of fear as Corsi floored the clutch pedal, raced the engine, and pulled the shift lever into reverse. Fully engaged in reverse when he methodically let up on the clutch pedal, the driver's right foot pressed on the accelerator to begin the tank's motion backward. It was a very slow and tedious roll back off the ramp and through the narrow slot. Cpl. Corsi knew his tank. More confidently, he knew his friend and tank commander, having swung his periscope 180 degrees to the rear, would be able to guide him safely back behind the ridgeline.

The Chinese, however, were not making it easy for F21, tracking the tank's reverse progress with continued mortar and artillery shots. This day, they do not find the mark. But in the not too distant future, flame tanks would suffer badly under similar enemy fury.

Safely through the slit in the ridge, Corsi continued backing the Flame Dragon into the small clearing that the Able Company dozer tank also had prepared for the smaller Sherman. Still in reverse, Corsi took his pigiron past Hedy's access road before he stopped. Double-clutching to shift into second gear, he then pulled back the right brake stick, pivoting F21 onto the access road and on its way off the Bunker Hill ridge.

Meeting F21 at the bottom of the hill was the napalm supply truck, ready to replenish the Dragon's belly with another 290 gallons of gasoline spiced with napalm. But F21 had done enough damage to the Gooks this day.

It was a good mission. There were seven confirmed Chinese killed—three scorched by the flames—and five estimated wounded. Much of the brush obstruction hindering infantry surveillance of the enemy approaches also was burned off.

Rumbling back to the tank park at Changdan, PFC Ravino had a chance to savor and feel a little pride about this burn mission. As usual, most of their fellow Flamers were there to greet F21 as it pulled into the tank park to refuel before slipping into its revetment.

The toughest part for the Dragon's crew at this point was convincing their audience that they had gotten orders directly from the commanding general of the First Marine Division. The doubters couldn't picture General Pollock bounding around the Jamestown line.

"Sounds like something MacArthur would do," cracked one unbeliever.

Deadly Friendly Fire

29Jan53:S-1 – Casualty: one (1) enl USMC KIA.
Command Diary Entry, January 1953,
1st Tank Battalion, 1st Marine Division, FMF

That terse cryptic summation—S.O.P. necessary to critique combat operations in a war zone—was the blunt military form typical of an accounting for a Marine's last day on earth. In the next eleven paragraphs of the *Command Diary of the First Tank Battalion's* activity of 29 January 1952, there was no mention who the "one (1) enlisted United States Marine Corps killed in action" was, or how that brave Marine died in action. It is just one cold, abbreviated fact of war that winds up on the battalion commander's field desk and is forwarded with the rest of the truncated reports up to Division.

Had Lt. Col. John I. Williamson, commanding officer of the First Tank Battalion, had his way, he would not have signed off on that report until he elaborated on the death of his popular and highly respected reconnaissance chief—M/Sgt. Charles J. "Tiny" Rhoades.

Tiny Rhoades, a veteran Marine who had become one of Colonel Williamson's favorite people, was killed in action on 29 January 1953 during a firefight with a Chinese Patrol. Rhoades was leading his own recon patrol back to the MLR after inspecting the area in front of Kum gok, about 1,000 yards into no man's land, where a major operation involving flame tanks was to take place a few days later.

Colonel Williamson, might, later, be prompted to supplement the 29 January Command Diary, but for the time being, he bared his feelings while describing the action in a letter to his wife, Buckie.

> *As you can gather from his nickname (Tiny), he was a mammoth of a man. He had a pugnosed, boyish face, always wreathed in good natured smiles. He had an awkward, lumbering gait, because of his size and carbuncles, which often pained him.*
> *. . . He was a simple, pleasant, and thoroughly likeable guy, exceptionally proficient in the work he was doing . . . a courageous and active man who seemingly enjoys combat.*
> *(JIW, Dearest Buckie)*

The irony of M/Sgt. Tiny Rhoades—a short-timer due to rotate back to the States within the next month—was that he had a premonition, as combat soldiers often do, that he might be tempting fate by continually going out on patrols. It was his second tour with Tank Battalion recon, which by its very nature is as hazardous a duty as it can get in a war zone. It was also his second tour in Korea, having landed on Wolmi-do Island as tank commander of a Sherman dozer ahead of the Inchon Landing in 1950. Dedicated as he was after his first tour, he volunteered to come back to the Land of the Morning Calm. For him, it was a fatal decision.

Two nights before his final mission, Tiny Rhoades had approached his former commanding officer, Lt. Michael McAdams, who had been transferred to the Flame Platoon. M/Sgt. Rhoades was going to ask out of recon.

> *Last night Lieutenant McAdams came in and told me what a grand job "Tiny" Rhoades had been doing prior to his death . . . getting several Lieutenants out of holes when their*

patrols were being clobbered. He also said that Tiny had told him a few nights before that he wanted to be transferred out of reconnaissance, as he felt that his luck had run out: Another instance of a warrior's fateful premonition of death that we usually view with such suspicion when encountered in fiction. (Dearest Buckie)

M/Sgt. Rhoades was back to patrol work in no man's land at his own choice. After his first tour with reconnaissance, he was reassigned as a first sergeant in one of the battalion's gun tank companies. It was not his cup of tea. He didn't like paperwork and was itching to get back with a more active combat unit. When the chance to rejoin the recon company opened, Rhoades jumped at it.

Capt. Clyde Hunter, commanding officer of Able Company, First Tank Battalion—who was coordinating the mission which would involve more than thirty tanks as well as infantry elements of the 5th Marine Regiment—was a longtime friend of M/Sgt. Rhoades. He was extremely happy to have Tiny and his recon team assigned to him about a week in advance of Operation Clambake.

"The two of us spent a lot time studying maps and photos," Captain Hunter said, "trying to locate obstacles, mine fields—both theirs and ours—as well as Chinese wire barriers and possible tank traps."

It was Rhoades' job to confirm as much of what he and Hunter had discussed, remove the impediments, and assure the C.O. that tanks would be able to follow the routes assigned them. "He also was to confirm known enemy positions and plot others he could locate," Hunter said. Such information was not only digested by the tank officer but was also passed along to unit leaders.

M/Sgt. Rhoades met with Captain Hunter each time he and his patrol returned to the Jamestown Line. Hunter would seek out Rhoades as he returned through the gate—slots bulldozed through lower portions of hills to give infantry or tanks passages of entry and return to and from no man's land. Or Rhoades would go right to the Able Company commander's tent and tell Hunter what he found, or did not find.

It was a few nights before the Operation Clambake that things began to go wrong. "I got a call," Capt. Hunter said, "that the patrol was in a serious firefight and had casualties they were trying to bring out."

Rhoades' patrol had been ambushed by a Chinese patrol, and they quickly exchanged fire. Along the MLR, the 5th Marines could hear the commotion, and see flashes of small arms fire, in open lowlands in front of them. As in previous missions by the Tank Battalion recon team, that night's patrol had been coordinated with the infantry company minding that area of the Jamestown. Either someone didn't get the word, or they got jumpy.

"They (the infantry) had been informed by Tiny (on the radio)," Captain Hunter, said angrily, "that the team was out there and those guys were coming back in."

But a Marine handling a 50-caliber machine gun on the Jamestown began to open up. M/Sgt. Tiny Rhoades was caught in the crossfire.

Sgt. Hank Amos, the Flame Platoon's mechanic, who doubled as the Platoon Commander's driver, had many friends in the recon unit. He got the straight scoop. "When they came under fire," Amos said, "they were ordered to get back to the MLR. Rhoades had sent his men back. Then he stood up to make sure they were safe, before he took off. That's when he got it." Two slugs had penetrated his upper body, piercing his lungs.

A couple of his buddies, braving the crisscrossing hail of bullets, scurried out to drag Rhoades back to the gate. He was quickly loaded onto the skid of a waiting chopper. As corpsmen were strapping him into the bubble on the skid, Captain Hunter hurried to his wounded friend.

"He told me that they were just about to come back through the wire when they engaged a Chinese patrol, and during the firefight a 50-caliber machine gun on the MLR opened on them."

There was no immediate determination who hit who, but Hunter felt anger beginning to boil in him.

After the chopper lifted and whirled up in a steep banking turn toward the rear, Captain Hunter went right to the infantry bunker. Seething with anger, he confronted the company commander, who apparently was well aware of what had happened. The tank officer was further infuriated with the infantry captain's response: "Well, sometimes everybody doesn't get the word."

His fury mounting, Hunter's reaction was immediate. "I felt like shooting him with my 45," he said. "I was so enraged with his response."

Fortunately for both men, Able Company's gunnery sergeant had followed his captain up the hill. The gunny pulled the angry Hunter out of the bunker and aimed him down the hill.

M/Sgt. Rhoades did not survive his wounds. "He died before they got him to the MASH unit," Sgt. Amos said.

One of Rhoades' buddies, who was among several of the recon team wounded in the foray, also died of wounds received that night.

Recalling Rhoades' exchange with Lt. McAdams a few days prior to that particular recon patrol, Lt. Col. Williamson lamented in the letter to his wife: "A guy who pushes his luck seems to run smack into the law of averages a lot quicker than most" *(Dearest Buckie)*.

M/Sgt. Charles J. "Tiny" Rhoades paid the ultimate price for Operation Clambake. It would be harbinger of the things to come.

Operation Clambake

"Operation Clambake was just one day in South Korea. There were many, many more, but that day was probably the most memorable that I can recall . . . seeing those flame tank crews up in the shit much like it was when I was on Iwo Jima."

Capt. Clyde Hunter, Commanding Officer,
Able Company, First Tank Battalion

Truce negotiations at Panmunjom were ongoing, and establishment of a permanent demilitarized zone (DMZ) was the big sticking point as the talks dragged into 1953.

Both sides were battling to seize key ground and the Nevada Outposts (Carson, Reno, Vegas) in front of the MLR, about midway up the First Marine Division's part of the Jamestown Line. The three outposts were so critical at this point of the war.

In early February, Col. Lewis Walt's 5th Marine Regiment was entrenched along the MLR with responsibility of the Nevadas and several smaller hills to their southwest. It was the Fifth's task to hold those outposts.

That led to Operation Clambake, a detailed coordinated mission that would bring a tank-artillery feint, with four flame tanks playing the major role, in the area of Hill 104, Kum gok and Red Hill, which were west of the main objective—Um gok. It was rehearsed, and rehearsed over and over during five weeks of preparation. At least, the records say it was rehearsed.

But nobody thought to include the Flame Platoon tankers in the rehearsals—and they were the ones who were going to carry out the major phase of the feint. They never got the word until the night before.

Routes were reconnoitered, mines cleared, and fire concentrations plotted and registered. MAG (Marine Air Group)–12 pilots studied the target areas from the nearby Marine MLR. Six rehearsals, including practice in casualty evacuation, uncovered potential problem areas. Final rehearsal was held 1 February, with artillery and air preparation made against the feint objectives. Four close air support strikes were conducted that day and the next as part of the plan to divert enemy attention from the Clambake destruction mission.

Shortly after first light on 3 February, three platoons of tanks rumbled across the MLR to assault the feint area. A heavy "false" artillery preparation by 1/11 (1st Battalion, 11th Marine Regiment) was also placed on the three western enemy hills as well as direct fire from gun and flame tanks. The two Marine assault forces, one against each hill, moved out armed with flamethrowers, 3.5-inch rockets, machine guns, grenades, satchel charges, bangalore torpedoes, and automatic weapons. Enemy forces occupying the positions made three separate counterattack attempts, which were blunted by Marine supporting arms. During the infantry attack, friendly air hovered on station and artillery fired continuous counter-battery and counter-mortar fire.

With the exception of the change of withdrawal route of one of the assault teams, the 5th Marines reported that the operation was carried out according to plan. Company A tanks had swung left across the frozen rice paddies to provide left flank security for the infantry and to interdict trenchlines that connected with the Un gok objective. Intense enemy fire lashed the armored vehicles as they approached Kum gok and Red Hill as well as those supporting tanks that remained on the MLR. Air, artillery, infantry, and tanks produced an estimated 390 Chinese casualties (including 90 known KIA) in addition to damaged or destroyed trenchlines, tunnels, caves, bunkers, and weapons of the enemy. Marine losses were 14 killed and 91 wounded. One flame tank was lost.

. . . Clambake was important not so much in accomplishing its primary mission

(actually, no POWs were taken) as in lessons learned. One of these was to reemphasize the fact that thorough preparation helped to ensure smooth coordination of infantry and supporting arms. In his report on the operation, Lt. Colonel (Jonas M.) Platt (commander of the 1/5, the reserve battalion) wrote, "minute planning to the last detail along with carefully executed rehearsals are basic to success in actions of this type . . . "confidence and enthusiasm stimulated by the rehearsals are assets which cannot be overlooked." The battalion commander also commented on the importance of planning for both troop withdrawal and maintaining a flexible schedule of fires by supporting arms. Air, artillery, and tanks all employed fire plans that could be readily adjusted to meet the changing tactical situation. (MCOinK, Volume V)

Yeah, well, that crap didn't wash with the Flame Platoon. As far as those brave tankers were concerned, "the best laid plans of mice and men often go awry." For the four flame tanks involved, they certainly did that day.

". . . minute planning to the last detail along with carefully executed rehearsals are basic to success in actions of this type . . ."

Well, why the hell wasn't the Flame Platoon brought in on "the minute planning to the last detail" and "carefully executed rehearsals?" Captain Hunter added a more practical observation when he talked to *MCOinK* historians:

On the ground, flame was found to be the best weapon for neutralizing the well-fortified CCF caves. From Company A, 1st Tank Battalion (Captain Hunter) came information about Chinese 3.5-inch rocket launcher teams used in antitank defense. Several of these tank-killer teams had run down the trenchline holding small bushes in front of them. The enemy then boldly advanced through a hail of bullets to within 15–20 yards of the Marine tank before opening fire with their rockets. Short bursts of flame from headquarters tanks soon caused even the most intrepid to beat a hurried retreat. (MCOinK, Volume V)

But not all of them beat a hurried retreat. Before it was all over, those tank-killer teams took their toll on the flame tanks in a mission gone very, very bad—as far as they were concerned. Nonetheless, what happened with the four flame tanks didn't seem to make much of an impact on the overall assessment.

Concluding his after-action report of clambake, the regimental commander, Colonel Walt, observed:

In addition to inflicting large numbers of casualties and destruction upon the enemy, the operation served a secondary purpose, none the less important. It provided excellent training and experience for the various infantry and supporting arms staffs involved, helping to develop them into a smoothly functioning infantry-air-artillery-tank team. (MCOinK, Volume V)

"Excellent training and experience!" You could not sell that bullshit to the crews of four flame tanks.

"Far too expensive!" would have been the better evaluation for the toll taken by the Flame Platoon—two men killed in the action, six others wounded, one tank burned and lost. A Navy Cross, two Silver Stars, and a Bronze Star were hardly enough consolation.

It was a massive display of rolling armor moving toward enemy outposts that Colonel Platt and Captain Hunter were watching from their command posts. Both were hoping—possibly, praying—that all their planning, rehearsals, and mockup strategy with infantry, tanks, a battery of 11th Marines 105s, would come off without much of a hitch.

The flame-throwing tanks were the key to this diversionary tactic—just like they were back in September at Bunker Hill and Siberia. While they occupied the Chinese Communists around Red Hill and Kum gok, the 5th Marines would take advantage of the distraction and assault Um gok to the northeast. The success of the feint by the Flamers depended on the gun tanks of Able Company and the 5th Anti-Tank platoon for protection.

Once again, the flame tanks were tasked to poke their fiery nozzles as close to enemy positions as they could get and bake Chinese clammed up in the bunkers and trenches of those threatening hills. "We were on our own," said PFC Jerry Ravino.

The four flame tanks were under the direct command of 1st Lt. Michael McAdams, who had become the platoon leader early in January, taking over from Lt. Henry Barry. Although he was relatively new to the Platoon, McAdams' personality and aggressiveness in behalf of his men quickly brought rapt respect from the ranks.

"There was something about McAdams that was noticeably special," Ravino said. "He was, as they say, an officer and a gentleman. He dressed like he was going to a general's inspection, and always took time at morning briefings to discuss why we were in Korea."

McAdams had been assigned to lead the Flame Platoon by Lt. Col. John I. Williamson, the First Tank Battalion commanding officer. Williamson had recognized the leadership qualities of the twenty-four-year-old Marine and figured he'd be a good fit for the Flame Platoon. McAdams quickly introduced himself to his crews, giving them his background, including telling them that he was married and the father of three boys, the youngest of whom was only six months and had not yet made his acquaintance. Ravino quickly came to the conclusion this was a good Marine officer, and his assessment was backed up by the number of recon Marines who constantly visited McAdams after he came to flame tanks.

"Their loss was our gain," Ravino said firmly.

McAdams had been spending a lot of time trooping the hills bugging Colonel Williamson to get his Flame Tankers back in action. And when the plan for Clambake started to unfold, it was a perfect spot for the flame tanks. But nobody, not even McAdams until the eve the operation, passed the word down to guys who would man the twin-barreled Shermans. They had no idea how big this operation was going to be. They suspected something was up because Lt. McAdams, and his new platoon sergeant, S/Sgt. Kenneth Miller, had been going up the MLR for about a week before the word came down.

Rehearsals?

"What rehearsals?" PFC Ravino asked sarcastically. "We never got the news until the night before."

The crews of the Flame Platoon, as usual, were enjoying the relative warmth of their squad tents after evening chow on 2 February. There was scuttlebutt, but still no solid skinny of any upcoming mission. As far as they were concerned, this was just another cold night in a warm tent to be spent writing letters home and listening to the music like Patti Paige's "You Belong to Me." That was complements of Ravino's little portable Zenith radio that was picking up a program from Kyushu, Japan.

The routine was interrupted when Sgt. Bob Rawlins, veteran of many missions and tank commander in F32 who was standing amid the tents, broke the relative quiet of the cold dark night:

"Listen up, people! The following crews report to Lt. McAdams . . . F12, F21, F31, and F32!" That was the first word the Flame Tankers heard on what pigirons were going to be involved in a forthcoming mission.

Knowing this was it, the relaxed attitude quickly changed to one of quiet anticipation of what was ahead of them as they strapped on their cartridge belts and 45s, put on their parkas, and made their way to the Platoon Leader's tent.

Though they had been chaffing at the bit to get back into action, there was no outward demonstration of satisfaction at being included again. The older "salts," veterans of previous actions, knew better. Gung-ho or not, war was not something taken lightly, and you didn't jump with joy when you knew you were going to be very involved with it.

Ravino just maintained an inner feeling of thanks to McAdams for making sure his Flame Dragons were going to take part in a major operation against the Chinese Communists. Little did the F21 loader realize it would be one of the most challenging and deadly close-combat missions in Flame Platoon history.

One by one, the crews came through the flap of McAdams' small tent and squeezed around a little table, which measured about three feet by five feet. McAdams and S/Sgt. Miller presided. The others listened intently. On hand were sergeants Henry D. Amos, Charles A. Foley, Richard C. Bauer, Rawlins; Corporals Marvin J. Dennis, Eugene J. DiPretoro, Clawson, John J. Corsi, Elmer R. Betts Jr., Charles J. Craig, Kennie L. Jones, and Arthur C. Burns; and PFCs James J. Oliveri, Jerry P. Ravino, Robert Clark, and Billy R. Baker.

Because of the complexity of the mission and seniority involved, there would be some jostling of the crews, which not always makes tankers happy. However, rank has its privilege and Marines were used to it. They may not have liked it, but they abided by it.

Lt. McAdams was taking command of F31 and leading the four flame tanks. This bumped 31's T.C., Sgt. Foley, into the bow gunner's seat next to Charlie Craig. Cpl. Dennis, newly married when he was on his boot camp leave, remained the loader in the command tank.

S/Sgt. Miller was relatively new to the platoon, but he took over F32, which was not a popular decision to the experienced Sgt. Rawlins, the tank's regular T.C. Rawlins, like Foley in the his tank, would do the mission as the bow gunner. The driving remained in the hands of Cpl. Burns while Sgt Bauer stayed in the turret with Miller.

F21 remained in tact—Cpl. Clawson in command, Cpl. Corsi driving, PFC Oliveri in the bow, and PFC Ravino in his usual loader's seat. F12 also was firm with Cpl. Betts in charge, PFC Billy Baker driving, PFC Clark in the right bow, and Cpl. Burns sitting in as loader.

Candles, a Coleman lantern—which was not a luxury in the squad tents—provided the light during the briefing in the command tent. Lt. McAdams had a flashlight and traced the map and pictures, which were spread out on the table.

"Gentlemen," the platoon leader said, his voice raised a little to make sure all could hear, "in the morning we will attack the enemy on his own turf with four of our flame tanks. For any of you who have not encountered him, or seen him—tomorrow will be your day!"

Sternly, he warned, because the Shermans would be breathing their flaming nostrils right down the throats of their trenches: "They will see us coming, and they will be ready to defend their positions. You can expect that because our four tanks will be so close to their trenchlines and bunkers, the Chinese will throw everything they have at us."

Lt. McAdams briefly added that Marine Corsairs would be in support with pre-attack bombing and strafing while artillery from the 11th Marines would be pounding into all three hills, Kum gok in particular. "You also will have the benefit of VT if needed," he said. VT is *variable time* fuse artillery, which can be called in to detonate in the air above a selected area. When friendly troops are in tight situations with the enemy, and the issue is in doubt, VT often is called in to scatter shrapnel. Friendly troops have time to seek concealment. The enemy, hopefully, is taken by surprise and left in the open.

It is one of the better methods of dispersing Gooks from around buttoned up tanks.

Looking at the maps, the Flame Tankers got their first glimpse of the area they would be trespassing. Although the maps were only about eight-by-ten inches, they presented a fair idea of the area encompassing Un gok, Kum gok, and Red Hill.

Red Hill was nearly 1,000 yards into no man's land from the MLR. To the northeast about 1,500 yards was Um gok. Kum gok lay slightly northwest of Red Hill, also about 1,500 yards out. Hill 104 was about 500 yards west of Kum gok.

Routes for each attacking platoon were marked and artillery registration points clearly shown by call numbers, pinpointing positions on the grid. Aerial photos afforded the tankers a distant visual look at their targets.

Lt. McAdams reviewed the whole show, making sure his men knew their jobs. Nothing was said about the so-called rehearsals from which the flame tanks, the key elements to the feint, had obviously been omitted.

The plan called for McAdams to command from F31 and lead the other three flame tanks up Kum gok's face. The lead tank would be followed slightly to the right by F21, commanded by Cpl. Clawson.

Cpl. Betts' F12, along with F32, now commanded by S/Sgt. Miller, would mount the higher ground to the left of the other two tanks. The tank operation would be coordinated by Capt. Clyde Hunter, Able Company's C.O.

"We were beginning to realize the magnitude of the operation," PFC Ravino said, "and were impressed by the number of other tanks that were going to be there." All told, thirty-five tanks would be involved, and it made Ravino think this was going to be one of the biggest operations by flame tanks since World War II. It appeared there would be plenty of protection for the flame tanks, which would be well out in front of their big brothers.

"Hit the rack," Lt. McAdams ordered as he closed the briefing. "I want everybody to be alert for this one."

There wasn't much conversation among the tankers as they walked back to their squad tents. Their minds were going in all directions, contemplating the attack and trying not to hazard thoughts of how dangerous this could be. As they stripped off their boots and outer cold weather gear to climb into sleeping bags, scattered whispers—unusually soft conversation—hung in the warmer air heated by potbelly stoves.

Some of the guys went back to the letters they were writing earlier, and quickly finished them, secretly hoping it wouldn't be their last. There were one or two wisecracks about packing gear so it could be sent home if someone didn't return.

"Remember, Jimmy," Cpl. Ravino said in a barely audible whisper to his best friend, "when we came here we thought we were coming into portable flamethrowers?" Ravino quickly answered his own question—strain of the obvious danger he knew was in the mission, turning what was intended as a wisecrack into a flat joke. "Jim, now we have one hell of a big flamethrower to use tomorrow."

"You gung-ho bastard," Olivieri said, somewhat in jest, using the term that was leveled on his friend way back in boot camp, "how do you feel, now? This is what you wanted, always looking for action."

Ravino knew his friend was rattling his chain.

"Jim, I came to this place because of my father, and I'm scared as anybody. All I can say is I'll take care of your ass just like I've done since we were in boot camp."

Ravino cut off the conversation. "Get some sleep! We'll be up at 0500."

Ravino couldn't get to sleep, and he was not alone. Some guys were rereading letters from girlfriends. There were only one or two married guys in the flame platoon

Cpl. Tom Clawson broke tension.

"Okay, you heard what the man said, hit the rack!"

Candles were extinguished and Ravino knew it was going to be bone-chilling cold when they got out of their racks in the morning. The potbelly stove probably would be near out of fuel and would not stand up to the single-digit temperatures seeping through the canvas during the night.

Still, he could not go right off to sleep. Few of the tankers could.

Ravino had a perfume-laced letter from Dotty Daly, his girl back in Boston, under his head. He began thinking about the two of them dancing to the music of Glenn Miller, Vaughan Monroe, Harry James, Arty Shaw.

Then his thoughts strayed from Dotty to Par, his father. *"Kill or be killed"* echoed in his mind. He recalled the elder Ravino telling him and his siblings stories of the experiences in World War I.

In the back of his mind, Ravino harbored the disappointment that this son could not live up to his father's expectations. He was forever trying to show his sire that he was just as good as his brothers, to whom he was constantly measured by his father. The recurring fear of not meeting those expectations, not so much the pending combat mission, brought a slight bead of sweat to his cold forehead.

Then, the reality of what lie ahead set in.

Will I be wounded, or killed? What will happen if I'm captured, or become separated from the crew—missing, maybe given up as KIA like Rocky De Rose (his hometown buddy, who disappeared from the 1st Marines last fall)?

Ravino thought of Big Paul Hannon, another friend from Platoon 113 at Parris Island, who was killed in action with the 11th Marines not long after he arrived in Korea.

His mind wandered again, for some reason thinking of Marine heroes of World War II—John Basilone, Barney Ross, Ira Hayes. As a teenager enthralled with patriotism at a War Bond Rally in Boston, Ravino got to shake hands with Hayes, the American Indian and reluctant hero who had gained fame in the Flag-raising at Iwo Jima. *I want to be as brave as those Marines if I have to face a life-or-death situation.*

Prayer finally took over as sleep began to dull PFC Ravino's rambling mind.

It was not unusual, in the apprehension of pre-combat, to *talk* to your Maker. You get a lot closer to Him when the shit starts hitting the fan. Prayers often come as fast as 30-caliber slugs ejecting from a machine gun. They would for PFC Jerry Ravino—a lot sooner than he could have imagined.

He finally dozed off.

Snow was falling lightly and the temperature already had dropped to about ten degrees. It was going to be a cold one in the morning. Then, Operation Clambake would heat up and sear most of these Flame Tankers like no other experience they would face in their lifetimes.

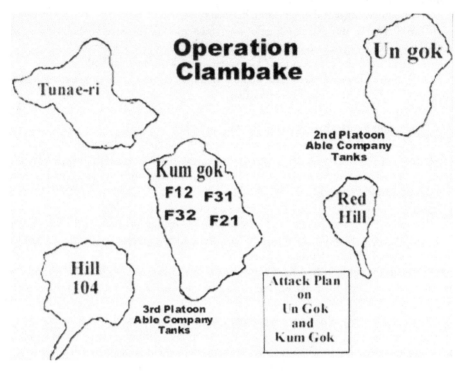

Four flame tanks sit on the side of Kum gok as all hell breaks loose, while five tanks of the Third Platoon, Able Company, are damaged and unable to provide flanking protection at Hill 104. (Graphic Jack Carty)

Operation Starts . . . Going Bad

E verybody Up!"
It was 0500 in the Flame Platoon tank park off the Changdan Road and the last duty guard was making his rounds—happily, if not sadistically—taking pleasure in rousting fellow tankers out of their slumber. He had been trooping around the park the last two hours in ten-degree weather, occasionally made colder by snow that had fallen most of the night.

I'm cold and miserable; why not share it with the rest of the guys?

Bleary eyes slowly opened. However, the anticipation of the day's mission quickly set in, and the Flame Tankers moved about their routine a little more quickly than usual. Soon, the potbelly stove was fired up till it glowed cherry red to beat off the raw damp air that seeped into the tent overnight. At least their clothes were warm—and needlessly pressed—after being between body-laden sleeping bags and the taut canvas of the racks all night.

A jerry can next to the stove provided water to quickly splash eyelids reluctant to fully open. A couple of the tankers took their seldom-used pots—infantry helmets—heated water, and shaved. Then, they braved the freezing outdoors for a brisk walk to the chow tent—hot coffee, cocoa, scrambled fresh eggs, fresh toast, and homemade buns for the special occasion of heading into battle. There wasn't much chatter, a little small talk.

When Cpl. Tom Clawson made sure his crew had eaten well, he summonded them to follow him to F21, which Cpl. John Corsi quickly cranked over. The Flame Dragon came alive without too much trouble. The rumbling of the engines quickly dominated the air, but it was still pitch dark.

"Mount up!" It was S/Sgt. Ken Miller ordering crews to get into the tanks. Clawson and his loader, PFC Jerry Ravino, climbed into the turret. PFC Jimmy Olivieri, the bow-gunner, already was in his compartment checking over his 30-caliber machine gun.

Weasel Switch, the master battalion communications center, passed along the radio frequency after crystals had been changed in all of the tanks radios.

The Flame Platoon's jeep—with Sgt. Hank Amos, the chief mechanic for the Shermans at the wheel—had pulled in front of F31 and slowly began moving out of the park. First Lt. Michael McAdams, just about visible in his turret, raised his right arm and then quickly dropped it.

"Move out!" Just in case the darkness prevented some of the tank commanders from seeing his signal, McAdams broadcast his order over the radio.

Lumbering under the strains of second gears, the parade of mighty M4A3E8 Sherman flame tanks began churning up the new crust of snow as they left the park and turned onto Changdan Road.

The sight of the convoy, the rumble of those thirty-five-ton monsters in the crisp, dark winter morning, kicked Cpl. Ravino into another one of his gung-ho moods. *There is nothing in the world that can compare to the feeling—esprit de corps—when a tanker, un-buttoned in his machine, is moving into the unknown of a combat mission.* Then he snapped back to reality and quickly came to the conclusion this was not going to be like any John Wayne war movie.

It was another freezing forty-five-minute ride to the MLR where the four flame tanks joined up with more than thirty other pieces of armor that would be involved in Operation Clambake.

Just as dawn was breaking over the back of the Jamestown Line, Capt. Clyde Hunter, was standing in the T.C. hatch of the Porcupine atop one of the highest crests of the MLR. The Porcupine was an M46 Patton communications tank, equipped with six radios, which provided voice contact with every unit in the mission. Several antennae poked into the sky from its turret, which Captain Hunter was using as a command center.

At the disposal of the veteran tanker of island warfare in the Pacific during World War II, were three platoons of his Able Companies tanks, to which the 5th Marines Anti-Tank Platoon was attached. Charlie Company and Dog Company each had a platoon involved in the mission.

As 5th Marines C.O., Lt. Col. Lewis Walt, ordered Operation Clambake into motion, he and Captain Hunter had a clear view of the thirty-five tanks rumbling from concealment behind the Jamestown Line through the gates into the open no man's land. *Gates* were breaks in the hills, either natural or carved by dozer tanks, to provide tanks and infantry access and return passages to and from no man's land.

As planned, Lt. Jim McMath led the way into the open with his five Able Second Platoon Pattons. His objective was to blow out the wire in front of Um gok, which he did, to allow Lt. McAdams' four flame tanks clear passage to the three targeted hills—Un gok, Red Hill, and Kum gok.

McMath let the Flames pass through to their designated staging position at Red Hill before he shuffled the rest of his tanks through them to set up protection from Um gok, behind Red Hill and northeast of Kum gok.

Meanwhile the third platoon of Lt. Hans Wilhelm Henzel, known by most of his fellow tankers as "Heinie," was trailing the four Shermans and swung his five M46s to the west as planned. This was to provide protection on the critical left flank of the flame tanks, which would be open to fire from Hill 104 if Henzel's guys weren't around to keep those Gooks pinned down.

Lt. Henzel was one of the newest platoon leaders in Able Company and was just getting his feet wet in combat. Instead of keeping his platoon on the slope above some rice paddies, he had ordered the five Pattons echelon left into the paddies, figuring to afford maximum concentration of firepower in coverage of the Flamers.

"Henzel got carried away with enthusiasm . . . and charged up the valley over the paddy dikes," Captain Hunter said.

Despite dawn breaking in the horizon behind him, Henzel said the visibility was poor. "It was dark and cold," he said and eventually was alerted by his driver that the tanks were picking up wire in their drive sprockets and tracks as they maneuvered west. Henzel had deviated from the plan.

"His platoon was to follow the flame tanks through the gap in the wire blown out by the Second Platoon," Capt. Hunter said. "Henzel's platoon then was to proceed on the left flank, staying on the slope of the rice paddy. Instead, he blew his own gap through the wire left of the intended passage and charged up the valley over the paddy dikes. He didn't get far!"

The crap in the tracks was not going to be Henzel's big problem. By sending his platoon into the rice paddies, Henzel had set up disaster.

Lt. Col. John I. Williamson was not just an interested bystander behind the MLR.

He was a quite concerned commanding officer of the First Tank Battalion, as he monitored the radio net, and the developing situation. He was dismayed by what he heard as things went from bad to worse.

> *Some of the tanks had reached their objectives, and the flame tanks were moving up onto the enemy-held hill. About this time the wind slacked off and shifted, and the field was literally obscured by the "fog of war"—all the smoke and dust raised by the (artillery) firing drifted over our troops and hid them from my view and from the view of each other, except (those) at close range. (JIW, Dearest Buckie)*

Lt. Henzel's platoon became victim of the devastating frosty mist.

"My platoon sergeant, S/Sgt. Joe Osieczonek, moved out as my lead tank to the left," Lt. Henzel said. "In as much as I was the new kid on the block, Captain Hunter very considerately assigned Osieczonek, a World War II tank veteran, to teach me some of the ropes."

Visibility was getting worse, and the tankers were only able to see as far as the Patton next to them. Being buttoned up with restricted forward vision, they had very little idea what was in their paths. "None of us were familiar with the ground over which we were riding, or its traffic ability," Henzel admitted. "There was a great sense of caution as we moved forward."

The staggered formation of the five tanks had moved out several hundred yards, the extreme left Patton extended the furthest. Lt. Henzel's command tank had lagged back in last position. Other than Henzel's driver reporting constant buildup of wire in the drive sprockets, which was making maneuverability of the tank difficult, there was no indication of other problems coming over the radio net.

Of course, Captain Hunter, Lt. Colonel Williamson, and everyone else listening on their radios could not see what was going on because of the pall of dust hanging over the scene.

Suddenly, S/Sgt. Osieczonek's panicked voice broke the silence of the radio net. "A35 beetle with a broken neck."

A prearranged series of code words had been authorized to indicate certain events that possibly would take place. "Beetle" was the tank. "Broken neck" meant there was failure of the elevating mechanism in the turret and a malfunction that would negate firing of the 90mm rifle and coax machine gun.

"Incredible," Henzel responded. "I could not believe what I was hearing."

He snapped back to Osieczonek: "Say again your last transmission!"

Osieczonek confirmed: "A35 beetle with a broken neck."

Henzel quickly ordered the other four tanks to keep moving because he knew he still had those 90mm rifles available to protect the flame tanks.

S/Sgt. Osieczonek radioed back to his platoon leader, warning the other T.C.s about the rice paddy dikes. The lieutenant was puzzled and wondered what Sergeant Joe was talking about.

Henzel radioed Hunter that he had lost the use of one tank. "I could tell by his voice that he was perplexed, too," Henzel said.

The problem was, Hunter's view of what was going on down on the deck was completely obliterated by the haze. He couldn't see where Henzel's Third Platoon was getting fouled up. It was a domino effect. The next third-platoon transmission was from A34: "Lieutenant, I have a broken neck." Then A33 checked in and Henzel was wondering what the hell was going on. It wasn't over. Minutes later, a similar report came from A32. Henzel would know what was going on very shortly.

"As A31 approached the paddy dike and lifted up," Henzel said, "all I could see with the tank commander's visual blocks was the morning's first light and the sky above."

Then, the fifty-ton M46 topped the rise of the dike and began plunging downward. "I heard a loud *clunk,* accompanied by a high-pitched metallic twang," Henzel said. It was the separating of steel as the elevating mechanism under the breach block snapped. Henzel then realized the long tube of the 90mm rifle, which extended far in front of the tank's bow, had hit the next dike as the tank rolled downward. It was fifty tons of steel pulling down on the tube, which was hung up horizontally in the dike. It had to snap something. Like the four other tanks before it, A31's rifle simply rocked up and down uncontrollably in the mount as it climbed the other dikes.

Not one of the third platoon's powerful rifles, or their turrrets' 30-caliber machine guns was left to protect the flame tanks. "For all intents and purposes," Henzel said, "we were five fifty-ton emasculated monsters."

At that point, Captain Hunter ordered Henzel to get all of his tanks back behind the MLR. "Hell, I did not want them out there like sitting ducks," Hunter said.

Lt. McAdams was totally unaware he had no protection to his left, and it was crucial that his flame tanks be covered on both sides.

A steep price was about to be paid by the Flame Platoon.

Four Flame Tanks in Trouble

"About this time we started to hear alarming transmissions over the radio:
'My tank's on fire!'
'One of the flame tanks is burning!'
'Tank has been hit. The hatch is open and all I can see is a bloody head sticking out of the turret, but there's at least one man left alive in the tank!'
'The enemy is closing in and within three yards of tank 31!'
'Have them close the hatch and we'll bring VT fire down on them!'"
—Lt. Col. John I, Williamson, Commanding Officer, First Tank Battalion
(JIW, *Dearest Buckie*)

While Able Company's Third Platoon of tanks was becoming incapacitated in the rice paddies to the west, Lt. Michael McAdams had reached the hills in F31 and began maneuvering his flame tanks into position at Kum gok. He had no idea that his left flank was being left wide open. It was somewhat ominous that a little trouble hit the Flame Platoon earlier.

As the four Shermans entered the gate to pass from the MLR, Cpl. Tom Clawson ordered the crew of F21 to button up.

"Tom," PFC Jerry Ravino, the 21 loader, hollered to the T.C., "my hatch pin won't lock." However, this was only a small glitch quickly solved. Ravino found the hammer used to pound end connectors on tracks and banged the pin with it.

"Test your 30s," Clawson order PFC Jimmy Oliveri, his bow gunner, and Ravino, who would handle the coaxial machine gun. "Just three short bursts."

Then, F21 ran afoul of a rice paddy. Going over one of the frozen dikes, the Sherman's bow dipped between two mounds, and something shorted out the radio, which was mounted on the back of the turret near the loader. Unlike the M46 with their 90mm rifles extending far in front of the tank's bow, the muzzle of the stubby 105s and flame guns of the Shermans only hung over about mid-bow, so there was no problem with those tubes being damaged.

"Sparks and flames poured out of the bottom of the radio," Ravino said. Before he could get out of the way in the confined loader's compartment, a streak of flame flashed over his right hand, inflicting a small but severe burn.

"What the hell was that, Jerry?" the alarmed Clawson asked. "Is your hand okay?"

"The radio blew out, Tom. It's gone. What do we do now?" Ravino's hand hurt like hell, but he told the T.C. he was okay.

Clawson knew the radio could not be repaired on the run. "Fuck it! We know what we have to do, so just keep your eyes open."

"Roger," Ravino replied, concentrating a little more on what he was picking up through his periscope as F21 rolled closer to the Chinese outpost.

"Jerry, look," Clawson said suddenly. "Lt. McAdams is out of his tank. He's pulling something out of his right drive sprocket. What the hell is he doing out there? The Gooks are looking right down his throat!"

F31 was also experiencing some of the problems that plagued Lt. Heine Henzel's Able Company Pattons west of the flame tanks. Strands of the barbed wire that had been blown to make paths for the tanks began to collect in the tracks and sprockets. It was giving drivers hell trying to maneuver their pigirons.

Lt. McAdams, after receiving information that the Able tanks on his left had run into trouble in the paddies, dismounted F31 and looked for a new route through the rice paddies.

The Platoon Commander was about 200 feet in front and to the left of F21. Looking toward Clawson's tank, he raised his arm and pointed to a clearer way through the wire. Then the lieutenant quickly clamored up the side of 31 and disappeared into his turret.

Through the wire and well into no man's land, the four flame tanks began to fan out to take their firing positions. F12 and F32 veered left to the high ground of Kum gok, slowly climbing the face of the small hill. F12 was near the top, and F32 stayed to right about thirty feet lower on Kum gok.

Cpl. Charles Craig was driving the command tank and as ordered, kept it below the other two Shermans, parallel to enemy trenches he could not see. Sitting across from Craig handling the bow gun in F31 was its T.C., Sgt. Charles Foley—who relinquished his normal place in the turret to Lt. McAdams. Cpl. Marvin Dennis was, as usual, in the loader's seat.

F21 was pulling up the rear about fifty feet behind the other tanks, before mounting the hill where Cpl. John Corsi brought it to a stop not thirty feet behind and slightly to the right of the command tank. Fortunately, some of the haze had cleared in the mission area, and the four flame tanks had good visual contact with each other. However, they could not see much beyond their own positions.

There was no sight within the restricted vision of the two-by-eight-inch periscopes of the Chinese soldiers. But the Gooks were there. Their concealment was excellent, and they waited until the tanks were just about on top of them. They were ready to pounce on the threatening Shermans with two-man teams manning shoulder-mounted powerful 3.5 rocket-launchers, which the Chinese plundered from equipment left by U.S. Army troops up North early in the war.

With the flame tanks just about set to ignite their tubes, all hell broke loose.

F31 was the first target. It took a rocket in the right side of the turret, parallel to the tank commander's main sight. The missile had a hard-steel piercing tip and delayed detonation timed to explode after penetrating the thick wall of the turret. It tore into Lt. McAdams' neck, then exploded and severely wounded Cpl. Dennis, the loader. No soldier manning a rocket could have made a better shot.

Immediately, another round from the right side came through the hull behind Sgt. Foley in the bow seat, seriously wounding the tank commander. When it exploded, Cpl. Charles Craig was blasted with shrapnel all over the back of his head.

Craig was still conscious when he turned to look up into the turret behind him.

"McAdams was leaned over—headless. And Dennis was seriously wounded with one leg torn apart and his arm was shattered. The inside of the tank was crimson red—all over the place," Craig said, describing the bloody scene.

The driver and his tank commander were shocked and dazed, but managed to get out of their bow hatches.

Meanwhile, F12 had just finished scorching the upper face of the hill with its load of napalm when Cpl. Elmer Betts, its tank commander, saw what was happening on his right. He immediately opened his hatch, climbed over the back of the turret, ran across the engine doors, and jumped off the side of the tank, sprinting to the smoking F31.

Quickly, he grabbed Foley and Craig and led them back to F12.

Through the loader's scope of F21, Ravino could see clearly what was happening. "Betts had already blasted the Gooks with a full load of napalm on the upper section of Kum gok," the shaken loader said. "His crew was able to pin more of those bastards back in the trenchline with their machine guns, or we all would have been overrun."

Then, Ravino and Clawson both saw the loader's hatch of F31 slowly open. Cpl. Dennis was straining to hold his .45 pistol high above his head. It was the tankers' signal that people inside were hurt and the tank was immobile. He stayed up in the hatch for about fifteen seconds, then disappeared into the turret.

Ravino would never forget the shocked expression on Dennis' face. "He still was wearing his glasses," Ravino said, not sure if his counterpart was hurt. "But I could see his eyes, pleading for help. Then he slumped back into the turret."

Ravino turned his scope so he could see forward of F31, which Lt. McAdams had been preparing to torch the well-concealed trenchline next to it. Ravino could not see any evidence that there was a trench—no excess dirt, no sandbags, certainly no trees. But sure as hell, it was there, because that's where one of the rockets came from.

No trees? Suddenly, Ravino saw something move—a branch. He knew it had to be a piece of Gook camouflage. "Get him, Tom," Ravino shouted to his tank commander.

Clawson rotated the turret and deflected the coax towards the branch. "Holy shit, do you believe this?" he shouted.

Ravino raked the area with the machine gun, but the stick kept bobbing up and down; then he hollered: "Tom, get the damn flame gun going!"

While the tank commander was getting the flame set up, Ravino continued to rake the trench with his 30. "The bastard was playing Russian roulette with me."

All of the sudden, two men rose out of the trench. They had a 3.5 rocket gun aimed right at F21. Ravino saw them immediately and laced them with the machine gun, blowing both against the side of the hill above them.

Cpl. Clawson reached over the 105 breech block with a friendly punch on his loader's left arm. "Good Jerry, we got them bastards."

But Ravino's eyes were trained on the boyish face of the Chinese rocket shooter. "It was covered with blood," he said, and turning to Clawson, "Tom, this is no time to be fucking around. Look for more of them."

Despite the gravity of the situation, Ravino had a quick reflection of the days when he was kid playing cowboys and Indians in the scrub fields around his home in Boston.

While Clawson traversed the turret toward F31, he and his loader both saw a Chinese soldier—bigger than the normal Gook—in a quilted uniform and a rifle slung over his back. He was on his belly, crawling along side of the immobile tank. He began to rise to his knees, reaching above volute spring mechanism of the forward bogey wheels. He was trying to place a satchel charge against the hull. The Chinese knew some of the crew was still inside and wanted to make sure they didn't get out.

Clawson and Ravino felt a ripple of panic. They couldn't depress the coax enough to fire on the Gook. In unison, they yelled to Jimmy Oliveri to get the Gook with the bow machine gun. Without the radio and intercom, shouting over all hell breaking loose around them was the only way the 21 crew was able to communicate. "Get him, Jim! Get him!"

Olivieri didn't respond, despite repeated pleas from the turret. For some unexplained reason, he couldn't fire the gun. John Corsi couldn't believe what was not happening and reached for Olivieri. "Jim, give me that fuckin' thing."

Gaining control of the machine gun, Corsi dipped the ball mount, immediately squeezing the trigger, stitching the Chinaman through the waist, just about cutting him in half. Corsi was so infuriated he continued firing into the body making it jump as the force of the fusillade drove the upper part of the remains into the small opening under the forward idler wheel.

"Good job, John," shouted Ravino, who had his eyes on the enemy soldier the whole time. Then Ravino pulled back from his periscope only to hear Clawson say, "What the hell is he doing out there, Jerry?"

Ravino looked back into the scope and saw Cpl. Betts, as calm as could be, walk up to the enemy soldier, whom he thought might have been alive—but was very dead. He began firing his 45 at the prone body, emptying a complete magazine of slugs into the corpse, and forcing it further into the track mechanism.

When Betts finished with the Gook, he reloaded his pistol and stood guard over the stricken tank, occasionally firing at anything he thought might be an enemy soldier trying to get near F31.

"Cpl. Betts has to be the coolest man I've ever known," Ravino said. Then, he lost sight of the F12 tank commander.

The F21 loader started rotating his scope to the left and cocking it downward to look along side his tank. He saw someone—only the back of the form—climb up on the hull, then crawl around the left side of the turret. Ravino reached into the burlap bag near his feet and grabbed a fragmentation grenade. He had his finger in the ring, ready to pull the pin and slip the grenade out the pistol port where loaders usually got rid of expended 105 shell casings.

"Hold it, Jerry," Clawson, in panic, yelled. "It's Elmer Betts!"

Ravino broke into a sweat, thinking he nearly killed one of his own tankers. Clawson cracked his hatch cover.

"Tom, come with me," Betts said, "we have to go get the mail." That meant they had to do something about getting F31 out of there. Clawson's crew had no idea how bad of shape the tank was in, nor the condition of Lt. McAdams and Cpl. Dennis. Betts knew the tank was out of commission. He knew, after talking to Foley and Craig, that the lieutenant was dead and Cpl. Dennis was badly wounded, possibly dead. Ravino could only hear Clawson's side of the conversation.

"Jerry," Clawson told his loader as he was climbing out of the hatch, "you take over the tank while I go with Elmer to see what's going on with McAdams' tank."

The two tank commanders ignored sporadic incoming falling around their tanks, and the rifle fire spitting from the Gook hill. But Ravino wasted no time securing the T.C. hatch once the Corporal left.

By the time he got into the T.C. seat and pressed his head against the scope, Ravino could see Cpl. Clawson standing behind 31's turret. He was arm-signaling F21 to have Corsi back F21 further down the hill. "Elmer Betts got into the driver's seat when we got to F31," Clawson said. "I climbed aboard to look in the turret. I looked down inside, and staring up at me was Cpl. Dennis. He was in shock and thought I was a Gook."

The severely wounded F31 loader still had his 45 in his hand. "If he had had the strength, he would have shot me," Clawson said.

That's when Clawson signaled PFC Ravino to have Corsi back F21 down the hill. He knew Betts needed plenty of room to turn F31 and get it down from the trench line of Kum gok.

In passing the order along to the driver, Ravino was surprised at his inner reaction: *Never did I think I would be given command of a tank in a situation like this!*

The thought quickly vanished when he saw, and a millisecond later heard, the blast of a mortar hitting alongside F31. It was as Clawson was looking into the loader's hatch at the carnage in the turret. When his tank commander looked up after the blast, Ravino could see his face was covered with blood. Yet the corporal managed to make his way around the turret and disappeared over the front of the tank.

Betts, sensing Clawson had been wounded by the blast that shook the tank, yelled for him to get into the bow gunner's seat.

Since Corsi had successfully backed F21 down the hill, Betts, who had gotten the engine of the command tank started, was able to turn 31 around and begin the agonizing trip back to the MLR. He had already ordered his own F12 to get the wounded Craig and Sgt. Foley back to the MLR. Betts hadn't bothered to be concerned about the body of the dead enemy soldier still wedged in the F31's right track. As Ravino watched in dismay, the Chinese soldier was being ground up as the upper part of the track dragged the body into the drive sprocket.

Although he felt a little relief to see F31 heading back to the friendly territory, the enormity of the job he had just inherited began to take hold of PFC Jerry Ravino. The Chinese were providing the grim reminder. Incoming mortars and 75mm rounds hitting on or near his tank sounded like the repetition of sledge hammers pounding on the turret.

The battle was far from over for the two remaining flame tanks.

Second Flame Tank Hit

As the information ebbed and flowed around us, our hopes were alternately plunged and raised. After another hour or so the haze began to lift, disclosing one of our flame tanks burning uncontrollably, and a few others disabled on the field. . . .

The flame tanks had it the worst. They ran into a veritable nest of close range anti-tank fire. Two took three solid hits each. One was set on fire and had to be abandoned by the crew.

JIW, *Dearest Buckie*

While Cpl. Elmer Betts slowly drove the battered F31 away from Kum gok, S/Sgt. Ken Miller's F32, still perched high on the hill, began saturating Gook fortifications with his flame gun. Sgt. Bob Rawlins, 32's regular T.C., was in the bow, squeezing tightly on the trigger of the 30-caliber machine gun, tracing Chinese soldiers frantically scurrying down the trench-line ahead of the scorching bead of orange flame.

PFC Jerry Ravino, with little time to ponder his new command in F21, acted instinctively and decided to keep his tank where it was low on the hill, knowing it may be needed to provide protection for the other Flame Dragon. "All hell was still erupting around us," Ravino said, "and I couldn't understand why our two tanks were left out there without any flanking support."

He kept looking for those Able Pattons on his left, then to the rear to see if help was behind them. Off in the distance, he did see one of the big gun tanks perched atop a good-sized hill. "You bastard," he yelled, "why the hell are you just sitting up there doing nothing to help us?"

The Patton overlooking the debacle down below was one of Dog Company's. Cpl. Harry Regan, a nineteen-year-old gunner, had been peering through the powerful scope mounted next to the 90mm rifle. His tank commander was seeing the same scene through his periscope. They couldn't do a thing at the time. There were too many friendly tankers out in the open.

My men were dismounting to work on the tanks, lead retrievers out to help, hooking up tows for those disabled, generally doing what had to be done and running around with the utter disregard for their personal safety. . . .

I never cease to marvel at this virtue, particularly in my tankers, who unflinchingly leave the comparative safety of those steel hulls to saunter about in the face of the enemy. (JIW, *Dearest Buckie*)

"Jerry," Cpl. John Corsi yelled up to the turret, "let's get the hell out of here!"

"No, John," Ravino snapped quickly. "We have to stay here!"

"Jimmy," Ravino hollered down to PFC Oliveri, who had regained his presence in the bow, "keep that 30 blasting at anything that moves."

Moving back and forth from the command seat to the loader's hatch, the new T.C. began barking more orders. He also told Oliveri to activate the pressure in the CO_2 bottles so the flame gun would be ready if there were any signs of enemy in force coming at the tank.

Ravino's hands were beginning to bother him. The right one was not very useful because of the burn he took when the radio blew out. The left hand was becoming sore from the recoil lever of the 30-caliber machine gun. Both hands were bleeding.

Suddenly there was a very loud *ping*, then a whine as incoming hit the curvature on the top of the turret and spun off into the air. It came from over his left shoulder, which caused Ravino to react by swinging the turret that way. He thought the shot had come from Tumae-ri and quickly elevated the coax to raked Gook position with the 30 by moving the turret back and forth.

Lack of protection from Able Company's Third Platoon of Pattons was starting to tell.

Another round hit the turret, rocking the tank so much Ravino bashed his head against the breech block of the 105. His nose began bleeding. He knew it was fractured.

When he came to his senses seconds later, Ravino looked into the scope and could see F32 still firing its napalm and machine guns up on the hill. As he watched, he knew his tank was not the only target of the Gooks on Tumae-ri. Still, 32 was okay—for the time being.

While scurrying back and forth in the turret, Ravino hadn't seen S/Sgt. Ken Miller's F32 take three direct hits from high velocity armor-piercing rounds coming from Hill 104. One of them ruptured the gasoline tank.

Immediately, Sgt. Richard Bauer, in the loader's seat, pulled the internal cord to activate the fire extinguishers in the engine compartment. Nothing happened. Bauer grabbed a small fire extinguisher in the turret, opened the hatch, and leaned out of the turret to spray through the grates of the engine doors. In the excitement, he didn't realize the extinguisher nozzle was pointing up when he squeezed the trigger. His face was blasted with white powder.

"Bail out!" S/Sgt. Miller screamed at the crew of F-32.

Miraculously, all of them were able to scramble from the burning tank and came rushing down the hill toward F21. Miller was carrying a Thompson sub machine gun in one hand, but being on the move like he was, he had little chance to fire it unless he stopped—which he didn't.

When Ravino saw the four tankers running toward 21, he waited to open the turret hatches until he was sure Miller and his men were mounting the tank and ready to climb inside the turret. Miller climbed in and stood on the tank commander's seat until the other three men managed to squeeze in the turret. As incoming increased, he lowered himself into the hatch. Quickly all the hatch covers were closed and secured. It was cramped, to say the least, and it may have had something to do with one of F32's crew panicking. "We're going to be killed!" he screamed.

Instinctively, Ravino grabbed the passenger's jacket with both hands, just under his neck, and shook him. The guy started to settle down, although he was trembling with fear.

About this time, Cpl. John Corsi, the driver, shouted, "Fuck this!" Corsi threw open his hatch, yanked the shift leaver down into second gear, stomped the accelerator pedal, and pulled deftly on the right brake, bringing the F21 slowly around to start descending Kum gok.

Corsi, once he got F21 to the bottom of the hill, kicked it into third gear and soon had the last surviving flame tank back within safety behind the MLR.

Relieved, the seven tankers dismounted the Sherman, hardly noticing the grim faces of their buddies. Relief soon would turn to grief.

Aftermath of Clambake

*My heart is heavy tonight . . . the operation, like most military operations, can be char-
acterized as successful. Only one who has experienced it can realize what mass melancholy can be concealed by the happy adjective 'successful' when used in reference to
battles. I believe that most military leaders are sentimental, if not sensitive, and therefore
deeply affected by what happens to the men placed in their charge . . . This commander's
melancholy is occasioned by the loss of one officer killed and six men wounded in today's
action.*

JIW, *Dearest Buckie*

When PFC Jerry Ravino, dismounted F21 after S/Sgt Ken Miller and his crew from
the burning F32 had hurriedly made their way to a group of fellow tankers, he did
as all tank commanders do following any exercise with the vehicle. He joined his crew for
a quick inspection of the tank.

Their minds occupied with trying to sort out the unbelievable experience they had
been through, Ravino, Cpl. John Corsi, and PFC Jimmy Oliveri were somewhat oblivious
of the other tankers who were gathering in the assembly area. What they did see was the
beating F21 had just taken.

Two fenders were gone—blown off. There was a visible indention where one round—
mortar or artillery—had ricochetted off the curvature of the turret. All kinds of pock
marks were peppered on the hull and turret from shrapnel and burp guns. By then, it set
in—three F21 tankers were visibly shaken.

As soon as they dismounted the battered Sherman, all three men automatically went
into their pockets for cigarettes and began chain-smoking. Oliveri finally broke the silence
among them. "How do you feel now, Ravino, you gung-ho bastard?"

Jerry Ravino looked at his friend. He was speechless, and just walked away. That's
when he first noticed the somberness of the other tankers. Oddly, he thought, there was
no big gathering around his tank, no inquisitive banter for the skinny of what happened—
normally S.O.P. when pigirons return from a run.

Without realizing where he was headed, Ravino began walking toward one of the
other flame tanks about fifty yards further back. He did see a grim-faced first lieutenant
striding toward him, obviously a bit angered over something. *He had to have been at the
party, that's for sure,* Ravino knew.

"You with the Flames?" the officer barked—crudely, Ravino thought, as his anger
began to build. He stifled the urge to ask the lieutenant: *What the fuck does it look like?*

"Yes, sir. That's my tank, F21, up forward."

The lieutenant could have cared less and barked, pointing to F31, "This is your responsibility, so get up on that tank."

"Yes, sir." PFC Ravino was wondering what the hell was going on. Were they sending
us back to Kum gok? Did something go wrong? Did he want the tank moved somewhere
else? Why me? He knew this wasn't my tank.

Ravino climbed up the side of the F31 and was standing a few feet in back of the
turret when he saw Sgt. Bob Rawlins mounting the stern up to the engine doors. He approached Ravino, seeing the confusion on the PFCs face. He put his hand on the younger
man's shoulder. "Jerry, here's the deal, so brace yourself," Rawlins said calmly. "I'm going

down into the turret because Lt. McAdams is dead. I will hand him up to you."

Ravino started to shake. This was the first he heard that the lieutenant had been killed.

"I will hand him up to you," Rawlins continued. "Get under his arms and pull him out, and lay him on the engine compartment doors."

Recovering momentarily, Ravino then realized why the other officer seemed so curt. *Responsible! Yes, it is my responsibility. He was one of us.* Par Ravino's familiar words were echoing in his son's head. Lt. McAdams was a Marine who *went to face the colors.*

"I'll give you a hand, Ravino." It was Sgt. Hank Amos, the Flame Platoon's mechanic, who also had climbed up on the tank.

Ravino turned and looked into the turret. He wasn't ready for what he saw and immediately his head jolted back. Lt. McAdams had no head, yet the silver bars on the shoulders of his jacket shined up at the shocked tanker.

Ravino grabbed the hatch cover, struggling to get his compusure. *I've got to do this. I can't lose it. He deserves my respect.*

Ravino found the inner strength, leaned into the tank commanders' compartment, and, as tenderly as he could be, got his hands under Lt. McAdams' arms as Sgt. Rawlins slowly struggled to force the body up through the hatch.

Sgt. Amos put his arms under the small of the lieutenant's back, and then slid them down to his legs as the body came out of the tank. As they were laying Lt. McAdams on the doors of the engine compartment, Ravino saw a Marine with a camera in his hand walking toward the tank. He was livid.

"Take one picture, you bastard, and I'll kill your ass. Go up the fuckin' hill if you want pictures."

As the Marine—he was not a tanker—turned, Amos and Rawlins grabbed Ravino, who turned as if he was going to go after the guy. "Slow down, Jerry," Sgt. Rawlins said.

Trembling, Ravino was near tears, and slumped down. "Things were bad enough without him showing up," he muttered.

When Lt. McAdams had been taken care of, PFC Ravino went back to F21 and told Corsi and Oliveri to mount up. They were following F12 back to the tank park.

Meanwhile, word was passed that Charles Craig, the F31 driver with a serious head wound, had been flown out to the USS *Repose,* a hospital ship anchored in Inchon Harbor. Sgt. Charles Foley, who was in 31's bow gunner seat, also suffered head wounds, and had been evacuated to a nearby MASH (Mobile Army Surgical Hospital).

Cpl. Marvin Dennis, who was in the turret of the command tank with Lt. McAdams, didn't make it. He died of his wounds in the hospital.

When the two tanks returned to the tank park at Changdan, they were met by Lt. Henry Barry, whom Lt. McAdams had replaced as Platoon Commander. The lieutenant had tears in his eyes. "Was it bad up there, Ravino?" he asked rhetorically, full well knowing what had happened.

"Yes, sir," the newest Flame Platoon tank commander replied wearily. "We did our best and got everybody off the hill. But I'm not sure about F32. It was still burning when we came back. We got plenty of those Chinese bastards, though!"

The survivors of Operation Clambake would spend a long, long time trying to rationalize the *success* of the mission against the price the Flame Platoon had to pay.

It was not lost on Henzel—the predicament he had caused. He was devastated by what happened.

"My out-of-action platoon would deprive the Flame Platoon of any close-in fire support," he admitted. "It was a total screw-up and all my fault. A total sense of failure and frustration came over me and the crews involved. Mistakes happen in combat, and the last thing any Marine in a combat situation looks for is being unsupportive of his brother Marines in battle."

Lt. Col. Williamson wanted Henzel's ass on the carpet. He was ready to court martial him.

Captain Hunter intervened. He knew his platoon leader had screwed up, but he also knew Henzel was a young, aggressive tanker whose experience had not yet matched the situation into which he was thrust. Henzel was not the only victim of the unexpected haze that gripped Operation Clambake at such a critical point.

"I had a problem with Colonel Williamson not having Heinie court martialed," Hunter said. "But he did relent and let me handle it my own way. And I did."

Hunter's instinct that Lt. Henzel would atone in some measure for his mistake was born out many times in the final months of the war. "Heine did a good job for me in later actions," Capt. Hunter said with pride.

Two days after Operation Clambake, the battalion commander made a point to visit the Flame Platoon and talked to the crews—again. He had met briefly with them the night after they returned from the mission, and left disappointed at his own "blue" feelings and inability to console the tankers. The second visit, though also tugging at his emotions, resolved some of his misgivings.

> Got them to rehash the whole story for me, and told them what a great job they'd done and how proud I and everyone else was of them. Several of them were very heroic, and I'll see that they get the proper awards. (JIW, Dearest Buckie)

The Colonel was true to his word.

Cpl. Elmer Betts earned the Navy Cross, the next highest award to the Medal of Honor, given in the Naval Service. Cpl. Marvin Dennis was awarded the Silver Star posthumously. F21 tank commander Cpl. Thomas Clawson also received the Silver Star, and S/Sgt. Kenneth Miller got the Bronze Star. Purple Hearts were presented posthumously to Lt. McAdams and Cpl. Dennis. Sgt. Charles Foley, Cpl. Charles Craig, Cpl. Clawson, and PFC Gerald Ravino also received Purple Hearts.

Colonel Williamson also passed along a comment from the Division C.O., Maj.Gen. Edwin A. Pollock, who had told the battalion commander that his "Flame Platoon was too aggressive."

Any combat tanker would take that as a flat-out compliment. "We certainly did," said PFC Ravino.

The loss of McAdams was particularly hard for Lt. Col. Williamson, who wrote to his wife, Buckie, the night of Operation Clambake.

> I brood a bit about Lieutenant McAdams, the lad who was killed, for he had three sons who were the apples of his eye, just as I do, one a six-month-old baby who he'd never seen.
>
> He, too, seems to have suspected that his number was up from the meticulous arrangements about his personal affairs he made just prior to going out. Ironically enough, it was he who was telling me about the premonition of disaster "Tiny" Rhoades had, and that not a week ago.
>
> He was a fine lad. (JIW, Dearest Buckie)

Back to Work

The Flame Platoon, despite its tragic experience in Operation Clambake, did not total-ly stand down. But for some reason—one that never was explained to the tankers—there were no firing or napalm missions for twin-barreled Shermans until mid-March.

Only one tank was kept busy, and for the time being it would be F13, commanded by Sgt.Donald DeWolf. Fox One-Three remained on station at Combat Outpost 2. DeWolf and his crew—Cpl. Robert W. Discenza, the driver; Cpl. Israel J. Garcia, the bow gunner; and Sgt. William Pierce, who usually was in the turret with his buddy, DeWolf, as the loader—had been on COP2 for a couple of weeks. It was the normal tour for rotating crews of flame tank on station.

COP2 was that heavily manned prime piece of real estate owned by the First Ma-rine Division to safeguard the Neutral Corridor between Munsan-ni, where the United Nations truce negotiators were billeted, and Panmunjom, site of the on-again, off-again negotiations. That corridor, part of the no-fire zone, ran right past the outpost's backdoor.

Indirect fire on the backside of enemy hills and direct shots into visible positions by rotating flame crews dealt daily harassment to Chinese Communist positions on both sides of the Panmunjom bubble. More so, those missions were a reminder to the Chi-Coms that they were being watched closely and dare not try any funny business around the neutral zone.

The importance of having that flame tank on station was emphasized when the First Tank Battalion Command Diary was filed with the First Marine Division in March 1952:

> One flame tank was maintained on position at COP 2 in order to counter any moves made by the CCF between COP 2 and the FREEDOM CORRIDOR. The use of flame and 105mm cannister is felt to be the best way to control enemy movement in this area as either can be fired without fear of violating neutrality restrictions.

That also was part of the reason that Division pushed through the replacement of the three flame tanks that had been lost early in February. Immediately after Clambake, there may have been some of the reluctance to call the Shermans since the Platoon's comple-ment of tanks was down from nine to six.

The ill-fated F31—in which Lt. Michael McAdams, the platoon leader, was killed, and Cpl. Marvin Dennis, the loader, was mortally wounded—was trucked to Service Company to be surveyed. The interior damage and carnage of the dead and wounded from the two rocket rounds that pierced the turret and the hull behind the bow gunner dictated that decision.

F32 never came back from the top of Kum gok, where it also took three rockets and caught fire. It had to be abandoned. Capt. Clyde Hunter, commanding officer of Able Company tanks, made sure the Sherman hulk would serve no purpose to the Chinese. He had his gunners tear it apart with their 90mm rifles.

F22, which had slid off into a ditch and could not be recovered at Outpost Hedy on 1 February, was nothing more than a mangled hulk. It also was put to lasting sleep by Patton 90s—only to be used as checkpoint for patrols roving in and out of no man's land.

Because of the injuries sustained in Operation Clambake, F12 and F21, which re-turned from Kum gok intact, also would be deadlined a short time. Personnel had to be reshuffled to realign some crews. So that left only F11, F13, F23, and F33 available for duty.

Although Battalion had put in a rush order for new tanks to bring the Flame Platoon up to T.O. (table of organization), there was no guarantee when that request would be filled. It would be sooner than later, however.

Within a week of the Clambake mission—9 February, to be exact—the Flame Platoon was brought up to T.O. The First Tank Battalion received three Shermans, type M4A3E8 POA (Pacific Operation Area) to replace F22, F31, and F32.

Battalion and Division had been quite concerned about not having a full complement of the specialized Shermans. They were well aware of the importance of having this unique outfit and its dual-faceted Shermans up to snuff. With winter about to pass into spring, there was no doubt the Chinese would become more active.

The Sherman's mobility and its capability of a two-pronged weapon to be thrust into position quickly when trouble spots flared up was a key weapon for the First Marine Division. The powerful Pattons could be summoned to level their 90s on the forward slopes of ChiCom strongholds. But they could not get to the reverse slopes like the flame tanks' 105s, which had the ability to loft ordnance over crowns of hills and into out-of-sight strongholds picked up by forward observers. Then, there always was the probability that the featured weapon—the flame gun—might be needed.

It took about a week to crew, check out, and bring the new equipment up to snuff before they were fully ready to go. But with the final stages of the 1952-53 winter, and the ongoing truce talks, still having a numbing effect on both sides of no man's land, there were no calls for Flame Platoon—other than on COP2.

The flame tank on the combat outpost would be moved into its firing slot at alternate times daily from a revetment on the reverse slope. Even while the four flame tanks were entangled in Operation Clambake, F13 was doing its job a few miles south. The daily fire mission routinely called for twenty rounds to be sent into Chinese positions known to be areas where the Gooks could pose a threat to the MLR, or could mount a a possible attack on United Nations negotiators traversing the crucial Corridor.

There was a minor problem, however, since the amount of ordnance the flame tanks were throwing at the Chinese from COP2 was predictable. Because twenty rounds were about as many of those 105 shells that could be squeezed into the crowded flame tank turret, that became the regular shoot. After a while, when Chinese knew that when the pudgy monster with the twin barrels pulled into its firing slot, they could hole up until they counted twenty rounds. Then the Chinks figured they could come out and return the favor because they knew that was the limit of incoming they could expect from the tank at that point.

Sgt. Jerry Ellis was one of the first Flame Tankers to screw up the Chinese arithmetic.

On 5 February, it was time to bring F13, which had been firing its 105 daily for more than two weeks, off the combat outpost to check the wear and tear on the gun tube. It had to be brought back to the Changdan Road Tank Park to have the howitzer and the rest of the Sherman given a thorough going-over.

It was that cold morning that Sgt. Jerry Ellis, F33, driven by PFC Andrew Pittmon, rolled out the Changdan Road and headed for the gate on the west side of Hill 229 where the 7th Marines were holding the Jamestown Line. There, under the protection of seven Charlie Company Pattons, Ellis' flame tank rumbled through the wire and mirrored the

Neutral Corridor west of outposts Marilyn and Star for the two-plus-mile trip to the gate at COP2.

Once F33 was in the clearing on the reverse slope, the Charlie gun tanks remained in the area. Sgt. Donald Dewolf, with Cpl. Robert W. Discenza driving, bought F13 down the hill. Discenza, with the gun tanks herding him home, traced Sgt. Ellis' route—in the opposite direction back though No Man's Land—to the relative safety behind the Jamestown.

It would be Ellis, Pittmon; PFC James S. Doyle, the bow gunner; and PFC Richard Courchaine, the loader, living the Spartan life in a bunker and feasting on C-rations some two miles out in no man's land for the next couple of weeks.

And that's when Jerry Ellis got creative.

Ellis was very aware the Chinese knew how to count without using their abacus—that when they checked the twentieth round coming from the Marine tank on COP2, they usually started coming out of their holes.

Early in the afternoon of 9 February, PFC Pittmon pulled F33 into the firing slot atop COP2. When the Chinese—in a valley on the north side of a small ridge a couple of thousand yards east of the Panmunjom bubble—sensed the first round of 105mm coming their way, they scurried into their holes and began counting.

Sgt. Ellis had a surprise for them. He had squeezed five extra rounds into the F33 turret. When he fired No. 20, PFC Courchaine slid another round into the breach. But Ellis waited several minutes until he thought the Chinese would venture out of their bunkers. Then, he tromped his foot on the floor trigger and sent the twenty-first round on its way. He quickly followed with the other four rounds.

There was no count on whether he dispatched any Chinese to their ancestors, but he set a precedent that the Flame Tanks could get off more than twenty rounds in one shoot and give the Gooks something to think about. Ellis would revert back to the normal load the rest of the time he had F33 up there, but he was sure he got the Gooks guessing a little. A few months later, he would find a way to really dump on them.

Of course, no matter how many rounds went north, there was usually retaliation. The Chinese reaction usually brought several rounds of mortar, often coupled with artillery, on the outpost. Seldom was the flame tank's volley unanswered. It didn't bother the buttoned-up tank crews too much, but every once in a while, a round hitting the right spot would cause some damage. And the concussions of the mortar pounding into the turret or hull sure as hell could shake up the guys inside. Of course, the counteraction wasn't very popular with the Marines in the trenches and bunkers of COP2. They didn't have a robe of steel around them.

Back at the Changdan Road Tank Park, there was some time allowed the remnants of the four crews who came back from Operation Clambake to shake off the effects of 3 February. Though the mission had a sobering effect on the entire Flame Platoon, after a couple of weeks many of the tankers were chaffing at the bit to do something about it. But there was nothing on the books for the Flame Platoon, other than replacing crews, and occasionally, the flame tanks on COP2.

The Flame Platoon tankers were beginning to feel like Battalion had put them on the shelf, and they began to grumble about it. But it didn't do any good. For the remainder of February and March, they could only take it out on the Gooks when it came time to pull their tour on COP2.

Next up on the strategic outpost was F21, with newly promoted Cpl. Jerry Ravino in the turret. Ravino was breaking in as tank commander under the tutelege of Sgt. Joe DeCoursie, a short-timer who would be heading home in a few weeks. DeCoursie had been T.C. of F22 before it wound up in the ditch near Hedy. That day, he had yielded command of the former *Roamin' Candle* to S/Sgt. Ken Miller, who took over the tank for the Hedy flame mission. DeCoursie, since he would be heading back to the States, hadn't picked up another command.

Ravino was thrust into the T.C. spot under fire at Kum gok, when Cpl. Tom Clawson left F21 to help recover the damaged F31—which still had the remains of Lt. McAdams and the mortally wounded Cpl. Marvin Dennis in the turret. Clawson was seriously wounded while standing behind the turret of the crippled F31, and Ravino remained in command of Two-One.

Lt. Charles A. Rosenfeld, who was given command of the Flame Platoon after Lt. McAdams' death, decided to have DeCoursie ride along with Ravino until the new T.C. got a good handle on running things from the turret. Cpl. John Corsi, the veteran driver and another short-timer, remained on the sticks with Cpl. Jimmy Olivieri still handling the bow gun.

By the time February eased into March, the three tanks that had worked on COP2 had sent nearly 600 rounds of 105mm ordnance into Chinese positions, ripping up trenchlines, bunkers, gun emplacements, caves, and crab holes, as well as counting an occasional KIA and many wounded Gooks. It was a two-way street, however.

"They had us zeroed in," said Cpl. Ravino, noting that hundreds of rounds of 60mm and 82mm mortars pounded COP2 in response to 105s going the other way. But they were more than fulfilling the need the First Marine Division saw for flame tank duty on the crucial outpost. Their very presence and added firepower were major factors in discouraging enemy troop movement in the vicinity of the Freedom Corridor.

The versatility of the unique M4A3E8 Sherman flame tank had long since proved it could protect a very sensitive area without violating very stringent neutrality restrictions.

CCF Comes Out of Hibernation

Winter still had the Korean War wrapped in relative inactivity until the thaw began to come in mid-March. It started turning roads and bare-faced hills into relative quagmires, and United Nations Command knew it was time to start looking for the Chinese Communist Forces to begin their annual rite of spring.

They did just that!

The Gooks started to come out of hibernation toward the end of the month. When they did, they launched their big offensive in front of the Jamestown Line in a pitched battle involving the Nevada Cities outposts, three of which—Carson, Reno, and Vegas—were in the hands of the 5th Marine Regiment.

> The Nevada Cities hill complex was located approximately 1,500 yards north of the MLR fronting the 5th Marines right sector . . . Ultimately, however, reverberations ran through nearly 10,000 yards of division front, from the two Berlin outposts, 1,000 yards east of Vegas, to COP Hedy, midpoint in the 1st Marines center sector. . . .
>
> The three Nevada outposts lay just below the 38th Parallel, approximately 10 miles northeast of Panmunjom and the same distance north of the Marine railhead at Munsan-ni. Possession of the area would give the Communists improved observation of I Corps MLR positions to the west. Indeed, the enemy had cast covetous eyes (an ambition translated into action through his well-known creeping tactics) on the semi-circular net of outposts since the preceding summer.
>
> Since they commanded the historic Korean invasion route to Seoul, 30 air miles south, the strategic importance of the Nevada outposts had been one of the reasons for transfer of the Marines from East Korea to the West, in 1952. Both Reno and Vegas, moreover, overlooked Chinese rear area supply routes. This was a matter of special concern to the enemy at this time since he had recently doubled his stockpiling efforts and wanted to prevent UNC intelligence from learning about the build-up. Possession of the Nevada hills would enable the Chinese to harass the Marines at even closer range and—hopefully—to conduct new thrusts at the MLR which would ultimately weaken the UNC position. (MCOinK, Volume V)

All hell began to break loose ominously around dusk of 26 March. First, machine guns and small arms peppered the Jamestown from small enemy hills in no man's land. Then came the mortars and artillery. There would be little letup as the battle ebbed and flowed in both directions. It was 30 March when it finally ended. Vegas was lost to the Commies, and retaken. The Gooks got Reno and never gave it up.

> Continuous attacks and counterattacks for possession of the key Vegas outpost raged unabated for five days. The action escalated into the bloodiest fighting to date in western Korea, resulted in loss of a major outpost (Reno), and the killing or wounding of nearly 1,000 Marines. It was a partial success for the enemy, but he paid a high price for the real estate: casualties amounting to more than twice the Marine losses, including 800 known killed and a regiment that was decimated by the Marine defenders. (MCOinK, Volume V)

Although Reno was lost, the 5th Marines took over Hill 47, southeast of Carson about 750 yards from the MLR. It was large enough to dig in a platoon, which could prevent the Chinese from controlling the patrol route to the MLR and also retard, at least temporarily, anything coming off Reno from the direct north.

When the dust began to settle on 31 March, numbers were staggering.

Recapture and defense of the Vegas outpost was one of the intense, contained struggles which came to characterize the latter part of the Korean War. The action developed into a five-day siege involving over 4,000 ground and air Marines and was the most bloody action that Marines on the western front had yet engaged in. Its cost can be seen, in part, by the casualties sustained by the 1st Marine Division. The infantry strength of two battalions was required to retake Outpost Vegas and defend it against successive Chinese counterattacks. A total of 520 Marine replacements were received during the operation. Marine casualties totaled . . . 116 killed, 441 wounded/evacuated, 360 wounded/not evacuated, and 98 missing, of which 19 were known to be prisoners. Losses for the critical five-day period represented 70 percent of division casualties for the entire month—1,488 killed, wounded, and missing (not including 128 in the KMC sector).

Enemy casualties were listed conservatively as 2,221. This represented 536 counted killed, 654 estimated killed, 174 counted wounded, 853 estimated wounded, and 4 prisoners. The Marines, moreover, in the five days of furious fighting had knocked out the 358th CCF Regiment, numbering between 3,000 and 3,500 men, and destroyed its effectiveness as a unit. (MCOinK, Volume V)

Marine air support dumped more than 425 tons of bombs and napalm. The 11th Marines expended 104,864 rounds of heavy and medium artillery, 4.5-inch rockets and 4.2 mortars. Able Company tanks, strung out in nine support positions and also helping mark targets for Marine air, went through 7,000 rounds of 90mm ordnance.

It was not a one-sided show of heavy firepower. The Chinese plastered the 5th Marines with an estimated 45,000 rounds of mortars and artillery.

As the month closed on the Vegas chapter, Marines on line and in the reserve companies who had just sweated through the bloodiest exchange of the war on the I Corps front to date added their own epitaph. With a touch of ungallantry that can be understood, they called the disputed crest of Vegas "the highest damn beachhead in Korea." (MCOinK, Volume V)

That *highest damn beachhead* was enough to bring the Chinese back to the truce table. They knew, at that point, they had just about shot their load and had very little to show for it. One of their regiments was decimated. It was 28 March—when the Communists decided they they had little more to gain—that the United Nations received word: the Chinese would be willing to talk about the return of sick and wounded prisoners. It was a proposal U.N. negotiators had been trying to bring to the table since December 1951.

Before April 1953 was a week old, the Chinese delegation once again returned to the truce table at Panmunjom to meet with U.N. negotiators and resume talks that had been deadlocked.

Finally, a Breakthrough!

The greatest accomplishment coming out of the resumption of the truce negotiations was the agreement on the first exchange of prisoners—Operation Little Switch.

On Monday morning, 20 April, a convoy of Chinese Communist ambulances, stretching five miles back to Kaesong, began arriving in Panmunjom from the north, and the exchange began. There were 149 Americans, 15 of them Marines, among the 684 haggard United Nations captives coming in from prisoner of war camps in North Korea.

It took six days for the exchange. On the surface, it seemed that less than 700 UNC prisoners was much too little compared to the more than 6,600 North Koreans and Chinese passing through the Freedom Gate going the other way. But it was a start.

Monitoring the entire operation from Combat Outpost 2 were an infantry company of the 1st Marine Regiment, the ever-present flame tank, and a platoon of Patton M46s from Dog Company.

> In the central part of Jamestown, the 1st Marines . . . continued to man the MLR and its 12 outposts, including the strategic COP-2 tucked down by the Panmunjom peace corridor. With the resumption of talks on 6 April, this position had again taken on renewed importance with its tank-infantry covering force of 5 armored vehicles and 245 Marines on call at all times. . . .
>
> This unit was on alert to evacuate the UN truce team from Panmunjom in the event of Communist hostile action or any threat to security . . . the Marine rescue force maintained close surveillance of the enemy and the Panmunjom peace corridor as well as the safe arrival and departure of the UN truce team shuttled in by helicopter or motor convoy. (MCOinK, Volume V)

The platoon of Pattons and the flame tank were there to make sure the Chinese were well aware that the United Nations truce team going into, and out of, the neutral zone would not be subjected to any Communist tricks. They could pounce on the Freedom Corridor in an instant.

To say the least, the prisoner exchange was big step in working out a truce, and it did inhibit the action on both sides for the time being—so much so that it was the beginning of a period the UNC labeled "Marking Time." Still, there were pockets of activity all along the line, and flame tanks finally got fairly involved in some of it. They expended more than 1,100 rounds of 105mm ordnance—mostly with indirect fire missions—during the month of April.

Fox 23, which had taken over the COP2 duty early in March, still was on station as spring began to seep through the pores of the Land of the Morning Calm in April. It continued to fire almost daily. The influence of Sgt. Jerry Ellis' little experiment back in February, appeared to have taken hold because the flame tanks now were regularly sending 25 rounds through the 105 tube once they got into the slot atop the critical combat outpost.

With the Flame Platoon now up to T.O.—nine fully-ready Shermans—assignments began to come with regularity. During the prisoner exchange, a section of the versatile stubby M4A3E8s were moved into blocking positions with Dog Company Pattons to provide further security around the Freedom Corridor.

Two flame tanks, from just inside the MLR southeast of outpost Hedy, went to work on 5 April and dropped an assortment of 105mm on machine gun positions on Hedy and outpost William, which was about 3,000 yards to the west. Meanwhile, F23 was working over two Chinese positions on outpost Molar and further north just on the fringe of the Panmunjom Bubble. That was fairly precise shooting for the 105 gunners—acting on good numbers from forward observers—because those targets were within 500 yards of the restricted zone. There was a report that two Chinese were killed in the barrage.

Six enemy soldiers never survived the wrath of F23 on its final shoot on station when its last mission in late afternoon of 8 April plastered a concentration of troops near Oksim-dong.

The next day, F11 came on station and remained there while the prisoner exchange was still taking place later in the month. By now, the tank was usually going into the firing slot twice a day and dispensing 25 rounds each time. There was some slackening of fire during the prisoner exchange, but before and after, it was mostly 50 rounds a day—two shoots.

It was a significant adventure on 11 April when the flame tanks got a shot at three Chinese T-34 tanks. It was the first time since early in the war that Commie tanks had come out of hiding and within striking distance of First Tank Battalion armor. Forward Observers spotted troop and tank movement in the vicinity of Tangmulsan-myo about five miles southwest of Panmunjom. There had been reports of T-34 sightings in the First Tank Battalion command diaries for several months, but this was the first time since early in 1951 that there was a chance for Marine tankers to get a shot at them.

The theory was that the Russian-made armor, one of the major reasons the Reds were able to turn the tables on the Germans in World War II, had been holed up in tunnel-type revetments behind Gook lines. Though the tank itself was a formidable piece of equipment, the Chinese and North Koreans did not show the expertise in handling them like the Russions did.

Early in the war when the T-34s were very active in the hands of North Koreans, they had initial success against undermanned U.S. Army troops. But once they ran into First Tank Battalion Pershing M26s and Marine anti-tank teams, they were no match. Their inexperienced crews appeared to have little or no idea how to handle them in a pitched battle. More often than not they were destroyed and left as rusted hulks.

After Inchon and the breakout from Pusan, U.N. forces saw relatively little of the T-34. Although there were sightings, they never came out to play in front of Marine lines until that one day in April 1953.

When they did, the four flame tanks, firing indirectly, lofted nearly fifty rounds from Wongdang-ni, below the Neutral Corridor, over Commie hills into the concentration. Though the Gook units were dispersed by the incoming, there was no count of any destruction of the enemy armor or Chinese casualties.

Meanwhile, one section of the Flames tied in with Dog Company in nightly blocking positions in the vicinity of the Corridor for a ten-day period.

It was "unlucky thirteen" for three Gooks who were confirmed KIA on the 13th day of April when F11 found the range on Hill 134 while tossing its daily 50-round allotment from COP2. The next day, the Gooks extracted a minor bit of revenge when an 82mm mortar hit near F11 and damaged a shock absorber.

The Flame Platoon put its primary weapon to work on 21 April when two of the Shermans rolled into no man's land to burn out some caves and bunkers on Hill 90, where the ChiComs often set up patrol activity west of COP2. Two days later, from COP2, F11 got an estimated two KIA with its 50-round direct shoot into Hill 134 and up towards Arrowhead.

A large direct fire shoot on 28 April—two days after Operation Little Switch concluded—involved four flame tanks called to set up east of the Imjin River in outpost Wisker area and supported the 1st Amphibous Tractor Battalion, which was probing the western shore. Sitting in pairs at positions near Tanhyon-Myon and Kimsan-ni inside the MLR south of the Corridor, the four Shermans lined 108 rounds directly across the river into enemy trenches and bunkers in a broad—nearly two square miles—area that included Sadong-ni, Karummu-gol, Narume, and Songan.

Four days later, they set up a little more to the north and, starting at 0745 until 1345, pummeled Huchon, Sadong-ni, Songan, Nureme, and the low lands of the Imjin south of Sikhyon-ni with more than 160 rounds of 105. Two houses were destroyed, and they took out two automatic weapon positions and an observation post.

With spring came more than changes in the weather.

The First Tank Battalion got a new commanding officer. Lt. Col. John I. Williamson, who was not shy about the use of flame tanks after he took over in May of 1952, turned over the unit's reins to Lt. Col. Charles W. McCoy, who also would keep the twin-barreled Shermans on the move.

But bigger things were to come for the entire First Marine Division after Lt.Gen. Maxwell Taylor, who assumed command of U.S. Eighth Army Korea (EUSAK) in February, began to get a handle on the situation. It was General Taylor's belief that his divisions needed eight weeks of upgraded training.

Thus, the First Marine Division, which had been in line since August 1951 when it was caretaker of a rugged mountainous stretch of the MLR in East Central Korea before it shifted west to hover over thirty-five miles of the Jamestown, was going to take a break.

General Taylor also took the "K" out of EUSAK, and it was now the Eighth U.S. Army. Gone also was the Jamestown Line—so was Missouri, Deluth, Minnesota, and CAT. Though the appearance of the MLR had not changed one bit, it would be known now only as the Main Line of Resistance from the east coast to the west.

But the major decision was the 1stMarDiv would not be anchoring it for the first time in twenty months.

By late April, plans had moved into high gear for relief of the 1st Marine Division by the 25th U.S. Infantry Division and transfer of the Marines to U.S. I Corps reserve at Camp Casey. Although the Marine division had been in active defense positions for 20 months (first in the eastern X Corps and, for the past year, on the western front), some observers noted that there was a reluctance to turn over their presently occupied positions and that the Marines were coming out "under protest" from commanders who wanted the Division to remain on the line.

For its part, the 25th Division . . . was to shift over to the I Corps far west coastal area from its own neighboring IX Corps sector on the right. Marine association with the Army division went back to the early days of the war. In August 1950, when the Korean Conflict was then only a few weeks old, the 25th Division, with the 1st Provisional Marine Brigade and the Army's RCT-5, had spearheaded the first UN counteroffensive on the far southern front, in the Sachon-Chinju area. Now fresh from its own recent period in reserve, the 25th Division, including its attached Turkish Brigade, was to take over the 33-mile 1st Marine Division line, effective 5 May. (MCOinK, Volume V)

There was one addendum to order:

Marine armor and artillery, however, would remain in support of the 25th Division and transfer to I Corps control. (MCOinK, Volume V)

It took four days to complete displacement of the First Marine Division—less the First Tank Battalion and the 11th Marines with their much-needed artillery support.

The idea that Marine tanks and artillery were to come under Army command didn't sit too well with a lot of Gyrenes. But on 5 May, the First Tank Battalion was under control of the 25th Division.

Companies, C and B, were assigned to the TAFC (Turkish Armed Forces Command) . . . in the left and right battalion areas, respectively. Company D vehicles came under command of the 35th Infantry Regiment, in the center sector; while A, the remaining company, was designated as the single reserve unit. This was a modification of the Marine system of maintaining two tank companies in reserve, one a short distance behind the MLR and the other, at the armored battalion CP near Munsan-ni. A change in tactics also took place when the Marine tanks came under Army operational control. It had been the Marine practice to retain the tanks at the company CP from where they moved to prepared firing slots at the request of the supported infantry unit. (MCOinK, Volume V)

This could have been the result of the First Marine Division doctrine of keeping anti-tank platoons of five very mobile M46 Pattons with each of its three infantry regiments. The ATs sat right up there on the MLR with their bunker buddies. If heavy firepower was needed, the ATs were able to dispense it right away. If the situation called for more support than they could give, it was easy enough to reinforce them with a platoon, or platoons, of First Tank Battalion gun company Pattons, sitting not too far from the front.

That the 25th Division didn't have any rolling armor of its own at the ready near the MLR probably necessitated the alternative disposition of Marine tanks when they came under command of the Army.

When the 1st Tank Battalion was attached to the 25th Division, the armored vehicles were shifted to firing slots near the MLR where they occupied semi-fixed positions. Armored personnel carriers (APCs) were assigned by the Army to Company B and used by both B and C as resupply vehicles to haul food, water, fuel, and ammunition to the tanks on line. Also as part of the relief, control of the KMC tank company was transferred from the Marine 1st Tank Battalion to I Corps, although the company still continued in its same location in the old KMC sector. (MCOinK, Volume V)

As for the Flame Platoon, it would remain under Headquarters Company, First Tank Battalion, and be assigned—as in the past—to the gun companies as needed.

Although the change in deployment of the Marine tanks met with some consternation at first, admittedly, it worked for the better.

A major advantage resulting from this change was that tanks effectively linked the MLR with rear area CPs. Through land line and radio. While initial preparatory fire often cut the phone lines, the radios worked well and this was "generally the only reliable means of communication with the scene of action." Capt. Robert J. Post, Company C Commanding Officer, First Tank Battalion (MCOinK, Volume V)

Around this time, there was a lull in the action virtually across the entire front. It was a lull before the storm. Even though the truce talks had resumed on 26 April, there was wary apprehension throughout the UN Command because it was no secret that Chinese Communist forces were gearing up for another big fight.

Through this relatively quiet "marking time," flame tanks remained active, mostly with indirect fire missions, all in addition to the Sherman on station at COP2, which remained part of the critical watchdog over what was going on in Panmunjom.

Marine Tankers Get New Boss

By late April and early May of 1953, the tenor of the war was changing. It was still dangerous along the MLR and, more so, among the outposts in front of it. But the breakthrough in the truce negotiations at Panmunjom that resulted in the initial exchange of prisoners had started to spread a little more hope that a truce could be worked out.

The tension that had prevailed during Operation Little Switch had passed, and there was renewed, if cautious, optimism that this was only the beginning of better things to come.

Despite the fact that all official papers and agreements had been concluded more than a week earlier, no one was absolutely sure until the last moment that the prisoner exchange would actually take place. The mechanics of the transfer operation itself, as it turned out, went off practically without hitch.

> One of the first things the liberated POWs saw was the big sign "Welcome Gate to Freedom" raised the preceding night over the Panmunjom receiving tents. Here they could get a cup of coffee and momentarily relax before starting the long one-and-a-half hour ambulance trip south to Freedom Village. The returnees were outfitted in blue Communist greatcoats, utilities, caps, and tennis shoes. Some of the men were bearded; some wore thin smiles; some had half-hidden tears in their eyes. . . .
>
> From Panmunjom all Allied prisoners were taken to Freedom Village at Munsan where they received a medical check, and the more seriously wounded were flown to a field hospital near Seoul. (MCOinK, Volume V)

At least, an encouraging start!

It wasn't long after that when, for the first time since the summer of 1951, the First Marine Division was coming off the line and going into reserve—that is, most of the 1st-MarDiv. The First Tank Battalion and the 11th Marine Regiment were detached from the Division and put under Army command and would stay at the front. The 11th Marines were needed for counter-battery support of the Army's 25th Tropical Lightning Infantry Division, which had been moved from its IX Corps responsibilities on the right of the Marines into I Corps. Similar assignments were laid on the First Tank Battalion.

It was a difficult pill to swallow for most Marines: coming under Army control. Intermingling of the Services is never easy, but putting Marines and the Army in one pot was mixing oil and water at best. Due respect, however, had to be paid the 25th Lightning. It was the one Army Division that stood its ground early in the war and linked with the 1st Provisional Marine Brigade to lead the initial offensive when United Nations troops were about to break out of the Pusan Perimeter.

But this was well before the current generation of Marine replacements, and all they had been fed through boot camp and subsequent training was a diet of the Army's "bug-out" reputation. That long since had been squared away, but you couldn't tell many Marines that in May 1953.

It did not seem to bother Sgt. Jerry Ellis, who was in command of the flame tank sitting atop Combat Outpost 2 (COP2). Sgt. Ellis figured he could do nothing about the situation and was going to make the best of it.

It was the Lightning's 2nd Battalion, 35th Infantry Regiment taking over the sector of the former Jamestown line, relieving the 5th Marines. So, suspicion, trepidation, and more than a touch of arrogance was running through the minds of the small detachment of tankers from the Flame Platoon and Charlie Company M46 Patton crews as they watched a company of Army infantry climb up the backside of COP2.

"They were not familiar with the number of CCF (Chinese Communist Forces) positions," a worried Sgt. Ellis said. "Nor," he added, "did they know which outposts we held and, no way could they know the sensitivity of the overall 'No Fire Zone,' which was right up against COP2. With Marines manning that hill for more than a year, we had that terrain down pat." Ellis and the rest of the Marines were very wary of the newcomers' unfamiliarity with the area. So, it was not unusual that they didn't have much truck with their new tenants. Like most Marines, they stayed to themselves and let the Army do its thing.

However, because Ellis was in command of the lone flame tank—which was crewed by PFC Andrew Pittmon Jr., the driver; PFC James S. Doyle at the bow gun; and PFC Richard Courchaine loading—on the outpost, he was required to have some interaction with the Army. But this was minimal since a Marine infantry lieutenant was left out on COP2 to help the 35th guys get acclimated, and also coordinate 105mm firing missions.

This was Ellis' second tour on COP2, and he had something else up his sleeve. He knew he had created some havoc among the Chinese when he altered the firing missions from twenty rounds to twenty-five on his first run up the hill. But he also knew the Chinks were counting to twenty-five now.

One day, preparing for the following day's mission, he decided to throw the Gooks another curve. He ordered his crew to find every pocket in the turret where they could set a round. There was some skepticism, but they managed to somehow cram in thirty-eight of those two-foot rounds and still leave room for Ellis and his loader, PFC Courchaine.

Come the next morning, there was a problem when Sgt. Ellis was confronted by PFC Pittmon. The driver thought the unsecured rounds would be bouncing and rolling around all over the place on the bumpy ride up to the slot. Pittmon told Ellis he didn't want to drive the tank under those conditions.

Respecting the valid concern of his driver, Ellis, simply said, "Okay, I'll take it up there. You get up in the turret."

With that, Sgt. Ellis climbed into the driver's compartment, started the engine, threw it into second gear, and slowly urged the tank up the slope. "Shit," he admitted, "only a few rounds slid down and hit me in the back. I just pushed them back onto the deck of the turret.

"Increasing our payload," Ellis said, "confused the hell out of the Gooks. They weren't quite sure when the hell they could come out of their holes after that." But Sgt. Ellis wouldn't be around too much longer to enjoy it.

Two days after the 35th Regiment moved into position on the hill, Ellis had been summoned to the COP2 command post late in the afternoon to review the day's results of a firing on the Gook hills. The bunker was filled with Army brass, who had been talking with the Marine officer. Ellis, walking from his tank, was about 20 feet from the entrance to the bunker when he heard it.

Pffft, pffft.

In a split second came the explosion into the soft soil behind him—soil that had been ground and powdered by more than a year's regular incoming. "It was like being in a sandstorm," Sgt. Ellis said.

But there also was rock and shrapnel mixed in that sand as the concussion blasted him into the entrance of the bunker.

The Marine officer immediately ran to fallen Ellis. "Sir," Ellis winced, "it feels like water in left boot."

Cutting away the shredded trouser, the lieutenant could see a gash running the length of the tank commander's left leg. Ellis also lost a piece of his left ear and had a wound under his chin. The only thing that may have saved his life was the flack jacket he was wearing. It had a sizeable piece of shrapnel wedge in the back of it. The metal surely would have ripped into the sergeant's upper body had it not been for the jacket.

The lieutenant wisely began to work on Ellis, applying a pressure pack to his hemorrhaging leg. "That Marine officer saved my life," Ellis said gratefully. A med-evac chopper soon arrived at COP2, and Ellis was put on helicopter skid and flown to Able Medical Company. "I would have bled to death if lieutenant hadn't taken care of that leg."

Three weeks later, Ellis was back with the Flame Platoon—much earlier than he was expected, and before doctors thought he was ready to return to duty. When he was feeling better, although limping quite noticeably, he asked the surgeon if he could return to his outfit.

"No, Sergeant," was the emphatic reply, "you still need more time to heal."

"Hell, sir," Ellis explained, "I'm in tanks and you know there's no walking in them."

Even the Sergeant was a little surprised that the doctor bought that line.

Turkish Tradition of Ears

It was toward the end of May when Lt. Charles A. Rosenfeld, commanding officer of the Flame Platoon, First Tank Battalion, summoned Cpl. Jerry Ravino, now one of the veteran tank commanders of the unit, to his tent.

The skeptical Ravino, who had taken over as T.C. of F21 in the middle of Operation Clambake, had been harboring some resentment since then because the flame tanks had not seen more action with their primary weapon. He was eager to extract some payback for the debacle at Kum gok, and indirect firing missions were not filling the bill.

Ravino was hoping Lt. Rosenfeld finally had come up with a flame mission. But based on the fact that only one such assignment—a comparatively benign operation at Hill 90—had been undertaken since early February, Ravino was not very confident this was the reason the platoon leader wanted him.

The NCO's mood changed immediately when Lt. Rosenfeld told him the Turkish Armed Forces Command (TAFC) had requested the First Tank Battalion to set up a torch mission on a couple of hills in the Nevada Cities outposts area.

When the 25th Infantry Division relieved the First Marine Division along the former Jamestown line a few weeks early, the Turkish Brigade was given responsibility of monitoring the Nevada hills as well as Berlin and East Berlin outposts, slightly south of the Hook. Charlie Company tanks had been assigned to the area in support of the TAFC.

"Corporal," Rosenfeld said, "I want you to go up to the MLR with me to help work out a flame mission in front of the Turks' positions."

Not only gratified that Lt. Rosenfeld had come up with a flame mission, Ravino got a shot to his ego because he was picked above more senior NCOs in the Platoon to stand in on the planning.

When Lt. Rosenfeld pulled the Flame Platoon's beat-up old jeep in behind the MLR, below the Turkish command post, the Marines were quickly met by two guards. The Turks took nothing for granted. They thoroughly, but respectfully, checked over the two Marines. One of the smaller units in the United Nations Command, the TAFC came to Korea with a centuries-old reputation as fierce warriors. Cpl. Ravino was beginning to see why. Later, he would know why.

When the tankers entered the command bunker, they were aware of an Army major and an Air Force major before they were introduced to the Turks commanding officer.

Not unlike the rest of the units along the MLR, the Turks were taking casualties almost daily from sniper and mortar fire coming from Chinese outposts beyond their own OPs. After going over the map, it was concluded that one flame tank, under the protection of a Charlie Company platoon of M46 Pattons, would move forward of the friendly outposts and burn out pockets of well dug-in Chinese on hills opposite the front. The mission would be set up by the 11th Marines artillery, followed by several strikes by Air Force Saberjets.

As the Marines left the command bunker, Cpl. Ravino was told by the lieutenant not to mention the mission to any of his fellow tankers until the plan was finalized. Then, Rosenfeld said, he would bring the tank commander in to help plan the flame tank's route and assignment before it would be laid out in a critique with the participating crew.

Lt. Rosenfeld and Cpl. Ravino were just about to climb into the old jeep when a

Turkish troop-truck pulled into the clearing behind the MLR. There were about twenty Turk infantryman screaming—nothing the two Americans could understand—as they jumped out of the back of the truck. After the Turks started walking up the hill, Cpl. Ravino looked back toward the truck and noticed something hanging from the forward post of truck bed. It looked like some kind of meat, and there was blood dripping to the ground. Looking closer, he saw it was a wire with several human ears skewered on it like a shish-kabob.

Almost losing his cookies, the Marine NCO recovered quickly enough to see the Turkish major watching him. The Corporal asked the major about the gory mess.

"Corporal," the major said rather firmly, but with a hint of a smile on his face, "last night, as is our custom, my men sneaked out into no man's land and attacked the Chinese when they least expected it.

"If a Turkish fighting man kills an enemy, he will cut off the enemy's ears as a sign that he has become a man in the Turkish Army. This has always been a part of our fighting tradition."

Ravino digested the story for a minute, then said, "Glad as hell you're on our side, Major!"

The Turks would be up to their own ears with the Chinese in days to come, and the flame mission never came off.

It all started when the CCF unleashed another offensive that targeted the Turkish holds on Carson, Elko, Vegas, Berlin, and East Berlin in the middle of May. With the help of Charlie Company tanks and artillery from the 11th Marines, the two-battalion Chink probe was beaten back.

But a little more than a week later, on 25 May after the United Nations negotiators made their final offer at the truce talks table, the Chinese began a broad offensive that stretched from the Freedom Corridor all the way east to the Hook area. By 28 May the 120th Chinese Division was completely involved. The Turks, defending the Nevadas hills, Berlin and East Berlin, took a beating.

It was so severe that two companies of the First Tank Battalion—and later, flame tanks—were among the support units rushed into forty-eight-hour fight.

Supported by heavy artillery fires, one CCF battalion moved in towards Carson and Elko. Another battalion, under cover of smoke, attacked central COP Vegas, while a third struck Berlin and East Berlin on the right flank. Three hours after the initial attack, defenders at Carson and Elko were engaged in hand-to-hand combat with the Chinese.

. . . The Turks . . . were still in possession of the two Berlin (platoon-strength) outposts, but Commonwealth forces were involved in a pitched battle at Ronson and Warsaw. The situation was even grimmer at this time in the Nevada Cities area outposted by the TAFC. Although the Turkish troops continued to hold Vegas, where 140 men were dug in, Carson (two-platoon size) had fallen and Elko (platoon-strength) was heavily besieged. Shortly thereafter, the 25th Division ordered that the TAFC withdraw from the latter position to its own MLR. The diversionary attack against Berlin-East Berlin had been broken off and the twin positions were secured.

During the first six hours of the attack, the night of 28–29 May . . . 11th Marines had sent 9,500 rounds crashing into Chinese strongpoints, while Marine air observers direct-ed eight missions against active enemy artillery positions. Ripples from the 1st 4.5-inch Rocket Battery, transferred to the Commonwealth sector to support the Hook defense, were fired on CCF troop activity there. Another curtain of flame engulfed the Carson in-truders. When the fighting started, 15 Marine tanks were positioned in the Turkish sector. Company B and C vehicles . . . relentlessly pounded the approaching CCF columns, while

Company D was put on a 30-minute standby. As the action developed, additional tanks were committed until 33 were on line at one time or another.

When savage Chinese pummeling of the 25th Division outposts continued the following day, Colonel (Wallace M.) Nelson's 1st Marines was transferred at 1315 to operational control of I Corps. The regiment's three infantry battalions, antitank, and heavy mortar companies . . . within two hours had relocated at 25th Division bivouac areas south of the Kansas Line . . . The 1st Marine Division Reconnaissance Company was similarly ordered to 25th Division control to relieve a 14th Infantry Regiment reserve company in position along the east bank Imjin River defenses.

Overhead, close air support runs were being conducted by . . . Marine Attack Squadrons . . .

During the 29th, control of the Vegas outposts–where 1st Division Marines had fought and died exactly two months earlier—changed hands several times between the indomitable Turkish defenders and the persistent Chinese. By dark, the CCF had wrested the northern crest from the TAFC which still held the southeastern face of the position. In the 24-hour period from 1800 on the 28th through the 29th, the 11th Marines had expended 41,523 rounds . . . At one point in the action Chinese counterbattery fire scored a direct hit on Turkish gun emplacements, knocking six howitzers out of action from the explosions of charges already loaded. As a result 2/11 . . . took over the direct support mission of the TAFC Brigade . . . . Although an Allied counterattack early in the day had restored Elko to friendly control, the enemy refused to be dislodged from Carson. (MCOinK, Volume V)

It was during the raging battle of 29-30 May that five flame tanks were summoned to join Charlie and Baker companies Pattons to give more support to the Turks. Three of the Shermans took up firing positions in the area manned by Charlie Company tanks on the backside of the MLR less than 1,500 yards directly south of Carson. From there their 105s unleashed 180 rounds into Commie positions on Vegas, Carson, and Reno. At least thirty enemy troops were killed by the devastation the flame tanks mixed into the battle. It was not a one-sided show, although there were no injuries among the Flame Tankers. The Chinese retaliated with nearly as much in a variety of 60mm, 82mm, and 120mm mortars.

Two other Shermans from the Platoon, working with Baker Company several thousand yards to the east, spread nearly 150 rounds of their ordnance on Vegas and the two Berlin outposts. At least three enemy troops were killed by the 105 barrage on Vegas. The flame tanks also worked out their 30-caliber machine guns to the extent of emptying ten cases of the ammo into nearby Gook trenches and bunkers.

An integral part of the defense was the successful use of the Leaflets on four of the gun tanks in the night fighting. Leaflets were the high-powered fighting lights, not only used to illuminate targets, but also to blind and confuse the enemy troops. With those things shining in their faces, the Chinese had difficulty seeing what was in front of them. "LEAFLETS illuminated the battlefield while the gun tanks incessantly pounded the CCF formations as they tried to storm the outposts" (Command Diary for May 1953, First Tank Battalion).

Still, the Turks had been beat up badly and were having trouble holding off the Chinese, who repeatedly threw fresh troops in the battle.

I Corps had previously regarded the defensive positions of the Nevada complex as "critical," with the TAFC having been "instructed to hold them against all enemy attacks." By midday on the 29th, however, the I Corps commander, General (Mark W.) Clark, and 25th Division CG, General (Samuel T.) Williams, had apparently had a change of mind. The Vegas strength was down to some 40 Turks. Altogether more than 150 men under the

25th command had been killed and another 245 wounded in defense of Nevada positions. It appeared that the Chinese, constantly reinforcing with fresh battalions despite estimated losses of 3,000, intended to retain the offensive until the outposts were taken.

With Carson and Vegas both occupied by the enemy, the Elko position became untenable without the support of its sister outposts. Six times the CCF had crossed over from Carson to Elko to try to retake the latter position, but had been thus far deterred by Allied firepower. Accordingly, at 2300, the 25th Division ordered its reserve 14th Regiment, earlier committed to the Elko-Carson counterattack, to withdraw from Elko and the Turks to pull back from Vegas to the MLR. By daybreak the withdrawal was completed and 25th Division and Turkish troops had regrouped on the MLR. (MCOinK, Volume V)

That was a bitter pill to be swallowed, particularly by Marines whose buddies had left blood spread all over those outposts in previous battles so the UNC could control the crucial ancient thruway to Seoul. Now, Eighth Army was letting it all go.

Yours is not to reason why, Marine.

But the Turks must have wondered why. It was an exhaustive, and expensive, battle in more ways than one.

The Army reported that more than 117,000 rounds of artillery and 67 close air support missions had buttressed the UNC ground effort. Official estimates indicated that in the three-day action the Chinese had fired 65,000 rounds of artillery and mortar, "up to this point an unprecedented volume in the Korean War." The Marine artillery contribution from its four active battalions during this 28–30 May period totaled 56,280 rounds in 835 missions.

During the three-day siege, 15 to 33 Marine tanks poured their lethal 90mm projectiles on the enemy from MLR firing slots. (MCOinK, Volume V)

There also was the contribution from the flame tanks that played a major roll in holding off the Chinese on their final seige.

At times the action was so heavy that the tanks were refueled on line. As they ran out of ammunition and fuel, "armored utility vehicles of the battalion, with a basic load of ammunition aboard, maneuvered beside the tanks in position and rearmed them on the spot," to permit virtually uninterrupted tank firing . . . Although 4,162 rounds of Chinese fire fell near the tank positions, no damage to material was reported. For their part the M46s and Flames were responsible for 721 enemy deaths, an estimated 137 more killed, 141 wounded, and an estimated 1,200 injured.

Ground action ceased the following day (30 May) as rain drenched the battlefield, although the 11th Marines reported sightings of more than 200 Chinese soldiers, most of them on the three recently lost outposts. Benched while the fierce battle was going on, the 1st Marines remained under operational control of I Corps as a possible contingency force from 29 May to 5 June. On the latter date, following the Eighth Army decision not to retake the Carson-Elko-Vegas outposts, the regiment reverted to Marine control and returned to Camp Britannia. The previous day the Communists had agreed on all major points of the UNC final offer and it appeared that a ceasefire was close at hand.

Diplomats and military leaders both felt this latest Chinese assault was to show a strong military hand and win dominating terrain features along the MLR. Thus the enemy would be able to improve his defensive posture when final battlelines were adjusted at the truce. It was not believed that the CCF effort was an attempt to expand their operations into a general offensive. In any event, the Nevada positions were downgraded from their previous designation as major outposts. I Corps also decreed no further effort would be made to retake them and that a "revaluation of the terrain in view of the destruction of the defensive work indicates these hills are not presently essential to defense of the sector." (MCOinK, Volume V)

With all said and done, and a tenuous probability of a truce in the offing, the overall defense and rigidity of the MLR did leave the Chinese frustrated and brought them back to the table to work out final negotiations.

The First Tank Battalion 's assessment put it this way:

The gun tanks (and Flame Tanks) and LEAFLETS kept the CCF continually off balance and accounted for seven hundred twenty-one (721) counted enemy KIA. The deadly, accurate and continued fire of the tanks may have prevented a successful penetration of the MLR by the CCF. (Command Diary for May 1953, First Tank Battalion)

The Final Weeks

The cautious expectancy of the war coming to an end had muted the activity along the front during June 1953, and it left the Flame Platoon relatively idle for the time being. But while the Flame Tankers were involved with a lot of preventative maintenance on their Shermans, the 90mm rifles of the gun companies of the First Tank Battalion were causing just enough nuisance to keep Chinese Communist Forces from getting too comfortable.

Although tanks were maintained in ML positions to support the static defense, this was a period of relative inactivity for tanks. Employment consisted of destruction fires against enemy positions and fires against targets of opportunity. (Command Diary for June 1953, First Tank Battalion)

For the most part, the Flame Platoon action was restricted to what the Sherman on COP2 was dishing out. It was hammering enemy positions east of the Freedom Corridor. One telling shoot was on 6 June when the daily allotment of twenty-five rounds went into the low hills north of Sonjang-ni, about 1,500 yards east of Panmunjom, and killed at least two Chinese.

The flame tank had its busiest day twenty-four hours later when it turned its guns eastward toward Three Fingers and, on two different trips up the hill and into the firing slot, unloaded forty-eight rounds of 105mm. Elsewhere along the line, it was relatively quiet—with one exception.

A rash of political activity in June markedly affected the tenor of military operations in Korea. Intensified Communist aggression broke out north of ROK sectors in the Eighth Army line, largely as a reaction to President Rhee's unprecedented action on 18 June of freeing, with the help of ROK guards, approximately 25,000 North Korean anti-Communist prisoners at POW camps in the south. Other anti-Communist POWs at Camp No. 10, near Ascom City, staged violent break-out attempts at that same time and Company A, 1st Amphibian Tractor Battalion passed to operational control of the camp commanding officer there to help prevent a repetition of any such incidents in the future. Following a recess of truce talks, pending a clarification of the status of the current military-diplomatic agreements, key delegates held crisis meetings at Panmunjom and Tokyo to get the beleaguered talks back on track.

Despite the furor, signing of the armistice agreement was expected shortly. (MCOinK, Volume V)

Things, however, would not be so mundane for the flame tanks and the rest of the First Marine Division during the final twenty-seven days of the war. The Chinese still had some irons in the fire and were going to make a couple of final stabs at picking up a little more real estate in no man's land. Ironically, or stupid planning by the Chinese, it appeared to be timed when the First Marine Division returned to its positions on the former Jamestown Line.

Still under command of the Army's 25th Lightning Division, the flame tank continued to work from Combat Outpost 2 where, with one or two exceptions, it was the usual twenty-five rounds going out, followed by the normal few rounds of retaliatory incoming. However, on 9 July there was some enemy activity detected in the configuration of Hill

67, Hill 134, and Three Fingers to the north and east of COP2. The Chinese there soon felt the fury of more than 50 rounds of 105. This was just after the First Marine Division was brought back on line and the CCF, for some reason, felt like flexing its muscles again.

By 6 July, the 7th Marine Regiment had begun moving into the right sector and relief of the 25th Lightning Division was underway. Next, the 5th Marines went into the center of the line, sending the Army's 35th Division into reserve. The 1st Marines would be held back as the 1stMarDiv's reserve regiment. Of course, the First Tank Battalion and the artillery of the 11th Marines, which had been detached and left on the line under Army command when the Marine Division was relieved, remained where they were—soon to be back in Gyrene control.

When the Marine infantry units returned to their old haunts, they could not have been blamed for showing a little chagrin at what they found. Sadly, outposts that had cost them much blood to wrestle from the Chinese, then maintain and stoutly defend, now were in enemy hands. The late May offensive by CCF forces had changed Eighth Army command's priorities, and the bitter battle left several of the key outposts to the Chinese.

The disturbing fact of giving up those hills was not lost on Maj. Gen. Randolph McCall Pate, who took command of the First Marine Division from Maj. Gen. Edwin A. Pollock in mid-June.

> *Vegas [had] dominated the enemy approaches to Berlin from the south and northwest and therefore made Berlin relatively secure. Berlin, in turn, dominated the enemy approaches from the south and northwest to East Berlin and made East Berlin relatively secure. The loss of Outposts Vegas to the CCF place Berlin and East Berlin in very precarious positions and negated their being supported by ground fire except from the MLR. (MCOinK, Volume V)*

It was like a row of dominos. Once one toppled there was a good likelihood the whole bunch would collapse.

> *Ground support fire from the MLR, moreover, tended to be only moderately successful in supporting the outposts because of the nature of the terrain. A major Communist stronghold, Hill 190, lay northeast of the Carson-Elko-Vegas complex. Since Berlin (COP 19) and East Berlin (COP 19-A) were sited on extensions of this same hill mass, the enemy could make sudden "ridgeline" attacks against the Berlins. With buffer outpost Vegas now lost, the likelihood of CCF success in such attacks was "immeasurably increased." (MCOinK, Volume V)*

Maybe the Chinese leaders had a death wish for their troops. They had felt the resolve of Marines many times and usually came out on the short end of the stick. They were going to try a couple more times before they ran and hid behind the Truce arrangements.

It was late on 7 July that the CCF began pounding into the outposts they had not successfully taken a little more than a month earlier. They were coming at Berlin and East Berlin, just 300-some yards from the MLR to the east of the Nevada Cities group. At this point, the Turks, who had taken such a beating at the hands of the Chinese in late May, were turning over the two outposts to elements of the 7th Marines.

The battle raged for two days. Baker Company M46 Patton tanks were in direct support and expended 800 rounds of 90mm on the Chinese. Some of that fire was critically placed just in front of Marine infantry in attempt to beat back the Gooks. Still they came. As General Pate feared, the Chinese were marshaling many of their forces from the once Marine-held Vegas.

East Berlin, to the far right on the same ridge as Berlin, was taken by the Chinese, then regained.

Five Baker Pattons crawled up Hill 129, the high ground just to the rear of the MLR and rifled 90mm over friendly heads into enemy positions. Charlie Company M46s began moving into position to join the fight, prior to relieving Baker. The newest armor on the scene did more with bow and turret machines guns than with the 90s, pouring more than 19,000 rounds of 30- and 50-caliber slugs into enemy attackers. By late afternoon of 9 July, the Gooks had enough and broke off the action.

The full reinsertion of the First Marine Division into its old haunts was completed in the next four days and that included bringing the First Tank Battalion and the 11th Marine Regiment back under 1stMarDiv control.

By the middle of July, the Land of the Morning Calm was drenched by days of rain—fortunately damping most aspirations either side had of heating up the war.

Spoonbill Bridge (crossing the Imjin River to the rear of the MLR) was submerged under 11 feet of water and destroyed by the pressure against it on 7 July. Flood conditions existed again on 14–15 July when the Imjin crested at 26 feet at Libby Bridge. Roads in the vicinity were impassable for three days. Resupply of forward companies was made via Freedom Bridge (crossing the Imjin further west). (MCOinK, Volume V)

It was about this time that something went wrong with the flame tank up at COP2. A mechanical problem shut it down. Efforts to get it back to the Changdan tank park were frustrated by the sloppy weather, and the fact the Chinese had somehow sneaked in between the outpost and the MLR to successfully mine the tank route. It sat up there until the truce was signed.

But the need for the 105s of the versatile Shermans was in demand elsewhere toward the middle of July. One flame tank went out between Hedy and Ingrid almost 300 yards in front of the MLR and scattered eighteen rounds on Yoke and Three Fingers. There was a similar shoot into Yoke from a few hundred yards inside the MLR a few days later.

A cadre of five other flame tanks were moved up and attached to the 1st Amphibian Tractor Battalion to protect the eastern banks of the Imjin River against enemy boats trying to cross the *gang* south of the Freedom Corridor in the middle of July.

The flame tanks worked from various slots on hills near Manu-ri overlooking the river about three miles south of Panmunjom. On 16 July, when the Chinese began testing Marine patrols in three different areas of the MLR, the Shermans poured more than 100 rounds across the gang into Sikhayon, Kkarumn-gol, and other concentrations of Gooks about 4,000 yards to the east.

Sgt. Jerry Ellis, still limping from his confrontation with incoming on COP2 in early May, and Sgt. Mackidy Love were two of the tank commanders who had their Shermans up near the Imjin. "We were in those slots on the high hills and firing at anything that moved," Ellis said. "It was all direct fire and sometimes we'd have four tanks up there on one hill."

That was on 17 July when they were sitting atop a hill near Sangdong-ni less than a thousand yards in from the mud flats. They expended more than 150 rounds with the area around Sikhyon-ni once again getting preferred treatment.

With the use of trailers—which the flame tanks towed behind them when they anticipated a long firing mission—the turrets were supplied with fresh, made-up ordnance as needed. That way they could remain in the slots, and not have to back down to restock the turrets.

Two of the flame tanks were set up near a blown out bridge. "We would shoot napalm onto the cement pillars," Ellis said, "and let the jelly burn off. We just wanted the Gooks to know they best not try to cross that river because fire was waiting for them."

That was one of the reasons the flame tanks pulled a lot of blocking missions on roads that were known routes used by the ChiComs. "It was a tactical move," Ellis said, "just to keep the bastards thinking they could be burned good."

The action by the flame tanks those two days accounted for at least three known enemy dead, but the biggest thing they accomplished was upsetting Chinese assembly areas and keeping the Gooks from trying to come across the Imjin.

All the while, scuttlebutt that a truce was coming was flying all over the place. But as far as the Marines along the MLR were concerned, they had to think that's all it was—*scuttlebutt*—because once again, the Chinese came storming at the key outposts of Berlin and East Berlin.

Agreement, But . . .

It was 19 July 1953 that negotiators in Panmunjom came to a final agreement on remaining disputed points. It was time to lay out the final parameters of the armistice agreement.

Common sense would have dictated that there would be almost an immediate easing of hostilities. But commanders of Chinese Communist Forces did not think that rationally.

Just after dark on the 19th, the relative quiet on Berlin and East Berlin, as well as the supporting positions along the MLR, was broken by heavy concentrations of mortar and artillery. The CCF came barging through no man's land and clamored up the faces of the Berlin complex. They also were putting pressure on Ingrid and Dagmar, Marine-manned outposts further west.

> Concentrating their main assault efforts on the Berlins, however, the Chinese forces swarmed up the slopes of the outposts at 2230, with more troops moving in from enemy positions on Jersey, Detroit, and Hill 139, some 700 yards north of Berlin. The Chinese struck first at East Berlin, where 37 Marines were on duty, and then at Berlin, held by 44 men. . . .
>
> By 2300 hostile forces were halfway up Berlin. Continuous volumes of small arms and machine gun fire poured from the defending MLR companies. Defensive boxes were fired by 60mm, 81mm, and 4.2-inch mortars. Eight Company C tanks augmented the close-in fires, with their lethal direct-fire 90mm guns tearing into Chinese troops and weapons. Within two hours after the initial thrust, the 11th Marines had fired 20 counterbattery and 31 countermortar missions. . . . Despite the heavy fire support, by midnight the situation was in doubt and at 0146 the twin outposts were officially declared under enemy control. Nearly 3,000 rounds of incoming were estimated to have fallen on division positions by that time, most of it in the 7th Marines sector.
>
> During the early morning hours of the 20th, Marine tank guns and continuous shelling by six artillery battalions wreaked havoc on Chinese hardware, reinforcing personnel, supply points, and fortifications. (MCOinK, Volume V)

A flame tank was brought into action and was credited with killing an estimated 15 attacking enemy. But it was not enough. The Berlins still were lost.

The 7th Marines had brought up reserves and had a counterattack in place to be launched early on the morning of 20 July. A half-hour before jump off, I Corps canceled the plan. The wisdom of Eighth Army once again prevailed. Berlin and East Berlin no longer were worth the fight.

> The outposts in front of the MLR had gradually lost their value in my opinion because, between the MLR and the outposts, minefields, tactical wire, etc. had made their reinforcement and counter attacks very costly . . . and holding poor real estate for sentimental reasons is a poor excuse for undue casualties."
> Lt. Gen. Bruce C. Clark, Commanding General, I Corps (MCOinK, Volume V)

General Clark's reasoning had been influenced by a meeting he attended with Maj. Gen. Randolph McC. Pate, commanding general of the First Marine Division, when they were called into conference with Eighth Army commanding general Lt. Gen. Maxwell D. Taylor. This was shortly after the early-July assault on the Berlins.

At that point, General Taylor could not see the value of that ridgeline against the cost of maintaining it:

> . . . *the positions could never be held should the Chinese decide to exert sufficient pressure against them and recommended instead that the sector be organized on a wide front defense concept. Actually, following the initial Berlins attack of 7–8 July, a discussion about possible readjustment of the Marine sector defense had been initiated by General Pate. A staff study recommending that just such a "strongpoint" concept (rather than the customary linear defense) be adopted had been completed by Marine Division officials on 15 July. I Corps staff members had concurred with the study and it was awaiting consideration by CG, I Corps when the Berlins were attacked for the second time on 19 July.*

Still, the Chinese weren't finished—even though the actual date for the ceasefire was set for 27 July.

Four days after the loss of the Berlins' ridge, the Gooks stirred up more trouble—this time all along the line involving elements of all three Marine regiments. Before it was over, the CCF had thrown an estimated 3,000 troops into Marine positions, but infantry with heavy support from the First Tank Battalion and 11th Marines artillery had stood their ground.

On the first night of the uprising, three flame tanks firing from two different positions threw nearly a hundred rounds into the attackers. The next day, a twin-barreled Sherman hooked up with two Able Company Pattons and another from the 5th Anti-tank Platoon. Among them, they sent more than 150 rounds into the Chinks' formations as they attacked outpost Esther, which was in the middle of the Siberia-Corrine-Dagmar hill mass within 500 yards of the 5th Marines center sector of the MLR.

Cpl. Jerry Ravino, tank commander of F21, would get a different view of what went on during the final Chinese push against the Marine front. Shortly before Lt. Charles A. Rosenfeld relinquished command of the Flame Platoon in anticipation of being rotated back to the States, he had been informed by the First Tank Battalion's Navy Corpsman that Cpl. Ravino was having a problem with his nose. He was being treated for persistent nosebleeds and the Corpsman thought he should be examined by a surgeon.

Ravino had suffered a broken nose during Operation Clambake when shifting from his loader's seat to the tank Commander's hatch after he had been given command of F21 while the battle was raging at Kum gok. Incoming—he suspected artillery, by the jolt of its impact—had hit the turret of the tank as he was navigating between the 105mm cannon and the back wall of the turret.

When the tank rocked because of the explosion, Ravino's head slammed into the breech block, breaking his nose. Although he was not incapacitated at the time, he had been suffering occasional nosebleeds since early February. Rosenfeld, on the suggestion of the Corpsman, immediately ordered Ravino to a MASH (Military Ambulatory Surgical Hospital). That was 16 July and the tank commander from suburbs of Boston thought he'd be back at Changdan tank park in a couple of hours.

Not so. Cpl. Ravino was quickly transferred to the USS *Repose,* one of two hospital ships anchored in Inchon Harbor, where he underwent evalutation by Navy doctors. Subsequently, he was sent to the USS *Haven* for extensive surgery.

It wasn't so much recovering from the operation that bothered Ravino, but the carnage of battle he was exposed to while on the *Haven.* "The only thing missing," Ravino said, "was the noise of combat. The suffering, the crying, the anguish that comes from being under fire and the mutilation it brings—that was there on those two ships."

When the shit hits the fan along the MLR, as it was doing in the final days of the war, an alert was immediately broadcast throughout the two ships: "Stand by to receive wounded."

Helicopters darted in and out of the hills, wind-milling their way to the landing pads on the afterdecks of the two huge brilliant-white floating hospitals with the enormous red crosses on their sides.

Thank God for those choppers!

They're like buzzing dragonflies, but they landed gently with their precious cargoes of severely wounded—too severely injured to be helped at field hospitals. Quickly the litters with mangled bodies were charged by hospitalmen, closely followed by nurses and doctors to be manhandled to triage.

What they immediately routinely saw was the carnage of battle—a uniform shredded, its color no longer green or dirt-stained. It was spattered deep black-red with blood. A torn arm or leg lay open with exposed pulsating tendons or veins. A face that once was handsome with a shock of blond hair might not be recognizable for the burned skin, or deep cuts and pock marks from shrapnel obliterating what used to be soft features of a cheek, nose, forehead.

As the medical team scurried from under the whirling overhead blades, the helicopter deftly began lifting, banking over the fantail toward the unknown in the hills well beyond and north of the port city of Inchon. It would soon return because the battle continued to rage.

Looking down on a wide ramp facing two large doors at the end of the landing pad, Cpl. Ravino watched many times when the entrance of the triage opened to take in the wounded. Nurses, doctors, and litter-bearers, their surgical gowns splattered with blood, quickly brought the wounded to the operating tables.

What tireless courage, compassion, and dedication these people give, the tank commander marveled. *Talk about above and beyond the call of duty. The word "love" was what that ship was all about!*

When the Chinese tore into the Berlins, Ravino took particular note. "All I could think of was 'blood bath' as chopper after chopper came on to the *Haven,*" Ravino said. "They were in and out all morning, bringing Marines."

The Corporal and other ambulatory convalescing patients were hearing all kinds of stories being relayed from the wounded by Corpsmen, nurses, and doctors.

"The hill was being pounded with precision mortar and rocket fire," Ravino said.

"It was incredible how accurate the Chinks were with their mortars," one wounded Gyrene told Ravino. "Marines were being blown all over the place. They destroyed all of our bunkers and trench lines."

It turned out not to be a fluke. Many line outfits, but more so in the rear, hired local natives to do their laundry. Keeping clean clothing in trenches and bunkers was extremely difficult. Having someone willing to take on the chore was a plus—most of the time. It was common to give young Korean boys—*Washy Washy Boys*—a few bucks of script to carry out this little chore.

On the morning of 20 July, one of the infantry outfits found its *Washy Washy Boy* hidden in some bushes. He had stolen one of the Marine field radios and was calling in enemy fire, which was hitting friendly positions on both the forward and reverse slopes of part of the MLR behind the Berlins outposts.

Incredible!

Ravino tried to get around to the wards on the *Haven* as much as he could, offering help to the wounded. "There was one sergeant," he said, "who took shrapnel to the face from a grenade which landed near him. His head was encased in a stainless-steel halo, and a brace ran up his back. There were wires strung from the halo attached inside his face to support the fractured bones."

Ravino felt a special tie to him because, for some reason, he immediately thought of his brother, Joseph, an Army sergeant, who had been wounded by incoming artillery in 1952 and still was undergoing treatment.

"Jerry," the wounded Marine sergeant asked Ravino one day, "would you do me a favor?"

"Sure, sergeant. You name it."

"I lost my right eye. Would you mind writing some letters to my family for me? But don't tell them what is going on. Just tell 'em I'm wounded, but okay."

Ravino knew the sergeant had lost his eye, but tried to conceal his concern from the Marine.

"By the way, Jerry," the sergeant asked one day, "what outfit did you come from off the line?"

When Ravino told him he was from flame tanks, the sergeant cracked, "Fuck them things. I've seen them operate and I wanted no part of them."

Ravino took that as a compliment.

The worst part of being on that hospital ship hit Ravino when the sounds of helicopters were replaced by the terse order coming from the loudspeakers: Attention on deck!" There were no other words, just the ever-emotional strains of a bugler's taps. It was ritual as flag-draped coffins were being lowered over the side of the ship into landing barges for transport of Marines to refrigerated holds in ships taking them home.

Cpl. Jerry Ravino left the *Haven* on 31 July and rejoined the Flame Platoon at Headqaurters Company of the First Tank Battalion. He was just in time to make the next rotation draft leaving Korea for the States on the USS *General Walker.*

He had wondered what happened on the final day of fighting and he got the scoop from his good buddy Jimmy Olivieri, who was the first one to welcome him back to the outfit. "Vinnie, we took every tank upon the line near the Berlins and let everything go all night until it was over."

Sgt. Jim Putnam of Fenton, Michigan, the machine-gun section leader in the 7th Marines, was there. "It was the most awesome display of firepower I was involved in," Putnam said. His section was attached to Fox Company and he was around the Berlin and East Berlin outposts, which had been lost about 300 yards southeast of the Hook.

"The Chinks hit the MLR," Putnam said. "In my platoon defense arc, which probably was no more than 100 yards in width, I counted twenty-one machine guns, two half tacks with quad 50s, and one halftrack with dual 40s.

"When everyone opened up, it was incredible. No illumination was necessary because tracers lit up the sky like it was daylight. I have no idea how may Chinks we killed, but no one could have lived through that hailstorm!"

Then it was official:

Cease fire at 2200. Commenced evacuating ammunition, equipment and supplies from installations North of IMJIN RIVER.

S-4, Command Diary, First Tank Battalion,
First Marine Division, 27 July 1953

Epilogue

Representatives of the Communist Forces and the United Nations Command signed the armistice agreement that marked the end of the Korean War in Panmunjom at 1000 on Monday, 27 July 1953. The cease-fire, ending two years of often fruitless and hostile truce negotiations, became effective at 2200 that night. After three years, one month, and two days the so-called police action in Korea had come to a halt.

MCOinK, Volume V

Although it was termed "the end of the Korean War," the war never was brought to a *final* conclusion. Nearly fifty years later, the Korean War remains a *truce*, an *armistice*.

Both sides pulled back from their Main Lines of Resistance, outposts were abandoned. No man's land was expanded into a 2,000-yard demilitarized zone that meandered southwest across the peninsula—mostly above the controversial 38th Parallel where it all started on 25 June 1950.

Marines on the line were still skeptical after word had come down that it would be all over at 2200 on 27 July. They would know for sure only when the star cluster shells signaled the end. After putting up with Chinese tricks throughout the war, there was more than a little apprehension.

But it was going to happen. Weary, but wary, Marines began believe.

> *Slowly at first, then with increasing rapidity the white star cluster shells began to burst over positions all along the line. Thousands of flares illuminated the sky and craggy hills along the 155-mile front, from the Yellow Sea to Sea of Japan.*
> *The war in Korea was over. (MCOinK, Volume V)*

Then, it really became a real "police action," the infamous label for which President Harry S. Truman was so vilified when a reporter suckered him into the two-word description a few days after the war had started. Patrols would *police* their beats along the barbed wire confines of each side of the DMZ. There would be flareups and more soldiers on both sides would die over the years. Real peace would never come to Korea.

But on the late night of 27 July 1953, the war, as it had been fought for three years, had stopped. Now, the most important thing for the United Nations Command lie at the end of a brief summary of the Armistice Agreement:

> *"Cease fire 12 hours (at 2200, 27 July) after signing of agreement;*
> *"Withdraw all military forces, supplies, and equipment from the demilitarized zone (2,000 yards from line of contact) within 72 hours after effective time of ceasefire;*
> *"Locate and list all fortifications and minefields in the DMZ within 72 hours, to be dismantled during a subsequent salvage period;*
> *"Replace combat personnel and supplies on a one-for-one basis, to prevent any buildup; and;*
> *"Begin repatriation of all POWs, with exchange to be completed within two months."*
> *(MCOinK, Volume V)*

It was Operation Big Switch, and it started 5 August when the first truckloads of United Nations Command prisoners of war began arriving in Panmunjom from North Korea in canvas-topped Communist trucks. From the start of Operation Little Switch in late April, through Big Switch, until the final American was repatriated on 6 September, 12,757 UNC military—some in captivity since the beginning of the war—returned through the Freedom Gate. An overwhelming 75,799 communist prisoners were repatriated—70,157 of them North Koreans.

Among the 3,597 American servicemen who came off those Communist trucks at Panmunjom in the two exchanges were 172 Marines. Some POWs did not return. The Marine count of men lost to Chinese captors was 221. That meant 49 did not survive the horrible camps in the north.

For the second time in less than a month, Cpl. Jerry Ravino was to see another disturbing side of war.

The *General Nelson M. Walker,* a troop ship, which made many trips between the United States and Korea the last three years, was sitting in Inchon Harbor on 6 August 1953. A few days early, several hundred Marines—who had arrived in Korea on the Walker with the 24th Replacement Draft the previous September—were back on board rotating home. So were hundreds of U.S. Army soldiers.

Cpl. Ravino, and his good buddy Cpl. Jimmy Olivieri, were about to complete their round trip to and from the Land of the Morning Calm. But like the rest of the troops who were whiling away time on the decks, Ravino and Oliveri were wondering why they had been sitting in the harbor day after day.

Finally, the ship's captain announced that the *General Walker* was standing by to take on former American Prisoners of War who had just undergone processing at the Freedom Village in Munsan-ni.

Okay! That was worth the wait for the two Marine corporals who, now, were eager to meet some of the Marine POWs. They even had faint hope one of them would be their friend Rocky DeRose, who was listed as MIA and later declared KIA two months after the 24th Draft arrived in Korea.

Eagerness began to be clouded by disappointment as landing craft after landing craft pulled up alongside the ship. The Marines only saw U.S. Army repatriates, more than 300 of them, came aboard. They were glad to see the released prisoners, but why were no Marines among them?

What the troops on the *Walker* did not know was that in the first day of Big Switch, only three Marines had come out of North Korea. And only three more returned the following day.

Finally, when the last LVP pulled alongside the *General Walker,* the Marines, lining the railing on the starboard deck, recognized the familiar herring-boned utilities worn by Gyrenes. "Here come the Marines!"

Emotion tugged at them as they watched five Marines—each them bandaged in one part of their body or another—come aboard. The greeting was in unison: "SEMPER FI, MARINES! SEMPER FI! WELCOME HOME!"

Ravino, like the rest of the Gyrenes on deck, was eager to talk to the former POWs about their experiences. But this was not to be.

No one was permitted to contact any of the former prisoners. It had been determined that all of them would undergo debriefing—either aboard the ship, or when they got back to the States—before they were allowed to have any conversation with anyone other than military and U.S. Government authorities. Civilian and military debriefers had come aboard the *General Walker* just before the former POWs.

The closest corporals Ravino and Oliveri got to the quarantined men would be on guard duty they pulled in the areas where the repatriates were billeted. But they were under strict orders not to attempt to talk to them. Any violation of those orders could be a court martial offense.

However, it was unavoidable for the guards—moving along the passageways where these men were being interviewed behind makeshift curtains—not to overhear explicit bitterness of having been a prisoner of war. Particular bitterness was aimed at some fellow prisoners.

"Rats, Rats, Rats,'" Ravino heard many times. *"We'll get them, one by one!"*

The reference was to collaborators from within the ranks of the prisoners in many of the camps in North Korea.

As in prison life everywhere, the POWs told of the hated stool pigeons, the so-called "progressives." These were the captives who accepted (or appeared to accept) the Communist teachings and who, in turn, were treated better than the "reactionary" prisoners who resisted the enemy "force feeding" indoctrination. (MCOinK, Volume V)

After thirteen days—south in the Yellow Sea, northeast through the Sea of Japan, and crossing the Pacific Ocean—the *General Walker* docked in San Francisco. The former POWs were met royally by military brass, political dignitaries, the press, and a military band as they debarked from the *Walker.*

The rotating Marines watched with pride as they waited their turn to set foot on good old American soil, even if the dock was covered by concrete. But by the time these Gyrenes retrieved their seabags and went down the gangplank, all the pomp and ceremony was gone. For them, the Korean War was on its way to becoming the Forgotten War.

Forgotten or not, it was a very costly war.

In the three years of the conflict, the Department of Defense put the toll at 33,629 military killed in action—27,704 U.S. Army, 4,267 Marines, 1,200 Air Force, and 458 Navy. There were 103,284 Americans wounded, including 26,038 Marines. South Korean losses were estimated at 70,000 killed. Other United Nations forces suffered 3,194 KIA.

More than 10,000 Americans were missing in action, or became prisoners of war. In the Courts and Gardens of the Missing at the National Memorial Cemetery of the Pacific in Honolulu, Hawaii, there are 848 unknown military among the 8,195 U.S. Korean War dead memorialized. Ironically, the hallowed Gardens are commonly known as the *Punchbowl,* though the name has nothing to do with the infamous Korean War battleground. It is noted: "In these Gardens are recorded the names of Americans who gave their lives in the service of their country and whose earthly resting place is known only to God."

For the North Koreans and Chinese Communists, the figures are staggering—an estimated 900,000 dead or wounded.

The Flame Platoon, as a unit of nine uniquely specialized Sherman M4A3E8 tanks, for all intents and purposes became history on 27 July 1953.

Modernization of military armor soon would outdate the "tank that won World War II" and earned a new and proud reputation in the First Tank Battalion as one of the major, and unique, weapons in the Korean War.

The flame tanks remained in Korea until 1955 before they returned to Camp Pendleton, according to 1st Lt. Antone "Tone" Hunter, the Flame Platoon's last commanding officer. Lt. Hunter, ironically, was the younger brother of Capt. Clyde Hunter, Commanding Officer of Able Company, First Tank Battalion. The M46 Pershings which were "loaned" to the First Tank Battalion were returned to the Army when the First Marine Division left Korea. A newer version of the flame tank fought in Vietnam after the Shermans were long gone from Marine Corps T.O.

But for three years in the Korean War, those magnificent Sherman M4A3E8s—uniquely equipped with their POA-CWS-H5 flame gun to work at close range on enemy positions, or sit back and fire 105mm ordnance indirectly or directly at targets—performed just the way they were designed. They went into no man's land and put their dual snouts right in the Gooks' faces, scorching bunkers, trenches, and anything that was in them. They sat in those slots up on hills and pummeled the enemy with the 105mm howitzer.

The flame tank had performed well beyond expectations because of its maneuverability and flexibility as a weapon. That's the proud legacy, true to United States Marine Corps tradition, of one virtually unknown fighting unit:

Flame Platoon,
Headquarters Company,
First Tank Battalion,
First Marine Division,
Korean War
1950-1953

Acknowledgments

In an effort to honor members of the Flame Platoon, Headquarters Company, First Tank Battalion, First Marine Division, who served in Korea during the three years of the war, we wanted to single out as many of them as possible. We are extremely grateful to those who helped us pay tribute to these few.

—Jerry Ravino and Jack Carty

Our Sincere Appreciation

Flame Tankers

Hank Amos	Lt.Col. Clement Buckley	Jerry Ellis
George F. Fish	Bill Kuykendall	Chuck Lasche
Werner J. Litzman	George Corky Manfull	Len Martin
Pat McDermott	Maurice Mo Sims	Chuck Wager

Tankers

Roger Chaput	Col. Walter MuMu Moore	Col. Walter Reynolds
Benjamin Gabijan	Heine Henzel	Clyde Hunter
Bob McDaniels	William B. Mentzel	Col. Harry T. Milne
Col. Phil Morrell	Dean Servais	Granville G.G. Sweet
John Wear		

Anti-Tanks

Chuck Batherson	Pete Clapper	John Cronin

M67A1 Flamers
Suez Canal*Lebanon*Vietnam

Don Masztak		John Wear

Infantry

Bob Atkinson	John Camara	Joe Discher
Bill Giguire	Jim Putnam	Robert Rosenthal
Lt.Col James B. Vanairsdale		

Authors

Col. Joseph Alexander	*Leatherneck Magazine*
Maj. Allan C. Bevilacqua	*Leatherneck Magazine*
Clay Blair	*The Forgotten War*
C. S. Crawford	*Four Deuces*
Fred W. Crismon	*U.S. Military TrackedVehicles*

James A. Field, Jr.   *History of United States Naval Operations — Korea*
George Forty   *United States Tanks of World War II — The Tank That Won The*
                                                                                    War

Andrew Geer   *The New Breed*
Don Knox   *The Korean War — An Oral History*
B. L. Kortegaard   *Battle of the Chosin Reservoir*
Lynn Montross   *Marine Corps Operations in Korea*
Russell Spurr   *Enter the Dragon*
John Toland   *In Mortal Combat—Korea 1950-1953*
Lt. Col. John I. Williamson   *Dearest Buckie*

Research

USMC Historical Center   Christine Laba   Danny J. Crawford
Marine Corps Operations   U.S. Naval Operations
in Korea   in Korea

Affiliations

Korean War Project   Korean War Veterans
                                                            Association

USMC Tankers Association   USMC Vietnam
                                                            Tankers Association
              Military Vehicle Collector's Club – Southern California

Special Thanks

The late Col. Edwin Imparato, whose initial support fueled the inspiration for this book.

Jo Ann Warden, who sustained Col. Imperato's support.

Len Martin and John Cronin for their steadfast encouragement and assistance along
the way.

Patricia M. McDermott, Psy.D.

Staff Psychologist, Stress Treatment Program, Bay Pines VAMC, Bay Pines, Florida

Barbara Graham for editing the rough and final drafts.

Super Special Thanks

Nona Ravino and Pat Carty, the patient and loving wives who endured a lack of attention to
Honey-do lists while we were holed up in our dens throughout this ongoing four-year project.

Appendixes

Reflections

It is down in history as the Forgotten War. At best, the Korean War is "generously" squeezed into a page—not more than a page and one-half—of high school history books. More than likely, it is reduced to a few paragraphs that, like most wars being reviewed for students, merely touches on the politics that surrounded the Korean War.

Nothing is written of the bitter battles that spilled American blood all over the Land of the Morning Calm. How many high school students, college students, or "baby boomers," for that matter, know that the Korean War is not over—that it is in a state of truce?

Why has it gone down as the Forgotten War?

Well, maybe it's partially our fault. Maybe the guys who were there are as much as anyone to blame for it being logged in as little more than an expanded footnote in history.

Most of us had grown up during World War II and proudly absorbed the massive feeling of patriotism that carried Americans through those unselfish five years. We were awed with pride what our fathers, brothers, and neighbors were doing to put down the fanatics in Europe and the Pacific Islands. When they came home, they had their fill of war. They put it behind them. They wanted to settle down, go to school, get a job, get married, raise families, and help rebuild our country—and yes, the rest of the world if need be—in Peace.

That was ingrained in our way of life as we grew up. Then, it was our turn when the first hot confrontation of a Cold War heated up in a strange place few of us had ever heard of.

Our country had called, and we went to Korea. Some of us were fortunate to endure, and we made it back home with no fanfare. In the tradition of our fathers, brothers, and neighbors, we settled down, went to college, got jobs, married, raised families, and were old enough, wise enough to pitch in with the burgeoning job of making America the world's beacon of hope for peace and prosperity.

We didn't quite forget the war we had just fought. But most of us did a damn good job of putting it in the far recesses of our minds, buried so deep that it took decades for the crust of inattention to peel away and expose the stains it made on our minds. It has only been of late that Korean veterans are baring their souls, finally beginning to talk about some of the hell that was the Korean War—the Forgotten War. They are talking about it, writing about it, and going into classrooms to make sure young people know just what happened in what was a godforsaken peninsula strangely called the Land of the Morning Calm.

When the past finally broke loose in Cpl. Jerry Ravino, this book was the result. A personal torment that plagued him for nearly fifty years kept emerging in the seared memory of pulling the headless body of his Platoon Commander out of a destroyed flame tank. It is reflected in these pages—*the phone call . . . after forty-nine years.*

In today's vernacular, it was partial closure for Ravino. In reality, something like that never is completely *closed* out of the mind. But a measure of relief takes hold because it finally has been brought out into the open.

Going back manifests itself in many ways.

We have been away from the Korean War more than fifty years.

In contributing to this book, men opened pockets of their minds that had been buttoned for most of the last half century. And after looking back at what happened to us in the Land of the Morning Calm, we no longer are reluctant to reveal what heretofore had been tightly sealed fragments in our memories.

Now, we can look back and wonder, and maybe marvel, why things happened the way they did such a long time ago.

* * * *

Sgt. Jim Putnam, the heavy machine-gun section leader from Dog and Fox Companies of the 7th Marine Regiment talked candidly about "Seeing the Elephant" many times when he was on patrol. He came out of the Korean War with his own share of memories that since have resurfaced. But he wonders if it matters.

"I enjoy talking with other Marines, especially about experiences we shared in our youth. No one else would understand and/or give a damn for that matter."

What does matter, however, is that he was not alone harboring some of his inner feelings.

"I was not, and am not, a deeply religious man," Putnam admits. "However, I certainly prayed on more than one occasion. It was never for my personal well-being. It was to give me the strength to not embarrass myself, and make my men have confidence in me as a combat leader. Most of all (I prayed) that none of my men would be killed or wounded."

His view on talking about the Korean War is not so far off the mark, and reflects, maybe, the attitude we encountered and held after returning from the land that rarely was calm in mornings we were there.

"It's very strange—in that, when one puts it down in black and white—it is difficult, if not impossible, to convey the adrenaline flow, fear, hopefully controlled, and trepidation one feels when he is out there in the dark, basically all by himself, and knowing that he is going to meet the enemy."

* * * *

Sgt. Len Martin went to Korea as an eighteen-year-old PFC. He wanted to be in the infantry but was trained to be a tanker. As fate would have it, he still managed to pull infantry-type duty in the historic Chosin Reservoir breakout before he ever climbed aboard a tank.

"The things that I saw and experienced in the thirteen months I spent in Korea," Martin said, "did more to shape my life than anything I had experienced in my previous eighteen years. I quickly learned that I was capable of doing, and enduring, much more than I thought. I also learned to accept responsibilities," he said, taking justified pride in rising to the rank of corporal, then sergeant, and ultimately tank commander. "Not everyone gets to be a tank commander at age nineteen."

Like many Flame Tankers looking back on their tour in Korea, he still wonders why things work out the way they did. "I thank the twist of fate that put me in Headquarters Company, First Tank Battalion and consequently in the safest place one could be in Korea—directly behind the Marine infantry. I do not regret the time that I spent in Korea, although I could have done without the cold."

Unlike many, who came back and went right back to work, Martin's youth delivered him somewhat unprepared for a non-regimented life. "I put the war behind me, although it took several years to fully adjust to civilian life."

Like his father before him, a proud Army veteran of World War I, Martin also savors his military experience. "I was, and still am, proud of the fact that I had the privilege of serving my country, and in particular, with the United States Marine Corps."

* * * *

It was June 27, 1985, when the floodgates opened for coauthor Jack Carty. "The saddest day of my life," he recalled.

Just before noon that sunny summer day, he had walked out the back door of his home in Haddon Heights, New Jersey, and slowly down into the yard. One of his five sons was sitting alone on the wooden steps leading up to the above-ground swimming pool. The Cartys' daughter and three of their other sons were in the family room, emotionally drained. That morning, their youngest brother, Billy, had lost a valiant on-again, off-again four-year battle with cancer.

As he walked toward the pool, the father knew the pain and the unanswered question that was tugging at the young man.

"Why, Dad?"

Jack Carty didn't have the answer.

Billy had been a college baseball player. He was engaged to be married. But, after beating testicular cancer into remission two years earlier and returning to college to play ball, he was stricken again. Nothing could help him this time. He was three months—to the day—shy of his 23rd birthday.

It wasn't until sometime later that day when Jack Carty began to think back, way back, to one very cold January day in 1952 in the rugged East Central Mountains of Korea. And he wondered. He had tucked the events of that day from long ago very deep into his memory. There was no reason to bring it back. But return it did this summer day in 1985.

When Carty left Korea in May 1952, he was going home to marry the love of his life, and it was easy to assign his brief brush with fate to the nether regions of personal history. As years went by, those times sank deeper into caverns, which he never expected to explore too deeply.

But thirty-three years later when Pat and Jack Carty lost their youngest son, Luke's Castle crawled from the crevices. He couldn't get the thought out of his mind that Billy being called by God was somehow entangled in the web spun a long time ago near an enemy hill called Luke's Castle. He knew that day, the Man Upstairs surely had been watching over this particular Marine Tanker.

"Never, ever, can I find a way to rationalize why Billy was taken from us," Carty said. "But the Good Lord made that decision, and I've always wondered if it had something to do with what happened that day in 1952. I'm not sure that I can put this the right way, but when I try to figure out why Billy had to die, I almost always go back to 1952 and wonder, Why did that mortar hit where it did, on the road, by the side of the tank, and not forward alongside my hatch, or on top of the tank near the turret where shrapnel surely would have gotten me?

"Why was the hatch cover exactly in the right position—protecting the back of my head—deflecting all that flying metal and rock. Why had Fred Castle taken the full impact of that blast, and not me?

"Why had I been called out of infantry training and sent to Camp Delmar to learn about tanks? Why, just before we got to Korea, did the war suddenly become one of non-aggression. Why, when I got there, was I assigned to a rear-echelon tank company instead of line-company tanks? And why was my particular tank outfit relegated to little more than extended training most of the time I was there?

"Why is it the sergeant went home in a flag-draped coffin, and I came back to marry a great girl, be blessed with six super kids and then nine priceless grandchildren?

"Was Billy the price God wanted me to pay for what He has showered on me the last fifty years? Did He look at me as the mortar was tracking our tank down that narrow dirt road and decide: *'Okay, Carty, I see you today and I'm going to cover your butt. But, I may want something from you sometime.'* Am I out in left field with all of this? Sacrilegious? I hope not! He's been extremely good to me."

With the experience of Korea once again out in the open, and forced to look at what had been his good fortune since then, Jack Carty eventually came to grips with a decision he mulled for years after Billy's passing.

His brush with fate in Korea was extremely minute compared to tens-of-thousands of other Marines and soldiers. But he had never told anyone—not even his wife, Pat, then his fiancée—about it. After Billy died, he eventually came to the conclusion it was time his family was made aware of their own good fortune.

But for a few feet, this particular Carty family may not be.

He wrote a book exclusively for his loved ones, detailing his three years in the United States Marine Corps—emphasizing the unusual circumstances woven throughout his enlistment that he considered key to his survival in the war. Excerpts were used in this book.

There are others out there who could tell more puzzling stories, and draw a myriad of stranger conclusions about their experiences. Living it is, maybe, understanding it a little better.

One thing is sure, the Korean War will never go away for those whose lives it impacted. It cannot be a Forgotten War to them.

Then and Now

Henry D. Amos

Clementon, New Jersey, high school student enlisted in Marine Corps at age 17 in Philadelphia. Sergeant at Naval Air Station in Morocco before joining 21st Replacement Draft for Korea in June 1952, Flame Platoon mechanic to 1953. 20 years in Marine Corps, retired as Captain. Teacher of the handicapped. Retired in 1995 from Lower Camden County (NJ) School District, where he was a student when he enlisted. Widower, five children.

Bob Atkinson

Enlisted February 1951 in Fitchburg, Massachusetts. 26th Replacement Draft to Korea, November 1952, PFC with Dog Company, 2ndBat7thMarines, Recon Company. Pulp and paper processor; engineer and incinerator manager City of Auburn, Maine. Retired 1997. Wife Phyllis Ann, children Suzan, Scott, Melissa, Jane.

Servart Standing Bear

Ranch-hand enlisted in Marine Corps in Millette County, South Dakota, February 1952. Korea 1952-53. Driver of D34, an M46 Patton with Dog Company, First Tank Battalion. Honorably discharged January 1954. Returned to former job working with cattle and breaking horses on Baxter Berry Ranch in South Dakota. After five years, drove school bus for Millette County until his retirement.

Clement Buckley

Enlisted August 1950 in Kmenia NY. 18th Replacement Draft March 1952, Baker Company First Tank Battalion, C.O. Flame Platoon, May 1952, Wounded in Action October 1952. Retired as Lt. Colonel. Silver Star, Legion of Merit, Bronze Star, Letter of Commendation, Purple Heart. Real estate executive. Wife Barbara.

Jack Carty

Sportswriter with Camden (New Jersey) Courier-Post enlisted October 1950, Philadelphia, PA. Hometown Runnemede, NJ. 10th Replacement Draft to Korea in June 1951, Flame Platoon, First Tank Battalion, PFC-Sergeant, Tank Commander. Discharged October 1953 as S/Sergeant, NCOinC Main Gate Philadelphia Naval Base. Sportswriter, columnist, section(s) editor with *Courier-Post* (Cherry Hill, NJ). Retired 1990. Continues to write college sports-notes column. Married Pat (July 1951). Six children, nine grandchildren. Resides in Barrington, NJ.

Roger W. Chaput

Wood pattern maker enlisted February 1950 in Nashua, New Hampshire. Stationed Camp Lejuene at start of Korean War. Able Company, First Tank Battalion during Inchon-Seoul campaign, PFC-Corporal. Twenty years in USMC, retired from Motor Transport at Camp Lejeune in 1970 at rank of Major. Wife Martha Jane, six children.

John Cronin

East Los Angeles Junior College student enlisted November 1950. 12th Replacement Draft to Korea, August 1951, Antitank Platoon, 5th Marines, PFC-Sergeant, Tank Commander. Aerospace engineering designer. Retired from Rockwell International April 1994. Wife Philomena, six children.

Jerry F. Ellis

Enlisted August 1950 in New York. Korea 1952-53, Sergeant and Flame Platoon tank commander. Wounded in Action May 1953, received Purple Heart. Retired carpenter. Wife Ruth.

George Fish

Enlisted in Falmouth, MA, in December 1950. 12th Replacement draft to Korea in August, 1951. PFC-Sergeant with Flame Platoon, First Tank Battalion. Two tours in Vietnam after training in tank turret artillery and various tracked vehicle courses at the Aberdeen Ordnance School. Special Forces training, Fort Bragg Special Warfare School. Commissioned 1969 between tours in Vietnam and rose to rank of Captain. Was retired as MGySgt in 1975 after 26 years in Marine Corps. Sixteen years in Civil Service as equipment specialist, quality assurance specialist, and supervisor at Fort Bragg and Marine Corps Logistics Base, Albany, GA. Deceased 2001. Wife Jean.

Benjamin Gabijan
  High school senior enlisted March 1949 in 11th Tank Battalion USMCR in Oceanside, California. Active duty July 1950. Inchon Landing with 3rd Platoon, Baker Company, First Tank Battalion. PFC-Sergeant. Ammunition, explosives teams U.S. Naval Weapons Station, Fall Brook, California. Retired as ordnance foreman at Fall Brook, California in 1981. Wife Shirley, seven children.

William P. Giguere
  High school student enlisted February 1952 in Laconia, New Hampshire. 31st Replacement Draft to Korea March 1953, Recon Company, PFC-Corporal. President of Giguere Electric, Inc. Retired 2000. Wife Rita, one son

Heine Henzel
  Enlisted 1943 and served as PFC to 1946. Re-entered Corps in 1949, was 2nd Lieutenant stationed at Quantico when Korean War started. 3rd Platoon Commander, Able Company, Charlie Company, Wolfpack Platoon First Tank Battalion 1953-54. Retired as Lt. Colonel in 1967 after 20 years.

Clyde Hunter
  High school student enlisted March 1942 in Cedar City, Utah. World War II: Fourth Tank Battalion, Siapan, Tinian, Iwo Jima. 1st Lieutenant at Camp Pendleton when Korean War started. 18th Replacement Draft to Korea, March 1952, Captain, Able Company Commanding Officer, First Tank Battalion. Two tours in Vietnam, Colonel C.O. 26th Marine Regiment. Retired as Colonel in 1973. Three Bronze Stars, three Purple Hearts. Real estate broker, owner of Two Rivers Realty, Fallbrook, California. Wife Fern died October 1990, one daughter.

Charles Lasche
  UPS truck driver enlisted in Marines in January 1951, Cascade, Iowa. 16th Replacement Draft to Korea, November 1951, Flame Platoon, PFC-Sergeant, Tank Commander, Section Leader. Retired Carpenter. Wife Parma, five children.

Werner Litzman
  Seismic surveyor enlisted March 1951 Hellersville, Texas. 15th Replacement Draft to Korea in October 1951, Flame Platoon, PFC-Sergeant. Two tours in Vietnam. Retired as 1st Lieutenant in October 1974. One child.

George Manfull
  Iron worker, enlisted May 1950 in hometown of Minerva, Ohio. Sixth Replacement Draft to Korea in February 1951, Flame Platoon, Tank Commander, PFC-Sergeant. Truck driver, maintenance foreman. Retired 1992. Wife Mary, four children.

Len Martin
  High school student enlisted in Marine Corps Reserve October 1949 in Forest Park, Illinois. 1st Replacement Draft to Korea, Headquarters Company, First Tank Battalion

during Chosin withdrawal, Flame Platoon January 1951, PFC-Sergeant, Tank Commander. Tool and die maker, purchasing agent, retired from Motorola, Inc. in 1995. Wife Kay, four children.

Pat McDermott

Construction worker and truck driver enlisted in Marines, January 1951, Epworth, Iowa. 16th Replacement Draft to Korea, November 1951, Flame Platoon, PFC-Sergeant, Tank Commander, Section Leader. Vietnam, Adjutant 3rd Tank Battalion. Two Bronze Stars w/Combat V, Joint Service Commendation Medal, Navy Achievement Medal. Retired from USMC as Major in 1972. Tree farmer. Wife Patricia, five children.

Jerry Ravino

Pfizer Chemical Plant worker enlisted in Marine Corps with John P. Hynes Platoon in Boston, February 1952. 24th Replacement Draft to Korea, September 1952, Flame Platoon, Tank Commander, Wounded in Action, PFC-Corporal. Returned to Pfizer in Groton, Connecticut, retired as shift foreman 1982. Retired substance abuse counselor State of Florida in 2000. Wife Dorothea, three children. Wife Nona.

Maurice Mo Sims

Enlisted in the Marine Corps Reserves in Oceanside in 1946 following service with the Seabees in World War II. Activated for Korean War. Flame tanks on Wolmi-do, Inchon, Seoul, Chosin Breakout. PFC-Corporal. Service station owner. Retired from Del Mar Race Track as public safety supervisor in 1998. Widower, three children.

James Putman

Enlisted January 1951, Guthrie, Oklahoma. Korea with 31st Replacement Draft, First Marine Division Reconnaissance Company. PFC-Sergeant. Home builder, antique auto dealer. Retired from antique auto business in 1985. Wife Div.

Granville "G.G." Sweet

Enlisted early 1930s while working with Civilian Conservation Corps in Chicago. Corporal in China prior to WWII. Gunner on U.S.S. *Nevada* during Japanese attack on Pearl Harbor, 7 December 1941, when bomb hit ship and blew him, wounded, into water. Tanks throughout World War II. 2nd Lieutenant at Camp Delmar when Korean War started. Commanded 3rd Platoon, Able Company, First Tank Battalion, 1st Provisional Marine Brigade in Pusan Perimeter defense. Took 3rd Platoon into Wolmi-do securing island for Inchon invasion. Spent year in Korea and served in Marine Corps until late 1950s.

Formed G.G. Sweet Co., Inc. of which he remains president. Organized the Third Platoon Association for veterans of the 3rd Platoon, Able Company in Korea. Association meets annually at Sweet's Pahrump, Nevada, estate, and publishes *The Centurion,* a monthly newsletter.

Charles P. "Chuck" Wager

Swift Packing Plant employee enlisted October 1950 in Hope, Kansas. 10th Replacement Draft to Korean, July 1951, Flame Platoon, Corporal-Sergeant, Tank Commander,

Section Leader, Platoon Sergeant. Commissioned 2nd Lieutenant 1953. made rank of Captain. Vietnam with Third Tank Battalion, 1966-67, C.O. Headquarters and Service Company. Retired from Marine Corps in 1970. Senior building inspector, Fairfax, VA, Retired 1992. Wife Betty Lou, two children.

Glossary

AKA – Assault Cargo Ship
APD – High Speed Transport
AT/5 – 5th Antitank Platoon
A-T – Anti-Tank
AT – Antitank
AP – Transport
AP – Armor Piercing
APA – Assault Transport
A/1/1 – Able Company, 1st Battalion, 1st Marines
BAR – Browning Automatic Rifle
CCF – Chinese Communist Forces
CG – Commanding General
CinCFE – Commander in Chief Far East
C.O. – Commanding Officer
COP – Combat Outpost
CP – Command Post
CWS – Chemical Warfare Servis
D.I. – Drill Instructor
EUSAK – Eight U.S. Army Korea
FMF – Fleet Marine Force
FMFPac – Fleet Marine Force Pacific
G-2 – Division Intelligence
JTF7 – Joint Task Force Seven
HE – High Explosive
KIA – Killed In Action
KMC – Korean Marine Corps
KP – Kitchen Police (Mess Duty)
LCVP – Landing Craft Vehicle, Personnel
LSD – Landing Ship, Dock
LST – Landing Ship, Tank
LSU – Landing Ship, Utility
LVT – Landing Vehicle, Tracked
MASH – Mobile Army Surgical Hosptal
MAW – Marine Air Wing
MCOinK – Marine Corps Operations in Korea
MIA – Missing in Action
MLR – Main Line of Resistance
MOS – Military Occupational Specialty
MSR – Main Supply Route
MSTS – Military Sea Transport Service
M-1 – Garand M-1 Rifle
NCO – Non-Commissioned Officer

NCOiC – Non-Commissioned Officer in Charge
NKPA – North Korean People's Army
S-1 – Regimental/Battalion Personnel
S-2 – Regimental/Battalion Intelligence
S-3 – Regimental/Battalion Supply
S.O.P– Standard Operating Procedure
M4A3E8 – Sherman Tank, U.S. Medium
M26 – Pershing Tank, U.S. Heavy
M46 – Patton Tank, U.S. Heavy
T-34 – Russian-Made Heavy Tank
M67A1 – Flame Tank Vietnam Era
TAFC – Turkish Armed Forces Command
T.C. – Tank Commander
T.O. – Table of Organization
TOT – Time on Target
UNC – United Nations Command
U.N. – United Nations
VT – Vertical Trajectory
WIA – Wounded in Action
WP – White Phosphorus
WWII – World War II
1stMarDiv – First Marine Division
1stBat1st – 1st Battalion, 1st Marine Regiment
4.2 – 106mm Mortar

Index